Third Edition

The Development of Language

EDITED BY

Jean Berko Gleason

BOSTON UNIVERSITY

Macmillan Publishing Company
New York
Maxwell Macmillan Canada
Toronto
Maxwell Macmillan International
New York *Oxford* *Singapore* *Sydney*

Cover art: Marsha McDevitt
Editor: Ann Castel
Production Editor: Christine M. Harrington
Art Coordinator: Lorraine Woost
Photo Editor: Anne Vega
Cover Designer: Cathleen Norz
Production Buyer: Patricia A. Tonneman
Illustrations: Steve Botts

This book was set in Century Old Style by Carlisle Communications, Ltd., and was printed and bound by Book Press, Inc., a Quebecor America Book Group Company. The cover was printed by Lehigh Press, Inc.

Printed in the United States of America

Macmillan Publishing Company
866 Third Avenue
New York, NY 10022

Macmillan Publishing Company is part of the
Maxwell Communication Group of Companies.

Maxwell Macmillan Canada, Inc.
1200 Eglinton Avenue East, Suite 200
Don Mills, Ontario M3C 3N1

Library of Congress Cataloging-in-Publication Data
The Development of language / edited by Jean Berko Gleason. —3rd ed.
p. cm.
Includes bibliographical references and index.
ISBN 0-02-344251-4
1. Language acquisition. 2. Psycholinguistics.
3. Sociolinguistics. I. Berko Gleason, Jean.
P118.D44 1993
401′.93—dc20 92-28907
CIP

Printing: 3 4 5 6 7 8 9 Year: 5 6 7

Photo credits: The Bettmann Archive, p. 261. Cleo Freelance Photographers, p. 81. Robert Finken, pp. 225, 245, 299, 307, 315, 427, 436. GSU/Yerkes Language Center, p. 16. Jean Claude LeJeune, p. 421. Barbara Schwartz/Macmillan, pp. 325, 350. Michael Siluk, pp. 129, 390. Anne Vega/Macmillan, pp. 1, 4, 39, 42, 46, 65, 95, 115, 123, 151, 175, 202, 239, 337, 369, 375. Gale Zucker, p. 195.

To my daughters and husband—Katherine, Pam, Cynthia, and Andrew—and to the memory of my brother Martin

Preface

This is the third edition of our text, which is intended for upper-level undergraduate or graduate courses in language development, or as readings to be used in conjunction with the study of psycholinguistics, cognitive development, developmental psychology, speech pathology, and related subjects.

This edition has been revised extensively and contains many new features that we have added in response to suggestions from those who, like most of us, have used the book in the classroom. In particular, we have reordered the chapters to reflect two things: (1) the overall developmental nature of language acquisition; and (2) the increasingly important emphasis in our field on both social factors and language use.

To enhance the developmental perspective, we have moved our chapter on language in later years to the end of the book, so that, although the text is basically topical in organization, there is also an underlying chronological framework. To highlight new theory and the importance of social factors, we have moved the extensively revised chapter on pragmatics to a more central position within the text. Our theoretical perspective has remained the same—both interactive and eclectic—but we have tried to add new material that represents the direction of the field. Theory remains a controversial area in psycholinguistics; the most important theoretical positions are presented here, along with their strengths and weaknesses, in what we hope is an evenhanded but thought-provoking approach.

Previous study of linguistics on the part of the reader is not assumed, and each chapter presents its material along with whatever linguistic background information is necessary to make it accessible. Most books on language development are concerned only with language acquisition by children, and have tended to assume that development is complete when the most complex syntactic structures have been attained. But linguistic development, like psychological development, is a lifelong process, and so we have set out to illuminate the nature of language development over the life span.

Since development is always the result of an interaction between innate capacities and environmental forces, we take an interactive perspective, one that takes into account both the biological endowment that makes language possible and the environmental factors that foster development. The study of language development has grown so rapidly that there are now many topics with their own considerable literatures. Fortunately, a number of researchers specializing in major subfields have agreed to contribute to this text; the chapters, therefore, are written by authors who not only know their topic well, but are known for their research in it. They present what they consider to be the salient ideas and the most recent and relevant studies in their own areas.

There are so many different topics that are now recognized in the study of language development that it is impossible to include them all in one text that students might be expected to assimilate during the course of a semester or a quarter. We have had to be selective in our choice of major topics, and have not attempted to include cross-cultural and bilingual studies that rely on knowledge of several languages. Rather, we have concentrated on topics that are central to our growing understanding of the processes that underlie development.

We also have a newly revised instructor's manual and computerized test bank prepared by Pam Gleason. These are available to instructors who use the text. The manual provides helpful outlines of the chapters, emphasizes key points, and provides suggestions for classroom activities.

A number of the authors here can be seen in the Public Broadcasting Service NOVA production on language development called "Babytalk," which students may enjoy watching; PBS has also made available a videotaped college course called "Discovering Psychology," with a half-hour program (#6) devoted to early language development.

It is impossible to edit a book without becoming indebted to many people; I am grateful, first of all, to the authors who agreed to contribute to this volume, all of whom have been willing and friendly colleagues in this round of revisions. Thanks also to Ann Castel and Christine Harrington, our administrative and production editors at Macmillan, and to Mary Perry at Boston University, who, as always, has been immensely helpful in every possible way. I thank the following for their comments and suggestions: Jacqueline Bauman-Waengler, University of South Alabama; Ron Gilliam, University of Missouri at Columbia; Jennifer Ryan Hsu, William Paterson College; Thomas Klee, University of Wyoming; and Beverly Otto, Northeastern Illinois University.

Contents

Language Development: An Overview and a Preview

1

Jean Berko Gleason *Boston University*

INTRODUCTION

Why do we study language development? This phenomenal yet basically universal human achievement poses some of the most challenging theoretical and practical questions of our times: How and why do young children acquire complex grammar? What if no one spoke to them—would children invent language by themselves? Are humans unique, or could language be taught to higher primates? Are there theories or models that can adequately account for language development? Is language a separate capacity, or is it simply one facet of our general cognitive ability? What is it that individuals actually must know in order to have full adult competence in language, and to what extent is the development of those skills representative of universal processes? What about individual differences? What happens when language develops atypically, and is there anything we can do about it? What happens to language skills as one grows older—what is acquired, and what is lost? These are some of the questions that intrigue language development researchers, and they have led to the plan of this book.

Children in every part of the world, regardless of the degree of grammatical or phonological complexity, acquire the major components of their native language by the time they are three or four years old. By the time they are of school age and begin the formal study of grammar, they already can vary their speech to suit the social and communicative nature of a situation, they know the meaning and pronunciation of literally thousands of words, and they use quite correctly the grammatical forms—subjects, objects, verbs, plurals, and tenses—whose names they learn only in the late elementary years. Language development, however, does not cease when the individual reaches school age, or, for that matter, adolescence or maturity—the developmental process continues throughout the life cycle. The reorganization and reintegration of mental processes that are typical of other intellectual functions can also be seen in language, as the changing conditions that accompany maturity lead to modification of linguistic capacity. This book, therefore, is written from a developmental perspective that encompasses the life span. Since most studies of language development have centered on children, this preponderance is reflected in the research reported here. The major questions addressed, however, are not limited to what can be learned from the study of children and, in fact, require the study of mature individuals as well.

This chapter is divided into four major sections:

The first section provides a brief overview of *the course of language development* from early infancy to old age. It contains a preview of the chapters that follow (the major topics included are treated at length in later chapters of the book).

The second section presents the unique *biological foundations* for language that make its development possible in humans. Biological factors are necessary, but they are not sufficient to ensure language development, which does not occur without social interaction.

The third section describes the major *linguistic systems* that individuals must acquire. No particular linguistic theory is espoused here; instead, descriptive techniques are used that have provided the framework for much basic research in language acquisition, and more technical linguistic material is presented in the appropriate substantive chapter. If there is a unifying perspective that the authors of this text share, it is the view that individuals acquire during their lives an **internalized representation** of language that is systematic in nature and amenable to study. This does not imply that inner representation could be established in the absence of social contact, or without several different types of learning (as Chapter 7 on theoretical perspectives makes clear).

The fourth and final section of this chapter focuses on the background and methods of the *study of language development*.

AN OVERVIEW OF THE COURSE OF LANGUAGE DEVELOPMENT

THE EMERGENCE OF INTENTIONAL COMMUNICATION

During their first months human beings begin to acquire the communicative skills that underlie language, long before they say their first words. They pay attention to adult faces and are responsive to the language spoken to them; they take their turn in conversation, even if the turn is only a burble (Lieven, 1978; Snow, 1977). If they want something, they learn to make their intentions known. In addition to possessing the social motivations for communication that are evidenced so early in life, data now show that infants are also physiologically equipped to process incoming speech signals; they are even capable of making fine distinctions among speech sounds that are both rare in the world's languages and previously unknown to them (Eimas, 1975; Trehub, 1976). The latest evidence available suggests that by the age of six months babies have already begun to categorize the sounds of their own language, much as adult speakers do (Kuhl, Williams, Lacerda, Stevens, & Lindblom, 1992).

Midway through their first year, infants begin to babble, playing with sound much as they play with their fingers and toes. There is considerable controversy over the relation between babbling and talking (Blake & Boysson-Bardies, 1992; Boysson-Bardies & Vihman, 1991; Jakobson, 1968); however, most researchers now believe that babbling blends into early speech and may continue even after the appearance of recognizable words. At approximately the same age that they take their first steps, many infants produce their first words. Like walking, early language appears at around the same age and in much the same way all over the world, regardless of the degree of sophistication of the society. The relative ease of pronunciation of a language and its degree of grammatical complexity do not appear to affect the age at which children begin to speak (Lenneberg, 1967). The early precursors of language that arise during the first year of life are discussed in Chapter 2.

PHONOLOGICAL DEVELOPMENT: LEARNING SOUNDS AND SOUND PATTERNS

Once infants have begun to speak, the course of language development appears to have some universal characteristics (Brown, 1973). Typically, toddlers' early utterances are only one word long, and the words are simple in pronunciation and concrete in meaning (Stoel-Gammon & Cooper, 1984). They refer to the objects, events, and people in the

Toddlers talk about familiar things.

child's immediate surroundings—words like *hi, doggie, mommy,* and *juice* (Bloom, 1970; Carey, 1982; Clark, 1973; Nelson & Lucariello, 1985). Here, as in other areas of linguistic research, it is important to recognize that different constraints act upon the child's **comprehension** and **production** of a particular form. A framework for the study of children's growing ability to both recognize and produce the sounds of their language is provided in Chapter 3.

LEARNING THE MEANING OF WORDS: SEMANTIC DEVELOPMENT AND BEYOND

The ways in which speakers relate words to their referents and their meanings are the subject matter of **semantic development.** Just as there are constraints on the phonological shapes of children's early words, there appear to be limits on the kinds of meanings that those early words embody—for instance, very young children are more likely to have in their vocabularies words that refer to objects that move (*bus*) than objects that are immobile (*bench*). Their vocabularies reflect their daily lives, and are unlikely to refer to events that are distant in time or space or to anything of an abstract nature. As they enter the school years, children's words become increasingly complex and interconnected, and children also gain a new kind of knowledge: **metalinguistic awareness.** This new ability makes it possible for them to think about their language, understand what words are, and even define them (Papandropoulou & Sinclair, 1974; Snow, 1990). Investigations of children's first words and their meanings, as well as the ways in which early meaning systems become elaborated into complex semantic networks, are discussed in Chapter 4.

PUTTING WORDS TOGETHER: MORPHOLOGY AND SYNTAX IN THE PRESCHOOL YEARS

Sometime during their second year, after they know about 50 words, most children progress to a stage of two-word combinations (Brown, 1973). Words that they said in the one-word stage are now combined into these **telegraphic** utterances, without articles, prepositions, inflections, or any of the other grammatical modifications that adult language requires. The child can now say such things as "That doggie," meaning "That is a doggie," and "Mommy juice," meaning "Mommy's juice" or "Mommy, give me my juice" or "Mommy is drinking her juice."

An examination of children's two-word utterances in many different language communities (Brown, 1973; Slobin, 1979) has shown that everywhere in the world children at this age are expressing the same kinds of thoughts and intentions in the same kinds of utterances. They ask for more of something; they say no to something; they notice something, or they notice that it has disappeared. This leads them to produce utterances like "More milk!" "No liver!" "Hi, kitty!" and "All-gone cookie!"

A little later in the two-word stage, another dozen or so kinds of meanings appear. For instance, children may name an actor and a verb: "Daddy eat." They modify a noun: "Bad doggie." They specify a location: "Kitty table." They name a verb and an object, leaving out the subject: "Eat lunch." At this stage, children are expressing these basic meanings but they cannot use the language forms that indicate number, gender, and tense. Even in a highly inflected language (such as Hebrew) in which it would be impossible to speak the root word without some of these markers, children settle on one form, which they use indiscriminately: girls, for example, frequently use the feminine form of words, regardless of the grammatical requirements (Dromi & Berman, 1982). Toddler language is in the here-and-now—there is no tomorrow and no yesterday in language at the two-word stage. What children can say is closely related to their level of cognitive and social development, and a child who cannot conceive of the past is unlikely to speak of it. As the child's utterances grow longer, grammatical forms begin to appear. In English, articles, prepositions, and inflections representing number, person, and tense begin to be heard. Although the two-word stage has some universal characteristics across all languages, what is acquired next depends on the features of the language being learned. English-speaking children learn the articles *a* and *the,* but in a language such as Russian there are no articles. Russian grammar, on the other hand, has features that English grammar does not, such as different past-tense endings depending on whether the verb's subject is male or female. One remarkable finding has been that children acquiring a given language do so in essentially the same order. In English, for instance, children learn *in* and *on* before other prepositions such as *under,* and they learn the progressive form with *-ing* before other verb endings such as the *-ed* of the past. After they learn regular plurals and pasts, like *horses* and *skated,* they create some **overregularized** forms of their own, like *mouses* and *eated.*

Researchers account for children's early utterances in varying ways, however. The work of the 1960s, inspired by new grammatical theory (Chomsky, 1957, 1965), interpreted early word combinations as evidence that the child was a young linguist, endowed with a cognitive impetus to develop syntax and a grammatical system. More recently, the child's intentions and need to communicate them to others have been looked to for explanations of grammatical development. But children's unique ability to acquire complex grammar, regardless of the motivation behind it, remains at the heart of linguistic inquiry. The learning of morphological systems, such as the plural or past tense (Berko, 1958), remains some of the strongest evidence we have that children are not simply learning bits and pieces of the adult linguistic system but are constructing generative systems of their own. Early sentences and the acquisition of morphology are examined in Chapter 5.

PRAGMATICS: LANGUAGE IN SOCIAL CONTEXTS

Language development includes acquiring the necessary ability to use language appropriately in a variety of social situations. The system of rules that dictates the way language is used to accomplish social ends is called **pragmatics.** An individual who acquires the phonology, morphology, syntax, and semantics of a language has acquired **linguistic competence.** A sentence such as "Pardon me, madam, but might I borrow your pencil for a moment?" certainly shows that the speaker has linguistic competence, since it is obviously **well formed** as far as English phonology and grammar are concerned. If, however, this sentence is addressed to a two-year-old, rather than something like "Give me the pencil—that's right, give it to me," it is just as certainly inappropriate. Linguistic competence is not sufficient; speakers must also acquire **communicative competence** (Hymes, 1972), or the ability to vary their language appropriately in a variety of situations; in other words, it requires knowledge of pragmatics. During the preschool years, young children learn to express a variety of **speech acts,** such as polite requests, or clarification of their own utterances. Their parents are particularly eager that they learn to be polite (Snow, Perlmann, Gleason, & Hooshyar, 1990). Speakers ultimately learn important variations in language that serve to mark their gender, regional origin, social class, and occupation. Other necessary variations are associated with such things as the social setting, topic of discourse, and characteristics of the person being addressed. These important aspects of pragmatics are discussed in Chapter 6.

THEORETICAL APPROACHES TO LANGUAGE ACQUISITION

In general, explaining what it is that children acquire during the course of language development is easier than explaining how they do it. Do parents shape their children's early babbling into speech through reinforcement and teaching strategies? Or is language, perhaps, a special capacity built into the human biobehavioral system, strengthened through the millennia by natural selection? Learning theorists and innatist theorists do not agree on these basic principles. Other groups of theorists, who adopt an interactional view, see language as influenced heavily by the child's developing cognition and the intervention of adult speakers. Cognitive interactionists believe that language is just one facet of human cognition, and that children in acquiring language are basically learning to put words to concepts they have already acquired. Social interactionists emphasize the child's motivation to communicate with others and the importance of **child directed speech** in their theories. Information theorists explain language acquisition by modeling it on the computer, and stress the importance of parallel processing. A discussion and an evaluation of the theories that have been put forth to explain language development are included in Chapter 7.

INDIVIDUAL DIFFERENCES IN LANGUAGE ACQUISITION

Even though this brief overview has emphasized the regularities and continuities that have been observed in the development of language, it is important to know that individual differences have been found in almost every aspect, even during the earliest period of development. In the acquisition of phonology, for instance, some children are quite conservative, and avoid words they have difficulty pronouncing; others are willing to take a chance. Early words and early word combinations reveal different strategies in acquiring language—whether the child is expressive or referential, analytic or holistic. In this book, individual differences are the topic of Chapter 8.

ATYPICAL LANGUAGE DEVELOPMENT

Language has been a human endowment for so many millennia that it is exceptionally robust; as we shall see, it is under most circumstances almost impossible to suppress. There are conditions, however, that may lead to atypical language development—for instance, sensory problems such as deafness. In this case the capacity for language is intact, but lack of accessible auditory input makes the acquisition of oral language difficult; deaf children who learn a manual language such as **American Sign Language** are able to communicate in a complete and sophisticated language.

Children who are diagnosed as mentally retarded, such as most children with Down syndrome, may show rather typical patterns of language development, but at a slower rate than normally developing children, whereas children with **autism** often exhibit patterns of language development that are atypical in multiple ways. Occasionally children suffer from **specific language impairment**, problems in language development accompanied by no other obvious physical, sensory, or emotional difficulties. Atypical language development, and its relation to the processes described in earlier chapters, is the subject of Chapter 9.

WORDS MOVE: THE INTERWOVEN DEVELOPMENT OF ORAL AND WRITTEN LANGUAGE

By the time they get to kindergarten, children have amassed a vocabulary of about 8,000 words and almost all of the basic grammatical forms of their language. They can handle questions, negative statements, dependent clauses, compound sentences, and a great variety of other constructions. They have also learned much more than vocabulary and grammar—they have learned to use language in many different social situations. They can, for instance, talk baby talk to babies, tell jokes and riddles, be rude to their friends, and act somewhat polite to their parents. Their communicative competence is growing.

During the school years, children are faced with the major task of learning another linguistic system: written language. This would be far more difficult if they did not already possess spoken language. Learning to read at a high level poses a particular problem for deaf children: imagine trying to learn to read Hungarian without having any idea of what it sounded like. Study of the cognitive processes involved in reading and the development of adequate models that represent the acquisition of this skill are two topics that actively involve researchers in developmental psycholinguistics. School and, in particular, the demands of literacy, remove a child's language from the here-and-now and emphasize those characteristics of displacement that many researchers consider the hallmark of uniquely human language. Literacy requires **decontextualized language** use: "An example of decontextualized language in the purely oral mode is giving metalinguistic judgments; for example, judging sentences as grammatical or ungrammatical, identifying ambiguity, and giving definitions" (Snow, 1983, p. 183). Children who come from literate households know a great deal about reading and writing before formal instruction begins, and thus are at an advantage in school. Once children have acquired the ability to read and write, these new skills, in turn, have profound effects upon their spoken language.

Learning to read is not an easy task for all children; this extremely complex activity requires intricate coordination of a number of separate abilities. Humans have been speaking since the earliest days of our prehistory, but reading has been a common requirement only in very modern times; we should not be surprised, therefore, that reading skills vary greatly in the population. Reading problems as exemplified in the **dyslexias** pose serious theoretical and practical problems for the psycholinguistic researcher. The acquisition of literacy skills and other aspects of language development during the school years are discussed in Chapter 10.

LANGUAGE DEVELOPMENT BEYOND CHILDHOOD

What if a child's early years were spent in silence, with no contact with any sort of language? The teen years may mark a crucial developmental watershed in the individual's ability to acquire language. Whereas studies of language development in young children have emphasized the ease and rapidity with which it occurs, a quite contrary situation prevails if, for some reason, language has not been heard or learned during those early years. Evidence obtained from the study of both feral and neglected children suggests that there may be a **critical period,** or **sensitive age** for first-language acquisition (Curtiss, 1977; Lane, 1979; Rymer, 1992). These cases are extremely rare, and conclusions drawn from them are inevitably controversial, since abandonment and neglect have pervasively devastating effects.

In the normal course of events, language development, like cognitive development, moral development, or psychological development, continues beyond the point where the individual has assumed the outward appearance of an adult. During the teen years, young people acquire their own special style, and part of being a successful teenager rests in knowing how to talk like one.

Language is also involved in psychological development: the psychiatrist Erik Erikson (1959) pointed out that one of the major life tasks facing young people is the formation of an identity, a sense of who they are. A distinct personal linguistic style is part of one's special identity. Further psychological goals of early adulthood that call for expanded linguistic skills include beginning an occupation and establishing intimate relations with others.

Language development during the adult years varies greatly among individuals, depending on such things as level of education and social and occupational roles. Actors, for instance, must learn not only to be heard by large audiences but to speak the words of others using varying voices and regional dialects. Working people learn the special tones of voice and terminology associated with their own occupational register or code.

With advancing age, numerous linguistic changes take place. For instance, some word-finding difficulty is inevitable—the inability to produce a name that is "on the tip of the tongue" is a phenomenon that becomes increasingly familiar as one approaches retirement age. But not all changes are for the worse—vocabulary increases, as does narrative skill. In preliterate societies, for instance, storytellers are typically older members of the community. Although most individuals remain linguistically vigorous in their later years, language deterioration becomes severe for some, and they may lose both comprehension and voluntary speech. The last words available for them may be as limited as those of young children. Language development in adolescence, adulthood, and old age is described in Chapter 11.

■ THE BIOLOGICAL BASES OF LANGUAGE

ANIMAL COMMUNICATION SYSTEMS

Human language has special properties that have led many researchers to conclude that such language is both **species specific** and **species uniform;** that is, it is unique to and essentially similar in all humans (Lenneberg, 1967; Marler, 1990). The characteristics that distinguish human language are illuminated when it is compared with animal communication systems. Animals are clearly able to communicate at some level with one another as well as with humans. Cats and dogs meow and bark for attention and are able to convey a variety of messages by such things as scratching at the door or looking expectantly at their dishes. Scratching, meowing, and hopeful gazes are clearly not language, however; the messages are very limited in scope and can be interpreted only in the context of the immediate situation.

Bee Communication

Insects such as bees have been shown to have an elaborate communication system. Ethologist Karl von Frisch (1950) began to study bees in the 1920s and won a Nobel prize in 1973 for his studies of communication among these highly social insects. Unlike the expressive meowing of a hungry cat, in many senses the communication system of the bee is referential: it tells other bees about something in the outside world. A bee returning to the hive after finding nectar-filled flowers collects an audience and then performs a dance that indicates the direction and the approximate distance of the nectar from the hive. Other bees watch, join the dance, and then head for the flowers. The bee's dance is actually a miniature form of the trip to the flowers, rather than a symbolic statement. There is nothing symbolic or arbitrary about dancing toward the north to indicate that other bees should fly in that direction. Moreover, although the movements of the dance have structure and meaning, there is only one possible conversational topic—where to find nectar. Even this repertoire is seriously limited: bees cannot, for instance, tell one another that the flowers are pretty or that gathering nectar is boring.

Sea Mammals and Birds

Many animals have ways of communicating with other members of their species. Whales and dolphins employ elaborate systems of whistles and grunts that are clearly meaningful to other whales and dolphins (Herman, 1981; Savage-Rumbaugh, in press). Some birds have been shown to have a variety of meaningful calls. Jackdaws, for instance, were studied by Konrad Lorenz (1971), who shared von Frisch's Nobel prize. Lorenz showed that these relatives of the crow have courting calls, a call for flying away, and one for flying home. They also have a warning rattle that they sound before attacking any other creature carrying a dangling black object. (He discovered this while carrying [dangling] his black swimsuit!)

All of these communication systems have clear utility for the animals that use them, and each one resembles human language in some respect, but they are all tied to the stimulus situation, limited to the here-and-now and a restricted set of messages. Human language has characteristics not found in their entirety in these other systems.

Researchers concerned with the question of criteria for language have produced lists of characteristics that vary somewhat in both length and scope. Most would agree, however, on at least these three cited by Roger Brown (1973): (1) true language is *productive* in the sense that speakers can make many new utterances and can recombine the forms they already know to say things they have never before heard; (2) it also has *semanticity:* that is, it can represent ideas, events, and objects symbolically; and (3) it offers the possibility of *displacement*—messages need not be tied to the immediate context.

Human language enables its users to comment on any aspect of their experience and to consider the past and the future as well as referents that may be continents away or only in the imagination. The natural communication systems of birds, bees, and lower animals do not meet these criteria of language.

Recent attempts to teach language to talking birds, however, have produced some extremely provocative results. For instance, an African grey parrot named Alex has been trained to recognize objects, colors, and shapes, and answer questions about them in English. Faced with an array of things, he is asked "What object is green?" Alex says, correctly, "wood." He is right about 80% of the time (Pepperberg, 1991). Is the bird responding to complex learned cues, or does an African grey parrot have the same sort of linguistic skill a child does? We shall have to withhold judgment on this one until more data are available.

Primate Language

During the past half-century a great deal of curiosity has focused on the possibility that the higher primates might be capable of learning human language. Chimpanzees are intelligent, social, and communicative animals (Maple & Cone, 1981; Miles, 1983). They use a variety of vocal cries in their life in the wild; for instance, a food bark and a danger cry. Chimpanzees possess genetic structures similar to our own, and are our closest relatives in the animal world, more closely related to us than they are to monkeys (Linden, 1974). There have been numerous attempts to teach language to chimpanzees and at least one major gorilla language project (Patterson, 1978). The chimpanzee studies have provided us with much useful and controversial data on the ability of nonhumans to acquire our language forms. Some of these studies, such as those of David and Ann James Premack (1976), have taught chimpanzees to manipulate artificial symbols (colored plastic tokens) in order to communicate with humans. In another study, researchers taught chimpanzees to use a computer console to send messages (Rumbaugh, 1977). We will concentrate here on some studies that have set out to teach natural language to chimpanzees.

Gua and Viki. In 1931, Professor and Mrs. W. N. Kellogg became the first American family to raise a chimpanzee and a child together (Kellogg, 1980). The Kelloggs brought into their home Gua, a seven-month-old chimpanzee, who stayed with them and their infant son Donald for nine months. No special effort was made to teach Gua to talk; like the human baby, she was simply exposed to a speaking household. During this period, Gua came to use some of her natural chimpanzee cries rather consistently; for instance, she used her food bark not just for food but for anything at all that she wanted. Although Gua was rather better than Donald in most physical accomplishments, unlike Donald she did not babble and did not learn to say any English words.

In the 1940s, psychologists Catherine and Keith Hayes (Hayes, 1951) set out to improve upon the Kelloggs' experiment by raising a chimpanzee named Viki as if she were their own child. They took her home when she was six weeks old, and she remained with them for several years. The Hayeses made every effort to teach Viki to talk; they had assumed that chimpanzees were rather like institutionalized retarded children, and that love and patient instruction would afford Viki the opportunity for optimal language development. After six years of training, Viki appeared to understand a great deal, but she was able to produce, with great difficulty, only four words: *mama*, *papa*, *cup*, and *up*. She was never able to say more, and in order to pronounce a /p/, she had to hold her lips together with her fingers. Since speech is an **overlaid function,** that is, the organs involved in its production (such as the tongue and lungs) all have primary functions other than language, it requires an extraordinary degree of physiological coordination to articulate while continuing with functions such as breathing and swallowing. From the Hayeses' research it became clear that chimpanzees do not have the specialized articulatory and physiological abilities that make spoken language possible.

In more recent times, other researchers have concluded that the inability to speak may not preclude the possibility of having language. The deaf community in the United States, for instance, uses a gestural rather than a spoken language, American Sign Language (ASL). ASL is a complete language, with its own elaborated grammar and a rich vocabulary, all of which can be conveyed by the shape and movement of the hands in front of the body; it is the equal of vocal language in its capacity to communicate complex human thought (Fischer, in press; Klima & Bellugi, 1979). A new appreciation of the richness of ASL led to innovative experiments with chimpanzees.

Washoe. The first attempt to capitalize on the ability to comprehend language and the natural gestural ability of a chimpanzee by teaching her signed human language (ASL) was made by Drs. Beatrice and Allen Gardner at the University of Nevada in 1966 (Gardner & Gardner, 1969). The Gardners moved a young chimpanzee named Washoe into a trailer behind their house and began to teach her ASL. Washoe was 10 months old at the time and had been captured in the wild in Africa. During the time she was involved in this project, she learned over 130 ASL signs, as well as how to combine them into utterances of several signs (Gardner & Gardner, 1980, 1983; see also 1984a, 1984b). On seeing her trainer, she was able to sign, "Please tickle hug hurry," "Gimme food drink," and similar requests.

Washoe was able to sign many of the same things that are found in the language of children in the very early stages of language acquisition, before they learn the grammatical refinements of their own language (Brown, 1970; Van Cantfort & Rimpau, 1982). She appeared to use her signs in a creative way: on seeing a duck for the first time, she signed "water bird." Since her utterances were typically answers to questions posed to her (e.g., "What is that?"), it is not clear whether she was attempting to make a new word, or simply saying that it was water AND a bird. Unlike English-speaking children, she did not pay attention to word order, and at the time her training ceased in the 51st month it was not clear if her sign language was actually grammatically structured in the sense that even a young child's is (Brown, 1970; Klima & Bellugi, 1972).

However, through vocabulary tests of Washoe, as well as of subsequent chimpanzee subjects named Moja, Pili, Tatu, and Dar, the Gardners were able to demonstrate that children's and chimpanzees' first 50 words are very similar (see Table 1.1).

Moreover, the chimpanzees extended or generalized their words in much the same way that humans do—for instance, once they knew the ASL sign, calling a hat they had never seen before *hat* (Gardner & Gardner, 1983; see also 1984a, b). The question of whether a chimpanzee was capable of syntax remained open. This is an important theoretical question, because syntax makes productivity possible. On the practical side, the remarkable successes attained with chimps have led to innovative programs that teach sign language to communicatively handicapped children.

Nim Chimpsky. An attempt to answer the question of whether chimpanzees can make grammatical sentences was made by Columbia University professor Herbert S. Terrace (1980). Terrace adopted a young male chimp, whom he named Nim Chimpsky. The plan was to raise Nim in a rich human environment, teach him ASL, and then analyze the chimp's emerging ability to combine signs into utterances, paying special attention to any evidence that he could indeed produce grammatical signed sentences. Nim began to sign early: he produced his first sign, "drink," when he was only four months old. But his later utterances never progressed much beyond the two- or three-sign stage. He signed, "Eat Nim," and "Banana me eat," but when he made four-sign utterances, he added no new information and, unlike even young children, he used no particular word order. He signed, "Banana me eat banana," in which the additional word is merely repetitive. Analyzing the extensive data collected in this project, Terrace concluded that there was no evidence that the chimp could produce anything that might be called a sentence.

An even more serious question regarding the chimpanzee's linguistic capability was raised after Terrace and his associates studied the videotaped interactions of young Nim and his many teachers. They found that Nim understood little about conversational turn-taking, often interrupting his teachers, and that very little of what Nim signed actually originated with the chimp. Most of what he signed was prompted by the teacher and contained major constituents of the teacher's signed utterance to him.

Terrace carried his study further by analyzing films made available to him by other ape-language projects, and arrived at the same conclusion: much of what the chimps signed had just been signed to them. The signing chimps appeared to be responding at least in part to subtle cues from their trainers. The question of the apes' potential was not completely settled by this study, since Terrace himself was aware of the inevitable shortcomings in his project. As Nim reached maturity, he became difficult to work with and faced an uncertain future. Animal lovers will be pleased to know that he is living out his life on Black Beauty Ranch in Texas, a guest of the Fund for Animals (Vittorini, 1991).

Kanzi. While for now it would appear that apes are not capable of language as we know it, the chimpanzee studies have indicated that there are substantial similarities between very young children's and chimpanzees' abilities to engage in symbolic communication (Greenfield & Savage-Rumbaugh, 1991).

TABLE 1.1 Item by Item Matches in the First 50 Vocabulary Items of Children and Chimpanzees (*From "Early Signs of Language in Children and Chimpanzees" [p. 49] by R. A. Gardner & B. T. Gardner, 1983. Adapted by permission.*)

	Chimpanzees					Children	
	W	M	P	T	D	1 Using Signs	8 Using Words
Names and Pronouns							
me	√	√	√	√	√		3
you	√	√	√	√	√		
own name	√	√	√		√		1
other names	√	√	√	√		√	8
General Nominals							
apple		√		√	√	√	1
baby	√					√	6
ball					√	√	5
banana	√			√			1
bed	√						1
berry				√	√		
bib		√	√	√	√		
bird	√	√	√	√	√		1
blanket	√						2
book	√						2
brush	√	√	√	√	√		
cat	√					√	5
clothes	√						
comb		√			√		
cookie				√	√	√	4
cow					√		1
diaper				√	√		
dog	√	√	√	√	√	√	7
drink	√	√	√	√	√	√	1
flower	√	√		√		√	
food	√	√	√	√	√	√	3
glasses		√					1
gum		√	√	√	√		
hankie					√	√	
hat	√	√	√	√	√		
hurt	√				√	√	1
ice cream				√		√	
key	√						3
light		√	√		√	√	2
lipstick		√	√				
milk		√	√	√	√		5
nut			√	√	√		1
oil	√	√	√	√	√		
pants	√						
pen	√	√					1
potty		√	√	√	√	√	1
shoes	√	√	√	√	√	√	3
shirt				√			
sweet	√				√		
toothbrush	√	√	√	√	√		
water			√			√	3
wiper	√	√	√	√	√		

	Chimpanzees					Children	
	W	M	P	T	D	1 Using Signs	8 Using Words
Actions							
catch	✓		✓		✓		1
chase			✓	✓	✓		
clean	✓				✓		1
come	✓	✓	✓	✓	✓		1
down	✓	✓	✓	✓	✓		2
go	✓	✓	✓	✓	✓		4
groom					✓		
hear	✓	✓	✓	✓	✓		
hug	✓	✓	✓	✓	✓		
hurry	✓	✓					
in	✓						2
jump			✓				
kiss		✓					
open	✓	✓	✓	✓	✓		
out	✓	✓	✓	✓	✓		3
peekaboo	✓		✓				1
see	✓		✓	✓			3
sleep			✓			✓	1
smell	✓	✓	✓				
tickle	✓	✓	✓	✓	✓		1
up	✓	✓	✓	✓	✓		4
Modifiers							
dirty		✓		✓		✓	2
finished			✓	✓		✓	1
funny	✓					✓	
hot		✓		✓	✓	✓	7
mine	✓	✓	✓	✓	✓	✓	2
more	✓	✓	✓	✓	✓		3
quiet		✓	✓	✓			
there	✓	✓	✓	✓	✓		2
Personal-Social							
can't		✓	✓	✓	✓		
don't know			✓				1
good		✓	✓	✓	✓	✓	1
good-bye		✓		✓			5
no		✓	✓	✓	✓		5
please	✓	✓	✓	✓	✓	✓	3
refusal			✓				
sorry	✓						
yes			✓				5
Functions							
that				✓			

Note: *W* = *Washoe*, M = *Moja*, P = *Pili*, T = *Tatu*, and D = *Dar*.

Kanzi can understand complex spoken language.

Current research by D. M. Rumbaugh and E. S. Savage-Rumbaugh with a pygmy chimp named Kanzi at the Yerkes Center in Atlanta (Savage-Rumbaugh, in press; 1990) has given rise to new hope and speculation about primate linguistic ability. Prior chimpanzee studies used the common chimp (*pan troglodytes*). The pygmy chimpanzee (*p. paniscus*) was virtually unheard of until the mid-1970s.

Pygmy chimpanzees are found only in the remote rain forests of Zaire. They are smaller, less aggressive, more social, more intelligent, and more communicative than the common chimp. Kanzi surprised his trainers when he acquired some manual signs merely by observing his mother's lessons. He is now the subject of an intensive longitudinal study. Kanzi now has a large, free area in which to roam, and many opportunities to learn both spoken and signed language.

Kanzi is 12 years old (in 1993), and weighs 130 pounds. Although he is sexually mature, the Rumbaughs believe they will be able to continue working with him. They are working on his understanding of spoken English, and find that he is able to understand many unusual utterances and carry out the acts described in them with remarkable accuracy. For instance, if asked to "Put the mushroom in the potty," Kanzi obligingly does so, proving that he is attending to language, and not simply carrying out activities that are evident from the nonverbal situation.

Current work with Kanzi on his understanding of pictures, including pictures that are described with passives, has led his trainers to be very optimistic about the chimp's ability to comprehend syntax. Whether the pygmy chimpanzee is the hope of the future in animal language studies remains to be seen.

THE BIOLOGICAL BASE: HUMANS

Language in humans is clearly dependent on their having a society in which to learn it, other humans to speak to, and the intelligence to make it possible; humans also appear to have evolved with specialized neural mechanisms that subserve language. Language is difficult or impossible to teach to nonhumans, and it is equally difficult to prevent humans from acquiring it (Lenneberg, 1967). Human beings who are physiologically and psychologically intact will acquire the language of those around them if they grow up among people who speak to them (Locke, 1990). This human interaction seems necessary; there is no evidence that infants can acquire language from watching television, for instance. There are some strong arguments for the case that human language is biologically determined—that it owes its existence to specialized structures in the brain and in the neurological systems of humans.

LANGUAGE AREAS IN THE BRAIN

Unlike our relatives the apes, humans have areas in the cerebral cortex that are known to be associated with language. The two hemispheres of the brain are not symmetrical (Geschwind, 1982). Most individuals, about 85 percent of the population, are right-handed, and almost all right-handers have their language functions represented in their left hemisphere. Of the left-handed population, perhaps half also have their language areas in the left hemisphere; therefore, the vast majority of the populace is **lateralized** for language in the left hemisphere. The right hemisphere, however, also participates in some aspects of language processing. For instance, recognition of the emotional tone of speech appears to be a right hemisphere function; moreover, when populations other than literate white males are studied, the cerebral asymmetry for language is less pronounced (Caplan, Lecours, & Smith, 1984).

Most of what we know about specialized areas comes from study of what happens when the brain is injured, either through a traumatic accident or from a stroke, aneurysm, or other cardiovascular event. Damage to the language areas of the brain results in **aphasia,** a generalized communication disorder with varying characteristics depending on the site of the lesion (Gleason & Goodglass, 1984; Goodglass, 1981). There are at least three well-established major language areas in the left hemisphere (see Figure 1.1).

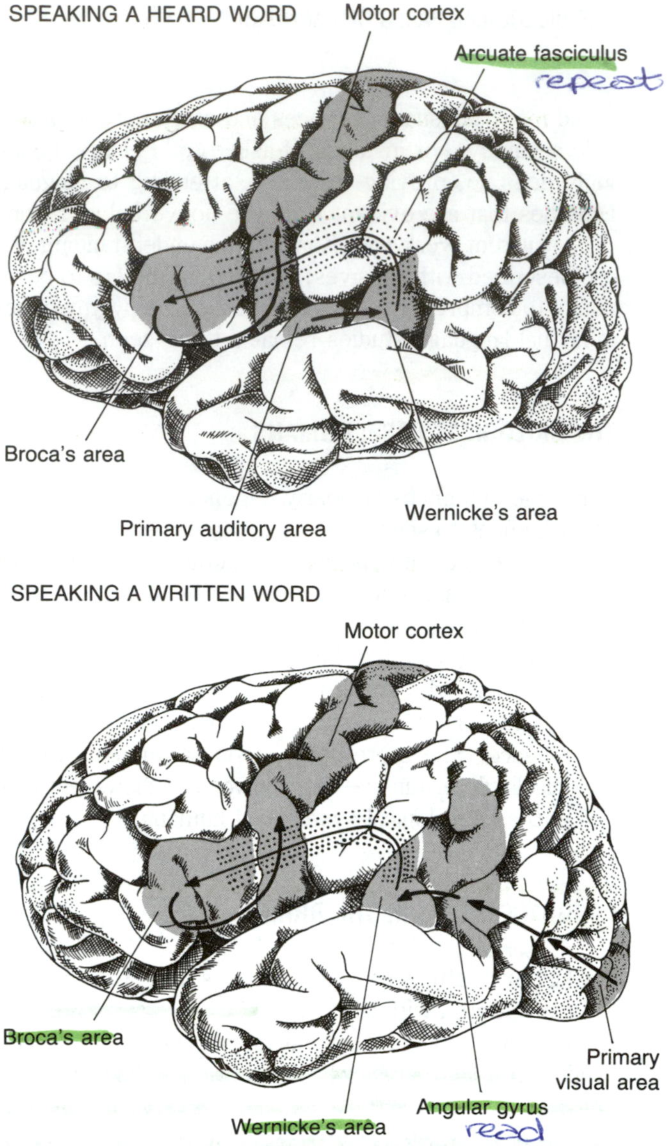

FIGURE 1.1 Language areas in the brain *(Note:* When a word is heard (upper diagram), the sensation from the ears is received by the primary auditory cortex, but the word cannot be understood until the signal has been processed in Wernicke's area nearby. If the word is to be spoken, some representation of it is thought to be transmitted from Wernicke's area to Broca's area, through a bundle of nerve fibers called the arcuate fasciculus. In Broca's area the word evokes a detailed program for articulation, which is supplied to the face area of the motor cortex. The motor cortex in turn drives the muscles of the lips, the tongue, the larynx and so on. When a written word is read (lower diagram), the sensation is first registered by the primary visual cortex. It is then thought to be relayed to the angular gyrus, which associates the visual form of the word with the corresponding auditory pattern in Wernicke's area. Speaking the word then draws on the same systems of neurons as before. (Adapted from "Specializations of the Human Brain," by Norman Geschwind. Copyright © 1979 by Scientific American, Inc. All rights reserved.)

Broca's area in the left frontal region is very near to that part of the motor strip that controls the tongue and lips, and damage to Broca's area results in a typical aphasic syndrome, called Broca's aphasia, in which the patient has good comprehension but much difficulty with pronunciation and producing the little words of the language, such as articles and prepositions. Speech tends to be *telegraphic*—it contains only the most important words. For instance, when one patient seen in Boston was asked how he planned to spend the weekend at home, he replied, with labored articulation, "Boston College. Football. Saturday."

Wernicke's area is located in the posterior left temporal lobe, near the auditory-association areas of the brain. Damage to Wernicke's area produces an aphasia that is characterized by fluent speech with many **neologisms** (nonsense words) and poor comprehension. One Wernicke's aphasic, when asked to name an ashtray, said, "That's a fremser." When he was later asked to point to the fremser, however, he had no idea what the examiner meant.

The **arcuate fasciculus** is a band of subcortical fibers that connects Wernicke's area with Broca's area. If you ask someone to repeat what you say, the incoming message is processed in Wernicke's area and then sent out over the arcuate fasciculus to Broca's area, where it is programmed for production. Patients with lesions in the arcuate fasciculus are unable to repeat; their disorder is called **conduction aphasia.** There are also areas of the brain known to be associated with written language: damage to the angular gyrus, for instance, impairs the ability to read.

These areas of the brain function in these ways in adults, but there is some evidence that in young children either the areas are not yet so firmly specialized or the nonlanguage hemisphere can take over in case of damage to the dominant hemisphere. A child of five or six who suffers left-brain damage will in all likelihood recover complete language, as the right hemisphere takes over language functions. However, adults who become aphasic are liable to remain so if they do not recover in the first half-year after their injury.

Special Characteristics

In examining the attempts to teach language to apes, we saw that language is probably species unique; the specialized areas of the brain contribute to that uniqueness. Human beings, of course, also have unique cognitive abilities and unique social settings in which to acquire language. These are discussed in subsequent chapters—the intent here is to describe briefly the neuroanatomical foundations that make language acquisition possible. As Eric Lenneberg (1967) has pointed out, language development in humans is associated with other maturational events. The appearance of language is a developmental milestone, roughly correlated with the onset of walking. In addition to possessing specialized brain structures, humans, unlike other creatures, have a long list of specializations in such things as the development of their vocal cords and larynxes and the ability to coordinate phonation with breathing and swallowing. Humans perform a remarkably complex set of activities when they engage in everyday activities, such as having a talk over lunch. Lenneberg (1967) cited a number of additional features as evidence that language is species specific and species uniform.

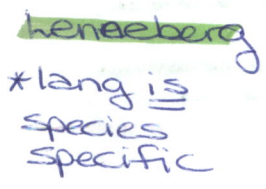

- *The regular onset of speech.* The order of appearance of developmental milestones, including speech, is regular in the species—it is not affected by culture or the language to be learned.
- *Speech is not suppressible.* Normal children learn to talk if they are in contact with older speakers. The wide variations that exist within and across cultures have all provided suitable environments for children to learn language.
- *Language cannot be taught to other species.* Lenneberg made this claim in the 1960s, before there were results from the chimpanzee studies, and time may have proven him right. However, it is also clear that chimpanzees can be taught sign language comparable to the language of very young children, and thus this claim depends on only one definition of language.
- *Languages everywhere have certain universals.* They are structured in accordance with principles of human cognition, and any human can learn any language. At the same time, there are universal constraints on the kinds of rules that children can learn. The universals that are found in all languages include phonology, grammar, and semantics. These systematic aspects of language, along with another universal, the existence of pragmatics (social rules for language use), provide the research arena for developmental psycholinguistics.

■ THE STRUCTURE OF LANGUAGE: LEARNING THE SYSTEM

COMPETENCE AND PERFORMANCE

A speaker who knows the syntactic rules of a language is said to have *linguistic competence.* Competence in this case refers to the inner knowledge of the rules, not to the way the person speaks on any particular occasion. The expression of the rules in everyday speech is *performance.* In the normal course of events, speakers produce errors, false starts, slips of the tongue, and utterances flawed in various other ways. These are performance errors and are not thought to reflect the speakers' underlying competence. There is also a general assumption that within a given linguistic community, all adults who are native speakers of the language, and not neurologically impaired in some way, share linguistic competence. It is possible to find out a great deal about adults' syntax by querying them about their language or asking them to judge the grammatical acceptability of a sentence. However, in studying children, researchers must either rely on performance for clues to competence or design clever experiments to probe inner knowledge, since young children are not able to discuss questions of "grammaticality."

When children learn language, what is it that they must learn? Language has many subsystems having to do with sound, grammar, meaning, vocabulary, and knowing the right way to say something on a particular occasion in order to accomplish a specific purpose. Knowing the language entails knowing its **phonology, morphology, syntax,** and **semantics,** as well as its **pragmatics.** The speaker who knows all this has acquired *communicative competence* (Hymes, 1972).

PHONOLOGY

sounds

What are the sounds of English? Although we all speak the language, without specific training it would be difficult to list all of the sounds we make when we speak, and even more difficult to list the rules for their combination. Phonology includes all of the important sounds, the rules for combining them to make words, and such things as the stress and intonation patterns that accompany them. If you have studied foreign languages, you know that there are many different sounds used in the languages of the world and that any given language uses only a subset of the possibilities. Each language has its own set of important sounds, which are actually categories of sounds that include a number of variations. For instance, in English we pronounce the sound /t/ many different ways: at the beginning of a word like *top* it is pronounced with a strong aspiration, or puff of air (you can check this by holding the back of your hand near your mouth and vigorously saying *top*). We pronounce a word like *stop* without the puff of air, unaspirated. Some speakers produce a different, unreleased /t/ when they say a word like *hat* at the end of a sentence: they leave their tongues in place at the point of articulation. Many speakers pronounce an even different kind of /t/ in a word like *Manhattan* by releasing the air through their noses at the end. A phonetician would hear these /t/ sounds as four different sounds: aspirated, unaspirated, unreleased, and nasally released. But for untrained English speakers, these are all just one sound. A group of similar sounds that are regarded as all the same by the speakers of a language are called phonemes. The different /t/ sounds just described are all part of one /t/ **phoneme** in English. In Hindi and many other Indian languages, the aspirated and unaspirated versions of /t/ are heard and treated as very different sounds, two different phonemes.

Children have to learn to recognize and produce the phonemes of their own language and to combine those phonemes into words and sentences with the right sorts of intonational patterns. Some parts of the system, such as consonant–vowel combinations, are acquired early on. Others are not acquired until well into the elementary school years: for instance, the ability to distinguish between the stress patterns of *hot dog* (sausage) and *hot dog* (warm canine) when the words are pronounced in isolation (Atkinson-King, 1973). The phonological tasks that face a young child can vary considerably from language to language. English and other Germanic languages, for instance, have quite complicated rules for the combination of consonants: we have many words like *risks* or *lengthy* that pose a challenge to anyone learning English. By contrast, Japanese has very few consonant clusters.

English has some sounds rarely found in other languages of the world, such as the *th* in *this;* but Czech has an even rarer sound, the medial sound /ř/ in the name *Dvořak,* which is a combination of an /r/ trilled on the tip of the tongue and the *z* in *azure,* said at the same time. Many African languages contain phonemic clicks rather similar to the sounds we make in English when we say what is written as "tsk tsk" or when we encourage a horse to go faster. In some languages tone is a phoneme: In Chinese, a rising or falling tone on a word can change its meaning entirely. When the tones are produced correctly, the sentence "Mama ma ma ma?" means "Did mother chide the horse?"

MORPHOLOGY

When a new word, such as *glitch,* or *dweeb,* comes into the English language, adult speakers can immediately tell what its plural is; they do not have to look it up in a dictionary or consult with an expert. They are able to pluralize a word that they have never heard before because they know the English inflectional morphological system. A **morpheme** is the smallest unit of meaning in a language; it cannot be broken into any smaller parts that have meaning. Words can consist of one or more morphemes. The words *cat* and *danger* each consist of one morpheme, which is called a **free morpheme** because it can stand alone. **Bound morphemes,** on the other hand, cannot stand alone and are always found attached to free morphemes; they appear affixed to free morphemes as prefixes, suffixes, or within the word as infixes: *happiness, unclear,* and *singing* contain the bound morphemes *-ness, -un,* and *-ing*. Bound morphemes can be used to change one word into another word that may be a different part of speech; for instance, *-ness* turns the adjective *happy* into the noun *happiness*. In this case, they are called **derivational morphemes** because they can be used to derive new words.

Other bound morphemes do not change the basic word's meaning so much as they modify it to indicate such things as tense, person, number, case, and gender. These variations on a basic word are inflections, and the morphemes that accomplish these changes are inflectional morphemes. Languages like Latin, Russian, and Hungarian are highly inflected. The verb *to love* (*amare*) in Latin has six separate forms in the present tense.

amo I love	*amamus* we love
amas you love (sing.)	*amatis* you love (pl.)
amat he loves	*amant* they love

Compared with Latin, English has few verb inflections in the present tense: an added *-s* for the third person (he *loves*) and no inflection for other persons (I, you, they *love*). Latin indicates the subject and object of its sentences using case inflections: *agricola amat puellam* and *puellam amat agricola* both mean "the farmer loves the girl"; the endings of the words indicate the subject and the object. English does not have case endings on its nouns: whether the girl loves the farmer or the farmer loves the girl is indicated entirely by word order. Grammar teachers, perhaps influenced by their knowledge of Latin, have tended to confuse the issue in English by referring to nouns as being in the subjective or objective case when, in fact, there are no separate noun case forms in English. Pronouns, on the other hand, have subjective, objective, and possessive forms: *I, me,* and *my.* Even with pronouns, however, word order is more important in English than it is in Latin: on hearing the sentence "Me saw it," most English speakers assume that "me" did the seeing, however ungrammatically it may be phrased.

English inflectional morphology includes the progressive of the verb (e.g., *singing*); the past, pronounced with /d/, /t/, or /əd/, (*played, hopped, landed*); and the third person singular verb and the noun plural and possessive, all of which use /z/, /s/, or /əz/ in spoken language (*dogs, cats, watches*). Whether one says, "He dogs my steps" (verb), "It's the dog's dish" (possessive), or "I have 10 dogs" (plural), the inflected form is pronounced in exactly the same way. The forms of the inflections vary depending on the last sound of the word being inflected, and, as stated earlier, there is a complex set of rules that adult speakers know that enables them to make a plural or past tense of a word that they have never heard before.

One task for the student of language development is to determine whether children have knowledge of morphology and, if so, how it is acquired and to what extent it resembles the rule system that adults follow.

SYNTAX

rules to form phrases/sentences

The syntactic system contains the rules for how to combine words into phrases and sentences, and how to transform sentences into other sentences. A competent speaker can take a basic sentence like "The cat bites the dog" and make a number of transformations of it: "The cat bit the dog," "The cat didn't bite the dog," "Did the cat bite the dog?" and "Wasn't the dog bitten by the cat?" Knowledge of the syntactic system allows the speaker to generate an almost endless number of new sentences and to recognize those that are not grammatically acceptable. If you heard a nonsense sentence like "The gorpy wug wasn't miggled by the mimsy zibber," you could not know what happened because the vocabulary is strange. On the other hand, the morphology and syntax of the sentence convey a great deal of information. A competent speaker of English could, with this information, make a number of new, perfectly grammatical and probably true sentences: "The wug is gorpy," "The zibber did not miggle the wug," and "The zibber is mimsy." If the words were presented randomly—"wug zibber mimsy by gorpy the miggled the wasn't"—the morphology would still convey some information, such as the likelihood that the action took place in the past, but in the absence of syntactic structure the sentence would truly be nonsense.

There is a great deal of controversy among researchers as to whether young children just learning language are acquiring syntactic structures, that is, grammatical rules, or whether it is more reasonable to characterize their early utterances in terms of the semantic relations they are trying to express (Bowerman, 1982). The child who says, "Doggie eat lunch," can be said to have learned to produce subject–verb–object constructions and to be following English syntactic rules specifying that the subject comes first in active sentences. (Even very young children do not say, "Lunch eat doggie.") To describe the language of young children, however, it is probably more useful to note the kinds of semantic relations the children are using. In this case the child is expressing her knowledge that an action is taking place and that there is an agent and an object.

Once children begin to produce longer sentences, however, they add the grammatical words of the language and begin to build sentences according to syntactic rules. They learn how to make *negatives*, *questions*, *compound sentences*, *passives*, and *imperatives*. Later, they add very complex structures, including embedded forms. The child who early on was limited to sentences like "Doggie eat lunch" can eventually comprehend and produce "The lunch that grandpa cooked the cleaning lady was eaten by the dog" in full confidence that the household helper was neither cooked nor eaten.

SEMANTICS

Semantic acquisition refers to the acquisition of vocabulary and the meanings associated with words. Word meanings are complicated to learn: words are related to one another in complex networks, and awareness of words comes later than does word use. A very young child may use a word that occurs in adult language, but that word does not mean exactly the same thing, nor does it have the same internal status for the child as it does for the adult (Clark, 1977). Two-year-olds who say "doggie," for instance, may call sheep, cows, cats, and horses "doggie," or they may use the word only in reference to a particular dog, without knowing that it refers to a whole class of animals. Vocabulary is structured hierarchically, and words are attached to one another in semantic networks. Dogs are a class of animals, and the adult who knows the meaning of *dog* also knows, for instance, that it belongs to a group known as domestic animals, it is a pet, it is related to wolves, it is animate, etc. Studying semantic development in children involves examining the ways in which they acquire the semantic system, beginning with simple vocabulary. Ultimately, it includes studying their metalinguistic knowledge, which enables them to notice the words in their language and comment on them. A young child does not know what a word is, but by the time children are in the primary grades, they not only notice words, they can provide definitions and tell such things as what their favorite words are.

PRAGMATICS

Linguistic competence resides in knowing how to construct grammatically acceptable sentences. Language, however, must be used in a social setting, to accomplish various ends. Speakers who know how to use language appropriately have more than linguistic competence; they have *communicative competence,* a term first used by Dell Hymes (1972). *Pragmatics* refers to the use of language to express one's intentions and get things done in the world. Even children at the one-word stage use language to accomplish various pragmatic ends; John Dore (1978), for instance, found that such children used their single words to ask, demand, and label. Adult pragmatics may include such additional functions as denying, refusing, blaming, offering condolences, flattering, and a host of others.

Communicative competence includes being able to express one's pragmatic intent appropriately in varying social situations. The importance of knowing the right forms becomes obvious when social rules are violated. Consider the use of directives. If you are seated in the aisle seat of a train, next to a stranger, and you are cold because the window is open, you can express your pragmatic intent in a syntactically correct sentence: "Shut that window." This could lead to a hostile reaction or, at the very least, to the impression that you are a very rude person. If, instead, you said, "I wonder if you would mind shutting the window?" compliance and the beginning of a pleasant conversation would probably follow. Knowing the politeness rules of language is part of communicative competence.

Research on pragmatics examines the way that children learn to use language appropriately in various social situations. Pragmatics includes important topics, such as the ability to make conversation. Pellegrini, Brody, and Stoneman (1987), for instance, studied the ways that children learn to make appropriate conversations with their parents. These researchers used a model provided by the philosopher Herbert Grice.

Grice (1975) provided a framework for the study of conversations by setting forth a number of cooperative principles or maxims that successful conversationalists must obey. These include:

1. *Quantity.* Be as informative as necessary, but not overly so. For instance, if someone asks a child what she would like to drink with dinner, she must know that it suffices to say "Orange juice, please" and that it would be inappropriate to say "Approximately eight ounces of juice squeezed from several oranges and placed in a glass here on the table at the right of my plate." Young children are, of course, likely to give too little rather than too much information.
2. *Quality.* This maxim requires that what one says be the truth. Children must learn that their interlocutors expect them not to lie.
3. *Relevance.* Contributions to the conversation are expected to be relevant. If a child responds to the question "What do you like for lunch?" by saying, "I like my kitty," she is violating the relevance principle (or exhibiting serious antisocial tendencies).
4. *Manner.* Speakers are expected to take their turns in a timely fashion and to present their words in a logical order. It is a violation of this principle, for instance, to say "We put on our pajamas and took a bath," since presumably bathing precedes putting on pajamas.

Adults, of course, violate these principles in order to achieve certain very human ends: to be ironic, for instance, or to make a joke, or perhaps to be deceptive or insulting. Every type of interaction between individuals requires observance of pragmatic conventions, and adults do not leave children's development of these rules to chance—whereas they may not correct syntactic violations except in the most superficial cases (see Chapter 5), they are active participants in their children's pragmatic socialization (Becker, 1990).

Just as there are phonological and grammatical rules, there are also rules for the use of language in social context. They are governed by such variables as the topic, the channel of communication (e.g., face-to-face, on the telephone, or over a CB radio), and the social situation—one might speak quite differently about the same topic at a funeral than at a wedding. There are also a number of speaker/hearer characteristics that affect the form of the communication; these include gender, age, rank, social class, and degree of familiarity. Mature language users have all of these variables under control. They know how to speak like men or women, to conduct discourse, to speak in appropriate ways to different people. They can talk baby talk to babies and be formal and deferential when appearing in court. All of these are part of communicative competence, which is the goal of language development.

■ THE STUDY OF LANGUAGE DEVELOPMENT

HISTORICAL TRENDS IN CHILD LANGUAGE STUDY

Probably the first recorded account of a language acquisition study is found in the work of the Greek historian Herodotus, who was a contemporary of the playwright Sophocles. Herodotus, sometimes called the father of history, lived from about 484 to 425 BC. In Book II of his *History*, he relates the story of the ancient Egyptian king Psammetichus, who wanted to prove that the Egyptians were the original human race.

In order to do this, Psammetichus ordered a shepherd to raise two children, caring for their needs but not speaking to them. "His object herein was to know, after the indistinct babblings of infancy were over, what word they would first articulate." Presumably, Psammetichus believed that the children would develop the language of the oldest group of humans all by themselves. This is perhaps the strongest version of an innatist theory of language development that one could have: babies arrive in the world with a specific language wired into their brains.

When the two children were about two years old, the shepherd went to their quarters one day. They ran up to him, with their hands outstretched, saying "Becos." Unfortunately for the Egyptians, *becos* was not a word that anyone recognized. The king, according to Herodotus, asked around the kingdom and eventually was told that *becos* meant "bread" in the Phrygian language, whereupon the Egyptians gave up their claim to being the oldest race of humans and decided that they were in *second* place, behind the Phrygians.

Even though interest in language development has ancient roots, the systematic study of children's language is new to our times, in part because the science of linguistics, with its special analytic techniques, has come of age in our own century. In earlier times, the structural nature of language was not well understood, and what studies there were tended to concentrate on the kinds of things that children said rather than on their acquisition of productive linguistic subsystems.

Studies in the Late Nineteenth and Early Twentieth Century

There were many studies of children, including notes on their language, published in Germany, France, and England during the latter half of the nineteenth century and the early years of the twentieth century. One of the main early figures in the United States in the field of developmental psychology, G. Stanley Hall, taught at Clark University in Worcester, Massachusetts. Hall (1907) was interested in "the content of children's minds," and he had been led to study children's language by the German philosopher Wilhelm Wundt. Hall, in turn, inspired a school of American students of child language (Bar-Adon & Leopold, 1971).

The kinds of questions that child language researchers asked during this period were primarily related to philosophical inquiries into human nature. (This was true of Charles Darwin (1877), who kept careful diaries on the language development of one of his sons.) Many of these early investigations included valuable insights into language. (A number of such studies are summarized in Bar-Adon and Leopold, 1971.) The early studies were almost invariably in the form of diaries, and were typically observations of the authors' own children. Notable exceptions were the studies of feral or isolated children who had failed to acquire language. Just as in antiquity, there was philosophical interest in the effects of isolation on language development; that interest has been sustained to the present day: *The Wild Boy of Aveyron,* a landmark study of a feral child, Victor, was written in the eighteenth century (Lane, 1979), and the study of Genie, an American girl who was kept isolated from other humans, was published not long ago (Curtiss, 1977; Rymer, 1992).

During the first half of the twentieth century, many psychologists still kept diary records of their children. In the educational world, children's language was studied in order to arrive at norms, delineate gender and social class differences, and pinpoint the causes and cures of developmental difficulties. Educational psychologists frequently used group tests with large numbers of children, and there was a great interest in such things as the average sentence length used by children at different grade levels, or the kinds of errors they made in grammar or pronunciation (McCarthy, 1954).

Contemporary Research

The mid-1950s saw a revolution in child language studies. Work on descriptive linguistics (Gleason, 1955) and the early transformational generative grammar of Noam Chomsky (1957) provided new models of language for researchers to explore. At the same time, a new behaviorist theory of language put forth by B. F. Skinner (1957) inspired other groups of investigators to design studies aimed at testing this learning theory.

Psycholinguistics came into being as a field when linguists and psychologists combined the techniques of their disciplines to investigate whether the systems described by the linguist had psychological reality in the minds of speakers. The linguistic description of English might, for instance, point out that the plural of words ending in /s/ or /z/ is formed by adding /əz/, for example, *kiss* and *kisses.* A task for the psycholinguist was to demonstrate that the linguistic description matched what speakers actually do, that speakers have a "rule" for the formation of the plural that is isomorphic (i.e., identical in form) with the linguist's descriptive rule. If speakers merely memorized the plural of each new word in their lexicon or vocabulary, there would be no evidence of internal rules.

In the decade of the 1960s, after the powerful, transformational model of Chomsky became widely known, there was an explosion of research into children's acquisition of syntax. The 1960s were characterized by studies of grammar; many projects studied a small number of children over a period of time, writing grammars of the children's developing language. At Harvard University, for instance, a group of researchers, many of whom were to become prominent individually, worked with Roger Brown (1973) on a project that studied the language of three children called Adam, Eve, and Sarah. These children were visited once a month in their homes by researchers who made tape recordings of their speech. The recordings were brought back to the laboratory and transcribed, and the resulting transcriptions were studied by a team of faculty and graduate students that met in a weekly seminar (DeCuevas, 1990).

As the 1960s drew to a close, the primacy of syntax in research gave way to a broadening interest that included the context in which children's language emerges and an emphasis on the kinds of semantic relations children are trying to express in their early utterances. The early 1970s saw a spate of studies on the language addressed to children; many of these were conducted to shed light on the innateness controversy—researchers wanted to know whether children had to discover the rules of language all by themselves, or whether adults provided them with help or even with language learning lessons.

Studies of the 1980s and thus far in the 1990s include all of the traditional topics: phonology, morphology, syntax, semantics, and pragmatics. There is also growing interest in cross-cultural research in language development, and in understanding how language development interfaces with other aspects of children's social and psychological development; in acquiring a language, children become members of a society, with all of its unique cultural practices and belief systems. Recent work has shown, for instance, that in a nonliterate society such as that of Gypsies in Hungary, parents' speech to children has special features that serve to preserve traditions and inculcate cultural values—for example parents tell even infants detailed stories about what their future life will be like (Réger & Gleason, 1991).

Social class and gender differences in language, stylistic variation in acquisition and use, the use of language in poetry and metaphor and in jokes and games, and the language addressed to children are examples of topics found in current journals devoted to the various branches of linguistics. Many of these topics are also explored in later chapters of this text.

RESEARCH METHODS

Equipment

Modern technology has made it possible to collect accurate data on children's everyday use of language. When developmental psycholinguistics was born in the 1950s, technology was very limited, and researchers had to rely on large reel-to-reel tape recorders and handwritten notes when they collected their data. Cassette audio recorders and palm-held video recorders have greatly simplified data collection, and computers have made analysis easier.

Studies of phonology require especially sensitive recording equipment, and must frequently use sophisticated laboratory hardware. Other studies, however, can usually be conducted with easily acquired equipment. A good cassette recorder is sufficient for most work, and if there is a great deal of data, a cassette transcriber is an invaluable aid. Some studies require a visual record as well; if, for instance, the researcher is interested in the gestural accompaniments of early language or the gaze behavior of subjects, low-light video cameras and lightweight video recording equipment are now widely available. This equipment makes it possible to film in subjects' homes with a minimum of intrusion. Video makes it possible to study the context of language acquisition. Most researchers use a back-up tape recorder in addition to their video equipment. Because the presence of equipment and observers will invariably have some effect on the behavior of subjects, it is possible in some naturalistic studies to leave a recorder with the subjects, instructing the subjects (for their parents) to turn it on at specified times.

Regardless of the method of recording, it is necessary to make a transcription of the data for analysis. This involves writing out as exactly as possible everything that is said on the tape. Transcripts can then be prepared in such a way that computer analyses are possible (see Figure 1.2).

One of the newest developments in child language research is the creation of a computerized child language data base on which researchers may draw. The Child Language Data Exchange System (CHILDES) was put into operation in 1984 at Carnegie Mellon University under the direction of Brian MacWhinney and Catherine Snow. Many powerful computer programs are available, along with data, from CHILDES (MacWhinney, 1991). The programs (CLAN, or Child Language Analysis programs) include programs that operate on any or all speakers' output and can automatically derive the mean length of utterance (see Chapter 5), a total list of all words used, as well as their frequency, and other data of immense value to the language researcher.

```
@Begin
@Participants:  CHI Charlie Child, MOT Mother, FAT Father
@Date:  7-JUL-1992
@Filename:  CHARLIE.CHA
@Situation:  Home Dinner Conversation
*CHI:   I-'m gonna eat some food.
*FAT:   you are?
*CHI:   I-'m gonna eat my spaghetti.
*CHI:   get big and strong.
*MOT:   so you-'ll be tall-er?
*FAT:   how big and strong do you want to be?
*CHI:   I-'m get-ing big-er and big-er and big-er.
*FAT:   and big-er and big-er.
*FAT:   how big are you go-ing to be?
*FAT:   uh oh.
*FAT:   do you want any sauce?
*FAT:   hm?
*CHI:   not this time.
*FAT:   you do-'nt like it this time?
*CHI:   I want some cheese.
*MOT:   is that gonna be enough for you?
*CHI:   I think so.
*MOT:   you can have more.
*CHI:   okay.
@End
```

FIGURE 1.2 Sample transcription suitable for computer analysis

By 1992, optical scanners had been used to enter data from many large studies, including Brown's famous work on Adam, Eve, and Sarah from the 1960s, thus making these data available to anyone who wants them. This system continues to collect data from researchers all over the world. Its advantages are that it allows (1) data sharing among researchers, who can test their hypotheses on many more subjects; (2) increased precision and standardization in coding; and (3) automation of many coding procedures.

Methods

Language development studies can be either ***cross-sectional*** or ***longitudinal*** in their design. Cross-sectional studies use two or more groups of subjects. If, for instance, you wanted to study the development of the negative between the ages of two and four, you could study a group of two-year-olds and a group of four-year-olds and then describe the differences in the two groups' use of negation.

Longitudinal studies follow individual subjects over time; one might study the same child's use of negatives at specified periods between the ages of two and four. Unless the researcher has ample funding, it is usually impossible to follow more than a few subjects in a longitudinal study.

Cross-sectional studies have the advantage of obtaining a great deal of data in a short time; one doesn't have to wait two years to get results. Having a sizable number of subjects also makes it more likely that the results of the study are generalizable to other children and not a reflection of the idiosyncratic behavior of a few. Longitudinal designs are used to study individuals over time when questions such as the persistence of traits or the effects of early experience are relevant. If, for instance, you wanted to know whether children who talk early also become early readers, you would have to use a longitudinal design. Longitudinal studies are expensive and time-consuming, and they depend on the willingness of subjects to be available for a period of weeks, months, or years. Their advantage is that they can provide fine and accurate data about what happens to individuals during the course of language development.

Both cross-sectional and longitudinal studies can be either *observational* or *experimental*. Observational studies involve a minimum of intrusion by the researcher. Naturalistic observational studies attempt to capture behavior as it occurs in real life; for instance, one might record and analyze family speech at the dinner table. Controlled observational studies can be carried out in various settings, including the laboratory; here the researcher provides certain constants for all subjects. Fathers might come to the laboratory with their daughters and be observed reading them a book provided by the researcher. Observational research can indicate what kinds of behaviors correlate with one another, but it cannot reveal which behavior might cause another.

Experimental studies involve some manipulation on the part of the researcher. In classic experimental designs, the researcher attempts to show that a particular manipulation causes a particular outcome. Typically, there is a *control group* of subjects that receives no special treatment, and an *experimental group* that receives the particular manipulation that the experimenter has chosen. If you wanted to see whether training makes a difference in the acquisition of the passive voice, for instance, you might take a group of 30 three-year-olds and randomly assign them to two groups, a control group and an experimental group of 15 children each. The experimental group would receive training in the passive; the control group, no special treatment. Finally, both groups could be asked to describe some pictures they had never seen before, and differential use of the passive would be recorded. If the trained group used passives and the control group did not, there would be evidence that training causes accelerated acquisition of one aspect of grammar.

In addition to clear-cut observational and experimental methods, language development researchers use a variety of research techniques. These include *standard assessment measures,* in which subjects can be compared or evaluated on the basis of their responses to published standardized language tests. These are useful for indicating whether a subject is developing at a typical rate or whether some facet of development is out of line with the others.

Imitation is a technique used by many researchers: you simply ask the child to say what you say. Imitation reveals a great deal about children's language, since they typically cannot imitate sentences that are beyond their stage of development (Slobin, 1979). This is true of adults as well—try imitating a few sentences in Bulgarian the next time you meet someone from Sofia who is willing to say them to you.

Elicitation is a technique that works well when a particular language form is the target, and you want to give your subjects all the help they need (short of the answer itself). In investigating the plural through elicitation, you might show your subjects a picture, first of one and then of two bird like creatures, and say, "This is a wug. Now there is another one. There are two of them. There are two _____?" The subject obligingly fills in "wugs." This technique works well with aphasic patients, especially severe Broca's aphasics who have very little voluntary speech.

The *interview* is an old technique, but one that can be very effective if the researcher has the time to do more than ask a list of questions and fill in a form. Researchers of the Piagetian school frequently use an interview type called the clinical method. This is an open-ended interview in which the sequence of questions depends on the answers the subject has given. In studying metalinguistic awareness, the investigator might ask a series of questions, such as "Is *horse* a word? Why? (Or why not?) What is a word? How do you know? What is your favorite word? Why?" The choice of method depends very much on the theoretical inclination of the investigator. Every method that has been mentioned here, as well as a few that have not, appears in the pages that follow.

SUMMARY

Before they are even one year old, babies are able to make fine discriminations among the speech sounds they hear, and they begin to communicate nonverbally with those around them. Young children acquire the basic components of their native language in just a few years: *phonology, morphology, semantics, syntax,* and *pragmatics*. By the time they are of school age they control all of the major grammatical and semantic features. Language development, however, proceeds throughout the life cycle; as individuals grow older, they acquire new skills at every stage of their lives, and in the declining years they are vulnerable to a specific set of language disabilities. To elucidate both the scope and the nature of language development, this book is written from a life-span perspective.

Babies begin to acquire language during their first months, long before they say their first words; language is built upon a prelinguistic communicative base. Midway through the first year, infants begin to babble, an event seen by many researchers as evidence of linguistic capacity. Near their first birthdays, infants say their first words. Early words, word meanings, and word combinations have universal characteristics, since toddlers' language is similar across cultures. Children's progress toward learning the particular grammatical structure of their own language follows a predictable order that is common to all children learning that language.

Although there are universal characteristics, there are also patterns of individual variation in language development. Different theories of language development emphasize *innate mechanisms; learning principles; cognitive prerequisites; social interaction;* and *parallel processing.*

During the school years, children perfect their knowledge of complex grammar, and they learn to use language in many different social situations. At the same time, they learn another major linguistic system: the written language. The demands of literacy remove a child's language from the here-and-now and emphasize *decontextualized language.* Not all children learn to read with ease.

Language development in adolescence is marked by a decrement in the ability to acquire a first language that has not been learned as a young child. Teenagers develop a distinct personal linguistic style, and young adults must acquire the linguistic register common to their occupations. With advancing age, numerous linguistic changes take place: there is some inevitable loss of word-finding ability, but vocabulary and narrative skill may improve.

Human language has special properties that have led many researchers to conclude that it is *species specific* and *species uniform.* Humans have a unique neurology and display unique cognitive and affective propensities. Insects may have an elaborate communication system but their conversational topics are very limited, whereas humans can talk about any part of their experience. Sea mammals employ communicative systems of whistles and grunts, and many birds have been shown to have a variety of meaningful calls. None of these systems are true language, however, which is *productive,* has *semanticity,* and offers the possibility of *displacement.*

During the past half century, many researchers have turned their attention to primates in an attempt to discover whether language is unique to humans or whether it can be learned by other species. The early studies, which tried to teach spoken language to chimpanzees, showed conclusively that primates cannot speak as humans do. More recent studies have attempted to teach American Sign Language (ASL) to chimpanzees, and have met with mixed results. The signing chimps appear to be responding at least in part to subtle cues from their trainers, but the question of the apes' potential is not completely settled. These studies have indicated that there are substantial similarities between very young children's and chimpanzees' abilities to engage in symbolic communication, and there is the possibility that the rare pygmy chimpanzee will reach new heights of linguistic achievement.

Language development requires social interaction, but language in humans is possible only because we have evolved with specialized neural mechanisms that subserve language. These include special areas in the brain, such as *Broca's area, Wernicke's area,* and the *arcuate fasciculus.* Other evidence of humans' unique biological disposition for language includes the regular onset of speech and the facts that speech is not suppressible, language cannot be taught to other species, and languages everywhere have universals.

The study of language development includes research into major linguistic subsystems: the *phonological system* is composed of the significant sounds of the language and the rules for their combination, the *morphological system* includes the minimal units that carry meaning, *syntax* refers to the rules by which sentences are constructed in a given language, and the meanings of words and the relationships between them are contained in the *semantic system.* Finally, to function in society, speakers must know the *pragmatic rules* for language use. Individuals must be able to comprehend and produce all of these systems in order to attain *communicative competence.*

Although interest in language development has ancient roots, the scientific study of this subject began in the 1950s, with the appearance of new linguistic and psychological theories of language that gave birth to the combined discipline now known as *developmental psycholinguistics.* Developmental psycholinguists use all of the research techniques, designs, and resources employed by psychologists and linguists, as well as a few that are unique, such as a new computerized data bank of child language materials.

SUGGESTED PROJECTS

1. Choose three related articles on language development from the *Journal of Child Language,* or from another journal such as *Child Development.* Write an introduction, explaining what the major questions of the research are, and then, for each article, describe the methods used by the authors, the subject population, any special equipment that was needed, and the nature of the results. In a separate discussion section, compare the results of the studies, and suggest other ways that the same question could be explored.
2. Tape record and transcribe a half-hour sample of a mother or father interacting with a one- or two-year-old child who does not yet combine words. Analyze the vocabulary used by the parent and the child, using categories similar to those listed in Table 1.1.
3. Read papers by the Premacks, Rumbaughs, and Terrace on their studies of the symbolic capacities of chimpanzees. Summarize the claims that are made for these animals, and provide a critique.

SUGGESTED READINGS

Brown, R. W. (1970). The first sentences of child and chimpanzee. In R. Brown (Ed.), *Psycholinguistics.* New York: Macmillan.

Curtiss, S. (1977). *Genie: A psycholinguistic study of a modern day "wild" child.* New York: Academic Press.

DeCuevas, J. (1990, September–October). "No, she holded them loosely." *Harvard Magazine,* 61–67.

Gardner, R. A., & Gardner, B. T. (1980). Two comparative psychologists look at language acquisition. In K. E. Nelson (Ed.), *Children's language* (Vol. 2). New York: Gardner Press.

Geschwind, N. (1982). Specializations of the human brain. In W. S.-Y. Wang (Ed.), *Human communication: Language and its psychobiological bases.* San Francisco: W. H. Freeman.

Greenfield, P. M., & Savage-Rumbaugh, E. S. (1991). Imitation, grammatical development, and the invention of protogrammar by an ape. In N. Krasnegor, D. M. Rumbaugh, M. Studdert-Kennedy, & R. L. Schiefelbusch (Eds.), *Biological and behavioral determinants of language developments.* Hillsdale, NJ: Lawrence Erlbaum.

Lane, H. (1979). *The wild boy of Aveyron.* Cambridge, MA: Harvard University Press.

Terrace, H. S. (1980). *Nim: A chimpanzee who learned sign language.* New York: Knopf.

REFERENCES

Atkinson-King, K. (1973). Children's acquisition of phonological stress contrasts. UCLA Working Papers in Phonetics (Department of Linguistics), 25.

Bar-Adon, A., & Leopold, W. (1971). *Child language: A book of readings.* Englewood Cliffs, NJ: Prentice-Hall.

Becker, J. A. (1990). Processes in the acquisition of pragmatic competence. In G. Conti-Ramsden & C. Snow (Eds.), *Children's Language* (Vol. 7). Hillsdale, NJ: Lawrence Erlbaum.

Berko, J. (1958). The child's learning of English morphology. *Word,* 14, 150–177.

Blake, J., & Boysson-Bardies, B. (1992) Patterns in babbling: a cross linguistic study. *Journal of Child Language, 19,* 51–75.

Bloom, L. (1970). *Language development: Form and function in emerging grammars.* Cambridge, MA: MIT Press.

Bowerman, M. (1982). Reorganizational processes in lexical and semantic development. In E. Wanner & L. Gleitman (Eds.), *Language acquisition: The state of the art.* Cambridge: Cambridge University Press.

Boysson-Bardies, B. de, & Vihman, M. M. (1991). Adaptation to language: Evidence from babbling and first words in four languages. *Language, 67,* 297–319.

Brown, R. W. (1970). The first sentences of child and chimpanzee. In R. Brown (Ed.), *Psycholinguistics.* New York: Macmillan.

Brown, R. W. (1973). *A first language.* Cambridge, MA: Harvard University Press.

Caplan, D., Lecours, A., & Smith, A. (Eds.). (1984). *Biological perspectives on language.* Cambridge, MA: MIT Press.

Carey, S. (1982). Semantic development: The state of the art. In E. Wanner & L. Gleitman (Eds.), *Language acquisition: The state of the art.* Cambridge: Cambridge University Press.

Clark, E. V. (1973). What's in a word? On the child's acquisition of semantics in his first language. In T. E. Moore (Ed.), *Cognitive Development and the Acquisition of Language.* New York: Academic Press.

Clark, E. V. (1977). Strategies and the mapping problem in first language acquisition. In J. MacNamara (Ed.), *Language learning and thought.* New York: Academic Press.

Chomsky, N. (1957). *Syntactic structures.* The Hague: Mouton.

Chomsky, N. (1965). *Aspects of the theory of syntax.* Cambridge, MA: MIT Press.

Curtiss, S. (1977). *Genie: A psycholinguistic study of a modern day "wild" child.* New York: Academic Press.

Darwin, C. (1877). A biographical sketch of an infant. *Mind, 2,* 285–294.

DeCuevas, J. (1990, September-October). "No, she holded them loosely." *Harvard Magazine,* 61–67.

Dore, J. (1978). Variation in preschool children's conversational performances. In K. Nelson (Ed.), *Children's language* (Vol. 1). New York: Gardner Press.

Dromi, E., & Berman, R. (1982). A morphemic measure of early language development: Data from modern Hebrew. *Journal of Child Language, 2,* 403–424.

Eimas, P. D. (1975). Auditory and phonetic coding of the cues for speech: Discrimination of the /r-l/ distinction by young infants. *Perception and Psychophysics, 18,* 341–347.

Erikson, E. (1959). Identity and the life cycle. *Psychological Issues, 1,* 1–171.

Fischer, S. (In press). The study of sign languages and linguistic theory. In C. Otero (Ed.), *Noam Chomsky: Critical assessments.* London: Routledge.

Gardner, R. A., & Gardner, B. T. (1969). Teaching sign language to a chimpanzee. *Science, 165,* 664–672.

Gardner, R. A., & Gardner, B. T. (1980). Two comparative psychologists look at language acquisition. In K. E. Nelson (Ed.), *Children's language* (Vol. 2). New York: Gardner Press.

Gardner, R. A., & Gardner, B. T. (1983). Early signs of language in children and chimpanzees. Draft of article to congratulate Benton J. Underwood on attaining his emeritus years. University of Nevada, Reno.

Gardner, R. A., & Gardner, B. T. (1984a). A vocabulary test for chimpanzees. *Journal of Comparative Psychology,* 381–404.

Gardner, R. A., & Gardner, B. T. (1984b). Signs of intelligence in cross fostered chimpanzees. *Philosophical Transactions in the Royal Society of London, B,* 1–34.

Geschwind, N. (1982). Specializations of the brain. In W. S.-Y. Wang (Ed.), *Human communication: Language and its psychobiological bases.* San Francisco: W. H. Freeman.

Gleason, H. A. (1955). *An introduction to descriptive linguistics.* New York: Henry Holt.

Gleason, J. Berko, & Goodglass, H. (1984). Some neurological and linguistic accompaniments of the fluent and nonfluent aphasias. *Topics in Language Disorders, 4,* 71–81.

Goodglass, H. (1981). The syndromes of aphasia: Similarities and differences in neurolinguistic features. *Topics in Language Disorders, 1,* 1–14.

Greenfield, P. M., & Savage-Rumbaugh, E. S. (1991). Imitation, grammatical development, and the invention of protogrammar by an ape. In N. Krasnegor, D. M. Rumbaugh, M. Studdert-Kennedy, & R. L. Schiefelbusch (Eds.), *Biological and behavioral determinants of language development.* Hillsdale, NJ: Lawrence Erlbaum.

Grice, H. P. (1975). Logic and conversation. In P. Cole & J. Morgan (Eds.), *Syntax and semantics.* (Vol. 3). New York: Academic Press.

Hall, G. S. (1907). *Aspects of child life and education.* New York: Appleton.

Hayes, C. (1951). *The ape in our house.* New York: Harper.

Herman, L. (1981). Cognitive characteristics of dolphins. In L. Herman (Ed.), *Cetacean behavior.* New York: Wiley.

Hymes, D. (1972). On communicative competence. In J. Pride & J. Holmes (Eds.), *Sociolinguistics.* Hammondsworth, G.B.: Penguin.

Jakobson, R. (1968). *Child language, aphasia, and phonological universals.* The Hague: Mouton.

Kellogg, W. N. (1980). Communication and language in the home raised chimpanzee. In T. Sebeok & J. Umiker Sebeok (Eds.), *Speaking of apes.* New York: Plenum Press.

Klima, E. S., & Bellugi, U. (1972). The signs of language in child and chimpanzee. In R. Alloway, L. Krames, & P. Pliner (Eds.), *Communication and affect: A comparative approach.* New York: Academic Press.

Klima, E. S., & Bellugi, U. (1979). *The signs of language.* Cambridge, MA: Harvard University Press.

Kuhl, P. K., Williams, K. A., Lacerda, F., Stevens, K. N., & Lindblom, B. (1992). Linguistic experience alters phonetic perception in infants by 6 months of age. *Science, 255,* 606–608.

Lane, H. (1979). *The wild boy of Aveyron.* Cambridge, MA: Harvard University Press.

Lenneberg, E. (1967). *The biological foundations of language.* New York: Wiley.

Lieven, E. (1978). Conversations between mothers and young children: Individual differences and their possible implications for the study of language learning. In N. Waterson & C. E. Snow (Eds.), *The development of communication.* New York: Wiley.

Linden, E. (1974). *Apes, men, and language.* New York: Pelican.

Locke, J. (1990). Structure and stimulation in the ontogeny of spoken language. *Developmental Psychobiology, 23*(7), 621–644.

Lorenz, K. (1971). *Studies in animal behavior.* Cambridge, MA: Harvard University Press.

MacWhinney, B. (1991). *The CHILDES Project: Computational Tools for Analyzing Talk.* Hillsdale, NJ: Laurence Erlbaum.

Maple, T. L., & Cone, S. G. (1981). Aged apes at the Yerkes Regional Primate Research Center. *Laboratory Primate Newsletter, 20,* 10–12.

Marler, P. (1990). Innate learning preferences: Signals for communication. *Developmental Psychobiology, 23*(7), 557–569.

McCarthy, D. (1954). Language development in children. In P. Mussen (Ed.), *Carmichael's manual of child psychology.* New York: Wiley.

Miles, H. L. (1983). Apes and language: The search for communicative competence. In J. deLuce & H. T. Wilder (Eds.), *Language in primates: Perspectives and implications.* New York: Springer-Verlag.

Nelson, K., & Lucariello, J. (1985). The development of meaning in first words. In M. Barrett (Ed.), *Children's single word speech.* Chichester, England: Wiley.

Papandropoulou, I., & Sinclair, H. (1974). What is a word? *Human Development, 17,* 241–258.

Patterson, F. (1978, October). Conversations with a gorilla. *National Geographic,* 438–465.

Pellegrini, A. D., Brody, G. H., & Stoneman, Z. (1987). Children's conversational competence with their parents. *Discourse Processes, 10,* 93–106.

Pepperberg, I. (1991, Spring). Referential communication with an African grey parrot. *Harvard Graduate Society Newsletter,* 1–4.

Premack, A. J. (1976). *Why chimps can read.* New York: Harper and Row.

Réger, Z., & Gleason, J. Berko. (1991). Romāni child-directed speech and children's language among Gypsies in Hungary. *Language in Society, 20,* 601–617.

Rumbaugh, D. M. (1977). *Language learning by a chimpanzee: The Lana project.* New York: Academic Press.

Rymer, R. (1992, April 13). Annals of science: A silent childhood—I. *The New Yorker,* 41–81.

Savage-Rumbaugh, E. S. (In press). Language learnability in man, ape, and dolphin. In E. Roitblat (Ed.), *Comparative cognition.* Hillsdale, NJ: Lawrence Erlbaum.

Savage-Rumbaugh, E. S. (1990). Language acquisition in a nonhuman species: Implications for the innateness debate. *Developmental Psychobiology, 23*(7), 599–620.

Skinner, B. F. (1957). *Verbal behavior.* Englewood, NJ: Prentice-Hall.

Slobin, D. (1979). *Psycholinguistics* (2nd ed.). Glenview, IL: Scott, Foresman.

Snow, C. E. (1977). The development of conversation between mothers and babies. *Journal of Child Language, 4,* 1–22.

Snow, C. E. (1983). Literacy and language: Relationships during the preschool years. *Harvard Educational Review, 55,* 165–189.

Snow, C. E. (1990). The development of definitional skill. *Journal of Child Language, 17,* 697–710.

Snow, C. E., Perlmann, R. Y., Gleason, J. Berko, & Hooshyar, N. (1990). Developmental perspectives on politeness: Sources of children's knowledge. *Journal of Pragmatics, 14,* 289–305.

Stoel-Gammon, C., & Cooper, J. (1984). Patterns of early lexical and phonological development. *Journal of Child Language, 2,* 247–271.

Terrace, H. S. (1980). *Nim: A chimpanzee who learned sign language.* New York: Knopf.

Trehub, S. E. (1976). The discrimination of foreign speech contrasts by infants and children. *Child Development, 47,* 466–472.

Van Cantfort, T. E., & Rimpau, J. G. (1982). Sign language studies with children and chimpanzees. *Sign Language Studies, 34,* 15–72.

Vittorini, L. (1991). Untitled report. *The Fund for Animals, 24,* 1. New York: Publication of The Fund for Animals.

Von Frisch, K. (1950). *Bees, their vision, chemical senses, and language.* Ithaca, NY: Cornell University Press.

The Emergence of Intentional Communication

2

Jacqueline Sachs *University of Connecticut*

■ INTRODUCTION

This chapter discusses communication development in the period before the child begins to use words. Although this stage is **preverbal,** we will see that the infant is responsive to language, vocalizes in a variety of ways, and, usually toward the end of the first year, discovers the possibility of communication through vocalizations and gestures. Not too many years ago most descriptions of child language, while probably containing some information about babbling, would have really started at the point that the child said the first word. (That is, after all, the big event that gets noted in the baby book!) We know now that there are many aspects of communication in the first year of life that establish the foundation for later stages in the acquisition of language.

We have seen in the first chapter that there is a biological basis for language. At birth, the infant's brain and sensory systems are prepared for the task of acquiring a language. The infant can hear even before birth. Sounds generated outside the mother's abdomen are experienced inside the amniotic sac (Querleu & Renard, 1981), and infants are affected by what they have heard before birth. They have heard their mothers' voices best, and at birth already prefer their mothers' voices over those of strangers (DeCasper & Fifer, 1980). DeCasper and Spence (1986) also showed that newborn infants preferred the acoustic properties of a speech passage that their mothers had recited while pregnant to a passage they had not heard before, and Mehler et al. (1988) found that four-day-old infants who had been exposed to French could distinguish utterances in their native language from those of another language (perhaps on the basis of prosodic characteristics).

Many of the sounds that are used in speech (including those in languages to which the infant has not been exposed) are well discriminated by the young infant (Aslin, Pisoni, & Jusczyk, 1983; Eimas, Miller, & Jusczyk, 1987; Eimas, Siqueland, Jusczyk, & Vigorito, 1971). Whether these discrimination abilities reflect special mechanisms for the processing of speech (Eimas, 1974) or are a characteristic of the mammalian auditory system (Kuhl, 1987) is as yet not completely resolved. However, even during the first year of life the infant's speech perception abilities are being shaped by the language she is hearing, so that the ability to discriminate sounds that are not used in the infant's language gradually disappear (Burnham, Earnshaw, & Clark, 1991; Werker & Tees, 1984). Although the infant will not show signs of beginning to comprehend the meaning of language until late in the first year, by that time she will normally have had a great deal of experience listening to speech. Table 2.1 shows the typical pattern of responses to sounds and speech in the first year of life.

At birth, the infant cries, producing the first of many signals that inform the caregiver about his needs. In the first year of life, the types of vocalizations that the infant can produce change dramatically. Table 2.2 shows the typical order of emergence of various types of vocalizations in the first year, with approximate ages. (There is considerable variability in the timing of the stages, and also overlap among them. For example, many infants continue to babble after they have begun to speak.) Chapter 3 will provide more detail on sound production during this period as it relates to the development of the ability to produce speech sounds.

TABLE 2.1 Examples of the Typical Order of Emergence of Responses to Sounds and Speech in the First Year, with Approximate Ages

Newborn	Is startled by a loud noise Turns head to look in the direction of sound Is calmed by the sound of a voice Prefers mother's voice to a stranger's Discriminates many of the sounds used in speech
1–2 mos.	Smiles when spoken to
3–7 mos.	Responds differently to different intonations (e.g., friendly, angry)
8–12 mos.	Responds to name Responds to "no" Recognizes phrases from games (e.g., "Peekaboo," "How big is baby?") Recognizes words from routines (e.g., waves to "bye-bye") Recognizes some words

TABLE 2.2 Examples of the Typical Order of Emergence of Types of Nonword Vocalizations in the First Year, with Approximate Ages

Newborn	Cries
1–3 mos.	Makes cooing sounds to speech ("oo," "goo") Laughs Cries in different ways when hungry, angry, or hurt Makes more speechlike sounds in response to speech
4–6 mos.	Plays with some sounds, usually single syllables (e.g., "ba," "ga")
6–8 mos.	Babbles with duplicated sounds (e.g., "bababa") Attempts to imitate some sounds
8–12 mos.	Babbles with consonant or vowel changes (e.g., "badaga," "babu") Babbles with sentencelike intonation (expressive jargon/conversational babble) Produces protowords

In terms of our focus in this chapter, the sounds made by infants can be viewed in terms of their role in the relationship between the infant and the caregiver. With that first cry begins an amazingly complex interactive process, the success of which depends both on the ability of the infant to signal messages clearly, and the ability of the caregiver to interpret those signals. While cries will alert the caregiver to the infant's physical needs, other vocalizations such as cooing, laughing, and babbling are a sign of the infant's inherent interest in social contact.

In recent years, there has been great interest in the caregiver–infant dyad. (We will use the term *caregiver* because, even though many studies have looked at mothers and their infants, other communicative partners, including older children, also play a role in the infant's development.) The infant seems helpless, and indeed is completely dependent on its caregivers. However, human infants have biologically given attributes

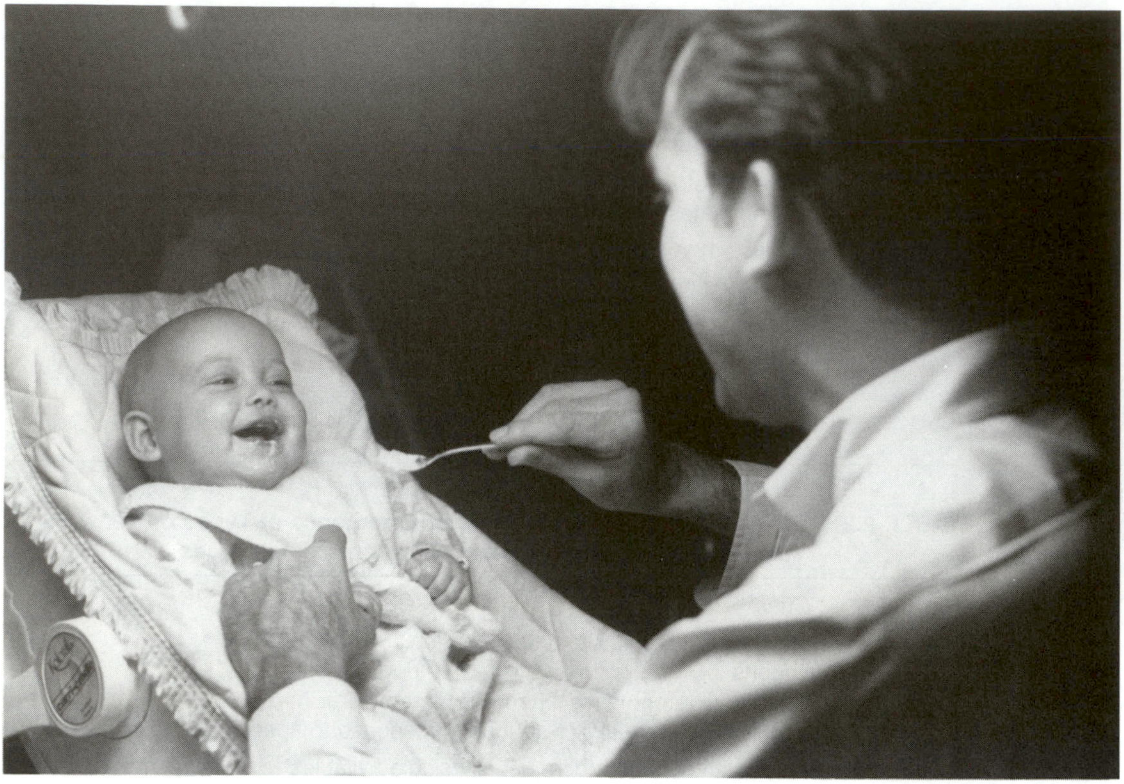

Gaze coupling in infancy is an important part of early communication development.

and behaviors that draw caregivers to them. They are not simply passive recipients of stimulation, but instead are active interactional partners who are equipped to obtain the experiences that they need to develop. How the infant acts affects the subsequent behavior of the caregiver (Lewis & Rosenblum, 1974; Worobey, 1989), as has been shown in studies of various aspects of communication, such as eye contact. For example, it has been found that eye contact is very important to caregivers in establishing an affective bond with the infant. Selma Fraiberg (1974) discovered that parents of congenitally blind children often had difficulty in relating to their infants for this reason. One of the first indications of abnormality noticed by parents of autistic infants is that the children avert their eyes (Stern, 1971). In contrast, the normally interacting dyad engages in "gaze coupling" that very much resembles conversational turn-taking (Jaffe, Stern, & Perry, 1973).

In vocal interaction, too, the caregiver is affected by the child's behavior. For example, in the course of carrying out research on young babies' vocalizations, Kathleen Bloom (1990) noticed that occasionally students and staff members who overheard the tapes made remarks like "That baby is really talking up a storm!" (p. 131). Thinking that perhaps the adults were responding to certain sorts of infant vocalizations, Bloom and Lo (1990) had adults rate videotapes of three-month-old babies who were making sounds that were more speechlike or less speechlike. The adults preferred the babies who produced sounds that were more like speech, rating them "cuddlier," "more fun," and generally more likable.

The crying, cooing, and babbling of a young infant are already communicative in the sense that the infant is a member of a social species and the signals are salient to caregivers. However, in the latter part of the first year of life, the normally developing infant makes an important discovery that provides a transition to language—that one can intentionally make a signal (a vocalization or a gesture) and expect that it will have a specific effect on the caregiver. Thus signals begin to have meanings arising out of the shared experiences of the child and the caregiver. In the next section, we will look in more detail at what typically occurs in the emergence of **intentional communication.** After that, we will look at some aspects of the social context of the emergence of these behaviors. Although we have divided what the infant does and what caregivers do into two sections for organizational purposes, keep in mind that the behaviors of the infants and caregivers mutually affect one another.

■ THE EXPRESSION OF COMMUNICATIVE INTENT BEFORE SPEECH

CHARACTERISTICS OF INTENTIONAL COMMUNICATION

Before about nine months of age, a child's behavior can be interpreted by adults, but there is little indication that the child deliberately behaves in a way that will obtain the adult's attention and help (Bates, Camaioni, & Volterra, 1975). There is not a distinct boundary between behavior without communicative intent and intentional communication, but rather the child moves gradually toward an understanding of goals and the potential role of others in achieving them (Harding, 1983a, 1983b).

Deciding whether any one instance of behavior is intentionally communicative or not is very difficult. Think, for example, of the behavior of a pet whose signals you interpret as meaning that the animal wants to be fed, let out, or petted. There has been much debate about the characteristics of intentional communication and the issue of whether the infant's behavior in the preverbal period is qualitatively different from that of other animals. Some researchers have suggested that, instead of using only one criterion for deciding whether a particular behavior is intentionally communicative, we use a set of criteria, applying them to the infant's entire behavior repertoire, to judge whether an infant is communicating with intentionality (Bakeman & Adamson, 1984; Bates, 1979; Bruner, 1973; Harding & Golinkoff, 1979; Scoville, 1983; Sugarman, 1984). The following are among the criteria that are often applied:

1. The child makes eye contact with the partner while gesturing or vocalizing, often alternating his gaze between an object and the partner.
2. The child's gestures and vocalizations become more consistent and ritualized. For example, a child named Annie used a gesture of opening and closing her hand rather than attempting to reach the object herself. The vocalization she used, "Eh eh," was one that she consistently used in situations in which she wanted something. Another child would probably have used a different

sound in the same situation, because this sound is not copied from adult speech but rather is a communicative signal invented by the child.

3. The child may gesture or vocalize and wait for a response from the partner.
4. The child persists in attempting to communicate if he is not understood and sometimes even modifies his behavior to communicate more clearly.

THE FUNCTIONS OF EARLY COMMUNICATIVE BEHAVIORS

Analyses of the functions of early communication stem from detailed observations of children's behaviors in various situations. For example, Michael Halliday (1975) studied his son Nigel's progress in attempting to communicate between 9 and 16 months, and found that several consistent nonword vocalizations seemed to convey meanings. Elizabeth Bates and her colleagues (Bates, 1979; Bates, Camaioni, & Volterra, 1975) reported on the gestures as well as preverbal vocalizations of the children they studied.

A number of different terms and systems of classification for early **communicative functions** have been proposed (e.g., Bruner, 1981; Chapman, 1981; Dore, 1974; Seibert & Hogan, 1982; Sugarman, 1984). Most systems distinguish at least among rejections, requests, and comments, often with further subcategories, as shown in Figure 2.1. The categories and examples of typical behavior cited in Figure 2.1 are:

1. *Rejection*. Consistent gestures or vocalizations are used to terminate an interaction. For example, the child pushes away an offered object and vocalizes, or uses a gesture or vocalization to end an action. (You may also see rejections referred to by some authors as one form of **behavioral regulation;** that is, communication that serves to get the listener to do something or stop doing something.)
2. *Request*. Consistent gestures or vocalizations are used to get the partner to do something or to help the child achieve a goal. (Requests are also viewed as a form of behavioral regulation.)
   a. *Request for social interaction*. Behaviors are used to attract and maintain the partner's attention. For example, a child might use a vocalization as a greeting.

Rejection
Request
  Request for social interaction
  Request for an object
  Request for action
Comment

FIGURE 2.1 Kinds of communicative functions that appear in the latter part of the first year of life

b. *Request for an object.* For example, an abbreviated reaching gesture might be used to indicate desire for an object. In our earlier example, Annie obtained something she could not get herself by her vocalization and gesture. Later, this communicative function might be carried out by a word or phrase.

c. *Request for action.* Consistent gestures or vocalizations are used to initiate an action by the listener. For example, the infant might lift her arms and use a vocalization when she wants to be picked up.

3. *Comment.* A consistent gesture or vocalization can be used to direct the partner's attention for the purpose of jointly noticing an object or event. For example, the infant might "show" an object to the caregiver by holding it out and vocalizing, or the infant might give an object to the caregiver. Pointing might be used not for the purpose of obtaining an object, but for directing the partner's attention to an object. (This function is also referred to as **joint attention.**)

All of these communicative functions are expressed by normally developing infants before they begin to use words (Wetherby, Cain, Yonclas, & Walker, 1988). When children begin to talk at around 12 months of age, their words emerge within a rich framework of communicative functions that have been established toward the end of their first year of life.

THE FORMS OF EARLY COMMUNICATIVE BEHAVIORS

As an example of a communicative gesture, consider pointing. Pointing is unlike reaching for something—the index finger is extended while the other fingers are curled. The appropriate response to a point is to look in the direction indicated by the finger, not at the end of the finger itself. (When you have a chance, observe the response of a dog or cat to pointing.) Infants begin responding appropriately to points by others and pointing at objects or pictures themselves around 10 months of age (Murphy, 1978; Zinober & Martlew, 1985). By 12 months, many infants point at an object and then shift their gaze to make eye contact with the listener (Bates, 1979; Masur, 1983).

The vocalizations used by children shortly before they begin learning conventional words have received much attention, because they form an interesting link between preverbal communication and speech. Intonation patterns can be used communicatively. For example, in the Halliday (1975) study mentioned above, his child used prelinguistic vocalizations with rising intonation contours for requests and falling contours for comments. Similar patterns have also been found in other children (Flax, Lahey, Harris, & Boothroyd, 1991; Menn, 1976).

Anne Carter (1979) studied a child named David over several months as he began to communicate intentionally, and noted that his preverbal vocalizations were initially quite variable in their pronunciation but were always linked with particular gestures. For example, several sounds similar to "ba" accompanied by waving hands seemed to signal that he did not want something, whereas sounds incorporating "mmm" accompanied by reaching meant that he did want it. Over time, the vocalizations became more phonet-

"Ba!" Protowords are the infant's unique but consistent vocalizations.

ically stable and less tied to a particular action. Other investigators have also noticed that vocalizations and gestures are originally linked together, but become more independent over time (e.g., Greenfield & Smith, 1976).

Preverbal vocalizations that contain consistent sound patterns and are used in consistent situations, but are unique to the child rather than based on the adult language, are referred to as **protowords.** For example, an infant might start using the vocalization "lala" when he is rubbing his blanket against his cheek, and then use "lala" when he wants his blanket. Walburga von Raffler Engel (1973) noticed that her son used the sound "eee" when he wanted an object, but used "uuu" for disapproval. Other investigators studying children about 11 months of age have also found many vowel sounds consistently used with certain affects (Dore, Franklin, Miller, & Ramer, 1976). These investigators used the term **phonetically consistent form (PCF)** for protowords (another term found for the same type of utterance is **vocable**) (Ferguson, 1978; Werner & Kaplan, 1963).

How strong is the evidence that protowords are really inventions of the infant rather than sounds copied (perhaps from some chance association) from caregivers' speech? One body of research that supports this view involves detailed observations of communicative behaviors in young, profoundly deaf children. Most deaf children are born of hearing parents, and some hearing parents choose not to expose their deaf child to sign language in order to motivate the child to learn speech (following an oral approach to education of the deaf), while providing the child with a supportive social environment. Susan Goldin-Meadow and her colleagues (e.g., Goldin-Meadow, 1979; Goldin-Meadow & Morford, 1985) have found that these children develop spontaneous gestures that are not based on gestures used by the parents. Such early gestures, invented by the child, would be analogous to protowords invented by hearing children (though in the case of protowords, these idiosyncratic forms soon drop out when the child learns the conventional word to signal the meaning, whereas the deaf child's spontaneous gestures may develop into a richer communication system).

THE ASSESSMENT OF COMMUNICATIVE INTENT

In order to assess whether a child is communicating intentionally, a method called **low structured observation** is sometimes used (Coggins, Olswang, & Guthrie, 1987). The caregiver plays with the child in a natural way, and a trained observer scores the child's behavior during the session or from a videotape. For example, the observer would look for instances of commenting, as indicated by the child's pointing, showing, or giving objects (sometimes accompanied by consistent vocalizations).

One can structure the situation somewhat to increase the likelihood of observing requests by providing some items for play that are designed to serve as **communicative temptation tasks**—tasks that entice the child to produce requests (Casby & Cumpata, 1986; Dale, 1980; Snyder, 1984; Sugarman, 1978). For example, the child might be presented with an attractive toy inside a tightly covered plastic container. An infant who is not yet communicating intentionally might bang the container and fuss or cry in frustration, while another preverbal infant might hand the container to an adult, make eye contact, point to the toy and/or vocalize, and persist in such behaviors that seem to be directed toward the adult. (Another type of toy good for eliciting requests is a mechanical toy that has to be wound up by the adult.)

One can see how the child expresses rejection by having some less desirable toys along. If such a toy is given to the child while more desirable toys are in view, the child may potentially produce rejection gestures and/or vocalizations (Olswang, Bain, Dunn, & Cooper, 1983).

COGNITIVE DEVELOPMENT AND THE EMERGENCE OF INTENTIONAL COMMUNICATION

In the course of the first year of life, the infant's ability to form and use mental representations appears to change, as indicated by behavior in the face of various sorts of natural or experimental problem-solving situations. For instance, a young infant might reach out to grasp an attractive toy, but when the toy is moved out of her view, she stops reaching and appears not to remember her interest in the toy. Such behavior has been taken as an indication that the infant did not hold a mental image of the toy in mind that would provide the basis for a continued effort to obtain the toy.

The child's developing ability to solve various types of problems was studied in great detail by the French psychologist Jean Piaget (e.g., Piaget, 1952). Piaget theorized that the infant is innately endowed with both certain reflexes and basic processes for learning from its interaction with objects in the environment, so that knowledge is constructed through a series of predictable stages in cognitive development. His descriptions of these stages in development have been very influential, and form the basis for much research about the relation between nonlinguistic thinking and language, as well as the basis for some clinical assessment of infants and children.

In the Piagetian framework, from birth until about 18 to 24 months the infant is in the **sensorimotor stage,** and is beginning the process of learning how to think. The infant can experience objects through his senses and his actions with the objects, but does not yet have functional mental representations of them. However, there are changes in the infant's cognition within this period, two of which involve an understanding of the concept of object permanence and seeing the relation between activities and results of those activities (means-ends relations).

The concept of **object permanence** refers to the understanding that things exist even when we are not currently experiencing them. As in the example given above, if we see an object and then it is hidden from us, we continue to know that the object exists; we have a mental representation of it. However, for an infant in Stage 3 of the sensorimotor stage (at four to eight months), if an object is taken from view, the infant does not look for it. (The ages given are averages—some infants are faster or slower in cognitive development, but they will still pass through the same stages.) A Stage 4 infant (8 to 12 months) will look for an object if it disappears behind a screen, showing that the notion of object permanence is emerging. However, at this stage development is not complete. For example, if an object has been frequently hidden in one location, the infant will look there even after he sees it being hidden somewhere else.

The concept of **means-ends** refers to the understanding that problems can be solved mentally, so that a goal can be attained by methods other than trial-and-error. At Stage 3, the infant may learn to make something happen again by repeating an activity that has led to the event, but does not seem to have a real sense of what could obtain the desired effect. During Stage 4, the infant begins to see the relation between actions and outcomes. For example, she may pull on a cloth to bring an object into reach. This is an example of primitive tool-using. At a later point the infant will experiment with actions to see what the result will be, and begin to be able to think ahead about what the result of an action might be. Also during this period, the infant will begin to anticipate what typically happens. For example, Piaget reported that at nine months his daughter would cry when someone stood up, because she had noticed that standing up was followed by leaving.

It has been found that the emergence of the ability to express communicative intent corresponds, at least temporally, with Stage 4 cognitive changes in the child such as those described above. For example, children do not begin to communicate intentionally until the time when they show, from other behaviors, that they understand something about means-ends relations. The child learns that it is possible to bring about changes through various means, and one of these means is to use another person to carry out one's goal. Thus the child is motivated to communicate to another person, rather than simply to attempt to achieve the goal himself (Bates, 1976; Harding & Golinkoff, 1979; Sugarman, 1978). [The interested reader should see Anisfeld (1984) for an extensive discussion of the relation between cognitive development and early language development.]

Although certain behaviors indicative of cognitive developments typically appear at the same time that certain language milestones do, we do not yet have convincing evidence that the cognitive changes are prerequisites for stages in language acquisition. There are at least two reasons to be cautious about conclusions regarding the relation between cognitive development and the emergence of specific aspects of language. One is that recent work in the field of cognitive development has shown that some abilities thought to develop at a certain time may be present much earlier. Jean Mandler (1990) states that "a good deal of evidence suggests that we have tended to confuse infants' motor incompetence with conceptual incompetence" (p. 240). For example, a series of studies on object permanence have involved a measure of infants' surprise rather than searching behavior (Baillargeon, De Vos, & Graber, 1989; Baillargeon, Spelke, & Wasserman, 1985). If four- and five-month-old infants see an object being hidden behind a screen, they are surprised when the screen appears to move backward through the object. In the Piagetian framework, they should, at this age, have no memory of the object that has disappeared from sight.

The second reason for caution about assuming too firm a link between stages in cognitive development and the emergence of intentional communication is that deaf children who are learning sign language begin to use conventional signs (analogous to words in a spoken language) at about six months of age (Bonvillian, Orlansky, & Novack, 1983; Prinz & Prinz, 1979), a full half-year before conventional spoken words appear. Future research on deaf children acquiring sign language should help to shed light on what nonlinguistic abilities are actually needed for the emergence of language.

■ THE SOCIAL CONTEXT OF THE PREVERBAL INFANT

Here we will look at some aspects of early communicative interaction between caregivers and preverbal infants. We will see that caregivers speak to infants in special ways, that they establish contexts for babies to take their turn at talk, and behave in other ways that may be supportive of the infant's attempts to communicate. We will not be able to describe all of the ways in which adults and infants communicate, but will concentrate on those aspects of communication that seem most closely related to later language development.

In describing the social context in which communication emerges, we are not arguing that social interaction causes the child to begin to communicate, or that adults teach their infants to communicate. Think, for example, of trying to be supportive of communicative development with your cat or dog. Clearly, one can not teach a cat or a dog to react like a baby! The infant has the **biological capacity** for certain sorts of behaviors and abilities to develop. However, that biological capacity will not be realized without certain kinds of environmental supports. An important goal of research concerning the social context of communicative development is to find out what kinds of experiences are sufficient to allow development, and how variations in experiences ultimately affect the communicative abilities of the child (by *communicative abilities* we mean all aspects of language, including pragmatics).

THE SOUND OF THE CAREGIVER'S SPEECH: "LISTEN TO ME!"

Speech addressed to babies is typically quite unlike the speech used to adults. We even have a name for it—**baby talk.** This term may initially merely bring to mind adult imitations of childlike speech ("Is ooo my tweetie-pie?") and special vocabulary words like *choo-choo* and *pottie,* along with strong denials that *you* would ever "use baby talk." However, as we will see here and in later chapters, there are actually many very interesting aspects of speech and language that are modified when we talk to infants and young children, and we make most of these modifications without even being aware of them. The primary difference between talk to babies and other speech is that "the **prosodic features** or 'music' appears to be more important than the words or 'lyrics' " (Stern & Wasserman, 1979, p. 3). Special intonation patterns with higher pitch, more variable pitch, and exaggerated stress have been found in baby talk in a variety of languages, including American English (e.g., Fernald & Simon, 1984; Garnica, 1977; Remick, 1976; Stern, Spieker, Barnett, & MacKain, 1983), Arabic (Ferguson, 1964), Marathi (Kelkar, 1964), Latvian (Ruke-Dravina, 1977), Mandarin Chinese (Grieser & Kuhl, 1988), and Japanese (Fernald et al., 1989).

Fathers as well as mothers use these special speech patterns (e.g., Papousek, Papousek, & Haekel, 1987), and so do men and women who are inexperienced with infants (Jacobson, Boersma, Fields, & Olson, 1983). Is there then one universal style of baby talk? No, because there are some differences in baby talk characteristics across cultures. Higher pitch and exaggerated intonation to infants was not found to be characteristic of rural African-American families in North Carolina (Heath, 1983), Kaluli families in New Guinea (Schieffelin, 1979), and Quiche-Mayan families in Guatemala (Bernstein Ratner & Pye, 1984). Perhaps there are some general tendencies, such as using higher pitch, but these tendencies can be affected by other aspects of the way language is used in a particular culture. For example, Quiche-Mayan speakers use higher pitch as a sign of respect, and thus might find higher pitch socially inappropriate for use with a baby.

Next we will look in a little more detail at some of the possible reasons for the baby talk characteristics that have been found in many cultures. (Keep in mind, though, that more research on diverse cultures and languages will be needed before we have a complete explanation.) Since certain prosodic features in speech to babies are common across many languages, it may be that these characteristics are used because they are especially appropriate. We can find out about babies' perceptual abilities and preferences by devising experiments in which they can "tell" us what they want to listen to. Infants cannot talk or press buttons, but they can turn their heads and control their eye movements, so a researcher might set up a situation in which a message plays only when the baby's head turns in a certain direction or when the eyes are fixated on a pattern, and measure the amount of time the baby thereby chooses to listen to one message or another. (A very important application of such techniques is for the testing of hearing in young infants.) A number of studies have shown that babies prefer baby talk intonation patterns (Fernald, 1985; Fernald & Kuhl, 1987; Sullivan & Horowitz, 1983; Werker & McLeod, 1989), even when only two days old (Cooper & Aslin, 1990). This neonatal preference suggests that baby talk intonation characteristics may mesh with some natural perceptual preference, but studies of babies' preferences in cultures in which these characteristics are not used would be valuable.

If babies are naturally responsive to speech that has certain features, such as the use of extremes of high and low pitch, adults may use these characteristics because they discover or know intuitively that infants pay more attention to them when they do. We will discuss two possible results of increasing the infant's attention to caregiver speech:

1. *Affective development.* By holding the infant's attention, the adult may help to cement the emotional bond between caregiver and child (Sachs, 1977). The attentive infant becomes quiet, faces the speaker, establishes eye contact, and responds to the adult. Of course, baby talk is not the only way a caregiver can attract and hold an infant's attention; for example, a signing deaf parent with a deaf or hearing child forms an emotional bond, as do parents and infants in cultures in which baby talk prosodic features are not used. What we do suggest is that an infant requires loving interaction of some sort for optimal development [for example, Cicchetti (1989) has reported significant language delays in maltreated toddlers] and that the speech of the caregiver is typically one source of that affectionate stimulation. [For more discussion of the relation between affective development and communicative development, see Prizant & Wetherby (1990).]
2. *Linguistic development.* A second possible result of the infant's increased attention to the speech of the adult is that the infant may begin to process and comprehend some aspects of speech considerably before the emergence of the first word. Anne Fernald (1989) has suggested that the exaggerated prosodic patterns of baby talk may help the infant become aware of the general communicative intent of a message, such as praising, getting attention, prohibiting, playing or comforting, before individual linguistic elements are understood. Also, higher pitch and exaggerated stress tend to be used together on important parts of an utterance, such as the label for an object (Fernald & Mazzie, 1991), perhaps ensuring the infant's attention to those words.

The prosody of baby talk may also make it easier for infants to begin to segment larger units of speech. In one study, when preverbal seven- to nine-month-old babies heard samples of baby talk, they preferred to listen to messages in which the timing matched the natural clause structure of English rather than samples with altered clause structure. When the researchers played adult-directed speech to the babies, the babies did not discriminate between samples with natural and altered clause structure (Kemler-Nelson, Hirsh-Pasek, Jusczyk, & Wright-Cassidy, 1989).

Keep in mind that most studies have thus far been carried out in America with babies of urban, middle-class families. Since babies everywhere learn to speak, one must be cautious about concluding that some particular feature of baby talk is necessary (or even very useful) for babies. We do not know enough yet to tell caregivers how they *should* talk to babies. Research on language learning environments in a wide variety of cultures is needed (Blount, 1990), as is research to discover whether there are causal links between certain features of the linguistic environment and language learning.

THE CONVERSATIONAL NATURE OF THE CAREGIVER'S SPEECH: "TALK TO ME!"

Another characteristic of caregiver talk to infants is that it creates a two-way interpersonal engagement. Based on her observations of mothers interacting with babies in England, Catherine Snow (1977) argued that the mothers' primary goal in talking with their infants seemed to be to have a "conversation" with them. Even at an early stage when the adult knows that the infant does not yet understand language, the adult behaves as if the child's response is a turn in the conversation. First, here is a little "conversation" between a mother and her three-month-old daughter, Ann (p. 12).

Mother	**Ann**
	(smiles)
Oh what a nice little smile!	
Yes, isn't that nice?	
There.	
There's a nice little smile.	(burps)
What a nice wind as well!	
Yes, that's better, isn't it?	
Yes.	
Yes.	
Yes!	(vocalizes)
There's a nice noise.	

In this example, the mother spoke in short, simple utterances, although of course the three-month-old could not understand the content of the speech. The mother responded to whatever her infant did, commenting on the various nonverbal and vocal behaviors that occurred and incorporating them into the conversation. It is as if she allowed the infant's behaviors to stand for a turn in the interaction and treated the behavior as if it were intentional communication on the part of the infant.

Snow also noticed that the mothers devoted many of their utterances to attempting to elicit some kind of behavior from the infant, such as coos and smiles. In contrast to adult–adult conversations, where we often must try very hard to get our own turn, each mother seemed intent on giving her child a turn in the conversation. Many of the mothers' utterances were followed by pauses, providing the opportunity for responses from the infant, as in this example (Snow, 1977, p. 13):

> Oh you are a funny little one, aren't you, hmm? Aren't you a funny little one? Hmm?

Although at three months the mother accepted almost any behavior on the part of the child as if it were an attempt to communicate, as the infants grew older, the mothers changed in what they accepted as a turn in the conversation. By seven months, when the babies had begun to be more active partners in the interactions, the mothers responded only to higher-quality vocalizations, such as a babbled sound, and not to sounds such as burps. Here is an example from a mutual babbling game, in which Ann's mother attempts to get her to imitate her vocalizations (Snow, 1977, p. 16).

Mother	**Ann**
Ghhhh ghhhh ghhhh ghhhh	
Grrrr grrrr grrrr grrrr	(protest cry)
Oh you don't feel like it, do you?	aaaa aaaa aaaa
No I wasn't making that noise.	
I wasn't going *aaaa aaaa.*	aaaa aaaa
Yes, that's right.	

In this episode, the mother continued to make an attempt to structure the conversation so that Ann could take her turn, even though she was more demanding about what constituted a turn.

At 12 months the mothers' criteria for a turn had changed again, and they now attempted to interpret their children's vocalizations as words (Snow, 1977, p. 17).

Mother	**Ann**
	abaabaa
Baba. Yes that's you, what you are.	

Having seen that adults interact conversationally in certain ways with infants in the first year of life, we now consider the effect of this interaction.

The adult's linguistic behavior has an effect on the infant's behavior in the immediate situation. When mothers speak to three-month-old infants, the most common infant response is a vocalization (Lewis & Freedle, 1973). Furthermore, if the caregiver uses a conversational pattern of interaction, where the adult responds in a turn-taking manner to infant vocalizations, the type of sound a three-month-old baby will produce becomes more speechlike in response (Bloom, 1988).

It has also been suggested that the adult's interpretation of the infant's vocalizations may help the child get the idea that communication is possible (Harding, 1983a, 1983b). Adults interpret infants' behaviors as communicative long before the children have an intention to communicate. A two-month-old baby who is crying may be described by her mother as "wanting her diaper changed." The infant at this age is not actually intending a particular message but is crying because of discomfort. However, the fact that the mother accepts the cry as conveying a particular message creates the possibility for the child to begin to communicate different messages with different cries, and eventually perhaps notice the correspondence between the vocalizations and the effect it has on others.

What about long-term effects? We cannot yet conclude that any particular style of caregiver–infant interaction is necessary for language development. Children learn to talk with a wide range of linguistic experiences. For example, Elinor Ochs (1988) observed childrearing in Samoa and found that infants were typically not spoken to until they began to speak themselves (although, of course, they heard the speech going on around them). However, some research carried out on American families suggests that caregivers' language usage does at least affect the rate of language learning. For example, looking at the 9-to-18-month period, Alison Clarke-Stewart (1973) found that the amount of talking that a mother did directly with her child (but not the amount of speech to others) was highly correlated with measures of the child's linguistic competence. This result would suggest that the overall quantity of speech that the child overhears is not so important for the rate of language development, but the quantity of direct adult-to-child talk is. Furthermore, infants whose mothers talk to them frequently using short utterances at nine months perform better on tests of receptive language abilities at 18 months than do infants of less vocally responsive mothers (Murray, Johnson, & Peters, 1990). Since lower socioeconomic-status mothers within the United States talk less to their infants than do middle-class mothers (Richman et al., 1988), one important question for future research is whether their less verbally interactive style, while sufficient for eventual language acquisition, slows the acquisition process and ultimately puts their children at a disadvantage in terms of some aspects of broader communicative abilities.

CONTEXTS FOR THE EMERGENCE OF OBJECT REFERENCE: "LOOK AT THAT!"

At about six months, infants begin to show a great interest in objects, perhaps reflecting both changes in their visual ability to scan their environment and their motor ability to grasp and manipulate objects. While earlier the infant was entertained by face-to-face social interactions, she now is drawn to investigate her surroundings. At this point, the caregiver will usually change the strategy of interacting with the infant, encouraging her to continue interpersonal interactions by jointly exploring objects and their potential (Adamson & Bakeman, 1984). For example, one might see a playful interaction in which an older sibling dramatically wiggles a toy cow, saying "Look at the *cow*! What does the cow say? The cow says 'mooooo.'" Caregivers label objects (and also the actions or characteristics of objects) in play, in caregiving situations, in looking at pictures in books, and in other social contexts of joint attention.

Research has shown, not surprisingly, that children whose mothers encourage joint attention to objects and supply labels develop their vocabularies faster in the early language acquisition period (e.g., Smith, Adamson, & Bakeman, 1988). Again, one could ask whether we can at this point tell caregivers what they *should* do. For example, it probably would not be a good idea to tell moms "Go around the house and label everything in sight." Michael Tomasello and his colleagues (Tomasello, 1988; Tomasello

& Farrar, 1986) have shown that words are most likely to be learned if the caregiver focuses on what the *child* is interested in, providing a word at that moment, rather than trying to direct the child's attention and actively teach the child vocabulary.

Also, as in other areas we have considered, there can be cultural differences in the pattern of joint attention involving objects. For instance, there are differences between American mothers and Japanese mothers in the way they interact with babies, even though both cultures are similar in paying a great deal of attention to infants and children. In one study, when infants of American mothers looked away from them, the mothers encouraged them with comments like "Want to look around? There you go," whereas Japanese mothers discouraged such looking away by saying things like "What's wrong with you?" and "Say, look at me" (Morikawa, Shand, & Kosawa, 1988, pp. 248–249). The researchers note that Americans tend to encourage independence in their children more than the Japanese do. Cultural values may begin to be transmitted by mother–infant interaction at a very early age, affecting subtle aspects of the mother–infant interaction. In another observation in a different culture, it was found that !Kung San caregivers in Botswana were more likely to interact with an infant when he was not focusing on an object. If the infant was attending to an object, the caregivers did not try to join in that interaction in the way seen in many studies of American mothers (Bakeman, Adamson, Konner, & Barr, 1990). [For additional information on the development of joint attention during infancy and the implications of variations in the environment for our understanding of this aspect of development, see Adamson & Bakeman (1991) and Adamson (1991).]

TALK IN STRUCTURED SITUATIONS: "HERE'S WHAT WE SAY."

Jerome Bruner and his colleagues (e.g., Bruner, 1983; Ratner & Bruner, 1978) have described the possible development of early communication signals in structured situations. Bruner has used the term **format** (also called **scaffold**) to refer to such potential learning situations. One such context would be games that are often played with babies. Suppose that in playing a game such as riding "horsie" on daddy's knee, the infant is completely passive initially; he simply hears the words of the game and is moved about. Gradually, however, as the child learns what happens in the game, the father's expectations change. He comes to expect the infant to take a part in the game. Over time the father "raises the ante" so that more and more ritualized or conventional means of expression are demanded at various points in the game. Where the baby was jiggled, he now bounces up and down. Where the father said all of the words, perhaps a word is omitted to be filled in by a vocalization by the child. Eventually, within the game context, both father and child are truly communicating with each other. Such interactions may help the child get the idea that it is possible to communicate, and eventually know what is said in particular communicative situations.

One problem with a view that places much emphasis on the role of play interactions with the caregiver, as in the example above, is that it is highly likely that children can learn language without such games. For example, Shirley Brice Heath (1983) has pointed out that even within American society there are speech communities in which games like pat-a-cake and peek-a-boo are not played. In some other cultures, play itself is not a central activity between mother and child (Ochs & Schieffelin, 1984).

Structured situations need not be games, however. Bruner (1982) has argued that though not all cultures will have play formats, they will have formats of some kind that facilitate the acquisition of language and culture. There may be certain things that are typically said in a feeding situation or when the infant is being dressed. Such routine events that occur frequently provide another way for the infant to begin noticing correspondences between sounds and meanings.

The explanation of development that Bruner and other researchers who study the social context of language acquisition propose is similar to that of Lev Vygotsky (1978). Vygotsky was a Russian psychologist who criticized Piaget's theory that cognition developed primarily through the child's learning about the physical world. Vygotsky argued that infants are innately social beings and that one must include the role of the caregiver, who serves as a support for the child's acquisition of knowledge and skills, in any study of development. One concept that has influenced many contemporary researchers is the **zone of proximal development.** The zone of proximal development refers to the difference between what the child can do acting alone and what she can do when acting with the guidance of a caregiver. In terms of the emergence of intentional communication, the caregiver who is sensitive to an infant's current level of functioning cooperates with the child in a way that fosters growth. (For more information about Vygotsky's theory and its application to children's development, see Rogoff & Wertsch, 1984.)

A complete explanation of the emergence of intentional communication in the infant undoubtedly will have to consider the interaction of many factors, including at least the following: (1) the biological basis for language and changes that take place because of maturation of the central nervous system and peripheral structures, (2) the nonlinguistic cognitive development of the child, and (3) the types of experiences the child has had with caregivers. [See Hardy-Brown (1983) for a discussion of the problems in disentangling maturational and experiential influences in development.] It is likely that there is both an inborn predisposition toward symbolic communication in the human infant and particular environmental experiences that interact with this predisposition to help bring about this important milestone in language development.

In this section on the social context of the infant, we have seen that caregivers typically speak in special ways to preverbal infants, behave as if infants are conversational partners well before they begin using language, and establish object and situationally focused contexts in which the correspondences between vocalizations and meaning can be discovered. Language normally has its beginning in a social communicative context, and patterns are established early that will continue to be used when a child's own speech emerges. There is some evidence that the specific characteristics of speech to prelinguistic infants play some role in their development. As one researcher in mother–infant communication put it, "The shared understandings which are built up between an infant and his familiars constitute the indispensable basic contexts for all his later interpersonal transactions, including the ones utilizing verbal language" (Bullowa, 1979, p. 12).

SUMMARY

The first year of life—though the infant may not say a single word—is a very important period for communicative development. The infant is inherently social, responsive to caregivers, and draws caregivers into communicational interaction.

Perhaps one reason that the child enters so naturally into communication is that she is well-equipped for perceiving speech sounds. Already at birth, infants appear to hear and discriminate speech sounds very well, and are thus well-prepared to begin the process of acquiring language. Because infants can also discriminate sounds that they have not heard before, it seems likely that they are born with the ability to hear many sound categories that are used in different languages. Whether this perceptual ability has evolved in humans especially for speech, or reflects a general characteristic of the auditory system, is still unresolved.

In the first year of life, there are dramatic changes in the ability of the infant to produce sounds, reflecting physical growth, neurological maturation, and experiences with speech sounds. As the infant comes to control his articulatory structures, he progresses from simple cries to babbling to expressive jargon.

Finally, toward the end of the first year, children begin to behave in ways that seem intentionally communicative. They make gestures and vocalizations in a consistent and persistent manner to achieve goals. These early gestures and vocalizations are not learned from adults but are the child's own inventions. Through such means a child can express various communicative functions, such as rejecting, requesting, or commenting. It seems likely that the child achieves the milestone of intentional communication through maturation, changes in his underlying cognitive abilities, and through his experience with others.

Caregivers in many cultures talk to infants in special ways, typically with higher pitch and more variable intonation patterns. Such speech provides one source of affectionate stimulation for the young child, and babies are responsive to such stimulation. This attention-holding speech may also help the child to become aware of the linguistic function of vocalizations. The caregiver, in turn, accepts the child's responses to speech as early attempts at communication. Thus, the caregiver and infant can engage in "conversations" that provide a rich social context for the child's learning about language. Talking while jointly attending to objects and actions, and talking in frequently repeated situations, also exposes the infant to language in a way that may support language acquisition. Through research in this culture and others, we are coming to understand the ways in which parents and other caregivers naturally provide a setting for their children's acquisition of communicative competence.

At the end of the first year, the child is finally ready for the accomplishment that her caregivers view as the beginning of language—the first word—but the child has been preparing for that day from the very beginning.

SUGGESTED PROJECTS

1. Locate infants of several ages (for example, four, eight, and twelve months) and observe the speech of the parents or caregivers to them. It is preferable to make a tape recording, so that

a transcript can be made and segments can be heard repeatedly. (It is difficult to listen for a number of features of speech at one time in a live observation session.) Choose particular features such as pitch, intonation patterns, rhythmic patterns, or repetition, and compare them in the tapes made at different ages. You might also want to compare caregivers—for example, observe both the mother and the father playing with the infant.

2. Locate babies at several ages, such as one, four, eight, and twelve months. Make tape recordings of the infants' vocalization in social settings with a caregiver. It is difficult to make transcriptions of infants' sounds even if you have had training in phonetic transcription. If you have had such training, attempt to transcribe some samples and see what problems you encounter. If you have not had such training, listen to the tapes and attempt to compare the sounds the babies make with the sounds used in your language. Do you hear changes in the types of sounds from age to age?
3. Locate two babies, one about seven months and one about eleven months but not yet talking in words. Observe these babies interacting with caregivers in a relatively unstructured, playful situation. Take notes on each baby's vocalizations and behaviors, watching for signs of intentional communication (described on pages 43–44). Do you notice any differences between the two ages?
4. The notions of "communication," "intentionality" in communication, and "language" make very interesting topics for discussion. Think of various ways in which information is transmitted, within and across species. For example, wilted leaves on a plant might indicate to its caregiver that the plant needs water, and we often say things like "Ferns like to be kept moist," but we would not ordinarily think of the plant as communicating to us. If an animal or baby is shivering, we might infer that it is cold, without calling the shivering "communication." What counts as communicative behaviors? Is a cat meowing by its food bowl an example of intentional communication? Is an infant's vocable "eh eh" different from the cat's meow? How is using the word *blanket* different from using an invented form such as *lala?*

SUGGESTED READINGS

Anisfeld, M. (1984). *Language development from birth to three.* Hillsdale, NJ: Lawrence Erlbaum.

Bates, E. (1979). *The emergence of symbols: Cognition and communication in infancy.* New York: Academic Press.

Bruner, J. (1983). *Child's talk: Learning to use language.* New York: Norton.

Bullowa, M. (Ed.). (1979). *Before speech.* New York: Cambridge University Press.

Feagans, L., Garvey, C., & Golinkoff, R. (Eds.). (1983). *The origins and growth of communication.* Norwood, NJ: Ablex.

Golinkoff, R. (Ed.). (1983). *The transition from prelinguistic to linguistic communication.* Hillsdale, NJ: Erlbaum.

Halliday, M. A. K. (1975). *Learning how to mean: Explorations in the development of language.* London: Edward Arnold.

Lock, A. (Ed.). (1978). *Action, gesture and symbol: The emergence of language.* New York: Academic Press.

Mandler, J. (1990). A new perspective on cognitive development in infancy. *American Scientist, 78,* 236–243.

Schaffer, H. R. (1977). *Studies in mother–infant interaction.* New York: Academic Press.

REFERENCES

Adamson, L. B. (1991). Variations in the early use of language. In L. T. Winegar & J. Valsiner (Eds.), *Children's development in social context: Vol. 1. Metatheory and Theory.* Hillsdale, NJ: Erlbaum.

Adamson, L. B., & Bakeman, R. (1984). Mothers' communicative acts: Changes during infancy. *Infant Behavior and Development, 7,* 467–478.

Adamson, L. B., & Bakeman, R. (1991). The development of shared attention during infancy. In R. Vasta (Ed.), *Annals of Child Development* (Vol. 8). London: Kingsley.

Anisfeld, M. (1984). *Language development from birth to three.* Hillsdale, NJ: Lawrence Erlbaum.

Aslin, R. N., Pisoni, D. B., & Jusczyk, P. W. (1983). Auditory development and speech perception in infancy. In M. M. Haith & J. J. Campos (Eds.), *Handbook of child psychology: Vol. 2. Infancy and developmental psychobiology.* New York: Wiley.

Baillargeon, R., De Vos, J., & Graber, M. (1989). Location memory in 8-month-old infants in a nonsearch AB task: Further evidence. *Cognitive Development, 4,* 345–367.

Baillargeon, R., Spelke, E. S., & Wasserman, S. (1985). Object permanence in five-month-old infants. *Cognition, 20,* 191–208.

Bakeman, R., & Adamson, L. B. (1984). Coordinating attention to people and objects in mother–infant and peer–infant interaction. *Child Development, 55,* 1278–1289.

Bakeman, R., Adamson, L. B., Konner, M., & Barr, R. (1990). !Kung infancy: The social context of object exploration. *Child Development, 61,* 794–809.

Bates, E. (1976). *Language and context: The acquisition of pragmatics.* New York: Academic Press.

Bates, E. (1979). *The emergence of symbols: Cognition and communication in infancy.* New York: Academic Press.

Bates, E., Camaioni, L., & Volterra, V. (1975). The acquisition of performatives prior to speech. *Merrill-Palmer Quarterly, 21,* 205–224.

Bernstein Ratner, N., & Pye, C. (1984). Higher pitch in BT is not universal: Acoustic evidence from Quiche Mayan. *Journal of Child Language, 11,* 515–522.

Bloom, K. (1988). Quality of adult vocalizations affects the quality of infant vocalizations. *Journal of Child Language, 15,* 469–480.

Bloom, K. (1990). Selectivity and early infant vocalization. In J. R. Enns (Ed.), *The development of attention: Research and theory.* North-Holland: Elsevier Science Publishers.

Bloom, K., & Lo, E. (1990). Adult perceptions of vocalizing infants. *Infant Behavior and Development, 13,* 209–219.

Blount, B. (1990). Parental speech and language acquisition: An anthropological perspective. *Pre- and Peri-natal Psychology Journal, 4,* 319–337.

Blount, B., & Padgug, E. (1977). Prosodic, paralinguistic and interactional features in parent–child speech: English and Spanish. *Journal of Child Language, 4,* 67–86.

Bonvillian, J. D., Orlansky, M. D., & Novack, L. L. (1983). Developmental milestones: Sign language and motor development. *Child Development, 54,* 1435–1445.

Bruner, J. (1973). Organization of early skilled action. *Child Development, 44,* 1–11.

Bruner, J. (1981). The social context of language acquisition. *Language and Communication, 1,* 155–178.

Bruner, J. (1982). The formats of language acquisition. *American Journal of Semiotics, 1,* 1–16.

Bruner, J. (1983). *Child's talk: Learning to use language.* New York: Norton.

Bullowa, M. (1979). Introduction: Prelinguistic communication: A field for scientific research. In M. Bullowa (Ed.), *Before speech.* New York: Cambridge University Press.

Burnham, D. K., Earnshaw, L. J., & Clark, J. E. (1991). Development of categorical identification of native and non-native bilabial stops: infants, children and adults. *Journal of Child Language, 18,* 231–260.

Carter, A. (1979). Prespeech meaning relations: An outline of one infant's sensorimotor morpheme development. In P. Fletcher & M. Garman (Eds.), *Language acquisition.* Cambridge: Cambridge University Press.

Casby, M. W., & Cumpata, J. F. (1986). A protocol for the assessment of prelinguistic intentional communication. *Journal of Communication Disorders, 19,* 251–260.

Chapman, R. S. (1981). Exploring children's communicative intents. In J. Miller (Ed.), *Assessing Language Production in Children.* Austin, TX: PRO-ED.

Cicchetti, D. (1989). How research on child maltreatment has informed the study of child development: Perspectives from developmental psychopathology. In D. Cicchetti & V. Carlson (Eds.), *Child maltreatment: Theory and research on causes and consequences of child abuse and neglect.* New York: Cambridge University Press.

Clarke-Stewart, K. A. (1973). Interactions between mothers and their young children: Characteristics and consequences. *Monographs of the Society for Research in Child Development, 38* (Serial No. 153).

Coggins, T. E., Olswang, L. B., & Guthrie, J. (1987). Assessing communicative intents in young children: Low structured observation or elicitation tasks. *Journal of Speech and Hearing Disorders, 52,* 44–49.

Cooper, R. P., & Aslin, R. N. (1990). Preference for infant-directed speech in the first month after birth. *Child Development, 61,* 1584–1595.

Dale, P. (1980). Is early pragmatic development measurable? *Journal of Child Language, 7,* 1–12.

DeCasper, A. J., & Fifer, W. P. (1980). Of human bonding: Newborns prefer their mothers' voices. *Science, 208,* 1174–1176.

DeCasper, A., & Spence, M. (1986). Prenatal maternal speech influences newborns' perception of speech sounds. *Infant Behavior and Development, 9,* 133–150.

Dore, J. (1974). A pragmatic description of early language development. *Journal of Psycholinguistic Research, 3,* 343–350.

Dore, J., Franklin, M. B., Miller, R. T., & Ramer, A. L. H. (1976). Transitional phenomena in early language acquisition. *Journal of Child Language, 3,* 343–350.

Eimas, P. D. (1974). Auditory and linguistic processing of cues for place of articulation by infants. *Perception and Psychophysics, 16,* 513–521.

Eimas, P. D., Miller, J. L., & Jusczyk, P. (1987). On infant speech perception and the acquisition of language. In S. Harnad (Ed.), *Categorical perception.* Cambridge: Cambridge University Press.

Eimas, P. D., Siqueland, E. R., Jusczyk, P., & Vigorito, J. (1971). Speech perception in infants. *Science, 171,* 303–306.

Ferguson, C. A. (1964). Baby talk in six languages. *American Anthropologist, 66,* 103–114.

Ferguson, C. A. (1978). Learning to pronounce: The earliest stages of phonological development in the child. In F. D. Minifie & L. L. Lloyd (Eds.), *Communication and cognitive abilities—Early behavioral assessment.* Baltimore: University Park Press.

Fernald, A. (1985). Four-month-old infants prefer to listen to motherese. *Infant Behavior and Development, 8,* 181–195.

Fernald, A. (1989). Intonation and communicative intent in mothers' speech to infants: Is the melody the message? *Child Development, 60,* 1497–1510.

Fernald, A., & Kuhl, P. K. (1987). Acoustic determinants of infant preference for motherese speech. *Infant Behavior and Development, 10,* 279–293.

Fernald, A., & Mazzie, C. (1991). Pitch-marking of new and old information in mothers' speech. Paper presented at a meeting of the Society for Research in Child Development.

Fernald, A., & Simon, T. (1984). Expanded intonation contours in mothers' speech to newborns. *Developmental Psychology, 20,* 104–113.

Fernald, A., Taeschner, T., Dunn, J., Papousek, M., de Boysson-Bardies, B., & Fukui, I. (1989). A cross-language study of prosodic modifications in mothers' and fathers' speech to preverbal infants. *Journal of Child Language, 16,* 477–501.

Flax, J., Lahey, M., Harris, K., & Boothroyd, A. (1991). Relations between prosodic variables and communicative functions. *Journal of Child Language, 18,* 3–19.

Fraiberg, S. (1974). Blind infants and their mothers: An examination of the sign system. In M. Lewis & L. A. Rosenblum (Eds.), *The effect of the infant on its caregiver.* New York: Wiley.

Garnica, O. (1977). Some prosodic and paralinguistic features of speech to young children. In C. Snow & C. A. Ferguson (Eds.), *Talking to children.* New York: Cambridge University Press.

Goldin-Meadow, S. (1979). Structure in a manual communication system developed without a conventional language model: Language without a helping hand. In H. Whitaker & H. A. Whitaker (Eds.), *Studies in neurolinguistics* (Vol. 4). New York: Academic Press.

Goldin-Meadow, S., & Morford, M. (1985). Gesture in early child language: Studies of deaf and hearing children. *Merrill-Palmer Quarterly, 31,* 145–176.

Greenfield, P., & Smith, J. (1976). *The structure of communication in early language development.* New York: Academic Press.

Grieser, D. L., & Kuhl, P. K. (1988). Maternal speech to infants in a tonal language: Support for universal prosodic features in motherese. *Developmental Psychology, 24,* 14–20.

Halliday, M. A. K. (1975). *Learning how to mean: Explorations in the development of language.* London: Edward Arnold.

Harding, C. G. (1983a). Acting with intention: A framework for examining the development of intention. In L. Feagans, C. Garvey, & R. Golinkoff (Eds.), *The origins and growth of communication.* Norwood, NJ: Ablex.

Harding, C. G. (1983b). Setting the stage for language acquisition: Communication development in the first year. In R. M. Golinkoff (Ed.), *The transition from prelinguistic to linguistic communication.* Hillsdale, NJ: Erlbaum.

Harding, C. G., & Golinkoff, R. M. (1979). The origins of intentional vocalizations in prelinguistic infants. *Child Development, 50,* 338–340.

Hardy-Brown, K. (1983). Universals and individual differences: Disentangling two approaches to the study of language acquisition. *Developmental Psychology, 19,* 610–624.

Heath, S. B. (1983). *Ways with words: Language, life and work in communities and classrooms.* Cambridge: Cambridge University Press.

Jacobson, J. L., Boersma, D. C., Fields, R. B., & Olson, K. L. (1983). Prelinguistic features of adult speech to infants and small children. *Child Development, 54,* 436–442.

Jaffe, J., Stern, D., & Perry, C. (1973). "Conversational" coupling of gaze behavior in prelinguistic human development. *Journal of Psycholinguistic Research, 2,* 321–330.

Kelkar, A. (1964). Marathi baby talk. *Word, 20,* 40–54.

Kemler-Nelson, D. G., Hirsh-Pasek, K., Jusczyk, P. W., & Wright-Cassidy, K. (1989). How the prosodic cues in motherese might assist language learning. *Journal of Child Language, 16,* 53–68.

Kuhl, P. (1987). Perception of speech and sound in early infancy. In P. Salapatek & L. Cohen (Eds.), *Handbook of infant perception: Vol. 2. From perception to cognition.* New York: Academic Press.

Lewis, M., & Freedle, R. (1973). Mother–infant dyad: The cradle of meaning. In P. Pliner, L. Krames, & T. Alloway (Eds.), *Communication and affect, language and thought.* New York: Academic Press.

Lewis, M., & Rosenblum, L. A. (Eds.). (1974). *The effect of the infant on its caregiver.* New York: Wiley.

Mandler, J. (1990). A new perspective on cognitive development in infancy. *American Scientist, 78,* 236–243.

Masur, E. F. (1983). Gestural development, dual-directional signaling and the transition to words. *Journal of Psycholinguistic Research, 12,* 93–109.

Mehler, J., Jusczyk, P., Lambertz, G., Halsted, N., Bertoncini, J., & Amiel-Tison, C. (1988). A precursor of language acquisition in young infants. *Cognition, 29,* 143–178.

Menn, L. (1976). *Pattern, control, and contrast in beginning speech: A case study in the acquisition of word form and function.* Unpublished doctoral dissertation, University of Illinois.

Morikawa, H., Shand, N., & Kosawa, Y. (1988). Maternal speech to prelingual infants in Japan and the United States: Relationships among functions, forms and referents. *Journal of Child Language, 15,* 237–256.

Murphy, C. M. (1978). Pointing in the context of a shared activity. *Child Development, 49,* 371–380.

Murray, A. D., Johnson, J., & Peters, J. (1990). Fine-tuning of utterance length to preverbal infants: Effects on later language development. *Journal of Child Language, 17,* 511–526.

Ochs, E. (1988). *Culture and language development: Language acquisition and language socialization in a Samoan village.* New York: Cambridge University Press.

Ochs, E., & Schieffelin, B. (1984). Language acquisition and socialization: Three developmental stories and their implications. In R. Shweder & R. LeVine (Eds.), *Culture theory: Essays on mind, self and emotion.* New York: Cambridge University Press.

Olswang, L., Bain, B., Dunn, C., & Cooper, J. (1983). The effects of stimulus variation on lexical learning. *Journal of Speech and Hearing Disorders, 48,* 192–201.

Papousek, M., Papousek, H., & Haekel M. (1987). Didactic adjustments in fathers' and mothers' speech to their three-month-old infants. *Journal of Psycholinguistic Research, 6,* 49–56.

Piaget, J. (1952). *The origins of intelligence in children.* New York: International Universities Press.

Prinz, P. M., & Prinz, E. A. (1979). Simultaneous acquisition of ASL and spoken English (in a hearing child of a deaf mother and hearing father). Phase I: Early lexical development. *Sign Language Studies, 25,* 283–296.

Prizant, B. M., & Wetherby, A. M. (1990). Toward an integrated view of early language and communicative development and socioemotional development. *Topics in Language Disorders, 10,* 1–16.

Querleu, D., & Renard, K. (1981). Les perceptions auditives du foetus humain. *Medicine et Hygiene, 39,* 2102–2110.

Ratner, N. K., & Bruner, J. S. (1978). Games, social exchange and the acquisition of language. *Journal of Child Language, 5,* 391–401.

Remick, H. (1976). Maternal speech to children during language acquisition. In W. von Raffler Engel & Y. Lebrun (Eds.), *Baby talk and infant speech.* Amsterdam: Swets and Zeitlinger.

Richman, A., LeVine, R., New, R., Howrigan, G., Wells-Nystrom, B., & LeVine, S. (1988). Maternal behavior to infants in five cultures. In R. LeVine, P. Miller, & M. West (Eds.), Parental behavior in diverse societies. *New Directions in Child Development* (No. 40), 81–98.

Rogoff, B., & Wertsch, J. V. (1984). *Children's learning in the "zone of proximal development."* San Francisco: Jossey-Bass.

Ruke-Dravina, V. (1977). Modifications of speech addressed to young children in Latvian. In C. Snow & C. A. Ferguson (Eds.), *Talking to children.* New York: Cambridge University Press.

Sachs, J. (1977). The adaptive significance of linguistic input to prelinguistic infants. In C. Snow & C. A. Ferguson (Eds.), *Talking to children.* New York: Cambridge University Press.

Schieffelin, B. B. (1979). Getting it together: An ethnographic approach to the study of the development of communicative competence. In E. Ochs & B. B. Schieffelin (Eds.), *Developmental pragmatics.* New York: Academic Press.

Scoville, R. (1983). Development of the intention to communicate: The eye of the beholder. In L. Feagans, C. Garvey, & R. Golinkoff (Eds.), *The origins and growth of communication.* Norwood, NJ: Ablex.

Seibert, J., & Hogan, A. (1982). *Procedures manual for the early social-communication scales.* Miami: University of Miami.

Smith, C. B., Adamson, L. B., & Bakeman, R. (1988). Interactional predictors of early language. *First Language, 8,* 143–156.

Snow, C. (1977). The development of conversation between mothers and babies. *Journal of Child Language, 4,* 1–22.

Snyder, L. (1984). Communicative and cognitive abilities and disabilities in the sensorimotor period. *Merrill-Palmer Quarterly, 24,* 161–180.

Stern, D. N. (1971). A micro-analysis of mother–infant interaction. *Journal of the American Academy of Child Psychiatry, 10,* 501–517.

Stern, D. N., Spieker, S., Barnett, R., & MacKain, K. (1983). The prosody of maternal speech: Infant age and context related changes. *Journal of Child Language, 10,* 1–15.

Stern, D. N., & Wasserman, G. A. (1979). Maternal language to infants. Paper presented at a meeting of the Society for Research in Child Development.

Sugarman, S. (1978). Some organizational aspects of pre-verbal communication. In I. Markova (Ed.), *The social context of language.* London: Wiley.

Sugarman, S. (1984). The development of preverbal communication. In R. Schiefelbusch & J. Pickar (Eds.), *The acquisition of communicative competence.* Baltimore: University Park Press.

Sullivan, J. W., & Horowitz, F. D. (1983). The effects of intonation on infant attention: The role of the rising intonation contour. *Journal of Child Language, 10,* 521–534.

Tomasello, M. (1988). The role of joint attentional processes in early language development. *Language Sciences, 10,* 69–88.

Tomasello, M., & Farrar, M. J. (1986). Joint attention and early language. *Child Development, 57,* 1454–1463.

von Raffler Engel, W. (1973). The development from sound to phoneme in child language. In C. A. Ferguson & D. Slobin (Eds.), *Studies of child language development.* New York: Holt, Rinehart & Winston.

Vygotsky, L. (1978). *Mind in society: The development of higher psychological processes.* Cambridge: Harvard University Press.

Werker, J. F., & Tees, R. C. (1984). Cross-language speech perception: Evidence for perceptual reorganization during the first year of life. *Infant Behavior and Development, 7,* 49–64.

Werker, J., & McLeod, P. J. (1989). Infant preference for both male and female infant-directed talk: A developmental study of attentional and affective responsiveness. *Canadian Journal of Psychology, 43,* 230–246.

Werner, H., & Kaplan, B. (1963). *Symbol formation.* New York: Wiley.

Wetherby, A., Cain, D., Yonclas, D., & Walker, V. (1988). Analysis of intentional communication of normal children from the prelinguistic to the multi-word stage. *Journal of Speech and Hearing Research, 31,* 240–252.

Worobey, J. (1989). Mother–infant interaction: Protocommunication in the developing dyad. In J. F. Nussbaum (Ed.), *Life-span communication: Normative processes.* Hillsdale, NJ: Lawrence Erlbaum.

Zinober, B., & Martlew, M. (1985). Developmental changes in four types of gesture in relation to acts and vocalization from 10 to 21 months. *British Journal of Developmental Psychology, 3,* 293–306.

Phonological Development: Learning Sounds and Sound Patterns

3

Lise Menn *University of Colorado*
Carol Stoel-Gammon *University of Washington*

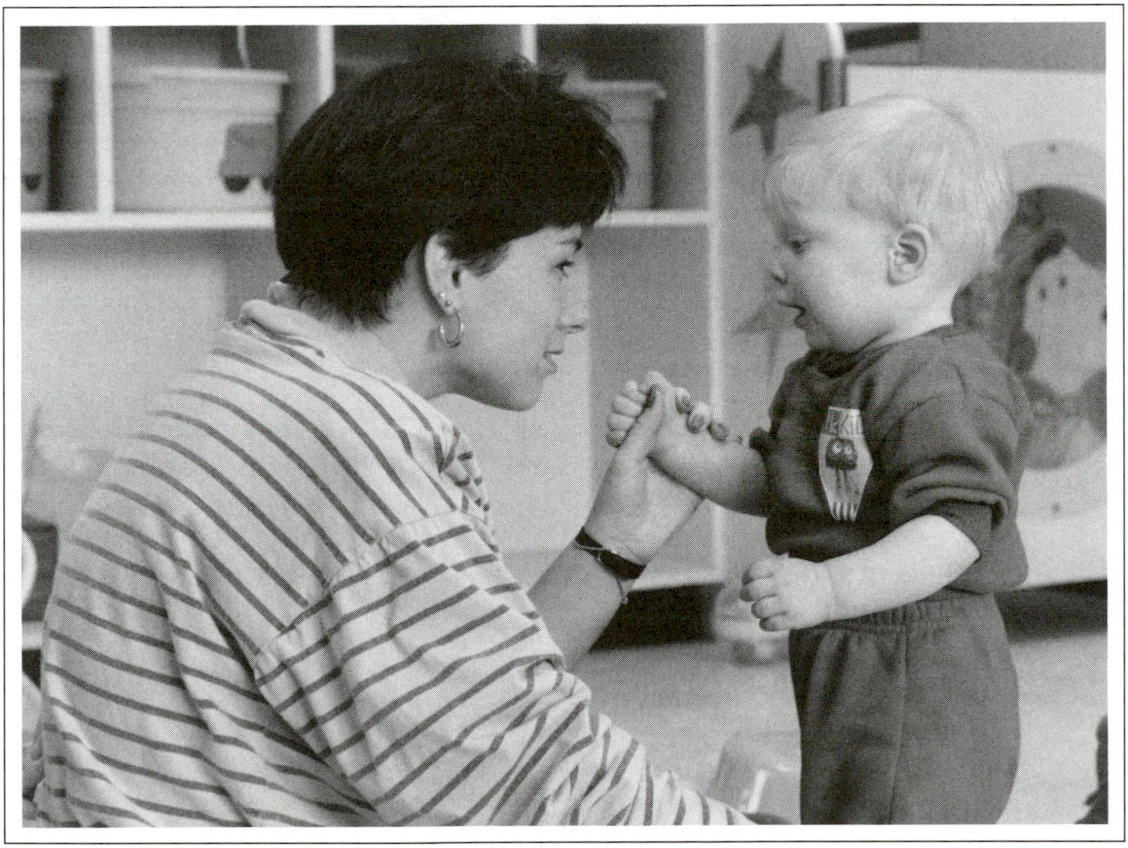

■ INTRODUCTION

Everyone knows that children's early attempts at words may sound quite different from adult pronunciations. We are familiar with some typical early word pronunciations, and we feel that they are somehow simplified (though it is not obvious why *wed* should be easier to say than *red*, or *tat* easier than *cat*). However, there are many other types of early pronunciations that adults are generally not aware of, such as *sore* for *store*, or *gig* for *pig*. Theories of phonetic and phonological development must explain why both the familiar and the less common early word forms may appear.

In this chapter, we describe and explain children's pronunciation in the first year or so after they begin to use words; then we look at some research on the later aspects of phonological development. To begin with, however, we must study the speech sounds themselves and see what is involved in learning to produce them, for adults tend to take this incredible skill for granted.

■ ENGLISH SPEECH SOUNDS AND SOUND PATTERNS

Our first step is to establish a way of referring to speech sounds that will avoid the ambiguities of the English spelling system. Descriptions of sounds in terms like *hard* and *soft*, *long* and *short* rapidly become too cumbersome. The ambiguity of the letter *c* is only one kind of mismatch between English spelling and English speech sounds. Another kind arises when English uses two letters to spell a unitary sound, like *sh*. A third comes about because there are multiple ways of spelling almost any given sound—for example, the *f* in *fat* can also be spelled *ff*, *ph*, and even *gh* (as in *cough*). Such mismatches make it misleading even to think of spoken words as being composed of letters; that term is therefore reserved for written words. This chapter, like much of the literature on language development and linguistics, will refer to speech sounds or to segments; technical terms for the elements that compose spoken words will be defined. For written reference to speech sounds, we will use a system called the International Phonetic Alphabet (IPA). The symbols presented in Table 3.1 represent the basic speech sounds of general American English.

PHONETICS: THE PRODUCTION AND DESCRIPTION OF SPEECH SOUNDS

The sounds of any language are cross-classified in a web of similarities and differences of pronunciation, and understanding the reasons for these similarities and differences is the key to understanding young children's speech patterns. One of these classifications, the division into vowel and consonant, is part of school grammar, and many of the others are reasonably straightforward. For example, the sounds [p], [b], and [m] have in common the property that they are all produced with the lips closed.

TABLE 3.1 General American English Phonemes

Vowels		Glides		Fricatives		Nasal Stops		Stops		Liquids	
/i/	bead	/j/	yet	/f/	fie	/m/	ram	/p/	pill	/r/	red
/ɪ/	bid	/w/	wet	/θ/	thigh	/n/	ran	/t/	till	/l/	led
/ej/	bait			/s/	sigh	/ŋ/	rang	/k/	kill		
/ɛ/	bet			/ʃ/	shy			/tʃ/	chill		
/æ/	bat			/v/	vat			/b/	bill		
/a/	tot			/ð/	that			/d/	dill		
/ɔ/	taught			/z/	Caesar			/g/	Gil(bert)		
/ow/	tote			/ʒ/	seizure			/dʒ/	Jill		
/ʌ/	putt			/h/							
/ʊ/	put			/ir/							
/uw/	boot			/or/							
/aj/	bite			/ar/							
/æw/	bout			/er/							
/ə/	about[1]			/ur/							

[1] *Unstressed syllables only, status as a phoneme arguable*

DESCRIPTIVE FEATURES: CLASSIFYING SOUNDS BY HOW THEY ARE PRODUCED

Descriptive features, as the name implies, are used to describe and classify each speech sound in terms of the *source* of the sound in the vocal tract and the *shape* of the vocal tract during sound production. Speech sounds are created as air passes through the vocal tract (larynx, pharynx, mouth, and nose); the shape is varied by moving the lips, tongue, and lower jaw. The sound waves that we hear are set in motion either by vocal cord vibration or by the friction of airstream turbulence. (Kissing and clucking mouth noises are examples of other oral sound sources.) Although they are not incorporated into English words, some other languages, such as Zulu and Xhosa (spoken in South Africa), do use such sound sources for their "click" consonants.

If the source of a speech sound is partly or entirely vocal cord vibration, it is called a **voiced** sound. It is easy to tell whether a sound is voiced: voiced sounds can be hummed or sung, at least for a fraction of a second, but unvoiced sounds cannot, since it takes vocal cord vibration to produce a singing tone.

Turbulence (airstream friction) has the sound of air hissing slowly out of a tire; we hear it in speech sounds like [s] and [f]. Turbulence occurs when air is forced through a narrow opening. In the vocal tract, the narrow opening is usually made by bringing the lower articulators (lower lip, teeth, and tongue) close to the upper articulators (upper lip, teeth, and roof of the mouth). The sound produced by the vocal cords or airstream friction takes on different qualities depending on the exact position of the lips, jaws, and tongue; thus, [f] sounds different from [s] even though both have friction as their source, and [a] sounds different from [i] even though both have the vibration of vocal cords as their source. The study of how the shape of the vocal tract gives sounds their distinct identities is **acoustic phonetics.**

THE MAJOR SOUND CLASSES

Vowel sounds are made with the vocal tract relatively unobstructed so that air moves through it smoothly; vocal cord vibration is the only sound source. Different vowel sounds result from varying the positions of the articulators: how wide the jaw opening is, whether the bulk of the tongue is held toward the front or the back of the mouth, and whether the lips are pursed, relaxed, or pulled out into a smile position. (Photographers ask their subjects to say "cheese" because the sounds of this word shape the mouth into a smile.)

Consonant sounds are made with a more constricted vocal tract. They are subdivided into several types, distinguished from one another by the tightness of that constriction. We have already mentioned some of the consonants whose sound source is airstream friction produced in the mouth; these are called fricatives. Besides [f] and [s], fricatives include [θ] (as in *think*) and [ʃ] (as in *shoe*). English has four other sounds made with oral turbulence—[v], [z], [ð] (as in *they*), and [ʒ] (as in the *si* sequence in *vision*); these four are produced with vocal cord vibration in addition to friction. Altogether these eight sounds are called the **fricatives:** the four fricatives made without simultaneous vocal cord vibration are called **unvoiced fricatives,** and the four made with both friction and vocal cord vibration are called **voiced fricatives.**

Another friction sound is [h], but the source of the turbulence for this sound can be quite variable, and it is usually put in a class by itself (which is why [h] is missing from Table 3.1). The narrow opening producing the friction can be the glottis (the space between the vocal cords), so [h] is sometimes called a **glottal fricative.**

The consonants made with the tightest vocal tract constriction are the stops, which are produced with the upper and lower articulators pressed together so tightly that no air can escape from the mouth. The **unvoiced stops** are [p], [t], [k], and [tʃ] (the sound of *ch* in *church*). The sound [tʃ] begins as an unvoiced stop similar to [t], but it trails off into the fricative sound [ʃ]. The **voiced stops** are [b], [d], [g], and [dʒ] (recall that [g] stands only for the *g* in *goat;* [dʒ] represents the *g* in *gem*). However, the timing of vocal cord vibration in English voiced stops is quite different from the timing in voiced fricatives, as discussed later. The stops [tʃ] and [dʒ] are given the special name **affricates** because of their fricative offset. The stops and fricatives together are called the **obstruents** because they fully or partially obstruct the oral airflow.

During normal breathing, air from the lungs exits from the nose. In the production of most speech sounds, however, including the ones already described, the passage from the pharynx to the nose is closed off by raising the **velum** (soft palate), a soft tissue extension of the roof of the mouth (hard palate), as shown in Figure 3.1. However, three speech sounds of English, the **nasal stops** [m], [n], and [ŋ], are made with the velum lowered so that air can escape through the nose; you can check that it does so by humming [m] or [n]. English speakers are often unaware of the third nasal stop listed here, the [ŋ], partly because it does not have its own symbol in the alphabet. It is the sound spelled *n* in *finger* and in *sink* (verify for yourself that this sound is not an [n]); it is also the final sound in words that end with the letters *ng,* such as *sing;* in most varieties of English, there is no [g] pronounced at the end of these words.

The **glides** [j] and [w] are made with little more vocal tract constriction than the vowels and are often called **semivowels.** Traditional English grammar groups the

FIGURE 3.1
The vocal tract

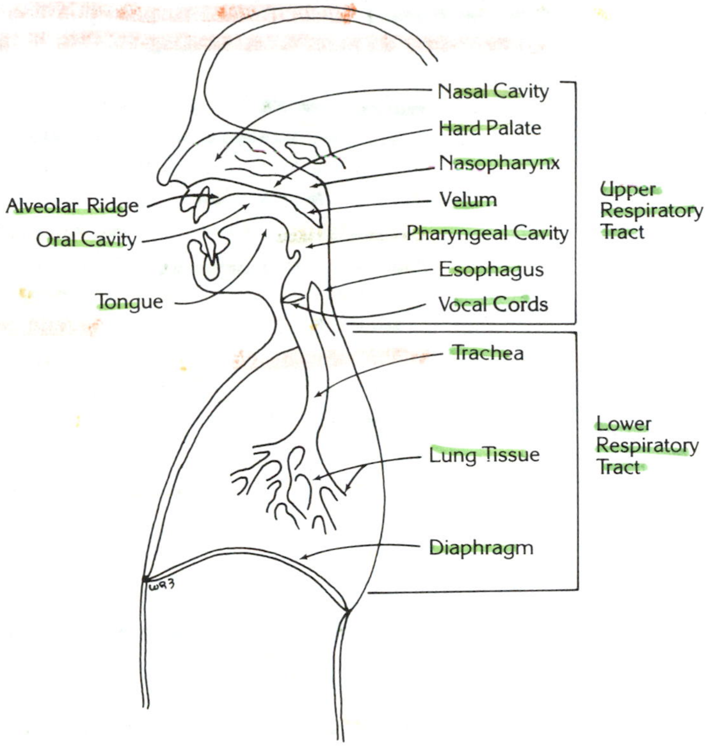

glides with the consonants, but phonologically they are usually considered as lying in between the true consonants and the vowels.

The **liquids** [r] and [l] are made with a little more constriction in the vocal tract than the glides, but still not enough to cause friction; they also have characteristics intermediate between vowels and obstruent consonants. One important vowel-like characteristic is the role that liquids can play in syllable structure: we usually think of a syllable as having to contain a vowel, but there are syllables in which a liquid is used as if it were a vowel. The second syllable of *legal* is spelled with an *a,* but what we say is /li-gl/ or /lig-l/; and in most varieties of American English, the noun *record is* /rɛ-krd/. The nasal sounds also have this capacity to serve in place of vowels in certain syllables: consider *random* /ræn-dm/ and *season* /si-zn/.

THE SHAPE OF THE VOCAL TRACT: POSITION OF ARTICULATION

The point at which the upper and lower articulators (upper lip, upper teeth, roof of the mouth; lower lip, lower teeth, tongue) touch or approach each other most closely is usually called the **place of articulation.** As mentioned, the sounds [p], [b], and [m] are all produced with the same mouth position: the lips are closed. They, therefore, are labeled as **labial** (or *bilabial*). Moving from the lips toward the back of the mouth, the other positions usually used in describing English sounds are:

> **Labiodental.** This term is used to describe sounds articulated with the lower lip resting lightly against the upper teeth. A slight space is left between the lip and teeth for the air to escape. This is the position of articulation for [f] and [v].
>
> **Interdental.** This term describes sounds made with the tongue lightly touching the upper teeth, perhaps projecting out slightly beyond them. This is the position of articulation for [θ], as in *thigh,* and [ð], as in *thy.*
>
> **Alveolar.** This term refers to sounds made with the tongue in contact with the alveolar ridge. This is the point behind the upper teeth where the front of the tongue makes contact in producing [t], [d], or [n] in English. The [s] and [z] sounds are also alveolar; they are made with the tongue in essentially the same position as [t], [d], and [n], but not quite in contact with the alveolar ridge since [s] and [z] are fricatives. The sound [l] (at the beginnings of syllables) is also made with the front of the tongue touching the alveolar ridge, but [l] is not a stop; in making [l], air escapes from the mouth by passing out between the side of the tongue and the upper teeth.
>
> **Palatal.** This term is used to refer to sounds articulated with the tongue contacting the hard palate and/or the slope leading up to it from the alveolar ridge. The tongue makes contact in the palatal area for the beginning of [tʃ] and [dʒ]. The fricatives [ʃ] and [ʒ] are also made in this position.
>
> **Velar.** This term refers to sounds made when the back of the tongue touches the velum, as in the production of [k], [g], or [ŋ].

English has no velar fricatives, but many other languages do, including German and Russian. There are many other descriptive features; some additional ones are needed for describing English, and even more are needed for sounds found in other languages of the world, and in children's babbling and speech. We will not attempt a larger catalog here but will define additional features as we need them.[1]

Variability in Production: Phonetic Detail

Laboratory measurements show that instances of "the same sound," like repetitions of any other natural event, are not completely identical. Instead, there is a range of tolerance for instances of, say, [d], which will all be taken as that sound despite variations in just where the front of the tongue touches the alveolar ridge, how long this closure lasts, and when the associated vocal cord vibration starts and stops. Outside

1. A primary object of linguistic research is to describe the precise minimal set of features sufficient to characterize all language sounds in a way that will bring out phonological patterns optimally; such a minimal set is called a set of *distinctive features*. In this chapter we are not concerned with whether a convenient descriptive feature is distinctive.

this range of tolerance lie sounds that may be taken for a /d/ pronounced with some kind of foreign accent: the tongue tip may have been used instead of the slightly broader area that lies just behind it, the upper contact point may have been the back of the teeth or the roof of the mouth instead of the alveolar ridge, or the timing of the contact may be outside the English range.

The range of acceptability is affected by many factors. Among them are the nearby sounds in the word and a sound's position at the beginning, middle, or end of a word. For example, measurements show that a voiced stop or fricative in the middle of an English word generally has vocal cord vibration extending throughout the whole period of oral closure. However, the voicing for an initial voiced stop need not begin until about a fiftieth of a second after the closure has actually been released, and the voicing for a final voiced stop or fricative may die away well before the end of the oral closure. Some of these fine details are audible to the trained ear, but many of them are not, and instrumental analysis is required to study them.

CONTRAST: THE PHONEME

On what grounds do we say that two audibly different sounds are both kinds of [t] but that another sound, objectively similar to them, is a [d] or a [k]? Native speakers of a language find such a question odd: we are normally quite sure that certain sounds are the same and others are different. Temporary confusion, however, may arise because of spelling, as in the two sounds [θ] and [ð], both spelled *th*. What we do to clear up that confusion is instructive. To show that there are two different sounds involved, we note that there are pairs of words, such as *thigh* and *thy*, that are kept distinct merely by the difference in pronunciation of the sounds in question. Such a pair of words, differing only with respect to one pair of sounds, is called a **minimal pair**, and two sounds are said to *contrast* if there is a minimal pair containing them.

A linguist studying an unknown language looks for minimal pairs to try to establish whether two similar sounds should be treated as variants of the same speech sound or as separate sounds. All the contrasting sounds in a language constitute its set of **phonemes.** The unvoiced [θ] and the voiced [ð] are separate phonemes in English, but there are other pairs of sounds differing in exactly the same way that are not in contrast and therefore do not represent separate phonemes. For example, the sound spelled *r* in *truck* or *cream*—more generally, *r* after any syllable-initial unvoiced stop—can be shown by instrumental analysis to be completely or largely unvoiced, although this is extremely difficult to hear. The voiced and unvoiced *r* do not contrast—there is no pair of words that is kept distinct by virtue of the fact that one contains a voiced *r* and the other contains its unvoiced variant, written with the symbol r̥. We speak of the two variants of *r* as being different **phones** but as representing the same phoneme, which we denote as /r/, using slanted lines. Square brackets are used to refer to phones; thus, the variants [r] and [r̥] are phones that represent the phoneme /r/. (Square brackets are also used to enclose the productions of young children.)

The distinction between phone and phoneme can be difficult to grasp, but the basic idea that some units of behavior are two concrete manifestations of the same abstract, socially defined unit can be found throughout anthropology. A dollar coin and a dollar bill are equivalent representations of a dollar value but contrast in value with coins and bills of other denominations; the queen on a chessboard plays the same role whether it is stamped of plastic or carved of ivory.

If any of several phones may be used to represent the same phoneme in a particular context, those phones are said to be in **free variation.** For example, in English, initial voiced stops may really have vocal cord vibration extending through their period of closure, but the voicing may also begin anywhere within about a fiftieth of a second after closure is relaxed. It makes no difference to the English listener whether the first (through-voiced) or the second (short-lag) phone is used. However, most linguistic variation is not free: some is stylistic and some is controlled by the linguistic context. We can go back to the "dollar" analogy: a vending machine will require coins, and a foreign currency exchange booth will accept only bills. Similarly, the unvoiced version of /r/ may be used only after unvoiced stops, and in fact it must be used there—English speakers typically have no control over the choice. In general, speakers find it very difficult to learn to hear the difference between two (or more) phones that belong to the same phoneme or to learn to override the automatic choice of which one to use in a given context. However, choice between separate phonemes is in general under voluntary control: one can choose to say "red" or to say "led." This is one of the reasons that the phoneme is taken as a basic behavioral unit of language and that many central questions in developmental phonology have been raised in terms of the phoneme.

PHONOTACTICS: POSSIBLE AND IMPOSSIBLE WORDS

So far we have talked about properties, such as voicing and the place of articulation, which are intrinsic characteristics of how each speech sound is made. Now we will consider the various sequences of English sounds that can be found and the positions of these sequences at the beginning, middle, or end of a word. This topic is called **phonotactics.**

Not every sequence of English sounds is a possible English word. No English word begins with the sound /ŋ/, which is why a set like *ram, ran, rang* had to be used to present the nasals in Table 3.1. If a new product were to be called Ngicekreem, it might be pronounced /nəgajskrim/ or /ɛŋgajskrim/, but only a few English speakers would be able to master the pronunciation /ŋajskrim/. We have the same problem with African names like Nkomo /ŋkomo/; this name is usually turned into /n-komo/ or /ɛnkomo/. And while English words frequently end with consonant clusters such as *lp* or *rt,* no English word can begin with either of these sound sequences: we can say *plot* and *true,* but we cannot have a word like *lpot* or *rtue.* Similarly, English words can begin with *pl* or *tr* but cannot end with those sequences, unless the *l* or *r* is used as a vowel as in *example* /ɛg-zæm-pl/. In French, however, words can end in such consonant clusters: the word *exemple* is pronounced /ɛk-sãmpl/ with the *l* an unvoiced consonant.

Phoneme sequence and position restrictions such as these are by no means random, although they do not seem to be completely regular. Therefore, instead of just listing permissible and impermissible sequences, we can make general statements with some notes of exception. The major initial consonant cluster restriction in English is that a word cannot begin with two stop consonants in a row, but most initial sequences of a stop followed by a liquid, /s/ followed by a stop, and /s/ plus stop plus liquid are pronounceable, as in *true, slew,* and *strew* respectively.

In a second language mastering a new cluster or a new word position for a familiar sound may require quite as much work as mastering an entirely new sound. English speakers learning Russian usually have problems with monosyllabic words like *rta* (mouth) and *lba* (forehead) as well as *vzglyad* (glance). It turns out, similarly, that learning new phonotactic arrangements is as central a part of the child's acquisition of phonology as is the learning of individual phonemes.

MORPHOPHONOLOGY

Morphemes

To understand morphophonology, we must also consider the important concepts of morpheme and allomorph. Words often can be seen to consist of smaller meaningful parts; the smallest units that carry meaning are called ***morphemes.*** Any word that cannot be subdivided into smaller parts with meaning is therefore a morpheme: *hat, run, big, how. Hatband, runner, biggest,* and *however* consist of two morphemes each: the *-er* of *runner* and the *-est* are separable, meaningful elements; *-er* here means "one who," and *-est* means "most." The inflectional endings, like the *-s* that signals plural and the *-d* that indicates past tense, are also morphemes that cannot stand alone. English has a much smaller set of these endings than languages like Latin, German, or French.

Allomorphy in Inflectional Endings

Some inflectional endings have the same shape regardless of the words they are attached to, like the progressive *-ing* of verbs like *giving;* others, however, have different shapes depending on the sound of the word or stem that they are attached to. These different shapes are called the ***allomorphs*** of the morpheme, and ***morphophonology*** describes the way that the choice among allomorphs is determined. The plural morpheme, for example, sounds like /s/ when it follows most unvoiced stops: *cats, rocks.* When the plural morpheme follows a vowel or most voiced stops, its sound is /z/: *days, kids, dogs.* There is one group of final sounds that requires still a third variant of this morpheme: words ending in the hissing or sibilant fricative sounds /s/, /z/, /ʃ/, /ʒ/, /tʃ/, or /dʒ/ take the variant /əz/—*kisses, sneezes, fishes, garages, churches,* and *judges.* These three variants of the plural morpheme are referred to as its ***regular allomorphs;*** regular, in this case, means that if one knows the sound of the singular noun, the choice among the three plural endings is automatic. There are also some irregular plural allomorphs, which have to be separately learned: for example, the *-en* of *oxen,* the *-ren* of *children,* and the internal vowel changes that signal the plural of words like *man.* (*Men,* therefore, consists of two morphemes, *man* and the plural, even though it can't be separated into stem and ending as *cats* can.) There are also some words like *sheep* and *deer* that are unchanged in the plural; such words are said to have a zero plural allomorph when they are used with plural meaning.

Allomorphy in Other Morphemes

English has other morphemes that are found almost entirely in words inherited or derived from Greek and Latin origins. Some of these also exhibit allomorphy: that is, the same morpheme will have several allomorphs. For example, the adjective ending *-ic* *(electric, toxic)* is found in the form /ɪk/ when it stands at the end of a word or before certain other endings, but in the allomorph /ɪs/ when the noun-forming *-ity* is added to it, as in *electricity* or *toxicity.*

The form variations that we have discussed so far have all involved forms of word endings: the inflections (plural, past) showed different allomorphs depending on what base word (stem) they were attached to, and the adjective ending *-ic* showed up as /ɪs/ when the additional noun-forming ending *-ity* was attached to it. The stem of a word may also vary when an ending is attached: consider the pronunciation (not the spelling) of the following verb–noun pairs, which show **stem allomorphy.**

Verb	Noun	Verb	Noun
inflate	inflation	abrade	abrasion
relate	relation	invade	invasion
pollute	pollution	delude	delusion
promote	promotion	corrode	corrosion

There seems to be an ending spelled *-ion* that turns these verbs into nouns, but the final consonant in the verb also changes in pronunciation when *-ion* is added. The morphemes ending in /t/, such as *promote,* show alternate forms with /ʃ/ in the related nouns; the morphemes ending in /d/, like *corrode,* show alternates ending in /ʒ/. We might try to link what happens to /t/ and what happens to /d/ by saying that alveolar consonants before *-ion* become palatal fricatives but do not change their voicing.

As we explore the English lexicon, however, we run into problems with formulating an explicit rule connecting a verb with its allomorph in an *-ion* noun. *Insert* gives *insertion,* with /ʃ/, but *invert* gives *inversion,* with /ʒ/; *degrade* gives *degradation,* not *degrasion; collect* gives *collection,* but *suspect* gives *suspicion,* not *suspection.* Many verbs have no *-ion* form at all (although one could imagine what such a related noun ought to be like): there is no *debation* or *debasion* to correspond to *debate.* Finally, there are many *-ion* nouns with no corresponding English verb: there is *vision* but not *vide, occasion* but not *occade.*

Recognition of Allomorphic Relations

In English, stem allomorphy involves many more irregularities and gaps than affix allomorphy. The question is often raised (Braine, 1974) as to whether English speakers apprehend these relationships at all since they have to memorize the proper noun and verb forms anyway. Furthermore, if speakers do sense correspondence between such pairs of words, can they be said to know rules expressing that correspondence in anything like the way they know rules linking the regular /s/, /z/, and /əz/ allomorphs of the plural?

Research (Jaeger, 1980; Myerson, 1975; Wilbur & Menn, 1975) indicates that speakers may indeed apprehend many of the less regular relationships between allomorphs, especially with the help of hints embodied in English spelling (the orthographic resemblance between *ignite* and *ignition* may facilitate recognition of their relationship). However, speakers do not have to extract the intricate patterns that we have just surveyed in order to become competent users of English since one does not have to make up new *-ion* words and, in fact, must refrain from doing so: spiting someone is not *spition,* nor is avoiding *avoision.* We say, therefore, that *-ion* is not a **productive** ending in English. In contrast, the regular plural, past, progressive, and possessive endings are productive: they can be added to almost any word, and especially to new words, if the semantics of the occasion demand.

Stress and Intonation Contour

The **stress** or accent pattern within a word is intimately related to the sounds in it, especially to the vowel sounds. In English, vowels are longer, louder, and often higher in pitch when they are in stressed (accented) syllables than when they are in unstressed syllables. In addition, if adding an ending to a word causes the stress to shift from one syllable to another, some of the vowels in the word may change more drastically and actually become different phonemes. These changes are often not reflected in spelling. For example, when the word *declare* /də-klér/ is used to make *declaration* /dɛ-kla-réj-ʃn/, the stress changes: /kléjr/ loses its stress, /də/ gains a little, and the strongest accent goes to the third syllable. Other examples of stress shifting when an ending is added can be seen in pairs like *méthod–methódical* and *nórmal–normálity;* in each case the vowels are affected. Endings may also trigger changes in vowels even when the stress does not shift; consider pairs like *vain–vánity* or *south–soúthern.*

In constructing sentences, stress has many uses that are beyond the scope of this chapter; the most familiar is probably contrastive or emphatic stress, as when one says, "I want the bláck book, not the greén book," with the strongest stresses on *black* and *green.* Compare this sentence with "I want the black book, not the black notebook"; in the latter the strongest stresses are on the first *book* and on *note.* Another use of stress in English is to distinguish compounds from phrases: *greénhouse* (transparent structure for growing plants) is a compound and is stressed on the word *green,* but a *green hoúse* is any house painted green, and when there is no occasion for emphasis on the color, the word *house* bears greater or at least equal stress—"At the end of this road there's a green hoúse and then a pond."

In this particular pair spelling distinguishes the compound *greenhouse* from the phrase *green house;* however, orthography is not reliable since, for example, the compound *hót dog* (frankfurter) is spelled the same as the phrase *hot dóg* (a very warm canine pet). There are also some items, like *apple pie* and *chocolate cake,* that can be thought of either as compounds or as phrases; some speakers stress these on the first word and some on the second.

The pitch or melody of the voice rises and falls during speaking, and the pattern of pitch changes accompanying a phrase or sentence is called its **intonation contour.** Strong final rises in pitch are found in many (but not all!) types of questions, and smaller rises are often found in tentative polite statements. A rise in pitch corresponds to an increase in frequency of vocal cord vibration, and this can easily be measured in the laboratory.

Conversational Speech and Regional Variants

In conversational speech, the pronunciation of words may differ very strongly from the way the same words are produced when they are read aloud carefully from a list, but speakers are generally quite unaware of this fact. For example, in the phrase "I have to leave now," the *have* and *to* are always run together as a single word, pronounced [hæftə]; *want to* and *going to* are rendered as *wanna* or *wannu* and *gonna* or *gonnu,* except when they are being specially emphasized. In the conversational insert phrase *y'know,* many speakers reduce the sounds to something like [jõ]; the word *no* has a huge set of variants, which we sometimes try to write in English orthography as *naw, nah,* and the like.

Other common casual speech rules or processes in English include simplification of various word–final consonant clusters depending on how the next word begins ("George an' Mary"; "cann' peaches"), omission of vowels in unstressed syllables, partial devoicing of phrase-final voiced stops and fricatives, omission of /ð/ and [h] in unstressed object pronouns ("I see *'er*"; "Push *'em* over here"), and so on.

Regional and Stylistic Variants

Most of us have lived only in a few areas of our native countries, and so we tend to have a very limited idea of the variations of English spoken in other regions, let alone in other English-speaking countries. Advertisement and entertainment media may give us a superficial acquaintance with stereotypes of the American southern, New York, Australian, or Cockney varieties of English, but such stereotypes represent only a few of the most striking differences between these varieties of English and what may be called the broadcasting network standard of the U.S. A few rough regional characteristics are listed below, but the best way to learn how people of a region really speak is to go there, tape, and listen to the fine details of their speech production.

A Few Regional Characteristics of American English. In the Midwest and West, the vowels [a] and [ɔ] contrast before [r]—*car* and *core* are distinct—but before sounds other than [r], these vowels are both produced as [a]: *cot* and *caught* are both [kat̪].

In the Middle Atlantic states, *cot* has the vowel [a] and *caught* has pretty much the same vowel [ɔ] as *core.*

In much of the Northeast, the vowels of *Mary, merry,* and *marry* are differentiated from one another as [meri], [mɛri], and [mæri], but in most of the rest of the country, two or all three of these words are homonyms, that is, are pronounced exactly the same way.

In much of the central part of the U.S., the vowels [ɪ] and [ɛ] are not distinguished before nasal consonants; *pin* and *pen,* for example, are homonyms, so that one may be asked, "Do you mean a [pɪən] to write with or a [pɪən] to fasten something with?"

In New York and New England, as well as much of the South, [r] is not pronounced at the ends of phrases nor before consonants. The [r] is often replaced by a lengthening, off-glide, or change of quality on the vowel preceding the position that it would have appeared in—for example, in some Boston-area speakers, the pronunciation of *shark* is [ʃa:k]: the vowel written [a:] is a long low front vowel, lower than the [æ] of *shack* [ʃæk] and farther front than the [a] of *shock* [ʃak].

In the New York area, a [g] is pronounced where it is written after [ŋ], but in the rest of the U.S., there is no [g] after [ŋ] at the ends of words, nor in nouns (e.g., *singer*) derived from verbs ending in [ŋ].

In the east, many words written with *or* (e.g., *orange, horrible*) are pronounced with [ar] rather than [ɔr]; however this is not true for all such words—*orchid* has [ɔr], for example.

In most of the U.S., [e], [i], [o], and [u] are **diphthongized,** that is, produced with a following off-glide as approximately [ej, ij, ow, uw], while [ɪ], [ɛ], and [ʊ] are **monophthongs**; however, in much of the South and Texas, the vowels in the first group are generally less diphthongized, while the vowels in the second set all tend to have a [ə] off-glide: *pan* is roughly [pæən].

In and near the large northern cities, the low vowels [æ] and [ɔ] are becoming more and more diphthongized, and the first part of the diphthong is becoming higher than it is in the rest of the U.S., so that they are approximately [eə] (or even [iə]) and [uə]. The names *Ann* and *Ian* are homophonous for many speakers in this region.

Stylistic Variation. A given person's pronunciation of a word also depends on the speech style being used at a given time: there is usually considerable variation between the highly self-monitored speech styles used for reading word lists aloud and presenting a new word to a young child, on the one hand, and the very unmonitored style used in a deeply involving conversation among family members or old friends, on the other hand. It is in the less monitored style that the most distinctive regional variations are most likely to be heard. Study of the details of such variations is one focus of the field of **sociolinguistics.**

■ INFANT SPEECH PERCEPTION[2]

To determine what infants perceive, researchers first needed to figure out a way of measuring babies' perceptual abilities. A number of ingenious techniques have been devised based on observations of the infant's physiological or behavioral responses to various sorts of auditory stimuli. One of the most successful techniques for studying the

2. This paragraph and the one that follows are adapted from Jacqueline Sachs' chapter in the previous (2nd) edition of this text.

abilities of infants in the first few months after birth is **high amplitude sucking** (HAS). In this method, the infant is given a pacifier to suck on that is connected to a sound generating system. Each suck causes a noise to be generated and the infant learns quickly that sucking brings about this noise. At first, babies suck frequently and the noise occurs often; then, gradually, they lose interest in hearing repetitions of the same noise and begin to suck less frequently. At this point, the experimenter changes the sound that is being generated. If the babies renew vigorous sucking, it can be inferred that they have discriminated the sound change and are sucking more, in response to their interest in a new and different sound.

With this technique, researchers have been able to gain information about perceptual abilities of very young infants. We now know that even in the first few months, infants can discriminate many fine distinctions between speech sounds. For example, Eimas and colleagues (Eimas, Siqueland, Jusczyk, & Vigorito, 1971) demonstrated that infants as young as one month of age are capable of perceiving the distinction between /b/ and /p/ in the syllables /ba/ and /pa/, although the difference in these sounds is minimal: /b/ differs from /p/ only in that vocal cord vibration starts sometime less than about one twenty-fifth of a second after the lips are opened for /b/, but sometime more than after one twenty-fifth of a second after the lips are opened for /p/. Interestingly, the infants' discrimination of these sounds was **categorical**, as it is in adults; that is, the infants discriminated the difference in vocal cord vibration delay **(voice onset time)** between /b/ and /p/, but ignored similar-sized timing differences involving different tokens within the categories of /b/ or /p/ (e.g., they did not start sucking more frequently when the sound changed from /ba/ with a through-voiced [b] to /ba/ with a short-lag [b]).

It has also been shown that infants under three months can detect differences in place and manner of articulation of consonants, and in contrasting intonational patterns [see Jusczyk (1992) for a summary of these studies]. The fact that infants can discriminate between very similar speech sounds at one month of age would suggest either that they have a built-in ability to make such distinctions or that they learn them very quickly. One way to test between these two alternative explanations is to look at a sound discrimination that infants could never have learned—that is, one that is not used in the language to which they have been exposed. Trehub (1976) ran such a study, testing Canadian infants who had not been exposed to any eastern European language for their discrimination of two fairly similar sounds used in Czech, [ʒa] and [řa]. Adult Canadian subjects were also tested for their ability to differentiate the two unfamiliar sounds. Although infants could discriminate [ʒa] and [řa] as well as they could English language contrasts such as [ba] and [pa], the English-speaking adults readily confused the Czech sounds.

The results of Trehub's study suggest not only that infants are born with the ability to hear the difference between the Czech phonemes, but that language experience may result in the loss of the ability to discriminate categories that are not functional in one's language. This possibility is supported by the results of another study of English-learning infants. Werker and Tees (1984) found that between six and eight months the infants could discriminate sounds that are used in Hindi or Thomson (a Salish language spoken in Canada) but not in English. By 10 to 12 months, this discrimination ability had disappeared, and the infants' performance was as poor as that of English-speaking adults.

It appears, then, that infants start out the language-acquisition process with the capacity to discriminate the phonetic contrasts of any of the world's languages. With exposure to their own language, they begin to focus on those contrasts that are relevant for that particular language, and to lose the ability to perceive certain contrasts not found in their native language. However, this does not mean that infants (or adults) fail to distinguish among all non-native contrasts; for instance, both English-learning babies of 14 months and English-speaking adults can perceive differences among clicks in Zulu, even though these sounds do not occur in English (Best, McRoberts, & Sithole, 1988). It appears, then, that the decline in discrimination abilities affects primarily those foreign sounds that are phonetically similar, though not identical, to sounds of the native language.

Some of the most intriguing findings in the field of infant speech perception involve studies of infants' abilities in the first week of life. DeCasper and Fifer (1980), for example, showed that three-day-old infants can identify their own mothers' voices when presented with voices of various mothers; moreover, there was evidence that they prefer listening to their own mother than to another mother. Mehler and his colleagues (Mehler et al., 1988) demonstrated that four-day-old infants can distinguish between utterances in their maternal language and those of another language. In both cases, it appears likely that the discrimination abilities are based primarily on prosodic cues in the utterances (such cues could be perceived in the uterus) rather than phonetic features of particular sounds.

PRODUCTION: THE PRELINGUISTIC PERIOD

During the first year of life, infants produce a variety of vocalizations, beginning with simple cries at birth and progressing through an ordered sequence of stages to complex babbling with identifiable syllables and adultlike intonation patterns. The productions can be divided into two general categories: (1) **reflexive** vocalizations—cries, coughs, and involuntary grunts that seem to be automatic responses reflecting the physical state of the infant—and (2) **nonreflexive** vocalizations, like *cooing* or *jargon babbling*—nonautomatic productions containing many phonetic features found in adult languages.

Regardless of the linguistic community in which they are being raised, all infants seem to pass through the same stages of vocal development. In this section, we will describe these stages and the approximate ages associated with each, using the frameworks of Oller (1980) and Stark (1980). (These are slightly more elaborate than the list presented in Chapter 2.) Although commonly referred to as "stages," the periods described here are not discrete; that is, vocalization types typically overlap from one stage to another. A new stage is simply marked by the appearance of vocal behaviors not observed in the preceding period.

Stage 1.

Reflexive vocalizations (birth to two months). This stage is characterized by a majority of reflexive vocalizations, such as crying and fussing, and vegetative sounds, like coughing, burping, and sneezing. In addition, some vowel-like sounds may occur. The vocalizations of this period are partially determined by the infant's anatomical structure: in newborn babies, the vocal tract resembles that of a nonhuman primate in that the oral cavity is small and almost totally filled by the tongue, and the larynx is high in the neck, with little separation of the oral and nasal cavities (Lieberman, Crelin, & Klatt, 1972). This configuration limits the range of sound types that can be produced. Rapid growth of the head and neck area in the stages that follow allow production of a greater variety of sounds.

Stage 2.

Cooing and laughter (two to four months). During this stage, infants begin to make some comfort-state vocalizations, often called *cooing* or *gooing* sounds. As indicated by this label, these vocalizations seem to be made in the back of the mouth, with velar consonants and back vowels. Crying typically becomes less frequent and, much to parents' delight, sustained laughter and infant chuckles appear.

Stage 3.

Vocal play (four to six months). In this period it seems as though babies are testing their vocal apparatus to determine the range of vocal qualities they can produce. The period is characterized by the appearance of very loud and very soft sounds (yells and whispers), and very high and very low sounds (squeals and growls). Some babies produce long series of raspberries (bilabial trills) and sustained vowels, and occasionally some rudimentary syllables of consonants and vowels occur.

Stage 4.

Canonical babbling (six months and older). The prime feature of this period is the appearance of sequences of consonant–vowel syllables with adultlike timing. For the first time, babies sound as though they are actually trying to produce words. Upon hearing a sequence such as [mama] or [dada], parents often report with delight that their baby has begun to call them by name. To be sure, it does sound as though the baby is saying *mama* or *daddy;* in most cases, however, there is no evidence that the productions are semantically linked to an identifiable referent, so for this reason these forms would not be considered words. Multisyllabic utterances in this period are often categorized as **reduplicated babbles** (i.e., strings of identical syllables like [bababa]) or **variegated babbles** (syllable strings with varying consonants and vowels, like [bagidabu]). While both types of utterances occur in the canonical stage, reduplicated babbles predominate initially; around 12 or 13 months, variegated babbles emerge as the more frequent type.

The infant's hearing of his own vocalizations and the vocalizations of those around him takes on increased importance during this period. We know this because although deaf infants engage in the earlier forms of vocalization, they fail to enter the canonical babbling stage at the appropriate time (Oller & Eilers, 1988). Moreover, during this period the variety of consonants in the vocalizations of deaf infants decreases with age, whereas the variety increases with age in the vocalizations of hearing babies (Stoel-Gammon & Otomo, 1986).

Stage 5.

Jargon stage (10 months and older). The last stage of babbling overlaps with the early period of meaningful speech, and is characterized by strings of sounds and syllables uttered with a rich variety of stress and intonational patterns. This kind of output is known by such names as *conversational babble, modulated babble,* or *jargon.* To many adults, it seems as though children are speaking in whole sentences—making statements, asking questions—but are using their "own" language rather than the standard language spoken by the older children and adults around them. This impression comes from more than the sounds themselves; it also comes from other aspects of the children's behavior. Many vocalizations are delivered with eye contact, gesture, and intonation so rich and appropriate that the person addressed typically feels compelled to respond, at least with a neutral "You don't say" or "How nice." More objectively, a child producing conversational babble seems to have a full grasp of the social nature of conversation and has merely missed the fact that the sounds in it have particular meanings. It is not generally correct, however, to call such conversational babble meaningless, because the gestures and the context often make it clear that the intonation—the rise and fall of the pitch of the voice—is indeed carrying meaning even if the articulated sounds are not. Thus, the term **modulated babble** is also used to refer to these conversational vocalizations. Conversational babble can clearly convey requests for aid, rejection of food or toys, or desire to direct attention to ongoing events (Menn, 1976). On the other hand, sometimes the child is apparently not conveying any meaning by her eloquent use of intonation contour; sometimes she appears to be simply imitating the outward form of adult conversation as an end in itself, for example, in pretended telephone conversations.

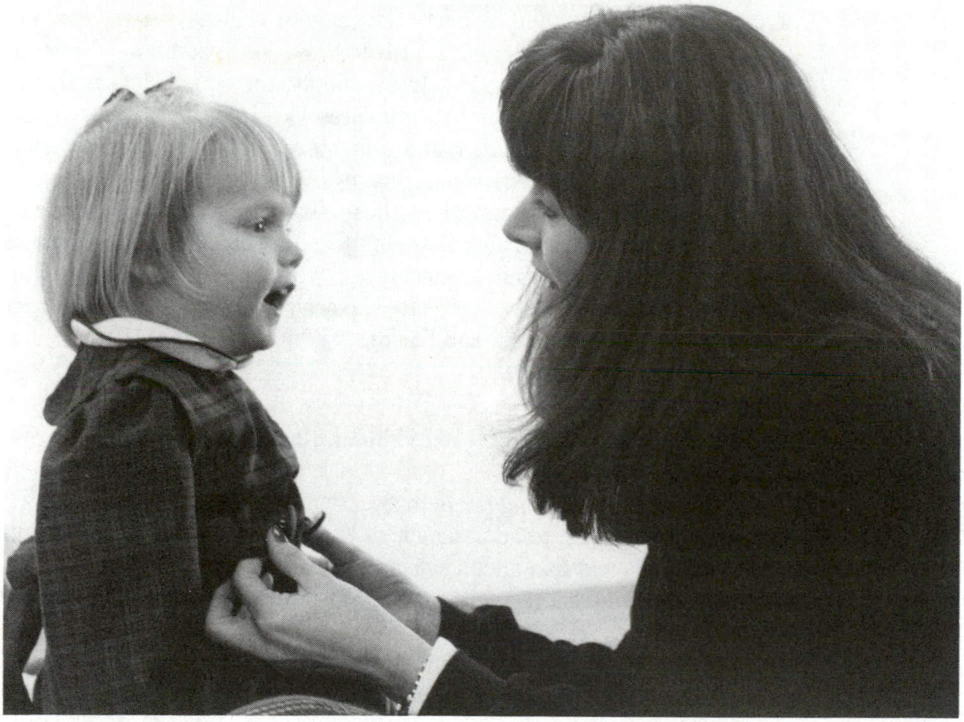

Adults respond to conversational babble with interest and attention.

Some vocalizations appear to be made for their own sake: the child does not appear to be "talking" to anyone, and there seems to be no connection between the sounds and any other ongoing activity. Such **sound play** may contain recurring favorite sound sequences, or even early words.

SOUNDS OF BABBLING

The speechlike sounds used by infants change dramatically during the first year of life. In the first six months, vowel articulations tend to predominate; as mentioned above, most consonantal sounds are produced in the back of the mouth (i.e., sounds like [k] or [g]). With the onset of the canonical babbling stage, there is a marked shift toward front consonants, particularly [m], [b], and [d].

Between 6 and 12 months, the sound repertoire expands considerably. However, claims that babies produce all the sounds of all languages of the world (Jakobson, 1941/1968) in this period have not been substantiated. In fact, studies have shown that a relatively small set of consonants accounts for the great majority of consonantal sounds produced. In his review of babbling data from 129 infants aged 11 to 12 months, Locke (1983) showed that 12 of the 24 consonantal sounds of English accounted for nearly 95 percent of the consonants produced. In terms of articulatory features, this set of sounds is characterized by particular manner classes, namely the **stops** [p, b, t, d, k, g], the **nasals** [m, n], and the **glides** [w, j]; in addition, the fricative [s] and the glottal [h] are included in the list. Interestingly, the sound classes that are missing from babble—fricatives like [v] or [ð], affricates like [tʃ], and liquids [l] and [r]—are precisely those classes of sounds that are mastered relatively late in the production of *real words;* in contrast, the consonants that are frequent in late babbling (the stops, nasals, and glides) are nearly identical to those that appear in the first adult-based words (Stoel-Gammon, 1985). Thus, it seems that the sounds of late babbling may serve as the building blocks for the production of words. Although there is a fair amount of individual variation, on average, stops, nasals, and glides appear in children's words before fricatives, affricates, and liquids.

THE RELATIONSHIP BETWEEN BABBLING AND SPEECH

At one time, it was suggested that early attempts at speech grew directly out of babbling, in response to adult language teaching. The idea was that infants babbled all possible sounds and that adults selectively reinforced those sounds that occurred in the input language and ignored sounds that did not (Mowrer, 1954; Winitz, 1969). There are several problems with this view. First, babies do not start out producing all possible sounds; they produce only a relatively small subset of them (Oller, 1980). Second, even though studies have shown that adult attention can increase the amount of babbling, it does not change the type of sounds that are produced (Dodd, 1972; Rheingold, Gerwitz, & Ross, 1959; Todd & Palmer, 1968; Wahler, 1969; Weisberg, 1963). Finally, babbled sounds do not markedly change to become more like the input language. A number of studies have examined whether listeners or spectrographic analyses could distinguish the babbled sounds of babies who have been exposed to different languages, and the results have consistently shown that the sounds are very similar, even with input languages as different as English, Arabic, Spanish, Japanese, and Chinese (Atkinson, MacWhinney, & Stoel, 1970; Nakazima, 1962; Olney & Scholnick, 1976). Only when judges listened to longer segments of babbling that contained intonational cues could they recognize babies from their own speech communities (Boysson-Bardies, Sagart, & Durand, 1984).

Another theory about the relationship between babbling and speech was that the two stages were essentially discontinuous. Jesperson (1925) proposed that babbling consisted of the playful exploration of the sounds that the baby could make, whereas speech involved the planful execution of particular sounds. Jakobson (1941/1968) developed this idea, suggesting that in babbling the infant randomly produced a wide range of sounds but could use only a restricted set of sounds when speech began. Furthermore, he had observed that some children had a "silent period" when babbling ceased just before true speech began.

More recently, evidence has suggested that the best way to characterize the relationship between babbling and speech is the *continuity* view. Detailed longitudinal studies of prelinguistic vocalizations have shown that children's phonological patterns in early meaningful speech are directly linked to the patterns they used in babbling. Although there are universal trends in terms of sound classes, as we noted above, the presence of individual preferences in babbling has also been documented, and these same preferences appear in the child's first words (Vihman, Macken, Miller, Simmons, & Miller, 1985; Vihman & Miller, 1988). Early words tend to use the same sounds that the child has preferred in babbling, presumably because these are the sounds that she has managed to bring under voluntary control. Early speech develops gradually out of babbling, and typically coexists with it for several months at least.

Another factor in support of the continuity view is the recent evidence showing an influence of the ambient language on babbling patterns. Studies of children acquiring French, English, Swedish, or Japanese have shown that they tend to use the same types of sounds, but that there are systematic differences in the frequency of occurrence of particular sound classes (Boysson-Bardies & Vihman, 1991). These differences in proportional occurrence mirror the proportional use of sounds in the children's early words, showing evidence, once again, of a continuity between the sound patterns of babbling and those of early speech.

■ THE BEGINNING OF PHONOLOGICAL DEVELOPMENT: PROTOWORDS

The beginning of speech seems easy to identify for some children: one day they make a sound that resembles an adult word, and they do it when that word would be appropriate. These first recognizable words are often greetings, farewells, or other social phrases, like "peek-a-boo." The situation is more problematic when the child has a recurrent form that doesn't resemble any appropriate adult word; for example, Halliday's (1975) subject Nigel created several of his own forms, such as the "na" used to indicate that he wanted an object. Does a word that the child has made up "count?"

It does, in at least two respects. First, the child who uses such a form has demonstrated an important level of voluntary control over his vocalizations, a level that is necessary (though perhaps not sufficient) for starting to say words that do have adult models. Second, a child using one or two invented words has acquired the difficult concept that sounds have meaning and is unclear only about the fact that you are supposed to find out what words exist instead of making them up for yourself.

The term **protoword** is often used for the invented words that may occur during the transition from prespeech to speech; it is also sometimes used for early words that have adult models but lack important semantic properties of those models. However, consideration of that topic will take us too far away from the acquisition of phonology. [The Halliday (1975) and Painter (1984) case studies are recommended for those who wish to explore this area further.]

Protowords (with or without adult models) often differ in another way from our usual notion of a word; although the sound sequences must be stable enough so that one can identify their recurrences (otherwise an adult would never realize that a child intended the sounds to have a particular meaning), they may be very poorly controlled, and individual instances may vary much more than repeated uses of a word do in adult usage. For example, Menn's (1976) subject Jacob had an identifiable protoword that he used to accompany the action of rotating anything that would turn (a wheel, a knob, a page of a book); the form of this "spinning song" varied from "ioioio" to "weeaweeaweea."

■ THEORIES OF THE ACQUISITION OF PHONOLOGY

Until about 1970, two kinds of theories of phonological development existed in sharp conflict, one **nativist** and the other **behaviorist.** A nativist theory of development holds that normal development proceeds like the development of an embryo; the environment provides raw materials that are assimilated and structured by the child according to an inborn program. The opposite theoretical pole is a behaviorist theory, which holds that the biological heritage is only anatomical—it determines, for example, the shape of the vocal tract, the auditory processing mechanism, and other physical characteristics that support language. All language behavior is held to be learned by stimulus-reward experience: children's word approximations are shaped by the reward of getting what they ask for until their forms match adult models.

NATIVIST THEORY

The best-known nativist theory was put forward by the late Roman Jakobson (1941/1968). Jakobson's theory was based on theoretical considerations drawn from adult language and from the few then-available reports of children's early words, and it is now known to be inadequate in several important respects. However, his work was of great importance because of the interest it aroused in child phonology, especially his claim that sounds that are acquired late in any given language are those that are relatively rare in the languages of the world.

Jakobson's theory was really rather limited in scope; it dealt only with the order of phonemic contrasts developed by children, and it does, indeed, appear to describe this in broad outline. His notion was that all children should show essentially the same order of acquisition of phonemic contrasts and that the earliest contrasts developed by the individual should be those that are most common in the languages of the world. Therefore, children would first learn to produce the consonant–vowel contrast since that is found in all languages—syllables like "pa-pa" and "ma-ma," which of course many children do say. He proposed that children would then proceed to subdivide both vowels and consonants, making finer and finer distinctions until they reached the full set of contrasts demanded by the language around them. The subdivision of consonants was supposed to begin either by distinguishing nasal from nonnasal stops or labial from nonlabial stops; after the labial–nonlabial contrast had been acquired, a child could learn to distinguish back (usually velar) consonants from dental or alveolar ones.

While this order of development is fairly common, counterexamples have been published. Menn (1976) followed a child named Jacob from age 12 to 21 months and showed that he acquired a contrast between dental and velar stops before learning to produce labials. Other children who have been studied—for example, Hildegard (Leopold, 1970)—have produced a word without any vowel, like "mmm" or "shhh," as a first word. This contradicts the mama-papa prediction. We note again that Jakobson's theory says nothing about phones in themselves but only as they represent phonemes, so the development of phonetic accuracy simply falls outside the scope of his theory.

BEHAVIORIST THEORY

The behaviorist approach to the acquisition of phonology is best exemplified by the work of Olmsted (1971). Olmsted was concerned with phones, not phonemic contrasts, and he tried to show that children tended to begin acquisition with the most frequent phones of their language and then proceed to the least frequent ones. It seems to have been assumed that the reward for improved approximation of each phone should be roughly equal. This theory, like Jakobson's, doesn't account for the degree of individual variation that children show in the order of acquisition of phones; in addition, it is contradicted by the fact that the very frequent phone [ð] is among the last to be acquired. Clearly, some phones, like [ð], are harder to learn to say than others, either for perceptual or articulatory reasons.

More importantly, there is a counterargument that works against both nativist and behaviorist types of theories, at least in the forms in which they have been advocated. Both nativist and behaviorist theories predict that development will follow a course of smooth, regular improvement toward an adult model, without any regression. But we know of clear cases of regression in the acquisition of phonology.

REGRESSION: KEY EVIDENCE AGAINST BOTH NATIVIST AND BEHAVIORIST THEORIES

Menn's (1971) study of the acquisition of phonology provides an example of a child who clearly showed **regression:** the pronunciation of two frequently used words actually got worse over time. Daniel established the words *down* and *stone* as [dæwn] (correct) and [don] ("doan"). Then, however, when he tried to say other words beginning with oral stops and ending in nasals, he produced them with nasals in both positions. For example, he produced *beans* as [minz] ("means") and *dance* as [næns] ("nance"). After a few weeks this nasal assimilation began to take over the established forms for *down* and *stone;* soon he was saying [næwn] ("noun") and [non] ("noan"). Behaviorist theories must assume that correct forms are rewarded more than incorrect ones; therefore, they cannot deal with the replacement of correct forms with incorrect ones.

Another type of regression doesn't involve a particular word getting worse, but rather the apparent loss of the ability to say a sound in new words, coupled with retention of the correct pronunciation in older words. This variability is also in itself evidence against a strong nativist theory. For example, many children acquire a word or two whose pronunciation is much closer to the adult model than that of their other words. These words were called **progressive phonological idioms** by Moskowitz (1980). Menn's Daniel had initial [h] only on his second and third words, *hi* and *hello;* all other adult words beginning with /h/, for example *horse, hose, hat*—indeed, all adult words beginning with glides, liquids, or fricatives—were produced without the initial semivowel or consonant. The ability to begin words with [h] appears to have been acquired and maintained for the two words *hi* and *hello* but to have been absent in all other cases. It would be impossible to speak of Daniel either as having learned to produce [h] or as not having done so. No strictly nativist model can be flexible enough to deal with this kind of word-to-word variation. There is no linguistic way to predict which words will become progressive phonological idioms and which words will not.

COGNITIVE APPROACHES TO THE ACQUISITION OF PHONOLOGY

The sort of theory of phonological development that seems to deal best with the data reported here is attributable to the work of a number of researchers, most of them associated at one time or another with Stanford University's Child Phonology Project, whose principal researchers have been Charles A. Ferguson, Marilyn M. Vihman, and Marlys A. Macken. This type of theory is called a *cognitive* or *problem-solving* theory, for in it the child is seen as a somewhat intelligent creature actively trying to solve a difficult problem: how to talk like the people around her do. She may adopt several general strategies that can provide temporary solutions: avoidance of difficult sounds or sound sequences, exploitation of favorite sounds, systematic replacement or less systematic rearrangement of the sounds in the target word. She may also have a general one-word-at-a-time approach or instead try to approximate whole phrases.

Within a child's general strategy, one can see characteristic components of problem solving: first, trial-and-error articulation attempts, but then the use of existing solutions to deal with new problems (generalization), and the temporary extension of these behaviors to situations where they are not quite the needed response (overgeneralization), like Daniel's use of "noun" for *down.* This sequence of events is typical of all areas of linguistic development and is a major reason for considering language development to be a part of general cognitive development.

Before leaving the discussion of the older theories, let us see what they do have of continuing value. Both contain elements that must be incorporated into any adequate approach. Nativist theories highlight the fact that the raw materials—the brain and the perceptual and motor systems, including their patterns of postnatal maturation—are biologically given. These put limits, some absolute and some probabilistic, on behavior, and many of the similarities among children are surely to be accounted for by this biological "substrate" for language. For example, the perceptual system will respond to the acoustic similarities between the fricatives /s/ and /ʃ/; a child learning to say them by trial and error may therefore be satisfied temporarily by the same sound for both of them. Another example: stops in general seem easier to produce than fricatives—perhaps because a stop can be produced by a fairly clumsy lip or tongue gesture since what is needed is a complete closure of the oral passage. However, the production of a fricative needs more delicate motor control: just the right distance to cause airstream turbulence must be maintained between the upper and lower articulators, and the right airstream speed as well. All this is a matter of physiology and physics.

Such considerations of innate predispositions and abilities are most often helpful when we look for explanations of what children tend to have in common. We need to modify the old absolute statements, however, giving them a probabilistic cast (e.g., "It is more likely that a child will use a stop for a fricative than vice versa" rather than "Stops are mastered before fricatives"). General statements about the order of acquisition of particular segments also have to be made in probabilistic terms; the order varies across children, and the actual ages of acquisition vary even more.

When we look for explanations of how children differ from each other, it is also not surprising to find that there is a useful role for behaviorist notions of trial-and-error shaped by reward. But again, the problem-solving theory gives the behaviorist idea an important new twist, for the notion of where rewards come from has changed. Traditional behaviorism assumes that the reward for correct behavior is external: the successful communication of a demand is rewarded when the child gets what he wants and thus learns to say the word(s) the same way the next time.

The real-life problems in this theory become glaringly obvious in any kitchen where a semi-intelligible child is trying to get a cookie: a child at this stage gets most of what she wants by whine, gaze, and gesture. This gives little occasion for differential reinforcement of any kind of articulatory improvement, and parental injunctions to "say *cookie*" are seldom heeded by the child who really wants one.

There is also a much stronger counterargument to the external-reward theory: if external reward were the principal shaper of behavior, prelingually deaf children would not have such a terribly difficult time learning to use spoken language. A deaf child in an oral training program is given intensive feedback from teachers, and yet many never learn to produce a useful amount of intelligible speech, although fully effective communication through manual sign language can be learned rapidly if the child has parents and companions who communicate with one of the sign languages used by the deaf community.

What is lacking in the deaf child's learning of speech but present in his acquisition of sign language? Clearly, because he cannot hear, he cannot monitor his own performance and match it against the models provided by others. The missing element, in other words, is *internal feedback*. Learning the intricate motor skill of speaking (like any other fine motor skill) requires the ability to assess one's own performance. Imagine learning to play tennis if you had to rely on someone else to tell you where the ball went! A deaf child can see his hands and the hands of others in order to judge the accuracy of his signs, but he cannot hear his words or compare them to the words of others and so cannot judge the accuracy of his sounds.

It is quite obvious why there is such a difference in effectiveness between internal and external feedback: there are literally dozens—even hundreds—of phonetic details that must fall within narrow tolerances for production of an adult-sounding word. The language learner must be able to tell, consciously or unconsciously, what part of a word is wrong and to play around with it, listening to it until she gets it better. So, the reward for a closer approximation of the adult form must be the child's own realization that she has "gotten" it; she must be pleased with herself for sounding more like her family or her friends. (For evidence that children practice their words and sounds, see Ferguson & Macken, 1980; Weir, 1962.)

The problem-solving theory, in summary, assumes that most of the reward is internal: the child is innately disposed to feel pleasure with behavior that he apprehends as successful emulation of adult or peer models. One current research endeavor is the attempt to construct computer models of the **self-organizing system** type, using internal feedback, to see if they can indeed simulate early phonological development (Leonard, 1992; Lindblom, 1992; Menn & Matthei, 1992; Stemberger 1992).

■ LEARNING TO PRONOUNCE

How do very young children really pronounce their words? Let us consider the examples from published literature found in Table 3.2. Some productions are quite accurate, others show overall resemblances between the target and the attempt, and some seem a little farfetched. But beyond displaying a list of examples, what more can be said? If there is some order behind this variety, how can it be elucidated?

REGULARITY IN CHILDREN'S RENDITIONS OF ADULT WORDS

One of the most important findings from the study of the acquisition of phonology is that most of the young children who have been studied have apparently developed rather systematic approaches to the reproduction of adult target words.[3]

---

3. Sometimes a particular word does seem to evoke an unsystematic series of potshots, and the difference between these words and others can be very striking. Ferguson and Farwell (1975) recorded a little girl's repeated attempts to say the word *pen* over the course of half an hour; they included the forms [mã^{ə}], [dɛ^{dn}], [hɪn], [^{m}bõ], [pɪn], [tntntn], [ba^{h}], [d^{h}au^{m}], and [buã]. (Transcription is simplified from the original: raised symbols indicate weak sounds, and the tilde [˜] over a vowel indicates a nasalized pronunciation.)

TABLE 3.2 Examples of Early Pronunciations of Common Words

	Jacob (approx. 19 months)	Hildegard (approx. 24 months)	Daniel (approx. 25 months)	Amahl (A) (approx. 25 months)	Amahl (B) (approx. 32 months)
apple /æpl/	æpw	ʔapa	æpu[1]	ɛbu	æpəl
bottle /badl/	gʌgʌ	balu	baw	bɔgu	bɔkəl
water /wɔdr/[2]	—	walu	ɔərs	wɔ:də	wɔ:tə
house /hæws/	—	haws	æws	aut	haut
dog/doggie /dɔg/ /dɔgi/	dadi	doti	gɔg	gɔgi	dɔg
cookie /kʊki/	kikʌ kʌki	tuti	guki	—	—
shoe /ʃu/	du ʃɪw	ʒu	u	du:	tu:
sock /sak/	sʌk	—	ak	gɔk	tɔk
stone /ston/	—	doɪʃ	non	du:n	—

Note: ʔ is the glottal closure phone heard between the syllables of the expression "uh-oh" /ʌʔow/.
: indicates lengthening of preceding vowel.

[1]Young children sometimes pronounce the vowels [u] and [o] without the [w] "off-glide" characteristic of adult pronunciation.

[2]Amahl's model was British "Received Pronunciation" /wɔtə/.

Source: Amahl's data in this chapter are from Smith, 1973; Hildegard's are from Leopold, 1970, and may also be found in Moskowitz, 1970.

Feature Changes

For most children's early speech we can find a core of words that show very clear patterns. Let us begin with two hypothetical examples, simplified for the sake of clarity. One might find a child who gives these pronunciations:

Child A

pot [bat] ("bot")	back [bæk] (correct)
top [dap] ("dop")	day [dej] (correct)
cat [gæt] ("gat")	game [gejm] (correct)

Child A seems to use voiced stops in word-initial position both when they are appropriate (in the righthand column) and when the corresponding unvoiced stop is required (in the lefthand column). The place of articulation in all of these words is correct, however.

Another hypothetical child might pronounce the same words this way:

Child B

pot [pat] (correct)	back [bæt] ("bat")
top [tap] (correct)	day [dej] (correct)
cat [tæt] ("tat")	game [dejm] ("dame")

Child B has voicing correct but is unable to manage the velar place of articulation; attempts at adult words containing /k/ come up with a [t] instead, and a [d] for /g/.

These hypothetical examples make it clear that there are two important benefits to be derived from thinking in terms of features as well as in terms of segments. First, instead of saying that the child uses this sound instead of that one, we can see that the child's attempt may be partly right and partly wrong. For example, hypothetical Child A gets position of articulation right but voicing wrong for unvoiced stops. Children in general get things partly right before they get them correct, so it is valuable to have a way of describing their attempts that deals with some of the attributes of a segment individually. In fact, even features can prove to be too crude a tool for some needs, as we shall see.

The second benefit of using features is that it allows one to see what several different-looking errors may have in common. Using a feature description, it is evident that the three mistakes of Child A were essentially identical: all were errors in which word-initial unvoiced stops were replaced by voiced stops. Similarly, the three mistakes of Child B were all a case of using the alveolar articulation when the target word required a velar. Patterns or families of errors like this are very common in child language (and also in second language acquisition).

Patterns are not always so regular, however. Sometimes a child may learn to get voicing correct for, say, /t/ and /d/, and yet still use [b] for /p/; another child may follow the general pattern of using voiced stops for unvoiced stops at the beginnings of words but have one or two words in which a word-initial /t/ appears to be produced correctly. An adequate theory of the acquisition of phonology must be able to accommodate both the regular and irregular relations between the child's attempt and the target word. We can thus rule out theories that try to describe the acquisition of phonology only in terms of the acquisition of features. The individual phonemes, and even individual words, often must be taken into account.

Cluster Reductions

Let's consider some other typical patterns of early pronunciation. Sequences of two consonants, or consonant clusters, appear to cause problems for most young speakers, and there are several patterns that children follow in dealing with them. Many children simply leave out one of the sounds. In English /s/ + stop consonant clusters are very common, and children often omit the /s/. Daniel, for example, would have produced the forms given in the first column of examples.

	Daniel	Stephen
spill	[pɪl] ("pill")	[fɪl] ("fill")
store	[tɔr] ("tore")	[sɔr] ("sore")
school	[kul] ("cool")	[sul] ("sool")

A less common pattern, found perhaps in 10 percent of children learning English, is to leave out the stop consonant, as we see in the treatment of *store* and *school* in the second column. Frequently, the children like Stephen, who omit alveolar and velar stops in these clusters, do something a little different with /sp/ clusters: they use [f], not /s/. This [f] appears to be an attempt to match the sound of the whole cluster within a single consonant: it has the fricative character of the /s/ but the labial character of the /p/. (English has no bilabial fricative; the labiodental /f/ is the closest a child can come to the bilabial fricative sound [ɸ] unless he teaches himself to make a segment that he has never heard, and some children do just this, using [ɸ] for /sp/ and also the non-English velar fricative [x] for /sk/.)

Other kinds of clusters may also be treated by omission of one of the sounds, as in column 1 of the example that follows. However, these stop + liquid clusters are sometimes broken up by an unstressed vowel, as in column 2 (Greenlee, 1974). We also find the use of [w] for the liquid, as in column 3.

	1	2	3
bread	[bɛd] ("bed")	[bərɛ́d"] ("buh-RED")	[bwɛd] ("bwed")
blue	[bu] ("boo")	[bəluˈ] ("buh-LOO")	[bwu] ("bwoo")

Writing Rules

We can write down abbreviated, explicit statements for regular patterns of correspondence between child and adult sound patterns when they occur; such statements are usually called *child phonology* rules. Those that are especially common among children and for which physiological rationales seem justified are also referred to as *natural processes* (Edwards & Shriberg, 1983; Ingram, 1989; Stampe, 1969).

Rules become particularly useful when we are trying to understand a child's form in which several different correspondence patterns are superimposed. For example, a child who has a pattern or rule of replacing velar stops with alveolars and another rule of approximating initial /sp/ with [f] would probably say the word *speak* as [fit] ("feet"); two separate rules have been applied independently.

Accuracy of Perception

Sometimes it is suggested that children who fail to pronounce particular sounds correctly have failed to perceive them accurately. Wholesale confusion of two similar adult phonemes may happen. Children learning English do appear to have some problems distinguishing between words that begin with a few pairs of extremely similar sounds, such as [f] and [θ], and this may contribute to the generally late acquisition of [θ]

(Velleman, 1988). But usually, children with normal hearing are able to perform such discrimination tasks quite well, provided they are thoroughly familiar with both test words in a pair (Barton, 1980). Hence, hypothetical Child A described earlier might well be able to point correctly to a coat and a goat even while calling them both "goat."

Although complete fusion of two similar adult phonemes appears to be relatively uncommon for children who have begun to speak, misidentification of one segment in an individual word is reported to occur quite frequently (Macken, 1980; see also Butler Platt & MacWhinney, 1983). This is usually discovered in the following way: a child who has been producing [f] for both /f/ and /s/ at last begins to get an [s]-like sound for almost all adult words that begin with /s/, including those that she used to say with [f]. However, there are still one or two words that begin with /s/ that she continues to pronounce with the old [f]. The usual explanation of this phenomenon is that in those one or two lagging words, the child had misidentified the initial segments; she really thought they began with /f/, either on first hearing them or after listening to her own erroneous renditions.

Suprasegmental–Segmental Interactions

In the early period of development, word pronunciations are often affected by length of the **word and stress patterns**. For example, it is quite common for young children to omit the initial syllable of a multisyllabic word when that syllable is unstressed. Thus, we have forms like "mato" for *tomato,* "zert" for *dessert,* and "posed" for *supposed*. Unstressed syllables in medial position may also be omitted in words like *telephone* [tɛfon] and *elephant* [ɛfənt]. In final position, however, it is much less common for unstressed syllables to be omitted.

Pronunciations of this type do not appear to be due to difficulties with production of particular sounds, but rather to problems with the stress patterns of the words. Since weakly stressed syllables are harder to perceive, the errors may be due to perception rather than production. However, since final unstressed syllables are usually not omitted, most such perceptual problems cannot simply be a matter of not hearing the unstressed syllable; they must instead have to do with selective attention—perhaps the child who makes such errors only "tunes in" to the word when the stressed syllable starts. Another pattern is found in children who use **dummy syllables**, such as [tə] or [rɪ], to take the place of many or all initial unstressed syllables (Menn, 1983; Smith, 1973). Obviously, in such cases the child knows that the initial unstressed syllable is present. In some instances, perhaps his knowledge of the sounds in the adult syllable may be incomplete; in others, the problem may be organizing the production of the sounds using this less common stress pattern.

Assimilation

So far we have talked about the ways in which children approximate the sounds of segments or clusters. However, in recent years we have come to understand that many of the ways in which children adapt adult words cannot be explained without taking the sounds of the whole target word into account. Daniel (Menn, 1971) showed the following pattern:

- Initial voiced stops usually showed correct position of stop articulation and correct voicing.

Set 1

bump	[bʌmp]	(correct)
down	[dæwn]	(correct)
gone	[gɔn]	(correct)

- Initial unvoiced stops usually showed correct position but incorrect voicing.

Set 2

pipe	[bajp]	("bipe")
toad	[dowd]	("dode")
car	[gar]	("gar")

However, when Daniel attempted to say a word that begins with a stop in one place of articulation and ends with a stop in a different place of articulation, a very striking kind of error occurred:

- Initial labial stops became [g] when the target word ended with a velar stop.

Set 3

bug	[gʌg]	("gug")
big	[gɪg]	("gig")
book	[gʊk]	("gook")
bike	[gajk]	("gike")
pig	[gɪg]	("gig")

- Initial alveolar stops and *s* + stop clusters also became [g] when the target word ended with a velar stop.

Set 4

dog	[gɔg]	("gawg")
Doug	[gʌg]	("gug")
duck	[gʌk]	("guck")
stick	[gɪk]	("gick")

- Initial alveolar stops and *s* + stop clusters became [b] when the target word ended with a labial stop.

Set 5

tub	[bʌb]	("bub")
top	[bap]	("bop")
step	[bɛp]	("bep")
stop	[bap]	("bop")

We cannot explain Daniel's changes in the initial consonants as an inability to pronounce the stops since he was able to get all three places of articulation correct individually (i.e., when there was only one stop in a word or two stops that shared the same place of articulation, as in *bump* or *pipe* in sets 1 and 2). However, when an adult word contained two stops with different places of articulation, he could only get one of the places right, and the place of the other stop was changed to match.

A change in one sound to make it more like another is called **assimilation.** (An example of nasal assimilation was given on p. 85–86.) One can see how rapidly a simple assimilation pattern like this one renders a child unintelligible to a person who is not familiar with the child's speech: who would know that to decode *gig,* one must consider whether the context called for *big, pig,* or *dig*? And of course, there are many frustrating times when such a child's utterances remain unintelligible because the context does not give enough cues.

Assimilation may also involve manner rather than place of articulation, with similar effects on intelligibility. As was mentioned in the section on regression, Daniel later made initial consonants nasal if the final consonant or consonant cluster contained a nasal.

bump	[mʌmp]	("mump")
beans	[minz]	("means")
dance	[næns]	("nance")
going	[ŋowɪŋ]	(cannot be spelled with English orthography)

Examples like these make it clear that tests or speech samples used for study of articulation must consider all the sounds in a target word. It would have been incorrect to say that Daniel, at either of the two stages just described, could not pronounce word-initial /b/ or /d/, which one might conclude from looking at his versions of *big, dog, duck, beans,* and *dance.* It is very important to use words with only one position and one manner of stop articulation—like *pipe, bib, daddy, papa, do, go, cake*—to assess stop production. Recent texts on functional articulation disorders (phonological disability) in children (Grunwell, 1987; Ingram, 1989; Stoel-Gammon & Dunn, 1985) make this point clearly. This quite normal two-year-old child's problem was in managing certain sound sequences, not in articulating the sounds themselves.

RULE ORIGIN

Discovery of Rules

We have seen that many children have regular ways of replacing sounds in adult words; and if there is a regularity, we can write a rule to describe it. If the child has mastered accurate productions of adult sounds, these are also to be counted among the child's regularities, and rules (trivial-sounding but often useful) like "adult /t/ becomes child [t]" can be written for them as well.

So far, we have discussed several error patterns that are regular enough to be abbreviated as rules: for example, a rule making all initial stops voiced (hypothetical Child A), a rule replacing all velar stops by alveolar ones (hypothetical Child B), a rule omitting [s] in word-initial consonant clusters, a rule changing initial stops to nasals if there is a nasal at the end of the word, and a more complex pattern involving rules of velar and labial assimilation (Menn, 1971). In general, it appears to be the case, as common sense would suggest, that children produce these patterns because they cannot yet produce any more accurate match to the adult target sound or sound sequence (except perhaps transiently dur-

Assimilation leads this child to say "tat."

ing imitation). There are exceptions to this commonsense view, however; a child who has finally learned to say a sound or sound sequence in some new words may continue in her habit of changing that sound or sequence to something else in old words and in new words that very closely resemble the old words. Rules, once acquired, appear to have a life of their own.

Many phonological error patterns that children use can be explained as fairly natural outcomes of imperfectly coordinated articulatory movements. For example, trouble in delaying the start of vocal cord vibration after the release of a stop would mean a tendency to produce all stops as voiced. The assorted errors that we see in early attempts at producing consonant clusters could be due to various ways of compensating for trouble in producing rapid shifts in manner and/or place of articulation. Such natural error patterns and the rules describing them are usually referred to as **natural processes** (Edwards & Shriberg, 1983; Ingram, 1989). However, individual children sometimes have error patterns which do not seem very "natural," such as use of [h] for a large number of different adult consonants.

Error patterns in a child's first handful of words are often not regular enough for rule writing. Early words typically include a few (progressive) phonological idioms and also a few grossly variable and inaccurate forms (e.g., "bye-bye" produced as [bæ-bæ], [ga-ga], and [ɣæ-ɣæ]; the symbol [ɣ] (gamma) denotes a voiced velar fricative). Apparently it generally takes a child some time to develop regular ways—accurate or inaccurate—of dealing with adult sounds. This suggests that rules, even natural ones, are discovered by trial and error rather than coming into play automatically as the child starts to speak. This view is basic to the cognitive/problem solving approach to developmental phonology, but it is at odds with the most strongly nativist versions of the "natural phonology" approach, which predict that natural processes will operate most generally at the beginning of speech and then gradually be overcome (e.g., Stampe, 1969).

Canonical Forms

We concluded earlier that children learn sound sequences, not just sounds. The beginning speaker appears to discover how to say certain word-length sequences of sounds and then to attempt similar approaches to other adult words that he perceives as being similar to his initial conquests. In cognitive terms the solution of a problem—how to say a particular word—is generalized to similar problems. This procedure, first described in exquisite detail in a diary study by Waterson (1971), results in the development of little groups of words; each group consists of the child's renditions of adult words that are somewhat similar and have usually become even more similar in the child's versions. Consider the following sets of words from Waterson's work:

Set 1		**Set 2**	
Randall	[ɲaɲo]	fish	[ɪʃ]
window	[ɲe:ɲe:]	dish	[dɪʃ]
finger	[ɲe:ɲe:] or [ɲi:ɲɪ]	vest	[ʊʃ]
another	[ɲaɲa]	brush	[byʃ]
		fetch	[ɪʃ]

Note. [ɲ] represents a palatal nasal, roughly the sound of *ny* in *canyon*.
[e] is used without [j] "off-glide."
[y] is the front rounded vowel spelled *u* in French and *ü* in German.
: indicates that the preceding phone was of relatively long duration.

Each little group can be described by abstracting out what the child's renditions have in common. The words in the first column are disyllables consisting of two palatal nasals [ɲ] and two vowels. The words in the second column all end with the palatal fricative [ʃ], contain a short vowel made with the tongue relatively high in the mouth, and begin with either a stop or that vowel. Using V to stand for any vowel and C to stand for any stop consonant, we can abbreviate the two patterns just presented: the first is [ɲVɲV], and the second is [(C)Vʃ]. (Putting the C in parentheses is a standard way of indicating that it is sometimes omitted.)

Such abstracted patterns for sets of words are called **canonical forms,** and each word that conforms to that pattern is then an instance of that canonical form. The output of children who have more than about five but fewer than perhaps a hundred words can generally be described as several sets of canonical forms plus a handful of other words, usually phonological idioms, that are relatively isolated.

This organization of children's early vocabulary is currently seen as the key to understanding most of their ways of dealing with adult words. A child's canonical forms represent the kinds of sound sequences that she has learned to produce at will up to that point; her rules are representations of the regular ways that she adjusts adult words to fit into those available sequences. Not all children arrive at regular ways to make these adjustments; Daniel did but Waterson's subject did not, and neither did the children reported by Macken (1979) and Priestly (1977).

Children who do use rules may start to do so at different points in their development. Some researchers distinguish a pre-rule period, "the stage of the first 50 words," from later rule-governed period, but we must be careful to bear in mind the great amount of individual variation across children and the fact that some aspects of a child's phonology can be quite rule-governed while other aspects remain irregular.

Instrumental Analyses of Children's Speech

An unanswered question thus far is whether the transcriber's ear is fully adequate to evaluate children's speech. We have described children's words with the same symbols that we use for adult phones and phonemes, but is this use really justified? Macken and Barton (1980) have shown that some degree of caution is necessary in transcribing a child's speech on the basis of adult perceptions. Some children who appear to be using voiced stops for initial unvoiced stops are actually trying to make the correct distinction, but they have not learned to do so in a way that is audible to the unaided ear. Their use of longer voicing onset timing for their unvoiced stops than for their voiced ones is detectable only by laboratory measurements of the sound waves they produce. This is a case where a description of the child's language in terms of features is too crude to give an accurate reflection of what is happening. A child who is making an inaudible but correct distinction between voiced and unvoiced stops has the correct phonological distinction but an inadequate version of the phonetic distinction; it would not be correct to describe him either as having mastered or as not having understood the voicing distinction for initial stops. He is at an intermediate stage.

STRATEGIES IN LEARNING TO PRONOUNCE

A major focus of research in child phonology, as in developmental psychology, has been the study of differences among children. The data presented so far have shown several differences in the rules describing the forms that various children use. If we look at the overall strategies that children adopt to deal with the problem of producing words, another type of difference becomes apparent. Some children might be thought of as relatively conservative: they seem not to use a word if they cannot produce at least the beginning sounds fairly accurately. In a list of the words such a child recognizes compared to the words she uses, there may be a very striking imbalance; for example, Jacob, who has been cited several times in this chapter, understood and responded to many words beginning with /b/, /k/, and /d/ but only attempted to say those beginning with /d/ (with the exception of "bye-bye," which he said under social pressure and which came out [da-da]). This state of affairs lasted for several months; then a group of /k/-initial words were observed, all produced with a correct first segment, and then initial /b/ was finally mastered.

Clearly, Jacob was sticking to what he knew how to pronounce and avoiding other words until he had figured out how to produce them to his own satisfaction. Other children have also been observed to avoid certain sounds (Ferguson & Farwell, 1975), although until quite recently few people thought it was possible for a child of, say, 15 months to have such a degree of phonological awareness. This skepticism was reinforced by the fact that many other children, often two years old or older, seem blissfully unaware of the discrepancy between what they are saying and the adult target. Most children probably fall between the extremes of selecting only what they can say, on the one hand, and casually adapting any adult word to fit their output repertoire on the other hand (see Schwartz & Leonard, 1982).

Another dimension of acquisition strategy seems closely related to Katherine Nelson's (1973) referential/expressive dimension (see Chapters 4 and 8). Some children attempt one word at a time, and these words generally have relatively clear and consistent (although possibly quite incorrect) pronunciation. Others use a more global approach to speech, approximating whole phrases with much less clear or consistent articulation (Branigan, 1979; Peters, 1977). The child's meaning may be understandable from context and tone of voice, and there may be enough recognizable phonetic material in the utterance to make it clear that particular words are intended; yet the phrase may be reduced to a virtually untranscribable mess.

There are other children who combine these approaches; for example, some embed one or two clear words in long, otherwise unintelligible strings. We know very little about why such differences among children exist or whether they correlate with any other developmental phenomena. However, as the selectors and the adaptors learn more sounds and as the one-worders start to put words together and the phrase-approximators become more precise in their articulation, the distinctions in strategy eventually blur and seem to disappear.

CHANGE OVER TIME: THE INCREASING IMPORTANCE OF CHILD-PHONOLOGY RULES

Let's review the developmental changes that we have seen up to now. A child's acquisition of phonology begins with trial-and-error attempts at isolated words, especially ones that match her favorite babble patterns. Some of these may be produced quite accurately, and these will become notable as progressive phonological idioms; others may be very loosely and variably approximated. Eventually, the child will be able to generalize some of his successes; thus, little groups of similar-sounding words form in his output repertoire. Canonical forms can be written to describe what the words in each group have in common; these help to capture the severe restrictions on what sounds can co-occur in the child's output.

A way of dealing with a group of adult words may be extended to a similar word that the child has already been pronouncing; if the old form was a closer approximation to the adult model than the new one, the change is a regressive one, as in Daniel's change from "down" to "noun" described earlier. If the adult words have regular correspondences to the child's words, rules can be written abstracting those regularities, and regression will be appropriately considered as a case of rule overgeneralization. This is the picture that we have described up to this point.

Now, gradually, an important change occurs: the child becomes able to combine a greater variety of sounds in a word. He no longer appears to be operating with little families of similar words but with segments, and so description in terms of canonical forms loses its usefulness. In psycholinguistic terms this development would reflect the ability to analyze a perceived word into segments and to pronounce those segments relatively independently. This development toward word segmentation is never complete, even in an adult, but the child moves toward whatever degree of combinatorial freedom the surrounding adults possess.

The developing ability to deal with individual segments increases the value of writing explicit rules to describe the child's renditions of those segments. N. V. Smith's child Amahl (Smith, 1973) gives a splendid example of this level of developing ability, and we will conclude this section with an account of his development of an initial /tʃ/ ("ch"). This portion of Smith's study is particularly interesting because it shows that one needs to consider the range of variation in a child's renditions of adult segments in order to decide which ones the child is treating as "the same" and which ones she is treating as distinct. The clinical and research importance of this example cannot be overemphasized: several elicitations of each test word are required to establish a child's ways of rendering the sounds in it. Gradual replacement of one way of saying a word with a new way of saying it, as illustrated here, is the norm, not the exception. However, if only a single sample of a word is obtained in a given observation, these orderly but gradual changes can be mistaken for wildly random variation.

At a certain point late in his second year, referred to as stage 19 in Smith's (1973) book, Amahl used a *t*-like phone correctly for the stop /t/ and incorrectly for the fricative /s/ and the affricate stop /tʃ/. The following data are taken (in simplified notation) from a table that summarizes the changes in the renditions of three words beginning with these sounds (p. 154).

Target:	toe	say	chair
	/tow/	/sej/	/tʃeʌ/
Output:			
Stage 19	[to]	[tej]	[teʌ]
20	[to]	[tej], [tsej]	[teʌ], [tseʌ]
21	[to]	[tsej], [sej]	[tseʌ], [seʌ]
22	[to]	[sej]	[seʌ]
26	[to]	[sej]	[seʌ], [tseʌ]
29	[to]	[sej]	[tseʌ]
			[tʃeʌ]

Note: The target dialect, British "Received Pronunciation," has no [r] in word-final position.

We see that Amahl said these three beginning sounds all as [t] at stage 19. At stage 20, however, he had separated the target /t/ from the other sounds and had begun to use [ts] for the friction sounds of /s/ and /tʃ/ in some productions of *say* and *chair.* He was at this point capable of *making* the output distinction between /t/ and the other two sounds but not of *maintaining* it.

At stage 21 he had clearly severed the connection of /s/ and /tʃ/ with /t/, for now the friction sound was always present in his renditions of the first two sounds. However, it becomes increasingly clear that as far as output is concerned, there is no distinction between /s/ and /tʃ/, for the sound [s] is appearing for both of these. By stage 22 and for the next three stages (not shown), [s] is used reliably for them both. Note that although this is fine for the true /s/ sound, it is an overcorrection for the target /tʃ/; [ts] was a more accurate rendition of this sound.

Finally, at stage 26 Amahl's productions start to represent the phonemic distinction between /s/ and /tʃ/: he starts to use [ts] again in *chair,* and by stage 29 the use of [s] for /tʃ/ has disappeared. The final phonetic detail of replacing the [ts] (which we may consider an alveolar affricate) with the palatal affricate /tʃ/ comes later.

■ DEVELOPMENT AFTER THREE YEARS

Although children's pronunciation patterns are not fully adultlike by three years of age, the basic features of the adult phonological system are present. Studies of groups of children tested at different ages (e.g., Prather, Hedrick, & Kern, 1975; Templin, 1957) provide a general picture of the acquisition of English during the period of *mastery.* These studies are important because they provide guidelines that speech therapists can use in identifying children whose phonological system is not developing normally (see Chapter 9). By three, most children can produce all the vowel sounds and nearly all the consonant sounds. This does not mean that their productions are 100 percent accurate, but rather that the sounds are produced correctly in at least a few words. Consonants that are likely to be in error, even at the age of four or five, are the liquids /r/ and /l/ and the fricatives /v/, /θ/ as in *thin,* and /ð/ as in *the.* As might be expected, correct pronunciation patterns are often more accurate in short words, like the /v/ of *vase,* while longer words like *vacuum cleaner* may cause mispronunciations. In most cases, correct production of all sounds is achieved by around seven years of age.

■ THE ACQUISITION OF ENGLISH MORPHOPHONOLOGY

Children begin learning some of the regularities governing the choice among English **allomorphs** fairly early. However, some aspects of English stress appear not to be mastered until age 12 or so, and some nonproductive regularities are still being learned well into adolescence. Much work remains to be done in this area, but we will discuss two pioneering experimental studies.

Myerson (1975) carried out a study that showed an increasing ability over the ages 8 through 17 to deal with three types of allomorphy: (1) the change from alveolar stop to palatal fricative when *-ion* is added, as in *explode–explosion;* (2) the shift in stress when *-ity* or *-ical* are added to words like *stupid (stupidity)* or *method (methodical);* and (3) the changes in vowels associated with such shifts in stress.

It had been known for some time (Krohn, Steinberg, & Kobayashi, 1972) that adults do not reliably make these changes in consonants, stress, and vowels when they are simply asked to tack on endings like *-ion* or *-ity* to nonsense words or to existing words that do not occur with these endings. This situation holds true for children as well. However, Myerson showed that older children and adolescents do gradually learn to make use of these relationships, which apparently reduce the load on long-term memory storage of words. Myerson taught 72 children (18 each from grades 3, 6, 9, and 12) 10 pairs of made-up words presented as meaningful. Each subject was presented with the same base "word" and one of two versions of that base word with an ending (*-ion, -ical,* or *-ity*) attached. One of those two versions followed an English pattern; for example, a base that rhymed with *distort* was paired with a derived form rhyming with *distortion.* The other version of the derived form just tacked the ending onto the base without change so that the subject was taught a base rhyming with *distort* and a derived form that was pronounced "distortean" (rather like what one would call a native of a place called Distortea). Each subject learned five pairs of words made up according to the English pattern and five pairs of words with the same endings just tacked on. The pairs were thoroughly taught in the first session and then tested for recall one day, one week, and six weeks later. The teaching procedure went according to the following example:

> A picture of a lion about to pounce on a pig is presented while the following paragraph is read aloud: "*Delort.* To delort means to attack. The lion is about to delort the pig. The lion is about to attack the pig. Now add *i-o-n* to *delort* to make a new word meaning an attack. The lion is about to delort the pig. Whenever a lion delorts a pig, he makes a (*version 1*) /dəlɔrtiʌn/ (*version 2*) /dəlorʒn/. What does a lion do when he delorts a pig? He makes a ____ . Whenever a lion delorts a pig, he makes a ____ ." Any errors are corrected. (Appendix p. xxix)

Similar presentations were used for pairs like *glane–glanity* (/gléjnəti/, /glǽnəti/) and *gathod–gathodical* (/gǽθədɪkl/, /gəθádɪkl/).

Myerson found that the forms with the tacked-on endings were harder to recall for all children. Furthermore, there was an overwhelming tendency for a child who had been taught a tacked-on form like *delortean* to recall it incorrectly as *delortion,* a form that had the appropriate allomorphic base change, whereas the opposite error of recalling a *delortion* form as *delortean* rarely occurred.

Atkinson-King (1973) also studied an aspect of word stress, the acquisition of the word-stress difference that distinguishes the noun *record* from the verb *record.* She found that kindergartners, the youngest children in her study, were able to listen to pairs of sentences like "I put the record (/rɛ́krd/) on the shelf" and "I put the record (/rəkɔ́rd/) on the shelf" and judge correctly that the first was better. They were also able to produce emphatic stress correctly, as in "I want the réd book, not the green book." The major portion of her study, however, was a large set of imitation, judgment, and production tests of children's ability to distinguish phrases like "a green hóuse" or "the red sócks" from compounds like "a gréenhouse" or "the Réd Sox" (the name of the baseball team from Boston, where the study was carried out).

For example, in one test the children were given pairs of pictures and asked to show which was the greenhouse and which was the green house. In a second task the children were given pairs of sentences, such as "I put mustard on my hót dog" and "I put mustard on my hot dóg," and asked which one was better. In a third task the children were given the pictures singly and asked to label them; adults heard tapes of their productions and attempted to decide which of the pair each child had intended. In a fourth test the children were given the pair of pictures together and asked to describe them so that the investigator could tell which was which. This one gave some curious results, for Atkinson-King found that

> some children knew that there was a difference between members of a pair but could not consistently and correctly signal that difference. For example, some used the same stress pattern on both members of a pair but said the entire first member very rapidly and the second extremely slowly (in this presentation, half the time the first member of the pair was the phrase and half the time it was the compound). A number of others were able to produce the two stress patterns correctly but always produced the compound and then the phrasal pattern, regardless of the order in which the pictures they were looking at appeared. (p. 111)

Note that this confusion did not indicate a general inability to control stress, since all of the children had been shown able to produce emphatic stress accurately.

All the children, even the kindergartners, could imitate each pair accurately, but the ability to deal with the other tasks at an adult level of performance (essentially perfect) developed gradually from first grade to sixth grade. Preference judgments were 80 percent correct by third grade; the ability to choose between two pictures given the label for one of them was acquired next, then the ability to produce the two labels accurately when presented with the paired pictures, and finally the ability to produce the label distinguishably when given only one of the pictures. The first two tasks (imitation and preference) may be seen as testing phonetic ability—can the child get the sound right and know how it should sound in context? The others require the ability to make a choice between stress patterns without the support of linguistic context; this can be considered a phonemic skill.

■ PARENTAL ROLE IN PHONOLOGICAL DEVELOPMENT

It is often said that overt correction by adults plays no role in the acquisition of language, at least with respect to phonology and syntax. Certainly it can fail to have any noticeable effect, and the arguments against external-reward behaviorist models of acquisition show that, in any case, the child's own self-monitoring, quite possibly taking place below the level of consciousness, must be responsible for the bulk of the acquisition of phonology. The general (but not total) resistance of phonological errors to overt correction appears to reflect the difficulty of modifying any aspect of habitual or automatic behavior, including slouching at the table and allowing the screen door to slam. Conscious efforts trickle down to automatic behavior slowly, if at all. Yet learning—in the case of phonology, incredibly precise learning—does take place over time; children adjust their production of words so that it approaches some composite of their parents and their peers (Deser, 1990; Payne, 1976).

They acquire the regional and stylistic variants that they hear—which of course has major clinical and research implications. We often cannot tell whether a child's form that differs from our own is correct or incorrect until we compare it with how the child's parents and/or slightly older friends would say the same word in the same setting. A child with parents from New York who pronounces *bang* as [bɭəŋg] or one from the West who says it as [beŋ] is just as correct as one from the Middle Atlantic who says [bæŋ]. We must not be misled by the fact that the last form matches the spelling of *bang* better; the child's target is the spoken word, not the written one.

Similarly, although young children are often given the opportunity to hear nouns in isolation in naming routines, they usually hear most other words in phrases, and the "targets" that they are trying to pronounce must be considered to be these phrasal forms (i.e., forms like *hafta, wan'em, couldja,* and so on).

Parents do seem to improve the precision of their articulation above normal conversational levels to help their children learn to speak, however. Two researchers, Malsheen (1980) and Bernstein Ratner (1984a, 1948b) have carried out major studies of this phenomenon using acoustic measurements to show that parents increase the articulatory precision of their speech to children in the first few years of their children's learning to speak. This adult behavior is probably not conscious either, except as an attempt to assure understanding; but there seems to be more to it than that, according to Bernstein Ratner.

Malsheen tape-recorded mothers of two children who had not yet produced any recognizable words (six and eight months old), two children who had produced one-word utterances (15 and 16 months old), and two children (two-and-a-half and five years old) who had used an average of several words per utterance. She compared the word-initial consonants (*b, d, g, p, t, k*) used by each woman in speaking to her child and in speaking to an adult, and she found that mothers clarified their pronunciation of initial consonants in speech to the children at the one-word stage but not to the prelingual children or to the older ones. She measured this clarification in terms of the same parameter used by Macken and Barton, the voice onset time (the period between the release of the oral closure and the onset of vocal cord vibration). Recall that voiced word-initial stops in English are not necessarily produced with concurrent vocal cord vibration but that voicing begins, on the average, well within two hundredths of a second after the release of closure (when a vowel follows); in the production of unvoiced stops, vocal cord vibration usually begins more than four hundredths of a second after the release. However, in normal adult–adult conversation consonant production is quite sloppy; for example, in Malsheen's adult–adult conversations as many as half of the instances of word-initial /t/ had voice onset time of less than two hundredths of a second, which means that they would have been heard as /d/ if they had been taken out of context. The same kind of sloppy control was also found in the mothers' speech to the prelingual children and to the children who were using multiword utterances. However, speech to the children in the one-word stage showed very few sloppy unvoiced stops; almost all were produced with a voice onset time of four hundredths of a second or more, and many were hyperdistinct with voice onset time of over a tenth of a second.

Bernstein Ratner studied vowel production of nine mothers speaking to their children (some at the one-word stage and some using an average of two to four words per utterance) as compared with the vowels in the same words excerpted from speech to other adults. Her findings indicate that mothers' clarification of vowel production is best seen as modeling words of the type that the child is currently learning to use, rather than increasing the distinctness of overall speech. What she found was that speech directed to children at the one-word stage showed clarification of vowels in nouns, verbs, and adjectives—that is, the sort of words being used most by the children themselves. Speech directed to children using several-word utterances showed clarification not only in nouns, verbs, and adjectives, but also in the function words that these children were just beginning to use: pronouns, prepositions, and conjunctions.

SUMMARY

Phonology concerns the relations among the speech sounds of a language: their phonetic resemblances due to the way they are produced, their distributions as shown by minimal-pair contrasts, the possible phonotactic sequences in which they occur, and the way that distinct phonemes correspond to one another in the several allomorphs that a morpheme can have. The child learning to talk must learn to produce the right sounds, to put them in the sequences demanded by the ambient language, to recognize variant phones as representative of the same phoneme, and to learn at least the productive allomorphic relationships.

Humans have an innate, biological basis for hearing and producing speech sounds; this is then shaped by language experience, including cognitive reactions to articulatory challenges. There is strong evidence to suggest that normal infants are born with the ability to hear many distinctions between speech sounds, but that around age 10 to 12 months their auditory perceptions become adultlike—that is, they become less sensitive to those differences that are subphonemic in whatever language is around them. Infants also appear to progress through the early months of sound production in a biologically determined way, for the detrimental effects of deafness on production only start to appear after babbling has begun. Individual differences and ambient language effects gradually appear in later babbling. The transition from babbling to speech is gradual; early words tend to utilize sounds that the child has been favoring in late babbling.

Nativist theories of phonological development emphasize the similarities among children; they have difficulty dealing with individual differences and with irregularities. In addition, the best-known nativist theory, that of Jakobson, deals only with the acquisition of phonemic contrast, not with phonetic targets or phonotactic patterns. Behaviorist theories that depend on external reward for improved pronunciation are inadequate; external reward is too crude to guide mastery of the myriad fine details of phonetics. Neither nativist nor behaviorist theories can deal with regression in accuracy of production; here, as elsewhere in language acquisition, the data require a cognitive problem-solving theory since only this type of theory predicts that there will be overgeneralizations.

With the aid of descriptive features, we can assess children's partial successes in pronunciation and see similarities linking their attempts at related sounds. Rendering all initial stops as voiced, using alveolar place of articulation for both alveolar and velar consonants, and assimilating nasality and/or place of articulation are common patterns in early child phonology, as are several varieties of cluster simplification. When such patterns occur regularly in a given child's speech, rules can be written to describe the relation between the adult word and the child's form, for both correct and incorrect renditions. Even when the adult–child correspondences are not regular enough to be called rules, early child words typically occur in little groups whose common properties can be abstracted and written in formulas called canonical forms. Often there are a few words whose pronunciation is much more adultlike than others; these isolated progressive phonological idioms do not, by definition, come under any of the child's canonical forms but are exceptions to the child's rules. They are usually among the child's earliest words; this supports that claim that rules for rendering adult words are discovered by the child through trial and error.

Not all of a child's progress is correctly assessed by the unaided ear; instrumental studies of tape recordings show that children's earliest steps toward mastering adult phonemic distinctions may be inaudible to adults.

Individual variation among children is found in the strategies they adopt as well as in their individual rules and canonical forms. Some children attempt whole phrases, others try words singly; some avoid (public) attempts at words they cannot pronounce, others rearrange adult words freely to fit them into their existing repertoire.

Eventually, as the child learns to put more different kinds of speech sounds together within one word, the small groups expand and merge; canonical forms become less useful as descriptors, while rules become more useful.

In the elementary school years, children learn to distinguish certain aspects of the English stress system, and in the later school years they become acquainted with some of the nonproductive relationships that prevail among words in the Latin-based portion of the English lexicon. These relationships strongly affect recall and presumably reduce the memory load required for learning new words.

Overt parental correction of pronunciation has perhaps the same effect on children as correction of any other habitual behavior. Yet mothers have been shown to increase the accuracy of their production of word-initial consonants just as children are learning to pronounce single words and to enhance the clarity of their vowels in content words during the same period. Furthermore, they later increase the clarity of function word production slightly, when their children are beginning to express the grammatical relations that adult grammar encodes in function words.

SUGGESTED PROJECTS

The first three activities are time-consuming and, if carried out in full detail, might well take several weeks to complete.

1. Tape-record the babbling or speech of a child between the ages of 12 and 30 months, keeping notes of the child's accompanying activities. As soon as possible after this session, transcribe the sounds the child made and try to classify them into the types of vocalizations discussed in this chapter: sound play, conversational babble, protowords, and words. What problems, if any, do you

face in making these distinctions? What additional information do you need? Are there any utterances about which you could never be sure? Are there any utterances that are none of the above? If yes, what keeps them from fitting into each of the four major categories? What would you call them?

2. Find a child whose speech is somewhat intelligible but whose pronunciation of words is still babyish. Tape-record and transcribe a half-hour of the child's speech during a play session. (A good-quality tape recorder will be needed for the best results; it will also help if you can get the child to wear a good external lavaliere microphone.) Can you find regularities in the way the child renders adult words? If not, can you find canonical output forms that the child seems to rely on? Are any adult sounds or sequences of sounds especially variable in the way the child produces them? If you do find some regularities, write rules to describe them. Do these rules have exceptions? Are the forms of these exceptions closer to the adult word or farther from it?
3. If you have no access to a child of the appropriate age for activities 1 or 2, go over the examples presented in this chapter, and write explicit rules to describe what the child is doing to the adult words. Which rules can be written simply as "Adult (target) segment X becomes child (output) segment Y"? Which ones must also mention other sounds in the target word? Which ones must mention whether the sound in the adult word is in initial, medial, or final position? If you can't answer the last question from the small number of cases presented for a given real or hypothetical child in this chapter, give two formulations: a general one, assuming that what you see is broadly representative of what the child does, and a narrow one, allowing for the possibility that the child does something quite different if the segments are not in the given word position. Consider formulating your rules in terms of features or in terms of phonemes. For each rule indicate which mode of formulation is more helpful in understanding what the child is doing, and explain why.
4. Consider the development of /s/ and /tʃ/ by N. V. Smith's child, as described on pages 98–100. Suppose you had only one sample of each word per stage. Show how you might get rather different ideas of what the child was doing, depending on which rendition of each word appeared in your data.

SUGGESTED READINGS

Allen, G., & Hawkins, S. (1980). Phonological rhythm: Definition and development. In G. Yeni-Komshian, J. F. Kavanagh, & C. A. Ferguson (Eds.), *Child phonology: Vol. 1. Production.* New York: Academic Press.

Barton, D. P. (1980). Phonemic perception in children. In G. Yeni-Komshian, J. F. Kavanagh, & C. A. Ferguson (Eds.), *Child phonology: Vol. 2. Perception.* New York: Academic Press.

Bloch, B., & Trager, G. L. (1942). *Outline of linguistic analysis.* Baltimore: Linguistic Society of America.

Braine, M. D. S. (1974). On what might constitute a learnable phonology. *Language, 50,* 270–299.

Clumeck, H. (1980). The acquisition of tone. In G. Yeni-Komshian, J. F. Kavanagh, & C. A. Ferguson (Eds.), *Child phonology. Vol. 1. Production.* New York: Academic Press.

Edwards, M. L., & Shriberg, L. D. (1983). *Phonology: Applications in communicative disorders* (pp. 123–199). San Diego, CA: College-Hill Press.

Fee, J., & Ingram, D. (1982). Reduplication as a strategy of phonological development. *Journal of Child Language, 9,* 41–54.

Ferguson, C. A., & Farwell, C. B. (1975). Words and sounds in early language acquisition. *Language, 51,* 439–491.

Ferguson, C. A., & Macken, M. A. (1980). Phonological development in children's play and cognition. In K. E. Nelson (Ed.), *Children's Language* (Vol. 4). New York: Gardner Press.

Ferguson, C.A., Menn, L., & Stoel-Gammon, C. (Eds.). (1992). *Phonological development: Models, research, implications*. Parkton, MD: York Press.

Fey, M., & Gandour, J. (1982). Rule discovery in early phonology acquisition. *Journal of Child Development, 9,* 71–82.

Grunwell, P. (1987). *The nature of phonological disability in children* (2nd ed.). London: Academic Press.

Grunwell, P. (1982). *Clinical phonology.* London: Croom Helm.

Halliday, M. A. K. (1975). *Learning how to mean: Explorations in the development of language.* London: Edward Arnold.

Hyman, L. M. (1975). *Phonology: Theory and analysis.* New York: Holt, Rinehart & Winston.

Ingram, D. (1974). Phonological rules in young children. *Journal of Child Language, 1,* 49–64.

Ingram, D. (1986). Phonological patterns in the speech of young children. In P. Fletcher & M. Garman (Eds.), *Language acquisition* (2nd ed.). Cambridge: Cambridge University Press.

Ingram, D. (1989). *Phonological disabilities in children.* London: Cole and Whurr.

Ingram, D., Christensen, L., Veach, S., & Webster, B. (1980). The acquisition of word-initial fricatives and affricates in English by children between 2 and 6 years. In G. Yeni-Komshian, J. F. Kavanagh, & C. A. Ferguson (Eds.), *Child phonology: Vol. 1. Production.* New York: Academic Press.

Jakobson, R. (1968). *Child language, aphasia, and phonological universals* (A. Keiler, Trans.). The Hague: Mouton.

Jusczyk, P. W. (1992). Developing phonological categories for the speech signal. In Ferguson, C. A., Menn, L., & Stoel-Gammon, C. (Eds.), *Phonological development: Models, research, implications.* Parkton, MD: York Press.

Kent, R. D. (1992). The biology of phonological development. In Ferguson, C. A., Menn, L., & Stoel-Gammon, C. (Eds.), *Phonological development: Models, research, implications.* Parkton, MD: York Press.

Labov, William. (1972). *Sociolinguistic patterns.* Philadelphia: University of Pennsylvania Press.

Ladefoged, P. (1971). *A course in phonetics.* New York: Harcourt Brace Jovanovich.

Leonard, L. B., Newhoff, M., & Mesalam, L. (1980). Individual differences in early child phonology. *Applied Psycholinguistics, 1,* 7–30.

Leonard, L. B., Schwartz, R., Folger, M. K., & Wilcox, M. J. (1978). Some aspects of child phonology in imitative and spontaneous speech. *Journal of Child Language, 5,* 403–416.

Lindblom, B. (1992). Phonological units as adaptive emergents of lexical development. In Ferguson, C. A., Menn, L., & Stoel-Gammon, C. (Eds.), *Phonological development: Models, research, implications.* Parkton, MD: York Press.

Locke, J. L. (1983). *Phonological acquisition and change.* New York: Academic Press.

Macken, M. A. (1979). Developmental reorganization of phonology: A hierarchy of basic units of acquisition. *Lingua, 49,* 11–49.

Macken, M. A., & Barton, D. (1980). The acquisition of the voicing contrast in English: A study of voice onset time in word-initial stop consonants. *Journal of Child Language, 7,* 41–75.

Macken, M. A., & Ferguson, C. A. (1982). Cognitive aspects of phonological development: Model, evidence, and issues. In K. E. Nelson (Ed.), *Children's language* (Vol. 4). New York: Gardner Press.

MacNeilage, P., & Davis, B. (1990). Acquisition of speech production: The achievement of segmental independence. In W. J. Hardcastle & A. Marchal (Eds.), *Speech production and speech modelling.* Dordrecht: Kluwer Press.

MacWhinney, B. (1978). The acquisition of morphophonology. *Monographs of the Society for Research in Child Development, 43,* 1–2.

Malsheen, B. (1980). Two hypotheses for phonetic clarification in the speech of mothers to children. In G. Yeni-Komshian, J. F. Kavanagh, & C. A. Ferguson (Eds.), *Child phonology: Vol. 2. Perception.* New York: Academic Press.

McCawley, J. D. (1977). Acquisition models as models of acquisition. In R. Fasold & R. Shuy (Eds.), *Studies in language variation.* Washington, DC: Georgetown University Press.

Menn, L. (1983). Development of articulatory, phonetic, and phonological capabilities. In B. Butterworth (Ed.), *Language production* (Vol. 2). London: Academic Press.

Menyuk, P., Menn, L., & Silber, R. (1986). Early strategies for the perception and production of words and sounds. In P. Fletcher & M. Garman (Eds.), *Language acquisition* (2nd ed.). Cambridge: Cambridge University Press.

Oller, D. K. (1980). The emergence of the sounds of speech in infancy. In G. Yeni-Komshian, J. F. Kavanagh, & C. A. Ferguson (Eds.), *Child phonology: Vol. 1. Production.* New York: Academic Press.

Painter, C. (1984). *Into the mother tongue: A case study in early language development.* London: Frances Pinter.

Payne, A. (1976). *The acquisition of a phonological system of a second dialect.* Unpublished doctoral dissertation, University of Pennsylvania.

Peters, A. M. (1977). Language learning strategies. *Language, 53,* 560–573.

Peters, A. M. (1983). *The units of language acquisition.* Cambridge: Cambridge University Press.

Priestly, T. M. S. (1977). One idiosyncratic strategy in the acquisition of phonology. *Journal of Child Language, 4,* 45–66.

Smith, N. V. (1973). *The acquisition of phonology: A case study.* Cambridge: Cambridge University Press.

Stoel-Gammon, C., & Dunn, C. (1985). *Normal and disordered phonology in children.* Austin, TX: Pro-Ed.

Velten, H. V. (1971). The growth of phonemic and lexical patterns in the infant. Reprinted in A. Bar-Adon & W. Leopold (Eds.), *Readings in child language.* Englewood Cliffs, NJ: Prentice-Hall. (Originally published in 1941 in *Language, 19,* 440–444.)

Vihman, M. M. (1981). Phonology and the development of the lexicon: Evidence from children's errors. *Journal of Child Language, 8,* 239–264.

Vihman, M., Macken, M. A., Miller, R., Simmons, H., & Miller, J. (1985). From babbling to speech: A re-assessment of the continuity issue. *Language, 61,* 397–445.

Vihman, M., & Miller, R. (1988). Words and babble at the threshold of language acquisition. In M. D. Smith and J. L. Locke (Eds.), *The emergent lexicon: The child's development of a linguistic vocabulary.* New York: Academic Press.

Wardhaugh, Ronald. (1986). *Introduction to sociolinguistics.* New York: Blackwell.

Waterson, N. (1971). Child phonology: A prosodic view. *Journal of Linguistics, 7,* 179–221.

Waterson, N. (1978). Growth of complexity in phonological development. In N. Waterson & C. E. Snow (Eds.), *The development of communication.* New York: John Wiley.

Werker, J. F., & Pegg, J. E. (1992). Infant speech perception and phonological acquisition. To appear in Ferguson, C., Menn, L., and Stoel-Gammon, C. (Eds.), *Phonological development: Models, research, implications.* Parkton, MD: York Press.

REFERENCES

Allen, G., & Hawkins, S. (1980). Phonological rhythm: Definition and development. In G. Yeni-Komshian, J. F. Kavanagh, & C. A. Ferguson (Eds.), *Child phonology: Vol. 1. Production.* New York: Academic Press.

Atkinson, K. B., MacWhinney, B., & Stoel, C. (1970). An experiment in the recognition of babbling. *Papers and Reports in Child Language Development, 1,* 71–76.

Atkinson-King, K. (1973). Children's acquisition of phonological stress contrasts. *UCLA Working Papers in Phonetics, 25.*

Bar-Adon, A., & Leopold, W. (Eds.). (1971). *Readings in child language.* Englewood Cliffs, NJ: Prentice-Hall.

Barton, D. P. (1980). Phonemic perception in children. In G. Yeni-Komshian, J. F. Kavanagh, & C. A. Ferguson (Eds.), *Child phonology: Vol. 2. Perception.* New York: Academic Press.

Bernstein Ratner, N. (1984a). Patterns of vowel modification in mother–child speech. *Journal of Child Language, 11,* 557–578.

Bernstein Ratner, N. (1984b). Cues to post-vocalic voicing in mother–child speech. *Journal of Phonetics, 12,* 285–289.

Best, C. T., McRoberts, G. W., & Sithole, N. M. (1988). Examination of the perceptual reorganization for speech contrasts: Zulu click discrimination. *Journal of Experimental Psychology: Perception and Performance, 14,* 245–360.

Bloch, B., & Trager, G. L. *Outline of linguistic analysis.* Baltimore: Linguistic Society of America.

Boysson-Bardies, B. de, Sagart, L., & Durand, C. (1984). Discernible differences in the babbling of infants according to target language. *Journal of Child Language, 11,* 1–15.

Boysson-Bardies, B. de, & Vihman, M. M. (1991). Adaptation to language: Evidence from babbling and first words in four languages. *Language, 67,* 297–319.

Braine, M. D. S. (1974). On what might constitute a learnable phonology. *Language, 50,* 270–299.

Branigan, G. (1979). *Sequences of words as structured units.* Unpublished doctoral dissertation, Boston University School of Education.

Butler Platt, C., & MacWhinney, B. (1983). Solving a problem vs. remembering a solution: Error assimilation as a strategy in language acquisition. *Journal of Child Language, 10,* 41–75.

Clumeck, H. (1980). The acquisition of tone. In G. Yeni-Komshian, J. F. Kavanagh, & C. A. Ferguson (Eds.), *Child phonology: Vol. 1. Production.* New York: Academic Press.

DeCasper, A. J., & Fifer, W. P. (1980). Of human bonding: Newborns prefer their mothers' voices. *Science, 208, 1174–1176.*

Deser, T. (1991). *Dialect transmission and variation: An acoustic analysis of vowels in six urban Detroit families.* Bloomington, IN: Indiana Linguistics Club Publications.

Dodd, B. J. (1972). Effects of social and vocal stimulation on infant babbling. *Developmental Psychology, 7,* 80–83.

Edwards, M. L., & Shriberg, L. D. (1983). *Phonology: Applications in communicative disorders* (pp. 123–199). San Diego, CA: College-Hill Press.

Eilers, R. (1980). Infant speech perception: History and mystery. In G. Yeni-Komshian, J. F. Kavanagh, & C. A. Ferguson (Eds.), *Child phonology: Vol. 2. Perception.* New York: Academic Press.

Eimas, P. D., Siqueland, E. R., Jusczyk, P., & Vigorito, J. (1971). Speech perception in infants. *Science, 171,* 303–306.

Fee, J., & Ingram, D. (1982). Reduplication as a strategy of phonological development. *Journal of Child Language, 9,* 41–54.

Ferguson, C. A., Menn, L., & Stoel-Gammon, C. (Eds.). (1992). *Phonological development: Models, research, implications.* Parkton, MD: York Press.

Ferguson, C. A., & Farwell, C. B. (1975). Words and sounds in early language acquisition. *Language, 51,* 439–491.

Ferguson, C. A., & Macken, M. A. (1980). Phonological development in children's play and cognition. In K. E. Nelson (Ed.), *Children's language* (Vol. 4). New York: Gardner Press.

Fey, M., & Gandour, J. (1982). Rule discovery in early phonology acquisition. *Journal of Child Language, 9,* 71–82.

Garnica, O. (1973). The development of speech perception. In T. E. Moore (Ed.), *Cognitive development and the acquisition of language.* New York: Academic Press.

Greenlee, M. (1974). Interacting processes in the child's acquisition of stop-liquid clusters. *Papers and Reports on Child Language Development, 7.*

Grunwell, P. (1981). *The nature of phonological disability in children.* London: Academic Press.

Grunwell, P. (1987). *Clinical phonology* (2nd ed.). Baltimore: Williams and Wilkins.

Halliday, M. A. K. (1975). *Learning how to mean: Explorations in the development of language.* London: Edward Arnold.

Hyman, L. M. (1975). *Phonology: Theory and analysis.* New York: Holt, Rinehart & Winston.

Ingram, D. (1974). Phonological rules in young children. *Journal of Child Language, 1,* 49–64.

Ingram, D. (1986). Phonological patterns in the speech of young children. In P. Fletcher & M. Garman, (Eds.), *Language acquisition* (2nd ed.). Cambridge: Cambridge University Press.

Ingram, D. (1989). *Phonological disabilities in children.* (2nd ed.). London: Cole and Whurr.

Jaeger, J. J. (1980). *Categorization in phonology: An experimental approach.* Unpublished doctoral dissertation. Berkeley, CA: University of California.

Jakobson, R. (1968). *Child language, aphasia, and phonological universals.* (A. Keiler, Trans.). The Hague: Mouton.

Jesperson, O. (1925). *Language.* New York: Holt, Rinehart & Winston.

Jusczyk, P. W. (1992). Developing phonological categories for the speech signal. In Ferguson, C. A., Menn, L., & Stoel-Gammon, C. (Eds.). *Phonological development: Models, research, implications.* Parkton, MD: York Press.

Krohn, R., Steinberg, D., & Kobayashi, L. (1972). The psychological validity of Chomsky and Halle's vowel shift rule. *20th International Congress of Psychology,* Tokyo (Abstract Guide, paragraph 1905).

Leonard, L. B. (1992). Models of phonological development and children with phonological disorders. In Ferguson, C. A., Menn, L., & Stoel-Gammon, C. (Eds.). *Phonological development: Models, research, implications.* Parkton, MD: York Press.

Leopold, W. (1970). *Speech development of a bilingual child, 1-4.* New York: AMS Press.

Lieberman, P., Crelin, E. S., & Klatt, D. H. (1972). Phonetic ability and related anatomy of the newborn, adult human, Neanderthal man, and the chimpanzee. *American Anthropologist, 74,* 287–307.

Lindblom, B. (1992). Phonological units as adaptive emergents of lexical development. In Ferguson, C. A., Menn, L., & Stoel-Gammon, C. (Eds.). *Phonological development: Models, research, implications.* Parkton, MD: York Press.

Locke, J. L. (1983). *Phonological acquisition and change.* New York: Academic Press.

Macken, M. A. (1979). Developmental reorganization of phonology: A hierarchy of basic units of acquisition. *Lingua, 49,* 11–49.

Macken, M. A. (1980). The child's lexical representation: The "puzzle-puddle-pickle" evidence. *Journal of Linguistics, 16,* 1–19.

Macken, M. A., & Barton, D. (1980). The acquisition of voicing contrast in English: A study of voice onset time in word-initial stop consonant. *Journal of Child Language, 7,* 41–75.

MacNeilage, P. (1980). The control of speech production. In G. Yeni-Komshian, J. F. Kavanagh, & C. A. Ferguson (Eds.), *Child phonology: Vol. 1. Production.* New York: Academic Press.

MacWhinney, B. (1978). The acquisition of morphophonology. *Monographs of the Society for Research in Child Development, 43,* 1–2.

Malsheen, B. (1980). Two hypotheses for phonetic clarification in the speech of mothers to children. In G. Yeni-Komshian, J. F. Kavanagh, & C. A. Ferguson (Eds.), *Child phonology: Vol. 2. Perception.* New York: Academic Press.

McCawley, J. D. (1977). Acquisition models as models of acquisition (pp. 51–64). In R. Fasold & R. Shuy (Eds.), *Studies in language variation.* Washington, DC: Georgetown University Press.

Mehler, J., Jusczyk, P. W., Lambertz, G., Halsted, N., Bertoncini, J., & Amiel-Tisson, C. (1988). A precursor of language acquisition in young infants. *Cognition, 29,* 143–178.

Menn, L. (1971). Phonotactic rules in beginning speech. *Lingua, 26,* 225–241.

Menn, L. (1976). *Pattern, control, and contrast in beginning speech: A case study in the acquisition of word form and function.* Unpublished doctoral dissertation, University of Illinois.

Menn, L. (1983). Development of articulatory, phonetic, and phonological capabilities. In B. Butterworth (Ed.), *Language production* (Vol. 2). London: Academic Press.

Menn, L., & Matthei, E. (1992). The "two-lexicon" account of child phonology: Look back, looking ahead. In Ferguson, C. A., Menn, L., & Stoel-Gammon, C. (Eds.), *Phonological development: Models, research, implications.* Parkton, MD: York Press.

Menyuk, P., Menn, L., & Silber, R. (1986). Early strategies for the perception and production of words and sounds. In P. Fletcher & M. Garman (Eds.), *Language acquisition* (2nd ed.). Cambridge: Cambridge University Press.

Moskowitz, A. C. (1970). The two-year-old stage in the acquisition of English phonology. *Language, 46,* 426–441.

Moskowitz, B. A. (1980). Idioms in phonology acquisition and phonological change. *Journal of Phonetics, 8,* 69–83.

Mowrer, O. H. (1954). The psychologist looks at language. *American Psychologist, 9,* 660–694.

Myerson, R. (1975). *A developmental study of children's knowledge of complex derived words of English.* Unpublished doctoral dissertation, Harvard Graduate School of Education.

Nakazima, S. A. (1962). A comparative study of the speech developments of Japanese and American English in childhood (1): A comparison of the developments of voices at the prelinguistic period. *Studia Phonologica, 2,* 27–46.

Nelson, K. (1973). Structure and strategy in learning to talk. *Monographs of the Society for Research in Child Development, 38.*

Oller, D. K. (1980). The emergence of the sounds of speech in infancy. In G. Yeni-Komshian, J. F. Kavanagh, & C. A. Ferguson (Eds.), *Child phonology: (Vol. 1). Production.* New York: Academic Press.

Oller, D. K., & Eilers, R. (1988). The role of audition in babbling. *Child Development, 59,* 441–449.

Olmsted, D. L. (1971). *Out of the mouth of babes.* The Hague: Mouton.

Olney, R. L., & Scholnick, E. K. (1976). Adult judgment of age and linguistic differences in infant vocalization. *Journal of Child Language, 3,* 145–156.

Painter, C. (1984). *Into the mother tongue: A case study in early language development.* London: Frances Pinter.

Payne, A. (1976). *The acquisition of a phonological system of a second dialect.* Unpublished doctoral dissertation, University of Pennsylvania.

Peters, A. M. (1977). Language learning strategies. *Language, 53,* 560–573.

Peters, A. M. (1983). *The units of language acquisition.* Cambridge: Cambridge University Press.

Prather, E., Hedrick, D., and Kern, C. (1975). Articulation development in children aged two to four years. *Journal of Speech and Hearing Disorders, 40,* 179–191.

Priestly, T. M. S. (1977). One idiosyncratic strategy in the acquisition of phonology. *Journal of Child Language, 4,* 45–66.

Rheingold, H. L., Gerwitz, J. L., & Ross, H. W. (1959). Social conditioning of vocalizations in the infant. *Journal of Comparative and Physiological Psychology, 52,* 68–73.

Schwartz, R. G., & Leonard, L. B. (1982). Do children pick and choose? An examination of phonological selection and avoidance in early lexical acquisition. *Journal of Child Language, 9,* 319–336.

Smith, N. V. (1973). *The acquisition of phonology: A case study.* Cambridge: Cambridge University Press.

Stampe, D. (1969). The acquisition of phonemic representation. *Proceedings of the Fifth Regional Meeting of the Chicago Linguistic Society,* pp. 433–444.

Stark, R. E. (1980). Stages of speech development in the first year. In G. Yeni-Komshian, J. A. Kavanagh, & C. A. Ferguson (Eds.), *Child phonology* (Vol. 1). New York: Academic Press.

Stemberger, J. P. (1992). A connectionist view of child phonology: Phonological processing without phonological processes. In Ferguson, C. A., Menn, L., & Stoel-Gammon, C. (Eds.), *Phonological development: Models, research, implications.* Parkton, MD: York Press.

Stoel-Gammon, C. (1985). Phonetic inventories, 15–24 months: A longitudinal study. *Journal of Speech and Hearing Research, 28,* 505–512.

Stoel-Gammon, C., & Dunn, C. (1985). *Normal and disordered phonology in children.* Austin, TX: Pro-Ed.

Stoel-Gammon, C., & Otomo, K. (1986). Babbling development of hearing-impaired and normally hearing subjects. *Journal of Speech and Hearing Disorders, 51,* 33–41.

Templin, M. C. (1957). Certain language skills in children: Their development and interrelationships. Minneapolis: University of Minnesota Press.

Todd, G., & Palmer, B. (1968). Social reinforcement of infant babbling. *Child Development, 39,* 591–596.

Trehub, S. E. (1976). The discrimination of foreign speech contrasts by infants and children. *Child Development, 47,* 466–472.

Velleman, S. (1988). The role of linguistic perception in later phonological development. *Journal of Applied Psycholinguistics, 9.*

Velten, H. V. (1971). The growth of phonemic and lexical patterns in the infant. Reprinted in A. Bar-Adon & W. Leopold (Eds.), *Readings in child language.* Englewood Cliffs, NJ: Prentice-Hall. (Originally published in 1941 in *Language, 19,* 440–444.)

Vihman, M. M. (1976). From prespeech to speech: On early phonology. *Papers and Reports on Child Language Development, 12.*

Vihman, M. M. (1981). Phonology and the development of the lexicon: Evidence from children's errors. *Journal of Child Language, 8,* 239–264.

Vihman, M. M. (1987, July). The interaction of production and perception in the transition to speech. Paper read at the Fourth International Congress for the Study of Child Language, Lund, Sweden.

Vihman, M. M., Macken, M. A., Miller, R., Simmons, H., and Miller, J. (1985). From babbling to speech: A re-assessment of the continuity issue. *Language, 61,* 397–445.

Vihman, M. M., & Miller, R. (1988). Words and babble at the threshold of language acquisition. In M. D. Smith and J. L. Locke (Eds.), *The emergent lexicon: The child's development of a linguistic vocabulary.* New York: Academic Press.

Wahler, R. G. (1969). Infant social development: Some experimental analyses of an infant–mother interaction during the first year of life. *Journal of Experimental Child Psychology, 7,* 101–113.

Waterson, N. (1971). Child phonology: A prosodic view. *Journal of Linguistics, 7,* 179–221.

Waterson, N. (1978). Growth of complexity in phonological development. In N. Waterson & C. Snow (Eds.), *The development of communication.* New York: John Wiley.

Waterson, N., & Snow, C. (Eds.). (1978). *The development of communication.* New York: John Wiley.

Weir, R. (1962). *Language in the crib.* The Hague: Mouton.

Weisberg, P. (1963). Social and nonsocial conditioning of infant vocalization. *Child Development, 39,* 377–388.

Werker, J. F., & Pegg, J. E. (1992). Infant speech perception and phonological acquisition. In Ferguson, C. A., Menn, L., & Stoel-Gammon, C. (Eds.), *Phonological development: Models, research, implications.* Parkton, MD: York Press.

Werker, J. F., & Tees, R. C. (1984). Cross-language speech perception: Evidence for perceptual reorganization during the first year of life. *Infant Behavior and Development, 7,* 49–64.

Wilbur, R., & Menn, L. (1975). *Towards a redefinition of psychological reality: The internal structure of the lexicon* (Occasional Papers in Linguistics). San Jose, CA: San Jose State College.

Winitz, H. (1969). *Articulatory acquisition and behavior.* New York: Appleton-Century-Crofts.

Yeni-Komshian, G., Kavanagh, J., & Ferguson, C. A. (1980). *Child phonology: Vol. 1. Production; Vol. 2. Perception.* New York: Academic Press.

Learning the Meaning of Words: Semantic Development and Beyond

4

Deborah Myers Pease
Jean Berko Gleason *Boston University*
Barbara Alexander Pan *Harvard Graduate School of Education*

INTRODUCTION

Even very young children understand the meaning of much that is said to them. A toddler who understands the meaning of his mother's saying "It's time for your bath now" may be responding to a variety of situational cues—it is a particular time of day, they are in a certain room, they are engaged in a familiar activity, or the parent may actually be pointing to the bathtub. Children understand the pragmatic intent of adults' utterances before they understand the individual words. Only very slowly do children come to understand and use words in adult fashion, to break them free of context and use them flexibly in a variety of situations. The acquisition of words, their meanings, and the links between them does not usually happen at once. During the course of this process, which is usually called **semantic development,** children's strategies for learning word meanings and relating them to one another change as their internal representation of language constantly grows and becomes reorganized.

In this chapter we will describe the relationship between words and their referents, and some of the theories that attempt to explain how children acquire and represent meaning. We will address what is known about early words and the ways in which contemporary researchers have attempted to interpret the data on children's early words and word meanings. We will also present research on later semantic development, which examines the ways that the semantic system is elaborated as words become related to one another in more complex semantic networks. Finally, we will describe children's growing awareness of words as physical entities independent of their meanings, and discuss the implications of such **metalinguistic development** for a variety of nonliteral language uses.

THE RELATIONSHIP BETWEEN WORDS AND THEIR REFERENTS

What does it mean to say that children acquire meaning? And what is it that adults share when they know the meaning of a word? First, it is important to note that the meaning of a word resides in the speakers of a common language, not in the world of objects. The word is a sign that signifies a **referent,** but the referent is not the meaning of the word. If, for example, you say to a child, "Look at the kitty," the referent, the actual cat, is not the meaning of *kitty*—if the cat ran away or were run over by a truck, the word would still have meaning because meaning is an act of cognition.

Let us assume that a child learns that the word *kitty* refers to her cat; in this case, the actual cat is the referent of the word *kitty.* But what is the relationship between the word and the cat? Cats can be called *kitty, cat, koshka, macska, katze,* or *chat,* depending on whether one is speaking English, Russian, Hungarian, German, or French. There is nothing intrinsic to cats that makes one or another name more appropriate or fitting—the relationship between the name and the thing is thus *arbitrary,* and it is by social convention in a particular language that speakers agree to call the animal by a particular word (Morris, 1946). This arbitrary relationship between the referent (the cat) and the sign for it (the word *cat*) is *symbolic.* Nonverbal signs can also share this symbolic nature: the red light that means stop, for instance, is purely symbolic because there is no obvious connection between the color red and the action of stopping. We could agree to have blue lights or even green lights mean *stop,* as long as we all agreed on the meaning of the light.

For a few words, the relation between word and referent is not arbitrary. If one says, for example, "The book fell with a *thud,*" the relationship between the word *thud* and the actual sound referred to is not arbitrary, since the word resembles the sound. As well, the name of the cuckoo bird is not arbitrary: it represents the sound that the bird actually makes. Although the study of semantic acquisition has concentrated on how children learn the meaning of symbols, we should not be surprised to learn that many of children's earliest words or protowords have a less-than-arbitrary relation to their referents: clocks are called *tick-tock,* and painful bumps become *owies.* Some of these words are in the baby talk lexicon that adults use when attempting to communicate with babies, and others are the children's own creations.

It is probably easier for children to learn a word that is obviously related to its referent than one that is totally arbitrary and symbolic; and, as some research has shown, young children believe that the name and the referent have more than a casual connection. They think that one cannot change the name of something without changing its nature as well; for instance, if one decided to call a dog a *cow,* a child might assume that the animal would begin to moo (Vygotsky, 1962).

This belief in the essential appropriateness of names was a subject of argument among ancient philosophers as well. Plato, writing in the fourth century B.C., discussed the question of whether there is a natural relation between names and referents in his Cratylus dialogue. The Anomalists of Plato's day believed that the relation was inexplicable, but the Analogists believed that through careful etymology the essential nature of words could be revealed (Bloomfield, 1933).

Using English examples, we might show that a blackberry is so called because it is a berry that is black, and a bedroom is so named because it is a room containing a bed. The ancient Greek Analogists would also claim that if we only looked hard enough, we would find the natural connections behind *gooseberry* and *mushroom* as well. This altogether human desire to produce order can be seen in many **folk etymologies** today, and explains why college students as well as young children, when asked why Friday is called *Friday,* may respond, "Because it is the day you eat fried fish," or why they may hold that a handkerchief is so named "Because you hold it in your hand and go *kerchoo*" (Berko, 1958).

MENTAL IMAGES

Although meaning is a mental event, we still have to specify what its exact nature is. One possibility is that meaning is a mental picture. As we have seen earlier (see Chapter 1), incoming language is processed in the part of the brain known as Wernicke's area, which is near the auditory association areas of the brain. The belief that the sound of a word evokes a mental picture of its referent and that the image is the meaning of the word has a long history (see Tichener, 1909). However, even though it is true that many people are able to visualize and can imagine quite vivid pictures, not everyone does so.

There are many other reasons that mental images cannot be the same as meaning (Brown, 1968). Many words, such as *happy* or *jealousy,* do not have picturable referents, and still we know their meanings. In addition, even if one has an image for a word, it is liable to be quite particularistic—*dog,* for instance, might evoke a picture of a black poodle you know. Yet anyone who knows the meaning of *dog* can recognize many hundreds of real dogs of all sizes and shapes, so the mental image would have to be a very complicated composite if it had to account for all instances. Clearly, this is not the case. Finally, images tend to be quite idiosyncratic; speakers who share meaning may hold very different internal images. One speaker's mental house may look like a mansion, whereas another's may be a simple cottage, yet both speakers recognize new instances of houses when they encounter them.

■ THEORETICAL PERSPECTIVES ON SEMANTIC DEVELOPMENT

ASSOCIATIONIST THEORY

One of the simplest explanations of how children learn the meanings of their first words is that they do so through association. This model is very similar to the classical conditioning model proposed by learning theorists for any kind of associative learning (see Chapter 7 for a complete discussion of this theory). In learning through association, there is first an unconditioned stimulus that produces a response. In Pavlov's famous experiments, dogs were first presented with meat powder (the unconditioned stimulus), which caused the quite natural response of salivating. Later, a bell was rung at the same time that the powder was presented. Eventually, the dogs salivated when the bell rang, even when there was no meat powder present. The dogs responded to the sound of the bell, at least in part, as they had responded to the meat powder. They had become conditioned to the bell, which had thus become the conditioned stimulus.

How might this model be extended to cover the acquisition of meaning? If we assume that the infant already has some responses to objects in the world, then through a similar process of association the names of the objects can be learned. For example, the baby is familiar with the family cat and has certain expectations whenever it appears. If the parent points and says "kitty," eventually the infant will react to the word alone (at least in part), as if the cat were there—looking around for it or feeling pleased and ready for play. The cat, in this model, is the unconditioned stimulus that gives rise to certain predispositions or responses in the child. Eventually, the word *kitty* becomes the conditioned stimulus that evokes much the same set of responses.

It is important to remember that the conditioned response is similar to, but not really the same as, the original response to the unconditioned stimulus (Lashley, 1954). Pavlov's dogs may have salivated at the sound of the bell as they had salivated at the sight of the meat powder, but they did not try to eat the bell. The infant may respond somewhat to the word *kitty* as if it were the actual cat, but not to the extent of patting the empty air. For learning to have taken place, it suffices that the word *kitty* and the actual cat have been associated so that they evoke at least some of the same responses. Association theory may explain the earliest and simplest kinds of linking between words and objects. Many of children's early words, such as *cookie* and *blanket,* have concrete referents and could be learned through association. The acquisition of more abstract early words, such as *more,* requires a more complex explanation.

DEVELOPMENTAL THEORIES

In contrast to the associationist model, developmental theories consider semantic development within the wider context of the child's general cognitive and linguistic skills. Such theories attempt to explain how the child may acquire first words, why the scope of reference to which children's early words are applied may not match that of adults, and how children's semantic systems become more adultlike over time. It is clear that young children first acquire meaning in a very context-bound way, as a part of their real-world expectations. As research on prelinguistic development has shown, by the time children begin to understand language and to talk, their cognitive development has made significant strides. Researchers like John Macnamara (1972) have pointed out that very young children map language onto a set of observations about the world that they have already made. They do not learn about taking baths because their parents say, "It's bath time"; rather, they already know that their daily routine contains such an item, and at some point they realize that the parent's phrase refers to that familiar activity. Similarly, Nelson (1974) has suggested that a **functional core** may underlie children's early words. For example, the child first learns that *ball* refers to an object one throws, and then extends the label *ball* to other objects that are perceptually similar.

Cognitive views of semantic development hold that the child's primary task is to acquire categorical concepts (e.g., to learn that the word *dog* refers to a whole class of animals). Theorists differ as to how they characterize the nature of children's categorical concept acquisition. One view is that children acquire categories defined by semantic features, a second is that they acquire probabilistic concepts, and yet another is that they acquire prototypes.

The **semantic feature** view is that children learn a set of distinguishing features for each categorical concept. For instance, children learn that the word *dog* refers to a category of animals that are alive and warm-blooded, have four legs, bark, and are covered with hair. According to Eve Clark (1974), when a child learns a new word, it is in the context of a specific situation: the word *dog* may at first be understood to apply only to the child's own dog, and only later comes the understanding that other creatures may also be called "dog" as long as they share the small set of critical features that uniquely define the category. Overextensions occur when the child infers category membership from a partial match of features. A toddler may, in this way, call a moose "doggie" because both animals have hair and four legs. According to feature theory, the child in this case does not yet know that antlers disqualify an animal from membership in the dog category.

Some researchers, notably Smith and Medin (1981), have pointed out that even if children are acquiring their concepts as categories, there are great differences in the nature of the concepts themselves. For instance, there are **classical concepts,** like "bachelor": every instance of this concept must have the qualities of being male, adult, and unmarried. One cannot meet, for instance, a married bachelor. The concept "triangle" is another example of a classical concept: all triangles must have three angles, otherwise they are simply not triangles.

In contrast to classical concepts, there are also **probabilistic concepts,** like "bird." Most birds have feathers and beaks, fly, chirp, etc., but not all do. For instance, a kiwi is a nonflying bird. Concepts that involve people are often probabilistic: "doctor," for example. All instances (doctors) share some characteristics, like some medical training, but other characteristics, like "has high self-esteem," are typical of only some doctors (Smith & Medin, 1981).

Some examples of probabilistic concepts have more of the qualities of the concept than others. For example, a robin has more typical "bird" characteristics than does a penguin—therefore, people see robins as better examples of birds, and they also can classify them faster when asked if a robin is a bird. These typical examples of the category, or **prototypes,** are more accessible in memory in adult subjects (Rosch, 1973). According to prototype theory (see Figure 4.1), children acquire these core concepts when they acquire meaning and only later come to recognize members of that category that are distant from the prototypes.

These theories have brought us a long way from the notion that meaning might be a little picture in one's brain. We do not know whether functional characteristics, perceptual features, or prototypes are what children most frequently use in acquiring word meaning. It is likely that individual differences in cognitive style may result in different children favoring particular strategies in semantic development. Moreover, it may be that children's semantic systems are best described by different models at different points in development (Lucariello, 1987; Nelson & Lucariello, 1985). Later in this chapter we will consider cognitive and linguistic operating principles that may help children in formulating hypotheses about word/meaning mappings.

■ EARLY WORDS

By their second year, children are using words to understand and communicate and have begun trying to figure out how the language system works. They begin with words related to what is intellectually and socially most meaningful to them, such as names for important people and objects in their lives. Thus *mommy, daddy, doggie,* and *blankey* are common early words, and *tree, vase,* and *policeman* are not. Subsequent patterns of word meaning and use reflect development not only within children's semantic systems, but also in other areas such as their cognition and memory, in addition to widened experience.

THE STUDY OF VOCABULARY

Examination of children's vocabulary is probably the oldest approach to the study of language acquisition. Beginning word use signals that children have a new tool that will enable them to learn about and participate more fully in their societies. Furthermore,

FIGURE 4.1
Some birds are more prototypical than others (From *Words in the Mind* [p. 54] by J. Aitchison, 1987. London: Basil Blackwell. Adapted by permission.)

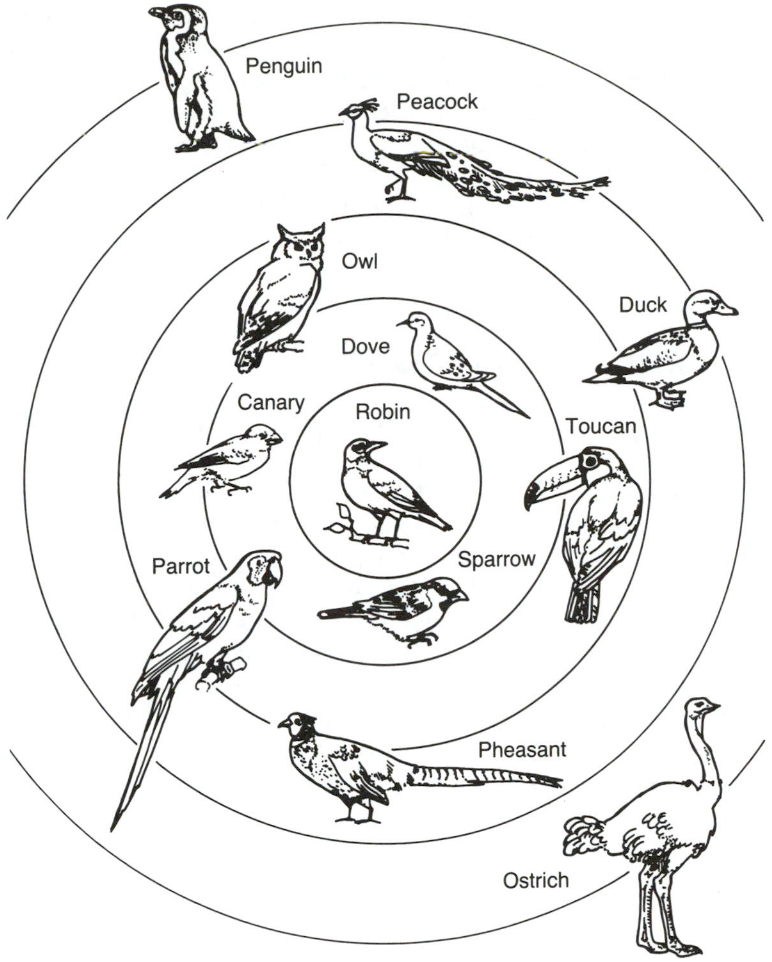

word use is thought to provide tangible indicators of the makeup and workings of children's minds. The first studies—some as early as the eighteenth century (e.g., Tiedemann, 1787)—were almost invariably based on observations of the authors' own children and were kept in the form of diaries. During the nineteenth century and the first half of the twentieth century, many psychologists kept diary records of their children's development. This remains a valuable way to trace the development of language in individual children. One of the most famous diary studies was conducted by Werner Leopold (1970), whose four-volume work traced the development of both English and German in his daughter Hildegarde:

> Hildegarde was from birth exposed to two languages, English and German, simultaneously, and built her own early speech from selected vocabulary items from both languages. . . . In examining Hildegarde's vocabulary it is necessary to keep in mind that meanings are necessarily hazy and vague at first. . . . (Leopold, 1948, p. 174)

Diaries can be a valuable adjunct to other research on children's language. By themselves, however, they can be misleading, since the temptation to write what is unusual or interesting, rather than what is daily and ordinary, is hard to resist. More recently, a number of researchers have found ways to augment and improve diary studies, by giving parents who are participating in a study checklists of the words that their children are likely to acquire during their first years (Dale, Bates, Resnick, & Morisett, 1989). The checklists help parents organize their observations and remind them of the more ordinary, but important, things their children say that they might otherwise overlook.

WHAT ARE EARLY WORDS LIKE?

By the time children begin to acquire a vocabulary, they have already been exposed to a great deal of language and have had a wide range of individual experiences. It is interesting, therefore, that children's initial productive or expressive vocabularies have been found to be quite similar, despite differences in upbringing and environment.

The words children acquire in their early productive vocabularies are influenced by many factors. One of these factors is phonological composition. Researchers have analyzed the phonology of children's first 50 words (Ferguson & Farwell, 1975; Stoel-Gammon & Cooper, 1984), studied children's imitations of words (Leonard, Schwartz, Folger, Newhoff, & Wilcox, 1979), and tried to teach new words to one-year-olds (Leonard, Schwartz, Morris, & Chapman, 1981; Schwartz & Leonard, 1982). The results of these studies show that words that are easier for children to pronounce are more likely to be included in their early productive vocabularies, and that favored sound patterns may vary greatly across children. Moreover, phonological composition continues to play a role in vocabulary through the early school years. Unlike adults, children aged five to seven tend to use few words that sound very similar to one another (Charles-Luce & Luce, 1990).

From the beginning, children's vocabularies appear to include words from a variety of grammatical classes; their first 50 words represent all of the major grammatical classes found in adult language. More importantly, children use the words in ways that reflect grammatical classes (Benedict, 1979). Nelson (1973) studied the vocabularies of 18 American children at the 50-word level. Attainment of the first 50 words marks an important developmental point, because most children begin combining words soon after their vocabularies have reached this size. Nelson asked the children's mothers to record the first time each new word was used. (Even though this study was informative and has inspired additional research, its conclusions are nonetheless subject to criticism; see Chapter 8, on individual differences in language acquisition.) Nelson's study revealed some marked similarities and some interesting differences among the children's vocabularies. Similarities were discovered in the relative proportions of word types. Nelson found that general nominals such as *doggie* (51 percent) were most prevalent, followed by specific nominals such as *Mommy* and *Fido* (14 percent), action words such as *up* and *give* (almost 14 percent), modifiers such as *dirty* and *mine* (9 percent), personal-social words such as *want* and *please* (8 percent), and function words such as *for* and *on* (4 percent).

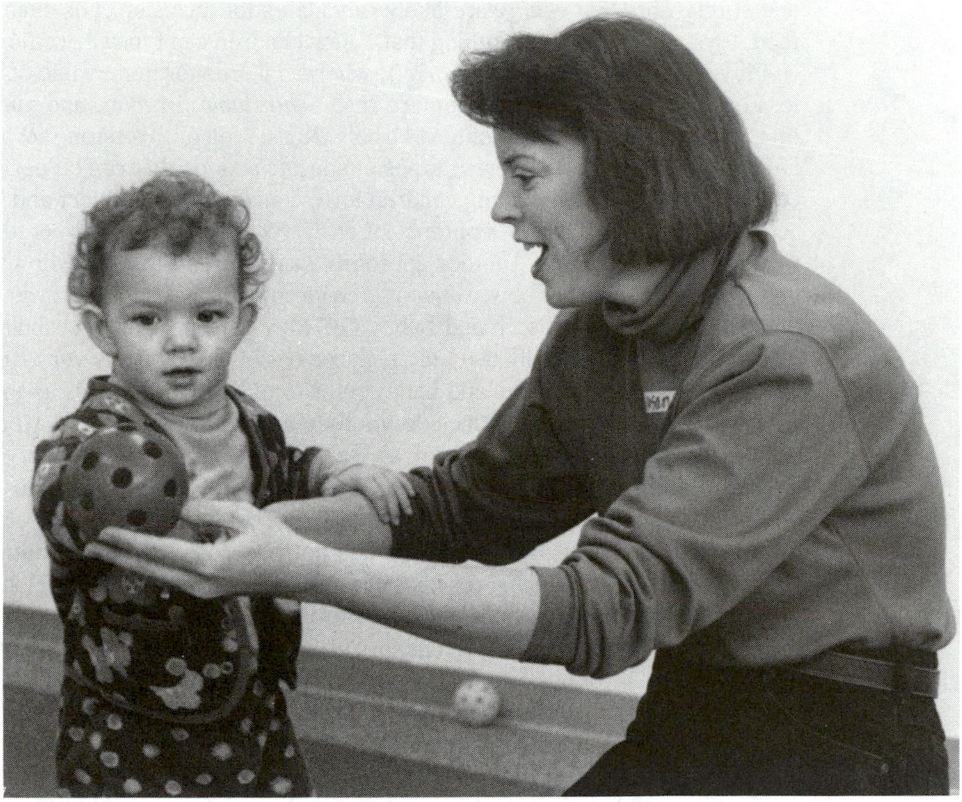

Words like "ball" that are easy to pronounce are likely to be in children's early vocabularies.

The preponderance of common nouns (or general nominals) in early vocabularies has been noted in many studies. Even though a particular noun may be used less frequently than a particular verb in the language, nouns appear to be acquired more easily and utilized when children are at a loss to remember a particular verb. For instance, a child who does not remember the word *drive* may say "car" instead, as in "Let's car to the store." Gentner (1983, 1988) suggests that nouns are favored over verbs in acquisition because verbs are more linguistically complex. In addition, the concepts referred to by nouns are clearer, more concrete, and more readily identifiable than those of verbs. Nouns tend to refer to the same concepts in different languages, but the particular aspects of meaning covered by verbs are not identical in different languages. Learning a verb's meaning requires a child to find out which of the possible aspects are included and which are not. Comprehension and production of **decontextualized** verbs (those that do not refer to the here-and-now) appear to be particularly late to emerge (Smith & Sachs, 1990).

Nelson has noted two principles that appear to affect which words are included in early vocabularies and which are not. Names of referents with which the child *interacts* and of referents that *change* are likely candidates for inclusion. For example, words for food, toys, and articles of clothing that young children can typically remove are common (*juice, cookie, ball, socks,* and *blanket*), whereas words for immovable objects and those less easily acted upon by children are rare (*wall, table, window,* and *mitten*). Research on young children's learning of novel labels (Ross, Nelson, Wetstone, & Tanouye, 1986) indicates that the more different types of specific actions that can be performed upon an object, the more readily young children form concepts of the object and learn its name.

Nelson's study of the contents of early vocabularies was directed toward determining what is included. Another approach was taken by Bloom, who used videotaped interactions to examine how frequently children actually use the words in their vocabularies. According to Bloom and Lahey (1978), children whose vocabularies are at the 50-word level may actually use only eight or ten of those words very frequently and in a variety of contexts. Bloom and Lahey refer to this group of words as the **core group.** Children's vocabularies also include another group of less favored words, somewhat greater in number, that are used at least once every day or two. The remaining vocabulary words are used rarely, perhaps as infrequently as once in a few months. Rescorla (1980) found in a longitudinal study that by the time her subjects had produced 445 words, 5 percent of those words had not been used for two months.

More recently, some researchers (Gopnik & Meltzoff, 1987) have noted the concurrent emergence of specific early words and specific cognitive developments. For example, just at the point where children acquire object permanence, that is, when they are mastering the notion that objects that disappear from sight continue to exist in some unseen location, they begin to mark such disappearances with words such as *gone*. Similarly, as children learn to use objects to achieve a desired result, success/failure terms such as *there* and *uh-oh* emerge. Studies such as these suggest that the early productive vocabularies of children may label meanings relating to specific cognitive problems on which the child is currently working.

UNCONVENTIONAL WORD/MEANING MAPPINGS

An **overextension** is said to occur when a child uses a word in a context or manner that is inconsistent with, but in some way related to, the adult meaning of the word, as when a dog is called "kitty" or a cotton ball "snow," or when a visitor is greeted with a hearty "bye-bye!" Thus, the term **overextension** derives from the fact that the child is extending the term beyond the adult word concept. An **underextension** is said to occur when a child uses a particular word for only a limited subset of the contexts allowed by the adult concept. A child who saw many breeds of dogs but referred only to basset hounds, dachshunds, and corgis as "doggie" would appear to be extending the term to a reduced set of referents. Clark (1987), Mervis and Mervis (1988), and others have pointed out that children's categories may not initially match those of adults: they may use "duck" for birds that swim, "bird" for those that fly, and "chicken" for those that don't fly (Clark, 1987). Both overextensions and underextensions are common in young children's speech; complete records of their occurrences could help reveal what children know about particular words.

What do children's extensions of words tell us? At best, they reveal how children categorize the world and what aspects of their experiences they find relevant to certain words. We might be able to detect ways in which children integrate their experiences differently as well as the course by which their word concepts approach ours. At the same time, some caution must also be exercised. As some researchers (e.g., Hoek, Ingram, & Gibson, 1986) have hinted, the extent to which the child's spoken word should be considered an accurate representation of her inner structuring of the world remains unclear.

Children's early utterances, consisting primarily of single words, were once considered to carry the meaning of whole sentences; they were labeled **holophrastic.** It was thought that children intended the more elaborate meanings of older individuals but were prevented from expressing them by nonsemantic factors, such as insufficient memory span (Greenfield & Smith, 1976). This position was difficult to support because it required attributing intention and semantic knowledge to young children on the basis of little evidence. It is now believed that young children come only gradually to understand and subsequently encode adult meanings in their words (Carey, 1982).

The processes of concept learning and **lexicalization,** or attachment of words and meanings, may occur at varying rates and overlap in time. While some overextensions occur because children's underlying word concepts differ from those of adults, other plausible explanations exist. As noted earlier, not all categories have clear-cut boundaries. Carabine (1991) found that most of the inappropriate labelling by two- and three-year-old children he studied consisted of labels applied to objects which were not uniformly categorized by adults either. In addition, some of children's overextensions may reflect retrieval problems, such that an older, better known label (e.g., "dog") may be inappropriately used in place of a more recently acquired, but more appropriate one such as "moose" (Hoek, Ingram, & Gibson, 1986). At other times, children may not yet have acquired the proper label, even though their concepts match those of adults. They may then opt to use words as analogies or as semantic stand-ins for the words they do not know. This view attributes significantly more semantic knowledge to children than the classical overextension view does.

Nelson and her colleagues (Nelson, Benedict, Gruendel, & Rescorla, 1977) have suggested that young children are actively engaged in the "classification and cross-classification of features of . . . objects and events" and use their single words analogically to comment on similarities they have noticed. Thus, the child who points to a Saint Bernard and says "cow" is thought to mean only that the dog is *like* a cow. Hudson and Nelson (1984) have shown that two-year-olds who correctly label an object in a naming task may misname or substitute another label in pretend play. Additional evidence that children are using analogy comes from the fact that they are seldom observed to use words in this fashion after they acquire syntax and can explain what they mean.

In other situations, children seem to overextend words as a humorous gesture. When our two-year-old friend Matthew was shown a flying helicopter by his father, who pointed and said "helicopter," Matthew grinned, giggled, and said "airplane." Matthew's demeanor and the fact that he had used the word *helicopter* previously suggest that he was using his knowledge of words to make a joke. Determining what a child's early words mean requires attention to the contexts in which they are spoken and understood, as well as information about how the child has referred to the concepts or used the words before.

INVENTED WORDS

In an experimental study, Berko (1958) found that preschoolers and first graders were often able to invent words to refer to meanings that were specified by an experimenter. In this structured situation, children and adults were asked questions like "What would you call a man who 'zibs' for a living?" Although children only rarely employed the typical adult strategy of **deriving** new words by adding suffixes (a *zibber* zibs for a living), they were frequently able to create words by using alternative techniques (e.g., making **compound words** like *zib-man*).

Children's strategies of word invention have also been explored by Clark (1981, 1982). She observed that young children between the ages of two and six invented new words to fill gaps in their vocabularies. These gaps occurred when the child had forgotten or did not know the usual word. Inventions such as *pourer* for *cup* and *plant-man* for *gardener* were common. Preschoolers frequently created needed verbs from nouns they knew, as when one almost-four-year-old said, while putting crackers in her soup, "I'm crackering my soup" (1981, p. 304).

Clark found that children's lexical innovations follow fairly regular principles of **productivity, semantic transparency,** and **regularization.** Productivity is shown in children's use of forms that are also used by adults as the basis of new words. Many English words meaning "people who do something," for instance, end in *-man* (*policeman, garbageman*), and that is children's first choice in making agentival nouns; they create a form like *plant-man* based on this principle of productivity. For three-year-olds, *plant-man* is also a more semantically transparent form than *gardener,* because it makes it easier to see the relationship between the word and the activity it denotes. Finally, children tend to regularize the new words they create just as they overregularize the words they already have in their lexicons (e.g., two *mouses* rather than two *mice*). Thus, a child may refer to a person who rides a bicycle as a *bicycler,* using the common *-er* agentive pattern rather than the rare, irregular, and unproductive *-ist* form to create *bicyclist.*

In a more recent study, Clark, Gelman, and Lane (1985) have shown that the ability to invent new words is preceded by understanding the principles of compound word formation at a very early age. In this study, children were shown pictures that might represent new compound words they heard, such as *apple-knife* (a knife for cutting apples) and *mouse-hat* (a hat for a mouse). Words of this type are common in English and serve to subcategorize larger categories. In order to understand them, it is necessary to know that the first term is a modifier and the second term is the head noun. Clark and her colleagues found that children as young as two-and-a-half had no difficulty understanding this modifier–head construction.

DIFFERENCES BETWEEN COMPREHENSION AND PRODUCTION

According to Nelson and her colleagues (1977), comprehension of a word requires that a child, on hearing the word, anticipate or do something. Production of a word requires on its most basic level that the child speak the word at an appropriate time and place.

It was once believed that a child's productive or expressive vocabulary did not differ from his receptive or comprehension vocabulary except in size. Productive vocabularies do indeed typically lag behind receptive vocabularies; the children studied by Benedict (1979) comprehended their first 50 words at about 13 months of age, but had not produced 50 words until about 19 months. The differences between receptive and expressive vocabularies, however, involve not only rate of acquisition, but strategies as well. Researchers including Gruendel (cited in Nelson, Benedict, Gruendel, & Rescorla, 1977), Huttenlocher (1974), Rescorla (1981), and Thompson and Chapman (1977) have observed numerous examples of accurate word comprehension with a concurrent lack of differentiation in the productive vocabulary. One of Rescorla's subjects, Rachel, was able to identify a motorcycle, bike, truck, plane, and helicopter; yet at the same time she referred to them all as "car!" Conversely, Rice (1983) has reported children's using a word quite accurately in production but not comprehending it when others use it. Clearly, then, the receptive and expressive systems do not overlap perfectly, and a clear understanding of the dimensions and features of each requires careful study.

■ FEATURES OF ADULT SPEECH THAT INFLUENCE CHILDREN'S SEMANTIC DEVELOPMENT

Even before children begin using words themselves, adults' labeling serves to focus children's attention on objects. Baldwin and Markman (1989) found that children between the ages of 10 and 20 months tended to focus longest on unfamiliar objects that adults pointed to or labeled for them. Later, during play intervals where adults were not present, children focused most on those toys that had been verbally labeled for them by adults.

The words adults use when they label objects for children are also reflected in children's vocabularies. When Western, middle-class children are noticed attempting to say a word, their parents engage them in naming games (Ninio & Bruner, 1978). In these interactions, the parent points to and names specific objects for the child and then helps the child say the name. The names adults provide for children are not always the ones they would use with adults or older children: Anglin (1977, 1978) showed that adults vary their object labeling according to the audience. When asked to label a set of pictures of objects for two-year-olds, adults used general names like *money* instead of *nickel,* and *dog* instead of *collie.* Anglin also gave the adults sets of words at different levels of generality and asked them to group them according to the way they thought two-year-olds would categorize them. The adults' picture labeling for the children had the same patterns as their ratings of two-year-olds' categorizations. Thus, it appears that adults have preconceived notions of the minds and activities of two-year-olds and use labels that reflect those notions.

Adults sometimes mislabel objects when speaking to very young children, teaching them in some cases to use labels that are incorrect by adult standards. Mervis and Mervis (1982) gave 10 mothers and their 13-month-olds sets of toys to play with and recorded their speech. The mothers named almost all of the toys for their children, and were observed quite often to misname some of them according to how their children might have categorized them. For example, a toy leopard was commonly referred to as "kitty-cat," and a toy tow truck was referred to as "car." Why would parents mislabel objects for their children? According to Mervis and Mervis, children provide their parents with signals indicating how they might categorize objects. Although babies first treat all objects in the same ways (mouthing, touching, shaking, and banging them), eventually they begin treating them differentially. At this point a doll might be held and a toy car pushed on the floor. Children's differential treatment of objects indicates on a fundamental level how they are categorizing the objects. By labeling the objects for children according to the children's own categories, parents are probably showing how words are used. That is, objects that differ in minor ways but are of the same category share names.

The naming practices of the mothers observed by Mervis and Mervis seem to be based on children's own ways of categorizing the world. The names chosen follow what Rosch et al. (1976) have called **basic level categories.** The first principle underlying such categories is that similarities within categories are emphasized, rather than similarities between categories. Thus, because leopards are more like cats than other objects, they are labeled "cats." The second principle defining the basic level is that it is the most general level at which objects are similar because of their forms, functions, or motions. Thus, although an owl bank and a Christmas ornament share neither name nor function for adults, because they are round objects that would most likely be treated similarly (i.e., rolled) by very young children, they were grouped with balls and identified as "ball" by the mothers studied by the Mervises.

Mothers' naming strategies also appear to influence their children's acquisition of the hierarchical nature of language. Mothers of two- to four-year-olds use different strategies when teaching their children basic level (e.g., *bath*) and superordinate terms (e.g., *toy*) (Callanan, 1985). For basic level words, they use **ostension:** they may point and say, "That's a tractor." When asked to teach superordinates, however, they employ a strategy of **inclusion,** mentioning both basic level terms and the superordinate term. For instance, they say things such as "A car and a bus and a train. All of them are kinds of *vehicles*." Because superordinates are generally used to refer to a class of objects, rather than a specific one, they may be more difficult to learn (Wisniewski & Murphy, 1989). Thus, it may be helpful to children when mothers provide additional information about superordinate terms.

Mothers' speech has also been shown to have an effect on the ways that children come to understand and use vocabulary relating to their own inner states (Beeghly, Bretherton, & Mervis, 1986). In a study conducted in Great Britain, Dunn, Bretherton, and Munn (1987) found that mothers talking with their young children routinely labeled a variety of the children's inner states, including quality of consciousness (e.g., "bored"), physiological states ("dizzy"), and emotional states ("happy"). By the age of two, the children used many of these inner state words themselves, particularly those relating to sleep, distress, dislike, temperature, pain, and pleasure. An even more intriguing finding of this study was that mothers used more of these labels with daughters, and, by the age of two, girls themselves referred to feeling states significantly more frequently than boys did.

In addition to the special vocabulary directed to young children, adults and even older children (Shatz & Gelman, 1973) seem to tailor other aspects of their language to the child's

Much of mothers' language to children focuses on shared activity.

ability level; some of the characteristics of input language may facilitate semantic development. Input language, especially when young children begin to understand and use words, is more clearly and slowly enunciated and is characterized by exaggerated intonation and clear pauses between utterances (Sachs, Brown, & Salerno, 1976). In addition, sentence elements are often uttered in an isolated fashion (Newport, 1975; Snow, 1972), and words that are being taught or focused on tend to be placed in sentence-final position with especially marked pitch and stress (Fernald & Mazzie, 1991). Thus, speech directed to young children tends to be better formed and more intelligible than that directed to other adults, which tends to be fraught with sloppily pronounced words, false starts, and ill-formed or incomplete sentences with unclear boundaries between words. This clearer, more precise, and simpler input language could assist children in separating words from the flow of speech and in perceiving correct pronunciation. Similarly, the consistent pronunciation could aid them in becoming familiar with new words and in picking out those words that map meanings they wish to express.

Speech to young children also simplifies the task of figuring out the meanings of words—adults speak to them about the here-and-now (Cross, 1977; Phillips, 1973; Shatz & Gelman, 1973; Snow, 1972). In this way, the immediate context that is shared by adult and child provides the meanings of the words that are spoken. Moreover, recent work by Tomasello and Farrar (1986) and by Akhtar, Dunham, and Dunham (1991) has shown that one-year-olds whose mothers typically talked about objects the children were already focused on in play situations had larger vocabularies than children whose mothers attempted to direct their attention elsewhere.

Input language is also typified by a reduced vocabulary containing more content words and fewer verbs, modifiers, pronouns, and function words than speech directed to adults. Thus, words with the simplest and most unambiguous meanings are more predominant. Words like *chair, shoe,* and *juice* are more common in child input language than words like *short, his, for,* or *by,* even though both groups of words are equally common in adult speech to adults. In addition, adults tend to repeat key words in subsequent utterances when addressing children (Newport, 1975).

In speaking to young children, adults and older children also modify the topics and content of their speech in ways that make it easier for children to recognize words and connect them to their meanings. Communicating and sharing information about social, emotional, and physical topics are the explicit reasons for talking to young children, but input language is clearly designed to teach about language as well.

In responding to young children's speech, older listeners provide feedback as to how well the children have represented their intended meanings. The older listener interprets the child's words according to their sounds and the context in which they are spoken. If the listener's subsequent actions show correct understanding, the child's words are confirmed, as when "mama" called from the crib brings mama to get the child out of the crib. One baby we know said "cracker" when she really wanted a cookie, and made a disappointing discovery when she received her saltine. Feedback from other people can also be in verbal form. For example, when a child labels a yo-yo "ball," the adult may provide the correct label. Chapman, Leonard, and Mervis (1986) found that adult corrections providing the correct label, accompanied by a description of critical features (e.g., "That's a yo-yo. See? It goes up and down"), were the most effective in correcting children's overextensions.

■ CHILDREN'S USE OF COGNITIVE AND LINGUISTIC INFORMATION IN WORD LEARNING

Children are remarkably quick and efficient word learners. During the peak preschool years, their vocabularies grow at an average rate of two to four new words a day (Smith,

1926). Yet the mapping task is not a simple one. As Rice (1990) points out, even an initial, incomplete mapping of a new word to a referent is a task that involves many components. First, the child must segment the incoming verbal stream into individual words. Next, she must identify any unfamiliar segment (the new word). Then, she must hypothesize what the referent of the new word might be and compare this word/meaning mapping to other words and meanings she already knows. And finally, she must store the new word/meaning mapping in semantic memory so that it can be retrieved and used when appropriate. How is it then that even very young children are able to perform this **fast mapping** of words to referents?

We have already discussed how features of adult speech may help children with the task. But children also may themselves bring to the task certain cognitive and linguistic **operating principles** that help focus their hypotheses about meanings of new words. For example, recent research has shown that when children hear a new word, they tend to hypothesize that the word refers to a whole object (or its shape), rather than to a part of the object, its color, material, or texture. Similarly, they tend to consider material a more likely candidate than color (Au, 1985; Markman & Wachtel, 1988; Taylor & Gelman, 1988).

In some contexts, children are able to bring linguistic information to bear on their nonlinguistic hypotheses about new words. For example, Au and Glusman (1990) found that children who heard the novel material term *rattan* contrasted with other material terms ("It's not paper, and it's not cloth; it's rattan") were more likely to learn the new material name than were children who simply heard rattan labeled. They also found that young children were better able to use linguistic information to learn a new label for something if they did not already have a label for it. For example, children had difficulty learning the label "crescent," even when given linguistic information like "It's not square, and it's not triangular; it's crescent." Instead, they tended to continue to label the crescent shape "moon." Eve Clark (1987) has called children's tendency to assume that no two words have the same meaning the **principle of contrast.** According to this principle, when a young child hears a novel label, he will cast about for a novel referent to which it might apply. Young children thus assign different labels to contrasting categories, and reject apparent synonyms (e.g., refusing the label "automobile" for a car because they already have it labeled "car").

Another constraint that has been suggested is that children avoid labeling an object at more than one level of generality at a time (e.g., maintaining that a dog is not "an animal," but "a dog"). This constraint or bias is called **mutual exclusivity** of categories.

These hypothesized constraints have generated a great deal of research and discussion in recent years. There is as yet no consensus as to whether these are constraints children are born with or develop later in life (MacWhinney, 1989; Markman, 1987; Markman & Wachtel, 1988; Merriman & Bowman, 1989), or indeed whether children's patterns of word learning are best described by such semantic constraints. Rice (1990), for example, has shown that even three-year-olds readily accept synonyms for known words (at least in comprehension). Other researchers (e.g., Gathercole, 1989) maintain that children rely extensively on their pragmatic understanding of the nature of human communication. For example, children may assume that adults will not use a new word for an old object without reason, thus leading children to search for a novel referent to which the new word might apply.

Use of the word in familiar contexts may also affect the child's comprehension and use of words. For example, Kavanaugh (1975) presented children between the ages of three-and-a-half and five with sentences containing temporal uses of *before* and *after,* and asked them to act out each sentence. The sentences were constructed so that *before* and *after* were found at the beginning of some sentences and after the main clause of others. In addition, in half of the sentences the events described had a natural, logically constrained order (e.g., "When a girl feeds a baby before putting it to bed"), and in half of the sentences the events described had no logical order and were therefore reversible (e.g., "When a girl puts the baby to bed before picking up a pencil") (p. 353). Sentences in which the order of events followed real life were significantly easier for the children to comprehend. In these sentences, *before* was also more likely to be understood by the children than *after.* In reversible sentences, however, *before* and *after* were equally well understood. The apparent developmental advantage of *before* over *after* was linked by Goodz (1982) to two linguistic strategies that had been considered previously: (1) the **order-of-mention strategy** leads the child to believe that the order in which events are mentioned in the sentence indicates their sequence of occurrence (Clark, 1971), and (2) the **main-clause-first strategy** leads to the belief that the event described in the main clause of a complex sentence occurs first. Goodz tested children between the ages of approximately three and four and found that their comprehension of *before* and *after* was equally good in sentences that did not violate the two processing strategies, but that *after* was more difficult for the children to understand in sentences in which the strategies did not lead to correct interpretation, such as "Put the boy in the box after you put the cat in the box." French and Nelson (1985), however, found that three- and four-year-olds were able to use relational terms such as *before* and *after* quite accurately when talking about familiar events in their own lives (e.g., "We eat our pizza after we have the salad").

■ LATER SEMANTIC DEVELOPMENTS

COMPLEX CONCEPTS

As we noted earlier, not all concepts are of comparable complexity; concrete object categories tend to be easier concepts to acquire than are action or affective categories, and superordinates are more difficult than are basic level categories. Other categories may be difficult to discriminate because they share many semantic features. **Kinship terms** exemplify this situation since many of them, such as *aunt* and *uncle,* share all but one feature.

Clark's semantic feature hypothesis would predict that terms whose meanings are defined by many features would be more difficult for children to master than terms that are semantically less complex. To test this hypothesis, Haviland and Clark (1974) asked children between the ages of three and eight to define English kinship terms. They asked questions like "What is an uncle?" or "What is a grandfather?" Terms that have only one relational component (e.g., *father:* a parent who is male) were expected to be less difficult than terms defined by many features (e.g., *aunt*). As expected, children learned the less complex kinship terms earlier, regardless of whether they had experience with the particular relationship. Haviland and Clark found that children's order of acquisition could be described in terms of adding component features, and that acquisition proceeded through four stages (see also earlier work by Danziger, 1957, and Piaget, 1928). At the earliest stage, one typical child (at three years, five months) has no component features:

Stage 1.

Q: "What's a cousin?"

A: "I have a cousin Daniel."

Q: "Are cousins big or little?"

A: "No."

Stage 2.

In the second stage, a child describes some features of the term but not relational ones, as in this example from a child of five years, ten months:

Q: "What's a father?"

A: "A father is somebody who goes to work every day except Saturday and Sunday and earns money."

Stage 3.

At the third stage, relational terms are used, but they are not yet reciprocal, as exemplified in this conversation with a child of six years, six months:

Q: "What's a mother?"

A: "It's a mommy. I have a mommy. It's somebody in your family."

Stage 4.

Finally, as with this seven-year-old, the child knows that the term is both relational and reciprocal:

Q: "What's a niece?"

A: "A niece is like a mother had a sister, and I'd be her niece."

Another type of complex concept that has received the attention of researchers is *deixis*. **Deictic terms** are pointers or contrasting relational terms that are used to indicate which of multiple objects is being referred to. The chief acquisitional challenge lies in the fact that the reference points for such terms depend upon who says them. Thus, for example, understanding the terms *I* and *you,* and *this* and *that*, requires that the speaker, rather than a fixed point, be assumed as the point of reference against which the meaning of the terms can be interpreted.

Some researchers have been interested in the acquisition of deictic terms for insights it might provide into the developmental relationship between cognition and language (deVilliers & deVilliers, 1974; Webb & Abrahamson, 1976). Comprehension of deictic terms would appear to require the type of multiple-perspective-taking ability that Piagetians maintain only becomes possible when children reach the stage of concrete operations, usually around seven years of age. However, deVilliers and deVilliers

(1974) reported that three- and four-year-old preschoolers were able to use different points of view to employ deictic terms such as *here* and *there*. They also found that differences in perspective-taking demands made by different pairs of relative terms had acquisitional consequences. Their three-year-old subjects could comprehend terms that required them to assume the speaker's perspective; their four-year-old subjects could, in addition, correctly produce terms that required them to assume the listener's perspective. In addition, even though the meanings of terms that do not usually require a shift in perspective (e.g., *in front of* and *behind*) were acquired first, they became less well understood for a time when the children were beginning to take into account the effect of perspective on the meanings of other relational terms.

Clark and Sengul (1978), in another study of deictic terms, focused on the different interpretive strategies children employ along the path to full comprehension. Noting that both shifting reference perspective and the proximity of the referent to the speaker and listener combine in the meanings of deictic terms, they developed hypotheses about possible developmental paths. Their data indicated three stages in the acquisition of the deictic contrasts they studied: (1) a stage in which the terms are used with no deictic contrast (*there* is thought to mean *all done,* and *here* is used as a general referent indicator, or *here* and *there* are thought to be synonyms), (2) a stage in which children include some of the necessary contrasts (i.e., they understand the terms in some contexts only), and (3) a stage in which the requisite contrasts are encoded in the lexicon. The active role children play in their own semantic development was highlighted in this study. It was observed that there were differences among children in their initial implicit hypotheses about the words' meanings, as indicated by their response strategies. In choosing a toy that was "here" or "there," some children always chose the one that was near them, whereas others always chose the one that was near the speaker, regardless of the term that was used. These early strategies determined how they later interpreted the deictic terms.

A third example of how children acquire concept-label mappings for complex concepts is their acquisition of **color terms.** Acquisition of color words and meanings has been studied by Bartlett (1977) and Carey and Bartlett (1978) for clues to how lexical development occurs. The conceptual knowledge required to learn the meanings of color terms includes being able, for analytic purposes, to isolate color from objects, differentiate among hues, and notice similarities among related shades. Linguistically, the child must know that color words refer to the dimension of color rather than, for instance, size (Bartlett, 1977). Carey and Bartlett (1978) were interested in finding out how a new color word and its meaning are normally acquired and how this is affected by, and in turn affects, the semantic domain of colors. After initial assessment of preschool subjects' and matched controls' knowledge of colors on a wide range of tasks, the subjects were introduced to a new color term (*chromium*) and its referent on several occasions. Between presentations they and their matched controls were retested to determine what they had learned about the new word and its referent and how the children integrated what they had learned into their lexicons. Carey and Bartlett found that if a first color word and its referent were already known, one or two isolated and brief exposures to a new color term were sufficient to affect children's naming of the color, and that children retained the knowledge sufficiently to build on it two months later. In addition, they documented a variety of strategies used by different children in integrating the new information into their lexicons. Color terms are somewhat unusual in that color names (like number terms) may be recognized by children before the terms are connected to their referents. For example, when asked, "What color is this?" even two-year-olds can supply color terms, though they may be the wrong ones. Rice (1980) has suggested that verbal interchanges with adults may supply the conceptual underpinnings for such knowledge. Andrick and Tager-Flusberg (1986) found a perceptual basis for color naming: **focal colors**—the bluest blues and the reddest red—were most easily named by children.

LEXICAL REORGANIZATION

Semantic system development consists of increases in the number of concepts and words a child knows and in the range of mappings the child has worked out within and between the conceptual and linguistic systems. Thus, semantic development consists of learning not only what individual words mean, but also how they are interrelated. These interrelationships are referred to as **semantic networks.** Most semantic network research suggests that semantic networks are formed relatively late, compared with other linguistic achievements (Aitchison, 1987; Francis, 1972; McNeill, 1966).

After examining diary data of young children, however, Bowerman (1978) has suggested that the formation of semantic networks is evident in younger children. According to Bowerman, children seek links, relationships, and conceptual wholes in everything they experience, including language. As a result, they add to their vocabularies not only words that will give them new communicative possibilities, but also synonyms that do not increase their communicative abilities. Other semantic links are evident in preschoolers' inappropriate use of certain words after they have learned the appropriate use. In such cases, Bowerman found elements of meaning shared by the misused word and the word called for in the context. An example of this phenomenon (appropriate use of a word interrupted by temporary inappropriate use) was given by two-year-old Christy, who said, "Daddy take his pants on" (p. 986) when previously in such cases she had used *put* instead of *take.* Both terms refer to actions that result in a change of location for an object, and Bowerman suggested that such substitutions can be interpreted most adequately as "incorrect choices among semantically related words that compete for selection in a particular speech context" (p. 979).

Another indication that words in children's vocabularies are becoming interconnected is developmental change that has been documented in children's **word associations.** Significantly, responses to such tasks have been shown to be indicative of other measures of linguistic sophistication (Brown & Berko, 1960). There are three general types of word association tasks that have been used. In **free-word-association** tasks, children are given a particular word and instructed to give the next word that comes to mind (see Palermo, 1971; Palermo & Jenkins, 1963). In **restricted-word-association** tasks, children are given additional semantic criteria for selecting responses; for example, the response must bear a particular relationship to the stimulus word, such as superordinate, opposite, or rhyming (see Riegel, Riegel, Quarterman, & Smith, 1968).

In **set tests,** children are given the name of a language category, such as "animals" or "furniture," and are asked to supply as many names of category members as they are able. On all three types of tasks, older individuals' responses represent a narrower, better-defined set than do those of younger children, and on set tests older children produce longer lists of group members. For example, Nelson (1974) found that eight-year-olds were able to supply nearly twice the number of responses of five-year-olds, and only the five-year-olds included "meat" and "ice cream" in the vegetable category and "wall" and "door" in the furniture category.

Young children respond to free word association tasks with words that are related in syntax to the stimulus word; that is, they give words that would typically follow the stimulus word in a normal sentence (Brown & Berko, 1960; Entwisle, 1966). For example, in response to the stimulus word *eat,* a child might say "lunch." In contrast, older individuals tend to respond with words that are of the same grammatical category as the stimulus word (e.g., *eat*—"drink"). Around age seven, children begin to respond with class-related words. While this trend in response pattern continues to evolve from first grade to college, it shows by far the greatest change between first and second grades. Explanations for the shift include general cognitive strategy shifts (Nelson, 1977), developmental changes in children's interpretation of the task, changes in knowledge of the features that define words (Lippman, 1971; McNeill, 1966), and cognitive reorganization that accompanies the acquisition of reading (Cronin, 1987).

■ METALINGUISTIC DEVELOPMENT

The primary focus of this chapter is on children's development of semantic knowledge, in which words symbolize, or stand for, particular meanings. Once we know the meanings of words, we do not need to notice the words themselves in order to appreciate the information they carry. However, along with the development of semantic knowledge, children come to appreciate that language has potential greater than that of simple symbols. Children first begin to notice words as objects, and later become able to manipulate them to learn to read and write and to accomplish a host of nonliteral ends such as using metaphors, creating puns, and using irony. These language uses depend on **metalinguistic knowledge,** or knowledge of the nature of language as an object. Metalinguistic awareness develops gradually through the middle school years.

Before children can engage in flexible, nonliteral uses of words, they must have at least an implicit understanding that words are separable from their referents. Without this understanding, words could only be used for direct, literal reference. But just as very young children are not able to think about the color of an object separately from the object itself, and are therefore unable to group objects by color, they often consider the name of an object another of its intrinsic attributes. During their second year, children gradually come to anticipate that a word is meant to refer to a related group of referents (Gruendel, 1977; Nelson & Bonvillian, 1973; Oviatt, 1982). As noted earlier, some overextensions of words may express intentional metaphoric comparisons of two objects (e.g., Nelson, Benedict, Gruendel, & Rescorla, 1977). Later, children learn that words themselves are not inherent attributes of objects, which allows them to move beyond literal word use and adopt a metaphoric stance.

Once children understand that a word and its referent are separable, they can begin to reflect on the properties of words and objects separately. What is challenging is that although words and their referents sometimes share properties, more often they do not. For example, *elephant* and *hippopotamus* are big words for big animals; however, other long words such as *mosquito* and *dragonfly* refer to very tiny insects. Similarly, while the sound of the word *silk* conveys perfectly the smooth, slippery quality of the fabric, the sounds of the words *rose* and *sunset* convey nothing of the sensual beauty of their referents.

Children's ability to compare and contrast such properties *explicitly*, in a formal way, develops only gradually over a period of several years, but even very young children on occasion are able to appreciate and reflect upon the physical attributes of words (cf. Sinclair, Jarvella, & Levelt, 1978). For example, preschoolers can recognize and sometimes comment that different pronounciations of words do not alter their meanings (Leopold, 1948). Children also engage in spontaneous rhyming, which involves implicit comparison and matching of phonological subsequences within words, and they recognize that some words include other words within them (e.g., *garden* includes *den*). Occasionally, children's awareness of phonological subsequences, combined with their tendency to assume a relationship between form and meaning, may lead them to predict incorrectly semantic correspondence between words that sound similar. Thus at four years of age, Phoebe, on the basis of her knowledge of *tomato*, believed that *tornadoes* were whirling masses of red air; and Polly, who knew the word *eagle*, wondered whether *beagle* referred to a kind of dog that could fly (Pease, 1986).

Many studies that aim to examine children's developing metalinguistic notions of the concept of "word" require that the child be able to verbalize such concepts. For example, in a seminal study of word awareness, Papandropoulou and Sinclair (1974) presented preschool and elementary school children with a variety of metalinguistic tasks, including one in which children were read a list of words, asked whether each was a word, and then asked for explanations for each response. The researchers observed improvement across the ages studied, both in children's recognition of words and in their ability to verbalize such concepts. Specifically, older children acknowledged both content and function words as words, while younger children sometimes rejected the latter; further, older children were more adept at articulating what constitutes a word.

It is likely, however, that well before children can demonstrate such explicit knowledge on demand, they have a rudimentary awareness of the nature of words. This view is supported, for instance, by a study by Bowey, Pratt, and Tunmer (1984), who found that preschoolers, first- and second-graders benefited significantly from a brief training session in correctly identifying single words from lists including phrases and nonspeech sounds. Another study (Pease, 1986) that attempted to examine children's implicit awareness of the concept of "word" took a somewhat different approach in order to minimize performance demands. Children between the ages of four-and-a-half and ten years were simply asked to tell what their favorite words and favorite things were. Even at the youngest ages, most children differentiated between the two questions, though they were sometimes unable to explain their responses. A few preschoolers failed to differentiate the two concepts, naming favorite things in response to both questions. For example, one child's favorite word was *toys* because "they are fun to play with" and her favorite thing was *car,* again because "it's fun to play with." In the kindergarten group, some children were even able to articulate the reason why a particular word was their favorite (e.g., the word *ear* because "it sounds neat"). The ability to differentiate between the two questions and to articulate metalinguistic aspects of words was even clearer at older ages, with children reporting favorite objects or activities (e.g., "swimming") for favorite things and giving words with interesting sound or spelling patterns (e.g., *petrified* or *Mississippi*) for favorite words. Furthermore, the oldest children reported that they and their friends had talked about words they liked, indicating that by the early school years children are actively and explicitly reflecting on and discussing words as objects.

SEGMENTATION

Children's awareness of words in context has also been investigated. Researchers have studied the development of children's ability to segment a stream of speech into words, syllables, and phonemes. The ability to correctly segment at the word level, in particular, would facilitate mapping of spoken language onto written language. Although literate adults may find the identification of word units in spoken language a trivial task, in fact boundaries between words in a stream of speech are not identifiable on the basis of pauses or other acoustic features. Thus, children must depend on a variety of other cues and information about semantics and syntax in order to identify word boundaries. The age at which children are able to segment utterances into adult word units varies depending on how the task is presented and on what response is required of the child (cf. Ehri, 1975; Fox & Routh, 1975; Hardy, Stennet, & Smyth, 1973; Huttenlocher, 1964). Sometimes children are asked to count the words in a spoken utterance, tap out each word in a phrase or sentence, or represent each word with a token. Such tasks involve auditory memory and the coordination of a verbal or motoric response, as well as metalinguistic awareness. Coordinating the various elements of the task tends to be difficult for preschoolers. Tasks in which children are asked instead to repeat smaller and smaller "bits" of an utterance are somewhat easier (Fox & Routh, 1975).

A different technique was used by Huttenlocher (1964), who presented children with pairs of words and asked them either to reverse the members of the pair or to pause between them. The pairs of words that were least likely to occur together in normal speech (e.g., *peach–apple*) were the easiest for children to separate, while those that often occur together (e.g., *happy–birthday*) were more difficult. Huttenlocher concluded that children as young as four are aware of words, but that their awareness is strongly related to the context in which the words appear. It may be that successful accomplishment of such "simpler" segmentation tasks relies more on perceptual skills than on a conceptual awareness of words; alternatively, it may be that when extraneous task demands are reduced in this way, children are better able to demonstrate their awareness of words.

More recently, when Chaney (1989) looked at the developing metalinguistic awareness of word boundaries in children between the ages of four-and-a-half and six-and-a-half, she found that children first were able to recognize phrase boundaries, then syllable boundaries, and finally were able to segment according to word boundaries. When children were faced with unknown or more abstract words, they tended to revert to a phrase strategy or to substitute common, known words for the unknown ones. Some substitutions made in repeating the Pledge of Allegiance were: "the night of states" instead of "the United States," "for witches stand" instead of "for which it stands," and "liver T" instead of "liberty." It is perhaps not surprising that children's first strategy is to segment at the phrasal level, since phrases are relatively self-contained units of meaning. Children's later segmenting at syllable and word boundaries may reflect their growing ability to attend to the physical, auditory properties of segments, rather than to semantic properties exclusively.

It is worth noting that all of these studies involved children who already had some experience with written language or who were in the process of learning to read. Because developmental change in children's word awareness tends to coincide with their beginning to read, researchers have been interested in exploring the role certain kinds of metalinguistic awareness may play in reading readiness and reading acquisition. Word segmentation skills in first graders, for example, have been shown to be strong predictors of later reading success (Evans, Taylor, & Blum, 1979). Of course, the converse is also possible: experience with seeing words represented on paper may facilitate children's segmentation of the speech stream into adult word units. Tentative support for the latter is found in research by Kolinsky, Cary, and Morais (1987) with illiterate adults and adults who had only recently learned to read. When their subjects were asked to produce long and short words and to match spoken words of different lengths to written words, those with some reading experience were better able to perform the task than those without. Like young prereaders, adults without reading experience tended to produce long and short phrases, rather than words. This research suggests that literacy and experience with printed matter may promote awareness of certain physical aspects of words.

HUMOR, METAPHOR, AND IRONY

From very young ages, children can be observed to play with semantic elements in syntactic structures for humorous effect, as in: "Daddy's proud of you; Grandma's proud of you; Uncle David's proud of you; Hamburger not proud of you, ha ha!" (Horgan, 1981). While toddlers and preschoolers find word play such as rhyming and intentional nonsensical talk amusing and at times even hysterical, delight in puns and riddles—like interest in favorite words—seems to become particularly intense in the middle elementary school years. In fact, many humorous uses of language such as puns and riddles depend on the speaker's ability to separate different facets of language (cf. Horgan, 1981; McGhee, 1979; Schultz, 1976; Slobin, 1978). Thus, what some elementary teachers have dubbed "third-grade humor" is an overt sign that children are actively practicing and consolidating their metalinguistic skills.

In addition to using language for humorous effect, children also learn to use language in other nonliteral ways, such as metaphor and irony. Winner (1988) has studied the development of **metaphor,** which she says generally serves to clarify meaning, and **irony,** which is usually used to evaluate or criticize. Initially, the ability to understand metaphoric uses of language is important because it offers children an additional strategy for clarifying communication, both in production and in comprehension. Even very young children spontaneously use and understand certain types of metaphor for communicative purposes, though their use becomes much more fluent and less context-specific with age (Pearson, 1990). Later, in addition to its clarifying function, metaphor also begins to be used as an important tool in grasping new concepts in relatively unfamiliar areas of knowledge. Winner (1988) cites examples from a variety of fields (art, science, medicine) in which analogy and metaphoric thinking greatly facilitated the generation of solutions to difficult problems. Both the clarifying and the problem-solving functions of metaphoric language and thinking continue to be crucial throughout the lifespan.

Using and understanding irony involves appreciating that words and phrases not only can have meanings different from their literal ones, but that the meaning the speaker intends to convey can in fact be precisely the opposite of what the surface meaning would suggest. In irony, as opposed to lying, stating the opposite of what is true can offer a pointed or funny way of commenting on the truth. Understanding and using irony requires a relatively high degree of cognitive and social sophistication, and is not typically observed in children before age seven or eight. Often the line between children who are able to use and appreciate irony and those who are not yet able to is poignantly clear to adults. One first grader we know got off the school bus with a big smile to report that a much-respected third grader thought his new notebook was really neat. When asked how he knew the older child was so impressed with the new possession, the first grader promptly replied, "because when I showed it to him he said, 'Big deal!' " Irony and sarcasm are probably other areas of metalinguistic awareness in which verbal interaction with peers provides the young language learner with important data and a forum in which to practice his developing communicative skills.

WORD DEFINITIONS

Defining a word involves metalinguistic skills as well as semantic knowledge. Children's ability to use linguistic context to deduce the meanings of new words was studied by Werner and Kaplan (1950). In this landmark study, children were presented with a number of sentences with a nonsense word in the place of a key word (e.g., "The painter used a *corplum* to mix his paints" or "A wet *corplum* does not burn"). The children were to figure out the meanings of the nonsense words from their linguistic contexts. Werner and Kaplan found age-related differences in the strategies children used to perform the task. For instance, five-year-olds, who tended to fuse the meaning of the word with the meaning of the sentence, might define *corplum* by saying, "A corplum is wet and painters use it," whereas an eleven-year-old might say, "A corplum is a kind of stick!"

Defining a word involves metalinguistic skills as well as semantic knowledge. With development, children become better able to define words as semantically unique by including critical types of information and using different approaches to organize it. For example, during the early school years children's definitions are concrete (descriptions of the referent's appearance or function), personal, and incidental (Snow, 1990). Through the elementary school years, these are gradually joined by abstract types of responses: synonyms, explanations, and specifications of categorical relationships (Al-Issa, 1969; Litowitz, 1977; Wolman & Baker, 1965). Swartz and Hall (1972) compared children's word definitions and their performance on a variety of tasks involving relational concepts. They found that children who were least able to consider relational concepts favored *functional* definitions, whereas older children (ages nine to eleven), who were most able to consider relational concepts, gave a majority of *abstract* definitions. Wehren, DeLisi, and Arnold (1981) found a developmental progression in word definitions among children aged five to eleven and college students, beginning with an emphasis on personal experience and moving toward information of a more general, socially shared nature. Snow (1990) has shown that knowledge of the conventional form for good definitions (the definitional genre), combined with frequent opportunities to practice hearing and giving definitions, are necessary for the development of adultlike definitional skills.

A LIFELONG ENTERPRISE

Semantic development continues apace throughout the life span. Not only do we as adults continue to add new words to our lexicons, but we also continue to fine-tune the extensions of old words in response to widening experience and to social and cultural changes in our linguistic community. Reflection on and analysis of language result in continual lexical reorganization, a flexibility that is essential if we are to use our language in the most adaptive and effective way to address a wide variety of communicative tasks throughout the life span.

SUMMARY

Vocabulary development involves the acquisition of new words and new meanings and the establishment of links between them. To learn a new word meaning, a child must learn how her language community has grouped and labeled the various aspects of experience; it is social convention—not individual experience or the world of objects—that defines words. Semantic development is characterized by both addition of new elements of meaning and reorganization of known elements.

At first, children seek clues to word meanings in the nonlinguistic and linguistic contexts in which words are encountered. Certain features of adult speech directed to children may facilitate their mapping of words to meanings. Later, children also rely on knowledge of syntax and other word meanings to generate and confirm hypotheses about the meanings of words.

Children's word meanings differ from adults', but not in a consistent fashion. In some cases children's initial meanings appear to be reduced versions of adult meanings, and in other cases they are different in content or internal organization.

In addition to semantic knowledge of words, children gradually come to understand that words themselves have properties that can be reflected on and discussed. This metalinguistic knowledge allows children to use language for nonliteral ends such as metaphor, irony, and humor.

SUGGESTED PROJECTS

1. Show adults and kindergarten children pictures of different kinds of birds and other flying creatures (e.g., bat, pterodactyl). Ask them to rank the pictures in order of bird-likeness. Compare the rankings of the adults and children. Did all the adults agree in their rankings, or were there fuzzy category boundaries?
2. Choose a passage of very technical language (e.g., legal document or technical manual). Practice reading it aloud until you can do it smoothly; then tape-record yourself reading it. Have five friends listen to the tape and write down what they hear. Examine their dictation samples to see if there are any incorrect segmentations.
3. Tape-record half-hour speech samples of a three-year-old and a five-year-old at play. Compare the topics they include and the words they use. What similarities and differences do you note?
4. Find a children's picture book with few or no words. Ask a parent of a child 18 to 24 months old to spend 10 or 15 minutes using the book with the child. Ask a parent of a three-and-a-half-year-old to four-year-old child to do the same thing. Record and compare the words the parents use with the two children.
5. Ask children of different ages to tell their favorite words and things, and explain their choices. Compare their choices and explanations.
6. Ask children of different ages to define what words are.
7. Ask children of different ages to tell you what particular words mean. Include some words with multiple meanings, such as *cold.*
8. Ask a few children to think of specific referents, such as *dog*, and tell what they "see."
9. Tell children of different ages a sentence with a new word in it, and then ask what the word means.

SUGGESTED READINGS

Aitchison, J. (1987). *Words in the mind: An introduction to the mental lexicon.* Oxford: Basil Blackwell.

Au, T. K. (1990). Children's use of information in word learning. *Journal of Child Language, 17,* 393–416.

Carey, S. (1982). Semantic development: The state of the art. In E. Wanner & L. R. Gleitman (Eds.), *Language acquisition: The state of the art.* New York: Cambridge University Press.

Clark, E. V. (1981). Lexical innovations: How children learn to create new words. In W. Deutsch (Ed.), *The child's construction of language.* London: Academic Press.

Haviland, S. E., & Clark, E. V. (1974). "This man's father is my father's son": A study of the acquisition of English kin terms. *Journal of Child Language, 1,* 23–47.

Mervis, C. B., & Mervis, C. A. (1982). Leopards are kitty-cats: Object labeling by mothers for their thirteen-month-olds. *Child Development, 53,* 267–273.

Nelson, K. (1974). Variations in children's concepts by age and category. *Child Development, 45,* 577–584.

Palermo, D. S., & Molfese, D. (1972). Language acquisition from age five onward. *Psychological Bulletin, 6,* 429–432.

Tunmer, W. E., Pratt, C., & Harriman, M. L. (1984). *Metalinguistic awareness in children.* Berlin: Springer-Verlag.

Werner, H., & Kaplan, E. (1950). Development of word meaning through verbal context: An experiment study. *Journal of Psychology, 29,* 251–257.

Winner, E. (1988). *The point of words: Children's understanding of metaphor and irony.* Cambridge, MA: Harvard University Press.

REFERENCES

Aitchison, J. (1987). *Words in the mind: An introduction to the mental lexicon.* London: Basil Blackwell.

Akhtar, N., Dunham, F., & Dunham, P. (1991). Directive interactions and early vocabulary development: The role of joint attentional focus. *Journal of Child Language, 18,* 41–49.

Al-Issa, I. (1969). The development of word definitions in children. *Journal of Genetic Psychology, 114,* 25–28.

Andrick, G. R., & Tager-Flusberg, H. (1986). The acquisition of colour terms. *Journal of Child Language, 13,* 119–134.

Anglin, J. (1977). *Word, object, and conceptual development.* New York: Norton.

Anglin, J. (1978). From reference to meaning. *Child Development, 49,* 969–976.

Au, T. K. (1985). Children's word learning strategies. *Papers and Reports on Child Language Development, 24,* 22–29.

Au, T. K. (1990). Children's use of information in word learning. *Journal of Child Language, 17,* 393–416.

Au, T. K., & Gusman, M. (1990). The principle of mutual exclusivity in word learning: to honor or not to honor? *Child Development 61,* 1474–1490.

Baldwin, D. A., & Markman, E. M. (1989). Establishing word–object relations: A first step. *Child Development, 60,* 381–398.

Bartlett, E. J. (1977). The acquisition of the meaning of color terms: A study of lexical development. In R. Campbell & P. Smith (Eds.), *Recent advances in the psychology of language* (Vol. 4a, pp. 89–108). New York: Plenum Press.

Beeghly, M., Bretherton, I., & Mervis, C. (1986). Mothers' internal state language to toddlers: The socialization of psychological understanding. *British Journal of Developmental Psychology, 4,* 247–260.

Benedict, H. (1979). Early lexical development: Comprehension and production. *Journal of Child Language, 6,* 183–200.

Berko, J. (1958). The child's learning of English morphology. *Word, 14,* 150–177.

Bloom, L., & Lahey, M. (1978). *Language development and language disorders.* New York: John Wiley.

Bloomfield, L. (1933). *Language.* New York: Henry Holt.

Bowerman, M. (1978). Systematizing semantic knowledge: Changes over time in the child's organization of word meaning. *Child Development, 49,* 977–987.

Bowey, J. A., Pratt, C., & Tunmer, W. E. (1984). Development of children's understanding of the metalinguistic term "word." *Journal of Educational Psychology, 76,* 500–512.

Brown, R. (1968). *Words and things.* New York: Free Press.

Brown, R., & Berko, J. (1960). Word association and the acquisition of grammar. *Child Development, 31,* 1–14.

Callanan, M. A. (1985). How parents label objects for young children: The role of input in the acquisition of category hierarchies. *Child Development, 56,* 508–523.

Carabine, B. (1991). Fuzzy boundaries and the extension of object words. *Journal of Child Language, 18,* 355–372.

Carey, S. (1982). Semantic development: The state of the art. In E. Wanner & L. R. Gleitman (Eds.), *Language acquisition: The state of the art.* New York: Cambridge University Press.

Carey, S., & Bartlett, E. (1978, August). Acquiring a single new word. *Papers and Reports on Child Language Development, 15,* 17–29.

Chaney, C. (1989). I pledge a legiance to the flag: Three studies in word segmentation. *Applied Psycholinguistics, 10,* 261–282.

Chapman, K. L., Leonard, L. B., & Mervis, C. B. (1986). The effect of feedback on young children's inappropriate word usage. *Journal of Child Language, 13,* 101–117.

Charles-Luce, J., & Luce, P. A. (1990). Similarity neighborhoods of words in young children's lexicons. *Journal of Child Language, 17,* 205–215.

Clark, E. V. (1971). On the acquisition of the meaning of before and after. *Journal of Verbal Learning and Verbal Behavior, 10,* 266–275.

Clark, E. V. (1974). Some aspects of the conceptual basis for first language acquisition. In R. L. Schiefelbusch & L. L. Lloyd (Eds.), *Language perspectives—Acquisition, retardation, and intervention.* Baltimore: University Park Press.

Clark, E. V. (1978). Strategies for communicating. *Child Development, 49,* 953–959.

Clark, E. V. (1981). Lexical innovations: How children learn to create new words. In W. Deutsch (Ed.), *The child's construction of language.* London: Academic Press.

Clark, E. V. (1982). The young word maker: A case study of innovations in the child's lexicon. In E. Wanner & L. R. Gleitman (Eds.), *Language acquisition: The state of the art.* New York: Cambridge University Press.

Clark, E. V. (1987). The principle of contrast: A constraint on language acquisition. In B. MacWhinney (Ed.), *Mechanisms of language acquisition.* Hillsdale, NJ: Lawrence Erlbaum.

Clark, E., Gelman, S., & Lane, N. (1985). Compound nouns and category structure in young children. *Child Development, 56,* 84–94.

Clark, E. V., & Sengul, C. J. (1978). Strategies in the acquisition of deixis. *Journal of Child Language, 5,* 457–475.

Cronin, V. (1987). Word association and reading. Paper presented at the meeting of the Society for Research in Child Development, Baltimore, MD.

Cross, T. G. (1977). Mothers' speech adjustments: The contributions of selected child listener variables. In C. Ferguson & C. Snow (Eds.), *Talking to children: Language input and acquisition.* Cambridge: Cambridge University Press.

Dale, P. S., Bates, E., Resnick, J. S., & Morisset, C. (1989). The validity of parent report instrument of child language at twenty months. *Journal of Child Language, 16,* 239–250.

Danziger, K. (1957). The child's understanding of kinship terms: A study in the development of relational concepts. *Journal of Genetic Psychology, 91,* 213–232.

deVilliers, P. A., & deVilliers, J. G. (1974). On this, that, and the other: Nonegocentrism in very young children. *Journal of Experimental Child Psychology, 18,* 438–447.

Dunn, J., Bretherton, I., & Munn, R. (1987). Conversations about feeling states between mothers and their young children. *Developmental Psychology, 23,* 132–139.

Ehri, L. C. (1975). Word consciousness in readers and prereaders. *Journal of Educational Psychology, 67,* 204–212.

Entwisle, D. R. (1966). *Word association responses of young children.* Baltimore: Johns Hopkins University Press.

Evans, M., Taylor, N., & Blum, I. (1979). Children's written language awareness and its relationship to reading acquisition. *Journal of Reading Behavior, 11,* 7–19.

Ferguson, C., & Farwell, C. (1975). Words and sounds in early language acquisition: English initial consonants in the first 50 words. *Language, 51,* 419–439.

Fernald, A., & Mazzie, C. (1991). Prosody and focus in speech to infants and adults. *Developmental Psychology, 27,* 209–221.

Fox, F., & Routh, D. K. (1975). Analyzing spoken language into words, syllables, and phonemes: A developmental study. *Journal of Psycholinguistic Research, 4,* 331–342.

Francis, H. (1972). Toward an explanation of the syntagmatic-paradigmatic shift. *Child Development, 43,* 949–958.

French, L. A., & Nelson, K. (1985). *Young children's knowledge of relational terms: Some ifs, ors, and buts.* New York: Springer-Verlag.

Gathercole, V. (1989). Contrast: A semantic constraint? *Journal of Child Language, 16,* 685–702.

Gentner, D. (1983, February). Nouns and verbs. Symposium presented at the meeting of the New England Child Language Association, Tufts University.

Gentner, D. (1988). Cognitive determinism: Object reference and relational reference. Paper presented at the Boston University Child Language Conference, Boston, MA.

Goodz, N. S. (1982). Is before really easier to understand than after? *Child Development, 53,* 822–825.

Gopnik, A., & Meltzoff, A. N. (1987). Early semantic developments and their relationship to object permanence, means-end understanding, and categorization. In K. E. Nelson & A. van Kleeck (Eds.), *Children's language* (Vol. 6). Hillsdale, NJ: Lawrence Erlbaum.

Greenfield, P. M., & Smith, J. (1976). *The structure of communication in early language.* New York: Academic Press.

Gruendel, J. M. (1977). Referential extension in early language development. *Child Development, 48,* 1567–1576.

Hardy, M., Stennet, R. G., & Smyth, P. C. (1973). Auditory segmentation and auditory blending in relation to beginning reading. *The Alberta Journal of Educational Research, 19,* 144–158.

Haviland, S. E., & Clark, E. V. (1974). "This man's father is my father's son": A study of the acquisition of English kin terms. *Journal of Child Language, 1,* 23–47.

Hoek, D., Ingram, D., & Gibson, D. (1986). Some possible causes of children's early word overextensions. *Journal of Child Language, 13,* 477–494.

Horgan, D. (1981). Learning to tell jokes: A case study of metalinguistic abilities. *Journal of Child Language, 8,* 217–227.

Hudson, J., & Nelson, K. (1984). Play with language: Overextensions as analogies. *Journal of Child Language, 11,* 337–346.

Huttenlocher, J. (1964). Children's language: Word–phrase relationship. *Science, 143,* 264–265.

Huttenlocher, J. (1974). The origins of language comprehension. In R. L. Solso (Ed.), *Theories in cognitive psychology.* New York: Erlbaum.

Kavanaugh, R. D. (1975). Observations of logically constrained sentences in the comprehension of "before" and "after." *Journal of Child Language, 6,* 353–357.

Kolinsky, R., Cary, L., & Morais, J. (1987). Awareness of words as phonological entities: The role of literacy. *Applied Psycholinguistics, 8,* 223–232.

Lashley, K. S. (1954). The problem of serial order in behavior. In L. A. Jeffress (Ed.), *Cerebral mechanisms in behavior.* New York: Wiley.

Leonard, L. B., Schwartz, R., Folger, M., Newhoff, M., & Wilcox, M. (1979). Children's imitations of lexical items. *Child Development, 50,* 19–27.

Leonard, L. B., Schwartz, R. G., Morris, B., & Chapman, K. (1981). Factors influencing early lexical acquisition: Lexical orientation and phonological composition. *Child Development, 52,* 882–887.

Leopold, W. (1948). Semantic learning in infant language. *Word, 4,* 179.

Leopold, W. (1970). *Speech development of a bilingual child* (Vols. 1–4). New York: AMS Press.

Lippman, M. Z. (1971). Correlates of contrast word associations: Developmental trends. *Journal of Verbal Learning and Verbal Behavior, 10,* 392–399.

Litowitz, B. (1977). Learning to make definitions. *Journal of Child Language, 4,* 289–304.

Lucariello, J. (1987). Concept formation and its relation to word learning and use in the second year. *Journal of Child Language, 14,* 309–332.

Macnamara, J. (1972). Cognitive basis of language learning in infants. *Psychological Review, 79,* 1–13.

MacWhinney, B. (1989). Competition and lexical categorization. In R. Corrigan, F. Eckman, & M. Noonan (Eds.), *Linguistic categorization.* Philadelphia: John Benjamins.

Markman, E. (1987). How children constrain the possible meanings of words. In U. Neisser (Ed.), *Concepts and conceptual development: Ecological and intellectual factors in categorization.* Cambridge: Cambridge University Press.

Markman, E. M., & Wachtel, G. F. (1988). Children's use of mutual exclusivity to constrain the meanings of words. *Cognitive Psychology, 20,*121–157.

McGhee, P. (1979). *Humor: Its origin and development.* San Francisco: Freeman.

McNeill, D. (1966). A study of word association. *Journal of Verbal Learning and Verbal Behavior, 5,* 548–557.

Merriman, W. E., & Bowman, L. L. (1989). The mutual exclusivity bias in children's word learning. *Monographs of the Society for Research in Child Development, 54:* 3–4.

Mervis, C. B., & Mervis, C. A. (1982). Leopards are kitty-cats: Object labeling by mothers for their thirteen-month-olds. *Child Development, 53,* 267–273.

Mervis, C. B., & Mervis, C. A. (1988). Role of adult input in young children's category evolution. I. An observational study. *Journal of Child Language, 15,* 257–272.

Morris, C. W. (1946). *Signs, language, and behavior.* New York: Prentice-Hall.

Nelson, K. (1973). Structure and strategy in learning to talk. *Monographs of the Society for Research in Child Development, 38.*

Nelson, K. (1974). Variations in children's concepts by age and category. *Child Development, 45,* 577–584.

Nelson, K. (1977). The syntagmatic-paradigmatic shift revisited: A review of research and theory. *Psychological Bulletin, 84,* 93–116.

Nelson, K., Benedict, H., Gruendel, J., & Rescorla, L. (1977). Lessons from early lexicons. Paper presented at the meeting of the Society for Research in Child Development, New Orleans.

Nelson, K. E., & Bonvillian, J. D. (1973). Concepts and words in the 18-month-old: Acquiring concept names under controlled conditions. *Cognition, 2–4,* 435–450.

Nelson, K., & Lucariello, J. (1985). The development of meaning in first words. In M. Barrett (Ed.), *Children's single word speech.* New York: John Wiley & Sons.

Newport, E. L. (1975). Motherese: The speech of mothers to young children (Tech. Rep. No. 52). San Diego: University of California, Center for Human Information Processing.

Ninio, A., & Bruner, J. (1978). The achievement and antecedents of labeling. *Journal of Child Language, 5,* 1–14.

Oviatt, S. L. (1982). Inferring what words mean: Early development in infants' comprehension of common object names. *Child Development, 53,* 274–277.

Palermo, D. S. (1971). Characteristics of word association responses obtained from children in grades one through four. *Developmental Psychology, 5*(1), 118–123.

Palermo, D. S., & Jenkins, J. J. (1963). *Word association norms: Grade school through college.* Minneapolis: University of Minnesota Press.

Papandropoulou, I., & Sinclair, H. (1974). What is a word? *Human Development, 17,* 241–258.

Pearson, B. Z. (1990). The comprehension of metaphor by preschool children. *Journal of Child Language, 17,* 185–203.

Pease, D. M. (1986). The development of semantic and metalinguistic knowledge. Unpublished doctoral dissertation, Boston University.

Phillips, J. R. (1973). Syntax and vocabulary of mothers' speech to young children: Age and sex comparisons. *Child Development, 44,* 182–185.

Piaget, J. (1928). *Judgment and reasoning in the child.* London: Routledge and Kegan Paul.

Plato. (1953). *Dialogues.* Translated into English with analyses and introduction by B. Jowett. 4th ed. Oxford: Clarendon Press.

Rescorla, L. A. (1980). Overextension in early language development. *Journal of Child Language, 7,* 321–335.

Rescorla, L. A. (1981). Category development in early language. *Journal of Child Language, 8,* 225–238.

Rice, M. L. (1980). *Cognition to language: Categories, meanings, and training.* Baltimore: University Park Press.

Rice, M. L. (1983). Contemporary accounts of the cognition–language relationship: Implications for speech-language clinicians. *Journal of Speech and Hearing Disorders, 48,* 347–359.

Rice, M. L. (1990). Preschooler's QUIL: Quick incidental learning of words. In G. Conti-Ramsden & C. E. Snow (Eds.), *Children's language* (Vol. 7). Hillsdale, NJ: Lawrence Erlbaum.

Riegel, K. F., Riegel, R. M., Quarterman, C. J., & Smith, H. E. (1968). An analysis of difference in word meaning and semantic structure between four educational levels. *Human Development, 11,* 92–106.

Rosch, E. (1973). Natural categories. *Cognitive Psychology, 4,* 328–350.

Rosch, E., Mervis, C. B., Gray, W. D., Johnson, D. M., & Boyes-Braem, P. (1976). Basic objects in natural categories. *Cognitive Psychology, 8,* 382–439.

Ross, G., Nelson, K., Wetstone, H., & Tanouye, E. (1986). Acquisition and generalization of novel object concepts by young language learners. *Journal of Child Language, 13,* 67–83.

Sachs, J., Brown, R., & Salerno, R. (1976). Adults' speech to children. In W. von Raffler Engel and Y. Lebrun (Eds.), *Baby talk and infant speech.* Lisse, The Netherlands: Swets and Zeitlinger.

Schultz, T. (1976). A cognitive-developmental analysis of humor. In A. J. Chapman & M. C. Foot (Eds.), *Humor and laughter: Theory, research, and applications.* New York: Wiley.

Schwartz, R. G., & Leonard, L. B. (1982). Do children pick and choose? An examination of phonological selection and avoidance in early lexical acquisition. *Journal of Child Language, 9,* 319–336.

Shatz, M., & Gelman, R. (1973). The development of communication skills: Modifications in the speech of young children as a function of the listener. *Monographs of the Society for Research in Child Development, 38* (No. 152).

Sinclair, A., Jarvella, R. J., & Levelt, W. J. (Eds.). (1978). *The child's conception of language.* New York: Springer-Verlag.

Slobin, D. I. (1978). A case study of early language awareness. In A. Sinclair, R. J. Jarvella, & W. J. Levelt (Eds.), *The child's conception of language.* New York: Wiley.

Smith, C. A., & Sachs, J. (1990). Cognition and the verb lexicon in early lexical development. *Applied Psycholinguistics, 11,* 409–424.

Smith, E. E., & Medin, D. L. (1981). *Categories and concepts.* Cambridge, MA: Harvard University Press.

Smith, M. E. (1926). An investigation of the development of the sentence and the extent of vocabulary in young children. *Studies in Child Welfare* (Vol. 3, No. 5). Iowa City: University of Iowa.

Snow, C. (1972). Mothers' speech to children learning language. *Child Development, 43,* 549–585.

Snow, C. (1990). The development of definitional skill. *Journal of Child Language, 17,* 697–710.

Stoel-Gammon, C., & Cooper, J. A. (1984). Patterns of early lexical and phonological development. *Journal of Child Language, 11,* 247–271.

Swartz, K., & Hall, A. (1972). Development of relational concepts and word definitions in children five through eleven. *Child Development, 43,* 239–244.

Taylor, M., & Gelman, S. A. (1988). Adjectives and nouns: Children's strategies for learning new words. *Child Development, 59,* 411–419.

Thompson, J. R., & Chapman, R. S. (1977). Who is "Daddy" revisited: The status of two-year-olds' overextended words in use and comprehension. *Journal of Child Language, 4,* 359–375.

Tichener, G. B. (1909). *Lectures on the experimental psychology of the thought processes.* New York: Macmillan.

Tiedemann, D. (1787). Über die Entwicklung der Seelenfahig-Keiten bei Kundern. *Hessiche Beitragzur Gelehrsamkeit und kunst.* Reprinted in English in A. Bar-Adon & W. Leopold (Eds.). (1971). Child language: A Book of readings. Englewood Cliffs, NJ: Prentice-Hall.

Tomasello, M., & Farrar, M. J. (1986). Joint attention and early language. *Child Development, 57,* 1454–1463.

Vygotsky, L. S. (1962). *Thought and language.* Cambridge, MA: MIT Press.

Webb, P. A., & Abrahamson, A. A. (1976). Stages of egocentrism in children's use of "this" and "that": A different point of view. *Journal of Child Language, 3,* 349–367.

Wehren, A., DeLisi, R., & Arnold, M. (1981). The development of noun definition. *Journal of Child Language, 8,* 165–175.

Werner, H., & Kaplan, E. (1950). Development of word meaning through verbal context: An experiment study. *Journal of Psychology, 29,* 251–257.

Winner, E. (1988). *The point of words: Children's understanding of metaphor and irony.* Cambridge, MA: Harvard University Press.

Wisniewski, E. J., & Murphy, G. L. (1989). Superordinate and basic category names in discourse: A textual analysis. *Discourse Processes, 12,* 245–261.

Wolman, R. N., & Baker, E. N. (1965). A developmental study of word definitions. *Journal of Genetic Psychology, 107,* 159–166.

Putting Words Together: Morphology and Syntax in the Preschool Years

5

Helen Tager-Flusberg *University of Massachusetts at Boston*

■ INTRODUCTION

After months of coaxing and prompting the meaningless babbles of their babies, parents are finally rewarded when the first word is produced. Several weeks after this important milestone is duly recorded, vocabulary begins to grow quite rapidly, as new words are learned daily. At this initial stage young children use their words in a variety of contexts, most frequently to label objects or to interact socially, but always limit their messages by speaking one word at a time. Still, parents and children together delight in showing off these earliest linguistic accomplishments that mark the beginning of the journey toward full mastery of language.

Within a few months, usually in the latter half of the second year, children reach the next important milestone: they begin putting words together to form the first "sentences." This new stage marks a crucial turning point, for even the simplest two-word utterances show evidence of **syntax;** that is, the child combines words to create sentences following certain rules rather than in random fashion. One of the remarkable features about the development of syntactic rules is that it seems to take place almost unnoticed, with no explicit instruction. Parents who quite consciously and conscientiously teach their children new concepts and words never presume to teach syntax. They focus more on *what* the child is saying rather than *how* the child says it (Brown & Hanlon, 1970).

Even though parents and others have essentially ignored the child's use and occasional misuse of syntactic rules, child language researchers and linguists have studied that usage closely all over the world. Years of careful and painstaking research have yielded a detailed, descriptive picture of the course of syntactic development in English and other languages, although the mechanisms that account for these accomplishments are still being hotly debated (see Chapter 7). In this chapter, we describe the main stages of syntactic development that take place during the preschool years, focusing on the order in which various constructions are acquired. At each stage we are concerned with extracting the universal and invariant features of children's language and characterizing the underlying knowledge of linguistic rules and categories that fit the language at that point in development.

THE NATURE OF SYNTACTIC RULES

Much of our understanding of the nature of syntactic rules has come from linguists who have been concerned primarily with characterizing the rules that underlie the well-formed sentences of adult language users—the natural end point of the acquisition process. The most influential linguistic framework is the one developed by Noam Chomsky, called the theory of **universal grammar,** or UG. Chomsky began developing this framework in 1957, but it has undergone several revisions since. The current version is known as **government and binding theory,** or GB (Chomsky, 1981, 1982). Because this theory has had such a significant influence on research on grammatical development, especially in recent years, we shall first describe briefly some of the major concepts and characteristics of this linguistic premise.

According to Chomsky, the goals of any theory of grammar, such as universal grammar, are that it is compatible with the grammars of all the world's languages (the goal of **universality**), and that it must, in principle, be compatible with the fact that children worldwide acquire the grammar of their language within a few short years, usually with little or no explicit training or correction (the goal of **learnability**). GB theory is a theory of language knowledge; essentially, it is a theory of how we represent language as a set of principles in our mind. Chomsky believes that our mental representation of grammar is autonomous of other cognitive systems, which means that the principles and rules of grammar are not shared with other cognitive systems but are in fact unique and highly specialized.

The central tenet of GB theory is that there are several components of the grammar that are linked at different levels of representation. Figure 5.1 provides a simplified view of the main components. Of key interest are the two levels: *d-structure,* which captures the underlying relationships between subject and object in a sentence (the basic unit of grammar); and *s-structure,* which captures the surface linear arrangements of words in a sentence. In order to see why these two levels are necessary, consider the following sentences:

John is easy to please.
John is eager to please.

Both sentences have virtually the same s-structures:

noun–verb–adjective–infinitive verb.

However, they mean quite different things. The subject of the verb "to please" is John in the second sentence, but someone else in the first. This difference in the underlying grammatical relationships of subject, predicate, and so forth would be captured by very different d-structures. From a developmental point of view, we must ask the question of how children come to grasp the underlying grammatical relations of sentences they hear (d-structures), when they are only presented with s-structures.

Figure 5.1 also shows that each level, s-structure and d-structure, has several components. The s-structure has two parts: *phonetic form,* which is the actual sound

FIGURE 5.1

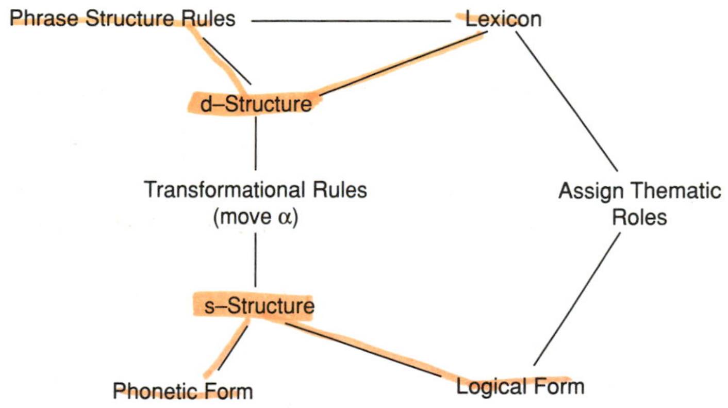

structure of the sentence; and *logical form,* which captures the meaning of sentences (this component connects the grammar to other aspects of cognition). The d-structure also has two parts: the *phrase structure rules,* which capture the basic subject/predicate structure of a sentence; and the *lexicon,* which specifies a number of important features (morphophonological, syntactic) for each lexical item in a sentence. Together, the lexicon and the phrase structure rules generate the d-structure of a sentence.

The phrase structures are often represented in "tree-diagrams" of the sort you see in Figure 5.2. They capture the underlying relationships of parts or *phrases* of the sentence, including *noun* or *determiner phrases* (phrases that usually begin with a determiner such as *the, a, this,* and always contain a proper or common noun), *verb phrases, adjectival phrases,* etc. The phrase structure of a sentence also includes some additional syntactic elements, such as *complementizers (that, what),* which introduces each sentence, and an *inflectional* category, which holds the auxiliary verb (*do, will, may,* etc.) and carries information about tense. Thus the basic structure of the sentence is organized in the d-structure by the phrase structure rules.

The lexicon provides the specific "words" or lexical items that get inserted at the end of the phrase structure trees. The lexicon contains information for each item about its syntactic category (noun, verb, adjective, etc.), much like a dictionary. It also contains information about what kinds of sentence structures the item requires, which is especially important for verbs. Consider the following set of verbs:

run
see
put

The lexicon would include different information for each verb because they all appear in different sentence structures, or *argument structure.* Thus the verb *run* only requires a subject; it does not require an object, but it could take a location as an optional argument:

John runs (to the store).

The verb *see* requires both a subject and an object, and it can take as an object either a simple noun phrase or a complete sentence:

FIGURE 5.2

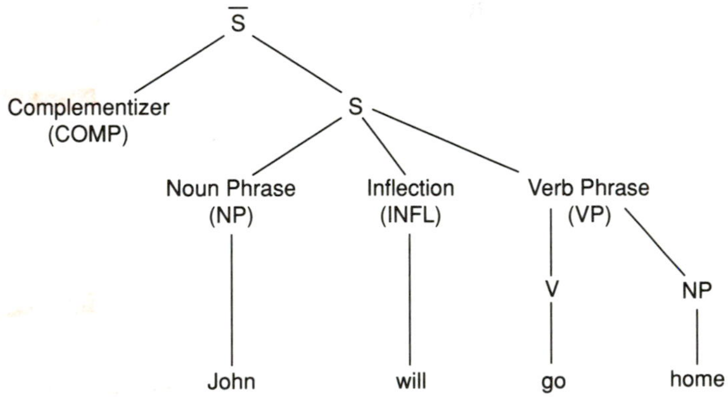

John sees Mary (writing her book).

The verb *put* not only requires a subject and object, but also needs a location specified:

John put the book on the shelf.

This information about the argument structure of different verbs is all contained in the lexicon, and is critical in organizing appropriate phrase structures.

The d-structure is connected to the s-structure by a rule that reorders the elements of the phrase structure into the linear arrangement of the surface form. This rule, called the *transformational rule,* is extremely general—"move any category anywhere"—which allows elements to get moved around. This movement rule is important in English; for example, in creating questions (as in the example in Figure 5.3) or passive constructions. Because the transformational rule is so general, the grammar also needs to have a set of rules, or *constraints,* on which elements may be moved and which may not, as well as where they may be moved to. Many of these restrictions are included in the numerous subtheories that form a part of the GB framework, but we will not go into these here. Some constraints are universal and apply to all languages; some are specific to each language (e.g., the English question-formation rule that moves the *wh-* word to the beginning of the sentence).

The lexicon is also connected to the logical form component of s-structure (see Figure 5.1) via the assignment of *thematic roles* (also called *semantic roles* in other linguistic systems). This assigns to each of the main noun phrases a role in the sentence like agent, patient, recipient, and location:

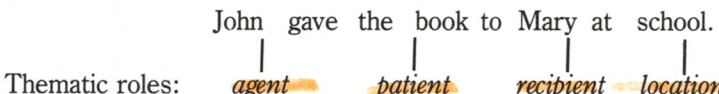

	John	gave	the	book	to	Mary	at	school.
Thematic roles:	*agent*			*patient*		*recipient*		*location*

All these components and rule systems are considered to be universal in UG. The grammar also has a system for handling the kind of syntactic and morphological varia-

FIGURE 5.3

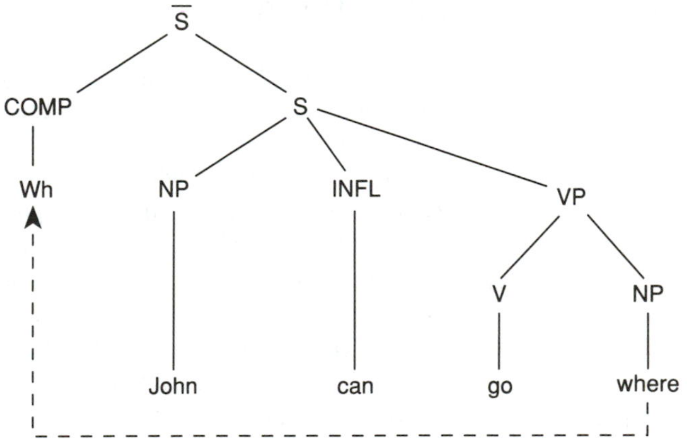

"Where can John go?"

tions that exist across languages of the world. UG includes a set of principles that vary as **parameters:** they operate one way for some languages and another way for other languages. These parameters are conceived of as a set of switches, with several settings (typically two) on each switch. In theory, at least, each language's grammar is captured by a unique combination of switch settings on all the main parameters. This is one of the exciting new ideas in UG, because it addresses the goal of universality, but so far not many parameters have been well worked out. It is also an important idea for researchers of language development, because one hypothesis that has been proposed is that in each child UG starts off with its collection of parameters. As a child is exposed to her native language the evidence from this input is used to guide which way the switches on each parameter should be set. Thus, the parameter setting hypothesis also addresses the goal of learnability.

One example of a parameter is called the *null-subject parameter* (sometimes also called *pro-drop*). In English, every sentence is required to have an explicit subject; however, languages such as Italian or Spanish allow sentences to drop their subjects in the s-structure. So, for example, one can say in Italian:

> *Sta piovendo.* (Is raining).

For this sentence to be grammatical in English, we must add an *It* as the subject, although the pronoun does not refer to anything at all. This kind of pronoun is called an *expletive,* and only languages that require subjects also have expletive pronouns. There are other differences between Italian and English that all covary under the null-subject parameter. In this way language variation is captured by an economical system that considers under a single parameter a range of correlated syntactic features. We shall see later in this chapter how this idea of parameters, especially the null-subject parameter, has motivated some interesting though not uncontroversial research into early child language.

STUDYING SYNTACTIC DEVELOPMENT

Much of what we know about the development of syntax comes, of course, from studying what children actually say. Longitudinal studies of children in their homes, talking with their mothers or fathers, have produced vast quantities of raw data in the form of transcripts. In order to find out what the child knows of syntactic rules at any given stage, the researcher must examine the full corpus of speech, looking for patterns and regularities, searching through what is said for what is left unspoken, and contrasting the language at this stage with what came earlier and what will come later. These studies of spontaneous speech can tell us a great deal about the language produced by the child, but they do not reveal much about what the child can or cannot understand. Nor do they tell us what the child might have been able to say but was never given the opportunity to do so. Because of these limitations, spontaneous speech data need to be complemented with more controlled, experimental studies that are designed to test children's comprehension of various syntactic forms, or their ability to produce or judge particular constructions in less natural but more controlled situations.

In this chapter we utilize both sources of evidence—spontaneous speech and controlled experiments—in describing the course of syntactic development. However, we depend more on spontaneous speech, which has been most widely used by researchers studying a variety of languages and provides us with the least problematic source of child language data since it is elicited in naturalistic contexts.

ENTERING THE COMPLEX LINGUISTIC SYSTEM

One of the most difficult issues about acquiring language that the child faces is how to break into the system. How do children manage to break up the steady stream of sounds they hear into basic units like words and morphemes? How do they learn to map specific sound sequences onto meanings? And how do they learn to figure out the basic grammatical categories of their language such as nouns, verbs, and adjectives? These are some of the fundamental questions about language acquisition that child language researchers must also address in their theories, even though young children at the earliest stages of development provide us with few clues.

One interesting hypothesis that has received some empirical support has been suggested by Morgan (1986), among others. According to Morgan, if adults were providing information in their speech to children about where boundaries exist, not only between words but also between phrases, the task of acquiring language would become feasible and simplified.

There does appear to be evidence that mothers and fathers provide strong intonational evidence about word and phrase boundaries, not only in English, but also in other languages, such as French and Japanese (Fernald et al., 1989). More importantly, there is also evidence that infants are sensitive to the salience of the information sent in pauses (Kemler Nelson, Hirsh-Pasek, Jusczyk, & Cassidy, 1989).

Once the child has broken the stream of speech into words, he may use other "bootstraps" into the syntactic system. Some researchers have suggested that meaning, or *semantics,* plays a key bootstrapping role for the child (e.g., Pinker, 1984); others suggest that the functions of language, or *pragmatics,* provide the primary route into the abstract grammatical system (e.g., Bates & MacWhinney, 1982). A third alternative is that grammar provides its own bootstrapping operation, suggesting that it operates as an independent cognitive system. We will consider the role that semantics, pragmatics, and grammar play in facilitating grammatical development at each of the different stages of the process.

MEASURING SYNTACTIC GROWTH

As children get older, their sentences grow longer. While age itself is not a good predictor of language development since children develop at vastly different rates, the length of a child's sentences is an excellent indicator of syntactic development; each new element of syntactic knowledge adds length to a child's utterances. Roger Brown (1973) introduced the major measure of syntactic development, the **mean length of utterance** or **MLU,** which is based on the average length of a child's sentences scored on transcripts of spontaneous speech. Length is determined by the number of meaningful units, or *morphemes,* rather than words. Morphemes include simple content words such as *cat, play, do, red;* function words such as *no, the, you, this;* and affixes or grammatical inflections such as *un-, -s, -ed.* The addition of each morpheme (or minimal unit carrying meaning) reflects the acquisition of new linguistic knowledge. So children who have similar MLUs are at the same level of linguistic maturity, and their language is at the same level of complexity.

In order to calculate the MLU of a particular child, one needs a transcript of a half-hour conversation. The child's language must be divided into separate utterances, and these utterances must be divided into morphemes. Brown (1973) provides detailed rules for judging what constitutes a morpheme for the child learning English (see Figure 5.4). For example, although compound words like *birthday* or *goodnight* contain two morphemes, they only count as one. The same is true for diminutives (e.g., *doggie, ducky*) and irregular past tense verbs (e.g., *got, did*). On the other hand, inflections (e.g., regular past tense *-ed,* plural *-s,* progressive *-ing*) and auxiliaries (e.g., *is, have, will*) count as separate morphemes. The number of morphemes in each of the first 100 fully transcribed utterances is counted, and the total is then divided by 100 (see Figure 5.4).

In longitudinal studies, the MLUs calculated at successive points in time gradually increase. Figure 5.5 shows the MLU plotted against chronological age for the three children studied by Brown and his colleagues. Clearly, MLU grows at different rates in different children. Of the children followed by Brown, Eve's MLU rose most sharply, indicating very rapid language development, whereas Sarah and Adam showed more gradual and less consistent increments in their MLU. According to the MLU norms developed by Miller and Chapman (1981), based on a sample of over 100 middle-class children in Madison, Wisconsin (see Figure 5.6), Adam and Sarah are about average for their age, whereas Eve is very much advanced for her age. Using the MLU, Brown subdivided the major period of syntactic growth into five stages, beginning with stage I when the MLU is between 1.0 and 2.0. Successive stages are marked by increments of .5; thus, stage II goes from 2.0 to 2.5, stage III is from 2.5 to 3.0, stage IV is from 3.0 to 3.5, and stage V is from 3.5 to 4.0. Beyond an MLU of about 4.0 some of the assumptions on which the measure is based are no longer valid, and longer sentences do not simply reflect what the child knows about language; so MLU loses value as an index of language development after this stage.

There are some questions that arise in calculating MLUs (e.g., should one include yes/no responses to adult questions?), and these have led to some criticisms of it as an index of syntactic development (Crystal, 1974). Nevertheless, it has proven immensely useful as a means of classifying children in the early stages of syntactic development, and it remains an important tool for research and clinical

1. Start with the second page of the transcription unless that page involves a recitation of some kind. In this latter case, start with the first recitation-free stretch. Count the first 100 utterances satisfying the following rules.
2. Only fully transcribed utterances are used; none with blanks. Portions of utterances, entered in parentheses to indicate doubtful transcription, are used.
3. Include all exact utterance repetitions (marked with a plus sign in records). Stuttering is marked as repeated efforts at a single word; count the word once in the most complete form produced. In the few cases where a word is produced for emphasis or the like (*no, no, no*) count each occurrence.
4. Do not count such fillers as *mm* or *oh*, but do count *no, yeah*, and *hi.*
5. All compound words (two or more free morphemes), proper names, and ritualized reduplications count as single words. Examples: *birthday, rackety-boom, choo-choo, quack-quack, night-night, pocketbook, see saw*. Justification is that no evidence that the constituent morphemes function as such for these children.
6. Count as one morpheme all irregular pasts of the verb (*got, did, went, saw*). Justification is that there is no evidence that the child relates these to present forms.
7. Count as one morpheme all diminutives (*doggie, mommie*) because these children at least do not seem to use the suffix productively. Diminutives are the standard forms used by the child.
8. Count as separate morphemes all auxiliaries (*is, have, will, can, must, would*). Also all catenatives: *gonna, wanna, hafta*. These latter counted as single morphemes rather than as *going* to or *want to* because evidence is that they function so for the children. Count as separate morphemes all inflections, for example, possessive {s}, plural {s}, third person singular {s}, regular past {d}, progressive {iŋ}.
9. The range count follows the above rules but is always calculated for the total transcription rather than for 100 utterances.

FIGURE 5.4 Rules for calculating mean length of utterance (Reprinted by permission of the publishers from *A First Language* by Roger Brown, Cambridge, MA: Harvard University Press, Copyright 1973 by the President and Fellows of Harvard College.)

assessment of English-speaking children. More serious problems are encountered in measuring the MLU in foreign languages, especially highly inflected and synthetic languages such as German, Russian, or Hebrew. In these cases it becomes difficult to decide what functions as a morpheme in the child's speech, and it is easy to obtain inflated numbers. Still, there have been attempts to extend the concept of MLU to structurally varied languages (Bowerman, 1973) or to modify the measure to account for cross-linguistic differences (Dromi & Berman, 1982). By using a similar index to chart language growth across a range of languages, we can search for the universal and invariant features that characterize the main stages of syntactic development.

Recently, there have been advances made in developing additional measures of syntactic development. One example is the **Index of Productive Syntax,** or **IPSyn,** introduced by Hollis Scarborough (1989). For this measure one also needs a transcript of 100 spontaneous speech utterances from a child. Using the scoresheet provided by

FIGURE 5.5
Mean length of utterance and chronological age for three children (Reprinted by permission of the publishers from *A First Language* by R. Brown, Cambridge, MA: Harvard University Press, Copyright 1973 by the President and Fellows of Harvard College.)

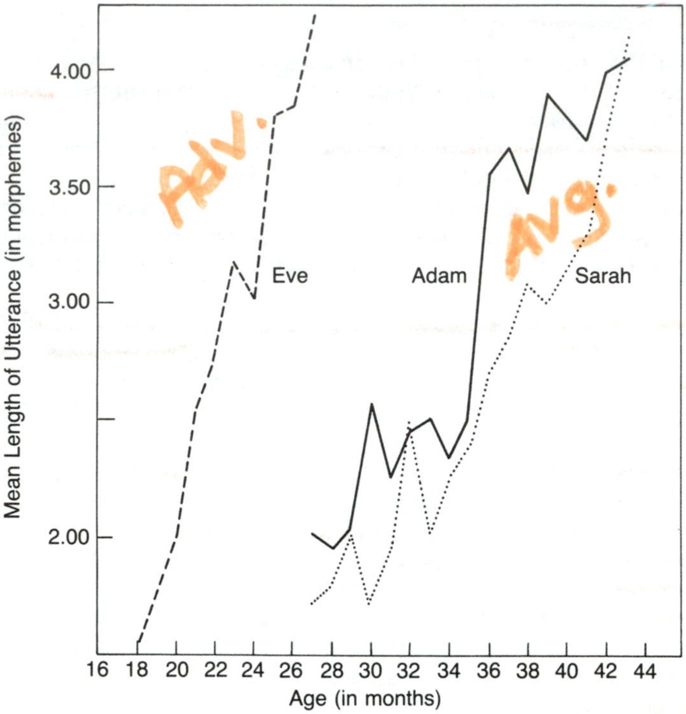

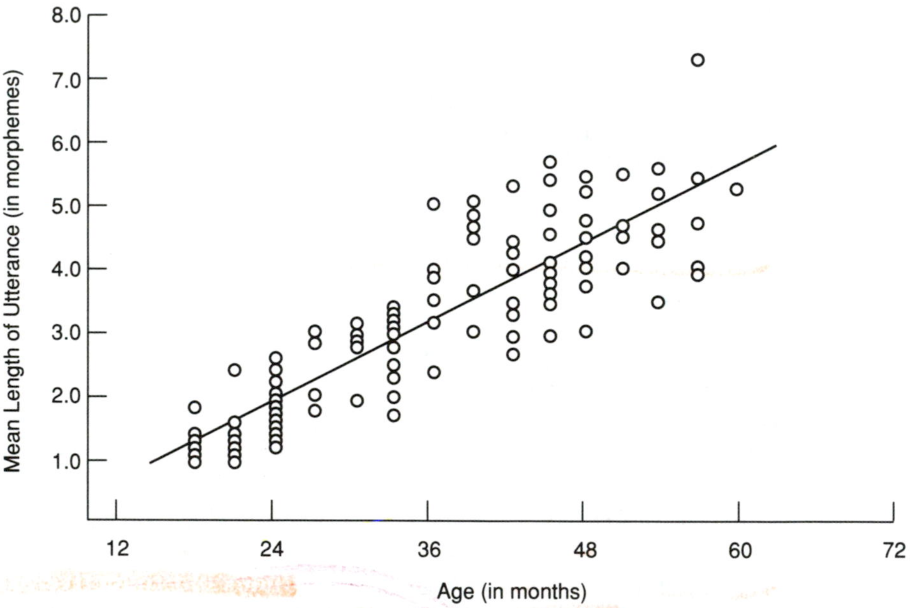

FIGURE 5.6 *Source:* From "The Relations between Age and Mean Length of Utterance" by J. F. Miller and R. S. Chapman, 1981, *Journal of Speech and Hearing Research, 24,* pp. 154–161.

Scarborough, the researcher marks the use, up to a maximum of two very different uses, of a variety of structures in four categories: in noun phrases (e.g., nouns, pronouns, articles, plural endings, compound nouns), verb phrases (verbs, prepositions, verb endings, auxiliaries, modals, tense), questions and negation forms (at various levels of complexity), and sentence structure (simple, complex, complements, conjunctions, infinitive forms). The score received is simply the total number of points, with points awarded for each structure used. The IPSyn measure correlates very highly with MLU, demonstrating its validity as a measure of grammatical development. However, it has the advantage of providing a measure that remains useful far beyond the MLU limit of 4.0, at least until around 5 years of age.

■ TWO-WORD UTTERANCES

The first stage defined by Brown follows children through their earliest attempts at multiword utterances, as the MLU grows from 1.0 to 2.0. Most of the child's sentences are two words long, although a few may be as long as three or even four words. Table 5.1 lists numerous examples of two-word sentences taken from separate children acquiring English as their first language. Examples from children learning other languages are very similar to these.

Looking at these examples, we can note a number of interesting features about children's early sentences. First, from the beginning the child's language is truly

TABLE 5.1 Examples of Two-Word Utterances

Andrew	Eve
more car	bye-bye baby
more cereal	Daddy bear
more high	Daddy book
more read	Daddy honey
outside more	there Daddy
no more	there potty
no pee	more pudding
no wet	Mommy stair
all wet	Mommy dimple
all gone	Mommy do
bye-bye Calico	Mommy bear
bye-bye back	eat it
bye-bye car	read it
bye-bye Papa	see boy
Mama come	more cookie
see pretty	

Note: Terms in column 1 are from Braine, 1976; those in column 2 are from Eve's transcripts and from Brown and Fraser, 1963.

creative: many of these sentences would never have been spoken by an adult. The particular word combinations spoken by stage I children are unique and novel rather than mere imitations of adult sentences. Second, these sentences are simple, compared to adult sentences, and simplicity is accomplished in a systematic way. Certain words called **content** or **open-class** words dominate the children's language. Thus, their sentences are composed primarily of nouns, verbs, and adjectives. These large word classes are called open since they freely admit new items and drop old ones as a language evolves. In contrast, **function words** or **closed-class** words are usually missing at this stage of language development. The closed word classes (including prepositions, conjunctions, articles, pronouns, auxiliaries, and inflections) are much smaller and do not change their composition readily. The absence of these grammatical terms lends to the impression of simplicity. We can also notice that some words are very frequent in a particular child's corpus (Andrew uses *more* and *bye-bye* often and in combination with many different words), and the order of the words appears quite regular. Finally, if we look at what the children are talking about, we can see that certain topics (such as possession, location, recurrence) are very prevalent.

Investigators of child language have spent the last 20 years trying to come up with the best, most accurate way of characterizing stage I language. There have been a number of changes in these characterizations as the focus shifted from one significant feature to another. However, these changes do not reflect differences in the data but in the kinds of categories imposed on the data by different researchers. The challenge is to ascribe neither too little nor too much knowledge of syntactic categories or rules to the child just beginning to acquire syntax.

TELEGRAPHIC SPEECH

The earliest characterizations of stage I language focused on the contrast between the open-class and closed-class words. Brown and Fraser (1963) called these two-word utterances *telegraphic* because the omission of closed-class words makes them resemble telegrams. In fact, not all of the words used are from the open classes. A small handful of functors like *more, no, you,* and *off* are scattered throughout the transcripts and can be seen in the examples in Table 5.1. Miller and Ervin (1964) suggested that children choose just those words that are highly stressed in adult language and are thus perceptually more salient. These include nouns, adjectives, and verbs and also some closed-class words, especially those that are syllabic and express semantic information (Brown, 1973). Gleitman and Wanner (1982) have suggested that children, in fact, learn open- and closed-class words quite separately. The earlier acquisition of open-class words is based on their perceptual salience, according to Gleitman and Wanner, and thus represents a good example of prosodic features helping the child to discover basic language structure.

The idea that stage I language consists exclusively of open-class words comes from research on the acquisition of English. More recent studies that have looked at

"My teddy." Possessives are acquired early.

children acquiring other languages, for example Italian (Hyams, 1986a, 1989), Turkish (Aksu-Koc, 1988), or Hebrew (Levy, 1988), which have much richer morphological systems and may be less reliant on words to express basic grammatical relations, have shown that even at the earliest stages children acquiring these kinds of languages are also beginning to acquire some of the closed-class morphology.

SEMANTIC RELATIONS

Studies of children from around the world in stage I, using two-word utterances, have shown that one universal feature of this stage is that only a small group of meanings, or *semantic relations,* is expressed in the children's language. Bloom (1970) first observed this in her study of three American children. Later, Brown (1973) extended her findings to children acquiring Finnish, Swedish, Samoan, Spanish, French, Russian, Korean, Japanese, and Hebrew. Table 5.2 lists the eight most prevalent combinatorial meanings found by Brown (pp.193–197) along with some examples of each.

From these examples we see that during stage I children talk a great deal about objects—they point them out and name them (demonstrative) and they talk about where the objects are (location), what they are like (attributive), who owns them (possession), and who is doing things to them (agent-object). They also talk about actions performed by people (agent-action), performed on objects (action-object), and oriented toward certain locations (action-location). Objects, people, and actions and their interrelationships thus preoccupy the toddler universally, and, as Brown points out, these are precisely the concepts that the child has just completed differentiating during what Piaget has called the sensorimotor stage of cognitive development.

EARLY GRAMMAR

Another important feature of children's two-word utterances is their consistent word order. In his study, Brown (1973) used the children's correct use of word order as evidence in support of the semantic relations approach to stage I. Braine (1963, 1976) also has documented the early productive use of word order rules for children acquiring a variety of languages. He noted, however, that early two-word combinations had more limited, lexical-specific scope than either Bloom or Brown had suggested, which he called *limited scope formulae.* Moreover, Braine (1976) showed that there were large individual differences in the order in which different semantic relations were acquired.

Pinker (1984, 1987) has taken the findings about stage I speech to argue that children use semantics to provide the key bootstrap into the linguistic system. The child

TABLE 5.2 Set of Prevalent Semantic Relations in Stage I

Semantic Relation	Examples
agent + action	mommy come; daddy sit
action + object	drive car; eat grape
agent + object	mommy sock; baby book
action + location	go park; sit chair
entity + location	cup table; toy floor
possessor + possession	my teddy; mommy dress
entity + attribute	box shiny; crayon big
demonstrative + entity	dat money; dis telephone

can use the correspondence between things and names to map onto the linguistic category of nouns. Names for physical attributes or changes of state are expressed as verbs. Because all sentence subjects at this stage are essentially semantic agents, children can use this syntactic-semantic correspondence to begin figuring out the abstract syntactic relations for more complex sentences that require the category of subject, but which are not clearly agents too.

Paul Bloom (1990a) provides some interesting evidence for this general idea that semantics may bootstrap the child directly into the grammatical system. He found that from the start children assign words to syntactic categories such as noun, verb, and adjective. Even in stage I, children learning English know that pronouns and proper nouns are different from common nouns because adjectives can only come before the latter. Thus the first sentence below is grammatical, but the other sentences (marked with an *) are not:

> The *big dog* runs away.
> *Small *she* goes home.
> *Happy Fred is here.

Looking through the transcripts from children in stage I, Bloom found that children almost never violated this word order rule of English, and seemed therefore to know the difference between common nouns, pronouns, and proper nouns. At the same time, Gleitman (1990) argues that very young children also seem able to use syntax to provide them clues about semantics or the meanings of words, and there is some evidence for this hypothesis (Naigles, 1990).

How does the evidence about very early child language fit in with the linguistic theory proposed in GB theory? One answer to this question comes from a British linguist, Andrew Radford (1990), who argues that much of the linguistic system is absent in stage I, but what the child does have at this stage is a lexicon and a limited set of phrase structure rules in d-structure. There is no transformational rule; however, the d-structure does get assigned thematic roles to yield the s-structure. These ideas are very similar to the other descriptions of stage I language that we have discussed earlier, but Radford uses the terminology and framework of the GB theory.

Another use of the GB framework to explain stage I grammar has been proposed by Hyams (1986a, 1989). If one looks at the examples of stage I utterances listed in Table 5.1 that contain verbs (e.g., *eat it*), one notices that these utterances lack a subject. Hyams suggests that this is the result of the null-subject parameter, which starts off in all children in the position for languages, like Italian, that allow subjectless sentences. According to Hyams, all children begin with the parameter set one way (e.g., the Italian way), and so English-speaking children eventually have to switch the setting of the parameter to the other position. During stage I, when English-speaking children often omit subjects and do not have any expletive pronouns in their language, their grammars conform to this setting.

Although Hyams's hypothesis is attractive because it is theoretically grounded, there have been some important criticisms raised by other researchers (O'Grady, Peters, & Masterson, 1989). Valian (1990) points out some logical problems with the claim that parameters start off in one particular setting. She also provides evidence that even though American children at the early stages of language development omit subjects, they do, in fact, include a sentence subject significantly more often than do Italian children at the same stage of development, suggesting that they know that subjects need to be expressed. But if they know that subjects must be included in a sentence, why do young children omit them frequently? Bloom (1990b) shows that the problem for young children is that they have a limited processing capacity—they can only cope with producing utterances of limited length, and this constrains which elements will be included in a sentence and which will be omitted. Subjects are omitted more frequently than objects (which are also occasionally absent) either because of processing limitations (since subjects come at the beginning of a sentence and this places a heavier processing load than do elements, like objects, which appear at ends of sentences) or for pragmatic reasons (the subject of a sentence is often provided by context, or has been established in prior discourse).

Controversies about the nature of children's early grammars, the role of GB theory, and the best way to conceptualize the child's early linguistic system have yet to be resolved. This extensive look at one stage in the acquisition of grammar highlights the importance of both theories in motivating new research and a closer, more detailed look at children's language, for English as well as other languages.

CHILDREN'S EARLY COMPREHENSION OF SYNTAX

Thus far we have presented a picture of early language development that is based entirely on studies of spontaneous speech production. These studies, however, leave unanswered a host of questions about young children's comprehension of syntax. We might ask, for example, when children begin to comprehend two or more word utterances. Is comprehension in advance of production or *vice versa*? What is the relationship between comprehension and production?

Parents generally believe that their children are understanding multiword utterances almost from the time they begin using their first words, and that comprehension is clearly in advance of production. Unfortunately, until very recently, research on this issue yielded conflicting results. For example, some studies supported the parents' view that children understand more than they can say (e.g., Fraser, Bellugi, & Brown, 1963; Huttenlocher, 1974; Sachs & Truswell, 1978), while others found that children could say more than they really understood (e.g., Chapman, 1977) or that the two abilities were at about the same level (e.g., Roberts, 1983). Of course, one difficulty in comparing different studies is that researchers have used very different methods for assessing comprehension while ensuring that children could not be relying on context to interpret the linguistic message (cf. Leonard, 1983). Different methods that have been used to assess comprehension include diary studies (which document conditions under which the child can or cannot understand); act-out tasks (in which the experimenter asks the child to act out a sentence using toys—e.g., "Make the girl kiss the duck"); direction tasks (in which the child is asked to carry out a direction, such as "Tickle the duck"); and picture-choice tasks (in which the child must select the picture that best represents the linguistic form being tested). There are serious limitations with each of these methods that have led to the confusion in the literature regarding children's comprehension abilities.

In recent years, Golinkoff and Hirsh-Pasek have pioneered the use of a new method for assessing language comprehension in infants as young as 12 months old, which avoids all the problems of other techniques. Using this new method, these researchers have found that even in the single-word stage, 17-month-old children can use word order to comprehend multiword utterances (Golinkoff & Hirsh-Pasek, 1987; Golinkoff, Hirsh-Pasek, Cauley, & Gordon, 1987). Their method (illustrated in Figure 5.7) involves setting the child on its mother's lap equidistant from two video monitors. While the mother closes her eyes and makes no attempt to communicate with her child, the child watches two simultaneously presented color videos. The linguistic message, presented over a centrally placed loudspeaker in synchrony with the videotaped scenes, directs the child to attend to one of the monitors. A hidden experimenter directly observes the child's eye movements and records the amount of time spent watching the two videos on each trial.

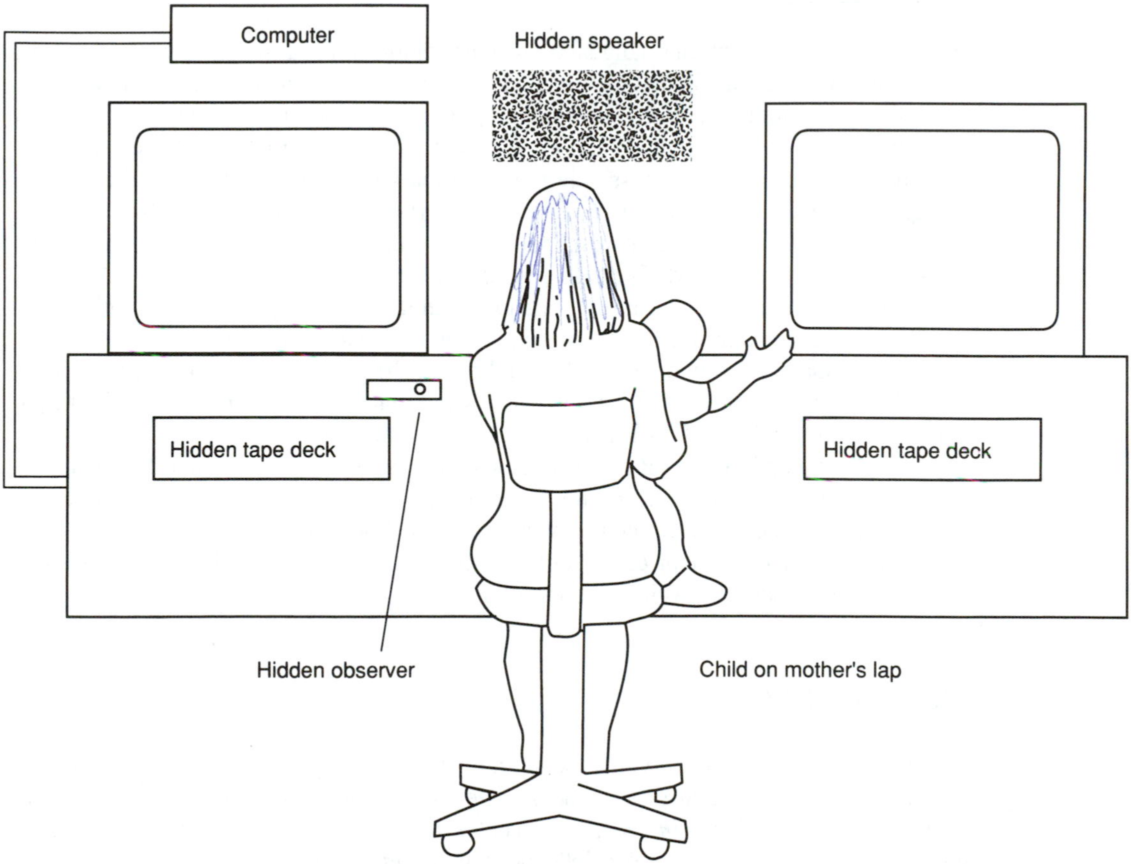

FIGURE 5.7 Experimental setup of the preferential looking paradigm (From Naigles, 1990)

Golinkoff and Hirsh-Pasek have used this paradigm to assess comprehension of various language features. For example, one key comparison they used to test comprehension of word order involved observing very young children while they heard the sentence "Cookie Monster is tickling Big Bird." One of the video scenes had Cookie Monster tickling Big Bird, while in the other scene, simultaneously presented, Big Bird was tickling Cookie Monster. Because children at 17 months of age reliably spent longer looking at the former scene, Golinkoff and Hirsh-Pasek concluded that children can comprehend word order before they even begin using two-word sentences.

These findings suggest that comprehension is indeed in advance of production, as parents have always known. Children are thus able to exploit knowledge gained from listening to adult speech to guide the acquisition of grammatical forms. Future studies perhaps will tell us whether comprehension development follows the same stages that have been found in the development of spontaneous speech.

DEVELOPING GRAMMATICAL MORPHEMES

When we look at children's language as it develops beyond stage I, we notice two important changes. One is that sentences get longer as children begin combining two or more basic semantic relations. For example, agent + action and action + object may be combined to yield agent + action + object, as in "Adam hit ball." In this way sentences also become progressively more complex in content. The second change is the gradual appearance of a few inflections and other closed-class terms that, "like an intricate sort of ivy, begin to grow up between and upon the major construction blocks, the nouns and verbs, to which Stage I is largely limited" (Brown, 1973, p. 249).

The process of acquiring the major grammatical morphemes is gradual and lengthy. Some are still not fully controlled until the child enters school (for example, certain irregular past-tense verbs). Nevertheless, the process begins early, as soon as the MLU approaches 2.0, and we will discuss the main research findings on the acquisition of a small subset of 14 English grammatical morphemes.

The development of these morphemes was studied by Brown and his colleague Courtney Cazden (1968) using the longitudinal data from Adam, Eve, and Sarah (Brown, 1973). The 14 morphemes were selected both because they were very frequent and because one can easily identify the contexts in which they are needed to produce a grammatically well formed sentence.

THE 14 MORPHEMES

Grammatical morphemes, even though they do not carry independent meaning, do subtly shade the meaning of sentences. The morpheme group studied by Brown included two prepositions (*in, on*), two articles (*a, the*), noun inflections marking possessive (*'s*) and plural (*-s*), verb inflections marking progressive (*-ing*), third person present tense of regular verbs (e.g., he walk*s*) or irregular verbs (e.g., he *has*), past tense of regular verbs (e.g., he walk*ed*) and irregular verbs (e.g., *had*), and the main uses of the verb *to be*—as auxiliary, both when it can be contracted (e.g., I *am* walking or I'*m* walking) and when it cannot be contracted (e.g., I *was* walking), and as a main verb or *copula* in its contractible form (e.g., I *am* happy or I'*m* happy) and its uncontractible form (e.g., This *is* it).

In order to chart the development of these morphemes, Brown closely examined each child utterance to identify whether it required any of the morphemes to make it fully grammatical by adult standards. Both the linguistic context (the utterance itself) and the nonlinguistic context can be used to decide which morphemes are necessary. For example, when a child says "that book" while pointing out a book, we know that there should be a copula (*'s* or *is*) and an article (*a*). Or if a child says "two book table" when there are a couple of books lying on the table, we know that *book* should have a plural *-s* and the preposition *on* and article *the* are required before the word *table*. In this way Brown went through the transcripts of his three subjects from stage I to stage V and identified all of the obligatory contexts for each morpheme. Then he checked how many of these contexts were actually filled with the appropriate morphemes at the different stages of development. From this he calculated the percentage of each morpheme actually supplied in its obligatory context for each child for each sample of spontaneous speech. This measure has the advantage of being independent of actual frequency of use since frequency may vary considerably from one child to another and from one point in time to the next.

The process of acquiring each of these grammatical morphemes is a gradual one—they do not suddenly appear in their required contexts all of the time. Rather, their appearance fluctuates, sometimes quite sharply, during the period when they are being acquired until they are almost always present. After this point is reached, there is rarely any regression (see also Mervis & Johnson, 1987, for a detailed case study).

ORDER OF ACQUISITION

The most important finding that Brown reports is the remarkable similarity among his three subjects in the order in which these morphemes were acquired: acquisition is defined as the time when the morpheme was supplied in 90 percent of its obligatory contexts. The first set of morphemes to be acquired included the two prepositions, the plural, and the present progressive inflection. The last morphemes were the contractible copula and auxiliary, which had not yet reached the acquisition criterion by stage V. Table 5.3 shows the average order of acquisition of all 14 morphemes.

A study by de Villiers and de Villiers (1973) examined the development of the same group of morphemes in a larger sample of 21 children who were of different ages and at different stages of language development. Each child was taped just once, and the transcripts were scored in the same way Brown had scored his subjects' transcripts. Their findings replicated the order of acquisition that Brown had reported. Thus, we now have strong evidence that English grammatical morphology develops in a more or less unchanging, predictable order.

EXPLAINING THE ORDER OF ACQUISITION

What accounts for this invariant sequence of development? Why do all children find the progressive inflection (*-ing*) easier than the past tense inflection (*-ed*) and articles (*a, the*) harder than the plural ending? One possible explanation is that the morphemes the children hear most often will be acquired earlier. Brown tested this *frequency hypothesis* in the following way. He examined the speech of each child's parents just before the child reached stage II and began using the morphemes. He tallied the number of times each morpheme was used by each parent and compared these frequencies with the order in which the morphemes were acquired by the children. But there was no relationship between these figures. For example, the most frequent morphemes in the parents' speech were the articles, but these were not among the earliest to be acquired. And even though prepositions were not so frequent in the parents' samples, they were acquired very early by all the children. So overall, frequency does not account well for the particular order in which the 14 morphemes develop. Some more recent attempts to demonstrate that frequency can account for the order in which grammatical morphemes are acquired (e.g., Moerk, 1980) have been criticized and shown to be quite incorrect both in the methodologies used and in the conclusions drawn (Pinker, 1981).

On the other hand, Brown (1973) did find that *linguistic complexity* predicted the order of acquisition very well. Complexity can be defined in two ways: *semantic* (the number of meanings encoded in the morpheme) and *syntactic* (the number of rules required for the morpheme). Brown defined complexity in a conservative way that he called cumulative complexity. Only morphemes that share common meanings or rules can be fairly compared: a morpheme that requires knowledge of both x and y is defined as more complex than a morpheme requiring knowledge of only x or y, but it cannot be compared to a morpheme requiring knowledge of w. When complexity is defined like this, not all the morphemes can be ordered, but those that can be predict well the order of acquisition found by Brown and the de Villierses.

If we look at cumulative semantic complexity, the plural morpheme encodes only number, the past tense (regular or irregular) morphemes encode "earlierness," and the present progressive morpheme encodes temporary duration. Since the copula verb and the third person singular morphemes encode both number and "earlierness," we would predict that these morphemes would be acquired later. This prediction is borne out by the order shown in Table 5.3. We would also predict that the auxiliary—which encodes number, "earlierness," and temporary duration—would be acquired after all of these since it entails all of these meanings. This prediction, too, is confirmed by the data.

Brown carried out a similar analysis for ordering the morphemes in terms of their cumulative syntactic complexity. In this case the rules needed to derive the morphemes were used to generate predicted orderings, which were also confirmed by the data in Table 5.3. Unfortunately, these two hypotheses—cumulative semantic complexity and cumulative syntactic complexity—cannot be teased apart; they make almost identical predictions for the set of English grammatical morphemes studied by

TABLE 5.3 Average Order of Acquisition of 14 Grammatical Morphemes by Three Children Studied by Brown

1.	present progressive
2/3.	prepositions *(in/on)*
4.	plural
5.	irregular past tense
6.	possessive
7.	copula, uncontractible
8.	articles
9.	regular past tense
10.	third person present tense, regular
11.	third person present tense, irregular
12.	auxiliary, uncontractible
13.	copula, contractible
14.	auxiliary, contractible

Brown and his colleagues. Research on other languages provides further support for these hypotheses.

PRODUCTIVITY OF CHILDREN'S MORPHOLOGY

Even though it is generally accepted that children cannot and do not learn the morphology of a language by repeating specific examples they have heard from others, what independent evidence do we have that children are indeed acquiring a rule-governed system? To start with, there are the charming mistakes that children make—mistakes in applying a morphological rule when it should not be applied. For example, children frequently add the plural *-s* to exceptional nouns (man*s*, foot*s*, teeth*s*, people*s*) or use the regular past tense *-ed* on irregular verbs (fall*ed*, go*ed*, brok*ed*), even when the correct irregular form has previously been used. *Overgeneralization* errors like these are an excellent source of evidence for the productivity and creativity of the child's morphology: these are the forms no child would have heard from an adult.

Other evidence for the productive use of morphological rules came from a pioneering study by Berko (1958). Berko designed an elicited production task in which children were shown novel creatures and actions that were given invented names. The children were then provided with the linguistic context for adding plural and possessive inflections to the novel nouns and progressive, third person present tense, and past tense endings to the novel verbs. Figure 5.8 shows two examples from this study. Overall, Berko found preschool and first grade children performed well with the nonsense words, although their performance was clearly constrained by the controlled, somewhat artificial conditions of the experiment (cf. Levy, 1983). Nevertheless, the ability to supply correct morphemes on novel nouns and verbs demonstrates beyond doubt that children have internalized knowledge about English morphological rules and have not simply learned the morphemes in a rote fashion by imitating others.

FIGURE 5.8
Two example items from the wug test (From Berko, 1958.)

This is a wug.
Now there is another one.
There are two of them.
There are two ___.
This is a man who knows how to rick.
He is ricking. He did the same thing
yesterday. What did he do yesterday?
Yesterday he ___.

CROSS-LINGUISTIC DATA

There is by now a growing literature on the acquisition of grammatical morphology in other languages, though not all of these studies use Brown's exact methodology. Nevertheless, some of his findings on English have been supported by data on children's acquisition of other languages. For example, records of children's acquisition of the morphology of Russian (Slobin, 1966), Hebrew (Berman, 1981), and many other languages all include abundant examples of overgeneralization errors (see the relevant chapters in Slobin, 1985).

Studies of other languages also yield some contrasting data. While English morphology is acquired slowly and in a piecemeal fashion, some aspects of Italian morphology, for example, are acquired very rapidly (Hyams, 1986b). Some verb endings, especially those marking person, appear regularly in the language of Italian-speaking children even at stage I (Pizzuto & Caselli, 1991). This may well be because verbs in Italian can never appear without some morphological marking (for person, number, gender, and tense), whereas in English verbs typically appear without suffixes, the exceptions being the past tense of most verbs, and third person singular present tense (e.g., he sing*s*).

There is also good evidence that both semantic and syntactic complexity play significant roles in determining the order in which grammatical morphemes are acquired. The best evidence for this comes from Slobin's monumental cross-linguistic project, in which the acquisition of Turkish, Italian, Serbo-Croatian, and English were studied with similar methods and in comparable groups of children. In one study (Johnston & Slobin, 1979) the acquisition of the morphology used to express location (such as the English prepositions *in* and *on*) was compared across these four languages, using an elicited production measure. There was some degree of similarity in the order of acquisition, which can be explained by the semantic complexity hypothesis. However, there were also some interlanguage differences that could only be accounted for by the syntactic complexity hypothesis.

We do not yet have data from other languages to confirm the findings from English that morphology is generally acquired in an invariant order. Nevertheless, morphology in all languages appears to be acquired in similar ways and at similar stages of development.

DIFFERENT SENTENCE MODALITIES

After stage II, when the grammatical morphemes begin to appear, the major changes in the child's language are in the development of different types of sentences, such as negatives, questions, and imperatives. Although children most certainly say no, ask questions, and make demands at the very earliest stages of language development, it is not until about stage III (when the MLU reaches 2.5) that they begin to acquire the adult forms for their expression. In this section we will follow the course of development of two different sentence modalities—negatives and questions.

NEGATIVES

Ursula Bellugi, one of Brown's students, undertook the analysis of the expression of negation in the longitudinal transcripts of Adam, Eve, and Sarah (Bellugi, 1967). Like most of the child language researchers during the 1960s, Bellugi focused exclusively on a syntactic analysis that was heavily influenced by the prevailing linguistic theories of the time. She identified three main periods in the acquisition of the full negative. In the first period a sentence was made negative by placing the negative marker, *no* or *not*, outside the sentence, usually preceding it. There were many utterances of this form:

No go movies.
No sit down.
No Mommy do it.

In the next period, the negative word was moved inside the sentence and placed next to the main verb; however, there was no productive use of the auxiliary system. During this period Bellugi reports examples such as these:

I no like it.
Don't go.
I no want book.

The final period (which is not usually reached until stage V) was marked by the appearance of different auxiliaries, and the child's negative sentences then approximated the adult forms. Negatives such as these are produced during this final period:

You can't have this.
I don't have money.
I'm not sad now.

Thus Bellugi's analysis of negation focused on the development of its syntactic form. Because of the complexity of the English auxiliary system, children take a long time to acquire full mastery over the expression of negation in English.

Bloom (1970) soon criticized Bellugi's approach. She argued that almost all of the sentences produced during the first period had no subjects anyway, and so, in fact, the negative marker was correctly placed next to the verb or predicate. In those few instances where there was a sentence subject and the *no* was outside the sentence (as in "No Mommy do it"), Bloom inferred that *no* was not negating the sentence but was *anaphoric;* that is, it referred back to a preceding utterance. In this example the meaning of the sentence would be "No, I want Mommy to do it." The thrust of Bloom's argument, then, was to question the existence of the first period of negative acquisition, even though some had claimed this was a universal first stage (see McNeill, 1970). But de Villiers and de Villiers (1979) pointed out that there were too few critical sentences in the existent literature on which to judge the issue. Fortunately, their own children had learned how to say *no* and, in the process, provided large numbers of these critical sentences (de Villiers & de Villiers, 1979).

The de Villierses found that their son, Nicholas, produced two kinds of negative sentences during the first period. One kind confirmed Bellugi's analysis of a *no* + sentence rule—where the *no* was not anaphoric but negated the sentence. However, at the same time he produced sentences that had the negative marker placed internally, next to the verb or predicate. Nicholas, therefore, appeared to use two different rules to generate negatives.

When these two groups of negatives were carefully analyzed, de Villiers and de Villiers saw that Nicholas used one form (*no* + sentence) to express one kind of negative meaning and the other form (internal *no*) to express a different negative meaning. Bloom herself had proposed that one could distinguish at least three semantic categories of negation in early speech. These categories include (1) nonexistence—when the child remarks on the absence of something, for example, "no cake" or "all gone cookie"; (2) rejection—when the child opposes something, for example, "no wash hair"; and (3) denial—when the child denies the truth of a statement made or implied by someone else, for example "that not Daddy." Both Bloom (1970) for English and McNeill and McNeill (1968) for Japanese found that these three semantic categories of negation appeared in children's speech in the order given here. De Villiers and de Villiers found that Nicholas used the *no* + sentence form to express rejection and the internal-*no* form to express denial. This same pattern was confirmed in their second child, Charlotte, and in Eve, but they did not find it in Adam's speech.

Where did this pattern come from? De Villiers and de Villiers suggest that the children picked it up from their parents' speech. Both Eve's parents and Nicholas and Charlotte's parents (but not Adam's) used a polite but indirect form to express rejection, which inadvertently modeled a *no* + sentence form. For example, they would say, "No, I don't think you should do that."

We see, then, that the development of negation reflects a complex interaction of syntactic, semantic, and input factors that may combine in different ways for different children learning various languages in the early stages. Clancy (1985) extended McNeill and McNeill's earlier work on the acquisition of the different negative markers in Japanese. She, too, found early acquisition of the negative marking nonexistence (*nai*) and rejection (*iya*), which was often overextended to include prohibition (*dame*). In the early stages *nai* and *iya* (but never *dame*) were overextended to express denial (*chigan*), which was a late-emerging negative morpheme.

"This isn't the kind that I wanted." Relative clauses appear late in the preschool period.

The late development of negative forms to express denial, and prohibition, contrasting with early appearing expressions of rejection and nonexistence, has also been demonstrated in a recent study on the acquisition of Tamil, a language spoken on the subcontinent of India and Sri Lanka (Vaidyanathan, 1991).

Just as young children differentiate negative sentences according to their semantic function, there is also evidence that they are sensitive to the *pragmatic* or contextual factors influencing negation. This was demonstrated in an elicited production study conducted by de Villiers and Tager-Flusberg (1975). Their study showed that children made fewer errors and were faster responding to negative sentences expressing denial when the context for the sentences was plausible rather than implausible. Thus nonlinguistic context can also influence young children's processing of linguistic forms such as negation.

QUESTIONS

In English and other languages we can ask different kinds of questions for different purposes in a number of ways. For example, we can simply use rising intonation on a declarative sentence to signal that we are asking a question: "Mommy is tired?" Children seem to rely on rising intonation in the earliest stages (Klima & Bellugi, 1966). We can also ask this question, called a **yes/no question,** since these are the responses that are called for, by reversing the subject of the sentence (*Mommy*) and the auxiliary verb (*is*). This syntactic rule is much more complex, and children only begin to master it in stage III.

A different group of questions is used for obtaining more than a simple *yes/no* answer. They are called the **wh-questions** in English since they begin with *what, where, which, who, whose, when, why,* and *how.* Answers to these questions will be more complex and contain more information. These questions also require the rule of inverting the subject and the auxiliary, as well as the correct placement of the appropriate *wh*-word at the beginning; for example, "When is dinner?" or "Why are we staying home?" Children initially ask *wh*-questions omitting the auxiliary altogether:

What that?
Where Daddy go?

They then include the auxiliary but do not consistently switch it around with the subject:

Where are you going?
What she is playing?

Finally, children are able to incorporate all of the syntactic rules necessary to produce well-formed *wh*-questions.

Klima and Bellugi (1966) hypothesized that since *yes/no* questions involved only one rule (inverting subject and auxiliary) and *wh*-questions required two rules (*wh*-word placement and subject-auxiliary inversion), one should find that children produce correctly inverted *yes/no* questions earlier than inverted *wh*-questions. Their analysis of questions asked by Adam, Eve, and Sarah confirmed this hypothesis; however, later studies, using larger groups of children, found no evidence for this (Erreich, 1980; Ingram & Tyack, 1979). Instead, many children employ the inversion rule for both kinds of questions at approximately the same time.

There is more agreement among researchers concerning the order in which children acquire the various *wh*-questions. Wootten, Merkin, Hood, and Bloom (1979) found that *what, where,* and *who* were the first questions asked by the children they followed longitudinally. Only later did their subjects ask questions about *when, how,* and *why.* And studies of children's comprehension of different *wh*-questions have found that *what, where,* and *who* are easier to understand and correctly respond to than *how, why,* and *when* (Ervin-Tripp, 1970; Tyack & Ingram, 1977; Winzemer, 1980). Erreich (1980) also found that her subjects inverted the subject and auxiliary more often in *what, where,* and *who* questions and less often in *how, why,* and *when* questions (but see Labov & Labov, 1978).

What factors account for this invariant acquisition order? One of the primary determinants appears to be semantic or cognitive complexity. The concepts that are required for encoding *how, when,* and *why* questions, including manner, time, and causality, are more abstract and develop later than the concepts encoded in *what, where,* and *who* questions, which are already incorporated into early stage I speech. A second important factor is linguistic complexity. Wootten, Merkin, Hood, and Bloom (1979) point out that children begin by asking (and answering) questions concerning objects, people, and locations that can be answered with a single word or short phrase. The later questions typically need whole sentences for an adequate response and thus require more sophisticated linguistic capacity.

Just as children are sensitive to the plausible contexts in which negatives are used, research has also shown that they are sensitive to the contexts in which various questions are plausible or implausible. Winzemer (1980) showed that children who were asked, "Where is the girl eating?" when shown a picture of a girl eating an apple made many more errors than they did when asked, "What is the girl eating?" The less plausible the question was in relation to the picture, the more frequent the errors. Thus, we find that the development of questions is determined not only by linguistic complexity, but also by semantic and contextual factors that interact with the acquisition of the requisite syntactic rules.

■ LATER DEVELOPMENTS IN PRESCHOOLERS

By the time children begin school, they have acquired most of the morphological and syntactic rules of their language. They can use language in a variety of ways, and their simple sentences, questions, negatives, and imperatives are much like those of adults. There are more complex grammatical constructions that children begin using and understanding during the preschool years, by early stage IV, but their acquisition is not complete until some years later. In this last section we will consider three such constructions: passives, coordinations, and relative clauses.

PASSIVES

The passive is a construction that is used relatively rarely in English for highlighting the object of a sentence or the recipient of an action. For example, one might say, "The window was broken by a dog," if the focus is on the window. Not surprisingly, passives are extremely rare in transcripts of children's spontaneous speech—too rare to study unless the researcher specifically tries to elicit them in an experimental situation. Nevertheless, a great deal of attention has been paid to how children handle passive sentences. Because the order of the agent and the object is reversed in passives in English, this particular construction can reveal a great deal about how children acquire word order rules that play a major rule in English syntax.

One of the few studies on children's production of passive sentences was carried out by Horgan (1978). She used a set of pictures to elicit passives from a group of children who ranged in age from 2 to 13. She found that the younger children produced full passives far less frequently than *truncated* passives, in which no agent is specified, as in "The window was broken." She also found that there were topic differences between the children's full and truncated passives. Full passives almost always had animate subjects (e.g., girl, boy, cat), whereas truncated passives almost always had inanimate subjects (e.g., lamp, windows). Because of these differences, Horgan argued that full and truncated passives develop quite separately and, at least for the young child, are unrelated. This contrasts with the typical grammar of adult language that considers truncated passives to be derived from full passives by deleting the agent. The child apparently relies on different syntactic rules to form truncated passives. One interpretation of the two different forms of the passive is given by Borer and Wexler (1987), who suggest that the early appearing truncating passives are really adjectival in form; whereas the later appearing full forms are complete verbal passives.

Most of the experimental research has focused on children's comprehension of passive sentences. The usual method to assess comprehension is the act-out procedure, in which the experimenter says a sentence and the child must act out its meaning with toys. One of the earliest studies on passive sentence comprehension was conducted by Bever (1970). He compared children aged two, three, and four on their understanding of active and passive sentences. Some of the sentences were semantically reversible; that is, both nouns could plausibly act as agent or object—"The boy kissed the girl" (active) or "The boy was kissed by the girl" (passive). And some of the sentences were semantically irreversible; that is, only one of the nouns could plausibly act as agent—"The girl patted the dog" or "The dog was patted by the girl."

Not surprisingly, Bever found that children could understand the irreversible passives earlier than the reversible ones. It was not until children were about four or five that they could act out correctly the reversible passive sentences. The most interesting aspect of Bever's results were the systematic mistakes that the three- and some of the four-year-olds made on the reversible passive sentences. They consistently reversed the agent and object: when they were given a sentence like "The car was pushed by the truck," they made the car push the truck, as if they had heard an active sentence.

Bever proposed that children by three or four years of age have developed a generalized abstract rule that the order of words in English signals the main sentence relations. They know that English uses predominantly noun-verb-noun sequences that, in the active voice, mean agent-action-object. Consequently, when they hear a passive sentence, they ignore the *was* and *by* and infer the meaning of the passive noun-verb-noun sequence to be active.

Many subsequent experiments have confirmed Bever's findings, and the strategy that children use at about three or four is usually called the word-order strategy. However, research conducted on children learning languages other than English has shown that this is not a universal strategy. English has a relatively fixed order of words in its sentences, and the order itself marks the main grammatical roles: subject-verb-object. Other languages like Russian, Japanese, and Turkish have much freer word orders because they rely on grammatical morphemes to mark these roles. For example, Japanese allows two word orders: subject-object-verb and object-subject-verb. Subjects are usually marked by *ga* placed at the end of the noun. Hakuta (1979) investigated the strategies that young Japanese children use when they are asked to act out different kinds of active and passive sentences. He found that three- and four-year-old Japanese children look for a combination of word order and morphemes to figure out the basic relations of a sentence. Their strategy is that the first noun of a sentence, if it ends in *ga* (subject marker), will serve as agent regardless of other markings, word order, or sentence voice. Children's strategies for handling complex syntax are tailored to the kind of language they are acquiring and indicate that three- and four-year-olds have already worked out the main way their language marks basic grammatical relations, whether it is word order alone, morphemes alone, or a combination of both.

Studies of the development of some non-Indo-European languages have found that children learning these languages in fact acquire the passive construction very much earlier than children learning languages like English (e.g., Demuth, 1990; Pye, 1988; Suzman, 1987). For example, Demuth's study of children acquiring Sesotho, a language spoken in southern Africa, found that these children began using the passive in everyday conversation by the time they were two years old, and it was quite frequent by the time they were four. Demuth (1990) suggests this is because in Sesotho, where subjects always mark the topic of a sentence, the passive is a very basic and quite frequent construction since most verbs can be passivized. She argues that the typology of a language, and the importance of the passive to a particular language, will influence the timing of its development.

Most of the studies on English-speaking children show that by age four or five they understand passive sentences. Typically, these experiments have used action verbs (*hit, push, kiss*) because of the nature of the act-out procedure. From these studies investigators have assumed that the acquisition of the passive was complete. However, it turns out that this is not true. Maratsos, Kuczaj, Fox, and Chalkley (1979) found that the type of verb used made a difference in whether five-year-old children could understand the passive voice. They assessed comprehension by asking children questions after they had heard short stories. To answer a question correctly, the children needed to have understood a critical sentence that was in the passive voice. Maratsos and his colleagues found that five-year-olds understood passives with action verbs but did not understand passives with nonaction verbs, such as "Donald was liked by Goofy." Thus, it seems that the acquisition of passives is not complete at five. Children do understand passive sentences with action verbs, but their knowledge of the construction is limited by the semantics of the verb. Only by middle childhood (the elementary school years) is the passive completely understood and used productively.

These findings have been confirmed by a number of other researchers both in studies of comprehension and production (e.g., de Villiers, Phinney, & Avery, 1982; Pinker, Lebeaux, & Frost, 1987; Sudhalter & Braine, 1985). Pinker and his colleagues suggest that children obey a semantic constraint on the kinds of verbs that they will passivize that requires the verb to have a physical object in the role of semantic patient, as indeed action verbs typically do.

In an alternative view, Lempert (1990) suggests that the animacy of the object is the single most important factor that predicts the child's ability to passivize a sentence. Thus, in her studies Lempert has noted that children find it much easier to process passive sentences that have animate objects (which also typically occur with action verbs) than those with inanimate objects (which typically occur with nonaction verbs).

COORDINATIONS

At very young ages, as early as two-and-a-half, children begin combining sentences to express complex or compound propositions. The simplest and most frequent way children combine sentences is to conjoin two propositions with *and.* Research on young children's development of coordination with *and* has demonstrated that, like many of the other constructions we have considered, its development depends not only on linguistic complexity, but also on semantic and contextual factors.

There have been a number of independent studies on the development of coordination in spontaneous speech. One of the questions that has interested researchers is the order in which different coordinations enter the child's speech. There are two main forms of coordination according to linguists: *sentential coordination,* in which two (or more) complete sentences are conjoined, as in "I'm pushing the wagon and I'm pulling the train," and *phrasal coordinations,* in which phrases within the sentence are conjoined, as in "I'm pushing the wagon and the train." There does not seem to be a strict sequence of acquisition for these two forms. Bloom and her colleagues (1980) reported that for three of the children they studied longitudinally both forms entered the children's speech at the same time. Their fourth subject, as well as Adam, Eve, and Sarah, who were studied by de Villiers, Tager-Flusberg, and Hakuta (1976, 1977), all used phrasal coordinations before sentential coordinations. The only constraint on acquisition order is that sententials generally do not develop before phrasals.

These developmental findings contradict some traditional linguistic accounts of coordination, which propose that phrasals are derived from their corresponding sentential forms by an extra syntactic rule of deletion (Chomsky, 1965). According to this account, a sentence like "I'm pushing the wagon and the train" is derived from "I'm pushing the wagon and I'm pushing the train" after deleting redundant elements. Certainly we would expect to find sentences involving more rules developing later. Since phrasals never begin appearing after sententials and since children do not find them any more difficult in comprehension and imitation (de Villiers, Tager-Flusberg, & Hakuta, 1976; Tager-Flusberg, de Villiers, & Hakuta, 1982), we must conclude that, in child speech at least, neither form of coordination is derived from the other. Instead, they develop independently, with children forming phrasal coordinations directly by joining phrases, not by deleting redundant elements.

From the beginning, children seem to be sensitive to the different contexts in which phrasal and sentential coordinations should be used. Jeremy (1978) examined the contexts in which children used these forms to describe events enacted by an experimenter. She found that sentential forms were used when the events took place at different times or in quite separate locations. But when the events occurred simultaneously and in the same location, phrasal forms were preferred at all ages.

In their longitudinal study Bloom et al. (1980) found that the course of acquisition of coordination was also influenced by semantic factors. All four of their subjects used *and* to encode a variety of meanings, and these meanings developed in a fixed order. The earliest meaning to develop was additive (no dependency relation between the conjoined clauses), as in "Maybe you can carry this and I can carry that." Several months later children began using *and* to encode temporal relations (the two clauses were related by temporal sequence or simultaneity); for example, "Jocelyn's going home and take her sweater off." Later still, *and* was used to encode causal relations; for example, "She put a bandage on her shoe and it maked it feel better." Some of the children went on to use *and* to encode other meanings—for example, object specification, "It looks like a fishing thing and you fish with it," and adversative relation (expressing opposition), "Cause I was tired and now I'm not tired"—but these were less frequent and more variable among the children. This study is important since it highlights the variety of meanings encoded by the single connective *and*. Thus, at the early stage of coordination development, children use *and* in a semantically limited way; however, as they progress, children add greater semantic flexibility as well as syntactic complexity to their language. It would be most interesting to see whether children acquiring languages other than English develop the meanings encoded by conjunctions in the same order that Bloom has found in her American subjects.

RELATIVE CLAUSES

Even though children begin producing and understanding some sentences with embedded relative clauses when they are about three years old, in stage IV, they do not develop the full structural knowledge of this construction until they reach school. In their longitudinal study, Bloom et al. (1980) reported that relativization developed much later than coordination, and it was used exclusively to specify information about an object or person. Limber (1973) and Menyuk (1971) also examined the emergence of relative clauses in the spontaneous speech of preschool children. They both found that initially all the relative clauses specified information about the object of the sentence; there were no subject relative clauses. Thus, children would say, "Let's eat the cake what I baked," or "Gimme the chair you sitting on." Often children omitted a relative pronoun (e.g., *that, who, which*), or they substituted an incorrect pronoun, usually *what*. Yet in all three studies the authors found that the actual number of sentences with relative clauses was disappointingly small. It seems to be difficult to capture a sufficiently large number of examples of relative clause sentences. Perhaps children avoid them since they are syntactically complex, or they may lack the occasion to use them in a naturalistic setting, where knowledge about the context is shared by listener and speaker and need not be made explicit.

To get around these problems, recent research has attempted to use elicitation techniques, providing children with the opportunity to use relative clauses for describing scenes. Both Hamburger and Crain (1982) and Tager-Flusberg (1982) asked children to describe a scene with nearly identical objects to a blindfolded listener. If children are to communicate successfully in this situation, they must use a relative clause or similar construction to clearly specify the object. Hamburger and Crain (1982) confirmed the earlier research on spontaneous speech and found that four-year-olds could perform successfully by using object relatives, such as "Pick up the walrus that is tickling the zebra." These studies of elicited production of relative clauses have also been conducted with Italian-speaking children (Crain, McKee, & Emiliani, 1990).

Tager-Flusberg (1982) provided children with the opportunity to use both subject and object relative clauses and found that once they used relative clauses (at about age four) they could produce both types equally well. However, if the main sentence was more complex and included a direct object and an indirect object phrase, such as "The boy gave the dog to the bear," the four-year-olds could add a relative clause only to the final object (the bear) and not to the subject or direct object. So they would say, "The boy gave the dog to the bear who is holding the wagon." It seems that children initially find it easiest to add a clause at the end of a sentence rather than in the middle, since this minimizes constraints on processing (see Hakuta, de Villiers, & Tager-Flusberg, 1982; Slobin, 1973).

Tager-Flusberg also gave this task to younger, three-year-old children who relied mostly on prepositional phrases to express restriction and used hardly any relative clauses. They would describe the same scene like this: "The boy gave the dog to the bear with the wagon." Children may be using their knowledge of a simpler construction to guide the acquisition of more complex constructions. In this task both forms, prepositional phrases and relative clauses, fulfill the functions adequately, but younger children used primarily simpler prepositional phrases, whereas older children used primarily more complex relative clauses. Perhaps the developmental roots of relative clauses lie in simpler constructions. This study, using production data, suggests that prepositional phrases are one such possible origin, although Tavakolian (1981), relying on comprehension data, has proposed that children initially treat relative clauses as if they were structurally equivalent to coordinations.

There have been quite a number of studies that have investigated children's comprehension of relative clause sentences. Overall, there is general agreement that preschoolers find all but a few difficult to understand, but there are contradicting theoretical claims about which kinds of relative clauses are easy for preschoolers. Probably none of the studies on relative clause comprehension provide a great deal of insight into children's full knowledge of the construction because there are many task variables that influence children's performance in these studies. Nonetheless, a number of studies (de Villiers, Tager-Flusberg, Hakuta, & Cohen, 1979; Goodluck & Tavakolian, 1982; Hamburger & Crain, 1982) have agreed that, as in production, children find object relatives easiest to understand. So preschoolers make the fewest errors on sentences like "The dog bit the cat that chased the rat."

De Villiers, Tager-Flusberg, Hakuta, and Cohen (1979) interpreted their findings as evidence of children using comprehension strategies in this experimental situation. Specifically, the surface order of nouns and verbs is taken by young children to signal the major grammatical relations in a sentence. When children hear a noun-verb-noun sequence, they interpret it as agent-action-object, even ignoring the relative pronoun *that.* This interpretation was confirmed by Hakuta (1981), who studied relative clause comprehension in Japanese preschoolers. It seems that processing constraints determine the strategies that children adopt in understanding very complex constructions in artificial, experimental situations. If structural complexity plays a role in relative clause comprehension in preschoolers, it is completely masked under these circumstances.

It is safe to conclude from all of the research conducted thus far that preschoolers are just beginning to use and understand relative clauses. Their knowledge of the syntactic structure of this construction is fairly incomplete, and their actual performance with relative clause sentences is highly constrained by processing limitations.

■ BEYOND THE PRESCHOOL YEARS

Before we leave the topic of syntactic and morphological development, we should note that even during the school years, children continue to develop in this domain of language. Certain constructions are not yet fully controlled by children at the time they enter school. One area that has received much attention in recent years, because of its centrality to GB theory, is the child's knowledge of co-reference relations in a sentence—how different pronoun forms link up with their referents in a sentence.

ANAPHORA

Consider the following sentences:

> John said that Robert hurt himself.
> John said that Robert hurt him.

We know that in the first sentence Robert was hurt—the reflexive pronoun *himself* is "bound" to the referent *Robert*. In the second sentence, Robert cannot be the one to get hurt; it must be John—here we note that the pronoun *him* is bound to the referent *John*. According to GB theory, this knowledge is encompassed in the *binding principles*, which are a part of our grammar. These sentences illustrate two of the binding principles (A and B), which are loosely defined here:

> *Principle A:* A reflexive is always bound to a referent that is within the same clause.
> *Principle B:* An anaphoric pronoun cannot be bound to a referent within the same clause.

These two principles explain our intuitions about the meanings of the two sentences above. The third binding principle (C) is concerned with "backwards" sentences, in which the pronoun comes before the referent. The following two sentences illustrate this principle:

> When he came home John made dinner.
> He made dinner when John came home.

In the first sentence, *he* can refer to John, or we could say that the pronoun is bound to the referent in the same sentence (backward co-reference) but in the second sentence *he* cannot be John—here, backward co-reference is not allowed. These intuitions are explained by the third binding principle:

> *Principle C:* Backward co-reference is only allowed if the pronoun is in a subordinate clause to the main referent.

From a developmental perspective, we can ask the question about when children seem to know these principles. Dozens of experiments have been conducted on children's knowledge of all three principles, using a variety of tasks and paradigms. One example is a recent study by Chien and Wexler (1990), which looked at children's knowledge of Principles A and B. In one experiment, children were asked to judge the truth of sentences paired with pictures. (Some of the test pictures and sentences used are shown in Figure 5.9.) In this study, the researchers found that by age six children knew Principle A, but were still making errors on pronouns, for example saying "yes"

THE "MATCH" CASES
THE "MISMATCH" CASES
Name-Reflexive
(41) This is Goldilocks; this is Mama Bear. Is Mama Bear touching herself?
Name-Reflexive
(45) This is Goldilocks; this is Mama Bear. Is Mama Bear touching herself?
Name-Pronoun
(42) This is Mama Bear; this is Goldilocks. Is Mama Bear touching her?
Name-Pronoun
(46) This is Mama Bear; this is Goldilocks. Is Mama Bear touching her?

FIGURE 5.9 *(From Chien & Wexler, 1990)*

to the sentence-picture illustrated in (46). Children's difficulties with Principle B have been confirmed in numerous other studies but they have been given different interpretations by different researchers. Some argue that the grammatical knowledge is absent until after the age of six or seven, others argue that children lack some important pragmatic knowledge (Grodzinsky & Reinhart, in press). Principle C also does not seem to be firmly controlled by children until the middle school years, which may be due either to grammatical limitations or to processing factors (Hsu, Cairns, Eisenberg, & Schlisselberg, 1991). Clearly, there is more research to be done in this interesting and important area of language acquisition and linguistic theory.

SUMMARY

We have followed the course of children's acquisition of syntax and morphology from its very beginnings in stage I until the end of the preschool years. During these few years children develop an extremely rich and intricate linguistic system. They go from expressing just a few simple meanings in two words to expressing abstract and complex ideas in multiword sentences. Yet the journey is not quite complete—children continue in the early school years to acquire full structural knowledge of constructions such as passives, coordinations, and relative clauses. And all of this is accomplished with no formal instruction and little informal guidance or correction. The course of development is influenced by linguistic, semantic, and contextual factors that together determine the order of grammatical development. The acquisition of grammar is, indeed, one of the most remarkable and mysterious achievements of childhood.

SUGGESTED PROJECTS

1. This project is highly recommended in order to appreciate fully the richness of a spontaneous speech sample and its utility as a source of data and insight into the child's linguistic system. First, you need to collect a speech sample. (Most researchers rely on tape recordings of naturalistic interactions between children and their mothers. About one hour is long enough to obtain a useful sample of child speech.) You should assemble a group of toys, such as a dollhouse with furniture and suitable occupants, a set of blocks, animals and a farmhouse, and play dough—toys that will elicit comment by both mother and child. After a few minutes warming up, during which the child can get used to your presence, turn on the tape and allow the child and mother to play naturally. Make sure that you are not intrusive. To facilitate coding later on, it is important to make detailed notes about the ongoing activity and context associated with the child's remarks.

   After the session is over, the tape should be transcribed as soon as possible, while your memories of the activities and the conversation are as fresh as possible. Divide the page down the middle into two halves. Keep the mother's speech on the right and the child's on the left. Contextual notes can be placed wherever relevant. Each new utterance should begin on a new line to make a transcript that is both easy to read and easy to code. It is not always simple to judge when a new utterance or sentence begins: try using falling intonation and pauses to mark breaks between utterances.

Once you have created the written transcript in this way, it is ready for analysis. First, you could compute the mean length of utterance (MLU) for the child in the sample. Just follow the rules set out in Figure 5.4. The MLU will provide some indication about the child's current stage. If the child speaks a language other than English, calculating the MLU will be much trickier. You will have to come up with a new set of rules, comparable to those for English, that will provide objective criteria for deciding what functions as a morpheme in the child's language.

The transcript can be used to analyze any number of syntactic forms, depending on the child's stage. You could examine the child's mastery of question syntax, for example, by pulling out all the examples of questions. Check whether the child has mastered the auxiliary system in both *yes/no* and *wh*-questions. If the child includes a relevant auxiliary only some of the time, try to see whether there is anything systematic (or rule-governed) about when the auxiliary is included or excluded. Be especially alert for semantic or pragmatic influences.

Any of the other forms described in this chapter can be similarly examined (i.e., grammatical morphemes, negatives, coordinations, relative clauses). If the child is a little older (four or more), other constructions not discussed here could also be analyzed; for example, pronouns, complements, past and future tenses.

2. It is becoming increasingly popular to use an elicited production technique to complement spontaneous speech samples as a source of production data. The main advantage of this method is that the experimenter can control which forms the children should produce, so that one can test the children to their limits. One way of reliably eliciting forms is using a puppet that has to say things in a certain way. In this project it is suggested that a puppet that always says the opposite could be used to elicit a variety of negative sentences from children aged two to five.

Select a sample of children between two-and-a-half and five-and-a-half. You should see each child individually. Introduce the child to a hand puppet and explain that he always likes to say the opposite of what you say. Then give some examples, encouraging the child to help the puppet.

Experimenter: She can drive.
Puppet: She can't drive.

Experimenter: He likes spaghetti.
Puppet: He doesn't like spaghetti.

Experimenter: You may have some marbles.
Puppet: You may not have any marbles.

Notice that each sample is slightly different. In the first, since there is an auxiliary, only *not* must be inserted. In the second, where there is no auxiliary, the puppet must put in a so-called dummy auxiliary *do.* In the third example the child must not only insert *not,* but also change the quantifier *some* to *any.*

After the examples have been given, ask the child to take the puppet. At this point present your own test sentences, one at a time. After each test sentence, have the child present the negative sentence in the role of the puppet. Provide the child with plenty of encouragement and praise. The test sentences, numbering between 10 and 20, should contain a variety of patterns and should not be too long. Try to make them all about the same length. Include some with auxiliaries (*can, shall, will, have*) and some without, which will require the child to add *do.* Have some sentences with quantifiers (e.g., *some, all*), which will need to be changed in the negative form. Present the test sentences in random order and tape-record what the child says.

You will need to transcribe your tapes before the data can be analyzed. Check which sentences the children get right and which ones have errors. Look for improvements with age. Examine the kinds of errors that children make at different age levels. Look for systematic patterns of correct and incorrect responses, both by subject and age group. What do your findings tell about the developmental course of the syntax of negation?

3. One of the most suitable ways for assessing children's understanding of language is to have them act out sentences or phrases, using toys. This project can be done with very young children (two- and early three-year-olds) who are still in the process of acquiring grammatical morphology. The purpose of this project is to find out whether children who omit inflections (such as articles, tense endings, and prepositions) understand sentences equally well that are presented with and without such inflections.

   You will need to select subjects who are still in their early stages of language development and are still omitting inflections. Try taping several young two- and three-year-olds for about 10 minutes and examine their speech for the presence or absence of the morphemes listed in Table 5.3. When you have your subjects picked out, you will need to demonstrate the procedure. You will need to see each child one at a time. First, give the child two toys and then tell the child that you will say something that she should show you with the toys. Then give a sample sentence: "The boy pats the dog." If the child doesn't know what to do, show her, and then have her repeat the action. Give several more examples using correct syntax.

   Once the child understands the task, present your test sentences. Half of these should be presented normally, including all of the relevant morphology. Because your subjects will be very young, you will need to make the sentences simple, with only a single clause. The other half of the sentences should be presented without relevant morphology, but in other respects they should be like the normal sentences.

   Normal:
   The boy puts the ball on the table.
   No inflections:
   Girl put book chair.
   Normal:
   The cow pushes the kangaroo.
   No inflections:
   Dog hit horse.

   Make up about eight sentences of each kind (normal and without inflections), and collect the toys you will need for all of them. Before giving the sentence, place the relevant toys in front of the child. Write down exactly what the child does with the toys.

   Code the children's responses as correct/incorrect. Compare within and across ages the percentage correct on normal sentences and that on sentences without inflections. What do your results tell you about young children's use of morphology in comprehension before they can produce that morphology?

4. One interesting project to illustrate some of the errors that even older children still make in interpreting and judging sentences would be to test children's knowledge of the binding principles. Select children between the ages of four and eight. You can use the set of pictures in Figure 5.9 or make up some of your own. Code the children's responses as correct or incorrect, and look at the percentage of children making errors at each age level.

You can also test children's knowledge of principle C using an act-out procedure with some toy animals. Make up a set of suitable sentences (using the animals you have) of the following form:

> After he touched the cow the horse ran away.
> He ran away after the horse touched the cow.

Again, code children's responses as correct or incorrect and look at the percentage of errors at each age. Do children seem to control principle B before or after principle C? What kinds of performance factors (e.g., pragmatics, test factors, processing load) may be accounting for the younger children's errors?

SUGGESTED READINGS

Brown, R. (1973). *A first language.* Cambridge, MA: Harvard University Press. This book provides the most detailed discussions of stages I and II.

Cook, V. J. (1988). *Chomsky's universal grammar: An introduction.* Oxford: Blackwell. An excellent introduction to Chomsky's theory (especially the GB framework), including some of the implications for first and second language acquisition.

Frazier, L., & de Villiers, J. (Eds.). (1990). *Language processing and language acquisition.* Dordrecht: Kluwer. A broad range of chapters, including both processing and linguistically oriented research on language acquisition.

Kessel, F. (Ed.). (1988). *The development of language and language researchers.* Hillsdale, NJ: Erlbaum.

Levy, Y., Schlesinger, I. M., & Braine, M. D. S. (Eds.). (1988). *Categories and processes in language acquisition.* Hillsdale NJ: Erlbaum. Covers a range of theoretical perspectives on the central issue of the early categories in child language.

Lust, B. (Ed.). (1987). *Studies in the acquisition of anaphora* (Vol. I–II). Dordrecht: Reidel. A detailed look from several research groups on the acquisition of anaphora in different languages, including signed languages.

MacWhinney, B. (Ed.). (1987). *Mechanisms of language learning.* Hillsdale, NJ: Erlbaum.

Maratsos, M. P. (1983). Some current issues in the study of the acquisition of grammar. In P. H. Mussen (Ed.), *Handbook of child psychology* (4th ed.): Vol. 3, J. H. Flavell & F. M. Markman (Eds.), *Cognitive development.* New York: Wiley. This is a thorough review of research and theories of syntactic development, with special reference to English.

Pinker, S. (1989). *Learnability and cognition: The acquisition of argument structure.* Cambridge: MIT Press. A detailed discussion, with a review of numerous original experiments, on how the young child can acquire the argument structure of verbs without negative feedback.

Radford, A. (1990). *Syntactic theory and the acquisition of English syntax.* Oxford: Blackwell. A theoretical linguistics approach to the earliest stages of grammatical development.

Slobin, D. I. (Ed.). (1985). *A cross-linguistic study of language acquisition.* Hillsdale, NJ: Erlbaum. This four-volume work presents an excellent survey of morphological and syntactic development covering a broad range of languages.

Wanner, E., & Gleitman, L. R. (Eds.). (1982). *Language acquisition: The state of the art.* Cambridge: Cambridge University Press. This covers a broad range of topics in language acquisition, with emphasis on syntax.

REFERENCES

Aksu-Koc, A. A. (1988). *The acquisition of aspect and modality.* Cambridge: Cambridge University Press.

Bates, E., & MacWhinney, B. (1982). Functionalist approaches to grammar. In E. Wanner & L. Gleitman (Eds.), *Language acquisition: The state of the art.* New York: Cambridge University Press.

Bellugi, U. (1967). *The acquisition of negation.* Unpublished doctoral dissertation. Harvard University.

Berko, J. (1958). The child's learning of English morphology. *Word; 14,* 150–177.

Berman, R. A. (1981). Regularity vs. anomaly: The acquisition of Hebrew inflectional morphology. *Journal of Child Language, 8,* 265–282.

Bever, T. G. (1970). The cognitive basis for linguistic structure. In J. R. Hayes (Ed.), *Cognition and the development of language.* New York: Wiley.

Bloom, L. (1970). *Language development: Form and function in emerging grammars.* Cambridge, MA: MIT Press.

Bloom, L., Lahey, J., Hood, L., Lifter, K., & Fiess, K. (1980). Complex sentences: Acquisition of syntactic connectives and the semantic relations they encode. *Journal of Child Language, 7,* 235–261.

Bloom, P. (1990a). Syntactic distinctions in child language. *Journal of Child Language, 17,* 343–355.

Bloom, P. (1990b). Subjectless sentences in child language. *Linguistic Inquiry, 21,* 491–504.

Borer, H., & Wexler, K. (1987). The maturation of syntax. In T. Roeper & E. Williams (Eds.), *Parameter setting.* Dordrecht, Holland: Reidel.

Bowerman, M. (1973). *Early syntactic development: A cross-linguistic study with special reference to Finnish.* Cambridge: Cambridge University Press.

Bowerman, M. (1976). Semantic factors in the acquisition of rules for word use and sentence construction. In D. M. Morehead & A. E. Morehead (Eds.), *Normal and deficient child language.* Baltimore: University Park Press.

Braine, M. D. S. (1963). The ontogeny of English phrase structure: The first phase. *Language, 39,* 1–13.

Braine, M. D. S. (1976). Children's first word combinations. *Monographs of the Society for Research in Child Development, 41* (Serial No. 164).

Brown, R. (1973). *A first language.* Cambridge, MA: Harvard University Press.

Brown, R., & Fraser, C. (1963). The acquisition of syntax. In C. N. Cofer & B. Musgrave (Eds.), *Verbal behavior and learning: Problems and processes.* New York: McGraw-Hill.

Brown, R., & Hanlon, C. (1970). Derivational complexity and the order of acquisition in child speech. In J. R. Hayes (Ed.), *Cognition and the development of language.* New York: Wiley.

Cazden, C. (1968). The acquisition of noun and verb inflections. *Child Development, 39,* 433–448.

Chapman, R. S. (1977). Comprehension strategies in children. In J. F. Kavanaugh & W. Strage (Eds.), *Speech and language in the lab, school, and clinic.* Cambridge, MA: MIT Press.

Chien, Y.-C., & Wexler, K. (1990) Children's knowledge of locality conditions in binding as evidence for the modularity of syntax and pragmatics. *Language Acquisition, 3,* 225–295.

Chomsky, N. (1957). *Syntactic structures.* The Hague: Mouton.

Chomsky, N. (1965). *Aspects of the theory of syntax.* Cambridge: MA: MIT Press.

Chomsky, N. (1981). *Lectures on government and binding.* Dordrecht: Foris.

Chomsky, N. (1982). *Some concepts and consequences of the theory of government and binding.* Cambridge: MIT Press.

Clancy, P. (1985). Acquisition of Japanese. In D. I. Slobin (Ed.), *The cross-linguistic study of language acquisition.* Hillsdale, NJ: Erlbaum.

Crain, S., McKee, C., & Emiliani, M. (1990). Visiting relatives in Italy. In L. Frazier & J. de Villiers (Eds.), *Language processing and language acquisition.* Dordrecht: Kluwer.

Crystal, D. (1974). Review of R. Brown, "A first language." *Journal of Child Language, 1,* 289–307.

Demuth, K. (1990). Subject, topic and Sesotho passive. *Journal of Child Language, 17,* 67–84.

de Villiers, J. G., & de Villiers, P. A. (1973). A cross-sectional study of the acquisition of grammatical morphemes in child speech. *Journal of Psycholinguistic Research, 2,* 267–278.

de Villiers, J. G., & de Villiers, P. A. (1978). *Language acquisition.* Cambridge, MA: Harvard University Press.

de Villiers, J. G., Phinney, M., & Avery, A. (1982, October). *Understanding passives from non-action verbs.* Paper presented at the Seventh Annual Boston University Conference on Language Development, Boston, MA.

de Villiers, J. G., & Tager-Flusberg, H. (1975). Some facts one simply cannot deny. *Journal of Child Language, 2,* 279–286.

de Villiers, J. G., Tager-Flusberg, H., & Hakuta, K. (1976). *The roots of coordination in child speech.* Paper presented at the First Annual Boston University Conference on Language Development, Boston, MA.

de Villiers, J. G., Tager-Flusberg, H., & Hakuta, K. (1977). Deciding among theories of the development of coordination in child speech. *Papers and Reports on Child Language Development, 13,* 118–125.

de Villiers, J. G., Tager-Flusberg, H., Hakuta, K., & Cohen, M. (1979). Children's comprehension of relative clauses. *Journal of Psycholinguistic Research, 8,* 499–518.

de Villiers, P. A., & de Villiers, J. G. (1979). Form and function in the development of sentence negation. *Papers and Reports on Child Language Development*, 17, 56–64.

Dromi, E., & Berman, R. A. (1982). A morphemic measure of early language development: Data from modern Hebrew. *Journal of Child Language, 9,* 403–424.

Erreich, A. (1980) *The acquisition of inversion in* wh-*questions: What evidence the child uses?* Unpublished doctoral dissertation, City University of New York.

Ervin-Tripp, S. (1970). Discourse agreement: How children answer questions. In J. R. Hayes (Ed.), *Cognition and the development of language.* New York: Wiley.

Fernald, A., Taeschner, T., Dunn, J., Papousek, M., de Boysson-Bardies, B., & Fukui, I. (1989). A cross-language study of prosodic modifications in mothers' and fathers' speech to preverbal infants. *Journal of Child Language, 16,* 477–501.

Fillmore, C. (1968). The case for case. In E. Bach & R. J. Harms (Eds.), *Universals in linguistic theory.* New York: Holt, Rinehart & Winston.

Fraser, C., Bellugi, U., & Brown, R. (1963). Control of grammar in imitation, comprehension and production. *Journal of Verbal Learning and Verbal Behavior, 2,* 121–135.

Gleitman, L. (1990). The structural sources of verb meanings. *Language Acquisition*

Gleitman, L. R., & Wanner, E. (1982). Language acquisition: The state of the art. In E. Wanner & L. R. Gleitman (Eds.), *Language acquisition: The state of the art.* Cambridge, MA: Harvard University Press.

Golinkoff, R., & Hirsh-Pasek, K. (1987, October). *A new picture of language development: Evidence from comprehension.* Paper presented at the Twelfth Annual Boston University Conference on Language Development, Boston, MA.

Golinkoff, R., Hirsh-Pasek, K., Cauley, K., & Gordon, L. (1987). The eyes have it: Lexical and syntactic comprehension in a new paradigm. *Journal of Child Language, 14,* 23–45.

Goodluck, H., & Tavakolian, S. (1982). Competence and processing in children's grammar of relative clauses. *Cognition, 11,* 1–27.

Grodzinsky, Y., & Reinhart, T. (in press). The innateness of binding and coreference: A reply to Grimshaw and Rosen. *Linguistic Inquiry.*

Hakuta, K. (1979). *Comprehension and production of simple and complex sentences by Japanese children.* Unpublished doctoral dissertation, Harvard University.

Hakuta, K. (1981). Grammatical description versus configurational arrangement in language acquisition: The case of relative clauses in Japanese. *Cognition, 9,* 197–236.

Hakuta, K., de Villiers, J. G., & Tager-Flusberg, H. (1982). Sentence coordination in Japanese and English. *Journal of Child Language, 9,* 193–207.

Hamburger, H., & Crain, S. (1982). Relative acquisition. In S. A. Kuczaj (Ed.), *Language development: Vol. 1. Syntax and semantics.* Hillsdale, NJ: Erlbaum.

Horgan, D. (1978). The development of the full passive. *Journal of Child Language, 5,* 65–80.

Hsu, J. R., Cairns, H. S., Eisenberg, S., & Schlisselberg, G. (1991). When do children avoid backwards coreference? *Journal of Child Language, 18,* 339–353.

Huttenlocher, J. (1974). The origins of language comprehension. In R. L. Solso (Ed.), *Theories of cognitive psychology: The Loyola symposium.* Potomac, MD: Erlbaum.

Hyams, N. M. (1986a). *Language acquisition and the theory of parameters.* Dordrecht: D. Reidel.

Hyams, N. M. (1986b). *Core and peripheral grammar and the acquisition of inflections.* Paper presented at the Eleventh Annual Boston University Conference on Language Development, Boston, MA.

Hyams, N. M. (1989). The null-subject parameter in language acquisition. In O. Jaeggli & K. Safir (Eds.), *The null-subject parameter.* Dordrecht: Kluwer.

Ingram, D., & Tyack, D. (1979). Inversion of subject NP and auxiliary in children's questions. *Journal of Psycholinguistic Research, 8,* 333–341.

Jackendoff, R. S. (1972). *Semantic interpretation in generative grammar.* Cambridge, MA: MIT Press.

Jeremy, R. J. (1978). Use of coordinate sentences with the conjunction "and" for describing temporal and locative relations between events. *Journal of Psycholinguistic Research, 7,* 135–150.

Johnston, J., & Slobin, D. (1979). The development of locative expressions in English, Italian, Serbo-Croatian, and Turkish. *Journal of Child Language, 6,* 531–547.

Kemler Nelson, D. G., Hirsh-Pasek, K., Jusczyk, P. W., & Cassidy, K. W. (1989). How prosodic cues in motherese might assist language learning. *Journal of Child Language, 16,* 55–68.

Klima, E., & Bellugi, U. (1966). Syntactic regularities in the speech of children. In J. Lyons & R. Wales (Eds.), *Psycholinguistic papers.* Edinburgh: Edinburgh University Press.

Labov, W., & Labov, T. (1978). Learning the syntax of questions. In R. N. Campbell & P. T. Smith (Eds.), *Recent advances in the psychology of language: Language development and mother-child interaction.* London: Plenum Press.

Lempert, H. (1990). Acquisition of passives: The role of patient animacy, salience, and lexical accessibility. *Journal of Child Language, 17,* 677–696.

Leonard, L. (1976). *Meaning in child language.* New York: Grune and Stratton.

Leonard, L. (1983, April). *Production before comprehension: Some methodological issues.* Paper presented at the Biennial Meeting of the Society for Research in Child Development, Toronto.

Levy, Y. (1983, October). *Berko's wug technique revisited.* Paper presented at the Eighth Annual Boston University Conference on Language Development, Boston, MA.

Levy, Y. (1988). On the early learning of formal grammatical systems: Evidence from studies of the acquisition of gender and countability. *Journal of Child Language, 15,* 179–187.

Limber, J. (1973). The genesis of complex sentences. In T. E. Moore (Ed.), *Cognitive development and the acquisition of language.* New York: Academic Press.

Maratsos, M., Kuczaj, S. A., Fox, D. E. C., & Chalkley, M. A. (1979). Some empirical studies in the acquisition of transformational relations: Passives, negatives and the past tense. In W. A. Collins (Ed.), *Children's language and communication.* Hillsdale, NJ: Erlbaum.

McNeill, D. (1970). *The acquisition of language: The study of developmental psycholinguistics.* New York: Harper & Row.

McNeill, D., & McNeill, N. B. (1968). What does a child mean when he says "no?" In E. M. Zales (Ed.), *Language and language behavior.* New York: Appleton-Century-Crofts.

Menyuk, P. (1969). *Sentences children use.* Cambridge, MA: MIT Press.

Menyuk, P. (1971). *The acquisition and development of language.* Englewood Cliffs, NJ: Prentice-Hall.

Mervis, C., & Johnson, K. (1987, October). *Acquisition of the plural morpheme: A case study.* Paper presented at the Twelfth Annual Boston University Conference on Language Development, Boston, MA.

Miller, J. F., & Chapman, R. S. (1981). The relations between age and mean length of utterance. *Journal of Speech and Hearing Research, 24,* 154–161.

Miller, W. R., & Ervin, S. (1964). The development of grammar in child language. In U. Bellugi & R. Brown (Eds.), The acquisition of language. *Monographs of the Society for Research in Child Development, 29* (Serial No. 92), 9–34.

Moerk, E. (1980). Relationships between parental input frequencies and children's language acquisition: A reanalysis of Brown's data. *Journal of Child Language, 7,* 105–118.

Morgan, J. L. (1986). *From simple input to complex grammar.* Cambridge, MA: MIT Press.

Naigles, L. (1990). Children use syntax to learn verb meanings. *Journal of Child Language, 17,* 357–374.

O'Grady, W., Peters, A. M., & Masterson, D. (1989). The transition from optional to required subjects. *Journal of Child Language, 16,* 513–529.

Pinker, S. (1981). On the acquisition of grammatical morphemes. *Journal of Child Language, 8,* 477–484.

Pinker, S. (1984). *Language learnability and language development.* Cambridge, MA: Harvard University Press.

Pinker S. (1987). Constraint satisfaction networks as implementations of nativist theories of language acquisition. In B. MacWhinney (Ed.), *Mechanisms of language learning.* Hillsdale, NJ: Erlbaum.

Pinker, S., Lebeaux, D. S., & Frost, L. A. (1987). Productivity and constraints in the acquisition of the passive. *Cognition, 26,* 195–267.

Pizzuto, E., & Caselli, M. C. (1991). *The acquisition of Italian morphology in a cross-linguistic perspective: Implications for models of language development.* Paper presented at the Workshop on Cross-Linguistic and Cross-Populations Contributions to Theory in Language Acquisition, The Hebrew University, Jerusalem, Israel.

Pye, C. (1988). *Precocious passives (and antipassives) in Quiche Mayan.* Paper presented at the Child Language Research Forum, Stanford, CA.

Radford, A. (1990). *Syntactic theory and the acquisition of English syntax.* Oxford: Blackwell.

Roberts, K. (1983). Comprehension and production of word order in stage I. *Child Development, 54,* 443–449.

Sachs, J., & Truswell, L. (1978). Comprehension of two-word instructions by children in the one-word stage. *Journal of Child Language, 5,* 17–24.

Scarborough, H. (1985, April). *Measuring syntactic development: The index of production syntax.* Paper presented at the Biennial Meeting of the Society for Research in Child Development, Detroit, MI.

Scarborough, H. (1989). Index of productive syntax. *Applied Psycholinguistics, 11,* 1–22.

Schlesinger, I. M. (1971). Production of utterances and language acquisition. In D. I. Slobin (Ed.), *The ontogenesis of grammar.* New York: Academic Press.

Slobin, D. I. (1966). The acquisition of Russian as a native language. In F. Smith & G. A. Miller (Eds.), *The genesis of language.* Cambridge, MA: MIT Press.

Slobin, D. I. (1973). Cognitive prerequisites for the development of grammar. In C. A. Ferguson & D. I. Slobin (Eds.), *Studies of child language development.* New York: Holt, Rinehart & Winston.

Slobin, D. I. (Ed.). (1985). *The cross-linguistic study of language acquisition: Vol. 1. The data.* Hillsdale, NJ: Erlbaum.

Sudhalter, V., & Braine, M. D. S. (1985). How does comprehension of passives develop? A comparison of actional and experiential verbs. *Journal of Child Language, 12,* 455–470.

Suzman, S. (1987). Passives and prototypes in Zulu children's speech. *African Studies, 46,* 241–254.

Tager-Flusberg, H. (1982). The development of relative clauses in child speech. *Papers and Reports on Child Language Development, 21,* 104–111.

Tager-Flusberg, H., de Villiers, J. G., & Hakuta, K. (1982). The development of sentence coordination. In S. A. Kuczaj (Ed.), *Language development: Vol. 1. Syntax and semantics.* Hillsdale, NJ: Erlbaum.

Tavakolian, S.L. (1981). The conjoined-clause analysis of relative clauses. In S. L. Tavakolian (Ed.), *Language acquisition and linguistic theory.* Cambridge, MA: MIT Press.

Tyack, D., & Ingram, D. (1977). Children's production and comprehension of questions. *Journal of Child Language, 4,* 211–224.

Vaidyanathan, R. (1991). Development of forms and functions of negation in the early stages of language acquisition: A study of Tamil. *Journal of Child Language, 18,* 51–66.

Valian, V. (1990). Null subjects: A problem for parameter-setting models of language acquisition. *Cognition, 35,* 105–122.

Wason, P. C. (1965). The contexts of plausible denial. *Journal of Verbal Learning and Verbal Behavior, 4,* 7–11.

Winzemer, J. A. (1980, October). *A lexical expectation model for children's comprehension of* wh-*questions.* Paper presented at the Fifth Annual Boston University Conference on Language Development.

Wootten, J., Merkin, S., Hood, L., & Bloom, L. (1979, March). Wh- *questions: Linguistic evidence to explain the sequence of acquisition.* Paper presented at the biennial meeting of the Society for Research in Child Development, San Francisco.

Pragmatics: Language in Social Contexts

6

Amye R. Warren *The University of Tennessee at Chattanooga*
Laura A. McCloskey *The University of Arizona*

■ INTRODUCTION

The major aim of this chapter is to place the young language learner back into the social, interactional, and conversational setting within which language normally develops. As Labov (1972) observed, "Children raised in isolation do not use language; it is used by human beings in a social context, communicating their needs, ideas, and emotions to one another" (p. 183). Although both children and adults sometimes do talk to themselves, this "private speech" appears to be a secondary development, derived from the social use of language (Vygotsky, 1962). In this chapter, we examine the development of communication rather than language *per se*. Even children with rather limited vocabularies and primitive syntax are able to make themselves understood by others. Conversely, children with extensive linguistic repertoires occasionally fail to make themselves clearly understood (Blank, Gessner, & Esposito, 1979). Thus, **communicative competence** and **linguistic competence** are interdependent but not equivalent skills.

The fact that many autistic children either never acquire language or have great difficulty in doing so indicates the importance of social factors in language development. Although autistic children may have normal intelligence, they suffer from severe social interaction deficits. Gleason, Hay, and Cain (1989) suggest that "autistic children may have little reason to talk," as they "may find no inherent satisfaction in social interaction, and consequently, may not be motivated to share their thoughts and feelings" (p. 174).

The social function of language is so important in determining the form of our utterances that some language researchers (e.g., Hymes, 1972) insist that any description of language is inadequate without it. Platt (1986) found that the order of acquisition of the verbs *to come* and *to give/bring* in Samoan could not be explained without reference to their respective social uses. Whereas English speaking children typically acquire *come* first (it is less semantically complex), the opposite is true for Samoan children because the use of the imperative form *sau* (*come*) is restricted to the speech of high-status to low-status persons.

Thus, in the process of language acquisition, children are simultaneously learning the social symbol system and how to modify their use of it depending upon the social and communicative demands of the situation. As Hymes (1972, p. 277) explains:

> We have to account for the fact that a normal child acquires knowledge of sentences, not only as grammatical, but also as appropriate. He or she acquires competence as to when to speak, when not, and as to what to talk about with whom, when, where, in what manner. In short, a child becomes able to accomplish a repertoire of speech acts, to take part in speech events, and to evaluate their accomplishment by others.

ADULT SOCIALIZATION OF CHILDREN'S LANGUAGE: ROUTINES

Children's entry into the social world of language is marked by the socialization of **routines** and verbal rituals. Routines and games such as "peekaboo" help the prelinguistic child acquire structures of social interaction, and "scaffold" her early experiences (Bruner & Sherwood, 1976). Whereas adults regularly impose regularity on action and speech, babies begin to internalize the events, and are eventually able to re-create the routines spontaneously. For example, even three-year-olds can verbally describe the sequence of events for familiar activities, such as going grocery shopping, going out to eat, or getting dressed (Nelson & Gruendel, 1986). Much of early childhood is spent in learning and internalizing these **scripts,** which serve to guide much of later social, cognitive, and communicative development.

Adults often laboriously teach children **social routines** as the child's first formal communicative acts (Gleason, 1973; Gleason, Perlmann, & Greif, 1984). Gleason and Weintraub (1978) watched adults repeatedly instruct their children in ritualistic Halloween routines, which include, of course, saying both "Trick or treat" and "Thank you." These interactions were so stylized that some children became hostile when the adults broke into the children's routine with questions like, "How old are you?" Although early in development children may not be able to fully grasp the social significance of verbally marking leave-taking by saying or waving "bye-bye" or acknowledging gifts with "thank you," adults use these routinized forms to socialize their children. Schieffelin (1982) observed Kaluli-speaking mothers in New Guinea teaching their children a social imitation routine: when Kaluli mothers wish their children to say something, they use an utterance ending with the word *elema* (meaning: "say it"). Among the Kaluli, food resources are scarce, and mothers socialize younger siblings to defend themselves against the proprietary moves of older siblings. In one exchange, Schieffelin described a mother with her two children; the oldest had just taken pandanus (a common food) from the baby. The mother repeated over and over to the baby, "That's not yours, it's mine, *elema*!" Although, when asked, Kaluli mothers acknowledge that babies cannot understand what they are directed to repeat, among the first acquired speech acts of Kaluli babies is the appropriate verbal response to an older sibling's aggression.

Japanese mothers attempt to teach children to have regard for the needs of others by "speaking" for others. For example, when a young child does not share his toys, a mother might say "The girls also say 'we want to play,' " or if one child has hurt another, "Older sister says 'Ouch ouch.' " The same routine is used to correct misbehavior, as in "Older sister is saying 'I'm surprised at Mako.' "

Eisenberg (1986) observed Mexican parents teasing their children, not just to have fun, but to induce them to behave a certain way or to pay attention to social rules. In one exchange, Uncle Carlos (C) is teasing a two-year-old girl, Maria (M), about her appearance. Her Aunt Amelia (A) prompts her to retort defensively, even though the girl probably does not understand the layers of sarcasm and meaning shared by the older participants:

C: [Wrinkling his nose and shaking his head] Fea, Fea!
A: "No es cierto," dile. "Soy bonita."
M: Soy bonito.
C: [Imitates her speech] "No nonito." No estas bonita?
A: "Si," dile, "soy bonita."
C: Estas fea.
M: bonita.

Translation:

C: Ugly, ugly!
A: "That's not true," tell him. "I'm pretty."
M: I'm pretty.
C: You're not pretty?
A: "Yes," tell him. "I'm pretty."
C: You're ugly.
M: Pretty.

(Eisenberg, 1986, p. 188)

It is evident from the above example that Aunt Amelia is trying to show her young niece how to defend and stand up for her attractiveness against male criticism. While these anecdotes suggest that young children are often oblivious to the underlying social significance of the speech acts they are taught to repeat, Miller (1986) observes that young children can appreciate and re-enact some jokes and teasing with both adults and other children. One of the little girls Miller observed at 20 months smiled at her mother while saying, "Shut up, punk."

Many parents are cognizant of using scripts, routines, and verbal play to socialize their children, and believe that training children in the social uses of language is an important aspect of child rearing (Becker & Hall, 1989). Bruner, Roy, and Ratner (1982) observe that parents will often use teasing or questions to tempt the child into making requests, as in "Look at this!" or "What *is* that?" uttered while withholding a desired object.

The content of routines varies with the cultural context. In middle-class American families and preschools, children are directly tutored in ways to issue "polite" requests, give thanks, and make apologies to resolve disputes (Becker, 1990; Mussen & Eisenberg-Berg, 1977). In Papua, New Guinea, inner-city Baltimore, and perhaps in Mexico, children are taught to defend themselves from others' aggressive acts, both physical and verbal. In Japan, mothers place emphasis on empathy and conformity in early interaction (Clancy, 1986). Although the specific routines are not universal, the importance of social processes in language development is.

■ PRAGMATIC DEVELOPMENT

An approach to language that accounts for social influences is called **pragmatics** (Austin, 1962; Grice, 1975; Searle, 1970). In a pragmatic analysis, every utterance has three aspects. First, there is an **illocutionary intent** of the speaker to accomplish some goal, such as informing, requesting, persuading, promising, etc. Second, there is the actual form of the utterance, called the **locutionary act,** which consists of the grammatical form of the sentence chosen for use. Lastly, there is the **perlocutionary effect** that the utterance has on the listener (for instance, the listener's compliance with a request).

Consider the following example (from Shuy, 1982): A five-year-old girl knocks on her neighbor's door one evening around dinnertime, and says, "Mr. Shuy, if you look across the street, you'll see that our car is gone." He replies, "Sure enough, Joanna, your car is gone." Joanna responds, "You know, Mr. Shuy, my mother worries if I miss meals," and he replies, "Joanna, would you like to come in?" After entering the house, Joanna says, "You know, Mr. Shuy, I eat almost anything." In a strictly linguistic analysis of this interaction, we would find that Joanna's *locutions* (or *locutionary acts*) were all declarative statements rather than requests, but it is clear from a pragmatic view that her *illocutionary intent* was to be invited to dinner, and that her indirect, roundabout way of doing so achieved the desired *perlocutionary effect*.

PREVERBAL INTENTIONAL COMMUNICATION

One simple but important idea embedded in *speech act theory* (Searle, 1975) is that language serves as a medium for the speaker's intentions. This point seems self-evident for adults, but the intentions underlying infant communication often are not transparent. Substantial research indicates that caretakers and infants take turns and coordinate gaze with vocalization (see Chapter 2), but these abilities do not indicate the presence of intentional communication. It is not until the child grasps some notion of "mind" and mutuality that communication is truly intentionally motivated. Bates, Camaioni, and Volterra (1975) offer the following example of a prelinguistic nine-month-old, Marta, and her concerted efforts to engage her father to help her:

> Marta is unable to open a small purse, and places it in front of her father's hand. . . . F. does nothing, so Marta puts the purse in his hand and utters a series of small sounds, looking at F. F. still does not react, and M. insists, pointing to the purse and whining. . . . Finally, F. touches the purse clasp and simultaneously says, "Should I open it?" M. nods sharply.
>
> (Bates, Camaioni & Volterra, 1975, p. 219)

Marta has a goal in mind, and employs a communicative means to attain that goal. She is capable of *repairing* or adjusting her request, by repeating it, whining louder, and correcting the misunderstanding her father has indicated. What is crucial in determining whether communication is truly intentional is that it is goal-directed, and the means to achieving that goal are exclusive or unique to the particular context. What is also clear from this episode is that Marta has a model of the physical and social world she is trying to share, that she expects to be understood and that her father will have the good will to assist her.

The emergence of expectations might be what distinguishes early turn-taking routines from intentional communicative exchanges. Sugarman (1984) argues that communicative intention appears as late as eight or nine months, when the infants "specify what was expected of the social environment . . . even if that expectation was limited to having the adult attend to some display." Sugarman separates the child's pragmatic development into three stages during the first year of life:

1. under 4.5 months
   simple, single orientations to person and objects; for instance, a single smile to another; or an asocial manipulation of an object.

2. 4.5–7 months
   complex single orientations to people and objects. The child will display several behaviors to a single person; i.e., a smile, touch and laugh.
3. over 7 months
   coordinated person-object orientation, e.g., the child looks at and touches the adult, the adult acknowledges the child, the child reaches towards objects in adult's lap, etc., as in the Marta example.

Although it is unlikely that three-month-olds mentally represent intention, it is clear that parents *attribute* intention to their infants' gestures and vocalizations almost from birth. The habit among caretakers in many cultures to treat their infants as intentional, regardless of their ability to coordinate means and ends may be the **bootstrap** enabling children to develop intentional structures of the mind, voice, and hands. However, mothers are not omniscient interpreters of their children's communicative efforts. Golinkoff (1986) observed frequent communication failures between infants and their mothers. She videotaped the interactions of three mothers and their 11- to 18-month-olds during lunchtime, while the babies were restrained in highchairs and therefore entirely dependent on their mothers to obtain what they might want. Babies expressed dissatisfaction with their mothers' comprehension failures, and tried to repair their (preverbal) messages with repetitions and alterations, as in the following example:

Baby (B.): looks above and behind Mother, leans and points in direction of look. [Coded as *initial signal*]
Mother (M.): looks at B., offers food, "Hmm?" [Coded as *comprehension failure; clarification request*]
B.: looks at food, bounces in high chair, pushes food away, then looks behind M. [Coded as *rejection*]
M.: offers food, "Want some?" [Coded as *comprehension failure*]
B.: withdraws from offer [Coded as *rejection*]
M.: "No?" [Coded as *comprehension failure*]

(Golinkoff, 1986)

Since not even mothers are all-knowing, children are forced into developing a **theory of mind** about others' beliefs and perspectives. These communicative failures, then, force prelinguistic—and eventually fully linguistic—children to modulate their messages.

Becoming Active Participants in Conversations

Piaget (1926) suggested that children's earliest conversations were not true conversations at all, but **monologues.** Even two children who appear to be talking to one another may be engaging in **collective monologues,** during which they take turns speaking, yet their utterances are completely unrelated to one another's, or related only by accident. Schober-Peterson and Johnson (1991) found that almost half of all verbalizations made by pairs of four-year-olds during free-play could be classified as "nondialogue", in that they were not clearly related to their partner's speech. Unlike Piaget, though, these researchers found that many nondialogue utterances were actually failed attempts to capture the partner's attention. Thus, although preschoolers may not always engage in coherent conversations with their listeners, it is not due to a lack of desire to do so, as Piaget believed.

Ochs (1986) argues that even before the age of three, children work to achieve coherent dialogues by constructing their own utterances to relate to the other party's prior conversational turn. She finds that even preverbal children often repeat another child's prior vocalization, either exactly (e.g., Child 1: "Tractor's comin"; Child 2: "Tractor's comin") or with slight modifications (e.g., Child 1: "bababababa"; Child 2: "dadadada"). Repetition thus serves as a primitive strategy for acknowledging a prior utterance, and it decreases as other, more sophisticated connective devices develop. Garvey and Hogan (1973) found that preschoolers were engaged in joint play or language a majority of the time, and responded appropriately to most of one another's utterances. Older children displayed longer contingent utterance sequences (in which one child speaks, the second responds, the first responds to the second's utterance, and so on) than younger children, and also had a higher proportion of socialized speech than did younger children. An example from a study of language play by Garvey (1977) demonstrates young children's abilities to maintain topics and take turns, as well as imaginative language manipulation:

Child 1: 'Cause it's fishy too. 'Cause it has fishes.
Child 2: And it's snakey too 'cause it has snakes and it's beary too because it has bears.
Child 1: And it's . . . and it's hatty 'cause it has hats.

(Garvey, 1977, p. 38)

In fact, turn-taking is so well established by late infancy that no age differences in turn-taking skill have emerged in repeated studies of children from one year of age up to school age (Berninger & Garvey, 1981; Garvey & Berninger, 1981). This early sophistication in turn-taking is rooted in the synchrony and turn-taking we see in mother–child nonverbal interactions beginning at birth (see Chapter 2). Moreover, the ability to follow a partner's gaze and maintain eye contact is related to conversational turn-taking, and a recent study indicates no differences in the amount of time two- and four-year-olds maintain eye contact with their mothers during conversation (Podrouzek & Furrow, 1988).

Although turn-taking is well established in very young children, *turnabouts*, in which speakers first comment on what their partners have just said and then add a request for another response from their partners, develop gradually over the preschool years (Goelman, 1986). Turnabouts and other strategies enable older children to maintain single topics of conversation for longer periods. Younger children's conversations are typically loosely organized, involving unrelated topics and abrupt topic shifts, and they do not always abide by Grice's (1975) **principle of relevance**, which states that conversational participants should make their contributions relevant to their partner's immediately prior utterances or to the overall topic. Older, school-aged children show greater **topic coherence** (Hobbs, 1990; Reichman, 1990) and more gradual topic shifts (Wanska & Bedrosian, 1985). By adolescence, children's conversations with peers may

Knowing how to talk to babies is part of communicative competence.

involve hierarchically organized superordinate and subordinate topics, and speakers may "topic hop" between levels with ease. The ability to maintain such complex, organized conversations may be related to: (1) improved listening skills, (2) improved memory ability—so that one may keep track of which topic or subtopic is currently under discussion (Hobbs, 1990), and (3) improved linguistic ability—usage of appropriate verbalizations to aid in topic transition, such as "Well" and "Getting back to . . .," (Reichman, 1990). Older children are also more active listeners during conversations, and more often indicate to speakers that they are following a topic by providing **back-channel feedback,** such as nodding or saying "Um hum" (Hess & Johnston, 1988).

THE ACQUISITION OF SPEECH ACTS

Although children have a great deal of practice making requests even during their prelinguistic months, they enter a new domain when language becomes their primary medium of communication. At this point, a new set of assumptions and standards becomes pertinent. For example, children must learn to make reasonable requests (i.e., not to "ask for the moon") and to be sincere in their desires. These two conditions fulfill what Grice (1975) has described as the conversational maxims of relevance and sincerity. In addition to these social conditions, the child must master the various subtle linguistic forms in which requests are couched.

Bruner, Roy, and Ratner (1982) traced the origins of two babies' requests from prelinguistic to linguistic forms. They observed that from 8 to 14 months the babies almost exclusively requested nearby objects in someone else's possession. Babies of this age are physically limited in what they can obtain and rely on adults to provide them with desired objects. During this period, the child often signals a request with a gesture, "reaching and stretching with arm extended and hand open towards the object . . ." (p. 98). As noted in Chapter 2, in order to be considered truly intentional communicative acts, such gestures must involve an attempt to attract another person's attention (e.g., looking back and forth from an adult to an object). When such requests or demands are made nonverbally (e.g., when Marta nonverbally requested her father's assistance in opening a purse) they are often called **protoimperatives** (Bates, 1976). At about 11 months, these gestural requests begin to be accompanied by vocalizations. Around 14 months, while children are still prelinguistic but vocal, they develop unique vocalizations that signify requests, usually nonsense syllables associated with specific intonational patterns. Halliday (1975) recalls that his son, Nigel, used the sounds "Nananana" uttered with singsong intonation only when requesting to play a particular game with his father (where Nigel would be tossed in the air). It is also about this age that children begin to request objects that are neither immediately visible nor available, and to use whole-body movements to signify their desires for more distant objects.

A third phase of requesting emerges around 22 months, marked by two-word verbal utterances such as "Richard's cake" or "more mouse." Sometime before this phase the children in Bruner, Roy, and Ratner's study began producing significantly fewer requests for objects (they are now more mobile and can obtain many of them for themselves) and uttering many more "invitations" for joint activity (Bruner, Roy, & Ratner, 1982). These invitations, such as "Mummy read" or "more slide," become pivotal to children's social interactions. Other request forms proliferate between 18 and 24 months, including negation, such as "No ride, no like." From about 18 months on, as mothers and children form shared social contexts, mothers demand clearer articulation, greater politeness, and greater conformity to cultural maxims governing the use of requests, including relevance, quality or clarity, and sincerity.

According to Searle (1970 & 1975), there are two meanings of any utterance, the direct (literal) and the indirect, or conveyed meaning; the conversational context determines which of the two interpretations the listener will use. In an investigation of how people generally process requests for information, Clark (1979) had students call various pharmacies to ask about closing times. Typically, the merchants answering the phone responded to both the literal and the implied meanings embedded in the caller's question, as in:

Merchant: Green's Pharmacy.
Caller: Hi. Do you close before seven tonight?
Merchant: Uh, no. (literal) We're open until nine o'clock (implied)

(Clark, 1979, p. 434)

Young children, however, often miss the conveyed meaning of indirect questions, responding only to the literal form, as in this example from Warren-Leubecker and Tate (1986):

Adult phone caller: What are you doing?
Child: Talkin' on the telephone.
Adult phone caller: Is your mother at home?
Child: Yes. (but does not retrieve mother)

Mothers and other caretakers appear to recognize that children become more sensitive to nonliteral, indirect meanings as they grow older, and they adjust their speech accordingly (e.g., Bellinger, 1979). However, Shatz (1978a) found that mothers and other caretakers frequently use indirect requests with their very young children, and that their children generally comply with them. Clancy (1986) also reports that Japanese mothers' speech to their children is very indirect. Rather than saying "Don't do that," the mothers say "That's no good," or "What are you doing?" For example, to get a child to stop taking another's toys, Japanese mothers might only hint "Is that yours?" (Clancy, 1986). Again, though, these children often comply even with such disguised requests.

This early ability to respond to indirect requests does not appear to be due to any appreciation of the differences between literal and conveyed meaning, however. Recent research indicates that children do not clearly distinguish a speaker's intended meaning from his message's literal meaning until the age of six years or later (Beal & Flavell, 1984; Mitchell & Russell, 1989). Instead, Shatz (1978a) and Shatz and McCloskey (1984) argue that children initially employ a "strategy" of responding with action to any adult utterance, simply on the basis of objects or actions mentioned in the utterance. For example, three-year-olds may respond to "Are you drawing?" by ceasing to draw, even if the utterance was not intended as a request, and five-year-olds may act upon even irrelevant remarks, such as "My pen is white," by handing the speaker their own pen (Ervin-Tripp, Strage, Lampert, & Bell, 1987). Young children do not need to analyze the grammar of the message or the context in order to respond to most requests. In fact, most requests made of children by their mothers are supported by gestures that direct the child's attention to the desired action (Schnur & Shatz, 1983). Over time, the action strategy develops to include a verbal response, although action still predominates as a fundamental response strategy until well into the third year. After the second year, children do seem to take social context into consideration when producing a response. If it appears that an adult is commenting, children will respond with "No" or "Yeah," versus responses of "Okay" to apparent directives (Shatz & McCloskey, 1984).

Attending to intonation is another potent early strategy for deciphering speakers' intentions. Fernald (1989) has shown that mothers mark their intentions with intonation in speech to infants more clearly than in their speech to adults. Even preverbal infants appear to use intonation to convey their intentions, for example, by babbling with a rising pitch to request an object (Marcos, 1987). The understanding of sarcasm, which develops much later in childhood, appears to be based first on intonation and only later on other cues. For example, a child may say "Nice catch" after watching another child drop a ball. Apparently, third-graders require sarcastic or mocking intonation to decipher the intended sarcastic meaning, whereas older children and adults can detect sarcasm from context alone (Capelli, Nakawaga, & Madden, 1990). Over time, as children develop more linguistic knowledge, their strategies change. Reeder and Wakefield (1987) found that the quantity of linguistic (versus nonlinguistic, contextual) information contained in a message affects four-year-old but not three-year-old children. Thus, older children appear to be using more linguistic and less contextual or paralinguistic cues to decipher illocutionary intent.

By the age of about four, most children are able to reproduce and comprehend most of the basic types of requests expressed in adult speech, including subtle hints. Children's use of request forms, however, differs from adults' use, as illustrated by Ervin-Tripp and Gordon (1986) in the case of "T." T. typically addressed requests to adults with "I want," a phrase that occurs only in special adult–adult contexts. "I want" expresses a presumption that the service will be delivered, as in:

> *Salesperson:* What'll it be?
> *Customer:* I'd like two . . .; I want a couple . . .; Gimme a couple . . .

Of course, for children, service from adults is an implicit assumption! Older children not only know the various linguistic forms for requests, but how to use them appropriately for listeners of varying status. This topic will be addressed in more detail in our section on politeness.

In sum, one of the first things children learn to accomplish, first with gestures and vocalizations, and later through linguistic means, is to meet their own needs. Perhaps this is why so much research has been devoted to children's production of requests. Although children clearly are sensitive to requests made by adults, they are considerably more attuned to adult speech when their own needs or desires are the subject. When Shatz and O'Reilly (1990) observed toddlers responding to adults' requests for clarification, the children were more likely to clarify their previous utterance if they had been requesting something rather than simply commenting or asking informational questions (Andersen, 1990).

OTHER SPEECH ACTS

Of course, children by about the age of four or five have mastered a wide range of speech acts. Children begin to learn, for example, how to persuade others to comply with their wishes by justifying their requests. Eisenberg and Garvey (1981) found that preschoolers knew that they had to justify their refusals to comply with requests, and were able to use verbal negotiation strategies. Ervin-Tripp and Gordon (1984) quote one four-year-old girl basing her requests on territorial rights, "Get out of my space. This is my space." In addition to justifying requests, children make attempts to negotiate, as "If you give me this for a while, you can have this for a while" (42-month-old to peer) (Ervin-Tripp & Gordon, 1986). In an experimental study, Montes (1981), cited in Ervin-Tripp and Gordon (1986), found age differences in preferred request forms, with 34 percent of nursery schoolers preferring requests that embedded a claim of rights (rights-oriented justification), 50 percent of kindergarteners, and nearly 80 percent of third-graders. The period between four and eight years is an important one for the child to develop the tools of argument, persuasion, and modulation of the social uses of language.

One understudied but interesting speech act, insofar as it reflects awareness of mutual responsibilities, is "promising." Children from an early age will retort "But you promised!" to adults who violate apparent child–adult contracts. Astington (1988a; 1988b) conducted a number of studies to determine children's awareness of promise violations. She found (1988a) that five- and six-year-olds determine whether someone "promised," depending on whether they kept the promise. If a speaker said "I promise to do . . ." but didn't do what she promised, the child claimed that a promise was not made. In other words, young children understand what a promise is as long as it is kept, but fail to follow the adage "a promise is a promise" if it goes unfulfilled.

In another study, Astington (1988b) read children a number of stories, such as the following:

> John is watching TV. Mom is going out to the grocery store. It is nearly dinner time. Mom says to John, "I'm in a hurry. Please set the table for dinner before I get back." John says, "I promise." Then Mom goes out. John's favorite show comes on. He wants to watch TV. He doesn't want to get the table ready. But he should do it, shouldn't he?
>
> (Astington, 1988b, p. 265)

When asked why John should set the table, most older children (eight through eleven) replied that he had made a promise. However, six- and seven-year-olds replied that he should because he would get punished, or because of other external reasons. They ignored the commitment generated by the promise. It is clear that the developmental changes in acquiring the promise reflect underlying social cognitive changes, which include the unfolding representation of mutual obligations and consistency in human relationships.

■ DEVELOPMENTAL SOCIOLINGUISTICS

In the overwhelming majority of language development research conducted prior to the 1970s, the focus was on a search for universal principles that applied across children, contexts, and cultures. Unfortunately, this quest for consistency led most researchers to ignore important differences between children and between the contexts in which language is learned and used every day. Variations both within and across languages and contexts have been dismissed as trivial, irrelevant, or simply coincidental.

However, in the field of **sociolinguistics,** the study of language variation is viewed as a worthy endeavor in its own right; an endeavor that serves as a necessary complement to the search for universals and broad developmental explanations (Hymes, 1972). We cannot ignore the fact that there are considerable differences in the way most languages are spoken (Halliday, 1970; Labov, 1966). The variety and prevalence of observed language differences make the concept of a **standard language** almost a myth (Foss & Hakes, 1978). Moreover, within each language, speakers modify their speech across differing communicative situations in predictable ways. In most cultures, speakers tend to talk to children differently than they talk to adults, and also vary their speech to friends versus strangers. Merely overhearing the conversations of others can inform the eavesdropper of the speakers' relative social positions, their gender, often their ages, and their intentions.

It is important for speech clinicians and educators to be aware of dialect diversity, and not to confuse language variation with language delay. For example, certain Boston dialects drop the terminal /r/ in words or consonant clusters, resulting in expressions that to outsiders may sound like "paahk the caah," etc. Without knowledge of regional differences in pronunciation, a young child with a Boston accent might be seen as phonologically impaired. This example might seem far-fetched, but African-American and Southern dialects have been penalized in Northern school systems (Burling, 1973). Further, the sociolinguistic rules governing adult–child interaction among Native Americans in Oregon differed from those of the Anglo-European educators, and teachers attributed low levels of effort and cooperation to the Native American children as a result (Philips, 1983). Finally, the single-word responses of children in the typical scientist–child interview may be taken as evidence of language delay when in fact there is none (Wells, 1979).

TYPES OF LANGUAGE VARIATION

Although several organizational models, each with many different dimensions of language variation, have been proposed (Hudson, 1980), we will limit our focus in this chapter to three levels of linguistic variation: the language, the dialect, and the register.

A **language** may be defined as a set of linguistic features (syntactic, semantic, and phonetic) that allows mutually intelligible communication within a group of speakers. Although languages often are identifiable as characteristic of different countries, only when two speakers are *not* able to understand each other do we say that they speak different languages. According to this definition, there are over 3,000 different languages still spoken today.

Languages are not spoken identically by all speakers. Systematic subvariants of a particular language that are spoken by a sizable group are often called **dialects.** Although the term *dialect* is typically associated with regional variations, it also encompasses **social dialects** based on the speaker's social class, gender, age, and race (Hudson, 1980). By definition, dialects within a language are mutually intelligible, although they may differ in certain aspects of grammar, lexicon, and pronunciation. In American English, the Southern dialect is easily discriminated from that of Brooklyn, New York, or Boston, yet speakers of each dialect (with patience) understand one another (usually).

Within both languages and dialects, **registers** occur as speech adaptations that depend upon the social and communicative demands of the situation. Registers refer to differences observable within the same speakers in different social situations. In other words, the term *register* refers to language variation according to *use,* whereas the term *dialect* refers to varieties according to *user* (Hudson, 1980). While most speakers in the United States spend their lives speaking a single language and often a single dialect, they must master several registers in order to be socially acceptable. The most elegant syntactic structures might not serve their purpose if used in a socially inappropriate fashion, such as the following addressed to a young child: "Notwithstanding what you recall having told the police, I suggest to you that what you said happened on that day is not only a mistake, but it is untrue, is it not?" (as might be heard in a courtroom cross-examination) (Brennan & Brennan, 1988).

REGISTERS AS SOCIAL ADAPTATION

Most people play many roles in society even within the course of a single day, and within the constraints of each role they must communicate their intentions appropriately. A woman may be a mother and a daughter, an employee and a supervisor, and a stranger to some and an intimate to others. Even if the content of a message is identical across these multiple roles, she will probably use different linguistic forms in each situation. For example, a woman might obtain a pencil in the following ways:

1. Excuse me, I don't have anything to write with.
2. Could you lend me your pencil, dear?
3. Give me that pencil, right now!

Although the intention (*illocutionary force*) of obtaining a pencil from the addressee is identical in all the above utterances, the forms (*locutionary acts*) differ radically. Sentence 1 is likely to be used with strangers or superiors, sentence 2 with an intimate, and sentence 3 with an immature subordinate, probably a child. If the same sentences were addressed to listeners in other contexts (e.g., if utterance 3 were addressed to an adult stranger), they could be inappropriate and might fail in their *perlocutionary effect* (Halliday, 1970). Thus, register variation may be primarily considered as the pragmatic adaptations of language to differing social and contextual demands of communicative situations.

Registers typically vary along (at least) two basic dimensions, as shown in Figure 6.1. [Lakoff (1977) has labeled these dimensions "clarity" and "politeness."] These dimensions reflect the dual nature of language itself; one a cognitive communication system, and second a social signaling system. The social signaling function varies between two extremes, a formal register used with social superiors and often strangers, and an informal register used with intimates and social inferiors. Adults know that some people should be addressed with deference while others may be spoken to more informally, and linguistically code such deference or informality in a variety of ways. For example, English speakers use less voice stress and higher or more variable pitch when speaking with intimates as opposed to strangers (Brown, 1977). Other languages, such as French, Italian, and Japanese, require different grammatical forms for formal and informal uses. For example, in Italian, when speaking to a professor, one must use the

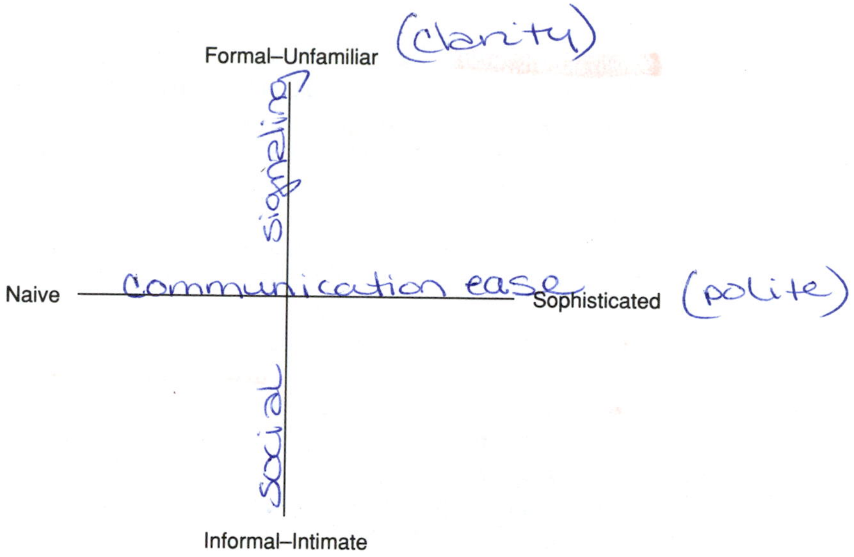

FIGURE 6.1. Two dimensions of listener characteristics that determine register variation.

third person verb form, but may use the familiar, second person when speaking to a fellow student.

The second, or horizontal, dimension in Figure 6.1 relates to the ease of communication between two individuals. At one extreme of this dimension, listeners may be sophisticated in both conceptual and verbal skills, as should be the case when adult members of the same profession converse. On the other extreme, certain speech adjustments (a *simplified register*) may be required when one's listener is naive in the speaker's language, or cognitively unable to understand the topic of discussion (or both, as when speaking to young children). When speaking to someone who, for whatever reason, is expected to have difficulty in comprehending, mainstream English-speaking adults typically speak more slowly and with more emphatic stress; use shorter, more concrete sentences; ask more questions; and repeat themselves more frequently (DePaulo & Coleman, 1986; Snow & Ferguson, 1977; Warren-Leubecker & Bohannon, 1982).

In summary, mature speakers are sensitive to many aspects of a communicative situation. They recognize their social position relative to their listeners, and detect cues from both their listeners and the context that demand register shifts. Mature speakers continually monitor the success of their communication, and readily modify their speech when they sense comprehension difficulties. How and when children acquire the ability to use various registers is the question that will be addressed in the following sections.

LEARNING TO ADJUST TO LISTENER STATUS: POLITENESS

Speech adjustments made to acknowledge the listener's status relative to the speaker are almost as basic to verbal interaction as the exchange of information itself. Lakoff (1977) argues that adults follow two general rules in conversational interactions: be clear, and be polite. Her rule of clarity may be considered as the reason for register variation along the naive–sophisticated dimension. The rule of politeness has several subcomponents: (1) do not impose, (2) allow the listener options (i.e., the right of request refusal), and (3) be friendly. Lakoff (1977) has even suggested that when the principles of clarity and politeness conflict, it is more important to avoid social offense than to communicate successfully. The result of this rule is evident when speakers try to make a request that truly imposes on the listener. In these awkward situations, the speakers will hesitate or "beat around the bush" so that their actual request is barely discernable.

Politeness can be marked linguistically in a variety of ways. Speakers can add certain polite words (called **semantic softeners**) such as *please* to their requests. Politeness may also be marked **paralinguistically,** with a "softer" tone of voice, or syntactically. For example, the relative politeness values of the imperative "Open the window," the direct request "Would you open the window?" and the indirect request "It's warm in here, isn't it?" are clear to adults, even though none contains the word *please*. Although we indicated in previous discussions that young children understand and comply with polite, indirect requests, considerable skill is required to produce them in appropriate situations.

Corsaro (1979) studied two- through five-year-old children in various settings, and found that they used more imperatives with peers and permission requests with social superiors, regardless of the setting. Becker (1982, 1986) asked children to pretend to request the return of borrowed items from a peer, in a "bossy way" and a "nice way." Although all the children could differentiate between the two, the five-year-olds relied more on semantic markers ("Let me have my ball back *right now,*" versus "Can you please give me my ball back?"), whereas ten-year-olds and adults used both semantic markers and syntactic directness. The "bossy" request supplied by one adult woman was "Could you please bring it back over here right now?" and her "nice" request was "I was just wondering if I could get my jacket back. . . but only if you don't need it anymore" (Becker, 1990, p. 12). McCloskey (1986) reported that while most preschoolers recognize both *please* and tone of voice as politeness markers independently, it is not until the age of about five that they select "Give me a cookie" uttered with falling intonation as less "nice" or polite than "Give me a cookie" uttered with a rising supplicant tone. These results support those reported by Bates (1976) for Italian children.

According to Ervin-Tripp and Gordon (1986), five skills are necessary for successful requests, including gaining the attention of the addressee, identifying the action or object desired, justifying the request or persuading the addressee if the desirability or necessity of the action is not obvious, choosing appropriate social markers to convey the request, and repairing the request if it fails. Given that social status can be marked (and, thus, politeness achieved) with very simple linguistic forms (such as *please*), learning the language necessary for requesting is not necessarily the most difficult part. What changes more with maturity is "the ability to adopt the viewpoint of someone else in manipulating information to change behavior, in recognizing when one is being intrusive, in assessing when to use social markings, and in avoiding intrusiveness without loss of effectiveness" (Ervin-Tripp & Gordon, 1986, p. 62).

Axia and Baroni (1985) asked children aged five to nine if they wished to use some pegs to make a figure on a pegboard. The adult experimenter kept the pegs, and told the children to ask when they wanted one. When a child did ask, the experimenter either ignored it or said that she was currently using that particular peg herself (even though there clearly were more pegs available). The five-year-olds almost never increased the politeness of their second requests, whereas the nine-year-olds almost always did. Ervin-Tripp, Guo, and Lampert (1990) found that if a child's first request to an adult was ignored (which happened most frequently for the youngest children), three-year-olds typically repeated their initial request, whereas five-year-olds softened their second requests syntactically (e.g., "Can you do this?" versus the initial "Do that again"). Five-year-olds also showed more deference in their requests when their listeners were preoccupied with another task or would otherwise be disturbed by complying with the request, and tried to gain the listener's attention before making the request. The oldest children in their study (six to eleven year olds) did not often soften or even attempt to justify their second requests to adults, but tended to speak with more urgency or aggravation after an adult ignored or refused their initial request.

As we noted earlier, preschoolers know that they should justify their refusals to comply with requests, and they use verbal negotiation strategies (Eisenberg and Garvey, 1981). A child as young as four may base her requests on territorial rights: "Get out of my space. This is my space" (Ervin-Tripp & Gordon, 1986). Mitchell-Kernan and Kernan (1977) reported that eight-year-old children may attempt to score social points by using direct imperatives with peers and social superiors. When a seven-year-old addressed an eleven-year-old with "Bring your l'il self here," the retort from a laughing third party was, "Who do you think you are?" The younger child replied, "I think I'm somebody big." If such an imperative is complied with, the children treat it as a coup of sorts. An eight-year-old girl interrupted an adult conversation with the statement, "I want that chair" (upon which one of the adults was leaning). The adult absentmindedly complied and gave the child the chair, which stimulated much animated discussion in the other observing children with comments such as, "You gon' let her talk to you like that?" When the adult acted as if she was going to retrieve the chair, the child hurriedly added, "Please."

How do children learn to vary their requests according to their addressee's status, rights (e.g., possession of a desired object), power, and other (often subtle) variables? One way is through direct instruction. Parents often insist that children use the semantic politeness markers *please* and *thank you.* The pedagogy is direct, forceful, and cued with the preceding verb *say,* as in "*Say* please" or in "What do you *say*?" (Gleason, Perlmann, & Greif, 1984; Gleason and Weintraub, 1978). Becker (1990) also has observed that parents use a variety of techniques, such as **modeling** and direct and indirect teaching, in their attempts to enforce their children's compliance with conventional politeness rules. In the following example, both indirect and direct tutelage is demonstrated:

Mother: I beg your pardon?
Child: What?
Mother: Are you ordering me to do it?
Child: Mmm, I don't know, Momma.
Mother: Can't you say "Mommy would you please make me some?"

(Becker, 1988, p. 178)

In addition, although parents are not obligated to be polite to their lower-status children in most contexts, they occasionally increase their politeness if the "cost" of their request to the child is over and above the usual, as in the following example:

> *Mother:* (to child, Martin) Martin, can Daddy have some of your milk for his coffee? 'Kay?
> *Child:* Yeah.
> *Mother:* Thank you.
>
> (Snow, Perlmann, Gleason, & Hooshyar, 1990, p. 296)

Interactions such as these may inform the child that one does not only increase politeness for higher-status listeners, but even for lower-status listeners if the request may infringe on their rights.

Gleason (1973) suggests that politeness may be an early accomplishment because parents insist upon it with direct consequences for appropriate performance, such as withholding a desired object until the child says *please*. Ervin-Tripp, Guo, and Lambert (1990) found that when children spoke to peers or older children, politeness did meet with greater compliance. However, politeness actually *reduced* adults' compliance. Mothers more often complied with requests uttered in a distressed or even aggravated voice. Given that infants use voice stress and intonation to control the behaviors of their caregivers, it is not surprising that young children still use these effective strategies even after acquiring language. Thus, politeness probably is not learned simply through its consequences in terms of compliance. The reward for being polite may instead come from sounding like a skilled speaker, and in getting attention (Ervin-Tripp, Guo, & Lambert, 1990).

The rudimentary forms of politeness, such as *please,* appear to be early developments. The more subtle aspects of indirectness and the cues that signal such shifts take more time to master. Ervin-Tripp and Gordon (1986) propose a developmental progression for polite requests: they suggest that two- to four-year-olds have little difficulty in identifying the appropriate action to be taken in a request, and can use some social markers appropriately (such as when speaking to someone who is older, more powerful, or in possession of a desired object). However, children of this age rarely attempt to gain the addressee's attention prior to making a request, nor do they often justify their requests or repair failed requests.

Between the ages of four and eight, children make extensive gains in strategies for gaining attention, in how to use persuasion, and in how to make repairs. Thus, by the time most children reach elementary school, they are accomplished social interactants who know how to mark relative status, shift request forms with different listeners, and even manipulate formal register cues in order to socially challenge their listeners. The development of these skills parallels children's mastery of the language code itself, but because of its importance, the acquisition of politeness adjustments may have a developmental course all its own.

Learning to Adapt to Listener Knowledge and Perspectives

Piaget (1926) argued that preschool children could not adapt their speech to meet their listeners' needs because of a form of cognitive immaturity called **egocentrism:**

> . . . he does not bother to know to whom he is speaking nor whether he is being listened to. . . . The talk is egocentric, partly because the child speaks only about himself, but chiefly because he does not attempt to place himself at the point of view of his hearer. Anyone who happens to be there will serve as an audience. . . . (Piaget, 1926, p. 9)

However, many researchers studying children's naturally occurring conversations (e.g., Garvey & Hogan, 1973) suggest that even preschool children are sophisticated social interactants who can readily fine-tune their speech to their listeners' requirements. Shatz and Gelman (1973) observed four-year-old children on the playground, and found that they consistently simplified their speech when addressing younger children versus peers and adults. Dunn and Kendrick (1982) demonstrated that even two-year-olds talk differently to their infant siblings than to adults, while Sachs and Devin (1976) observed the same phenomenon in speech to dolls.

More recently, Guralnick and Paul-Brown (1989) demonstrated that three- and four-year-olds adjusted their speech to mildly developmentally delayed peers. Clearly, then, children are not nearly as insensitive to listener characteristics as Piaget believed. However, exactly which aspects of the context or listener's behaviors that children use in making these adjustments is unclear in most studies of naturally occurring conversations. For example, do four-year-olds speak differently to two-year-olds because they "automatically" know that younger children have less knowledge, or do the younger children give explicit feedback that they do not understand? In the next sections we review studies of more fine-grained types of speech adjustments (rather than global measures such as "simplified speech") and specific aspects of conversational contexts that may require those adjustments.

Adjusting to Others' Physical and Visual Perspectives and Speech Roles

Young children display abilities to adjust to their listeners in their use of **deictic terms.** **Deixis** (derived from a Greek term meaning "to point") involves drawing attention to some feature of the spatio-temporal context. For instance, **deictic pronouns** label the speaker (*I*) and listener (*You*) in a setting. Children apparently acquire first- and second-person deictic pronouns early in development. Charney (1980) found that children virtually never confuse *my* with *your* when speaking about themselves, but that they tend to undergeneralize these pronouns to specific people. For example, one girl appeared to think that the term *you* applied only to her mother. However, Chiat (1982) observed a two-year-old who was able to use *I* correctly when referring to himself, but overextended the pronoun to refer to the other:

> *Shula:* What will happen if you cut my hair?
> *Matthew:* I'll cry.
> *Shula:* Who'll cry?
> *Matthew:* Shula cry.

Later, children produce *my* correctly, and understand when another person uses *your* to refer to the *child's* possessions, but they do not comprehend *my* said by another person to refer to that person's possessions, nor do they correctly produce *your* to refer to the *other's* possessions. Thus, children cannot produce these pronouns correctly in all situations because of their limited understanding of the way such terms vary in use across conversational roles (speaker versus listener). It is no wonder that mothers, possibly realizing the potential confusion inherent in the ever-changing status of *I* and *you* according to conversational role, often label objects simply as "Mommy's" or "baby's", rather than "my" and "your."

Other deictic expressions (e.g., *here, there, this, that*) function to place the speaker and listener within a spatio-temporal context. For instance, a child who points to a doll, or says, "That doll" distinguishes the doll from other dolls partly by location. Clark and Sengul (1978) found that when preschoolers sat opposite an adult experimenter they often failed to grasp the adult's use of *there* to mean nearer the child, or *here* to mean closer to the adult. However, Charney (1979) found that when the child and adult sat next to one another, the confusion disappeared. Preschoolers were able to take the perspective of the speaker as long as the speaker and child were not in direct perspective-taking conflict. Correct production of these deictic terms follows a similar pattern. De Villiers and de Villiers (1974) asked two- to four-year-old children, "Is the candy on this side of the table or that side of the table?" The terms were used correctly more often when the child and the experimenter sat beside one another. Garton (1986) found that three-year-olds were more likely to say "that one," picking up and proffering a more distant object to an adult experimenter who sat opposite them. They appeared, then, to be aware of the need to add gestures to their verbal use of deictic terms in order to make things clear for their listener.

Adapting to another's perspective not only requires consideration of what role they play in the conversation and how close or far they may be from the objects under discussion, but also their visual access to those objects. In one early innovative study of visual perspective-taking, Flavell and his colleagues (Flavell, Botkin, Fry, Wright, & Jarvis, 1968) compared children's messages to blindfolded listeners and "sighted" listeners. Second-graders often produced messages that were inadequate for the blindfolded listeners, by pointing or referring to objects using visual features or deictic terms such as "that one." However, Maratsos (1973) found that even three- and four-year-olds gestured less often when speaking to blindfolded listeners. In other studies, pairs of children were separated by a screen, and the "speaker" child was asked to explain to the "listener" how to stack some colored blocks, or to select one from among several objects (Glucksberg, Krauss, & Higgins, 1975). Again, younger children sometimes pointed, and provided less informative messages to their peers.

Although such studies are informative, they scarcely resemble natural conversations. Two more recent studies have managed to visually separate speakers from listeners in a less artificial way—through telephone communication. Lloyd (1991) required children to give route directions over the telephone, and found that seven-year-olds were significantly poorer at this task than either ten-year-olds or adults. Warren and Tate (1991) videotaped preschool children talking on the telephone to familiar relatives. The children often referred to nonshared visual information inappropriately (e.g., responding to Grandmother's question "What are you doing?" by pointing, or saying "Look at that"). However, the children did modify their communications in other ways, by gesturing less and using less deixis on the telephone (where they are less useful) than in face-to-face interactions.

Adjusting to Listener Knowledge: The Given-New Principle

Using the various forms of definite reference correctly (e.g., the definite article *the;* the definite pronouns *he, she, it*) requires an assessment of whether a listener shares certain aspects of the speaker's knowledge. According to another maxim from Grice (1975), which we will refer to as the **given-new principle,** cooperative speakers refer to an object or person with a definite article or pronoun only if they can safely assume that the information is already "given" (shared by the listener). **Exophora** involves referring to information that is given in the nonlinguistic context, such as objects that are physically present. **Anaphora** (derived from another Greek term meaning "to recall back") involves linking a pronoun or an article back to its prior referent or mention in the linguistic context, as in, "Elissa went to school where *she* learned to read," or "*A* girl was riding her bike in the countryside. *The* girl got lost." Note that such sequences cannot be reversed (i.e., "The girl was riding her bike. A girl got lost.") without confusing the addressee.

Early pronoun usage appears to be largely *exophoric* rather than *anaphoric.* Nelson (1975) found that over 90 percent of the pronouns used by two-year-olds referred either to physically present objects or to those which could be understood from the nonlinguistic context. Van Hekken, Vergeer, and Harris (1980) studied four- to six-year-olds' use of third person pronouns, and found that they often used nonverbal means (e.g., pointing) to indicate the referent to which the pronoun referred.

Ochs (1986) reported that her two children's use of anaphoric pronouns increased greatly in the latter half of the third year. For example, before the age of 30 months, one child would repeat exactly what the other had just said: when one child said "Tractor's comin,' " the other repeated his partner's utterance. As the children grew older, a response of "It's comin' " was more likely. Ervin-Tripp and Mitchell-Kernan (1977) showed that three-year-olds understand that pronouns substitute for specific, previously introduced nouns. They showed pictures and asked questions such as "What's happening to Kate?" which children answered using the pronoun *she.*

However, understanding of pronoun substitution is not fully developed at this age. Wykes (1981) asked children to act out sentence sequences such as "Jane wanted Susan's pencil. She gave it to her." Five-year-olds always understood *she* to substitute for the first name in the sequence. Bamberg (1987) asked German children and adults to narrate a series of pictures that featured two characters, a boy and a (male) dog. When switching reference from one to the other, adults reintroduced the character with a noun (e.g., "the boy" or "the dog," or by name), but used the pronoun *he* to maintain reference. In contrast, children under age five almost always used the pronoun *he* to switch reference to the boy, and even the nine- and ten-year-olds used pronouns to reintroduce the boy more often than adults did. Bamberg (1987) argues that young children do not use pronouns anaphorically. They seem instead to use pronouns to refer to a "main" or focal character (in this case, the boy), while primarily using nouns to refer to secondary characters. Given that adult listeners do not share this strategy, violations of the given-new principle and misunderstandings occur.

Comprehension of anaphoric use of definite articles emerges fairly early. Maratsos (1974; 1976) engaged children in a doll-play experiment in which a doll went up to three dogs in cars, and began talking to one of the dogs. After being told either that suddenly "the" or "a" dog drove away, the children were asked to indicate which dog. The majority of three- and four-year-olds (who were using articles in their own spontaneous speech) correctly chose the dog to whom the doll had been talking in answer to "the" dog, and one of the two other dogs for "a" dog. Even without toys for contextual support, youngsters appear to understand that definite articles are for *given* information and indefinite articles for *new* information (Maratsos, 1976). However, when children do make errors, they err in assuming that more information is shared than actually is.

Correct production of definite and indefinite determiners appears to follow a similar developmental pattern. Menig-Peterson (1975) engaged children in a play session with an adult, and then had them return to the same room a week later to interact with the same or a different adult. In describing the events of a week earlier, three-year-olds did not use any more definite or indefinite articles with the new listener than with the familiar listener, but four-year-olds appropriately used more definite reference with the familiar adults. Emslie and Stevenson (1981) asked preschoolers to narrate a picture-story for another child who could not see the pictures. The children correctly used the indefinite article when first mentioning each referent and the definite article for subsequent mentions. In a similar study, Warden (1976) found that preschoolers almost always, and seven-year-olds always, referred to given information with definite articles. However, they also occasionally used definite articles when referring to new information, and even nine-year-olds did so around 20 percent of the time. Finally, Martin (1983) had children describe a set of pictures and then later retell a story about the pictures. In both tasks, the younger children (six- and seven-year-olds) depended more on exophora, and more often inappropriately treated information that had been given in the first task as given in the second. They seemed less willing to treat the second task as a distinct context that required reintroductions of information. Again, the errors made were in the direction of assuming a shared referent when none existed.

Karmiloff-Smith (1979) argues that children's overuse of definite articles comes from their faith in adults as omniscient—they believe that adults know everything, so all referents are shared. Moreover, she suggests that their more frequent use of definite articles and determiners can actually be interpreted as *sensitivity* to listener needs. In one of her studies, the experimenter introduced an object with the description "In my hand I've a tiny little church." Children were then asked to tell the experimenter where to put the church. Nine-year-olds typically deleted the modifiers and simply said "You put the church into the tin," whereas five- and seven-year-olds retained the superfluous modifiers, saying "You put the tiny little church into the tin." Such redundancy may be unnecessary, but certainly makes things clear for the listener.

In addition to proper usage of definite and indefinite articles and pronouns, adapting to a listener's knowledge may require providing more elaborate, redundant, or informative messages to those who share less information with the speaker. In the Menig-Peterson (1975) study described earlier, even the three-year-olds supplied more elaborate descriptions and talked more about an earlier event to the adults who had not participated in those events. Sonnenschein (1986; 1988) demonstrated that six- and seven-year-olds are more likely to give redundant messages both to strangers and to familiar listeners with whom they have had no shared experience than to familiar listeners with whom specific experiences have been shared. However, the messages of older children better meet the differing needs of their listeners by providing different types of redundancy.

RESPONDING TO LISTENER FEEDBACK

In many early studies, children failed to modify their speech appropriately when their listeners (often adults) signaled communicative difficulty. Glucksberg and Krauss (1967) found that third- and fifth-grade children and adults lengthened and elaborated their initial statements when listeners supplied noncomprehension feedback (i.e., "I don't understand"), whereas kindergarten children responded with silence or merely repeated their initial utterances. Wilcox and Webster (1980) studied children aged 17 to 24 months in their own homes. Adults responded to the children's requests either with a query ("What?") or by inappropriately treating the requests as simple statements. Even the youngest children responded differentially to these types of feedback, as they were more likely to repeat their initial utterances when asked "What?" Children with larger vocabularies also tended to recode their utterances more, reflecting the obvious fact that larger vocabularies allow children a broader response selection when an initial communicative effort has failed, especially when children are limited to one- or two-word utterances. Wellman and Lempers (1977) videotaped two-year-old children playing together, and noted that they reacted differently depending on whether their listener indicated comprehension, lack of comprehension, or inattention. Further, Warren-Leubecker and Bohannon (1983) had three- to five-year-olds converse with both an adult experimenter and a "talking" doll (wired to a speaker and microphone system that allowed full two-way conversation). The adult and doll gave cues of both comprehension ("Uh-huh" and "I understand") and noncomprehension ("What?" and "I don't understand") during the conversations. All children shortened their utterances to the child-like doll listener but not to the adult. Also, the older children exactly repeated themselves more with the adult listener than with the doll, whereas the younger children repeated themselves equally often with both listeners. This reflects the older children's greater understanding that listeners who appear younger and act less mature may require considerably more register adaptation than an adult whose comprehension failure probably is not due to a lack of linguistic skill.

JUDGING THE ADEQUACY OF A SPEAKER'S MESSAGE

In many early studies, when communication clearly failed, young child speakers typically assigned the blame for the failure to their listeners (Robinson, 1981), regardless of the adequacy of their own original communication. However, Lloyd, Baker, and Dunn (1984) found that when children are later allowed to view their communicative performance on videotape (thus free from the simultaneous social, cognitive, and linguistic demands involved while originally communicating), they are more likely to correctly assign the blame to themselves rather than their listeners.

Children often fail to detect ambiguity or misinterpret messages due to prior assumptions about the speaker's intentions and honesty (Beal & Belgrad, 1990). Younger children assume that speakers are honest and cooperative, and, therefore, when asked to select an object from an ambiguous array, select the first item that meets the description without requesting more identifying information (Ackerman, 1981; Bonitatibus, Godshall, Kelley, Levering, & Lynch, 1988).

Older children (fourth-graders), although realizing that messages can be ambiguous, appear to assume that speakers conform to Grice's (1975) **first maxim of quantity**—making their messages only as informative as is required for a specific circumstance. In other words, if a speaker says "I am thinking of the happy clown" when there are pictures of a clown with a smiling face, a clown with a smiling face holding a red flower in his hand, and a clown with a frowning face, the older child listener will pick the clown with the smiling face (not holding a flower), under the assumption that the flower would have been mentioned if necessary (Pynte, Girotto, & Baccino, 1991; Surian & Job, 1987). Children who are told that a speaker may be uncooperative, dishonest, or may be referring to more than one object are significantly better at detecting inadequate messages (Bonitatibus et al., 1988).

Even if children detect ambiguous or inadequate messages, they often fail to alert the speaker to the problem. Although children may hesitate in responding or display puzzled facial expressions, they frequently do not accompany these nonverbal indicants of comprehension difficulty with more salient verbal markers (Whitehurst & Sonnenschein, 1985). Over time, children become more responsive and active listeners, assisting speakers in their job of providing speech fine-tuned to their listeners' knowledge and perspectives.

Summary

Clearly, adaptation to a listener's perspective and knowledge is *not* an all-or-none, suddenly acquired skill. Communicative competence appears in some areas sooner than others. There are many reasons for children's apparent failures to modify speech, only one of which is egocentrism. Children (and adults) are limited in their ability to process information simultaneously and from several sources. When a communicative situation places cognitive, social, and linguistic demands upon a child, certain skills probably suffer so that others may be adequately performed. For instance, if a child is trying to remember the rules of a new game in order to inform another child, the child-speaker may not exhibit the most sophisticated social behaviors (Shatz, 1978b).

Appropriate variation of registers requires several different skills. First, one must have mastered enough language and have enough conceptual knowledge so that variation is possible. Whitehurst and Sonnenschein (1985) identify several *enabling skills* (such as vocabulary, memory, and perceptual processes) that may be required for communicative competence. For example, a young child who only knows one word for an object cannot refer to it in another way, even if her listener indicates noncomprehension of the word, and a child who does not remember whether an object has been referred to in prior discourse may violate the given-new principle (DeHart & Maratsos, 1984). Next, one must be aware of the features of the listener or context that demand registral shifts. For example, young children tend to think that adult listeners can understand everything they say, and they might not make adjustments even for noncomprehending adults. Finally, children must know what types of adjustment are appropriate for specific listener characteristics. Even if children realize that they need to be informative or that a listener has misunderstood their message, they may not know *how* to be informative or *how* to change their message to increase comprehension.

Whitehurst and Sonnenschein (1985) call the means by which speech is adapted *procedural rules,* and suggest that most of the deficits observed in preschoolers' communicative behaviors are due to ignorance of these rules. *Listener rules* involve the necessity for speakers to produce informative messages sensitive to a listener's status, knowledge, and abilities. The *difference rule* refers to the need to distinguish for the listener the items being discussed from other items with which it might be confused. For example, if two items share color but not shape, the informative message would refer to shape. Although many listener rules may be mastered by preschoolers, only elementary school children demonstrate knowledge of the difference rule (Sonnenschein, 1986).

In addition to children's perspective-taking and enabling skills and knowledge of procedural rules, McDevitt and Ford (1987) have outlined numerous other factors that may be equally important for communicative performance. These factors include arousal (the child's involvement in the task), speaker and listener goals, information storage and acquisition skills, and conversation-monitoring abilities (attention and utilization of feedback). Moreover, they suggest that children could demonstrate communicative competence for many very different reasons—by simply imitating adult speech in similar situations; through listener feedback of communication effectiveness; by using previously effective, stored routines; or by preplanning strategies based on expectations of listener needs. For example, a child speaking to another, well-acquainted child listener about a familiar topic (as opposed to one just learned) might appear more competent than in other situations because of greater reciprocity in speaker–listener goals, greater arousal, more reliance on stored or routine information, or less need for complex syntactic forms, among other things. It should be remembered that children are busy developing all these component skills simultaneously, yet not all at the same rate.

In sum, young children are not entirely egocentric, in that they seem to be aware that their listeners may not completely share their perspectives or their knowledge. However, they may not know exactly how their listeners' perspectives and knowledge differ from their own, or that such differences require different speech. Thus, it takes some time before children can reliably coordinate their choice of speech forms in accordance with their listeners' knowledge or perspective (DeHart & Maratsos, 1984). Although even the youngest children can sometimes adjust their speech when the communicative context places little stress on their developing social and linguistic skills, there is much room for improvement. These abilities gradually improve over time, possibly even into and throughout adulthood, increasing the range of register variations at the speaker's command.

DIALECTS: SPEAKER DIFFERENCES

Although we noted earlier that speakers of different languages cannot understand one another, whereas speakers of differing dialects within a language can, the distinction between the two terms is actually more a matter of degree than an absolute. Some dialects are so different that the speakers cannot understand one another (e.g., the Mandarin and Cantonese dialects of Chinese), and some languages are mutually intelligible (e.g., Norwegian and Swedish). Whether a particular set of linguistic features will be called a language or a dialect may depend upon the geopolitical status of its speakers—some have facetiously suggested that a dialect acquires the status of a language once its speakers have acquired their own army and navy (Foss & Hakes, 1978).

Whereas different languages share some universal features (i.e., they all consist of sentences, which are composed of nouns and verbs), they typically do not share common vocabularies, grammatical constructions, or phonemes. For example, the sound represented by the letter *h* in English is not found in Italian, and English does not contain the nasalized vowel phonemes found in French, even though all three languages are related. In other words, languages often differ with respect to the presence or absence of linguistic features. In contrast, dialects within a language share most linguistic features, but differ from one another primarily according to the frequency of usage of certain features. For example, speakers with a Boston accent understand and occasionally pronounce the terminal /r/, but less frequently than speakers of other dialects.

Just as languages are naturally associated with a speaker's geographic origin, dialects tend to be associated with relatively stable characteristics of the speaker, including race, gender, age, social class, and geographic origin. These factors remain fairly constant (obviously, some more than others) throughout the life of an individual speaker. Age-related speech patterns, of course, change over time (see Chapter 11). Typically, adolescents in each generation have their own jargon or special vocabulary (e.g., *cool* or *groovy* in the 1960s or 1970s, or more contemporary but short-lived expressions such as *gnarly* and *totally tubular*). With the exception of these age-related and profession-related jargons (e.g., the technical vocabulary of doctors or lawyers), most people do not change their dialect much over time, particularly in phonological and syntactic features. Only when people change their status or role with respect to important characteristics do they find it necessary to acquire a new dialect (e.g., females who wish to be sportscasters may learn to use the "male" dialect, or southerners who move north may acquire a northern accent and dialect). However, many speakers never have any need to learn more than one dialect in a single language.

LINGUISTIC CHAUVINISM

The process of **language standardization** is a conscious, deliberate selection of one form of a language that becomes fixed and regulated in spelling, grammar, and pronunciation. This standard facilitates oral and written communication across a wide variety of situations, and becomes the one form of language taught in school or taught to foreigners. The form of a language that becomes the standard typically is *not* selected by virtue of any inherent linguistic features, but because it is used by people with higher social status. In other words, the standard language is not the one that "wins out" due to simple or clear rules or even frequency of use, but because of the political clout of its speakers (e.g., English is the so-called "international" language, even though there may be more native speakers of other languages). Bolinger (1980) describes an incident from a television show produced during President Carter's administration—when a New Yorker commented on one character's southern accent, he replied "We don't have an accent anymore, you do" (p. 45).

An unfortunate side effect of standardization, however, may be what is called **linguistic chauvinism,** in which speakers frequently assume that their own or the standard dialect is the only proper way of speaking. Differing dialects are considered either incorrect (i.e., degenerate, illogical, or simpler as compared to the standard) or quaint, depending on the prestige of their speakers (Luhman, 1990). Romaine (1984) reports that to someone who does not speak English at all, the difference between "RP" (received pronunciation, or the Queen's English) and local varieties such as Birmingham or Glasgow English, would be virtually undetectable. The native British English speaker will, however, quickly dismiss both local dialects as unpleasant, incorrect, and sloppy. As far as linguists are concerned, all dialects are equally valid exemplars of a language. Some dialects may share more features with the standard dialect than others, but this makes them no more correct.

According to Luhman (1990), although speech is only one of many markers we may use to infer someone's social position, it carries more weight than most since it is not as easily changed as others (e.g., clothing). Unfortunately, social judgments about speakers are frequently made based solely upon their languages or dialects. In countries where one language predominates (either in prevalence or by being spoken by those in power), speakers of the minority or nondominant language are typically viewed as less intelligent, less ambitious, and less attractive (e.g., Gardner & Lambert, 1972; Lambert, 1967). In one study, college students in Kentucky were asked to rate speakers who were **bidialectal** in both Appalachian English (AE) and standard English (SE) on several dimensions. Even the students who spoke AE themselves rated others as lower in education, intelligence, and ambition, and less wealthy and successful, when they spoke in AE dialect than when they spoke SE. Williams (1970) asked teachers to rate the voices of African-American, white, and Mexican-American children; children with nonstandard speech were rated as less competent than those with speech closer to the standard. This holds true in other countries as well; Edwards (1981) found that lower-class Irish children received much more unfavorable ratings than their middle-class peers when rated by speech samples alone. What's more, even children seem to be somewhat aware of these stereotypes, and by their midteens share adults' opinions of which speech variants are socially preferable (e.g., Ervin-Tripp, 1973; Labov, 1971; Romaine, 1984).

Rating children's personality and competence from their dialects alone is not only unfair but inaccurate, since a child's competence and skills are not easily predicted from his dialect. It is more probable that teachers who expect problems with some children, based upon judgments of their dialects, may deal with those children differently (Cherry, 1981; Edwards, 1981; Ervin-Tripp, 1973).

BLACK ENGLISH

The most studied nonstandard English dialect is often called **Black English (BE).** Although this form is associated with its speakers' race, variants of this dialect are actually spoken in many sections of the south, and by lower, working-class speakers regardless of their racial origin. Thus, BE is actually a misnomer for a fairly common dialectic variant of English. Differences between SE and BE are not great (although BE is less similar to SE than most other nonstandard English dialects for historical reasons; see Stewart, 1970); they share most of their lexicons, pronunciation, and basic syntax.

Some who believe that BE is a degenerate form of SE explain that because of their impoverished backgrounds, African-American children have little opportunity to learn "correct" speech patterns. However, many of the examples of BE dialect that are commonly taken as evidence of its illogicality or degenerate nature are, in fact, logical linguistic rules for speech production. For example, SE can change "I have seen no one" into "I have not seen anyone," marking the negative either on the verb or with the indefinite noun, but not both. In BE, the rule is that indefinites (e.g., *someone, something*) are negated with the verb, so the sentence becomes "I have not seen no one." This is a straightforward rule (so long as the listener also knows it), which is quite similar to one in Russian. In fact, the BE rule might be considered more complex than the SE rule because BE marks the negative twice rather than just once.

BE also employs a syntactic device known as **aspect,** which is not found in SE. When a speaker of BE wishes to express a continuing state in contrast to a temporary condition, the speaker includes the auxiliary *be.* For example, if a man is usually employed and is currently working, he would be described with "He be working," but for the usually unemployed man working on a temporary job, the form "He working" would be used.

Unfortunately, children who have acquired the complex grammatical marker for aspect may actually be penalized on certain language tests. For example, one commonly used sentence-maturity rating method allows no points to be given for sentences that omit the copula or auxiliary *be,* so resulting scores favor SE speakers (Lively, 1984). The true language abilities of young BE speakers may be significantly underestimated when tests are administered only in SE, or scored only according to SE rules (Adler, 1990; Wheldall & Joseph, 1986).

But SE is the **school dialect,** spoken by teachers and used in written texts. It appears that most BE-speaking children understand more SE pronunciation and grammar than they use (e.g., Ervin-Tripp, 1973; Melmed, 1971). What aspects of SE they do not understand may be relatively superficial, at least from a linguistic standpoint (although perhaps not from a social one; see Ervin-Tripp, 1973). The greater problem may be that their SE-speaking peers and teachers do not understand BE (Weener, 1969). According to Heath (1989) and DeStefano (1984), African-American children typically arrive at school not only with nonstandard rules for pronunciation and grammar, but with nonstandard pragmatic rules and linguistic experiences as well. For example, Heath (1989) finds that African-American working-, or lower-class parents rarely ask children questions to which they (the parents) already know the answers—so-called **test questions.** White, middle-class parents and, of course, teachers, on the other hand, frequently ask young children such questions in attempts to get the children to display their knowledge. Michaels (1981) and Gee (1989) note that lower-income African-American and middle-income white children also have differing narrative styles. Whereas white children use a tightly organized, *topic-centered* style that focuses on a single topic or series of related topics, African-American children use a *topic-chaining* style that flows easily from one topic to another (also see Chapter 10). Not only do white teachers have difficulty following the latter style, it does not translate well into "good writing" (Gee, 1989). Thus, to be academically successful, native BE speakers may need to become bi-dialectal in SE and BE (e.g., Adler, 1990).

How is this accomplished? Labov (1971) hypothesized that there are several stages in the child's acquisition of dialects. The particular native language and dialect that children acquire obviously depends on the language to which they are exposed. Typically, they learn the language spoken by their parents, which is in turn determined by the parent's geographical origin and social class. The first stage consists of learning the basic rules of grammar, lexicon, and phonetics from one's parents. While some aspects of BE are learned from the parents at this stage, Labov argues that from the ages of five to fifteen years, children learn the local dialect from their peers, and that peer influence supercedes parental influence in the use of **vernacular.** It is only late in this second stage (around age 15) that the adolescent becomes aware of the social significance of dialect differences and begins to use more standard forms. Unfortunately, such relatively late acquisition of a second dialect may result in non-native competence in that dialect. Labov (1971) believes that even when the standard forms have become part of a speaker's repertoire, the speaker may still make slips, being unable to maintain a consistent choice between standard and nonstandard alternatives. Similarly, Scarcella (1983) suggests that older foreign language learners may have **discourse accents,** meaning that they are not as competent as native speakers in such pragmatic factors as topic choice, sequencing, and provision of feedback.

Studies of **code switching** in children whose original dialect is BE support the claim that children gradually acquire a second dialect during the school years. DeStefano (1972) recorded the classroom and nonschool speech of eight- to eleven-year-old African-American children, finding many distinctions. Classroom speech appeared to be more formal or careful, containing a greater frequency of standard features than non-school speech. Further, in a repetition task, BE-speaking first-graders responded in standard English 56 percent of the time, but fifth-graders used SE responses 70 percent of the time. Either these students were learning more of the standard forms over time, or they already knew the forms and were learning, instead, to use them in the appropriate contexts. A study by Melmed (1971) found that third-grade African-American children used SE 70 percent of the time in school-related tasks.

Although Labov (1971) may have been correct about the importance of exposure to peers and formal learning situations for acquisition of new dialects, it appears that he may have greatly underestimated the code-switching abilities of young children. The studies just presented indicate that even young elementary school children (not just older adolescents) code-switch in certain situations. Romaine (1984) reports that during the later stages of primary school, children in Edinburgh, Scotland, show an increasing awareness of the differences in "posh" and "rough" speech, and an increasing tendency to style-switch according to the formality of the situation.

By the age of four or five, bilingual children appropriately switch between languages according to the context and listener (McLaughlin, 1984). When children become proficient in more than one dialect or language and begin to use them appropriately in differing social contexts, the dialects and languages have become more like registers. Thus, children who are bilingual or bidialectal have the advantage of a greater repertoire of stylistic variation available for their use.

GENDERLECT

Another speaker characteristic commonly associated with dialect variation is gender. In American English, there are strong stereotypes concerning the gender-role appropriateness of particular speech patterns, or **genderlects** as Kramer (1974) has termed them. Robin Lakoff (1973) was among the first to describe gender differences in speech. She claimed that women are more polite and other-oriented in speech style, more often saying "Thank you" or "Goodbye" (Greif & Gleason, 1980), using more indirect requests, and adding tag questions at the end of statements (e.g., "This is a hard exam, *isn't it?*"), presumably revealing their insecurity at making assertions. Lakoff and others also observed that women use some lexical items more than men, such as *adorable* or *cute,* and more euphemisms and mild expletives (e.g., *oh dear*), whereas men more commonly use swear words and obscenities. The average adult male also speaks more loudly and in a much lower pitch than the average adult female, and women tend to vary their voice pitch more than men (are more expressive), while men are more monotonic. These differences are only partly determined by physiology; men are capable of producing much larger ranges of voice pitch (such as when they speak to young children; see Warren-Leubecker & Bohannon, 1984) than they normally do.

Many of Lakoff's initial claims have not been confirmed by subsequent research (Crosby & Nyquist, 1977). She actually described the stereotypes more than the reality; however, these stereotypes persist in the ways in which we perceive men's and women's speech. For example, Edelsky (1977) asked first-, third-, and sixth-grade children and adults to decide whether certain sentences were spoken by a male or female. Even the youngest children held genderlect stereotypes (albeit inconsistent ones), but older children's stereotypes more closely approximated the adults' views. Garcia-Zamor (1973) found that even preschoolers could distinguish whether a doll was male or female depending on how it "uttered" a sentence. For instance, the euphemism "drat" was attributed to the female doll, whereas an obscene expression, "s—t," was attributed to the male doll.

Some of these differences have been found in studies of children's actual social interactions, rather than studies of judgments or role-playing with dolls. Sheldon (1990) reported gender differences in children as young as three, where girls' conflict was more mitigated while boys' arguments were more coercive and apparently competitive. Sachs (1987) observed same-sex two- to five-year-old child dyads in pretend play as "doctors." Boys almost always chose the role of doctor for themselves, and "assigned" their partners to other roles, whereas girls usually asked their partners what role they would like to play. Regardless of the role played, however, boys used more imperatives

"Well I know a funnier story!" Boasting is common when boys talk with one another.

and prohibitions (e.g., "Don't touch nothing") than girls, and girls made heavier use of tag questions and joint utterances (e.g., "Let's sit down"). Goodwin and Goodwin (1987), studying the patterns of play among African-American elementary school children in Philadelphia, also found that girls asked more questions and used more enjoining suggestions such as "We can . . ." or "Let's" than the boys. These findings are corroborated by Leaper's (1987) study of children playing with puppets. He found that girls' speech was in general aimed at establishing *communion* or collaborative goals ("Let's play store"), and that boys' speech was more coercive ("I'm gonna hit you!").

While Lakoff and other researchers (Thorne & Henley, 1975; Thorne, Kramarae, & Henley, 1983) view gender differences in speech as reflecting differences in underlying power relations between the sexes, another possibility, proposed by Maltz and Borker (1982), is that these differences develop simply as cultural speech registers, a result of sex segregation in childhood and adolescence. That children are segregated in childhood either by choice or design is well established (Thorne & Luria, 1986). McCloskey and Coleman (in press) compared conversations between same- and opposite-sex third-graders, and found few sex differences unique to mixed sex interaction. That is, they found no evidence that boys interrupted, talked more, commanded, insulted, or verbally controlled the girls in mixed-sex exchanges. However, they did find that when children were paired with same-sex partners, differences emerged—in particular, girls talked more about personal topics and boys bragged and boasted more with each other. Haas (1979) also found that over three age groups (four-, eight-, and twelve-year olds), girls talked significantly more about school and boys talked more about sports.

It appears then that there are separate genderlects, although it is unclear whether they emerge from the status imparity between the sexes in our society or from segregated social lives, as Maltz and Borker suggest. Insofar as children's play and social lives are determined by the adult gender roles surrounding them, both explanations have virtue. It should also be noted that although McCloskey and Coleman found little evidence for boys dominating girls in conversations in the third grade, considerable evidence (Thorne, Kramerae, & Henley, 1983; West & Zimmerman, 1983) is available for adults indicating **conversational asymmetry.** It would be important to explore gender differences in speech beyond the third grade, especially into late childhood and adolescence (Eckert, 1990), when gender role identification and stereotyping become more pronounced (Galambos, Almeida, & Petersen, 1990; Martin, Wood, & Little, 1990).

One factor likely to play an important role in the child's acquisition of genderlect is differential treatment by adults. Cherry (1975; Cherry & Lewis, 1976) found that mothers and preschool teachers interacted with boys and girls differently, for example, using longer utterances, more repetitions, and more questions with girls, and more directives with boys. Gleason (1987) reported that fathers use more imperatives as well as jocular or insulting terms with their sons than their daughters. For example, little girls were called "honey" and "sweetie," whereas little boys were called "dingaling" or "nutcake." Parents use a greater number and a wider variety of diminutives (e.g., "blankie," "doggie") to infant and young girls than to boys (Gleason, Perlmann, Ely, & Evans, in press). Further, both mothers and fathers are more likely to interrupt their daughters than their sons.

Regardless of the gender of the child listener, mothers and fathers provide different models for gender-appropriate speech. Although mothers' and fathers' speech to children is quite similar in many ways (both simplify their speech and use higher voice pitches when addressing children), Gleason (1987) asserts that there are also many differences, related to differing roles within the family and society. For instance, fathers use more direct imperatives and implied imperatives (e.g., "Shut the door" or "It is getting cold in here") while mothers use polite, question-form imperatives ("Could you shut the door?"). Fathers are more likely than mothers to interrupt their children, and fathers do not appear to adjust their speech to their child's language level as well as mothers do. Gleason concludes therefore that fathers are more demanding conversational partners than mothers.

Lakoff (1975) suggested that all children speak "women's language" (having been exposed more to their mother's speech) up until the ages of five or six years. However, from evidence reported earlier, it appears that boys and girls already speak differently by three or four years of age. Although differences in mothers' and fathers' speech to boys and girls have been documented, at this time the effects of these differences on genderlect acquisition are unknown.

Section Summary: Dialects

In summary, dialects vary with features of speakers—with geographical origin, gender, social class, race, and age. The various dialects that make up different languages have more common than unique features. Dialect differences, especially those of syntax or pronunciation, follow similar generative rules as the standard versions of the language. Lastly, dialects seem to be acquired, in most cases as the "mother tongue," and a single dialect will probably be spoken until such time as the child becomes aware of dialect differences and their social consequences. Therefore, researchers interested in normative language acquisition should be aware of the speaker characteristics that lead to dialectic variation.

SUMMARY

The study of developmental pragmatics spans an array of linguistic, cognitive, and social domains of achievement. Pragmatic knowledge relies on linguistic competence, particularly in the integration of linguistic form and social interpretive function. Children need to acquire the rudimentary principles governing question-asking and answerhood conditions, deixis and anaphora, and discourse cohesion, before they can modify these forms to meet social goals. Children also must retain perspective when speaking and listening. Their developing awareness of others' minds, as represented by their understanding of intentionality and shared knowledge, shapes their use of language in multiple ways. Perspective-taking is a universal cognitive skill that enables the child to acquire culture-specific speech codes, expressing social place and attitude. We have reviewed how children encode the forms necessary for different speech acts within interpersonal contexts, and the features of speech registers and dialects framed within a broader context. Children acquire all these social uses of language remarkably early in development; indeed, it is virtually impossible to separate in time the development of communicative and linguistic competence. Children learn language within the context of social relationships and community, and are as ready to code-switch as they are to acquire grammatical morphemes. Humans are able to apply a unique, generative linguistic symbol system to the demands of a highly complex and political social existence, and it is this character of expression that gives us identity and a sense of shared knowledge and culture.

SUGGESTED PROJECTS

1. Attempt to identify the features of adolescent language that differ from "standard" speech. Develop a lexicon, complete with definitions, of the special jargon used by this age group.
2. Record your own speech in different situations, such as to a friend versus a professor, to a peer versus a child, to a member of the opposite sex versus a same-sex peer, and to a familiar versus a stranger. Note differences in your pronunciation, grammatical forms and complexity, in the types of semantic items used, and in paralinguistic features such as volume, stress, intonation, and rate of speaking. Compare your findings with those reported in this chapter.
3. Examine newspaper comics or television programs for evidence of speech stereotypes associated with sex roles, geographic origins, or age. Write down the speech features that are most frequently associated with these speaker characteristics.
4. Watch someone talking on the telephone. Observe how much they make use of gestures, or use color or deictic terms (such as "over here"). Also listen for the routines of opening and closing the conversations, and examine them for politeness according to who the conversational partner is.

SUGGESTED READINGS

Gleason, J. B., & Perlmann, R. Y. (1985). Acquiring social variation in speech. In R. Sinclair & H. Giles (Eds.), *Recent advances in language, communication, and social psychology* (pp. 86–111). Hillsdale, NJ: Erlbaum.

Lloyd, P. (1990). Children's communication. In M. Hughes & R. Grieve (Eds.), *Understanding children: Essays in honour of Margaret Donaldson* (pp. 51–70). Oxford: Blackwell.

Schiefelbusch, R. L., & Pickar, J. (Eds.). (1984). *The acquisition of communicative competence.* Baltimore: University Park Press.

Wells, G. (1979). Variation in child language. In P. Fletcher & M. Garman (Eds.), *Language acquisition.* New York: Cambridge University Press.

Dialects

Labov, W. (1972). *Sociolinguistic patterns.* Philadelphia: University of Pennsylvania Press.

Romaine, S. (1984). *The language of children and adolescents: The acquisition of communicative competence.* London: Basil Blackwell.

Thorne, B., Kramerae, C., & Henley, N. (Eds.). (1983). *Language, gender, and society.* Rowley, MA: Newbury House.

Registers

Becker, J. (1982). Children's use of requests to mark and manipulate social status. In S. Kuczaj (Ed.), *Language development: (Vol. 2) Language, thought, and culture.* Hillsdale, NJ: Erlbaum.

Dickson, W. P. (Ed.). (1981). *Children's oral communication skills.* New York: Academic Press.

McDevitt, T., & Ford, M. (1987). Processes in young children's communicative functioning and development. In M. E. Ford & D. H. Ford (Eds.), *Humans as self-constructing living systems: Putting the framework to work* (pp. 145–175). Hillsdale, NJ: Erlbaum.

Whitehurst, G. J., & Sonnenschein, S. (1985). The development of communication: A functional analysis. In G. J. Whitehurst (Ed.), *Annals of Child Development* (Vol. 2, pp. 1–48). Greenwich, CT: JAI Press.

REFERENCES

Ackerman, B. P. (1981). Performative bias in children's interpretations of ambiguous referential communications. *Child Development, 52,* 1224–1230.

Adler, S. (1990). Multicultural clients: Implications for the SLP. *Language, Speech, and Hearing Services in Schools, 21,* 135–139.

Andersen, E. S. (1990). *Speaking with style: The sociolinguistic skills of children.* London: Routledge.

Astington, J. W. (1988a). Children's understanding of the speech act of promising. *Journal of Child Language, 15,* 157–173.

Astington, J. W. (1988b). Promises: Words or deeds? *First Language, 8,* 259–270.

Austin, J. (1962). *How to do things with words.* Oxford: Oxford University Press.

Axia, G., & Baroni, M. (1985). Linguistic politeness at different age levels. *Child Development, 56,* 918–927.

Bamberg, M. (1987). *The acquisition of narratives: Learning to use language.* New York: Mouton de Gruyter.

Bates, E. (1976). *Language and context: The development of pragmatics.* New York: Academic Press.

Bates, E., Camaioni, L., & Volterra, V. (1975). The acquisition of performatives prior to speech. *Merrill-Palmer Quarterly, 21,* 205–226.

Beal, C., & Belgrad, S. (1990). The development of message evaluation skills in young children. *Child Development, 61,* 705–712.

Beal, C., & Flavell, J. (1984). Development of the ability to distinguish communicative intention and literal message meaning. *Child Development, 55,* 920–928.

Becker, J. (1982). Children's strategic use of requests to mark and manipulate social status. In S. Kuczaj (Ed.), *Language development: Language thought and culture* (Vol. 2). Hillsdale, NJ: Erlbaum.

Becker, J. (1986). Bossy and nice requests: Children's production and interpretation. *Merrill-Palmer Quarterly, 32,* 393–413.

Becker, J. (1988). The success of parents' indirect techniques for teaching their preschoolers pragmatic skills. *First Language, 8,* 173–182.

Becker, J. (1990). Processes in the acquisition of pragmatic competence. In G. Conti-Ramsden & C. Snow (Eds.), *Children's language* (Vol. 7, pp. 7–24). Hillsdale, NJ: Erlbaum.

Becker, J., & Hall, M. S. (1989). Adult beliefs about pragmatic development. *Journal of Applied Developmental Psychology, 10,* 1–17.

Bellinger, D. (1979). Changes in the explicitness of mothers' directives as children age. *Journal of Child Language, 6,* 443–458.

Berninger, G., & Garvey, C. (1981). Questions and the allocation, construction, and timing of turns in child discourse. *Journal of Psycholinguistic Research, 10,* 335–342.

Blank, M., Gessner, M., & Esposito, A. (1979). Language without communication: A case study. *Journal of Child Language, 6,*(2), 329–352.

Bolinger, D. (1980). *Language. The loaded weapon: The use and abuse of language today.* London: Longman.

Bonitatibus, G., Godshall, S., Kelley, M., Levering, T., & Lynch, E. (1988). The role of social cognition in comprehension monitoring. *First Language, 8,* 287–298.

Brennan, M., & Brennan, R. (1988). *Strange language.* Wagga Wagga, New South Wales, Australia: Charles Stuart University—Riverina.

Brown, R. (1977). Introduction. In C. Snow & C. Ferguson (Eds.), *Talking to children: Language input and acquisition.* Cambridge, MA: Cambridge University Press.

Bruner, J., Roy, C., & Ratner, N. (1982). The beginnings of request. In K. E. Nelson (Ed.), *Children's language* (Vol. 3, pp. 91–138). Hillsdale, NJ: Erlbaum.

Bruner, J., & Sherwood, V. (1976). Early rule structure: The case of peekaboo. In J. S. Bruner, A. Jolly, & K. Sylva (Eds.), *Play: Its role in development and evolution.* Harmondsworth, England: Penguin.

Burling, R. (1973). *English in Black and White.* New York: Holt, Rinehart & Winston.

Capelli, C., Nakagawa, N., & Madden, C. (1990). How children understand sarcasm: The role of context and intonation. *Child Development, 61,* 1824–1841.

Charney, R. (1979). The comprehension of "here" and "there." *Journal of Child Language, 6,* 69–80.

Charney, R. (1980). Speech roles and the development of personal pronouns. *Journal of Child Language, 7,* 509–528.

Cherry, L. J. (1975). Teacher-child verbal interaction: An approach to the study of sex differences. In B. Thorne & N. Henley (Eds.), *Language and sex: Difference and dominance.* Rowley, MA: Newbury House.

Cherry, L. J. (1981). Teacher–student interaction and teacher's expectations of student's communicative competence. In O. Garnica & M. King (Eds.), *Language, children, and society.* New York: Pergamon Press.

Cherry, L. J., & Lewis, M. (1976). Mothers and two-year-olds: A study of sex-differentiated aspects of verbal interaction. *Developmental Psychology, 12,* 278–282.

Chiat, S. (1982). If I were you and you were me: Analysis of pronouns in a pronoun reversing child. *Journal of Child Language, 9,* 359-379.

Clancy, P. (1986). The acquisition of communicative style in Japanese. In B. Schieffelin & E. Ochs (Eds.), *Language socialization across cultures* (pp. 213–250). Cambridge, England: Cambridge University Press.

Clark, E. V., & Sengul, C. J. (1978). Strategies in the acquisition of deixis. *Journal of Child Language, 5,* 457–475.

Clark, H. H. (1979). Responding to indirect speech acts. *Cognitive Psychology, 11,* 430–477.

Corsaro, W. (1979). Young children's conception of status and role. *Sociology of Education, 52,* 46–59.

Crosby, F., & Nyquist, L. (1977). The female register: an empirical study of Lakoff's hypotheses. *Language in Society, 6,* 313–322.

DeHart, G., & Maratsos, M. (1984). Children's acquisition of presuppositional uses. In R. L. Scheifelbusch & J. Pickar (Eds.), *The acquisition of communicative competence* (pp. 237–293). Baltimore: University Park Press.

DePaulo, B. M., & Coleman, L. M. (1986). Talking to children, foreigners and retarded adults. *Journal of Personality and Social Psychology, 51,* 945–959.

DeStefano, J. (1972). Social variation in language: Implications for teaching reading to Black ghetto children. In J. A. Figurel (Ed.), *Better reading in urban schools* (pp. 18–24). Newark, DE: International Reading Association.

DeStefano, J. (1984). Learning to communicate in the classroom. In A. D. Pelligrini & T. D. Yawkey (Eds.), *The development of oral and written language in social contexts* (pp. 155–165). Norwood, NJ: Ablex.

de Villiers, P. A., & de Villiers, J. G. (1974). On this, that, and the other: Nonegocentrism in very young children. *Journal of Experimental Child Psychology, 18,* 438–447.

Dunn, J., & Kendrick, C. (1982). The speech of two- and three-year-olds to infant siblings: "Baby talk" and the context of communications. *Journal of Child Language, 9,* 579–595.

Eckert, P. (1990). Cooperative competition in adolescent "girl talk." *Discourse Processes, 13,* 91–122.

Edelsky, C. (1977). Acquisition of an aspect of communicative competence: Learning what it means to talk like a lady. In S. Ervin-Tripp & C. Mitchell-Kernan (Eds.), *Child discourse.* New York: Academic Press.

Edwards, J. (1981). Ratings of Black, White and Acadian children speech patterns. Unpublished manuscript, Mount St. Vincent University, Halifax, Nova Scotia.

Eisenberg, A. (1986). Teasing: Verbal play in two Mexicano homes. In B. B. Schieffelin & E. Ochs (Eds.), *Language socialization across cultures* (pp. 182–198). Cambridge, England: Cambridge University Press.

Eisenberg, A. R., & Garvey, C. (1981). Children's use of verbal strategies in resolving conflict. *Discourse Processes, 4,* 149–170.

Emslie, H., & Stevenson, R. (1981). Preschool children's use of the article in definite and indefinite referring expressions. *Journal of Child Language, 8,* 313–328.

Ervin-Tripp, S. (1973). Children's sociolinguistic competence and dialect diversity. In A. Dil (Ed.), *Language acquisition and communicative choice: Essays by Susan M. Ervin-Tripp* (pp. 262–301). Stanford: Stanford University Press.

Ervin-Tripp, S., & Gordon, D. (1986). The development of requests. In R. L. Schiefelbusch (Ed.), *Language competence: Assessment and intervention* (pp. 61–95). San Diego: College Hill.

Ervin-Tripp, S., Guo, J., & Lampert, M. (1990). Politeness and persuasion in children's control acts. *Journal of Pragmatics, 14,* 307–331.

Ervin-Tripp, S., & Mitchell-Kernan, C. (1977). *Child discourse.* New York: Academic Press.

Ervin-Tripp, S., Strage, A., Lampert, M., & Bell, N. (1987). Understanding requests. *Linguistics, 25,* 107–143.

Fernald, A. (1989). Intonation and communicative intent in mothers' speech to infants: Is the melody the message? *Child Development, 60,* 1497–1510.

Flavell, J. H., Botkin, P. T., Fry, C. L., Wright, J. W., & Jarvis, P. E. (1968). *The development of role-taking and communication skills in children.* New York: Wiley.

Foss, D., & Hakes, D. (1978). *Psycholinguistics: An introduction to the psychology of language.* Englewood Cliffs, NJ: Prentice-Hall.

Galambos, N. L., Almeida, D. M., & Petersen, A. C. (1990). Masculinity, femininity and sex role attitudes in early adolescence: Exploring gender intensification. *Child Development, 61,* 1905–1914.

Garcia-Zamor, M. A. (1973, December). Child awareness of sex-role distinctions in language use. Paper presented at the Linguistic Society of America Meeting.

Gardner, R. C., & Lambert, W. E. (1972). *Attitudes and motivation in second language learning,* Rowley, MA: Newbury House.

Garton, A. F. (1986). The production of "this" and "that" by young children. *First Language, 6,* 29–39.

Garvey, C. (1977). Play with language and speech. In S. Ervin-Tripp & C. Mitchell-Kernan (Eds.), *Child discourse.* New York: Academic Press.

Garvey, C., & Berninger, G. (1981). Timing and turn-taking in children's conversations. *Discourse Processes, 4,* 27–57.

Garvey, C., & Hogan, R. (1973). Social speech and social interaction: Egocentrism revisited. *Child Development, 44,* 562–568.

Gee, J. P. (1989). Two styles of narrative construction and their linguistic and educational implications. *Discourse Processes, 12,* 287–307.

Gleason, J. Berko. (1973). Code switching in children's language. In T. E. Moore (Ed.), *Cognitive development and the acquisition of language* (pp. 169–177). New York: Academic Press.

Gleason, J. Berko. (1987). Sex differences in parent–child interaction. In S. U. Philips, S. Steele, & C. Tanz (Eds.), *Language, gender, and sex in comparative perspective* (pp. 189–199). New York: Cambridge University Press.

Gleason, J. Berko, Hay, D., & Cain, L. (1989). Social and affective determinants of language acquisition. In M. Rice & R. L. Schiefelbusch (Eds.), *The teachability of language* (pp. 171–186). Baltimore: Paul H. Brookes.

Gleason, J. Berko, Perlmann, R. Y., Ely, D., & Evans, D. (In press). Aspects of babytalk: Parents' use of diminutives in speech to infants and children. In J. L. Sokolov & C. E. Snow (Eds.), *Handbook of research in language development using CHILDES.* Hillsdale, NJ: Erlbaum.

Gleason, J. Berko, Perlmann, R. Y., & Greif, E. B. (1984). What's the magic word: Learning language through routines. *Discourse Processes, 6,* 493–502.

Gleason, J. Berko, & Weintraub, S. (1978). Input language and the acquisition of communicative competence. In K. Nelson (Ed.), *Children's language* (Vol. 1, pp. 171–222). New York: Gardiner Press.

Glucksberg, S., & Krauss, R. M. (1967). What do people say after they have learned how to talk? Studies of the development of referential communication. *Merrill-Palmer Quarterly, 13,* 309–316.

Glucksberg, S., & Krauss, R., & Higgins, T. (1975). The development of referential communication skills. In F. D. Horowitz (Ed.), *Review of child development research* (Vol. 4, pp. 305–345). Chicago: University of Chicago Press.

Goelman, H. (1986). The language environments of family daycare. In S. Kilmer (Ed.), *Advances in early education and daycare* (Vol. 4, pp. 153–179). Greenwich, CT: JAI Press.

Golinkoff, R. (1986). "I beg your pardon?": The preverbal negotiation of failed messages. *Journal of Child Language, 13,* 455–476.

Goodwin, M. H., & Goodwin, C. (1987). Children's arguing. In S. U. Philips, S. Steele, & C. Tang (Eds.), *Language, gender and sex in comparative perspective* (pp. 200–247). Cambridge University Press.

Greif, E. B., & Gleason, J. Berko. (1980). Hi, thanks, and goodbye: More routine information. *Language in Society, 9,* 159–166.

Grice, H. P. (1975). Logic and conversation. In P. Cole & J. L. Morgan (Eds.), *Syntax and semantics: (Vol. 3) Speech acts.* New York: Academic Press.

Guralnick, M., & Paul-Brown, D. (1989). Peer-related communicative competence of preschool children: Developmental and adaptive characteristics. *Journal of Speech and Hearing Research, 32,* 930–943.

Haas, A. (1979). The acquisition of genderlect. *Annals of the New York Academy of Sciences, 237,* 101–113.

Halliday, M. A. K. (1970). Functional diversity in language as seen from a consideration of modality and mood in English. *Foundations of Language, 6,* 322–361.

Halliday, M. A. K. (1975). *Learning how to mean.* London: Edward Arnold.

Heath, S. B. (1989). Oral and literate traditions among Black Americans living in poverty. *American Psychologist, 44,* 367–373.

Hess, L., & Johnston, J. (1988). Acquisition of back channel listener responses to adequate messages. *Discourse Processes, 11,* 319–335.

Hobbs, J. (1990). Topic drift. In B. Dorval (Ed.), *Conversational organization and its development* (pp. 3–22). Norwood, NJ: Ablex.

Hymes, D. (1972). On communicative competence. In J. Pride & J. Holmes (Eds.), *Sociolinguistics.* Hammondsworth, G.B.: Penguin.

Hudson, R. A. (1980). *Sociolinguistics.* Cambridge, England: Cambridge University Press.

Karmiloff-Smith, A. (1979). *A functional approach to child language.* Cambridge, England: Cambridge University Press.

Kramer, C. (1974). Women's speech: Separate but unequal? *Quarterly Journal of Speech, 60, 14–24.*

Labov, W. (1966). *The social stratification of English in New York City.* Washington, DC: Center for Applied Linguistics.

Labov, W. (1971). Stages in the acquisition of standard English. In W. Labov (Ed.), *Readings in American dialectology.* New York: Appleton-Century-Crofts.

Labov, W. (1972). *Sociolinguistic patterns.* Philadelphia: University of Pennsylvania Press.

Lakoff, R. (1973). Language and woman's place. *Language and Society, 2,* 45–80.

Lakoff, R. (1975). *Language and women's place.* NY: Harper & Row.

Lakoff, R. (1977). What can you do with words: Politeness, pragmatics, and performatives. In A. Rogers, B. Wall, & J. Murphy (Eds.), *Proceedings of the Texas conference on performatives, presuppositions, and implicatures.* Arlington, VA: Center for Applied Linguistics.

Lambert, W. (1967). A social psychology of bilingualism. *Journal of Social Issues, 23,* 91–109.

Leaper, C. (1987). Agency, communion, and gender as predictors of communication style and being liked in adult male-female dyads. *Sex Roles, 16* (3/4), 137–149.

Lively, M. (1984). Developmental sentence scoring: Common scoring errors. *Language, Speech, and Hearing Services in the Schools, 15,* 154–168.

Lloyd, P. (1991). Strategies used to communicate route directions by telephone: A comparison of the performance of 7-year-olds, 10-year-olds, and adults. *Journal of Child Language, 18,* 171–189.

Lloyd, P., Baker, E., & Dunn, J. (1984). Children's awareness of communication. In L. Feagans, C. Garvey, & R. Golinkoff (Eds.), *The origin and growth of communication.* Norwood, NJ: Ablex.

Luhman, R. (1990). Appalachian English stereotypes: Language attitudes in Kentucky. *Language in Society, 19,* 331–348.

Maltz, D. N., and Borker, R. A. (1982). A cultural approach to male-female miscommunication. In J. Gumperz (Ed.), *Language, interaction, and social identity* (pp. 196–216). Cambridge: Cambridge University Press.

Maratsos, M. (1973). Nonegocentric communication abilities in preschool children. *Child Development, 44,* 697–700.

Maratsos, M. (1974). Preschool children's use of definite and indefinite articles. *Child Development, 45,* 446–455.

Maratsos, M. (1976). *The use of definite and indefinite reference in young children: An experimental study of semantic acquisition.* Cambridge, England: Cambridge University Press.

Marcos, H. (1987). Communicative functions of pitch range and pitch direction in infants. *Journal of Child Language, 14,* 255–268.

Martin, C. L., Wood, C. W., & Little, J. K. (1990). The development of gender stereotype components. *Child Development, 61,* 1891–1904.

Martin, J. R. (1983). The development of register. In J. Fine & R. O. Freedle (Eds.), *Developmental issues in discourse* (pp. 1–40). Norwood, NJ: Ablex.

McCloskey, L. A. (1986). Prosody and children's understanding of discourse. Unpublished doctoral dissertation, University of Michigan, Ann Arbor Microfilms.

McCloskey, L. A., & Coleman, L. (in press). Difference without dominance: Children's talk in mixed- and same-sex dyads. *Sex Roles.*

McDevitt, T., & Ford, M. (1987). Processes in young children's communicative functioning and development. In M. E. Ford & D. H. Ford (Eds.), *Humans as self-constructing living systems: Putting the framework to work* (pp. 145–175). Hillsdale, NJ: Erlbaum.

McLaughlin, B. (1984). *Second language acquisition in childhood: (Vol. 1) Preschool children* (2nd ed.). Hillsdale, NJ: Erlbaum.

Melmed, P. J. (1971). Black English phonology: The question of reading interference. *Monographs of the Language-Behavior Research Laboratory, 1.*

Menig-Peterson, C. L. (1975). The modification of communicative behavior in preschool aged children as a function of the listener's perspective. *Child Development, 46,* 1015–1018.

Michaels, S. (1981). "Sharing time": Children's narrative styles and differential access to literacy. *Language in Society, 10,* 423–442.

Miller, P. (1986). Teasing in a white working-class community. In B. B. Schieffelin & E. Ochs (Eds.), *Language socialization across cultures* (pp. 199–212). Cambridge, England: Cambridge University Press.

Mitchell, P., & Russell, J. (1989). Young children's understanding of the say-mean distinction in referential speech. *Journal of Experimental Child Psychology, 47,* 467–490.

Mitchell-Kernan, C., & Kernan, K. (1977). Pragmatics of directive choice among children. In S. Ervin-Tripp & C. Mitchell-Kernan (Eds.), *Child discourse* (pp. 189–208). New York: Academic Press.

Montes, R. (1981). Extending a concept: Functioning directively. In *Children's functional language and education in the early years.* Final report to the Carnegie Foundation.

Mussen, P. H., & Eisenberg-Berg. (1977). *Roots of caring, sharing, and helping: The development of prosocial behavior in children.* San Francisco: W. Freeman.

Nelson, K. (1975). The nominal shift in semantic-syntactic development. *Cognitive Psychology, 7,* 461–479.

Nelson, K., & Gruendel, J. M. (1986). Children's scripts. In K. Nelson (Ed.), *Event knowledge: Structure and function in development.* Hillsdale, NJ: Erlbaum.

Ochs, E. (1986). Evolving discourse—The next step. In B. B. Schieffelin & E. Ochs (Eds.), *Language socialization across cultures* (pp. 40–49). Cambridge, England: Cambridge University Press.

Philips, S. (1983). *The invisible culture: Communication in classroom and community on the Warm Springs Indian Reservation.* Research on Teaching Monograph Series. New York: Longman, Inc.

Piaget, J. (1926). *Language and thought of the child.* New York: Harcourt, Brace and World.

Platt, M. (1986). Social norms and lexical acquisition: A study of deictic verbs in Samoan child language. In B. Schieffelin & E. Ochs (Eds.), *Language socialization across cultures* (pp. 127–152). Cambridge, England: Cambridge University Press.

Podrouzek, W., & Furrow, D. (1988). Preschoolers' use of eye contact while speaking: The influence of sex, age, and conversational partner. *Journal of Psycholinguistic Research, 17,* 89–93.

Pynte, J., Girotto, V., & Baccino, T. (1991). Children's communicative abilities revisited: Verbal versus perceptual disambiguating strategies in referential communication. *Journal of Child Language, 18,* 191–213.

Reeder, K., & Wakefield, J. (1987). The development of young children's speech act comprehension: How much language is necessary? *Applied Psycholinguistic Research, 8,* 1–18.

Reichman, R. (1990). Communication and mutual engagement. In B. Dorval (Ed.), *Conversational organization and its development* (pp. 23–48). Norwood, NJ: Ablex.

Robinson, E. J. (1981). The child's understanding of inadequate messages and communication failure: A problem of ignorance or egocentrism? In W. P. Dickson (Ed.), *Children's oral communication skills* (pp. 167–188). New York: Academic Press.

Romaine, S. (1984). *The language of children and adolescents: The acquisition of communicative competence.* London: Basil Blackwell.

Sachs, J. (1987). Preschool boys' and girls' language use in pretend play. In S. U. Philips, S. Steele, & C. Tanz (Eds.), *Language, gender, and sex in comparative perspective* (pp. 178–188). New York: Cambridge University Press.

Sachs, J., & Devin, J. (1976). Young children's use of age appropriate speech styles in social interaction and role-playing. *Journal of Child Language, 3,* 81–98.

Scarcella, R. C. (1983). Discourse accent in second language performance. In S. Gass & L. Selinker (Eds.), *Language transfer in language learning* (pp. 306–322). Rowley, MA: Newbury House.

Schieffelin, B. (1982). Cross-cultural perspectives on the transition: What difference do the differences make? In R. Golinkoff (Ed.), *The transition from prelinguistic communication: Issues and implication.* Hillsdale, NJ: Erlbaum.

Schnur, E., & Shatz, M. (1983). The role of maternal gesturing in conversations with one-year-olds. *Journal of Child Language, 10,* 22–34.

Schober-Peterson, D., & Johnson, C. (1991). Non-dialogue speech during preschool interactions. *Journal of Child Language, 18,* 153–170.

Searle, J. (1970). *Speech acts.* Cambridge, England: Cambridge University Press.

Searle, J. (1975). Indirect speech acts. In P. Cole & J. Morgan (Eds.), *Speech acts: Syntax and semantics* (Vol. 3). NY: Academic Press.

Shatz, M. (1978a). On the development of communicative understandings: An early strategy for interpreting and responding to messages. *Cognitive Psychology, 10,* 271–301.

Shatz, M. (1978b). The relationship between cognitive processes and the development of communication skills. In C. B. Keasey (Ed.), *Nebraska Symposium on Motivation* (Vol. 25, pp. 1–42). Lincoln: University of Nebraska Press.

Shatz, M., & Gelman, R. (1973). The development of communication skills: Modifications in the speech of young children as a function of listener. *Monographs of the Society for Research in Child Development, 38*(5, Serial No. 152).

Shatz, M., & McCloskey, L. (1984). Answering appropriately: A developmental perspective on conversational knowledge. In S. Kuczaj (Ed.), *Discourse development: Progress in cognitive development research* (pp. 19–36). New York: Springer-Verlag.

Shatz, M., & O'Reilly, A. W. (1990). Conversational or communicative skill? A reassessment of two-year-olds' behavior in miscommunication episodes. *Journal of Child Language, 17,* 131–146.

Sheldon, A. (1990). Pickle fights: Genderlect talk in preschool disputes. *Discourse Processes, 13,* 5–31.

Shuy, R. (1982). The importance of understanding function. . . . In L. Feagans & D. Farran (Eds.), *The language of children reared in poverty* (pp. 261–264). New York: Academic Press.

Snow, C. E., & Ferguson, C. A. (Eds.). (1977). *Talking to children: Language input and acquisition.* Cambridge, MA: Cambridge University Press.

Snow, C. E., Perlmann, R. Y., Gleason, J. Berko, & Hooshyar, N. (1990). Developmental perspectives on politeness: Sources of children's knowledge. *Journal of Pragmatics, 14,* 289–305.

Sonnenschein, S. (1986). Development of referential communication skills: How familiarity with listener affects a speaker's production of redundant messages. *Developmental Psychology, 22,* 549–552.

Sonnenschein, S. (1988). The development of referential communication: Speaking to different listeners. *Child Development, 59,* 694–702.

Stewart, W. A. (1970). Toward a history of American Negro dialect. In F. Williamson (Ed.), *Language and poverty.* Chicago: Markham.

Sugarman, S. (1984). The development of preverbal communication: Its contributions and limits in promoting the development of language. In R. L. Schiefelbusch & J. Pickar (Eds.), The acquisition of communicative competence (Vol. 8). Baltimore: University Park Press.

Surian, L., & Job, R. (1987). Children's use of conversational rules in a referential communication task. *Journal of Psycholinguistic Research, 16,* 369–382.

Thorne, B., & Henley, N. (Eds.). (1975). *Language and sex: Difference and dominance.* Rowley, MA: Newbury House.

Thorne, B., Kramerae, C., & Henley, N. (Eds.). (1983). *Language, gender, and society.* Rowley, MA: Newbury House.

Thorne, B., & Luria, Z. (1986). Girls and boys together . . . but mostly apart. In W. W. Hartup & Z. Rubin (Eds.), *Relationships and development* (pp. 167–184). Hillsdale, NJ: Erlbaum.

Van Hekken, S. M. J., Vergeer, M. M., & Harris, P. L. (1980). Ambiguity of reference and listener's reaction in a naturalistic setting. *Journal of Child Language, 7,* 555–563.

Vygotsky, L. (1962). *Thought and language* (translated by E. Hanfmann & G. Vakar). Cambridge, MA: MIT Press.

Wanska, S. K., & Bedrosian, J. L. (1985). Conversational structure and topic performance in mother–child interaction. *Journal of Speech and Hearing Research, 28,* 579–584.

Warden, D. A. (1976). The influence of context on children's use of identifying expressions and references. *British Journal of Psychology, 67,* 101–112.

Warren, A., & Tate, C. S. (1991). Egocentrism in children's telephone conversations. In R. Diaz & L. Berk (Eds.), *Private speech: From social interaction to self regulation.* Hillsdale, NJ: Erlbaum.

Warren-Leubecker, A., & Bohannon, J. (1982). The effects of expectation and feedback on speech to foreigners. *Journal of Psycholinguistic Research, 11,* 207–215.

Warren-Leubecker, A., & Bohannon, J. (1983). The effects of verbal feedback and listener type on the speech of preschool children. *Journal of Experimental Child Psychology, 35,* 540–548.

Warren-Leubecker, A., & Bohannon, J. (1984). Intonation patterns in child-directed speech: Mother-father differences. *Child Development, 55,* 1379–1385.

Warren-Leubecker, A., & Tate, C. (1986, October). Is preschoolers' speech egocentric? Evidence of pragmatic errors and routines in telephone conversations. Paper presented at the Boston University Conference on Language Development, Boston, MA.

Weener, P. D. (1969). Social dialect differences and the recall of verbal messages. *Journal of Educational Psychology, 60,* 194–199.

Wellman, H. M., & Lempers, J. D. (1977). The naturalistic communication abilities of two-year-olds. *Child Development, 48,* 1052–1057.

Wells, G. (1979). Variation in child language. In P. Fletcher & M. Garman (Eds.), *Language acquisition.* New York: Cambridge University Press.

West, C., & Zimmerman, D. (1983). Small insults: A study of interruptions in cross-sex conversations between unacquainted persons. In B. Thorne, C. Kramarae, & N. Henley (Eds.), *Language, gender and society* (pp. 103–118). Rowley, MA: Newbury House.

Wheldall, K., & Joseph, R. (1986). Young black children's sentence comprehension skills: A comparison of performance in standard English and Jamaican Creole. *First Language, 6,* 149–154.

Whitehurst, G. J., & Sonnenschein, S. (1985). The development of communication: A functional analysis. In G. J. Whitehurst (Ed.), *Annals of Child Development* (Vol. 2, pp. 1–48). Greenwich, CT: JAI Press.

Wilcox, J., & Webster, E. (1980). Early discourse behavior: An analysis of children's responses to listener feedback. *Child Development, 51,* 1120–1125.

Williams, F. (1970). *Language and poverty.* Chicago: Markham Publishing.

Wykes, T. (1981). Inference of children's comprehension of pronouns. *Journal of Experimental Child Psychology, 32,* 264–279.

Theoretical Approaches to Language Acquisition

7

John Neil Bohannon III *Butler University*

■ INTRODUCTION

Developmental psycholinguists have been accumulating facts about language acquisition for almost 30 years. Unfortunately, the development of a coherent theory that accounts for all these facts has lagged far behind. In fact, some noted researchers have described the process of language acquisition as seeming "magic" (Bloom, 1983) or "mysterious" (Gleitman & Wanner, 1982). Perhaps the task of constructing a general theory of language development is hindered by the broad scope of "language" behavior. The breadth of the preceding chapters illustrates this complexity. "Language" includes such diverse topics as phonology, semantics, syntax, and pragmatics. There are few explanatory principles common to all these domains. A true theory of how language develops should, in some sense, organize the facts from these varied sources, generate testable and verifiable hypotheses, and provide an explanation of the acquisition process. It appears that none of the extant "theories" qualifies according to these requirements.

Another reason many have despaired of organizing the current mass of data is that some of the facts appear to be contradictory or even irrelevant to particular research issues. Researchers, therefore, have typically focused upon narrowly circumscribed problems within each area (phonology, semantics, etc.). This allowed limited explanations specific to the problem without reference to broader issues. Other researchers have devised *models* of the language acquisition process (e.g., MacWhinney, 1978, 1987; Pinker, 1984, 1989; Wexler & Culicover, 1980). A model differs from a theory in that it is an analogy based upon some known mechanism. A model describes a process by simulation, invoking similarities between some already understood process and the phenomenon under investigation. For example, computers are often used to model the human memory system. Models generally do not explain the actual process or mechanism, nor are they meant to. While models may be useful in the eventual understanding of phenomena, they often prove misleading or inaccurate. This is especially true when the real mechanism ultimately turns out to be only superficially similar to the model, because important underlying differences may be obscured or overlooked. Regarding the previous example, the computer model of human memory has stimulated a tremendous amount of research, but many researchers now agree that human memory is grossly different from computer memory in almost every respect (Estes, 1980).

Chomsky (1957, 1965) proposed that descriptions, models, and theories are all part of an overall taxonomy of theoretical adequacy. His first level of **descriptive adequacy** requires cataloging all behaviors relevant to language and distinguishing them from nonlanguage behaviors. Language acquisition research in the past 20 years has gone a long way toward fulfilling this descriptive goal. On the other hand, children's language is creative and, potentially, infinitely variable. Therefore, an exhaustive list of all possible language productions, even from children, might be impossible to complete. Even if an exhaustive list were compiled, it would lack explanatory power, conveying little understanding of the mechanisms that produced the behavior. The second level, **model adequacy,** is achieved when some finite number of unifying principles are identified that account for the appearance of the various language behaviors. These principles predict the known facts of development, but are not necessarily the principles by which language-learning children actually operate. This second level is, in fact, theoretical modeling such as learnability approaches. Most grammars written from transcripts of children's speech are attempts to determine the rules that account for the observed data. However, few researchers would insist that their grammars are the actual rules children use when speaking or understanding speech. The last and most ambitious level of **theoretical adequacy** is achieved when a finite set of principles is discovered that not only accounts for all the language behaviors observed, but also is the actual set of mechanisms used by language-learning children.

A theory of language acquisition must explain not only why children say what they do, but also why they eventually speak like adults. This developmental perspective obviously presents researchers with additional concerns. Derwing (1973) argued that without a complete understanding of the developmental implications of a particular theory of adult language, the theory would be inadequate. In contrast, Gleitman and Wanner (1982) argued that any theory of child language would be similarly impaired unless it takes mature language behavior as its ultimate goal. The trouble with the current state of affairs is that few can agree on what either adults or children are doing when they speak and understand (Gleitman & Wanner, 1982).

DISTINGUISHING FEATURES OF THEORETICAL APPROACHES

Despite the bleak picture presented above, language acquisition research and speculation goes on undiminished. These speculations may be grouped into several general theoretical approaches to the problem. The rest of this chapter will attempt to outline these competing approaches and compare them on several critical features relevant to their explanations of both steady-state language behavior and language development. These features include distinctions between: (1) **structuralism** versus **functionalism,** (2) **competence** versus **performance,** and (3) **nativism** versus **empiricism.** In addition, the methods and relevant data for each approach will be considered. It is important to note that the distinctions to be described are, in a sense, artificially bipolar dimensions. As will be apparent, some of the extreme positions are complementary rather than truly opposite (see Segal, 1977; or Zimmerman & Whitehurst, 1979; for a discussion of structuralism versus functionalism). However, these features should facilitate recognition of critical similarities and differences between various approaches, thus providing a clearer picture.

Structuralism versus Functionalism

A *structural* description of behavior attempts to discover *invariant* processes or mechanisms underlying observable data. Structuralists emphasize the form or organization of behavior that is common across many individuals and situations. Chomsky's rules of grammar and Watson's stimulus-response bonds are examples of structures that are used to explain observable behavior. *Functional* accounts of behavior seek to establish predictive *relationships* between environmental or situational variables and language.

The aim of a functional account of language is the prediction and control of verbal behavior in *different contexts* and individuals.

The structural–functional distinction may be illustrated by the following example. If a child said, "I want milk," structuralists would analyze the form of the utterance, finding it to be composed of a subject (*I*), a main verb (*want*), and an object (*milk*). They might then take this sentence as evidence that the child knows the English word-order rule governing active, declarative sentences (i.e., subject–verb–object). Knowledge of this rule should enable the child to create an unlimited number of similar sentences from it. Functionalists would examine the situation in which the utterance "I want milk" occurred. They might determine that this particular utterance, if said in the presence of the mother, is frequently followed by a glass of milk. The occurrence of the utterance, then, is jointly determined by the context (presence of mother) and the consequences of the behavior (receiving a glass of milk). The exact form of the utterance is considered unimportant. Notice that in this case, structuralists and functionalists are describing different aspects of language behavior, the former accounting for syntax and the latter explaining the pragmatic, social use of language. These perspectives are complementary, and both are necessary to fully explain the child's language behavior.

Competence versus Performance

Competence refers to the individual's knowledge of language, or the underlying rules that may be deduced from language behavior. *Performance* refers to actual instances of language use. In other words, competence and performance distinguish the individual's abstract linguistic knowledge and the use of this knowledge. For example, mature speakers of English might say "She will be home yesterday," although they know, upon reflection, that such an utterance violates the rule of tense agreement. Mistakes of this type are typically attributed to performance problems, such as lapses of attention or memory, rather than a basic ignorance of the rules of English grammar. This concept is important because of the concept of competence. For example, one must be very careful that the utterances used for determining grammatical rules are not cluttered with performance mistakes. For this reason, many researchers use judgments of grammaticality rather than language use to discover a speaker's linguistic competence (e.g., de Villiers & de Villiers, 1972; Gleitman, Gleitman, & Shipley, 1972). In addition, notice that only structuralists are typically concerned with competence, since functionalists are more concerned with particular instances of language use (performance).

Nativism versus Empiricism

The third dimension concerns the emphasis placed upon either the child or the environment in the process of language acquisition. This is another example of the old nature–nurture issue. On the one side, *nativists* insist that language is too complex and is acquired too rapidly to have been learned through any known methods (e.g., imitation), so some critical aspects of the language system must be innate. In contrast, *empiricists* place the majority of the responsibility for language acquisition upon *environmental* agents. Proponents of this view feel that language is not essentially different from any other behavior. Therefore, it is learned like any other behavior and subject to all the laws and principles of learning derived from the study of simpler behaviors and simpler organisms.

Language researchers typically do not adhere strictly to either extreme position on the nativistic–empiricistic continuum. Few will disagree that language acquisition is determined both by the organism's innate capacities and its linguistic experiences. The course of early development is too invariant across many languages and contexts not to have some innate component. Similarly, some type of experience is clearly essential for language growth. Regardless of the child's biological predispositions to acquire language, children with no linguistic experience, such as normal children of deaf parents (Sachs & Johnson, 1972), do not learn to speak. The recognition of the necessity of both factors has not inhibited theorists from stressing the role of one factor at the expense of the other. Rarely are the two factors given equal credit.

EVALUATING RESEARCH METHODS

The major approaches to language acquisition may also be compared with respect to the methods frequently used and the data that each theory attempts to explain. The approach followed by researchers usually determines the data and methods they consider relevant. Unfortunately, this sometimes leads to a complete separation of research efforts, with one group pursuing longitudinal observations of the changing grammars of a small number of children, and others performing experiments on sizable groups of children to change the frequency of occurrence of particular verbal behaviors. The developmental perspective and the subjects chosen for study are also dependent upon the researchers' theoretical views. For example, those who agree that language is uniquely human, largely maturational, and composed of syntactic structures would observe maturing grammars in human children. Studies of adults or nonhuman subjects would be considered irrelevant, and experimentation fruitless. In contrast, those who believe that language differs little from other motor activities and is learned in much the same way might try to reinforce communicative behavior in chimpanzees.

At first glance, it may appear that the approaches outlined in this chapter are so different that they don't even attempt to answer the same questions. Is agreement possible when the theoretical approaches differ so drastically? In any scientific endeavor, diversification of research methods and strategies should ultimately lead to *convergent validity.* That is, the more one examines a problem from different angles, the more likely it is that a solution will be discovered. Moreover, the broad range of language behavior needing explanation (phonology, semantics, etc.), may require just as much diversity to answer all the resulting questions. These points justify the hope that some unifying principles will be discovered, despite the splintered nature of current language development research.

In the sections to follow, some of the competing approaches offering explanations of language acquisition will be outlined. They are organized into three main groups—the *behavioral, linguistic,* and *interactionist.* The interactionist position is further subdivided into the cognition/language interaction approach and the social/language interaction approach. Each area will be outlined according to the distinctions previously delineated (e.g., structural–functional). Finally, after presenting each approach and its tenets, a brief evaluation of the approach will be presented, in order to highlight its strengths and weaknesses.

■ BEHAVIORAL APPROACHES

GENERAL ASSUMPTIONS

There are many different hypotheses concerning language acquisition that come under the general heading of *behaviorism.* In spite of their differences, all share a common focus on the observable and measurable aspects of language behavior. Whenever possible, behaviorists avoid mentalistic explanations of language behavior that rely on such constructs as intentions or "implicit knowledge" of grammatical rules. Because these mental processes are not easily defined nor accessible for measurement, behaviorists search for observable environmental conditions (stimuli) that co-occur and predict specific verbal behaviors (responses). This is not to say that behaviorists deny the existence of internal mechanisms—they recognize that overt behavior has an internal physiological base, and that research into these physiological processes is necessary for a better understanding of behavior (e.g., the relationship between language dysfunction and specific brain structures; see Springer & Deutsch, 1981). What behaviorists reject are internal structures or processes with no specific physical correlate, such as grammars (Zimmerman & Whitehurst, 1979).

Clearly, behaviorists emphasize performance over competence. In fact, few would even acknowledge the existence of competence, or any knowledge that is separated from observable behavior. Eschewing the structure of language, behaviorists focus on the functions of language, the stimuli that evoke verbal behavior, and the consequences of language performance. Skinner (1957) argued that behavioral psycholinguists should not accept traditional categorizations of linguistic units (e.g., words and sentences), but should examine language as they would any other behavior; searching for the functional units as they naturally occur, then discovering the functional relationships that predict their occurrence. Traditional linguistic approaches were seen as being irrelevant to this task.

Behaviorists also focus on learning because they regard language as a skill, not essentially different from any other behavior. For example, Watson (1924) stated that "Language as we ordinarily understand it, in spite of its complexities, is in the beginning a very simple type of behavior. It is really a manipulative habit." Skinner (1957) argues that language is a special case of behavior only because it is behavior that is reinforced exclusively by other organisms. Apart from the effect that language has on someone else, verbal behavior does not produce any reinforcement or serve any biological function. Lee (1981) suggests that the term *language* itself is misleading, because it connotes an entity, something that children possess and use, rather than something that children do. Thus, many behaviorists prefer the term *verbal behavior* to *language,* emphasizing the similarity of linguistic skills to all other learned behaviors.

Behavioral theory regards language as a skill, similar to other learned behaviors.

The emphasis on learning places behaviorists toward the empirical end of the nativism–empiricism continuum. Although they admit that humans have specialized physiological structures (e.g., fine motor control of the lips, tongue, larynx, etc.) that allow them to speak, speaking is assumed to be learned through the same principles as rats learn to run mazes. Speaking (and understanding speech) must be brought under the control of stimuli in the environment by reinforcement, imitation, and successive approximations to mature performance (sometimes known as *shaping*). The child is typically viewed as a passive recipient of environmental pressures, much as a malleable piece of clay is molded into new shapes. Behaviorists rarely acknowledge that children, in turn, may affect their environment. In fact, Skinner (1957) states that the speaker should be considered as merely an "interested bystander," having no active role in the process of language behavior or development.

BEHAVIORISTIC LANGUAGE LEARNING

One of the simplest ways of explaining changes in behavior is through the connection or association of stimuli in the environment and certain responses of the organism. The process of forming such associations is known as *classical conditioning* (see Chapter 4). The associations formed between arbitrary verbal stimuli and internal responses are often cited as the source of word meanings (Staats, 1971). For example, a child may learn the word *milk* in the following manner: Milk (UCS) fed to a hungry infant usually results in physiological responses in the infant (UCR). When the infant's mother says the word *milk* prior to or during feeding, this word (CS) becomes associated with the primary stimulus of the milk and gradually acquires the power to elicit a response (CR) in the child that is similar to the response to the milk itself.

Once a CS (a word) has come to elicit a CR, it can then be used as a UCS to modify the response to another CS. For example, if a new CS, such as the word *bottle,* frequently occurs with the word *milk,* it may come to elicit a CR similar to the response to *milk.* The associations formed between several stimuli (CSs) and a single response lead to the formation of associations between the stimuli themselves. Thus, not only may arbitrary verbal CSs be associated with specific internal meanings (CRs), but the words themselves may be connected by stimulus–stimulus associations. In this way, classical conditioning is used to account for the interrelationship of words and word meanings.

Whereas behaviorists use the principles of classical conditioning to account for the child's development of receptive vocabulary, additional learning principles must be applied to explain productive speech. *Operant conditioning* is the form of learning most often used to fill this role (Moerk, 1983; Mowrer, 1960; Osgood, 1953; Staats, 1971). Operant conditioning concerns the changes in voluntary, nonreflexive behavior that arise due to environmental consequences contingent upon that behavior. Simply put, behaviors that most frequently result in rewards tend to be repeated, whereas behaviors that result in punishment do not tend to recur. All behavioristic accounts of language acquisition assume that children's productive speech is shaped by differential reinforcers and punishments supplied by environmental agents (e.g., parents). Behaviorists assume that children's speech that more closely approximates adult speech will be rewarded, while meaningless or inappropriate speech will be ignored or punished. Gradually, the response unit will change from simple sounds to whole words as the parents change their reinforcement practices, eventually restricting rewards to only those utterances that are meaningful and adultlike.

Throughout development, behaviorists assume that children's caretakers industriously train children to perform verbal behaviors, usually after the parent has provided an example: "Say bye-bye. Bye-bye." In this way, the adult provides the child with both mature speech exemplars and training in imitation of adult speech. When children successfully imitate what the adult just pronounced, the children are rewarded. In addition, the word *dog* is provided in the presence of dogs, *boy* in the presence of boys, and so on. Thus, the acquisition of both receptive and productive vocabulary begins to accelerate as all the types of learning—classical, operant, and imitative—converge to direct and control the child's language behavior. Behaviorists assume that the course of language development is largely determined by the course of training, not maturation.

Children's word combinations are assumed to be acquired in much the same ways as single words. Parents train simple word combinations through shaping and imitation training, rewarding successive approximations to adultlike word strings. Some behaviorists explain these word combinations as response chains, with the first word and current context serving as a stimulus for the second word, which with the context serves as a stimulus for the next word, and so forth. These word chains are also known as *Markov models of sentences* (Mowrer, 1960). Some theorists (Osgood, 1953, 1963) include internal stimuli within the system that may alter the chain by eliciting different overt responses, but they are, in essence, still Markov models. Clearly, the child need not have heard every possible chain or string of words in order to produce and understand them. It is only necessary for the child to have associations between pairs of words, between individual words and the environmental context, and between words and possible internal mediating stimuli.

Behavioral interpretations assume increasing complexity in the response unit. Just as sounds were shaped into words in infancy, such that words became the functional response unit, combinations of words come to serve as new, larger response units. Whitehurst (1982) argues that some word patterns (e.g., the boy's shoe, the boy's bike, the boy's dog) become grammatical frames (the boy's *X*), where insertion of novel lexical items with similar properties is allowed (the boy's toothbrush). It should be noted, however, that most behaviorists do not view such grammatical frames as true grammatical rules. A "rule," according to Skinner (1969), is a special verbal behavior that allows extensive responding without direct exposure to established contingencies. The fact that children eventually come to speak in accordance with formal linguistic rules does not imply to Skinner that children's early speech is indeed rule-governed. Because young children cannot verbalize or make explicit the rules (e.g., "You add *-ed* to the verb stem to create past tense"), Skinner assumes that children's speech is not rule-governed, but directly shaped by the contingencies alone.

The basic processes of learning (i.e., classical and operant conditioning) are assumed to direct and control the increasing complexity of children's verbal behavior. While all these processes continue to function into adulthood, the accelerated rate of learning during childhood seems to require additional learning principles that facilitate the rapid acquisition of complex behaviors. Thus, behaviorists rely on imitation as an especially important factor in language learning, because it allows a short cut to mature behavior without laborious shaping of each and every verbal response. Imitation may be an exact copy of observed behavior, but it is not limited to exact copies (Bandura & Walters, 1963). Children may perform behaviors through imitation that only partially resemble the modeled behavior. Whitehurst and Vasta (1975) suggest that children can acquire grammatical frames through imitation, substituting their own words appropriate to the new context in which the utterance occurs. Nor is imitation limited to behaviors that follow modeled behavior closely in time; imitations may occur after a considerable delay. When children successfully imitate new words and forms, behaviorists assume that reinforcement occurs, either from adults or from the children themselves. The fact that the process of imitating in itself becomes reinforcing suggests that children will use imitation more frequently over time. Thus, imitation serves as a relatively flexible and frequently used learning strategy that enables rapid learning of complex language behaviors.

In summary, behaviorists focus on simple learning of stimulus–response associations. Language development is considered to be a problem of linking various stimuli in the environment to internal responses, and these internal responses to overt verbal behavior. Language development is viewed as a progression from random verbalizations to mature communication through the simultaneous application of classical and operant conditioning and imitation. The time it takes children to acquire language is seen as a limitation of the training techniques of the parents rather than maturation of the child. Moreover, behaviorists typically do not credit the child with knowledge of rules, with intentions or meaning, or with the ability to abstract important properties from the language environment. Rather, certain environmental stimuli evoke and strengthen certain responses in the child. The sequence of language acquisition, then, is determined primarily by which environmental stimuli are most salient at any point in time, and by the child's past experience with those stimuli. The learning principle of reinforcement, according to the behavioral approach, plays the major role in the process of language acquisition.

■ EVALUATION OF THE BEHAVIORAL APPROACH

SUPPORTING EVIDENCE

Many recent accounts of word meaning have shown that networks of interstimulus and stimulus–response associations of varying qualities and strength may be involved in semantics (Smith, 1978). The question remains, though, how are these associations learned initially, and are word meanings actually acquired through these associations? The behaviorists suggest that classical conditioning is primarily responsible. Staats, Staats, and Crawford (1962) asked adult subjects to learn a list of words, during which they received intermittent electric shocks. The words that preceded the shocks eventually came to be rated as unpleasant and generated emotional reactions similar to the shock itself. Staats (1971) argued that similar conditioning processes during the course of development are responsible for the differential reactions to words, such as *horror, ugly* and *disaster* versus *graceful, gift,* and *pretty.* Moreover, word stimuli may modify each other through occasional pairing. Staats and Staats (1957) paired nonsense syllables (GIW, WUH, etc.) with either pleasant or unpleasant words. Those syllables paired with the negative words (*ugly, bitter*) were rated significantly more unpleasant by college-aged subjects than those syllables paired with positive words (*beauty, gift*). Thus, the principles of classical conditioning may alter the meanings of words.

Behaviorists have explored the power of reinforcement to alter verbal behavior. Typically, as adults converse with an experimenter, the experimenter provides a verbal reinforcer (*good* or *umm-humm*) after the subject has emitted a response of the desired class. Usually, the rate of responding increases during the reinforcement phase, and drops when reinforcement ceases. Plural nouns, passive sentences, and relative pronouns are just a few of the verbal constructions that have been manipulated in this way (for a review, see Salzinger, 1959). Similar techniques involving shaping and reinforcement have also proven successful in some cases with retarded and autistic children (Lovaas, 1977; Sailor, 1971).

The effects of imitation have also been studied extensively by behaviorists (for a review, see Speidel & Nelson, 1989; Whitehurst & Vasta, 1975). These studies usually involve an adult model who uses particular grammatical forms in differing sentential contexts. Unfortunately, the simple provision of novel grammatical exemplars by adult models has not yielded convincing evidence that children will always learn the modeled form (Bandura & Harris, 1966; Liebert, Odum, Hill, & Huff, 1969). Whitehurst and Novak (1973) demonstrated new grammatical forms to children under two conditions. In the first condition, an adult simply modeled the target rule for the child. The second condition involved "imitation training," which encouraged the child to try to reproduce the form if imitation had not occurred spontaneously. Such imitation training is much more effective in getting the children to use the targeted linguistic rule in novel sentences.

Behaviorists often have trained adults in miniature artificial languages in attempts to model the processes involved in children's language learning. Palermo and Eberhart (1968) asked adults to learn a language of nonsense syllables with both regular and irregular forms. Mirroring the patterns of occurrence in English, the experimental language used the irregular forms more frequently than the regular forms. The pattern of adult acquisition of the experimental language parallelled children's progress in learning English, in that the adults began using the frequent irregular forms correctly until they learned the regular rules. After discovering the regular forms, the adults overgeneralized the regular rule to the irregular items. The authors concluded that children's overgeneralizations in language were due to typical learning patterns that result from the frequency of occurrence of the materials to be learned.

CONTRARY EVIDENCE

The problem with much of the above research concerns a very important distinction between changing levels of performance and acquiring new behaviors. Clearly, to increase adults' use of known grammatical structures is quite a different proposition from teaching children new grammatical rules. Thus, getting an adult to use more prepositions through verbal reinforcement (*umm-humm*) tells us little about how children originally come to use prepositions in the first place. Moreover, the adults in the Palermo and Eberhart (1968) study had extensive experience with the distributional frequencies of regular and irregular verb forms in English, which may have caused the similar patterns of acquisition. In other words, the behaviorists must test their assumptions and relationships in experiments on the subjects about whom they theorize, namely children. Further, they must search for evidence of their critical factors (e.g., shaping and reinforcement) in children's natural home environments.

If a factor proven to be effective in increasing learning in the lab does not exist in the child's natural environment, then that factor cannot be relied upon to explain language acquisition. Many researchers (McNeill, 1966; Pinker, 1984; Wexler & Culicover, 1980) have argued that children are not carefully shaped and tutored in the home, regardless of the effectiveness of these techniques in the lab. McNeill (1966) cited the following example as reflecting the importance of maturation in the acquisition process:

Child: Nobody don't like me
Mother: No. Say, "Nobody likes me."
Child: Nobody don't like me.
(Eight repetitions of the above)
Mother: Now listen carefully. Say, "Nobody likes me."
Child: Oh! Nobody don't likes me. (p. 69)

The failure of careful, patient tutoring is clear in this instance, but this evidence is only anecdotal. Further studies of naturally occurring conversations between children and parents have drawn similar conclusions from much more data. Several studies (Brown & Hanlon, 1970; Hirsh-Pasek, Treiman, & Schneiderman, 1984; Penner, 1987) found that parents do not verbally reward or praise their children for producing grammatically correct utterances, nor do they punish them for producing ungrammatical statements. Instead, these researchers found that parents were more likely to respond with praises such as "Right" or "Good" when the content of an utterance (the semantic relationships) was true, whether or not the utterance was syntactically appropriate. Parents were more likely to say "No" or "Wrong" when the semantic content of an utterance was false, even if it had been expressed in grammatically correct form.

The assumption that language is "just another behavior" is also seriously questioned. There is simply too much data to suggest that humans are uniquely constructed to detect language stimuli in the environment and process language information differently from other information. Condon and Sander (1974) found that newborns moved in synchrony with human voices but not with other sounds. Molfese (1977) found that the brains of newborns responded asymmetrically to speech and nonspeech stimuli. He reported greater left hemisphere responses to speech sounds and greater right hemisphere responses to nonspeech sounds. Last, human language behavior is clearly not sequentially organized such as the S-R chains used to explain other behaviors (Ervin-Tripp, 1971). Sequential Markov models cannot account for the hierarchical organization and recursive nature of sentences with multiple embedded clauses (McNeill, 1970). As Miller (1965) pointed out, the total number of possible sentences in a language is so great that it would be almost impossible to learn each one through association with a particular set of environmental stimuli.

In summary, the behavioral approach has belied its original promise of prediction and control of language behavior. Although language performance has been shown to be responsive to shaping in the lab, researchers are hard put to: (1) find clear instances of successful tutelage in the home, and (2) prove that children's language gains are equally susceptible to manipulation via reinforcement. One reason for this failure may be that behaviorists have rarely tested their assumptions in relevant contexts (i.e., with language-learning children in natural settings), thus making generalizations difficult or impossible. In spite of the major failures of the behavioral approach, it should be remembered that language acquisition is a form of behavioral change over time. As such, the study of language acquisition must incorporate some aspects of general learning mechanisms, which the behavioral approach has studied extensively. To totally neglect the learning approach would be tantamount to "throwing the baby out with the bathwater."

■ LINGUISTIC APPROACHES

GENERAL ASSUMPTIONS

All linguistic approaches assume that language has a structure or grammar that is somewhat independent of language use. This independent rule system determines the sentences that are "grammatical," or permissible in any particular language. Grammars consist of a finite set of rules, shared by all the speakers of that language, which allow the generation of an infinite set of mutually comprehensible sentences. The rules of grammar are not unlike the rules that govern mathematics (e.g., associativity, commutativity, etc.), which allow the solution of an infinite number of problems with a finite set of theorems. The grammatical rules described by linguists are simply descriptions of the regularities present in the language. All native speakers of a language are assumed to know these rules without being overtly taught, although they may not be aware of their knowledge. Language acquisition, according to this view, is largely a process of children discovering these regularities in their native language.

Chomsky (1957) argued that an adequate grammar must be generative or creative in order to account for the myriad of sentences that speakers can produce and understand. Adult speakers of any language can produce and understand sentences they have never said or heard before, simply by using a single grammatical rule and inserting various lexical items. Considering the large number of grammatical rules and the extensive vocabulary of most languages, the number of possible combinations is endless. The rules of the grammar must also account for the fact that speakers can produce sentences of (theoretically) unlimited length. Of course, speakers do not actually produce such sentences. Chomsky (1957) argued, however, that a true grammar should describe the speaker's knowledge of all permissible utterances (competence) rather than just the utterances typically produced (performance).

The grammar that Chomsky (1957, 1965, 1979, 1980, 1982) devised to account for these possibilities is known as *transformational generative grammar (TGG)*. TGG includes phrase structure rules, which specify the permissible constituent structures or elements of phrases. For example, $S \rightarrow NP + VP$ means that a sentence may be a noun phrase followed by a verb phrase. There are further rules specifying the elements of the noun phrase, the verb phrase, and so on. TGG also includes lexical insertion rules, which specify the semantic and phonological features of each lexical item in the vocabulary of the language, as well as the syntactic category to which they belong.

Lexical insertion rules essentially describe the restrictions on placement of lexical items into particular phrase elements. Lexical items from the appropriate syntactic category and with the appropriate features are placed into the nodes of a phrase structure "tree" diagram, resulting in a deep structure. These deep structures (also known as *remote, underlying,* and *conceptual structures*) may be further modified. Transformational rules, such as [move X] meaning move any part of the sentence to a new position, applied to the underlying structure produce various syntactic surface forms while retaining the meaning or intent of the original. For example, the passive form of [move X] may be applied to the string "She hit me" to produce "I was hit by her." The sentences that result after all transformational rules have been applied are called *surface structures*. The surface structure is the form that most closely resembles the actual utterance of a sentence. A single deep structure may be transformed into many different surface structures. Conversely, a single overt surface structure, such as, "She was killed by the river" may be interpreted (or produced from) two different deep structures (i.e., "The river killed her," or "Someone killed her near the river"). Thus, one of the most important tasks confronting the language-learning child is how to map meaning onto the ambiguous surface structure exemplars provided by the language environment (Gleitman & Wanner, 1982; Pinker, 1984).

Those following a linguistic approach maintain that language is innately human. Their argument is based upon several assumptions. First, language behavior is a species-specific behavior, unique to humans. Corollaries to this assumption are: (1) such behavior has a strong genetic basis, (2) patterns of language development will be similar across different languages and cultures, and (3) the environment should play a minor role in the maturation of language. The second assumption is that language is acquired quite rapidly, such that the speech of four-year-old children already resembles adult speech. Third, it is assumed that the language environment of the child does not provide sufficient data from which a complex, adult grammar could be discovered through known learning principles. These assumptions about the nature of language and the learning situation confronting children have profound implications. First, there is a "formal chasm between the input and output of language learning" (Pinker, 1987). In general, this means that what the child hears in speech is only indirectly related to the formal grammatical rules that are assumed to be the end product of language learning. If language learning consists of children forming a succession of hypotheses about these rules, there is simply too much ambiguity between different meanings and various surface structures for language to be learned. Second (and contrary to the behaviorists), linguists assume that children are never specifically taught the forms of language. Stated another way, children are never told which sentences are correct and incorrect, either in the speech they hear or through correction of their own productive errors (McNeill, 1970; Pinker, 1984, 1987; Wexler & Culicover, 1980; and many others).

LAD AND DEVELOPMENT

The innate language component has been defined as a **language acquisition device,** or **LAD** (Chomsky, 1965; Lenneberg, 1967), that bestows upon the child a host of information about grammatical classes, deep phrase structure, and possible transformations (McNeill, 1966, 1970). The LAD operates on the raw linguistic data in children's language to produce the particular abstract grammar of the children's native tongue. The LAD is assumed to be a physiological part of the brain that is a specialized language processor. Just as wings allow birds to fly, the LAD allows children enough innate knowledge of language to speak (Chomsky, 1979). The innate knowledge must consist of aspects of language that are universal to all languages. Since children initially have the capacity to learn any language, the properties of the LAD cannot be specific to any one tongue, such as English. The exact nature of the LAD and its attendant mechanisms is a matter of great debate.

In an early formulation, McNeill (1970) argued that children are innately endowed with "strong linguistic universals" such as the concepts of "sentence" and grammatical classes, and some aspects of phonology, all of which are necessary for the proper development of a grammar. More recently, others have confined the innate linguistic capacities to some inherent constraints and biases to treat the language environment in special ways. Children are regarded as "little cryptographers," who must employ their inherent knowledge of languages to decipher their mother tongue. As children are exposed to their native language, a series of linguistic "parameters" are set. For example, a child hearing English would be "set" to use word order to signal relations between words, whereas someone hearing Latin might be "set" to use word endings (inflections). Slobin (1979) describes the natural linguistic tendencies as "operating principles" that facilitate the acquisition of grammar. For example, Slobin argues that children "pay attention to the ends of words," which ensures that they will note grammatical morphemes that cause changes in word meaning, such as the addition of the morpheme *-s* to denote plurality. Another proposed operating principle is that "there are linguistic elements that encode relations between words." This principle argues that children know that separate words, when strung together, not only relate to the environment but also to each other. These two important operating principles, when taken together, should aid the child in decoding the relations between spoken strings of words and their deep structure meanings.

Obviously, the linguistic approach is biased toward the structural and nativist ends of the continuum. Linguists search for commonalities across children, cultures, and languages to discover the inherent organization that can be deduced from features that are universal to all languages. These universal features, it is suggested, are the innate structures upon which language is based. It should be noted here that the linguistic approach recognizes the need for experience with the language environment. However, this approach insists that the environment merely triggers the maturation of a physiologically based language system (LAD), or sets certain parameters, but does not shape or train verbal behavior. In addition, the linguistic approach favors competence over performance, although both concepts are considered acceptable topics of research. Competence is emphasized because it consistently reflects the formal organization of grammar, whereas children's performance is too susceptible to errors of attention, memory, and general processing problems irrelevant to the structure of language.

The child's task of acquiring a language, within this view, is made considerably simpler when certain critical aspects of the task are assumed to be present at birth within the LAD. Newborns immediately begin to detect the sounds in the environment that are linguistically significant. As their ability to control the articulatory mechanisms matures, they begin to produce only those sounds that have been present in their linguistic environment. This process may be facilitated by some innate imitative tendencies, through which the child automatically reproduces facial motor movements (lip and tongue configurations that correlate with different sounds) seen in adults (Field, Woodson, Greenberg, & Cohen, 1982). As the skills of phonetic production mature, children are simultaneously forming primitive, unlabeled concepts for referents in their environment, such as milk (Golinkoff, Hirsh-Pasek, Bailey, & Wenger, 1992; Nelson, 1981). At some point, the child may hear an adult say, "Do you want some milk?" and conclude that *milk* is the label that refers to the primitive concept of milk, even though this word was not taught specifically. The reason that the word *milk* was chosen by the child to represent the concept, rather than the other words in the string, is that the child possesses mechanisms for categorizing words into appropriate grammatical classes. In other words, children can, almost automatically, differentiate nouns from verbs by their differing patterns of usage in adult speech.

Many have speculated that children are particularly sensitive to commonalities in usage and meaning (Pinker, 1984, 1989). For example, nouns usually refer to things, and verbs to actions or relations. Moreover, these classes of words, things versus acts, tend to occur in predictable combinations with other words. Thus, the word "snurt" used in the medial position in the sentence, "He snurt himself" conveys considerable information about the permissible uses of the word in other sentences, such as "Can I snurt the bread?" or "I snurted until my brains fell out." These critical combinatorial cues may also derive from examples of how the word combines with grammatical morphemes, such as *-ed,* usually meaning that the root is a verb (Landau & Gleitman, 1985; Maratsos & Chalkley, 1980; Pinker, 1991). This may be an example of one of the mechanisms responsible for Slobin's (1979) second operating principle that searches for linguistic elements that encode changes in meaning.

Children move rapidly from the acquisition of their first word to the realization that "everything has a name" (Dore, 1978; McShane, 1979; Stern, 1930), which leads to great increases in vocabulary size. In spite of the fact that children now know many words, they use only one word per utterance during this stage. Although each word occurs in isolation, the linguistic approach assumes that each word is governed by grammatical relations or rules. That is, each word constitutes a sentence, and is assumed to be a direct expression of children's intentions or deep structure. The child does not string more words together in this stage only because of performance limitations, such as memory or attentional factors. The child's notion of a hierarchically organized sentence structure is further differentiated over time into noun phrases, verb phrases, etc. Thus, children move from the one-word stage to two words at a time to multiword utterances by testing their own evolving grammars against the data provided by the environment. Some have called this process *hypothesis testing* to highlight the child's active role in the acquisition of syntactic rules.

There is considerable disagreement within the linguistic approach relating to the actual grammars children use over the course of development. Some (Gleitman &

Wanner, 1982; Wexler, 1982) insist that there must be continuity in grammatical structures, with an eye to the target—adult grammar the child will eventually use. Others (Bloom, 1970; Bowerman, 1982; Pinker, 1984, 1987, 1989) argue that children's grammars undergo reorganization as increasing linguistic sophistication proves immature grammars inadequate. The argument does not seem to concern the fact that grammars change over time, but exactly what forms the grammar attains at any one time. Gleitman and Wanner (1982) insist that the grammar must always be some primitive subset of adult grammar. In contrast, Bowerman (1982) holds that the earlier grammatical structures may be qualitatively quite different from more mature forms. As previously stated, there is a considerable gap between what children hear and the abstract rules of grammar that are assumed to govern adult language. Early versions of language may have nothing to do with grammatical relations such as "subject of sentence," but instead may rely on the semantic properties of the words, such as *actor—action—acted upon.* The meanings of the words themselves may allow children to gain an initial toehold into a more abstract grammatical system (see Pinker, 1987, 1989).

■ EVALUATION OF THE LINGUISTIC APPROACH

SUPPORTING EVIDENCE

Research supporting the linguistic approach has essentially followed two lines, one supporting the concept of grammatical rules and the other searching for evidence of innate linguistic characteristics in humans. The former attempts to back up Chomsky's (1957, 1965) distinction between underlying structure and the overt surface structure. Besides the intuition that underlying structures are necessary to account for ambiguous sentences, some empirical data have been sought to confirm the existence of grammatical structures.

Several classic studies (Clifton & Odum, 1966; Savin & Perchonock, 1965) demonstrated that simple sentences more closely approximating base structures were processed more quickly and were easier to recognize than more complex, transformed sentences. For example, in early versions of Chomsky's TGG, the passive sentence was considered to be more complex than the active, because it involved at least one transformation. Thus, a passive sentence should be psychologically more complex, and take longer to process for comprehension, which was confirmed by a number of studies (e.g., Gough, 1965, 1966; Slobin, 1966). Sachs (1967) found that regardless of the surface form of a sentence, only the baselike meaning of the sentence was remembered, suggesting that subjects somehow transform surface structures back into deep structure in order to comprehend sentences. Lastly, in two studies, if subjects heard a "click" while processing a sentence, they perceived the sound as having occurred at the nearest constituent boundary, regardless of when it actually occurred (Fodor & Bever, 1965; Garret, Bever, & Fodor, 1966). Thus it appears that perception of sentences is determined by the principles of syntactic organization (parsing into constituents) that linguists have described. Taken together, the above research suggests that comprehending a sentence consists of actively processing the hierarchical sentence structure to determine the major syntactic units, and deriving the transformations of those structures to attain the base structure meaning (Bock, 1982).

Evidence of the emergence of linguistic rules was also sought in children's spontaneous speech, primarily using longitudinal, in-depth observations of small numbers of children. (For an extensive review of these studies, see Brown, 1973.) Many focused on the phenomenon of overregularization, defined as the inappropriate application of a grammatical rule. For example, a child might say, "I taked a cookie." This utterance may be taken as evidence that the child knows the rule for the formation of past tense for regular verbs (add *-ed* to the root), and has overapplied this rule to irregular forms. Brown and Bellugi (1964) concluded that children must be inducing the latent structure of language since they could never have heard these errors in adult speech. Moreover, many studies have found evidence of similar rule use in children from a wide range of languages and cultures, including Finnish (Bowerman, 1973), Turkish (Slobin, 1982), Russian (Slobin, 1966), and Japanese (Hakuta, 1977). The orderly patterns of rule appearance in these varied contexts and cultures resembled the simple maturation of motoric development (Lenneberg, 1967).

The cross-cultural or cross-linguistic perspective also has proven to be a rich source of data concerning the biological basis of language (Slobin, 1986). Because the LAD is assumed to function in all children, it must allow the acquisition of any language (Pinker, 1984, 1989), so similar patterns of development across several languages are taken as evidence of the LAD's operation. Slobin (1982) found that young children use subject–object word order, regardless of the order used by mature speakers of their native language, and thus it may be a universal. McNeill (1966) argues that the LAD also allows children to presuppose the existence of grammatical classes, such as nouns, verbs, etc., because these classes are common to all languages and are acquired relatively early in development. Other "innate" language biases may take the form of Slobin's principles such as "look at the ends of words." Kuczaj (1979) taught children an artificial language which either encoded grammatical information in word suffixes or prefixes, and found that children learned the suffix cues more readily.

The surprising abilities of infants to perceive relevant acoustic dimensions may also bolster the maturational view of language development. Many studies (for reviews, see Eimas, 1974; Molfese, Molfese, & Carrell, 1982; Morse, 1974) document categorical perception of consonants and vowels within months of birth. Molfese (1977) even found that infants' brains responded asymmetrically to language sounds versus nonlanguage sounds. Thus, children seem to be especially sensitive to the sounds characteristic of human language and quickly achieve adultlike sound discrimination abilities. Moreover, the early patterns of babbling in infancy are comparable over many languages and situations.

Further support for the nativistic position comes from two additional sources. First, the available data on "wild children" suggests that language may indeed have a critical period, after which acquisition becomes difficult or impossible (Lenneberg, 1967). Recent studies of Genie, who was almost totally deprived of linguistic input until age 13, show that she still has not acquired syntax after years of intensive training, even though her semantic (and cognitive) development has advanced normally (Curtiss,

1981). Studies of cerebral lateralization show that post-pubescent damage to the left hemisphere frequently results in severe language deficits, whereas earlier left hemisphere damage typically results in much less serious language problems (Springer & Deutsch, 1981). It is presumed that before puberty, the right hemisphere may take over the functions of the left if damage occurs, whereas after puberty lateralization is complete. Second, those concerned with the species-specificity of language have determined that only humans have the ability to create and understand potentially infinite combinations of linguistic symbols (Terrace & Bever, 1976). The communication systems of other animals are thought to be stimulus-bound and not generative or creative (Umiker-Sebeok & Sebeok, 1980).

Some linguists have tried to test the formal learnability of certain grammars, much as mathematicians test the adequacy of a set of axioms in proving a theorem. Learnability theorists (Pinker, 1984, 1989; Wexler & Cullicover, 1980) reason that if languages are acquired by learning syntactic rules, then those rules must be learnable or, in some sense, discoverable from the raw linguistic data provided by the environment. Their basic assumption is that the sample strings of words that children hear are all positive exemplars or "true" instances of permissible constructions, and they are given no information about unacceptable strings. This type of learning situation is called *text presentation* (Gold, 1967). Wexler (1982) argued that there are many possible alternative hypotheses or rules that could account for the language the child hears. Pinker, Lebeaux, and Frost (1987) found that when children are presented with syntactic rules, they usually generalize them, resulting in overregularization. Without any information concerning their errors, children would never arrive at the correct rules, so some rules must be innate, or some alternatives must be ruled out *a priori*. The general conclusion, given the assumption of text presentation, is that grammar is unlearnable through any known principles, and must largely be innately programmed.

CONTRARY EVIDENCE

Ironically, the same assumptions thought to be the strong points of the linguistic approach in the 1960s have recently been the targets of serious criticism. A major tenet of the "standard" theory of generative grammar developed by Chomsky (1957, 1965) was that grammars are made up of abstract categories that are only distantly related to surface structures and meaning. At first, this was viewed as a milestone, because a context-free grammar was seen as being much more flexible and useful across situations and languages. Gradually, though, this idea began to bother those who could not imagine grammar or language as anything else besides the mapping of meaning onto an acoustic code (Bates & Snyder, 1985; Pinker, 1984, 1989). A theory of language that was so far removed from meaning, and from the child's actual performance, began to seem irrelevant to the task of explaining the known facts of language acquisition. Many now view Chomsky's original TGG as an inadequate treatment of semantics (Pinker, 1984, 1989). As evidence accumulates that the major part of language acquisition involves semantic, not just syntactic, processes, this becomes an especially damaging flaw in the traditional linguistic approach (see Maratsos, 1983; Pinker, 1984, 1989, for thoughtful discussions of this issue).

To circumvent the problems noted with Chomsky's original TGG, many other grammars have been developed. Currently there are at least four competing generative grammars (Fodor, 1977), and a few grammars based upon semantics (Fillmore, 1968; Katz, 1972; Pinker, 1984, 1989). Instead of solving the problems, however, the fact that so many different descriptions of adult grammar exist has created more problems. Which of these grammars are children supposedly acquiring? Moerk (1989) suggests that if linguists, after extensive training, cannot adequately or consistently describe the grammar of English, then it is quite unlikely that young children are acquiring formalized grammars at all. The problem is exacerbated by some linguists' excessive adherence to the concept of competence that discards much of the data from adults and children as irrelevant to linguistic theory (e.g., Bever, 1982). Many now agree that because linguistic grammars do not correspond well to processes observed in language performance (Palermo, 1978), these grammars are untestable as psychological theories.

Whether TGG has any "psychological validity" has been seriously questioned. Early studies seemed to suggest that surface structures that had been transformed were more difficult to process than their corresponding underlying structures, and that sentences were stored in a form similar to deep structure. However, there are many problems in concluding that either deep structure or transformational rules are actually used in comprehension or production. For example, the early studies that found that passive sentences took longer to verify than active sentences were based on the earlier versions of Chomsky's TGG. Later versions of TGG assumed that passive and active sentences are equally complex, and later studies have provided support for this idea, directly contradicting the earlier results. Moreover, a study by Olson and Filby (1972) demonstrated that passive sentences are sometimes more easily processed than active sentences, depending on the context. Many (e.g., Glucksberg & Danks, 1969; Matthews, 1968) have since shown that nonlinguistic, performance factors (e.g., sentence length, delay between presentation and recognition test) may have accounted for the earlier results. Due to such conflicting results, and the fact that the numerous existing generative grammars have markedly different assumptions about the nature of underlying structure, the attempt to verify its psychological validity has been largely abandoned.

A similar problem exists with Wexler's (1982; Wexler & Culicover, 1980) formal test of the "learnability" of the standard generative grammar (i.e., Chomsky's). Any of a number of alternative grammars, such as those mentioned above, might have proven to be more learnable. Rather than concluding that grammar is by nature unlearnable (Wexler, 1982), it is just as likely that the grammar tested was a false description of language. Wexler and his colleagues (Wexler & Culicover, 1980; Wexler, Culicover, & Hamburger, 1975) further assumed several unlikely axiomatic conditions for his formal theorem test. They postulated that children parse their language environment into sentences as minimum units, despite the fact that infants can detect the acoustic cues of clause boundaries in sentences (Hirsh-Pasek et al., 1987). This sensitivity to units within sentences makes sentence structure more transparent and learnable to the listening child (Garnica, 1978; Hirsh-Pasek et al., 1987). Moerk (1989) further suggests that the most informative unit is not the sentence, but relations or contrasts between utterances. Moreover, concluding that grammar is not learned through any known principles is not equivalent to concluding that it is innate. Pinker (1984) calls this the *poverty of imagination* postulate, meaning that just because someone cannot imagine how a particular behavior might have been learned, it does not necessarily follow that it was not learned (is innate).

Probably the most damaging point to the linguistic approach concerns the assumption of text learning or the lack of negative evidence (Gold, 1967; Pinker, 1984, 1989; Wexler & Culicover, 1980). This postulate is so central to learnability theory that it may be the "smoking gun" (Moerk, 1989; Pinker, 1984, 1989). If children are provided any information at all about the acceptability of sentences in their language, then the elaborate arguments of learnability fall apart. Several recent reports have clearly questioned the negative evidence issue.

Hirsh-Pasek, Treiman, and Schneiderman (1984) found that the mothers of two-year-olds were much more likely to repeat and expand children's ungrammatical utterances than well-formed utterances. Two further studies (Demetras, Post, & Snow, 1986; Penner, 1987) found that parents were also more likely to question children after a grammatical error than a well-formed utterance. Last, Bohannon and Stanowicz (1988) examined both parents and nonparents conversing with children. They found over 90 percent of adult exact imitations followed children's well-formed speech, whereas over 70 percent of adults' recasted or expanded imitations followed children's language errors. In this study, the adults, both parents and nonparents, rarely reproduced a child's language error; instead, children's language errors were *changed* into correct alternative forms and presented immediately following the child's error, especially when the child's utterance contained solitary versus multiple language errors. Perhaps children can only deal with one error at a time. For example, in McNeill's (1970) "Nobody don't like me" anecdote, the interaction terminates with the child correcting a single grammatical contrast (see previous section). Bohannon and Stanowicz (1988, 1989) and others (Farrar, 1987, 1992; Furrow & Moore, 1991; Sokolov, 1991) also report that children are more likely to imitate their parent's recasts and expansions than any other utterances. Thus, children seem to be sensitive to the adult responses that follow their errors. In summary, the most basic assumption of the linguistic approach seems to be false. Adults do respond differentially to well-formed versus ill-formed child utterances, and children, in turn, respond to the adult's feedback.

Some of the other assumptions of the linguistic approach also seem to be false. Language does not develop as rapidly as had been supposed (McNeill, 1966), as the acquisition of complex rules (e.g., relative clauses) and the subtleties of syntax continues well past age four and possibly through adulthood (Chomsky, 1969; Menyuk, 1977). Furthermore, no neurological basis for such rapid early development and slower to nonexistent later developments (i.e., the critical period notion) has been clearly identified. Recent studies indicate that language lateralization occurs fairly early and not during adolescence (Molfese, Molfese, & Carrell, 1982), and that languages can be learned after adolescence (e.g., Krashen, 1975). Last, Chomsky's (1979) assertion that human language is due to a species-specific structure (LAD), is controversial. As described in Chapter 1, chimpanzees and gorillas have learned a variety of communication systems. Depending upon one's definition of language, then, there is research to support either a species-specific argument or the position that human language is merely one end of a continuum of symbolic communication (Bohannon, 1982; Marler, 1977).

The linguistic approach has generally minimized the effects of differing language environments. Taken to its extreme (e.g., Bever, Fodor, & Weksel, 1965), this view suggests that the LAD could construct a grammar from any kind of linguistic textual presentation, no matter how abstract, complex, or errorful. However, children exposed to language only through the medium of television do not learn a language (Sachs & Johnson, 1972).

Probably the most dangerous tendency, which appears all too frequently in the linguistic approach, is an excessive willingness to resort to the innateness explanation without giving serious consideration to alternative hypotheses. As pointed out earlier, this may be due to a "poverty of imagination." Many researchers (e.g., Gleitman, Newport, & Gleitman, 1984; Goldin-Meadow, 1982; Goldin-Meadow & Feldman, 1977; Hoff-Ginsberg & Shatz, 1982; Landau & Gleitman, 1985; Shatz, 1982) are quick to accept the "null hypothesis," gravitating to nativistic biases whenever any environmental factor appears not to have an effect upon children's language, although there could be many other explanations for such findings (Bohannon & Warren-Leubecker, 1988; Moerk, 1989; Whitehurst, 1982).

■ INTERACTIONIST APPROACHES

GENERAL ASSUMPTIONS

If the behavioristic and linguistic approaches are radical complements on the ends of each theoretical continuum, then the interactionist might be considered a moderate compromise. This approach recognizes and often accepts the more powerful arguments from both camps. Interactionists, as the name implies, assume that many factors (e.g., social, linguistic, maturational/biological, cognitive, etc.) affect the course of development, and that these factors are mutually dependent upon, interact with, and modify one another. Not only may cognitive or social factors modify language acquisition, but language acquisition will in turn modify the development of cognitive and social skills (Vygotsky, 1962). Thus, not only are these variables interactive, the causal relationships among them are reciprocal.

There are three basic types of interactive approaches. First, the cognitive theory of Jean Piaget has a number of important implications for the development of language. Second, our growing knowledge of human cognition (perception, problem solving, memory) has encouraged applications of the information processing paradigm to language behavior. We will focus on one of the newer cognitive models, the so-called *competition model* (Bates & MacWhinney, 1987). Finally, the fact that language acquisition emerges from and develops within social interaction demands that social factors be explored as causal candidates in language development.

PIAGET'S COGNITIVE APPROACH

The cognitive theory of Jean Piaget shares many important features with the traditional linguistic account of language acquisition. Both emphasize internal structures as the

Jean Piaget.

ultimate determinants of behavior. They also agree upon the basic nature of language, as a symbolic system for the expression of intention or meaning. The distinctions between competence and performance, and between underlying (deep) structure and surface structure, are typically retained by cognitive researchers. In spite of these similarities, there are also some major theoretical differences between the two. Most important is Piaget's assumption that language *per se* is not a separate innate characteristic, but is rather only one of several abilities that result from cognitive maturation. According to Piaget (1954), language is structured or constrained by reason; basic linguistic developments must be based upon or derived from even more basic, general changes in cognition (Bates & Snyder, 1985). The sequence of cognitive development, then, determines the sequence of language development.

In 1975, Piaget and Chomsky met and debated the issue of nativism in language, with Chomsky asserting that the general mechanisms of cognitive development cannot account for the abstract, complex, and language-specific structures of language. Moreover, he stated (as discussed previously) that the linguistic environment is also unable to account for the structures that appear in children's language. Therefore, language, or at least aspects of linguistic rules and structure, must be innate. Piaget, on the other hand, insisted that the complex structures of language might be neither innate nor learned. Instead, these structures emerge as a result of the continuing interaction between the child's current level of cognitive functioning and her current linguistic, and nonlinguistic, environment. This interactive approach is known as *constructivism* as opposed to strict nativism or empiricism. Bates and Snyder (1985) explain that the resulting structure in language may not resemble either the structure of external reality or the structure of the simple, innate cognitive schemas with which the child began exploring his environment. Instead, the structure is:

> an inevitable emergent solution to a series of interactions. Because that structure is inevitable, it does not have to be innate. There is no reason for nature to waste perfectly good genes on an outcome that is going to happen anyway. Applied to language, this approach suggests that the semantic and grammatical structures of language are the inevitable set of solutions to the problem of mapping certain non-linguistic, cognitive meanings and social intentions onto the highly constrained linguistic channel, and vice-versa. (Bates & Snyder, 1985)

Another, related point of contention between traditional linguistic and cognitive interactionist approaches is the data which each regard as relevant to the explanation of child language acquisition. Whereas both approaches preserve a distinction between competence and performance, typically linguists insist that performance factors are simply annoying complications. To Piagetians, on the other hand, performance "limitations" provide some of the most useful data. The child's cognitive capacities are assumed to be qualitatively, as well as quantitatively different from those of adults. Thus, the different way in which the child reasons about the world will affect the way in which she approaches the language acquisition task. Children's linguistic performance, including their errors, may reveal not only their knowledge of the structure of language, but also the structure of their knowledge. The cognitive constraints and abilities that determine linguistic performance are assumed to be the same that underlie the child's language competence as well.

To illustrate the relationship between cognitive and linguistic developments, we will examine the earliest stage of Piaget's (1954) account of intellectual development. In this account, the infancy period (from birth to approximately 18 months or two years of age) is described as the stage of sensory-motor intelligence. This stage is assumed to be prelinguistic, since children have not yet begun to use symbols to represent objects in their environment. According to Piaget, sensory-motor children understand the world only through direct sensation of it (sensory) and the activities they perform upon it (motor). These children do not yet recognize the separate existence of objects, apart from their own direct experience of them. Objects that are out of sight are also out of mind, ceasing to exist as soon as they are not in the child's immediate perceptual environment. During the second year of life, children establish the concept of object permanence, understanding that objects have a permanence and an identity apart from their own perception of them.

Sinclair-deZwart (1969) argued that children in the sensory-motor stage have no need for symbols to represent objects in the environment, since the objects are either present, hence serving as their own referents, or they are totally absent and nonexistent for the child. Once object permanence is achieved, the child may begin to use symbols to represent objects that are no longer present, and these symbols become the child' first true words. In this view, then, object permanence is a necessary precursor for language acquisition.

Similarly, other cognitive developments are assumed to occur before they are reflected in the child's linguistic skills. For example, children's first word combinations have been posited to be dependent upon the child's perception of semantic relations among objects and people in the world (Bowerman, 1973, 1982). With the realization that animate beings typically act upon inanimate things, the child then combines the symbols for these concepts in a similar fashion. Thus the child's first grammar is composed of semantic classes, with animate actors (subject) followed by actions (verb), and inanimate acted-upons (object). It is only later in the course of development that the more abstract grammatical classes of subjects, predicates, noun phrases, verb phrases, etc., are formed through the reorganization of the more primitive semantic categories. This linguistic reorganization is assumed to reflect an underlying restructuring of cognitive schemas.

In summary, the Piagetian cognitive approach suggests that language is only an expression of a more general set of human cognitive activities. Proper development of the cognitive system is considered a necessary precursor of linguistic expression. The major task facing the cognitive interactionist, then, is to identify the sequence of cognitive maturation, and to explain how these cognitive developments are reflected in language acquisition.

■ EVALUATION OF THE COGNITIVE PERSPECTIVE

SUPPORTING EVIDENCE

The cognitive approach has sought evidence that some basic cognitive concepts precede the expression of those concepts in language. Early linguistic attainments do correlate with many nonlinguistic measures, such as symbolic play with objects, imitation of gestures and sounds, and aspects of problem solving through tool use (for reviews, see

Bates et al., 1979; Bates & Snyder, 1985; Corrigan, 1978). Bates (1976) found that children's first words typically occurred after the realization that other people may serve as agents. As discussed previously, Sinclair-deZwart (1973) suggested that development of the object concept should precede the child's first words. As a general rule, this does not appear to be the case. However, there is a growing body of evidence (Corrigan, 1978; Gopnik, 1984; Gopnik & Meltzoff, 1984, 1986, 1987; Halpern & Aviezer, 1976) that more specific cognitive attainments do correlate with particular linguistic milestones. For example, the development of "disappearance" words (e.g., *allgone*) is related to object permanence, "success and failure" terms (e.g., *There!, uh-oh*) appear around the same time as means-end understanding (solving problems through insight rather than trial and error), and certain ways of categorizing or grouping objects, which develop around 18 months of age, appear to coincide with the "naming explosion" (the precipitous increase of referential words in children's vocabularies).

Nonlinguistic accomplishments related to later stages of language acquisition also have been demonstrated. Corrigan (1978) discovered that the appearance of two-word combinations was related to Piaget's final level of sensory-motor intelligence. Others (e.g., Branigan, 1979; Case, 1980; Fenson & Ramsey, 1980) report that children begin joining two or more words into a single intonational contour, or two or more gestures into single, planned motor units around age 20 months. Further, Shore, O'Connell, and Bates (1984) found significant correlations between multiword speech and multischeme gestures. Taken together, these results indicate that the transition from one-word to multiword speech is part of a more general shift toward "chunking" and the planning of higher order motor schemes (Bates et al., 1983).

The work of Slobin (1979) and others (e.g., Block & Kessel, 1980) further suggests that the acquisition of a particular productive morpheme (e.g., tense or plural markers) follows the child's understanding of the semantic properties that the morpheme encodes. In other words, children do not grammatically mark relationships in their spontaneous productive speech until they know the concept that the marker denotes. On this basis, Slobin (1982) suggests that new functions are first expressed in old forms and new forms first express old functions. For example, children must first grasp the primitive concept of past before they will talk about past events using old forms (e.g., "the other day" to refer to a displacement in time), and after this they may use the new form (e.g., past-tense markers to the main verb). A related argument (Bowerman, 1982; Sinclair-deZwart, 1973) suggests that cognitive-semantic categories of agent, action, and patient more adequately describe early sentences than the strict syntactic forms of subject, verb, and object. Bates et al. (1983) concluded that children use cognitively based meanings to decipher the grammatical code in their language. Indeed, early grammars based upon cognitive-semantic categories seem to be the strongest asset of the cognitive-interactionist approach (Pinker, 1984, 1989).

CONTRARY EVIDENCE

The cognitive-interactionist approach avoids many of the problems inherent in the extreme nativistic position, by assuming that language in and of itself is not innate, but that nonlinguistic, cognitive precursors of language are. However, there are several other criticisms that may be levelled at the Piagetian cognitive view. Many of the studies relating cognitive and language development implicitly assume that abilities that emerge at the same point in development (e.g., first words and object permanence) share underlying cognitive mechanisms. In addition, positive correlations between cognitive and linguistic achievements are often taken as reflections of causal relationships. As Curtiss (1981) and others (Newport, Gleitman, & Gleitman, 1977) have pointed out, age-related correlations and codevelopments occur frequently, such as first molar teeth appearing around the time of first words, yet such co-occurrences are rarely assumed to be causally related. A better method of sorting out these relations is to identify cognitive achievements that always precede particular linguistic attainments. Then, if any child develops the linguistic skill without also displaying the supposedly prerequisite cognitive skill, the hypothesis would be clearly disproven. Unfortunately, as Bates and Snyder (1985) point out, such clear negative instances are nearly impossible to find given current measurement limitations; thus, we resort to comparing the probabilities that A leads to B versus B leads to A, which is still only weak evidence for a causal interpretation. Moreover, there are certain developments that always precede others (e.g., teething precedes puberty), yet, as Bates and Snyder (1985) point out, is one necessary for the onset of the other?

The best method to test for causal connections between cognition and language would be experimental manipulations of the assumed prerequisite cognitive skills to look for effects on linguistic skills. In an extensive review of the literature, Bates and Snyder (1985) identified only one such study. Steckol and Leonard (1981) trained children in various Piagetian cognitive skills, and this training did facilitate gestural communication. However, we should be cautious in generalizing these results to language-learning children within their ordinary environments. Is this particular cognitive skill truly necessary for language development, or just helpful? Moreover, is it possible that training in the linguistic skill might have produced corresponding improvement in the cognitive skill, rather than vice versa? In fact, Vygotsky (1962) might argue for this latter position; that linguistic attainments often predate corresponding cognitive concepts, as language development proceeds according to the move from external to internal, private speech.

Gopnik and Meltzoff (1984, 1986, 1987), as advocates of the "specificity hypothesis," avoid some of these pratfalls by simply asserting that children learn specific words related to the very specific cognitive problems that interest them at any point in time. They do not attempt to answer the chicken or egg question—"Which came first?"—but focus on the fact that certain cognitive and linguistic events do coincide.

Finally, the work of Curtiss and her colleagues (Curtiss, 1977, 1981; Curtiss & Yamada, 1978; Curtiss, Yamada, & Fromkin, 1979) has identified situations in which language and cognitive skills may be separable. Children with Turner's syndrome score quite poorly on cognitive tasks yet exhibit normal language skills. The case study of Genie suggests that semantic and cognitive development are parallel (both were proceeding normally with training), but syntax and morphology are quite different (these were delayed). In other cases, syntax and morphology are normal or even advanced, whereas semantic development lags, apparently due to cognitive disabilities. Thus,

Curtiss (1981) argues that acquisition of syntax and morphology must be somewhat independent of other cognitive developments. More recently, Bates (1986) and others (e.g., Newport, 1986) have suggested that after infancy and early childhood, during which cognitive and linguistic development proceed more or less in tandem, they begin to take different paths. Although these case studies of abnormal language development cannot provide compelling counter evidence, they should caution us against making general, sweeping statements about the cognitive bases of language acquisition.

In summary, the broad assertion that cognitive development determines language development remains virtually untested. Despite an abundance of correlational evidence, methodological problems prevent a clear causal interpretation of the data. However, the studies so far indicate that continued research efforts attempting to explicate the relations between cognition and language will be even more rewarding.

INFORMATION PROCESSING APPROACH

One of the newest cognitive approaches to language learning is derived from the information processing paradigm. This paradigm is common in experiments on human memory, perception, and problem solving. In essence, the human information processing system is viewed as a mechanism that encodes stimuli from the environment, operates on interpretations of those stimuli, stores in memory representations of stimuli and results of operations on them, and allows retrieval of information stored. As previously stated, one way of approaching language learning is to ascertain the nature of mature language use and then backtrack developmentally to see how such a system might develop (Gleitman & Wanner, 1982). There is considerable extant evidence about the nature of adult language processing and memory (Bock, 1982), and this approach views children, however naive and primitive they may be, as qualitatively similar to adults. Simply put, children are information processors in transition from novices to skilled processors of linguistic information.

Although there are several new information processing approaches to language, we will focus on one of these, known as the *competition model* (Bates & MacWhinney, 1987; MacWhinney, 1987). This model emphasizes both structure and function in learning language, but in a novel way. Specifically, the functions are communicative devices, such as establishing topicality, requesting, and identifying location. The structures are language mechanisms that produce strings of spoken words that encode those communicative functions. To a certain extent, structure and function are opposite sides of the same language coin. As Bates and MacWhinney (1987) argue, the structure emerges from the communicative function the structure serves. "The idea that grammars routinely . . . spawn forms that play no role in facilitating communication is foreign to . . . the position" (p. 160). In a similar way, information processing models, such as the competition model, are meant to exclusively address language performance rather than competence. But it is their position that the same structures that produce language performance at any point in time, even during development, are the same structures that allow the linguists to make grammatical judgments (competence). Thus, although this approach explicitly models language performance, it may also account for the nature of linguistic competence.

Before further elaborating on the details of the competition model, it will be necessary to understand the difference between two basic types of information processing. In *serial processing,* decisions or operations are performed one at a time, sequentially, whereas in *parallel processing,* multiple operations may occur simultaneously. The linguistic approach discussed previously relies largely on serial processing, in that deep structure relations are formulated first, prior to application of transformations (e.g., passive, question, etc.), which are also performed in order. Moreover, current conceptions of the linguistic approach suggest that innate linguistic parameters such as word order versus inflections are set sequentially through exposure (see Pinker, 1989).

More recent cognitive approaches employ parallel processing. In parallel processing, networks of processors are mutually linked or connected such that many operations or decisions may proceed concurrently. These networks have come to be called *parallel distributed processors,* or PDPs for short (McClelland & Rummelhart, 1987). An example of a PDP network is shown in Figure 7.1. PDP models consist of a series of processing units, called *activation nodes.* These are meant to resemble or model individual neurons or assemblies of neurons in the brain. Each unit is connected to other units by pathways that vary in the "strength" of their connections. These pathways are meant to model the dendrites and axons that connect neurons in the brain. The strength of the connections is seen as reflecting the extent of a neural connection, the number of axon terminals, dendritic spines, etc. Activation nodes, like neurons, are decision mechanisms. They receive input from other nodes across pathways of varying strength, weigh the input, and "decide" whether or not to activate. This is seen as similar to the process by which neurons sum all incoming signals and "fire" or not depending upon the amount of stimulation. If sufficient input has occurred across the pathways, the unit may activate itself, thus sending activating information out its own output pathways to other nodes.

What is important to understand about such PDP systems is that even though they are computer models, they do "learn." That is, when confronted with a pattern of input (e.g., words in Figure 7.1), they generate an output (e.g., the past tense of the word in Figure 7.1), which may be correct or incorrect. When the correct output occurs, the system does not change itself; when the output is wrong, the pathways leading to activated units within the network are decreased in strength and pathways leading to inactive units are increased in strength. Thus, unlike typical computer models that have to have preprogrammed correct answers and algorithms, PDP models are "taught" the correct answers over time. Researchers rarely know beforehand how the network of units will configure themselves in order to arrive at the right answers. For example, some networks are presented with pairs of names as input (e.g., Bill and Martha) and it must guess at their familial relationship as the output (Martha is Bill's sister, aunt, grandmother, etc.). As more and more names are presented along with their correct relations, the network will start to get its answers right more often. In the final stages of learning, the network will correctly guess relations that it was never presented, for example when presented with "Bill is Martha's brother," and "Bill is Ted's grandfather," the network will correctly conclude that "Martha is Ted's great aunt." When the individual nodes are examined, sometimes a network such as this will have a "gender detector" node that turns on in the presence of a female and stays off

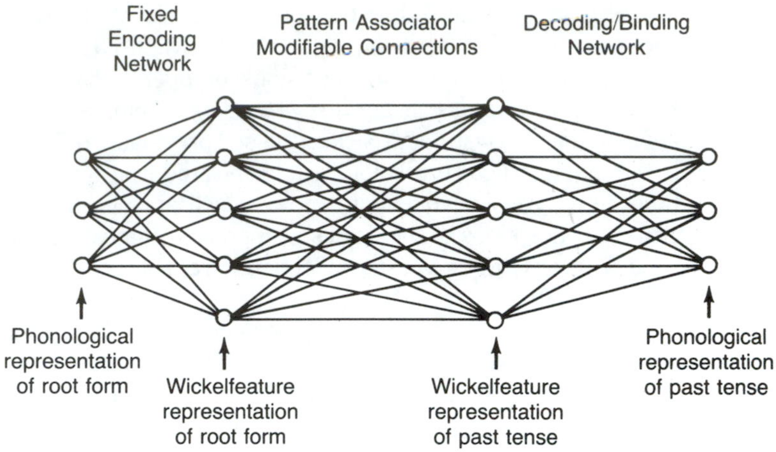

FIGURE 7.1 The basic structure of the model (from *"Learning the Past Tense of English Verbs: Implicit Rules or Parallel Distributed Processing" [P. 201] by D. Rummelhart & J. McClelland, 1987, in B. MacWhinney (Ed.),* Mechanisms of Language Acquisition, *Hillsdale, NJ: Erlbaum. Reprinted by permission.)*

in the presence of a male relationship. Other times, networks have generated unusual nodes, such as units that activate only in the presence of a two-generation maternal relation (i.e., a "grandmother detector"!). These networks are sometimes called *dynamical systems* because the patterns of their connection strengths can vary so widely over the course of learning.

Figure 7.1 shows a network used by McClelland and Rummelhart (1987) to learn the past tense of English verbs. Information concerning the pattern of sounds that make up a present tense verb (e.g., *eat*) would be fed to the earliest input level (far left in Figure 7.1). The resulting pattern of activation (decisions of each node) is passed to an associator network (the middle set of units in Figure 7.1). At the pattern associator level, these activation patterns are known by the curious name of *wickelfeatures* (which are abstract patterns unrelated to the phonetic or syntactic features you learned in earlier chapters). The initial wickelfeatures are further modified, when passed to the second level of the pattern associator. The fixed output connections, known as a *decoding network,* take these modified wickelfeatures and generate another pattern of activation that represents the output pattern (e.g., *eated*) (far right portion of Figure 7.1). The place where all learning occurs is within the connections of the pattern associator.

The way the system learns new patterns, such as formation of the past tense, is to change the way input patterns are transferred to the output level. Depending upon whether or not the output pattern generated by the system successfully matches a criterion (in the above example, *eat* must generate *ate,* not *eated* or *ated*), the relative strengths of the connections between the associator nodes are adjusted. For example, the system might be taught to generate plurals. In this example, the word *house* is fed into the associator network as a pattern of activation strengths. The associator network sends another pattern of activation to the decoding network. If the system, in fact, generated the match *houses,* then the connections in the patterns associator responsible for that guess are left alone. If, on the other hand, the system generates a mismatch (e.g., presented the word *mouse,* it generates the response *mouses,* which would not match the criterion plural of *mice*), it would result in an adjustment of the connections in the pattern associator. With enough presentations of root word forms, such as *mouse, house, horse, moose,* etc., and their corresponding correct plural forms (*mice, houses,* etc.), the system will eventually converge, through these incremental adjustments, on the correct plural representation for each root item. Notice that the system would also proceed through an error stage, as similar-sounding words would lead to overgeneralization errors. In the example above, a PDP network, after being presented with *house* and *houses,* is likely to respond with *mouses* when presented with *mouse,* due to the similar activation patterns. This would hold true even though the system may have been previously exposed to *mice.*

Using PDP models as a base, Bates and MacWhinney (1987) have proposed their derivative *competition model.* They argue that PDP networks may be thought of as allowing all known syntactic forms, words, and phonetic patterns to simultaneously compete to represent any particular meaning and communicative function. For example, *mice* and *mouses* are both present as possible activation patterns. Which of these is ultimately used depends upon the current levels of activation of each. Over the course of development, the patterns that most successfully match the various criteria are more likely to occur again (are strengthened) and errorful, primitive patterns will eventually disappear. This critical matching function takes place when children's responses are matched against the criteria of adult speech that the children hear. Thus, PDP models in general, and the competition model specifically, are empirical and not nativistic. Children learn speech from the exemplars provided to them. Few if any innate biases or constraints are necessary for them to eventually learn to process language similarly to adults.

Very specific predictions about the course of language development may be derived from the competition model. Learning occurs dependent upon the probability of form–function matches. Therefore, those forms most frequently addressed to children will be learned over rarer forms. This is known as *cue availability* and accounts for both the fact that children from English-speaking homes learn English forms and not Spanish, and less obviously, that children learn highly frequent verb forms (*is—was—were*) prior to less frequent forms (*walk—walked*). Children learning English acquire word-order forms relatively early in comparison to Italian-speaking children, because word order in Italian is not a good indicator of the word's role in a sentence.

In summary, the competition model of language performance is a specific adaptation of a PDP information processing system. The language-learning mechanism within this model employs cognitive structures radically different from any previously proposed. They are not behavioristic stimulus-response associations, neither are they interrelated rule systems as suggested by linguists. Rather, they consist of multilayered networks of connections that function to interpret linguistic input and generate speech. The way PDP networks function allows predictions to be made concerning the course of language development. According to the competition model, the rate at which a particular linguistic form is mastered is determined by the nature of the form–function relations in that language system, and the way these relations are presented to children. Language learning within this system is, therefore, empirical—the only innate structure required is a powerful PDP learning mechanism.

■ EVALUATION OF THE INFORMATION PROCESSING APPROACH

SUPPORTING EVIDENCE

There is considerable evidence from research with adults that suggests the viability of the information processing approach, in general. The application of PDP to language acquisition, namely the competition model, has some support, but it is so new that a solid body of relevant research has yet to accrue. Despite the novelty of the area, some positive preliminary findings are presented below.

PDP-like processes have been frequently implicated in adult cognition. *Mental dictionaries* (semantic memories) may be organized as networks of varying semantic relations (Smith, 1978). When a word is presented, a host of related words immediately becomes active or more available. For example, after being exposed to the word *nurse* people more quickly recognize related words, such as *woman* or *doctor* (Meyer & Schwaneveldt, 1971), and phonologically related words, such as *purse* or *hearse* (Rubin, 1975). Thus, prior processing causes some spreading activation throughout the system or network of information related to the priming stimulus.

This phenomenon can be easily demonstrated. Say the word *silk* out loud five times, then quickly answer this question: "What do cows drink?" Most people readily respond with "milk," although upon reflection one realizes that cows rarely drink what they produce. The word *milk* was doubly primed, first with the similar sounds in *silk* and then with semantic association to *cows*. This priming subtly changes the current state of the language network, such that one particular response (*milk*) becomes more likely than any other response. Syntactic priming has been demonstrated as well (Bock, 1986). Prior exposure to passive sentences makes subsequent passive use more likely, even when topics and lexical items change.

The PDP model has been tested in a simulated acquisition of past tense forms. Rummelhart and McClelland (1987) presented a PDP simulation with over 400 different verbs and their past tense forms. The frequency of presentation was matched to what a child might be exposed to, namely irregular verbs (e.g., *take—took*) were presented more frequently and prior to the presentation of regular verbs (e.g., *walk—walked*). Although the simulation never learned any rules per se (i.e., add */-ed/* to form the past tense), the pattern of learning was remarkably similar to that found in children by Bybee and Slobin (1982). The system initially used every verb correctly, then passed an overregularization "stage," ultimately regularizing only regular verbs, and correctly producing exceptions. Any completely novel verbs were also regularized. Moreover, the child's tendency to overregularize varies with verb class, making *blowed* for *blew* more common than *singed* for *sang* (Bybee & Slobin, 1982), and the PDP simulation displayed similar patterns. One of the great strengths of the PDP model is these very specific predictions in this domain, in stark contrast to the often vague predictions of linguistic theory, on the order of "overregularizations will occur and eventually disappear" (Sampson, 1987, p. 878).

The strongest data in support of this approach come from its application in the competition model. Within the competition model, the statistical properties (availability and reliability) of syntactic forms determine their rate of acquisition, so that cues that consistently signal particular meanings should be learned first. An extensive review of several candidate cues (case marking, word order, semantics) across a number of different languages (French, English, Italian, Turkish, and Hungarian) supports this prediction, virtually without exception (Bates & MacWhinney, 1987; MacWhinney, 1987). This was true even in cases where predictions were contrary to supposed "universals." For example, Pinker (1984) proposed that all children will rely on word order as an initial cue to sentence meaning over other cues, such as case markings, but Turkish children, whose language has an extremely reliable case marking system, have been shown to master case marking considerably sooner than word order (Slobin & Bever, 1982). Examinations of sentence processing strategies in bilinguals also provide support for the competition model (e.g., Harrington, 1987). For example, Dutch speakers acquiring English initially use valid Dutch cues to interpret English, but gradually shift to appropriate English cues with increasing exposure (MacDonald, 1987).

CONTRARY EVIDENCE

Again, because the competition model is so new, not only are there little supporting data, no contrary data exist at all. However, we can identify potential problems with this approach. To the extent that this model shares assumptions with the linguistic position, it is susceptible to the same criticisms. For example, the competition model also assumes *text presentation* (no corrective feedback of language errors, Gold, 1967); thus, the child must be endowed with extremely powerful learning mechanisms. Given the new evidence that negative evidence or corrective feedback does occur regularly (although at this point we cannot be positive that every child receives it), these learning mechanisms may be overly powerful. According to the principle of parsimony, theorists should use the simplest of the available alternative explanations, given they all describe the data equally well. Whenever information in the environment can account for children's behavior, it may be inefficient or redundant to credit them with internal processes designed to achieve identical goals. Although the competition model is based on language cues actually available to children, it is woefully underspecified with respect to the social context within which those cues are embedded.

One of the factors that makes PDP networks so appealing may ultimately prove to be misleading. PDP models seductively resemble the organization of neurons in the brain. Thus, we may be tempted to adopt this model because of its superficial resemblance to the biological system, when in fact closer inspection of the operation of neurons and PDP nodes reveals vast differences (Grossberg & Stone, 1986). Sampson (1987) suggests that PDP writers "make too much" of the brain metaphor, though the strong points in favor of their theory are independent of it.

Finally, Fodor and Pylyshyn (1988) have attacked this approach on theoretical grounds. Imagine, they argued, that there are networks that implement linguistic theory. Although there are no linguistic rules, parameters, or binding principles as such within the system, the input–output relations behave as if there were just such a set of rules. In this view, PDP systems are mere pathways that implement linguistic relations, in the same way that sets of computer chips implement calculations of elegant differential equations. Thus, PDP approaches are inherently uninteresting as mere mechanical tools of linguistic laws. Further, PDP models handle a wide range of phenomena, if the stimuli to be processed are presented all at once (i.e., in parallel), such as pictures, arrays of words, etc. What PDP systems handle poorly are things presented in sequence, one after another. Unfortunately, language is just such a phenomenon. Words are generated and understood, in sequence. Indeed, until recently the sequential nature of sentence processing seemed to be the one hurdle PDP systems could not handle. However, this last barrier may have been overcome as well—Elman (1991) has generated a looping PDP model that retains information about past words to influence the processing of current words in sentences. His model has correctly generated hierarchical sentence structures after being presented simple sentences. Interestingly, Elman's model only works if it is presented in short simple sentences in the beginning of training. As you will see below, this mirrors the situation with children to a surprising degree.

SOCIAL INTERACTION APPROACH

The social interaction approach also combines many aspects of both the traditional behaviorist and linguistic positions. For example, social interactionists typically agree with linguists who stress that language has a structure and follows certain rules that make it somewhat unique from other behaviors. However, this approach shares with the behaviorists an emphasis on the role of the environment in producing such structure. Specifically, the social interactionist believes that the structure of human language may have arisen due to the social-communicative functions language plays in human relations (Bates & MacWhinney, 1982). Conversely, a more mature linguistic structure allows more varied and sophisticated ways of socially relating to others. In Figure 7.2, the directions of possible causal relations emphasized by the behavioristic, linguistic, and social interactionist positions are outlined.

The behavioral approach views children as passive beneficiaries of the language-training techniques employed by their parents. In this view, children's language development from one time to another (arrow *c* in Figure 7.2) is considered to be the exclusive result of parental action (arrow *a* in Figure 7.2). The linguistic approach sees children as active and specialized language processors, whose maturing neural systems guide development. Linguistic approaches acknowledge that although children may affect what their parents say (arrow *b* in Figure 7.2) at any one time, whatever the

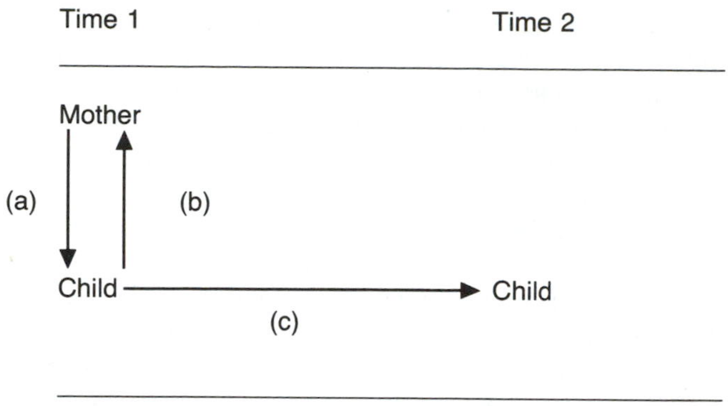

FIGURE 7.2 Possible directions of effects within language acquisition.

parents provide children in the way of language experience only triggers the maturation of children's innate tendencies. In contrast to these views, the social interactionist argues that children cue their parents (arrow *b*) into supplying the appropriate language experience (arrow *a*) that the child requires for language advancement (arrow *c*). Interactionists see children and their language environment as a dynamic system, both requiring the other for: (1) efficient social communication at any point in development, and (2) improving the child's linguistic skill.

Social interactionists assume that language development is equivalent to the acquisition of grammatical rules much as the linguists have suggested. They too search for common forms across children, cultures, and languages (DePaulo & Bonvillian, 1978). On the other hand, these rules may have developed from much simpler rote associations and imitations learned within the social context (Moerk, 1975). Therefore, although this approach tries to explain language structure, it is simply less committed to the form of the structure and to the time of its development than the linguistic approach.

Simultaneously, the functions of language in social communication are considered to be important throughout development. The linguistic approach attempts to abstract children's language development away from the day-to-day functions emphasized by behaviorists. Yet, the intricate grammatical structures described by linguists are useless to a child (and probably would not occur) unless they have a practical function, such as understanding and making oneself understood. Humans are such social organisms that it would be odd indeed if there were no relationship between language and social skills in the acquisition of a communicative system (Bates, Bretherton, Beeghly-Smith, & McNew, 1983). The social interactionist approach might be taken as an attempt to account for children's changing linguistic abstractions by examining how those abstractions might be derived from functioning social communication (Gleason, 1977).

The competence–performance issue is considered more moderately by this approach. Since interactionists acknowledge grammatical structure, they also pursue explanations of the child's language competence. In contrast, what children actually know about language (competence) can only be measured through what they say and understand (performance) within the context of social conversation. In general, it might be said that interactionists require more performance data than do the linguists, in order to conclude that children know a particular grammatical rule. For example, interactionists realize that children's parents usually bear the burden of communication, phonetically emphasizing important content words, slowing the rate of their speech, frequently repeating themselves, and supplying critical nonverbal cues such as pointing, in order to aid communication (Gleason, 1977; Snow, 1972, 1977a). Some say that parents supply a "scaffold" or supportive communicative structure (Bruner, 1978) that allows efficient communication despite the young child's primitive linguistic system. Thus, children often look much more linguistically sophisticated than they actually are (Lloyd, Baker, & Dunn, 1984). Vygotsky (1962) argued that for the young child, language is at first only a tool for social interaction. Gradually, the child begins to use language in his own private interactions with the environment, by talking aloud during play, or verbalizing intended actions. As a result, language eventually becomes the source for structure of the child's actions, governing or directing thought. Thus, the role of language changes over the course of development from a social tool to a private tool, as the child internalizes linguistic forms.

Social interactionists might also be said to adhere to both sides of the nature–nuture controversy. They recognize that humans are physiologically specialized as language users, and that some language abilities may require the maturation of physiological systems in order to appear. Thus, interactionists agree with the assertion that maturation is critical, and that children cannot acquire language until a certain level of cognitive development has been attained. On the other hand, interactionists, like the behaviorists, insist that the environment, particularly the social interactive system, is the place to look for the emergence of language. Proponents of this view insist that some specific types of experience and even training are probably necessary for children's language skills to develop. The social interactionist argues that innate mechanisms alone cannot explain children's mastery of language, and moreover, that linguistic competence goes beyond conditioning and imitation to include nonlinguistic aspects of interaction: turn-taking, mutual gaze, joint attention, context, and cultural conventions. Many social interactionists point to the special nature of the speech directed to children (sometimes known as *motherese* or *child-directed speech—CDS*) as an important experience, which may simply facilitate, or even be required for, normal language development. Again, the innate linguistic predispositions must interact with the environment in order to mature.

SOCIAL INTERACTIVE LANGUAGE LEARNING

As previously stated, the mother's role in providing the child with appropriate language experience is emphasized by the interactive approach. The mother's unusual vocal behavior (motherese or CDS) is seen to be as important as the child's innate linguistic discriminations in explaining children's eventual ability to segment the soundstream appropriately. During the child's infancy, mothers also spend a great deal of time in face-to-face social interaction with their infants, performing the vocal behaviors described above. Social interactionists believe that children's maturing ability to control their vocal apparatus is assisted by watching their mothers produce the exaggerated sounds characteristic of baby talk (Field et al., 1982). Moreover, the maturing patterns of social play interaction between mothers and infants are believed to be the basis of later conversational patterns (i.e., conversational turn-taking) (Stern, Beebe, Jaffe, & Bennett, 1977).

Interactionists believe that language has an underlying structure and that children express intentions in their speech. Yet, how do children map their intentions onto the linguistic code? Many in this view suggest that children's caretakers (usually the mother) impute intentions and meaning to the child's speech regardless of what the child says. Even when a child is simply babbling, mothers will attempt to interpret their vocalizations as if they were quite meaningful. As mothers continue in their attempt to decipher these vocalizations, critical events begin to occur. These events, which Golinkoff (1983) calls *conversational bouts,* consist of meaning negotiations between the child and the mother. For example, the child might babble "glub" while hungry. The mother interprets *glub* through the present context and her knowledge of the child's past history, and offers the child milk. The child continues to fuss because milk is not the object of her intention. The mother continues to offer different food items until the child stops fussing, and concludes that the child's utterance "glub" was a request for the item that terminated the conversational bout. From there on, the mother should treat the utterance "glub" as a request for the food item that terminated the prior bout. Thus, underlying structure mapping is not innate, but negotiated or conventionalized through social interaction.

The social interaction approach also suggests that some early language may be taught by the parents and learned through rote or imitation by the children. Despite some obvious failures to teach grammatical forms (e.g., McNeill, 1970), parents insist on teaching children social conventions such as "bye bye" and politeness routines (Gleason & Weintraub, 1976). It is not known yet whether such deliberate instruction is critical for the rest of language development, but it is believed that social use of language is assisted by such teaching. Moreover, the success of teaching social routines suggests that instruction in other forms of language might be of equal benefit.

The role of the child's language environment is stressed throughout development. It is assumed that the child's maturation and current level of grammatical skill interact with the language data provided the child to determine the further course of development. Assuming that children deduce grammatical rules from the consistencies in their linguistic environment (e.g., subjects come before verbs, plurals are signaled with a terminal *-s,* etc.), the child's task is made easier by pacing the complexity of the data or problem to be solved with the child's language level. That is, children who are linguistically naive will receive grammatically simple input (CDS). As the child grows older and increases in language skill, the data provided by the environment also increase in complexity. This is probably not due to any conscious effort on the part of parents to give specific language instruction, but simply an effort to facilitate communication. When the child fails to comprehend a parental utterance, the statement is usually simplified and repeated. Since the complexity of the speech addressed to the children is largely determined by cues from the children themselves (Bohannon & Marquis, 1977), one might think of language acquisition in this view as a self-paced lesson.

The parent also may have an effect upon the child independent of the interactive conversational system described above. The interactive view of language acquisition suggests that there may be some instances when the parents provide language exemplars that are particularly salient to the child. Snow (1979) argues that the process of mapping meaning onto the language code is assisted when the code provided by the parent closely parallels the young child's attention. Not only must parents talk about things in the child's immediate environment, but they must also focus their comments upon the objects their children are attending to. It is thought that the mapping of meaning, for example, between a ball and the word *ball* is enhanced when the word is used frequently while the child is holding or playing with a ball. It is possible that the extensive occurrence of this phenomenon in infancy through early childhood is necessary for the normal development of children's vocabulary and early syntax.

In a similar fashion, children might notice the difference between their own immature sentences and more mature versions if the two closely co-occur. Nelson (1977) insists that parental recasts of their children's utterances are particularly powerful events that children use to modify their grammars into more mature versions. He argues that children's attention is focused upon the relevant aspects of the environment and their own intentions, which together result in an utterance. For example, a child may feel thirsty, see mom open the refrigerator, want a glass of milk, and utter, "Want milk." The mother expands and recasts the child's utterance immediately in several forms, "Oh, do you want a glass of milk? Please, may I have some milk?" It is thought that the contrast between the mature and primitive forms may highlight syntactic differences for the child at a time when there is a close correspondence between the environmental context, the child's intentions, and the linguistic form which encodes those intentions and referents.

The interactive approach also recognizes the possibility that simple imitation may have important functions in language development. Although it may not be as important as the behaviorist approach insists, children may test linguistic hypotheses gained through the imitation of forms (Snow, 1978; Stine & Bohannon, 1983). Children are most likely to imitate forms which they only partially understand (Bloom, Hood, & Lightbown, 1974; Clark, 1977). This may be an interaction between the process of acquiring the form and the social-conversational role imitation plays. Stine and Bohannon (1983) argue that partially understood forms (e.g., dependent clauses) are imitated as a possible test of the grammatical rule that generates that form. At the same time, imitation is a conversational signal of partial comprehension that usually results in a recast of the full original sentence. For example, an adult tells a child, "The man who opened the door was your uncle." The child imitates, "Man who opened the door?" The parent then responds, "Yes, your uncle opened the door." It is possible that such conversational interactions, involving imitation, hypothesis testing, and recasts, combine to demonstrate new forms and their equivalent transformations.

In summary, the social interactive approach assumes that language development is the result of acquiring grammatical rules. The child is also assumed to bring a number of innate predispositions to the language learning situation that constrain children in their search for linguistically relevant distinctions. On the other hand, the environment is believed to be almost as constrained as the children, in order to supply children with the types of language experience necessary for development. Language development is viewed as an orderly, although complex, interactive process where social interaction assists language acquisition and the acquisition of language allows more mature social interaction.

■ EVALUATION OF THE SOCIAL INTERACTIONIST PERSPECTIVE

SUPPORTING EVIDENCE

One of the strengths of this approach is its eclectic nature. Because the interactionist believes that language emerges from the interplay between children's linguistic and cognitive capacities and their social language environment, this position borrows from the methods and strengths of the other areas. Therefore, much of the supporting evidence for this approach has been presented previously. The point of departure of this position pivots about the role played by the language addressed to children (motherese or CDS). In contrast to other positions, the social interactive approach has sought evidence from mother–child conversations that the simplified and fine-tuned nature of CDS assists the process of acquisition.

The adult's tendency to use a special form of language apparently begins within minutes of the child's birth. Despite infants' ability to differentially respond to speech and nonspeech stimuli (Molfese, Molfese, & Carrell, 1982), child-directed speech simplifies and highlights (through differential prosodic stress) important phonological distinctions (Ferguson, 1977; Garnica, 1977). Rheingold and Joseph (1977) observed nurses in hospital neonatal nurseries who cooed and simplified the phonological features of their speech when speaking to neonates. Fernald (1981, 1983) found similar cooing, repetition, and simplification in German mothers regardless of the mother's amount of experience with infants. In addition, CDS has been observed in 14 different languages, and it is used by all adult speakers (including fathers) when addressing children (Gleason & Weintraub, 1978). The role of CDS becomes even more important in light of recent research that shows that children prefer to listen to this type of speech from birth (Fernald, 1981, 1983) throughout infancy (Friedlander, 1970) and childhood (Rileigh, 1973). Moreover, DeCasper (1980) found that infants prefer to hear their own biological mother's CDS over another mother's CDS. Clearly, infants prefer this type of speech and, if given a choice, will seek the voice of their mother.

Several questions emerge from the data on CDS. First, what variables control the linguistic modifications observed in CDS? The answer seems to be the most obvious and intuitive; simplified and exaggerated speech is required when communicating with someone who is less linguistically sophisticated. The exact amount of simplification required for more efficient communication seems to be determined by feedback from the listener, informing the speaker of the adequacy of the listener's comprehension of prior statements. Gleason (1977) argued that children rarely yield the little nods and *uh-huhs* that periodically punctuate adult conversations, and mark successful communication. The lack of these listener's signals may cue a speaker to simplify.

Bohannon and his colleagues (Bohannon & Marquis, 1977; Bohannon, Stine, & Ritzenberg, 1982; Bohannon & Warren-Leubecker, 1988; Warren-Leubecker & Bohannon, 1982, 1983) insist that listeners play a more active role in controlling the speech they hear. They have found comprehension feedback to be a powerful signal that elicits simplified speech from both adults and children as young as three years. Simply put, children are less likely to signal comprehension of longer, more complex sentences, and when children signal such failures ("what?" "Huh?"), adults tend to shorten and simplify their next utterances. This pattern of conversational interaction has been observed in all but one of 49 adults in both English and Spanish (Bohannon, 1989). This process works equally well when the listener is a "foreigner" and understands little of the native language. The summary effect of this system seems to be a fine-tuning of the syntactic and conceptual complexity of the speech addressed to any child. Moreover, because children control the speech addressed to them, most speakers should use similar CDS, thus avoiding possible confusing variability in the linguistic environment. As children grow in their ability to comprehend more complex sentences, their success is signaled and their linguistic environment keeps pace.

An example of this process was reported by Sachs (1982) who observed her daughter, Naomi, acquiring past tense markers. Before Naomi's spontaneous use of the past tense, Sachs found little evidence of her own use of the form when addressing her daughter. But just prior to the first appearance of *-ed* marked verbs in Naomi's speech, Sachs found that her own use of that form increased markedly. Was this a random event where a mother suddenly and inexplicably chose to use the past tense when addressing her child? Obviously, it was not. The interactionist explanation suggests that Naomi's signals of noncomprehension limited the use of the form by her mother until Naomi began to struggle with a primitive concept of "displacement in time" (see earlier discussion of the cognitive approach). As Naomi began to signal comprehension of the few past-tense tokens used by her mother, the mother's use of the form increased. This possibly provided Naomi with the linguistic data on the past tense, within characteristically simple sentences of CDS, that were required to master the form.

Another question involves the possible benefits of CDS to the developing child. The benefits of CDS may assist with the "meaning mapping" problem addressed earlier by the linguistic approach (e.g., Gleitman & Wanner, 1982). One characteristic of CDS is that the topic of discussion is usually something concrete and the object of children's transitory attention (Cross, 1978; Tomasello & Farrar, 1988). Adults use both the direction of the child's gaze and topics of her speech to determine conversational content. In their review of the literature, Tomasello and Farrar (1986) conclude that those mothers who spend more time talking about the object of the child's visual gaze patterns had babies who (1) used their first words earlier, and (2) had larger initial vocabularies. As the majority of semantic forms are provided when the child's attention is focused on the meaning of that form, maybe "meaning mapping" is not as mysterious as some have suggested.

Recent correlational studies have delineated some of the features of CDS that may be important for child language acquisition (e.g., Barnes, Gutfreund, Satterly, & Wells, 1983; Cross, 1977, 1978; Newport, 1976; Newport, Gleitman, & Gleitman, 1977). One study (Furrow, Nelson, & Benedict, 1979) examined six holophastic 18-month-olds and their mothers over the course of nine months. They found that the mothers who used longer and more complex speech when speaking to their children had children who showed the least language gains at the end of the study. In other words, the more the mothers used CDS, the more rapidly their children acquired language. High frequencies of deictic utterances in mother's speech have been associated with larger child vocabulary size and greater noun phrase elaboration. In addition, synergistic sequences (where mother expands, extends, or imitates the preceding child utterance and then repeats, reduces, or elaborates on her own utterance) have also been related to greater child language gains (Cross, 1977, 1978). Imitation plus expansions, and extensions (Barnes et al., 1983; Newport, Gleitman, & Gleitman, 1977) are positively associated with language development, as are simple recasts (Nelson, 1981; Nelson, Denninger, Bonvillian, Kaplan, & Baker, 1983). As previously mentioned, these types of adult responses also tend to follow children's utterances that contain language errors (Bohannon & Stanowicz, 1988). It is possible that adult recasts may be essential in assisting children to converge on the correct form of their native language.

CONTRARY EVIDENCE

One problem with the social interactionist position derives from its relative youth. It simply has not been around long enough to be adequately assessed. As with the cognitive and information processing approaches, social interaction theory has outstripped data collection "to a startling degree" (Bates et al., 1983). Thus many of its explanations rest on untested intuitions and assumptions. Because the details of this approach have yet to be specified, true counterevidence may be difficult to find. On the other hand, some of the basic assumptions about CDS have been addressed.

Newport, Gleitman, and Gleitman (1977) questioned whether CDS was truly a simple subset of speech. They pointed out that imperatives and questions, which form a solid proportion of speech to children, are more complex than active, declarative sentences. Imperatives delete the sentence subject and questions move parts of the verb phrase in front of the sentence subject. Although CDS is generally simpler than speech to adults, they argued, it is not a simple language. Shatz (1982) found that the form–function relations in maternal speech are not materially simplified. Hoff-Ginsberg and Shatz (1982) also argued that claims that CDS improves the child's data base for language learning are theoretically vacuous unless they describe a mechanism by which those modifications would support acquisition.

Another complaint weakening a strong CDS position is that not all features of CDS are found in all languages. (For a review see Bohannon & Warren-Leubecker, 1988; DePaulo & Bonvillian, 1978.) If these features are necessary for language development shouldn't they be present in the speech addressed to all children regardless of the native language? Further, Snow (1979) suggested that language is too important a developmental accomplishment to depend upon a single acquisition mechanism such as a precisely fine-tuned and simplified syntax. She argued that children may tolerate a fairly wide window of simplified linguistic data, some very simple sentences and some quite complex, and still acquire language normally.

There are several studies (Hoff-Ginsberg, 1986; Newport, 1976) that investigated the necessity of simplified speech using designs similar to the Furrow, Nelson, and Benedict (1979) study. They found the complexity of maternal speech addressed to the children was unrelated to the children's language gains. Despite the fact that these children were, on the average, older than Furrow's, this suggests that the simplifications within CDS may not predict children's language growth in the simple, linear fashion suggested by the Furrow study (for a review of this research, see Bohannon & Hirsh-Pasek, 1984; Bohannon & Warren-Leubecker, 1988).

Although researchers consistently have documented certain features in CDS that differ from adult–adult speech patterns, the mere presence of these differences does not, in itself, suggest that CDS is necessary or even helpful to the language-learning child. Instead, correlational studies relating the relative prevalence of CDS features in mothers' speech with their children's language growth provide only hints to the effects of specific input features. Moreover, Baker and Nelson (1984) argue that the positive correlations obtained from these studies may reflect a substantial impact of the child on the mother. In other words, it is impossible from such studies to determine "who is leading whom" in language development. Only experimental studies that manipulate the presence or frequency of usage of speech features and examine the effects on child language acquisition can circumvent these problems. The experimental studies of recasts by Nelson and his colleagues (Baker & Nelson, 1984; Nelson, 1977; Nelson, Carskaddon, & Bonvillian, 1973; Nelson, Denninger, Bonvillian, Kaplan, & Baker, 1983) represent an initial attempt at solving this dilemma. Their results have shown that certain linguistic input, specifically recasts, can facilitate the acquisition of previously unused syntactic forms. Unfortunately, other features of CDS have not been as closely, experimentally examined, so conclusions regarding their effects are, at this time, premature.

Another problem with CDS relates to the great variety of features that differentiate CDS from other speech registers (see Chapter 10). Even if CDS is required by the language-learning child, it is entirely possible that only a few features are really critical in this function. Most CDS studies have focused on global measures, such as mean length of utterance, or frequency of usage of particular grammatical types, and similarly general measures of child language growth. Although the sheer amount of language stimulation provided by the mother is significantly correlated with children's language growth (e.g., Bates, 1975), Bates et al. (1983) justifiably argue that these quantitative relationships do not prove the hypothesis that CDS teaches the child language structure. In order to test these claims, one must examine very specific types of linguistic input and relate them to specific measures of child language output. Once we have narrowed our focus in this way, we may find that some aspects of child language are quite malleable and sensitive to linguistic input, whereas others are relatively immune (e.g., Gleitman, Newport, & Gleitman, 1984; Goldin-Meadow, 1982).

Another problem with the correlational studies reported here is the statistical assumption of linearity, which has been addressed by many critics (e.g., Bates et al., 1983; Bohannon & Hirsh-Pasek, 1984). One conceptual implication of the linearity assumption is that "if some maternal input is good, then more is better" (Bates et al., 1983, p. 43). This may be true up to a point, in that a minimal or threshold value of linguistic input is required, but additional input is irrelevant. Second, when the age range of the children studied is broad, it is inappropriate to assume that the oldest children should benefit from more CDS in the same way that the youngest children would. For example, the greatest simplification in MLU would dictate that mothers use single-word speech. While this may be the best level of complexity to use to a one-year-old (Furrow, Nelson, & Benedict, 1979), it would certainly hinder further language acquisition in a four-year-old (Bohannon & Hirsh-Pasek, 1984).

In summary, despite the methodological problems involved in testing its fundamental assertion, the social interactionist approach seems to hold a great deal of promise. It employs the empirical perspective of the behaviorists by acknowledging the importance of environmental sources of language data. It also recognizes children as specialized language processors who must not only acquire the language code, but, in turn, must teach it to their children through conversation.

SUMMARY

Admittedly, no developmental psycholinguist seriously believes that magic is at the root of language acquisition, despite our frustrated attempts to identify the actual processes involved. One of the reasons that we have failed to discover simple and easily observable processes in language learning may be that they do not exist, due to the importance of the phenomenon to the developing child. In other words, there is simply so much pressure placed on children to communicate successfully that there are probably many routes to the goal, and within each route, a great deal of variability may be tolerated (e.g., Snow, 1978, 1979).

The behaviorist approach probably has suffered most from an overreliance on presumably simple principles to explain language development. Although reinforcement may explain food searching in rats, it has failed to explain the average human child's search for communicative competence. If the child's parents and peers do industriously shape verbal behavior, then we must have overlooked it somehow, or it must be much more subtle and indirect than the laborious tutelage performed in laboratory settings. On the other hand, some of the behaviorist mechanisms, such as imitation, continue to show promise as an integral part of the language-learning process (Whitehurst & Vasta, 1975). In fact, modern definitions of imitation postulate a process by which observers can learn new behaviors vicariously, by watching others being rewarded or punished without direct consequences to the observers themselves. Even the most ardent supporters of the nativist, linguistic position would agree that children need to be exposed to the language behavior of others in order to acquire it themselves. Thus, even linguists appear to espouse a general imitation model as the basic process responsible for language acquisition.

This unacknowledged agreement among the competing camps goes further. The more articulated model of imitation (Bandura & Walters, 1963) includes a process called *general disinhibition,* wherein the observing learner is more likely to perform a behavior in the general class of behavior as that observed in the model. This suggests that the learner had access to the behavior all along and imitation merely disinhibited it, allowing the behavior to be performed. Viewed in this way, imitation seems to play a "releasing" function to innate language devices, which seems remarkably similar to the most recent innatist position (Gleitman & Wanner, 1982), and to the "priming" effects used to support PDP models. Clearly, researchers from either camp would be perturbed at the liberties of comparison we have taken. Yet the point to be made here is far from frivolous. The behaviorist approach offers much to the concerned developmental psycholinguist. Just as Piaget (1926) argued that cognitive development is epigenetic (complex cognitive processes arise from simpler functions), it is probable that language learning at least partially depends on simpler skills such as those described by behaviorists (Moerk, 1991). Indeed, when examined closely, some of these basic principles are featured in most of the theoretical approaches. For example, Nelson's (1977) recasts could be considered a special form of imitation or modeling that comes into play as feedback to children when they make language errors (Bohannon & Stanowicz, in press).

The linguistic approach also currently suffers several maladies. The first concerns the nativism–empiricism issue and the nominalist fallacy. Researchers fall into this fallacy when they think that giving a phenomenon a special name sufficiently explains the phenomenon. When an observer is at a loss to explain the origin of a form in children's speech, it would behoove him to realize that simply labeling it as innate neither helps us determine its relation to other forms, nor to predict when it should appear in the developmental progression (Atkinson, 1982). On the other hand, employing information theory to determine the formal learnability of a particular grammar seems promising if the nominalist fallacy can be avoided. The work of Wexler and Culicover (1980) and Pinker (1984) has attempted to model the minimal necessary principles for the acquisition of grammar. They found grammar unlearnable unless the children were either given information about impermissible sentences, or that some aspects of grammar are innate. If this approach is utilized to test new grammars and other assumptions, then some of the possible combinations of psychological processes and competing grammars may be excluded *a priori*.

Before students of developmental psycholinguistics reject the linguistic approach outright, they should reflect upon the logical nature of grammar. The internal structure of the rules used to produce and understand language will probably be discovered within the linguistic approach. As long as researchers in this approach allow children's performance data to bear upon conclusions concerning the child's language competence, then a coherent explanation that achieves Chomsky's (1965) third level of theoretical adequacy (psychological reality) will be achieved. Without such a system describing the organized nature of adult language or the progression of emerging grammars in children, any explanation of language or its acquisition will remain as a disorganized array of accumulated data.

The obvious solution to the controversy between the behaviorist and linguistic approaches lies in the contribution of the various interactional approaches, each of which provides important foci for research. The cognitive approach stresses that language is only one of many complex cognitive skills that children acquire. Moreover, the structure of language and the processes involved in its learning are constrained by the nature of the child's thought at the time of acquisition. The information processing theorists emphasize cognitive processing demands of language learning. They look to the availability and reliability of linguistic cues that signal important communicative functions. It is their position that the nature of the information to be processed determines the course of development. The social interactionist approach highlights the social context in which language is learned, without which language learning seems impossible and perhaps unnecessary. This approach seeks the critical aspects of social interaction that allow normal language learning to proceed.

These varied interactional approaches seem to hold the most promise for the future, perhaps due to their eclectic natures. Recognizing the strengths of the historically prior theoretical camps, the interactionist borrows freely from each. By avoiding a strict insistence on simple associations or strong innate mechanisms, interactionists may circumvent the more obvious pitfalls. On the other hand, both interactionist positions are relatively new and largely untested. Until language theories incorporate a general learning model that accurately specifies both the psychologically valid structure of language, and the environmental variables required for children to develop language in natural settings, then the language acquisition process will continue to be mysterious and magical.

To recap some of the important differences between each of the major theoretical approaches discussed herein, consider the following metaphor. As children begin the developmental journey from birth to mature language users, we can examine the initial state of the child and nature of the trip itself. Within the behaviorist approach, children start out naked, and helplessly lost. Behaviorists insist that children remain in this sorry state until an adult grabs the child's hand, and drags her all the way to the appropriate destination language. Behaviorists might state, "Children can't be trusted to go anywhere by themselves—leave the driving to us." According to the linguistic approach, children are not helpless but simply initially ignorant of their destination. Therefore, linguists equip the diminutive travelers with a great deal of durable luggage and maps. This allows children to recognize all of the significant routes to their native language, and moreover, to arrive with little or no help from passersby. Using their extensive maps and baggage, children eventually recognize when they have made wrong turns (overregularization errors), and they can get back on course without delay or assistance. Linguists might say, "We've packed everything you need. Follow your maps and don't talk to strangers along the way. You're on your own, kid." In the cognitive approaches, children are equipped with a minimum of baggage, and the maps are fairly global. After all, the main routes are the paths of least resistance, defined by the cognitive topology. When routes diverge, there are easily read street signs in the environment to guide the child to the home language. They ask, "Why burden the child with excessive baggage when such may be purchased from the environment along the way?" In the social interactionist approach, children require even less baggage. Innate baggage is seen as unnecessary because adult guides freely give children what they need along the way. Adults gladly point out the main routes and shortcuts that they themselves have discovered through experience. Children do not have to worry about wrong turns, either; any adult will provide assistance to return the child to the correct path. Social interactionists ask, "Why weigh children down when we will *give* them what they need during the trip?"

The problem for researchers and theorists is to chart the path of children from linguistic naiveté to sophistication. The use of theory in this endeavor reminds me of the "lost keys" parable. Walking down the street one night, a distraught fellow was observed dashing from street light to street light, searching frantically around each lamp pole. When asked what he was doing, the man replied, "Searching for my keys. I lost them." When he was asked, "Did you lose them under a streetlamp?" the man replied, "No, but the light is better here." In a similar way, our current limited set of approaches and methods often seems to leave us looking only where the theoretical and methodological light is good, though the object of our search may be far away indeed. Thus, unless we can develop decent theoretical flashlights, children's progress to language maturity will continue to seem mysterious.

SUGGESTED PROJECTS

1. Read Skinner's *Verbal Behavior.* Write a synopsis of his position on the problem of language description and acquisition. Compare Skinner's terms, such as "tact," "mand," and "autoclitic," with traditional grammatical categories devised by linguists.
2. Select some friends to play the following games. Using the figure provided (p. 285), see if they can solve the puzzles you present. The figure is a simple concept formation problem with the top set of stimuli serving as "maternal exemplars" and the bottom set of stimuli serving as opportunities for "child responses." Notice that the stimuli are an aggregate of orthogonal dimensions of size (large, medium, and small), shape (circle, triangle, and square), pattern (open, vertical stripes, and horizontal stripes), and position (left, middle, and right). You begin the game by selecting one of the 12 stimuli values as "correct," without telling the "child" subject. For example, if "left" is going to be the correct "linguistic" rule, you should now point to the left-most stimulus in the top "maternal" array. The subject should then try to guess the modeled form in the successive numbered arrays in Figure 7.3. Various forms of language learning assumptions can then be tested.
   a. *No negative evidence assumption.* Regardless of what the subject chooses, act totally delighted that they chose anything at all and record their choices. Never correct the subject if they choose the wrong stimulus. Offer to call Grandma to tell her the "baby" has uttered its first word. After several subjects, compare the resultant patterns of responses to see if they converged on the same solution (e.g., "left").
   b. *Implicit negative evidence.* Do the same behaviors as in a above, except for two of the subjects' responses. When the subject makes a correct choice, point to the choice they made and say, "that one." When the subject makes an error (e.g., any choice other than the left stimulus), point to the left stimulus and say, "That one." Never tell the subjects that they are right or wrong and act delighted that they are "speaking" (i.e., playing the game). After several subjects, compare the pattern of their choices. Did they converge on the rule you selected? How did they do this if you never told them right or wrong? Compare your data to the theoretical positions of formal language learning theorists such as Pinker or Wexler. Read Farrar (1992) and briefly discuss the negative evidence issue in comparison to your data.
3. Record a child in normal conversation. Observe and describe as completely as possible the contextual situation in which the conversation occurred (if videotaping is possible, even better). Select at least 30 utterances by the child and analyze them according to the various theoretical perspectives: behaviorist, linguist, cognitive, and social interactionist. Try to account for the data that each position would consider important.

FIGURE 7.3

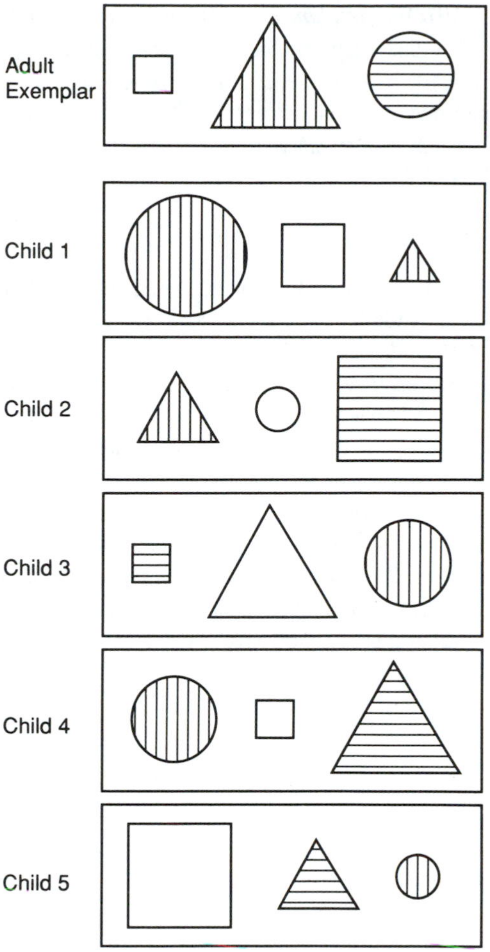

SUGGESTED READINGS

Behavioral Approaches

MacCorquodale, K. (1970). On Chomsky's review of Skinner's *Verbal Behavior. Journal of the Experimental Analysis of Behavior, 13,* 83–99.

Skinner, B. F. (1957). *Verbal behavior.* Englewood Cliffs, NJ: Prentice-Hall.

Linguistic Approaches

Atkinson, M. (1982). *Explanations in the study of language acquisition.* Cambridge: Cambridge University Press.

Brown, R. (1973). *A first language: The early stages.* Cambridge, MA: Harvard University Press.

Chomsky, N. (1982). *Lectures on government and binding.* New York: Foris.

Derwing, B. (1973). *Transformational grammar as a theory of language acquisition.* Cambridge: Cambridge University Press.

Pinker, S. (1989). *Learnability and cognition: The acquisition of argument structure.* Cambridge, MA: MIT Press.

Cognitive Interactionist

Bates, E., & MacWhinney, B. (1982). Functionalist approaches to grammar. In E. Wanner & L. Gleitman (Eds.), *Language acquisition: The state of the art.* Cambridge, MA: Cambridge University Press.

Grossberg, S., & Stone, G. (1986). Neural dynamics of word recognition and recall: Attentional priming, learning, and resonance. *Psychological Review, 93,* 46–74.

MacWhinney, B. (1987). The competition model. In B. MacWhinney (Ed.), *Mechanisms of language acquisition.* Hillsdale, NJ: Erlbaum, 249–308.

McClelland, J., Rummelhart, D., & the PDP Research Group. (1986). *Parallel distributed processing: Explorations in the microstructure of cognition.* Vol. 2, Cambridge, MA: Bradford Books.

Piaget, J. (1926). *The language and thought of the child.* New York: Harcourt Brace Jovanovich.

Pinker, S., & Prince, A. (1988). On language and connectionism: Analysis of a parallel distributed processing model of language acquisition. *Cognition, 28,* 73–193.

Social Interactionist

Bates, E., Bretherton, I., Beeghly-Smith, M., & McNew, S. (1983). The social basis of language development: A reassessment. In H. Reese & L. Lipsitt (Eds.), *Advances in child development.* New York: Academic Press.

Bohannon, J., & Warren-Leubecker, A. (1988). Recent developments in child-directed-speech: You've come a long way, baby-talk. *Language Science, 10*(1), 89–110.

Gleason, J. Berko, & Weintraub, S. (1978). Input language and the acquisition of communicative competence. In K. Nelson (Ed.), *Children's language* (Vol. 1). New York: Gardiner Press.

Moerk, E. (1983). *The mother of Eve—as a first language teacher.* Norwood, NJ: Ablex.

Snow, C. (1979). The role of social interaction in language acquisition. In W. A. Collins (Ed.), *Minnesota symposia on child psychology,* Vol. 12. Hillsdale, NJ: Erlbaum.

REFERENCES

Atkinson, M. (1982). *Explanations in the study of child language development.* New York: Cambridge University Press.

Baker, N., & Nelson, K. (1984). Recasting and related conversational techniques for triggering syntactic advances by young children. *First Language, 5,* 3–22.

Bandura, A., & Harris, M. (1966). Modification of syntactic style. *Journal of Experimental Child Psychology, 66,* 341–352.

Bandura, A., & Walters, R. (1963). *Social learning and personality development.* New York: Holt, Rinehart & Winston.

Barnes, S., Gutfreund, M., Satterly, D., & Wells, G. (1983). Characteristics of adult speech which predict children's language development. *Journal of Child Language, 10,* 65–84.

Bates, E. (1975). Peer relations and the acquisition of language. In M. Lewis & L. Rosenblum (Eds.), *Friendship and peer relations.* New York: Wiley.

Bates, E. (1976). *Language and context: Studies in the acquisition of pragmatics.* New York: Academic Press.

Bates, E. (1986, October). Discussion. In H. Tager-Flusberg (Chair), Theoretical issues in the acquisition of grammar: Evidence from children with sensory, cognitive, or neurological deficits. Symposium conducted at the Boston University Conference on Language Development, Boston.

Bates, E. (1991, April). Language development research in the nineties. Address at the biennial meeting of the Society for Research in Child Development, Seattle, WA.

Bates, E., Bretherton, I., Beeghley-Smith, M., & McNew, S. (1983). Social basis of language development: A reassessment. In H. Reese & L. Lipsitt (Eds.), *Advances in child development and behavior* (pp. 8–75, Vol. 16). New York: Academic Press.

Bates, E., Benigni, L., Bretherton, I., Camaioni, L., & Volterra, V. (1979). *The emergence of symbols: Cognition and communication in infancy.* New York: Academic Press.

Bates, E., & MacWhinney, B. (1982). Functionalist approach to grammar. In E. Wanner & L. Gleitman (Eds.), *Language acquisition: The state of the art* (pp. 173–218). New York: Cambridge University Press.

Bates, E., & MacWhinney, B. (1987). Competition, variation, and language learning. In B. MacWhinney (Ed.), *Mechanisms of language acquisition* (pp. 157–194). Hillsdale, NJ: Erlbaum.

Bates, E., & Snyder, L. (1985). The cognitive hypothesis in language development. In I. Uzgiris and J. M. Hunt (Eds.), *Research with scales of psychological development in infancy.* Champaign–Urbana, IL: University of Illinois Press.

Bever, T. G. (1970). The cognitive basis for linguistic structures. In J. Hayes (Ed.), *Cognition and the development of language.* New York: Wiley.

Bever, T. G. (1982). Some implications of the nonspecific bases of language. In E. Wanner & L. Gleitman (Eds.), *Language acquisition: The state of the art.* Cambridge, MA: Cambridge University Press.

Bever, T., Fodor, J., & Weksel, W. (1965). On the acquisition of syntax: A critique of "contextual generalization." *Psychological Review, 72,* 467–482.

Block, E., & Kessel, F. (1980). Determinants of the acquisition order of grammatical morphemes: A reanalysis and reinterpretation. *Journal of Child Language, 7,* 181–189.

Bloom, L. (1970). *Language development: Form and function in emerging grammars.* Cambridge, MA: MIT Press.

Bloom, L. (1983). Of continuity, nature, nurture, and magic. In R. Golinkoff (Ed.), *The transition from preverbal to verbal communication.* Hillsdale, NJ: Erlbaum.

Bloom, L., Hood, P., & Lightbown, P. (1974). Imitation in language development: If when and why? *Cognitive Psychology, 6,* 380–420.

Bock, K. (1982). Towards a cognitive psychology of syntax: Information processing contributions to sentence formulation. *Psychological Review, 89,* 1–47.

Bock, K. (1986). Cognition in language production: A plague on both your houses. Paper presented at the meeting of the Conference on Human Development. Nashville, TN.

Bock, K. (in press). Syntactic persistence in language production. *Cognitive Psychology.*

Bohannon, J. N. (1982). Close encounters of the primate kind. *American Journal of Primatology, 3,* 353–358.

Bohannon, J. (1989). Control of adult speech in Spanish. *Acta Paedologica, 2*(1), 48–60.

Bohannon, J., & Hirsh-Pasek, K. (1984). Do children say as they're told? A new perspective on *motherese.* In L. Feagans, C. Garvey, & R. Golinkoff (Eds.), *The origins and growth of communication* (pp. 176–195). Norwood, NJ: Ablex.

Bohannon, J. N., MacWhinney, B., & Snow, C. E. (1990). Negative evidence revisited: Beyond learnability or who has to prove what to whom? *Developmental Psychology, 26,* 221–226.

Bohannon, J., & Marquis, A. (1977). Children's control of adult speech. *Child Development, 48,* 1002–1008.

Bohannon, J., & Stanowicz, L. (1988). Adult responses to children's language errors: The issue of negative evidence. *Developmental Psychology, 24,* 684–689.

Bohannon, J., & Stanowicz, L. (1989). Bidirectional effects of imitation: A synthesis within a cognitive model. In K. E. Nelson & G. Speidel (Eds.), *A new look at imitation in language acquisition* (pp. 122–150). Norwood, NJ: Ablex.

Bohannon, J., Stine, E. L., & Ritzenberg, D. (1982). The effects of experience and feedback on motherese. *The Bulletin of the Psychonomic Society, 19,* 201–204.

Bohannon, J., & Warren-Leubecker, A. (1988). Recent developments in child-directed speech: You've come a long way, baby-talk. *Language Science,* 89–110.

Bonvillian, J., Nelson, K. E., & Charrow, V. (1976). Languages and language-related skills in deaf and hearing children. *Sign Language Studies, 12,* 211–250.

Bowerman, M. (1973). Structural relationships in children's utterances: Syntactic or semantic? In T. Moore (Ed.), *Cognitive development and the acquisition of language.* New York: Academic Press.

Bowerman, M. (1982). Reorganizational processes in lexical and syntactic development. In E. Wanner & L. Gleitman (Eds.), *Language acquisition: The state of the art.* Cambridge, MA: Cambridge University Press.

Branigan, G. (1979). Some reasons why some successive single word utterances are not. *Journal of Child Language, 6,* 411–421.

Brown, R. (1973). *A first language: The early stages.* Cambridge, MA: Harvard University Press.

Brown, R., & Bellugi, U. (1964). Three processes in the child's acquisition of syntax. *Harvard Education Review, 34,* 133–151.

Brown, R., & Hanlon, C. (1970). Derivational complexity and the order of acquisition in child speech. In R. Brown (Ed.), *Psycholinguistics* (pp. 155–207). New York: Free Press.

Bruner, J. (1978). The role of dialogue in language acquisition. In A. Sinclair, R. Jarvella, & W. Levelt (Eds.), *The child's conception of language.* New York: Springer-Verlag.

Bybee, J., & Slobin, D. (1982). Rules and schemas in the development and use of the English past tense. *Language, 58,* 265–289.

Case, R. (1980). Intellectual development in infancy: A neo-Piagetian interpretation. Paper presented at the International Conference for Infant Studies, New Haven, CT.

Chapman, K., Leonard, L., & Mervis, C. (1986). The effects of feedback on young children's inappropriate word usage. *Journal of Child Language, 13,* 101–117.

Chomsky, C. (1969). *The acquisition of syntax in children from 5 to 10.* Cambridge, MA: MIT Press.

Chomsky, N. (1957). *Syntactic structures.* The Hague: Mouton.

Chomsky, N. (1965). *Aspects of a theory of syntax.* Cambridge, MA: MIT Press.

Chomsky, N. (1972). *Language and mind.* New York: Harcourt Brace Jovanovich.

Chomsky, N. (1979). Human language and other semiotic systems. *Semiotica, 25,* 31–44.

Chomsky, N. (1980). On binding. *Linguistic Inquiry, 11,* 1–46.

Chomsky, N. (1982). *Lectures on government and binding.* New York: Foris.

Clark, E. (1977). Strategies and the mapping problem in first language acquisition. In J. MacNamara (Ed.), *Language learning and thought.* New York: Academic Press.

Clifton, C., & Odum, P. (1966). Similarity relations among certain English sentence constructions. *Psychological Monographs, 80,* 1–35.

Collins, A., & Loftus, E. (1975). A spreading activation theory of semantic processing. *Psychological Review, 82,* 407–428.

Condon, W., & Sander, L. (1974). Synchony demonstrated between movements of neonate and adult speech. *Child Development, 45,* 465–472.

Corrigan, R. (1978). Language development as related to stage six object permanence development. *Journal of Child Language, 5,* 173–190.

Cromer, J. (1987). Language growth without experience with feedback. *Journal of Psycholinguistic Research, 16,* 223–231.

Cross, T. (1977). Mothers' speech adjustments: The contribution of selected child listener variables. In C. Snow & C. Ferguson (Eds.), *Talking to children: Language input and acquisition.* Cambridge: Cambridge University Press.

Cross, T. (1978). Mothers' speech and its association with rate of linguistic development in young children. In N. Waterson & C. Snow (Eds.), *The development of communication.* New York: Wiley.

Curtiss, S. (1977). *Genie: A psycholinguistic study of a modern-day "wild child."* New York: Academic Press.

Curtiss, S. (1981). Dissociations between language and cognition: Cases and implications. *Journal of Autism and Developmental Disorders, 11,* 15–30.

Curtiss, S., & Yamada, J. (1978). Language = cognition. Paper presented at the Third Annual Boston University Conference on Language Development, Boston.

Curtiss, S., Yamada, J., & Fromkin, V. (1979). How independent is language? On the question of formal parallels between language and cognition. Conference on Human Development, Alexandria, VA.

DeCasper, A. (1980, April). Newborn preference for maternal voice: An indication of early attachment. Paper presented at the meeting of the Southeastern Conference on Human Development, Alexandria, VA.

Demetras, M., Post, K., & Snow, C. (1986). Feedback to first language learners: The role of repetitions and clarification questions. *Journal of Child Language, 13,* 275–292.

DePaulo, B., & Bonvillian, J. (1978). The effect on language development of the special characteristics of speech addressed to children. *Journal of Psycholinguistic Research, 7,* 189–211.

DePaulo, B., & Coleman, L. (1986). Talking to children, foreigners, and retarded adults. *Journal of Personality and Social Psychology, 51,* 945–959.

Derwing, B. (1973). *Transformational grammar as a theory of language acquisition.* Cambridge: Cambridge University Press.

de Villiers, P., & de Villiers, J. (1972). Early judgments of semantic and syntactic acceptability by children. *Journal of Psycholinguistic Research, 1,* 299–310.

Dore, J. (1978, September). Concepts, communicative acts, and the LAD. Paper presented at the Boston Child Language Conference.

Eimas, P. (1974). Linguistic processing of speech by young infants. In R. Schiefelbush and L. Lloyd (Eds.), *Language perspectives—Acquisition, retardation, and intervention.* Baltimore: University Park Press.

Elman, J. (1991, April). Incremental learning and the projection problem: The importance of starting small. Paper presented at the biennial meeting of SRCD, Seattle.

Ervin-Tripp, S. (1971). An overview of theories of grammatical development. In D. Slobin (Ed.), *The ontogenesis of grammar.* New York: Academic Press.

Estes, W. (1980). Is human memory obsolete? *American Scientist, 68,* 62–69.

Farrar, J. (1987, April). Immediate effects of discourse on grammatical morpheme acquisition. Paper presented at the meeting of the Society for Research in Child Development, Baltimore.

Farrar, J. (1992). Negative evidence and grammatical morpheme acquisition. *Developmental Psychology, 28,* 90–98.

Fenson, L., & Ramsey, D. (1980). Decentration and integration of the child's play in the second year. *Child Development, 51,* 171–178.

Ferguson, C. (1977). Baby talk as a simplified register. In C. Snow & C. Ferguson (Eds.), *Talking to children: Language input and acquisition.* Cambridge: Cambridge University Press.

Fernald, A. (1981, April). Four month olds prefer to listen to motherese. Paper presented at the meeting of the Society for Research in Child Development, Boston.

Fernald, A. (1983). The sound of meaning in early mother–infant interaction. In L. Feagans, K. Garvey, & R. Golinkoff (Eds.), *The origins and growth of communication.* Norwood, NJ: Ablex.

Fernald, A., & Kuhl, P. (1987). Acoustic determinants of infant preference for motherese speech. *Infant Behavior and Development, 10,* 279–293.

Field, T., Woodson, R., Greenberg, R., & Cohen, D. (1982). Discrimination and imitation of facial expressions by neonates. *Science, 218,* 179–181.

Fillmore, C. (1968). The case for case. In E. Bock & R. Harms (Eds.), *Universals in linguistic theory.* New York: Holt, Rinehart & Winston.

Fodor, J. (1977). *Semantics: Theories of meanings in generative grammar.* New York: Thomas Y. Crowell.

Fodor, J., & Pylyshyn, Z. (1988). Connectionism and cognitive architecture: A critical analysis. *Cognition, 28,* 3–71.

Fodor, J., & Bever, T. (1965). The psychological reality of linguistic segments. *Journal of Verbal Learning and Verbal Behavior, 4,* 414–420.

Friedlander, B. (1970). Receptive language development in infancy. *Merrill-Palmer Quarterly, 16,* 7–51.

Furrow, D., Nelson, K., & Benedict, H. (1979). Mothers' speech to children and syntactic development: Some simple relationships. *Journal of Child Language, 6,* 423–442.

Furrow, D., & Moore, C. (1991, April). Mother's feedback to children's utterances: The role of context. Paper presented at the biennial meeting of the Society for Research in Child Development, Seattle, WA.

Garnica, O. (1977). Some prosodic and paralinguistic features of speech to young children. In C. Snow & C. Ferguson (Eds.), *Talking to children: Language input and acquisition.* Cambridge: Cambridge University Press.

Garnica, O. (1978). Non-verbal concomitants of language input to children. In N. Waterson & C. Snow (Eds.), *The development of communication.* New York: Wiley.

Garrett, M., Bever, T., & Fodor, J. (1966). The active use of grammar in speech perception. *Perception and Psychophysics, 1,* 30–32.

George, B., & Tomasello, M. (1984). The effect of variation in sentence length on young children's attention and comprehension. *First Language, 5,* 115–128.

Gleason, J. Berko. (1977) Some notes on feedback. In C. Snow & C. Ferguson (Eds.), *Talking to children: Language input and acquisition.* Cambridge, MA: Cambridge University Press.

Gleason, J. Berko, & Weintraub, S. (1976). The acquisition of routines in child language. *Language in Society, 5,* 129–136.

Gleason, J. Berko, & Weintraub, S. (1978). Input language and the acquisition of communicative competence. In K. Nelson (Ed.), *Children's language* (Vol.1). New York: Gardiner Press.

Gleitman, L., Gleitman, H., & Shipley, E. (1972). The emergence of the child as grammarian. *Cognition, 1,* 137–164.

Gleitman, L., Newport, E., & Gleitman, H. (1984). The current status of the motherese hypothesis. *Journal of Child Language, 11,* 43–79.

Gleitman, L., & Wanner, E. (1982). Language acquisition: The state of the state of the art. In E. Wanner & L. Gleitman (Eds.), *Language acquisition: The state of the art.* Cambridge: Cambridge University Press.

Glucksberg, S., & Danks, J. (1969). Grammatical structure and recall: A function of the space in immediate memory or of recall delay? *Perception and Psychophysics, 6,*113–117.

Gold, E. (1967). Language identification in the limit. *Information and Control, 10,* 447–474.

Goldin-Meadow, S. (1982). The resilience of recursion: A study of a communication system developed without a conventional language model. In E. Wanner & L. Gleitman (Eds.), *Language acquisition: The state of the art.* Cambridge: Cambridge University Press.

Goldin-Meadow, S., & Feldman, H. (1977). The development of language-like communication without a language model. *Science, 197,* 401–403.

Golinkoff, R. (1983). The preverbal negotiation of failed messages: Insights into the transition period. In R. Golinkoff (Ed.), *The transition from preverbal to verbal communication.* Hillsdale, NJ: Erlbaum.

Golinkoff, R., Hirsh-Pasek, K., Bailey, L. & Wenger, N. (1992). Young children and adults use lexical principles to learn new nouns. *Developmental Psychology, 28,* 99–108.

Gopnik, A. (1984). The acquisition of "gone" and the development of the object concept. *Journal of Child Language, 11,* 273–292.

Gopnik, A., & Meltzoff, A. (1984). Semantic and cognitive development in 15- to 21-month-old children. *Journal of Child Language, 11,* 495–513.

Gopnik, A., & Meltzoff, A. (1986). Relations between semantic and cognitive development in the one-word stage: The specificity hypothesis. *Child Development, 57,* 1040–1053.

Gopnik, A., & Meltzoff, A. (1987). The development of categorization in the second year and its relation to other cognitive and linguistic developments. *Child Development, 58,* 1523–1531.

Gough, P. (1965). Grammatical transformations and speed of understanding. *Journal of Verbal Learning and Verbal Behavior, 4,* 107–111.

Gough, P. (1966). The verification of sentences: The effects of delay of evidence and sentence length. *Journal of Verbal Learning and Verbal Behavior, 5,* 492–496.

Grimshaw, J., & Pinker, S. (1989). Positive and negative evidence in language acquisition. *Behavioral and Brain Sciences, 12,* 341–342.

Grossberg, S., & Stone, G. (1986). Neural dynamics of word recognition and recall: Attentional priming, learning, and resonance. *Psychological Review, 93,* 46–74.

Hakuta, K. (1977). Word order and particles in the acquisition of Japanese. *Papers and Reports on Child Language Development* (Stanford University), No. 13, 110–117.

Halpern, E., & Aviezer, L. (1976). Psycholinguistic skills and sensory-motor development within Piaget's theoretical framework. Paper presented to the 21st International Congress of Psychology, Paris.

Hamburger, H., & Crain, S. (1984). Acquisition of cognitive compiling. *Cognition, 17,* 85–136.

Harding, C. (1983). Acting with intention: A framework for examining the development of the intention to communicate. In L. Feagans, C. Garvey, & R. Golinkoff (Eds.), *The origins and growth of communication.* Norwood, NJ: Ablex.

Harrington, M. (1987). Processing transfer: Language-specific processing strategies as a source of interlanguage variation. *Applied Psycholinguistics, 8,* 351–378.

Hirsh-Pasek, K., Nelson, D., Jusczyk, P., Cassidy, K., Druss, B., & Kennedy, L. (1987). Clauses are perceptual units for young infants. *Cognition, 26,* 269–286.

Hirsh-Pasek, K., Treiman, R., & Schneiderman, M. (1984). Brown and Hanlon revisited: Mothers' sensitivity to ungrammatical forms. *Journal of Child Language, 11,* 81–88.

Hoff-Ginsberg, E. (1986). Function and structure in maternal speech: Their relation to the child's development of syntax. *Developmental Psychology, 22,* 155–163.

Hoff-Ginsberg, E., & Shatz, M. (1982). Linguistic input and the child's acquisition of language. *Psychological Bulletin, 92,* 3–26.

James, L., & Singh, B. K. (1978). An introduction to the logic, assumptions, and basic analytic procedures of two-stage least squares. *Psychological Bulletin, 85,* 1104–1122.

Katz, J. (1972). *Semantic theory.* New York: Harper & Row.

Krashen, S. (1975). The critical period for language acquisition and its possible basis. *Annals of the New York Academy of Sciences, 263,* 211–224.

Kuczaj, S. (1979). Evidence for a language learning strategy: On the relative ease of acquisition of prefixes and suffixes. *Child Development, 50,* 1–13.

Landau, B., & Gleitman, L. (1985). *Language and experience: Evidence from the blind child.* Cambridge, MA: Harvard University Press.

Lee, V. (1981). Terminological and conceptual revision of the experimental analysis of language development: Why? *Behaviorism, 9,* 25–55.

Lenneberg, E. (1967). *Biological foundations of language.* New York: Wiley.

Liebert, R., Odum, R., Hill, J., & Huff, R. (1969). The effects of age and role familiarity on the production of modeled language construction. *Developmental Psychology, 1,* 108–112.

Lloyd, P., Baker, E., & Dunn, J. (1984). Children's awareness of communication. In L. Feagans, C. Garvey, & R. Golinkoff (Eds.), *The origins and growth of communication.* Norwood, NJ: Ablex.

Lovaas, O. I. (1977). *The autistic child: Language development through behavior modification.* New York: Irvington Publishers.

MacDonald, J. (1987). Sentence interpretation in bilingual speakers of English and Dutch. *Applied Psycholinguistics, 8,* 379–414.

MacWhinney, B. (1978). Processing a first language: The acquisition of morphophonology. *Monographs of the Society for Research in Child Development, 43,* Serial No. 174.

MacWhinney, B. (1987). The competition model. In B. MacWhinney (Ed.), *Mechanisms of language acquisition* (pp. 249–308). Hillsdale, NJ: Erlbaum.

MacWhinney, B. (Ed.). (1987). *Mechanisms of language acquisition.* Hillsdale, NJ: Erlbaum.

Maratsos, M. (1983). Some current issues in the study of the acquisition of grammar. In P. Mussen (Ed.), *Charmicheal's manual of child psychology.* New York: Academic Press.

Maratsos, M., & Chalkley, M. A. (1980). The internal language of children's syntax: The ontogenesis and representation of syntactic categories. In K. Nelson (Ed.), *Children's Language* (Vol. 2). New York: Gardner Press.

Marler, P. (1977). Primate vocalization: Affective or symbolic? In G. Bourne (Ed.), *Progress in ape research.* New York: Academic Press.

Matthews, W. (1968). Transformational complexity and short-term recall. *Language and Speech, 11,* 120–128.

McClelland, J., & Rummelhart, D. (1981). An interactive activation model of context effects in letter perception: An account of the basic findings. *Psychological Review, 88,* 375–402.

McClelland, J., Rummelhart, D., & the PDP Research Group. (1986). *Parallel distributed processing: Explorations in the microstructure of cognition* (Vol. 2). Cambridge, MA: Bradford Books.

McNeill, D. (1966). Developmental psycholinguistics. In F. Smith & G. Miller (Eds.), *The genesis of language.* Cambridge, MA: MIT Press.

McNeill, D. (1970). *The acquisition of language: The study of developmental linguistics.* New York: Harper & Row.

McShane, L. (1979). The development of naming. *Linguistics, 17,* 879–905.

Menyuk, P. (1977). *Language and maturation.* Cambridge, MA: MIT Press.

Meyer, D., & Schwaneveldt, R. (1971). Facilitation in recognizing pairs of words: Evidence of a dependence between retrieval operations. *Psychological Review, 90,* 227–234.

Miller, G. (1965). Some preliminaries to psycholinguistics. *American Psychologist, 20,*15–20.

Moerk, E. (1975). Verbal interactions between children and their mothers during the preschool years. *Developmental Psychology, 11,* 788–794.

Moerk, E. (1983). *The mother of Eve—As a first language teacher.* Norwood, NJ: Ablex.

Moerk, E. (1985). A differential interactive analysis of language teaching and learning. *Discourse Processes, 8,* 113–142.

Moerk, E. (1989). The LAD was a lady and the tasks were ill-defined. *Developmental Review, 9,* 21–57.

Moerk, E. L. (1991). *Language training and learning: Processes and products.* Baltimore, MD: Paul Brookes.

Molfese, D. (1977). Infant cerebral asymmetry. In S. Segalowitz & F. Gruber (Eds.), *Language development and neurological theory.* New York: Academic Press.

Molfese, D., Molfese, V., & Carrell, P. (1982). Early language development. In B. Wolman (Ed.), *Handbook of developmental psychology.* Englewood Cliffs, NJ: Prentice-Hall.

Morse, P. (1974). Infant speech perception: A preliminary model and review of the literature. In R. Schiefelbush & L. Lloyd (Eds.), *Language perspectives—Acquisition, retardation, and intervention.* Baltimore: University Park Press.

Mowrer, O. H. (1960). *Learning theory and the symbolic processes.* New York: Wiley.

Nelson, K. (1981). Acquisition of words by first-language learners. In H. Winitz (Ed.), *Annals of the New York Academy of Sciences, 379,* 148–160.

Nelson, K. E. (1977). Facilitating children's acquisition of syntax. *Developmental Psychology, 13,* 101–107.

Nelson, K. E. (1981). Toward a rare-event cognitive comparison theory of syntax acquisition. In P. Dale & D. Ingram (Eds.), *Child language: An international perspective.* Baltimore: University Park Press, 229–240.

Nelson, K. E., Carskaddon, G., & Bonvillian, J. (1973). Syntax acquisition: Impact of experimental variation in adult verbal interaction with the child. *Child Development, 44,* 497–504.

Nelson, K. E., Denninger, M., Bonvillian, J., Kaplan, B., & Baker, N. (1983). Maternal input adjustments and non-adjustments as related to children's linguistic advances and the language acquisition theories. In A. D. Pelligrini & T. D. Yawkey (Eds.), *The development of oral and written languages: Readings in developmental and applied linguistics.* New York: Ablex.

Newport, E. (1976). Motherese: The speech of mothers to young children. In N. Castellan, D. Pisoni, & G. Potts (Eds.), *Cognitive theory* (Vol. 2). Hillsdale, NJ: Erlbaum.

Newport, E. (1986, October). The effect of maturational state on the acquisition of language. Paper presented at Boston University Conference on Language Development, Boston.

Newport, E., Gleitman, L., & Gleitman, H. (1977). Mother I'd rather do it myself: Some effects and non-effects of motherese. In C. Snow & C. Ferguson (Eds.), *Talking to children: Language input and acquisition.* Cambridge: Cambridge University Press.

Olson, D., & Filby, N. (1972). On the comprehension of active and passive sentences. *Cognitive Psychology, 3,* 361–381.

Osgood, C. (1953). *Method and theory in experimental psychology.* New York: Oxford University Press.

Osgood, C. (1963). On understanding and creating sentences. *American Psychologist, 18,* 735–751.

Palermo, D. (1978). *The psychology of language.* Glenview, IL: Scott, Foresman.

Palermo, D., & Eberhart, V. (1968). On the learning of morphological rules: An experimental analogy. *Journal of Verbal Learning and Verbal Behavior, 7,* 337–344.

Penner, S. (1987). Parental responses to grammatical and ungrammatical child utterances. *Child Development, 58,* 376–384.

Piaget, J. (1926). *The language and thought of the child.* New York: Harcourt Brace Jovanovich.

Piaget, J. (1954). *Origins of intelligence.* New York: Basic Books.

Piatelli-Palmerini, M. (Ed.). (1980). *Learning and language.* Cambridge, MA: Harvard University Press.

Pinker, S. (1979). Formal models of language learning. *Cognition, 7,* 217–283.

Pinker, S. (1984). *Language learnability and language development* Cambridge, MA: Harvard University Press.

Pinker, S. (1987). The bootstrapping problem in language acquisition. In B. MacWhinney (Ed.), *Mechanisms of language acquisition.* Hillsdale, NJ: Erlbaum.

Pinker, S. (1989). *Learnability and cognition: The acquisition of argument structure.* Cambridge, MA: MIT Press.

Pinker, S. (1991). Rules of language. *Science, 253,* 530–535.

Pinker, S., Lebeaux, D., & Frost, L. (1987). Productivity and constraints in the acquisition of the passive. *Cognition, 26,* 195–267.

Pinker, S., & Prince, A. (1988). On language and connectionism: Analysis of a parallel distributed processing model of language acquisition. *Cognition, 28,* 73–193.

Rheingold, H., & Joseph, J. (1977, March). Speech to newborns by nursery personnel. Paper presented at the meeting of the Society for Research in Child Development, New Orleans.

Rileigh, K. (1973). Children's selective listening to stories: Familiarity effects involving vocabulary, syntax, and intonation. *Psychological Reports, 33,* 255–266.

Rubin, D. (1975). Within word structure in the tip-of-the-tongue phenomenon. *Journal of Verbal Learning and Verbal Behavior, 13,* 392–397.

Rummelhart, D., & McClelland, J. (1987). Learning the past tense of English verbs: Implicit rules or parallel distributed processing. In B. MacWhinney (Ed.), *Mechanisms of language acquisition* (pp. 195–248). Cambridge, MA: MIT Press.

Sachs, J. (1967). Recognition memory for syntactic and semantic aspects of connected discourse. *Perception and Psychophysics, 2,* 437–442.

Sachs, J. (1982). Talking about there and then: The emergence of displaced reference in parent–child discourse. In K. Nelson (Ed.), *Children's language.* New York: Gardner Press.

Sachs, J., & Johnson, M. (1972). Language development in a hearing child of deaf parents. Paper presented at the International Symposium on First Language Acquisition, Florence, Italy.

Sailor, W. (1971). Reinforcement and generalization of productive plural allomorphs in two retarded children. *Journal of Applied Behavior Analysis, 4,* 305–310.

Salzinger, K. (1959). Experimental manipulation of verbal behavior. *Journal of General Psychology, 61,* 65–94.

Sampson, G. (1987). Review of *Parallel distributed processing: Explorations in the microstructure of cognition, Vol. 1: Foundations,* by D. Rummelhart, J. McClelland, and the PDP Research Group, *Language, 63,* 871–886.

Savin, H., & Perchonock, E. (1965). Grammatical structure and immediate recall of English sentences. *Journal of Verbal Learning and Verbal Behavior, 4,* 348–353.

Segal, E. (1977). Toward a coherent psychology of language. In W. K. Honig & J. E. R. Staddon (Eds.), *Handbook of operant behavior.* Englewood Cliffs, NJ: Prentice-Hall.

Shatz, M. (1982). On mechanisms of language acquisition: Can features of the communicative environment account for development? In E. Wanner & L. Gleitman (Eds.), *Language acquisition: The state of the art.* Cambridge: Cambridge University Press.

Shore, C., O'Connell, B., & Bates, E. (1984). First sentence in language and symbolic play. Personal communication.

Sinclair-deZwart, H. (1969). Developmental psycholinguistics. In D. Elkind & J. Flavell (Eds.), *Studies in cognitive development: Essays in honor of Jean Piaget.* New York: Oxford University Press.

Sinclair-deZwart, H. (1973). Language acquisition and cognitive development. In T. Moore (Ed.), *Cognitive development and the acquisition of language.* New York: Academic Press.

Skinner, B. F. (1957). *Verbal behavior.* Englewood Cliffs, NJ: Prentice-Hall.

Skinner, B. F. (1969). *Contingencies of reinforcement: A theoretical analysis.* New York: Appleton-Century-Crofts.

Skinner, B. F. (1974). *About behaviorism.* London: Jonathan Cape.

Slobin, D. (1966). The acquisition of Russian as a native language. In F. Smith & C. A. Miller (Eds.), *The genesis of language: A psycholinguistic approach.* Cambridge, MA: MIT Press.

Slobin, D. (1979). *Psycholinguistics* (2nd ed.). Glenview, IL: Scott, Foresman.

Slobin, D. (1982). Universal and particular in the acquisition of language. In E. Wanner & L. Gleitman (Eds.), *Language acquisition: The state of the art.* Cambridge: Cambridge University Press.

Slobin, D. (1986). Crosslinguistic evidence for the language-making capacity. In D. Slobin, (Ed.). *The crosslinguistic study of language acquisition.* Vol. 2. Hillsdale, NJ: Erlbaum.

Slobin, D., & Bever, T. (1982). Children use cannonical sentence schemas: A cross-linguistic study of word order and inflections. *Cognition, 12,* 229–265.

Smith, E. (1978). Theories of semantic memory. In W. K. Estes (Ed.), *Handbook of learning and cognitive processes* (Vol. 6). Hillsdale, NJ: Erlbaum.

Snow, C. (1972). Mother's speech to children learning language. *Child Development, 43,* 549–565.

Snow, C. (1977a). The development of conversation between mothers and babies. *Journal of Child Language, 4,* 1–22.

Snow, C. (1977b). Mothers' speech research: From input to interaction. In C. Snow and C. Ferguson (Eds.), *Talking to children: Language input and acquisition.* Cambridge: Cambridge University Press.

Snow, C. (1978). The conversational context of language acquisition. In R. Campbell and P. Smith (Eds.), *Recent advances in the psychology of language* (Vol. 4a). New York: Plenum Press.

Snow, C. (1979). The role of social interaction in language acquisition. In W. A. Collins (Ed.), *Minnesota symposia on child psychology* (Vol. 12). Hillsdale, NJ: Erlbaum.

Snow, C. E. (1981a). Social interaction and language acquisition. In P. Dale and D. Ingram (Eds.), *Child language: An international perspective.* Baltimore: University Park Press.

Snow, C. (1981b). The uses of imitation. *Journal of Child Language, 8,* 205–208.

Sokolov, J. (1991, April). A reverse analysis of implicit negative feedback: Exact, expanded, and reduced parental imitation. Paper presented at the biennial meeting of the Society for Research in Child Development, Seattle, WA.

Speidel, G. E., & Nelson, K. E. (Eds.) (1989). *The many faces of imitation in language learning.* New York: Springer-Verlag.

Springer, S., & Deutsch, G. (1981). *Left brain, right brain.* San Francisco: W. H. Freeman.

Staats, A. (1971). Linguistic–mentalistic theory versus an explanatory S-R learning theory of language development. In D. Slobin (Ed.), *The ontogenesis of grammar.* New York: Academic Press.

Staats, A., Staats, C., & Crawford, H. (1962). First-order conditioning of meaning and the parallel conditioning of a GSR. *Journal of General Psychology, 67,* 167–195.

Staats, C., & Staats, A. (1957). Meaning established by classical conditioning. *Journal of Experimental Psychology, 54,* 74–80.

Steckol, K., & Leonard, L. (1981). Sensorimotor development and the use of prelinguistic performatives. *Journal of Speech and Hearing Research, 24,* 262–269.

Stern, D., Beebe, B., Jaffe, J., & Bennett, S. (1977). The infant's stimulus world during social interaction: A study of caregiver behaviors with particular reference to repetition and timing. In H. Schaffer (Ed.), *Studies in mother–infant interaction.* New York: Academic Press.

Stern, W. (1930). *Psychology of early childhood.* New York: Holt.

Stine, E. L., & Bohannon, J. N. (1983). Imitation, interactions and acquisition. *Journal of Child Language, 10,* 589–604.

Terrace, H., & Bever, T. (1976). What may be learned from studying language in the chimpanzee? *Annals of the New York Academy of Sciences, 280,* 579–588.

Tomasello, M. (1988). The role of joint attentional processes in early language development. *Language Sciences, 10,* 69–88.

Tomasello, M., & Farrar, J. (1986). Joint attention and early language. *Child Development, 57,* 1454–1463.

Umiker-Sebeok, J., & Sebeok, T. (1980). Introduction: Questioning apes. In T. Sebeok & J. Umiker-Sebeok (Eds.), *Speaking of apes: A critical anthology of two-way communication with man.* New York: Plenum Press.

Vygotsky, L. S. (1962). *Thought and language.* Cambridge, MA: MIT Press.

Warren-Leubecker, A., & Bohannon, J. (1982). The effects of expectation and feedback on speech to foreigners. *Journal of Psycholinguistic Research, 11,* 207–215.

Warren-Leubecker, A., & Bohannon, J. (1983). The effects of verbal feedback and listener type on the speech of preschool children. *Journal of Experimental Child Psychology, 35,* 540–548.

Warren-Leubecker, A., & Bohannon, J. (1984). Intonation patterns in child-directed speech: Mother-father differences. *Child Development, 55,* 1541–1548.

Watson, J. (1924). *Behaviorism.* Chicago: University of Chicago Press.

Wexler, K. (1982). A principle theory for language acquisition. In E. Wanner & L. Gleitman (Eds.), *Language acquisition: The state of the art.* Cambridge: Cambridge University Press.

Wexler, K., & Culicover, P. (1980). *Formal principles of language acquisition.* Cambridge, MA: MIT Press.

Wexler, K., Culicover, P., & Hamburger, H. (1975). Learning theoretic foundations of linguistic universals. *Theoretical Linguistics, 2,* 215–253.

Whitehurst, G. (1982). Language development. In B. Wolman (Ed.), *Handbook of developmental psychology.* Englewood Cliffs, NJ: Prentice-Hall.

Whitehurst, G., & Novak, G. (1973). Modeling, imitation training, and the acquisition of sentence phrases. *Journal of Experimental Child Psychology, 16,* 332–335.

Whitehurst, G., & Vasta, R. (1975). Is language acquired through imitation? *Journal of Psycholinguistic Research, 4,* 37–59.

Zimmerman, B., & Whitehurst, G. (1979). Structure and function: A comparison of two views of the development of language and cognition. In G. Whitehurst & B. Zimmerman (Eds.), *The functions of language and cognition.* New York: Academic Press.

Individual Differences in Language Acquisition

8

Beverly A. Goldfield *Rhode Island College*
Catherine E. Snow *Harvard Graduate School of Education*

■ INTRODUCTION

Children acquiring a first language exhibit striking similarities in the content and sequence of development. Earlier chapters have documented these universals in phonology, morphology, semantics, and syntax. Although commonalities have been stressed, there is also evidence for considerable diversity among young language learners. There is linguistic variation, for example, that can be related to the child's *gender, social class,* and *cultural community.* Children also vary in the *age of onset* of speech and *speed of acquisition.*

However, qualitative differences that cut across these traditional distinctions are now well documented. These differences include the *kinds of words* children begin to acquire, the *combinatorial patterns* of their earliest sentences, and the *strategies* they prefer to employ in learning to talk.

This chapter examines these individual differences in language development. We begin with a look at the status of individual differences in the history of child language research. This is followed by a discussion of variation in children's early words and sentences and later differences among second language learners and beginning readers. Final sections discuss the implications of individual differences for a theory of language development and suggest areas in which future research is needed.

■ THE HISTORY OF INDIVIDUAL DIFFERENCES IN CHILD LANGUAGE RESEARCH

Although the topic of individual differences currently generates considerable study and theoretical interest among child language researchers, this has not always been the case. Until recently, language development texts would scarcely have mentioned the topic, much less devoted an entire chapter to its discussion. This change can best be understood by considering the history of child language research.

Interest in individual differences follows almost two decades of research committed to documenting universal patterns of acquisition. Even though researchers during this period typically reported (and dismissed as unimportant) variations in the *rate* of language development, they placed greater emphasis on *similarities* among children in the sequence of development. At one level emphasis on commonalities among language learners grew out of a practical need for basic information about the nature and sequence of development. Another contributing factor, however, was the influence of linguistic theory on child language research. In the early 1960s Chomsky's (1957) theory of **transformational syntax** offered a new and coherent way of accounting for structural principles of adult linguistic competence that cut across inter- and intralinguistic diversity. For the next 10 years the kinds of questions asked and the methods used to study child language were direct outcomes of applying the new theory to problems of acquisition. Child language research focused on questions of *structure,* with the intent of documenting the *rules* governing children's early sentences; for example, *stages* were hypothesized to characterize the acquisition of *negative sentences,* of *wh-questions* (Bellugi, 1967), and of *noun* and *verb inflections* (Cazden, 1968).

The focus on linguistic universals during this period carried with it certain assumptions about the methods that could be used to investigate child language. For instance, since all normally developing children were assumed to construct similar rule systems, longitudinal study of a single child or a few children was a typical research paradigm (e.g., Braine, 1963; Brown, 1973). Many studies looked cross-linguistically for common structures and stages of acquisition (e.g., Bowerman, 1973; Slobin, 1968). While this paradigm guided much research and outlined the major dimensions of language development, it also biased us toward seeing shared patterns of development in the data. Children in some studies were selected for inclusion because of the ease with which the researcher could understand and record their speech (e.g., Brown, 1973). Children with less clear articulation or "messy," jargonlike strings in their early speech were less likely to be included (Peters, 1983). Similarly, utterances that appeared to be advanced, imitative, or nonrule-generated in an otherwise predictable corpus of child utterances were often relegated to the anomalous or miscellaneous category and were excluded from further study.

Several factors are responsible for the paradigm change represented by the current interest in variation in the pattern of language acquisition for individual children. First, linguistic theory grew more attentive to *semantic* and *pragmatic aspects* of adult language, and child language research also began to shift away from an exclusive emphasis on syntax. In the 1970s investigators became interested in the *meanings* of early words and sentences and in the ways in which language was used before the onset of word combinations. As the scope of child language research broadened, departures from a universal acquisition sequence began to be noticed and accorded some significance. Using larger samples of children to study the *meaning* and *function* as well as the *form* of early language, investigators have since observed that children vary along all three dimensions.

Another factor contributing to increased reports of variation is the attention now paid to children and child utterances previously excluded from study. Children with poor articulation and early jargonlike sentences have begun to appear in the literature (Adamson, Tomasello, & Benbenisty, 1984; Peters, 1977, 1983). Some investigators have made deliberate methodological decisions not to select children on the basis of a priori decisions about the representativeness of their language or language environment (Lieven, 1980).

We also have the benefit of recent studies of children from *diverse language communities* (e.g., Slobin, 1985) and *varied cultural* and *socioeconomic groups* (e.g., Heath, 1983; Lieven, Pine, & Barnes, 1991; Miller, 1982). The finding that some children, more than others, imitate the language they hear and that such imitation is selective (Bloom, Hood, & Lightbown, 1974; Clark, 1974, 1976; Snow, 1981, 1983) has encouraged researchers to consider how imitative utterances may help children induce the rules of language structure, in addition to serving as a means of conducting a conversation with limited linguistic resources.

Finally, the growing literature on individual differences among children acquiring a second language (Fillmore, 1979; Hatch, 1974) has been a major impetus for similar work in first language research. The variation reported among second language learners is striking and has provided investigators with clues to the kinds of strategies that younger and less advanced first language learners may likewise employ.

Serious attention to individual differences began in the 1970s, with a few studies that reported variation in children's first words (Dore, 1974; Nelson, 1973) and early sentences (Bloom, Lightbown, & Hood, 1975; Starr, 1975). Since then, research into individual differences has explored one or more of the following questions: (1) In what *ways* do children vary? (2) what *factors* contribute to individual differences? and (3) what are the *implications* of individual differences for understanding the process of acquisition, for devising an adequate theory of language development, and for clarifying the complex interdependence of cognitive, social, and linguistic factors in development?

■ INDIVIDUAL DIFFERENCES IN EARLY LEXICAL DEVELOPMENT

Nelson's (1973) study was the first to draw attention to differences in early lexical development. Nelson collected diary data on the productive vocabularies of 18 children (7 boys and 11 girls). The first 50 words of each child were assigned to form classes (nominals, action words, modifiers, personal-social items, function words) based on content or the child's first use of a word. Nelson found that all of the children acquired words for familiar people, animals, food, toys, vehicles, and household objects. The children varied, however, in the proportion of nominals in their vocabulary. Ten "**referential**" children had early lexicons that were dominated by words for *objects*. Referential children moved predictably from single words to a two-word stage. A sudden spurt of new words near the 50-word level often preceded the appearance of word combinations. An early preference for object labels was positively related to talk about objects and negatively related to talk about self in a follow-up speech sample at 24 months of age.

Eight **expressive** children followed a different route. They had fewer object labels but more pronouns and function words than the first group. They also acquired many more personal-social expressions, which were usually longer than a single word. From early on, these children used phrases such as "go away," "stop it," "don't do it," and "I want it." Their transition into syntactic combinations was less clear and not marked by a rapid increase in new vocabulary items.

Although there was no difference in the age at which the two groups acquired 50 words, children in the referential group included both early and late talkers who tended to learn words at a faster rate than children in the expressive group, who evidenced a slower, steadier rate of acquisition.

Nelson argued that these differences reflected the children's differing hypotheses about how language is used. Referential children were learning language to talk about and categorize the objects in their environment. Expressive children were more socially oriented and were acquiring the means to talk about themselves and others.

Although Nelson introduced a new approach to the study of language development, it is important to note that the referential–expressive dimension is not a dichotomy, but rather a continuum along which individual children vary. Most children appear to acquire a relative balance of referential and expressive items; only a few children acquire a distribution extreme enough to be called a distinct "style" (Bretherton, Mc-

New, Snyder, & Bates, 1983; Goldfield, 1985/86, 1987; Nelson, 1981). Moreover, we must also consider how children actually use their words.

As Nelson recognized, there is no direct correspondence between form class and usage. Although Nelson defined nominals in her classification scheme as words that referred to the "thing world," they included pronouns, substances, and names for people as well as objects, and could be used to *demand* as well as to *label*. Moreover, even object labels may mediate social interaction, especially during shared, familiar routines such as looking at and naming pictures in a book.

A few studies have examined *functional* differences in children's early speech. Dore (1974) examined how two children used their single-word utterances in videotaped conversations with their mothers and nursery school teachers. One child used clearly articulated single words to label, repeat, and practice, and her speech involved others 26 percent of the time. The second child produced fewer words but used prosodic features to communicate in more ways. His utterances included others 63 percent of the time. Dore suggests that the first child's language was **code-oriented,** concerned with *representing* things in the environment. The second child was **message-oriented,** more often using language to manipulate the *social* situation. Thus, Dore finds some support for Nelson's hypothesized functional differences, but it is not clear if his two subjects also differed with respect to the kinds of words (e.g., nominals versus personal-social words) they used.

Pine (1992), on the other hand, collected diary data on the first 100 words of seven children, and coded audiotaped speech samples for various functions, including attention, labeling, description, demand, and protest. Although children varied considerably in the proportion of common nouns in their lexicon (a range of 28 percent to 54 percent at 50 words, and 35 percent to 67 percent at 100 words), there was no relationship between referential vocabulary and any functional category at either vocabulary level.

Bowerman (1976) also points out that word usage may *shift* over time. She cites an example from Ferrier (1975), who reports that her daughter initially used *phew* expressively, to greet her mother in the morning. The word was originally an imitation of her mother's own routine comment on the odor she invariably encountered on these occasions. The same word was later used by her daughter referentially, as a name for diapers, clean or soiled.

A related issue is the *frequency* with which children use the various types of words in their lexicons. Even in cases where nouns account for about half of children's reported vocabulary, they may be used less often than other words (Pine, 1990). Three children Lieven (1980) observed, for example, acquired more nominals than any other word class. Thus, Lieven's subjects, Jane, Kate, and Beth, seem similar to Nelson's referential group. But taking into account the frequency of a word's use produced a different pattern. Jane used general nominals more frequently than any other word class, whereas Kate used almost as many personal-social items as general nominals. Beth used many more specific nominals, nonclassifiables (ambiguous utterances such as "there"), and action items than the other two children. The relative weight of these categories was due to Beth's frequent use of a few words (*Mommy, Julian, look, there, more*) to win attention from others. Even though Beth could be described as socially directed, this classification did not depend on her use of personal-social items, which distinguished the expressive group in Nelson's study. Rather, Beth was using many of her words, including words Nelson would have called referential, in an expressive way.

Thus, although children may vary in the kinds of words they acquire, there is no consistent support for the notion that children with relatively more nouns use language in more naming and fewer social contexts. Many, if not most, early words serve a variety of functions, and the *distribution, function,* and *frequency* of word usage are related but separable aspects of early lexical development.

Another line of research suggests that children differ with respect to the *length* of the linguistic unit that they segment from adult speech. As previously described, both Nelson's expressive children and Dore's message-oriented child tended to produce longer, phraselike utterances during the single-word stage. Minh, the child studied by Peters (1977, 1983), began producing phrases at 11 months that were largely unintelligible yet were marked by stress and intonation that conveyed "an impression of sentencehood" (1977, p. 564). At 14 months, Minh began to use single words that increased in number and phonetic accuracy over time. Peters termed these two kinds of speech *gestalt* and *analytic,* respectively.

Plunkett (1991) observed that different *segmentation strategies* distinguished the early speech of his two subjects. One child relied heavily on longer, formulaic expressions, whereas the second child tended to use shorter, lexically reduced forms. Plunkett suggests that these two strategies are alternative solutions to the problem of segmenting lexical units in adult speech. Formulaic expressions represent solutions that overshoot a target adult word, whereas lexically reduced forms represent undershooting solutions. Both children experimented briefly with the alternative strategy prior to a spurt in their vocabulary.

A distinction that may be related to these differing segmentation strategies occurs in children's early *phonological* systems as well. Some children's early utterances seem to be generated on the basis of an elegant and orderly set of phonological rules, such that the child-form of any adult word is highly predictable. Such children (e.g., Smith's subject Amahl, 1973) either apply their rule system consistently to imitated as well as to spontaneous forms or else resist imitating words that would constitute violations of the restrictions on their output. Other children, in contrast, operate with fairly sloppy phonological systems, showing alternation among several ways of producing most words and applying their phonological rules optionally. Typically, the children with sloppy phonological systems incorporate imitated (and thus progressive) forms into their lexicon quite easily and may be more likely to show improvement in production as a result of direct modeling (Macken, 1978).

■ INDIVIDUAL DIFFERENCES IN EARLY SENTENCES

Variation in children's early word combinations has been reported by Bloom, Lightbown, and Hood (1975) in a study of four children recorded at three- to six-week intervals during the early stages of multiword speech. Bloom, Lightbown, and Hood found that a common set of *semantic categories* (utterances expressing action, locative action, state, locative state, existence, recurrence, negation, possession, attribution, notice, *wh*-question, place, action and place, intention, dative, instrument) and a similar order of emergence characterized the early sentences of all four children. The form of the children' s combinations varied, however.

All four children used a *pivot strategy* to encode negation and nonexistence (*no* + *X*, *no more* + *X*) and recurrence (*more* + *X*, *'nother* + *X*). This strategy consisted of combining one of a small class of *function words* and any one of a larger, varying set of *content words*. The meaning of the entire utterance was thus determined by the meaning of the function word. Eric and Peter used this same approach to express action, location, and possessive relations. To encode these semantic notions, the two boys tended to combine all-purpose pronouns with content words. They produced utterances such as "I finish," "play it," "sit here," and "my truck." During this same period Kathryn and Gia expressed the same set of semantic relations by combining content words, as in "Gia push," "touch milk," "sweater chair," and "Kathryn sock."

Bloom, Lightbown, and Hood claim that the children were using two different strategies for breaking into the language system. The pronominal approach used by the two boys allowed them to begin encoding relationships between objects and events without relying on specific lexical items. Since they used a varied lexicon in single-word utterances and in functional relations with *no* and *more,* their strategy could not be attributed to simply not knowing enough labels. The two girls, on the other hand, preferred to encode the same meanings using specific labels for particular objects. When the MLU approached 2.5, the two systems began to overlap. Children using a *pronominal strategy* combined more content words, whereas the *nominal* children incorporated more pronouns into their utterances.

The child observed by Goldfield (1982) also exhibited an early pronominal style, but close examination of her multiword speech over time revealed that a few specific combinatorial patterns accounted for the relative dominance of pronouns. For example, the roles of agent and possessor were initially limited to the child herself and encoded by pronouns *I* and *my,* respectively. These semantic roles later broadened to include others, and in these cases nominals were used to encode the constituent. Earliest action utterances ("I'll do it," "I found it") were initially unconstructed phrases marked by particular intonation contours and used in specific situations. Later action utterances took the form of agent + action + *it* and appeared to have evolved from the earlier pattern.

Braine (1976) also observed that children's first word combinations are generated by a small number of specific, concrete formulas. Braine examined cross-linguistic data from 11 children and found considerable variation in the kinds of early formulas individual children acquired, with no overlap in some cases. These formulas typically encoded a limited semantic domain (e.g., *big/little* + *X*, *hot/cold* + *X*), and each pattern was acquired independently. Consolidation of individual patterns into broader, more abstract semantic categories, such as attribute, was a later development. Braine would argue, then, that children show considerable variation in the specific meanings they encode but considerable universality in their common beginning with specific, concrete patterns.

It is possible that the individuality of children's early combinatorial patterns has often been obscured by the level of analysis applied to the data. A single, broad, abstract category, such as attribute, may subsume several more specific patterns. This more general level of analysis is congruent with the implicit goal of most child language research: to identify universal aspects of development. An analysis that focuses on individual patterns requires more detailed description and finer distinctions. Thus, the more general and abstract the categories of analysis, the more one child will look like another. More specific patterns will distinguish the individual child.

■ INDIVIDUAL DIFFERENCES ACROSS LEVELS OF LANGUAGE DEVELOPMENT

We have discussed, thus far, variation among children acquiring either first words or the beginnings of language structure. A related issue is the *relationship* of these differences across *developmental stages,* that is, from first words through early sentences. Do children with a preference for object labels tend to develop a nominal strategy for their early word combinations? Do children with relatively more expressive speech prefer a pronominal approach?

There is some evidence that children's early *lexical preferences* are reflected in the form of their first word combinations. Nelson (1975) followed the later language development of her original referential–expressive sample. Using transcripts of speech recorded when the children were 24 and 30 months of age, she found that referential speakers began with a high proportion of nouns in early sentences. With increasing MLU, the use of pronouns increased while nouns decreased for these children. Children from the original expressive group began with a balance of noun and pronoun use. Pronoun use changed very little for this group, but nouns increased with advanced MLU.

Functional differences that extend from single words to word combinations have also been reported. Starr (1975) observed 12 children in a longitudinal study of language development from one to two-and-a-half years of age. She found that children who preferred to label objects in single-word speech tended to produce two-word sentences encoding object-attribute relations. A second group of children described objects less frequently but used more interjections (conventional social responses such as "hi," "bye," "ouch") and made more self-references (e.g., "want ball") in their early sentences.

Similarly, Lieven (1980) reports that early sentences of the three children she observed appeared to derive from characteristics of their single-word speech. For one child both single words and early constructions (e.g., "there," "mommy," "there Julian," and "there mommy") were used to gain adult attention rather than to convey reference. The other two children were more likely to describe attributes and actions of people and things in both their single- and multiple-word utterances.

The tendency to produce whole phrases in the one-word stage is characteristic of an expressive style, but it is not clear how these early units are related to grammatical development. Evidence based on age-related correlational measures, on the one hand, suggest that early phrasal speech is unrelated to later analyzed productions (Bates,

Evidence shows that children's early lexical preferences are reflected in the form of their first word combinations.

Bretherton, & Snyder, 1988). Pine and Lieven (1990), however, argue that age-related measures of individual differences confound strategy and variation associated with developmental level. They argue, instead, for continuity between early phrases and later pivot constructions. In a sample of 12 children (Lieven, Pine, & Barnes, 1992), phrasal speech correlated negatively with common nouns in the first 50 and second 50 words. Moreover, children's productive combinations at 100 words correlated positively with earlier phrasal speech, and negatively with common nouns. Lieven, Pine, and Barnes (1992) suggest that nouns and formulaic phrases represent two distinct strands in early lexical development, and that early phrases are potential patterns for eventual analysis and use in productive combinations.

An alternative view of variation that predicts some stability across language levels identifies *imitativeness* as a central dimension of individual differences. Children who have a strong tendency to imitate adult utterances may, as a result, acquire phrasal units as well as single words during the one-word stage, produce more high-frequency items of low semantic value (such as pronouns) during the early sentence stage, and have messier phonological systems all along. Relationships between imitativeness and the tendency to be expressive, to produce longer utterances, and to show high levels of unintelligibility have been reported (Bloom, Hood, & Lightbown, 1974; Ferguson & Farwell, 1975; Nelson, 1973), but other studies that have found that referential children imitate more suggest that differences between expressive and referential children lie more in what they imitate than in how much. Whereas expressive children imitate large units and social expressions, referential children tend to imitate object labels, particularly those they do not already know (Leonard, Schwartz, Folger, Newhoff, & Wilcox, 1979; Nelson, Baker, Denninger, Bonvillian, & Kaplan, 1985).

Children who acquire many phrases during the one-word stage appear to be intent on sounding like the adult speech they hear. Nelson's expressive speakers, for example, early on acquired phrases such as "go away," "stop it," "don't do it," and "I want it." Bloom's subject, Eric, was also notable for his ability to produce the "acoustic aspects of heard speech" (Bloom, 1970, p. 102). In the early sessions he often produced unintelligible, extended strings of sound with adultlike intonation contours. He usually directed his utterances to a listener and appeared to expect a response. Eric's intelligible utterances were also, at times, multimorphemic, most often a single word extended phonologically with a dummy [ə]. Three boys studied by Ramer (1976) relied heavily (13.5 to 63.9 percent of all multiple-word productions) on utterances extended with empty phonetic forms and continued to use such "presyntactic" forms throughout the period of syntactic acquisition. These boys began by specifying predicate structures only, rather than the full range of possible syntactic relations. A group of four girls used fewer presyntactic forms (.0 to 31.0 percent) and specified more varied syntactic relations.

In his use of gestalt language, Peter's (1977, 1983) subject Minh appeared to be aiming at whole phrases or sentences. Peters suggests that these phrasal utterances may be stored, retrieved, and used as single lexical items that are later analyzed and broken down into productive components. This implies an *alternative strategy* for learning about language structure, one that proceeds from the whole to parts, with the parts later recombined in novel utterances. Children who tend to imitate this kind of phrasal language may be sensitive to the social functions that such language can serve, while at the same time they are accumulating instances of structured utterances that are the basis of later rule induction. The term *analysis for reproduction* describes this strategy of making use of larger segments of the input, in contrast to *analysis for understanding*, which instead looks for smaller linguistic units that can be used in other combinations. A series of studies by Bates and her colleagues (Bates, Bretherton, & Snyder, 1988; Bretherton, McNew, Snyder, & Bates, 1983; Snyder, Bates, & Bretherton, 1981), suggests that the operation of these two strategies may be reflected in dissociable "strands" or related clusters of language abilities that emerge at various developmental stages. In their longitudinal study of 27 children, these researchers found that measures of MLU and morphology at 20 months were related to unanalyzed productions at 13 months, suggesting that early grammar is largely a rote process that depends most heavily upon analysis for reproduction. At 28 months, however, MLU was associated with earlier measures of comprehension and analyzed production, suggesting that later grammatical constructions are largely under the control of analysis for understanding. Although both strategies may be necessary in the course of acquisition, individual children may differentially exploit one or the other at any point in the process. This research also points out that a measure of MLU may mean very different things at different developmental stages.

The qualitative differences described thus far may also be related to a more traditionally accepted dimension of variation: **rate of acquisition.** Children who emphasize nouns in their early speech have typically been described as faster or more advanced language learners than their less referential peers. This characterization, however, depends heavily on the indices used to assess linguistic skill. Measures based solely on the number of words produced may underestimate both comprehension and the multiplicity of factors involved in effective communication. For example, the child observed by Adamson, Tomasello, and Benbenisty (1984) made relatively slow initial progress in terms of the number of distinct words she acquired, but her communicative skills included a high rate of vocalization with varied prosody, and she used her few single words to serve a variety of functions, including labeling.

Goldfield and Reznick (1990) also suggest that differences in rate are due to differing approaches to word learning. Thirteen of their subjects evidenced a *vocabulary spurt,* during which three-quarters of the words added were nouns. These children appeared to concentrate their efforts on learning object names, a strategy that might allow them to accumulate words rapidly. Five other children evidenced a more gradual learning curve, acquiring a more balanced distribution of nouns and other word classes. These children appeared to favor an alternative strategy, one that attempts to encode a broad range of experience with a more varied lexicon, resulting in less dramatically accelerated lexical growth.

Horgan (1981) examined the relationship between rate and *pattern* of development by comparing the speech of children who were categorized as slow or fast learners. Fifteen pairs of children were matched on MLU but differed in age by at least six months. Horgan compared the language of the younger (faster) and older (slower) children on several measures. The faster learners tended to use more nouns and more complex noun phrases and to talk more about people and things. These children also tended to make more grammatical errors. The slower learners used fewer and less elaborate noun phrases but more and more complex verb phrases. These same children, however, were more advanced on a comprehension task.

Horgan suggests that the slower children were more cautious language learners, with good receptive abilities but a more guarded approach to displaying their verbal skills. They may also have been focusing their attention on the details of language structure, as evidenced by their use of more auxiliaries and more kinds of constructions. The faster children, with their more frequent errors, were "more willing to take risks" (p. 636), especially with the finer points of grammatical structure. Their attention was focused instead on the task of describing in detail the objects and people in their environment. This same distinction between a *cautious/conservative* and a *risk-taking/error-prone* approach to acquisition has been proposed to account for style differences in second language learners.

■ SOURCES OF VARIATION

Investigators have suggested two sources for the variation observed in children's early language: differences in the way children *organize information* and act on the world and/or differences in *environmental influence,* particularly *language input.*

COGNITIVE ORGANIZATION

Nelson (1973) proposed that differences in children's prelinguistic conceptual organization contribute to their early preferences for a referential or expressive vocabulary. She hypothesized that some babies organize their world around objects, whereas others focus on people. Children's differing hypotheses about what language is for (to organize and categorize objects or to talk about self and others) derive from these differing organizations of experience. Mothers of referential children more often reported that their children favored manipulative toys, supporting the notion that preexistent cognitive differences may influence children's speech style.

Studies of children's language and play have not found consistent support for linguistic differences that map onto object and social preferences. On the one hand, there is evidence that children who are more attentive to toys learn more nominals, whereas children who orient more toward adults learn more personal-social words (Rosenblatt, 1977). Similarly, Wolf and Gardner (1979) report that some children, termed **patterners,** preferred to exploit the possibilities of the object world, particularly physical characteristics and spatial arrangements. These children excelled at constructing two- and three-dimensional displays. The early vocabulary of patterners had a high proportion of names of objects, animals, and locations. Later vocabulary emphasized color, size, and number words and terms for physical relationships.

A second group, called **dramatists**, was more involved in the social world. These children preferred to reproduce aspects of human interaction in their symbolic play and chose materials and activities (e.g., puppets and toy telephones) that lent themselves to their concerns. Dramatists had more early words that were proper names, greetings, and expressions of feeling. Later vocabulary emphasized words for emotions, moods, and qualities of people.

Goldfield (1985/86, 1987), however, suggests that episodes of *shared attention* to objects may contribute more to the acquisition of referential language than the sheer quantity of object or social behavior. Goldfield observed 12 children during play sessions in the home at 12, 15, and 18 months of age. Mothers kept a diary record of children's first 50 words. Children who acquired relatively more nominals did not differ from their less referential peers on measures of time in toy play or frequency of social behaviors. Children with more nominals, however, did use objects more frequently to engage their mothers' attention. These children, for example, often held out a toy to show their mother. Children with more expressive speech, on the other hand, were not necessarily less interested in objects nor more sociable than their peers. They did, however, tend to overlap the two domains less often. These children were more likely to interrupt or leave their toy play to seek social attention, rather than to share or show a toy. Differences in the use of objects to mediate social interaction may, in turn, influence the language parents address to children. Child pointing typically elicits a maternal label (Masur, 1982), and children who more frequently point to objects acquire more nouns (Goldfield, 1990).

THE LANGUAGE ENVIRONMENT

Although adult speech to children shares many features, there are also clear differences in how parents talk to children, and encourage their children to talk. Stable differences have been noted in maternal conversational style, including mothers' preferred use of language to direct behavior, elicit conversation, or instruct their children (Olsen-Fulero, 1982). Moreover, at least some aspects of maternal style appear to influence children's acquisition of referential or expressive speech. Referential language has been associated with maternal utterances that refer to and describe objects, and that request and reinforce names for things (Brown, 1973; Della Corte, Benedict, & Klein, 1983; Furrow & Nelson, 1984; Nelson & Bonvillian, 1972). A socially expressive lexicon, on the other hand, is related to maternal speech that refers to persons rather than objects and that directs or regulates the child's behavior (Della Corte, Benedict, & Klein, 1983; Furrow & Nelson, 1984; Nelson, 1973). The number of nouns versus pronouns in maternal talk, however, is unrelated to children's speech style (Furrow & Nelson, 1984; Nelson, 1973). Thus the *pragmatic focus* of maternal speech (i.e., what mothers talk about and for what purpose) appears to be more influential than the quantity of a particular part of speech.

These differences suggest that mothers of referential and expressive children are seeking out different opportunities for interaction and conversation. A good deal of children's referential language, for example, may originate in certain *routinized naming games*. Dore (1974) found that most of the labeling and repeating of the code-oriented baby he observed occurred in verbal routines established by the caregiver:

> M's mother set up routines in which she would pick up one item, label it, and encourage her daughter to imitate the label. There were animal-naming routines . . . utensil-naming and people-naming routines also occurred frequently. (p. 348)

Nelson (1973) also observed that 28 percent of the first 50 words acquired by referential children referred to body parts, almost surely learned in this kind of routine, whereas none of the expressive children had acquired labels for parts of the body. Expressive children, on the other hand, learn many conventional social expressions (e.g., "hi," "bye," "please," "thank you," "let's go," and "oh dear") that typically mark events such as arrivals, departures, and exchanges. Mothers of children with more expressive speech tend to use many such stereotypical utterances (Nelson, 1973; Lieven, 1980; Plunkett, 1991). Urwin (1978) observed that the parents of two visually handicapped children differed in the activities they organized and the language they used with their children. The parents of one child utilized his limited vision by encouraging attention to and labeling of objects, whereas the parents of a totally blind child more often engaged him in physical activities and social games. The latter child's early utterances were dominated by requests for and expressions of these games and routines.

CONTEXT: THE INTERACTION OF CHILD AND CAREGIVER BEHAVIOR

Although there is evidence supporting the contributions of both the child's unique organization of experience and aspects of maternal input to individual differences in early language, these variables and the complex relationships between them have not been sufficiently explored. Some investigators have emphasized the role of child variables, whereas others have implicated environmental determinants. Snyder, Bates, and Bretherton (1981), for example, suggest that referential children have made the conceptual discovery that words name things prior to the onset of speech. The preponderance of object labels in their early lexicon reflects a developmental shift from functional, context-bound language to language that refers to classes of objects and events. McShane (1980), on the other hand, proposes that this same precocious grasp of the concept of reference is a result of referential children's frequent participation in naming games, such as pointing to and labeling objects in a book. As we noted earlier, both Nelson (1973) and Dore (1974) have observed such maternal–child naming rituals among their label-oriented children. There may be other, similarly routine contexts that provide opportunities for learning the kind of personal-social language characteristic of expressive children.

Bornstein (1989) identifies a number of categories of parent–child interaction, and suggests that, among these, social and didactic interactions are particularly significant. The *social mode* consists of "physical and verbal strategies parents use to express their feelings and to engage their young in primarily interpersonal exchanges," whereas the *didactic mode* includes parental efforts for "stimulating and arousing their offspring to the world outside the pair, in encouraging attention to properties, objects, or events in the environment" (p. 199). Moreover, specific modes of interaction can be expected to influence developmental outcomes in specific ways. The challenge for research is in specifiying the mechanisms that regulate these interactive modes at different points in development.

It seems important, then, to examine how contexts vary for different caregiver–child pairs in attempting to account for variation in early language. Episodes of *joint object attention*, for example, are associated with more child labels and more maternal comments (Tomasello & Farrar, 1986; Tomasello & Todd, 1983). Book reading may be a particularly effective context for acquiring object labels (Ninio, 1980; Ninio & Bruner, 1978). Other situations in the child's life (eating, dressing, playing with siblings and peers, playing with toys, rough-and-tumble playing, and listening to and singing nursery rhymes and songs) provide quite different contexts for input and acquisition. As Nelson (1981) has observed, the context in which language is used determines the form and function of the input. Thus, as the range of contexts varies, opportunities for language learning will differ for individual children.

The interests of both child and caregiver, moreover, will influence the kinds of contexts that make up the daily events and routines of a particular mother–child pair. Goldfield (1987) found that children's lexical differences were best predicted by a combination of child and caregiver variables. More referential language was acquired by children who more often used objects to elicit maternal attention and who had mothers who more often labeled and described toys. More expressive speech was acquired by children in dyads ranking low on these two measures. Children in mixed dyads (mother ranking high, child ranking low; child ranking high, mother ranking low) acquired a relatively balanced distribution of object labels and expressive speech. Thus, children with more object labels may have a developmental history of consistent interaction and conversation around objects. Johanna, the most referential child in this sample, for example, gave clear evidence that shared attention to objects was a familiar and enjoyable interactive context. During the play sessions, almost half (48 percent) of her attempts to engage her mother involved showing or giving a toy. Johanna's mother, moreover, clearly and consistently supported the acquisition of labels. Talk about toys was the largest category of maternal speech (41 percent), and the mother highlighted names for things during all types of play, from bookreading ("egg in the hole book/look/see the tree") to ball games ("ayy it's a ball") and pretend play ("here's a woman—you can put the woman in the truck"). Johanna learned labels for body parts (e.g., "eyes," "ears," "nose," "mouth," "teeth," and "hair"), food (e.g., "juice," "banana," "milk," "pear," and "cheese"), clothing ("sock," "shoes," "hat," and "diaper"), and household items and toys ("light," "book," "chair," and "dolly"). Only one of her first 50 words was a phrase ("get you").

Other children may experience relatively more contexts in which the focus is on the child's behavior, performance, or nontoy play. Caitlin, a child with highly expressive speech, for example, included a toy in only 18 percent of her social initiations. She was more likely to pause in her play to look and smile at her mother. Caitlin's mother, moreover, often engaged her baby in social play, using conversational formulae and routines more than any other mother in the sample. Almost half (48 percent) of her utterances were questions and directives used to prompt her daughter's performance and to engage her participation in shared play. Sixty-one percent of Caitlin's first 50 words consisted of social-centered expressions, many of them phrasal units (e.g., "hi kitty," "thank you," "hey you guys," "let's go," "where are you," "lemme see," "don't touch," and "sit down").

Most children, however, are likely to learn a more balanced mix of referential and expressive speech, acquired through participation in a range of contexts with an object or personal/social focus. Peters (1983) observed that Minh's use of analytic and gestalt language was often tied to specific contexts. One-word utterances were likely in situations such as naming pictures in a book, whereas gestalt language was often copied from songs and storybook rhymes.

Even the same context, however, may be negotiated quite differently by different mother–child pairs. Ninio (1980), for example, observed different interaction styles for mother–child pairs engaged in looking at picture books. An *eliciting* style, characterized by frequent maternal what's-that questions, was used with active infants and was related to a large productive vocabulary. A high proportion of where's-*X* questions occurred with less talkative infants with a larger comprehension vocabulary. Maternal labeling statements were frequent for mothers with infants least likely to participate and were related to higher imitative responding. The different content and structure of a given context for different mother–child pairs also need to be considered in accounting for children's language differences.

■ LATER DIFFERENCES

We have seen that extreme exploitation of one style or another in language acquisition is likely to be the product of a convergence between a child tendency and some characteristic of the linguistic or social interaction available in the child's environment. The question arises, then, how stable these dimensions of individual difference in language acquisition are when the child is faced with a similar task—such as learning a second language, or learning to read—in a somewhat different environment. The stability of style from the one-word stage through early sentences suggests the differences might be persistent, but the influence of environmental factors suggests that they would not persist if the conditions for the new learning were quite different.

One cross-language case study (Bates, Bretherton, & Snyder, 1988) is available, of a child who was highly referential in her English one-word vocabulary but looked very expressive in the Italian she acquired at a later age. The caretakers providing the major sources of input in English and Italian were different, and this may account for the child's style shift. Unfortunately, no larger groups of children have been followed from first language acquisition through second language acquisition or reading—the study that is required to answer questions about stability of individual differences. However, the dimensions of individual differences that have been noted within groups of second language learners and groups of beginning readers map enticingly well onto the dimensions of differences in first language acquisition.

SECOND LANGUAGE ACQUISITION

Hatch (1974) was the first to suggest that second language learners fall into two groups—*rule-learners* and *data-gatherers*. The rule-learners maintain rather limited and orderly systems for generating utterances, produce utterances easily classified within their systems, develop in an orderly way through stages, and resist using utterances they have not fully understood or analyzed. Data-gatherers, on the other hand, use a mixture of rule-generated and imitated utterances, are more willing to take risks by using expressions they have heard but have not fully parsed, and have language systems less easily characterized by a discrete set of rules. They seem to be oriented toward using language socially rather than operating on the linguistic system itself.

Fillmore (1979) points out that the major dimension of individual differences in second language acquisition is *speed of learning:* some of us are slow and laborious second language learners, whereas others pick up languages quickly and easily. She

Second languages are learned in a wide variety of settings.

explains such differences as the product of differential utilization of a series of social and cognitive strategies that support second language learning. The most successful learner in her study was motivated to be a member of the second language social group, tended to be playful and experimental with language, used newly acquired expressions extensively, and imitated formulaic expressions but also analyzed and parsed her own imitative utterances quickly. The least successful learner avoided social contacts, postponed using expressions until he understood them fully, and used formulaic expressions with little tendency to analyze or modify them. As described earlier, first language learners may also be distinguished by their tendency to proceed slowly and cautiously or quickly and with more errors. Similar differences in the application of social and cognitive resources may underlie the relationship between rate and pattern of development in first language acquisition.

An aspect of individual variation in second language acquisition that has much less impact for first language acquisition is the interaction between learners' differences and the learning situation. Second languages are learned in a wide variety of settings and approaches—in bilingual classrooms, in immersion programs (i.e., programs that "immerse" a group of students in the second language for the entire school day), from "submersion" in a group that speaks the language, or through formal teaching using one of a variety of methods. There is evidence (Wesche, 1981) that certain learners do better in particular formal settings (e.g., audiolingual classrooms rather than explicit grammar and translation classrooms) and furthermore, that those who find learning in certain settings very difficult can be identified on the basis of aptitude profiles even before they start their language studies.

Another aspect of individual differences that is heightened by second language acquisition is learners' relative proficiency at different components of language ability. For example, Genesee and Hamayan (1980) found that field-independence (the tendency to analyze or impose structure on a visual perceptual field) and English reading ability predicted French immersion students' abilities in French language arts and in listening comprehension but not in oral production. Snow and Hoefnagel-Hohle (1978) found that after learners had one year's exposure to a second language, their pronunciation and auditory discrimination ability were clearly differentiated from grammar and vocabulary, with some learners scoring very high on one but low on the other factor. It is tempting to suggest that learners who are relatively high on phonological and low on grammatical ability turn out to be data-gatherers or imitators, whereas those with stronger grammatical skills look like rule-learners. There is at the current time, however, no firm basis for linking up these various dimensions.

READING

Reading is also susceptible to different approaches. In early reading instruction, for example, **phonics methods** focus on phoneme–grapheme correspondences, rule-governed patterns, and analytic skills, whereas **whole-word,** look-and-say methods rely on the gestalt ability to perceive and recall larger, meaningful units. The success of both methods suggests that most children must be able to operate with both strategies, at least to some extent.

However, Bussis, Chittenden, Amarel, and Klausner (1984) present evidence that children bring their own stylistic preferences to the task of learning to read. These investigators conducted a longitudinal study of beginning readers in first through second grade and observed systematic differences in children's approaches to reading and other classroom activities. One group of children was relatively more oriented to the imaginative possibilities of various media and was more likely to explore and experiment with the materials themselves than to fashion a predetermined product. These same children minimized classroom "boundaries," seeking to connect their own activities with those of their classmates or their own experiences with characters and events they encountered in books. They moved easily in and out of classroom spaces, changed activities frequently, skipped around on workbook pages, and typically previewed reading selections by thumbing through pages to look at pictures and read ahead. In their oral reading these children focused on maintaining the pace and storyline of the text. They would approximate or skip over unknown words and fabricate whole segments of a difficult passage. These children often appeared to scan the print ahead of their actual place in the text, using this information to further their understanding of the meaning of the text.

A second group of children focused on reproducing conventional structures and meanings. They worked carefully and methodically to depict accurate representations of reality in their drawings and block designs. They preferred a contained working space and approached tasks one at a time. These children were particularly adept at recalling details in proper sequence, and their story retellings were typically factual accounts of chronologically ordered events. On oral reading tasks these children also concentrated on faithfully translating the text. They rarely skipped or slurred over trouble spots and were reluctant to guess at a word. With unknown words these children simply paused for however long it took to sound it out themselves or to obtain the teacher's assistance. Despite reading in this step-by-step fashion, these children were nonetheless able to construct and retain the meaning of the story.

The two patterns of classroom behavior noted by Bussis et al. are strikingly similar to the distinctive profiles of the Wolf and Gardner (1979) dramatist and patterner groups. Children in both studies differed in their approach to materials and in the direction and tempo of their activities, with apparent consequences for early language and the language-related task of learning to read. Further longitudinal research is needed to determine whether these are indeed stable and related patterns that children differentially exhibit across contexts and over time.

■ IMPLICATIONS OF INDIVIDUAL DIFFERENCES FOR A THEORY OF LANGUAGE ACQUISITION

The fact of individual differences in language acquisition has implications for theories of language development. Assessing the extent and the type of individual differences in language acquisition helps us to construct a theory that incorporates the full range of patterns children exhibit and processes they employ in the task of learning to talk.

One way we might begin to test our view of language development is by examining data that have previously been neglected or considered less than typical. Children whose early language consists of clearly articulated single words are well represented in the bulk of language development research. Nelson's referential speakers evidenced the classic pattern of a clearly defined one-word stage with a sharp increase in vocabulary coinciding with the emergence of word combinations. The expressive style, however, was characterized by a mixture of single words and multimorphemic phrases and a more gradual transition into combinatorial speech. One of Nelson's expressive speakers, for example, produced "I do," "you do," "I want it," "I don't want it," "do it," "I love you," "I don't know," "what do you want," and "go away." This kind of appropriation of communicatively useful phrases in the early stages of language learning has been less well described and is less well understood. Children's early use of such multimorphemic utterances, however, suggests that a theory of acquisition must account for the possibility that (1) imitation is a mechanism for acquiring the use of structured utterances well before the onset of combinatorial speech and (2) for those children who use phrasal language, one aspect of syntactic learning may consist of finding regularities in the surface forms of phrases they already use, gradually decomposing these larger chunks into smaller units, and inducing the structural rules for generating similar utterances in the process. Peters (1983) suggests the term *fission* for the eventual breakdown of these multimorphemic forms and distinguishes this process from the complementary one of building sentences by combining units, which she calls *fusion*.

The early use of phrasal utterances may be more common than has been previously acknowledged. Longer, expressive phrases occur throughout the one-word period (Branigan, 1977; Lieven, Pines, & Barnes, 1992; Stokes & Holden, 1980; Thomas, 1979). Lieven, Pines, and Barnes suggest that research would reveal more nonreferential children if samples were more often expanded to include a wider range of social backgrounds. Five out of 12 children in their sample of families from varied socioeconomic groups had 25 or more phrases in their first 100 words. Attention to phrasal speech has resulted in improved methodologies and criteria for determining the length and productivity of children's linguistic units (Lieven, Pines, & Barnes, 1992; Plunkett, 1991). Cross-cultural studies also reveal that non-nominals figure more prominently in the early speech of children learning languages other than English. In Japanese and Korean, for example, verbs are more perceptually salient than in English (word order in the two languages is typically verb-final, and nominal referents are often omitted), and children learning these languages acquire verbs and verbal inflections earlier than children learning English (Clancy, 1985; Gopnik & Choi, 1991; Tanouye, 1979).

In addition to alerting us to aspects of acquisition that universalist models ignore, studies of children who display a particular style of acquisition to an extreme degree can give us hints about how the related mechanism of acquisition works in other children who show more balanced acquisitional styles. A tendency that begins as a simple preference—for instance, imitating an adult utterance when no other response is available—may reveal its value to the learner as a support for learning and become a skilled strategy for the acquisition of new information (Snow, 1989). It is important to note that different cultures vary in the degree to which they encourage and support various child tendencies. The highly referential child is appropriate and rewarding to a middle-class American mother who sees naming as a sensible and intelligent way to use language, but not to a Kaluli mother, who would view naming as "talking to no purpose" (Schieffelin, 1986). The skill of imitation may be relatively little valued by American mothers, but it is crucial for children whose caregivers instruct them to repeat modeled utterances as a way both to learn and to function socially, as do Kaluli (Schieffelin, 1986), Kwara'ae (Watson-Gegeo & Gegeo, 1986), and Basotho (Demuth, 1986) mothers. The existence of cultural variation in the language-learning environment has been proposed by many as an argument against a strong environmental influence on language acquisition; we see variation instead as a fact that must be understood, in the light of information from studies of individual differences, as evidence that children have many mechanisms available for the acquisition of language that are differentially exploited in different cultural contexts.

SUMMARY

It is important to reiterate that even though individual differences in styles or strategies for language acquisition are striking, the differences observed may reflect preferences or tendencies rather than dichotomies. Children who are classified as highly *imitative* produce many nonimitated utterances. *Pronominal* children produce some nominal word combinations. *Referential* children are not incapable of socially expressive speech. Language acquisition is a remarkably buffered process with a high rate of success; clearly, most children control many different strategies and mechanisms that contribute to language development.

We are left with the question of where the differences originate. It has been suggested that children's varying approaches to language and other cognitive problem areas reflect basic *temperamental* differences—differences, for example, in risk-taking tendencies, wariness, and inhibition. Such hypotheses await further, more interdisciplinary investigations to test them adequately. Hardy-Brown (1983), for example, suggests that we employ research designs from the field of behavioral genetics to disentangle the effects of heredity and environment on individual differences in rate and style of acquisition. These methodologies would include adoption studies, which assess the cognitive and linguistic abilities of both birth and adoptive parents and compare these measures to the child's developing linguistic skills. Meanwhile, the fact of individual differences has implications not only for theory, but for *research* and *educational practice* as well. We can apply what we know about individual differences to amend and improve our methods of *collecting language data, intervening* with children at risk for language delay or deviance, and *teaching* reading and foreign languages.

Methods for collecting data on language acquisition have been developed on the assumption that all children go about it much the same way. Thus, for example, most published analyses are based on utterances elicited in the context of play with toys, usually a set of novel toys provided by the experimenter. If, as seems to be the case, some children are more object-play-oriented than others, then this setting is particularly appropriate for them but less suitable for the socially oriented children. Children who rely on imitation and routine contexts as sources of their utterances are also relatively disadvantaged in this novel situation and need to be observed during familiar, everyday events in order to gain an adequate basis for judging their communicative effectiveness. Individual differences in children are compounded by *social class, ethnic,* and *cultural differences* in the ways children are expected to interact and be socialized, thus further complicating the problem of assuring that a standard observational situation eliminates variability in what is observed.

Finally, the recognition that there are many ways to learn a language and that normally developing children may differ from one another in how they accomplish the task should help us to think more creatively about *therapy, intervention,* and *education.* A single therapeutic or educational method is unlikely to work for all children, and the failure of one method does not imply that success is impossible. The delayed or language-handicapped child, like the normally developing child, may exploit or avoid imitation, may search cautiously for rules or recklessly try out utterances, may be more easily involved in social games, or may demand a referential vocabulary. All of these preferences are compatible with successful language acquisition, and all can be utilized by therapists, teachers, and parents.

SUGGESTED PROJECTS

1. Analyze the speech of one child with two different adults, one familiar and one unfamiliar, in a variety of situations to determine how much intrachild variability occurs on percentage of imitative utterances, use of pronouns, and use of object- versus social-oriented utterances.
2. Analyze the oral reading errors of five children reading at early to middle grade-one level, all reading the same passage, to determine to what extent they all make errors in the same places and whether their strategies for reading (guessing at) difficult words are the same or different.
3. In three half-hour sessions, teach two preschool children as much as you can of some language you know and they don't. Try varied teaching methods—sing songs, recite verses, read books, name toys, name pictures in books, etc. Tape the sessions so you have a record of what you have taught. At the end, assess whether the children have learned social or referential expressions and whether they have learned more from imitative or analytic strategies.

SUGGESTED READINGS

Bates, E., Bretherton, I., & Snyder, L. (1988). *From first words to grammar: Individual differences and dissociable mechanisms.* Cambridge: Cambridge University Press.

Bloom, L., Lightbown, P., & Hood, L. (1975). Structure and variation in child language. *Monographs of the Society for Research in Child Development, 40,* (2, No. 160).

Fillmore, C., Kempler, D., & Wang, S.-Y. (Eds.). (1979). *Individual differences in language ability and language behavior.* New York: Academic Press.

Nelson, K. (1981). Individual differences in language development: Implications for development and language. *Developmental Psychology, 17,* 170–187.

Peters, A. (1983). *The units of language acquisition.* Cambridge: Cambridge University Press.

REFERENCES

Adamson, L. B., Tomasello, M., & Benbenisty, L. L. (1984, April). An "expressive" infant's communicative development. Paper presented at the International Conference on Infant Studies, New York.

Bates, E., Bretherton, I., & Snyder, L. (1988). *From first words to grammar: Individual differences and dissociable mechanisms.* Cambridge: Cambridge University Press.

Bellugi, U. (1967). *The acquisition of negation.* Unpublished doctoral dissertation, Harvard University.

Bloom, L. (1970). *Language development: Form and function in emerging grammars.* Cambridge, MA: MIT Press.

Bloom, L., Hood, L., & Lightbown, P. (1974). Imitation in language development: If, when and why. *Cognitive Psychology, 6,* 380–420.

Bloom, L., Lightbown, P., & Hood, L. (1975). Structure and variation in child language. *Monographs of the Society for Research in Child Development, 40.*

Bornstein, M. H. (1989). Between caretakers and their young: Two modes of interaction and their consequences for cognitive growth. In M. H. Bornstein & J. S. Bruner (Eds.), *Interaction in human development* (pp. 197–214). Hillsdale, NJ: Erlbaum.

Bowerman, M. (1973). *Early syntactic development: A cross-linguistic study with special reference to Finnish.* London: Cambridge University Press.

Bowerman, M. (1976). Semantic factors in the acquisition of rules for word use and sentence construction. In D. Morehead & A. Morehead (Eds.), *Directions in normal and deficient child language.* Baltimore: University Park Press.

Braine, M. D. S. (1963). The ontogeny of English phrase structure: The first phase. *Language, 39,* 1–13.

Braine, M. D. S. (1976). Children's first word combinations. *Monographs of the Society for Research in Child Development, 41.*

Branigan, G. (1977, September 30). If this kid is in the one-word period, so how come he's saying whole sentences? Paper presented at the Second Annual Boston University Conference on Language Development, Boston.

Bretherton, I., McNew, S., Snyder, L., & Bates, E. (1983). Individual differences at 20 months: Analytic and holistic strategies in language acquisition. *Journal of Child Language, 10,* 293–320.

Brown, R. (1973). *A first language.* Cambridge, MA: Harvard University Press.

Bussis, A. M., Chittenden, E. A., Amarel, M., Klausner, E. (1984). *Inquiry into meaning: An investigation of learning to read.* Hillsdale, NJ: Erlbaum.

Cazden, C. (1968). The acquisition of noun and verb inflections. *Child Development, 39,* 433–438.

Chomsky, N. (1957). *Syntactic structures.* The Hague: Mouton.

Clancy, P. M. (1985). The acquisition of Japanese. In D. I. Slobin (Ed.), *The cross-linguistic study of language acquisition, Vol. 1: The data.* Hillsdale, NJ: Erlbaum.

Clark, R. (1974). Performing without competence. *Journal of Child Language, 1,* 1–10.

Clark, R. (1976). What's the use of imitation? *Journal of Child Language, 4,* 341–358.

Della Corte, M., Benedict, H., & Klein, D. (1983). The relationship of pragmatic dimensions of mothers' speech to the referential-expressive distinction. *Journal of Child Language, 10,* 35–44.

Demuth, K. (1986). Prompting routines in the language socialization of Basotho children. In B. Schieffelin & E. Ochs (Eds.), *Language socialization across cultures.* New York: Cambridge University Press.

Dore, J. (1974). A pragmatic description of early language development. *Journal of Psycholinguistic Research, 4,* 343–351.

Ferguson, C. A., & Farwell, C. (1975). Words and sounds in early language acquisition. *Language, 51,* 419–439.

Ferrier, L. J. (1975, September). Dependency and appropriateness in early language development. Paper presented at the Third International Child Language Symposium, London.

Fillmore, L. W. (1979). Individual differences in second language acquisition. In C. J. Fillmore, D. Kempler, & W. S.-Y. Wang (Eds.), *Individual differences in language ability and language behavior.* New York: Academic Press.

Folger, J., & Chapman, R. (1978). A pragmatic analysis of spontaneous imitations. *Journal of Child Language, 5,* 25–38.

Furrow, D., & Nelson, K. (1984). Environmental correlates of individual differences in language acquisition. *Journal of Child Language, 11,* 523–534.

Genesee, F., & Hamayan, E. (1980). Individual differences in second language learning. *Applied Psycholinguistics, 1*(1), 95–110.

Gleitman, H., & Gleitman, L. (1979). Language use and language judgment. In C. J. Fillmore, D. Kempler, & W. S.-Y. Wang (Eds.), *Individual differences in language ability and language behavior.* New York: Academic Press.

Goldfield, B. (1982, October 9). Intra-individual variation: Patterns of nominal and pronominal combinations. Paper presented at the Seventh Annual Boston University Conference on Language Development, Boston.

Goldfield, B. (1985/86). Referential and expressive language: A study of two mother–child dyads. *First Language, 6,* 119–131.

Goldfield, B. (1987). The contributions of child and caregiver to referential and expressive language. *Applied Psycholinguistics, 8,* 267–280.

Goldfield, B. A. (1990). Pointing, naming, and talk about objects: Referential behavior in children and mothers. *First Language, 10,* 231–242.

Goldfield, B. A., & Reznick, J. S. (1990). Early lexical acquisition: Rate, content, and the vocabulary spurt. *Journal of Child Language, 17,* 171–183.

Gopnik, A., & Choi, S. (1991). Do linguistic differences lead to cognitive differences? A cross-linguistic study of semantic and cognitive development. *First Language, 11,* 199–215.

Hardy-Brown, K. (1983). Universals and individual differences: Disentangling two approaches to the study of language acquisition. *Developmental Psychology, 19,* 610–624.

Hatch, E. (1974). Second language learning-universals? *Working Papers on Bilingualism, 3,* 1–18.

Heath, S. B. (1983). *Ways with words: Language, life, and work in communities and classrooms.* Cambridge: Cambridge University Press.

Horgan, D. (1981). Rate of language acquisition and noun emphasis. *Journal of Psycholinguistic Research, 10,* 629–640.

Leonard, L., Schwartz, R., Folger, M., Newhoff, M., & Wilcox, M. (1979). Children's imitations of lexical items. *Child Development, 59,* 19–27.

Lieven, E. V. M. (1980). *Language development in young children.* Unpublished doctoral dissertation, Cambridge University.

Lieven, E. V. M., Pine, J. M., & Barnes, H. D. (1992). Individual differences in early vocabulary development: Redefining the referential-expressive distinction. *Journal of Child Language, 19,* 287–310.

Macken, M. (1978). Permitted complexity in phonological development: One child's acquisition of Spanish consonants. *Lingua, 44,* 219–253.

Masur, E. F. (1982). Mothers' responses to infants' object-related gestures: Influences on lexical development. *Journal of Child Language, 9,* 23–30.

McShane, J. (1980). *Learning to talk.* Cambridge: Cambridge University Press.

Miller, P. J. (1982). *Amy, Wendy, and Beth: Language learning in South Baltimore.* Austin: University of Texas Press.

Nelson, K. (1973). Structure and strategy in learning to talk. *Monographs of the Society for Research in Child Development, 38.*

Nelson, K. (1975). The nominal shift in semantic–syntactic development. *Cognitive Psychology, 7,* 461–479.

Nelson, K. (1981). Individual differences in language development: Implications for development and language. *Developmental Psychology, 17,* 170–187.

Nelson, K. E., Baker, N., Denninger, M., Bonvillian, J., & Kaplan, B. (1985). Cookie versus do-it-again: Imitative-referential and personal-social-syntactic-initiating language styles in young children. *Linguistics, 23,* 433–454.

Nelson, K. E., & Bonvillian, J. D. (1972). Concepts and words in the 18-month-old: Acquiring concept names under controlled conditions. *Cognition, 2,* 435–450.

Ninio, A. (1980). Picture book reading in mother-infant dyads belonging to two subgroups in Israel. *Child Development, 51,* 587–590.

Ninio, A., & Bruner, J. (1978). The achievement and antecedents of labeling. *Journal of Child Language, 5,* 1–15.

Olsen-Fulero, L. (1982). Style and stability in mother conversational behavior: A study of individual differences. *Journal of Child Language, 9,* 543–564.

Peters, A. M. (1977). Language learning strategies: Does the whole equal the sum of the parts? *Language, 53,* 560–573.

Peters, A. M. (1983). *The units of language acquisition.* Cambridge: Cambridge University Press.

Pine, J. M. (1990). Individual differences in early language development and their relationship to maternal style. Unpublished doctoral dissertation, University of Manchester.

Pine, J. M. (1992). The functional basis of referentiality: Evidence from children's spontaneous speech. *First Language 12,* 39–55.

Pine, J. M., & Lieven, E. V. M. (1990). Referential style at thirteen months: Why age-defined cross-sectional measures are inappropriate for the study of strategy differences in early language development. *Journal of Child Language, 17,* 625–631.

Plunkett, K. (1991). The segmentation problem in early language acquisition. Paper presented at Child Language Seminar, University of Manchester, Manchester, England.

Ramer, A. L. (1976). Syntactic styles in emerging language. *Journal of Child Language, 3,* 49–62.

Rosenblatt, D. (1977). Developmental trends in infant play. In B. Tizard & D. Harvey (Eds.), *Biology of play.* London: William Heinemann Medical Books.

Schieffelin, B. (1986). *How Kaluli children learn what to say, what to do, and how to feel.* New York: Cambridge University Press.

Slobin, D. I. (1985). *The cross-linguistic study of language acquisition.* Hillsdale, NJ: Erlbaum.

Slobin, D. J. (1968). *Early grammatical development in several languages, with special attention to Soviet research* (Working Paper No. 11). Berkeley: University of California, Language-Behavior Research Laboratory.

Smith, N. (1973). *The acquisition of phonology: A case study.* London: Cambridge University Press.

Snow, C. E. (1981). The uses of imitation. *Journal of Child Language, 8,* 205–212.

Snow, C. E. (1983). Saying it again: The role of expanded and deferred imitations in language acquisition. In K. E. Nelson (Ed.), *Child language* (Vol. 4). Hillsdale, NJ: Erlbaum.

Snow, C. E. (1989). Imitativeness: A trait or a skill? In G. Speidel & K. E. Nelson (Eds.), *The many faces of imitation in language learning.* New York: Springer-Verlag.

Snow, C. E., & Hoefnagel-Hohle, M. (1978). The critical period for language acquisition: Evidence from second language learning. *Child Development, 49,* 1114–1128.

Snyder, L. S., Bates, E., & Bretherton, I. (1981). Content and context in early lexical development, *Journal of Child Language, 8,* 565–582.

Starr, S. (1975). The relationship of single words to two-word sentences. *Child Development, 46,* 701–708.

Stokes, W. T., & Holden, S. (1980, October). Individual patterns in early language development: Is there a one-word period? Paper presented at the Fifth Annual Boston University Conference on Language Development, Boston.

Tanouye, E. K. (1979). The acquisition of verbs in Japanese children. *Papers and Reports on Child Language Development, 17,* (Department of Linguistics, Stanford University), 49–56.

Thomas, E. (1979). It's all routine: A redefinition of routines as a central factor in language acquisition. Paper presented at the Fourth Annual Boston University Conference on Language Development, Boston.

Tomasello, M., & Farrar, M. J. (1986). Joint attention and early language. *Child Development, 57,* 1454–1463.

Tomasello, M., & Todd, J. (1983). Joint attention and lexical acquisition style. *First language, 4,* 197–212.

Urwin, C. (1978). The development of communication between blind infants and their parents. In A. Lock (Ed.), *Action, gesture, and symbol.* New York: Academic Press.

Watson-Gegeo, K., & Gegeo, D. (1986). Calling-out and repeating routines in Kwara'ae children's language socialization. In B. Schieffelin & E. Ochs (Eds.), *Language socialization across cultures.* New York: Cambridge University Press.

Wesche, M. B. (1981). Language aptitude measures in streaming, matching students with methods, and diagnosis of learning problems. In K. C. Diller (Ed.), *Individual differences and universals in language learning aptitude.* Rowley, MA: Newbury House.

Wolf, D., & Gardner, H. (1979). Style and sequence in symbolic play. In M. Franklin & N. Smith (Eds.), *Early symbolization.* Hillsdale, NJ: Erlbaum.

Atypical Language Development

9

Nan Bernstein Ratner *University of Maryland*

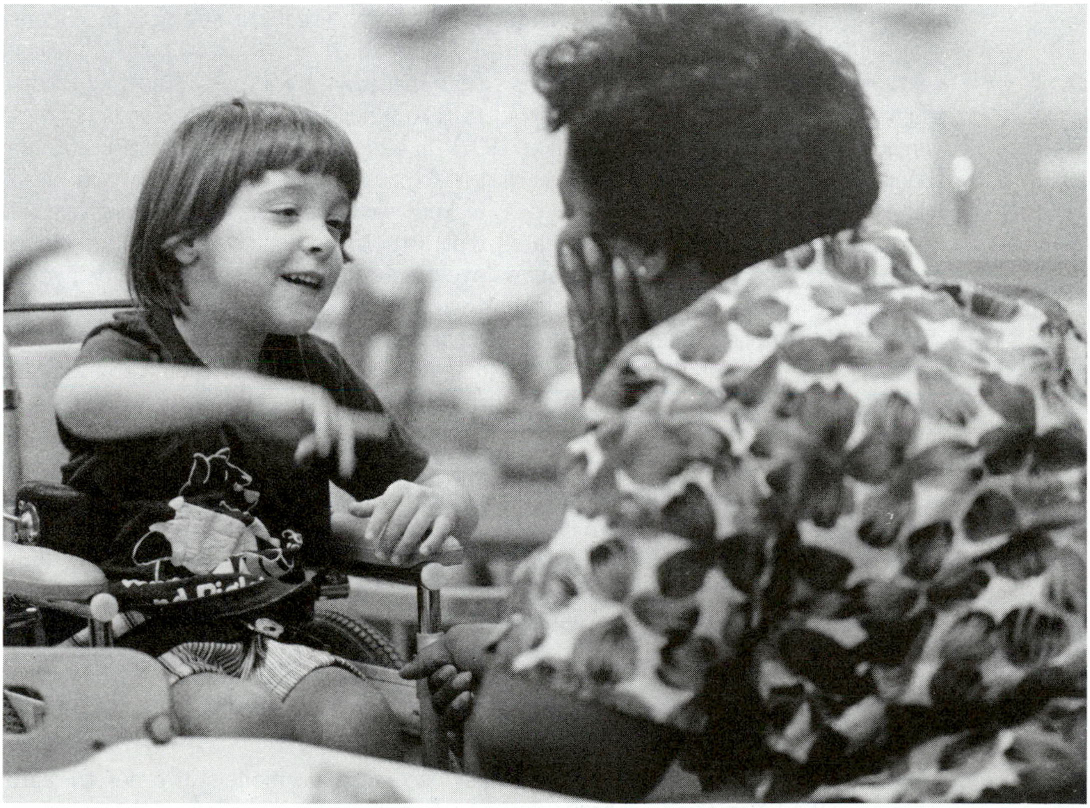

INTRODUCTION

Not all children acquire language easily and well. In this chapter, we examine some major causes and patterns of language delay and disorder in children. The study of childhood language disorders is important for a number of reasons. First, the case of individuals who fail to learn language normally allows us to evaluate possible prerequisites for the normal acquisition process. For instance, when a mentally retarded child does not learn to use language rapidly or appropriately, we may test hypotheses about the possible role that cognitive development plays in language development. Likewise, the role of the environment in fostering language learning is highlighted when we examine patterns of language difficulty experienced by deaf children. This type of speculation is not without its problems. For example, very often quite reasonable hypotheses about the role of certain factors in normal development do not necessarily predict the nature of some children's disorder in learning language.

Second, the study of language disorders in children represents one attempt to apply findings about the normal language acquisition process to a practical problem: what can be done to aid children who experience difficulty in learning and using language? By examining the specific patterns of delay and disorder certain children encounter during their language development and by reviewing what we already know about the sequence and nature of normal language development, we can more effectively target our attempts to remediate their difficulties.

Finally, as we learn more about the factors that may play a role in hindering children's language development, we hope to discover that, to some degree, certain disorders are preventable (U.S. Department of Education, 1987). In other words, if we find that certain environmental or physical factors predispose children to communicative disorder, we may begin to address how we can reduce the number of children who display difficulty with language skills.

Some researchers have estimated that 8 to 10 percent of school-aged children demonstrate patterns of communicative development that may be termed "delayed" or "disordered" (Silva, 1980). In this chapter, we describe four major patterns of language disturbance. In each case, we review what is known about affected children's development, how current theory attempts to explain the nature of their communicative difficulty, and what can be done to aid such children in improving their language skills. These major syndromes of language disorder involve children with *hearing impairment, mental retardation, autism,* and *specific language impairment.* We will also briefly describe the effects of *blindness* on the process of language development. Finally, we will note some conditions that lead to difficulty in producing speech, as opposed to language. Such *speech disorders* include delayed or deviant articulation and stuttering.

SEVERE HEARING IMPAIRMENT

THE EFFECTS OF SENSORY DEPRIVATION

We know that it is necessary to be exposed to linguistic models in order to learn a language. We know this at a basic level because we recognize that we learn only the language or languages we hear spoken around us, rather than any possible human language. At a deeper level, however, we become aware that if certain conditions limit linguistic exposure, language development may be severely hindered. Such is the case with significant hearing impairment. Children who are born with hearing impairment that limits their perception of sounds to those exceeding 60 *decibels* (dB), or about the

TABLE 9.1 Handicapping Effects of Hearing Loss

Average Hearing 500–2,000 (ANSI)	Description	Possible Condition	What Can Be Heard without Amplification	Handicapping Effects (If not Treated in 1st Year of Life)	Probable Needs
0–15 dB	Normal range	Conductive hearing losses	All speech sounds	None	None
15–25 dB	Slight hearing loss	Conductive hearing losses, some senso-rineural hearing losses	Vowel sounds heard clearly; may miss un-voiced conso-nant sounds	Mild auditory dysfunction in language learn-ing	Consideration of need for hearing aid; speechreading, auditory training, speech therapy, preferential seating
25–40 dB	Mild hearing loss	Conductive or sensorineural hearing loss	Only some of speech sounds, the louder-voiced sounds	Auditory learn-ing dysfunction, mild language retardation, mild speech prob-lems, inattention	Hearing aid, speechreading, au-ditory training, speech therapy
40–65 dB	Moderate hear-ing loss	Conductive hearing loss from chronic middle ear dis-orders; senso-rineural hearing losses	Almost no speech sounds at normal con-versational level	Speech prob-lems, language retardation, learning dys-function, inatten-tion	All of the above, plus consideration of special class-room situation
69–95 dB	Severe hearing loss	Sensorineural mixed losses due to a combi-nation of middle ear disease and sensorineural involvement	No speech sounds of nor-mal conversa-tions	Severe speech problems, lan-guage retarda-tion, learning dysfunction, in-attention	All of the above; probable assign-ment to special classes
95 dB +	Profound hear-ing loss	Sensorineural or mixed losses due to a combi-nation of middle ear disease and sensorineural involvement	No speech or other sounds	Severe speech problems, lan-guage retarda-tion, learning dysfunction, in-attention	All of the above; probable assign-ment to special classes

Source: Human Communication Disorders (p. 432) by G. H. Shames and E. H. Wiig, 1986, Columbus, OH: Merrill/Macmillan.

intensity level of a baby's cry, generally will not be able to develop spontaneous oral language that approximates that of normal children. Children born with losses exceeding 90 dB are considered deaf and will not develop speech and language skills spontaneously (without educational and therapeutic intervention). Just as importantly, such children will eventually demonstrate language comprehension difficulties, even when the mode of language presentation (e.g., writing) bypasses their problems of auditory reception.

Figure 9.1 illustrates typical loudness and frequency levels for common environmental and speech sounds. It is possible for hearing to be impaired such that only small subtleties (such as whispering) might be missed; it is also possible for hearing impairment to be severe enough to limit reception of almost all important linguistic and environmental information. Generally, the extent to which a child is handicapped by hearing loss depends upon the severity of the loss (see Table 9.1), the utility of hearing aids in restoring some hearing ability, and the age at which the hearing loss occurred. Obviously, large hearing losses are more detrimental to language development than lesser losses. Additionally, while amplification may provide the child with the ability to hear some otherwise inaudible sounds, it cannot restore normal hearing function, especially in cases of severe loss. Even recent clinical experience with **cochlear implants,** which are capable of directly stimulating the auditory nerve to restore a sense of hearing, does not suggest that deafness can be fully overcome by assistive devices. Only a handful of children have received such implants, and their benefits are being weighed against the risks of implantation (Staller, 1991). Though their progress has been promising (Boothroyd, Geers, & Moog, 1991), it also appears to be dependent upon strong oral educational support, which we will discuss in a following section. Finally, an NIH consensus statement (1990) warns that implantation carries surgical risk, and that the long-term effects of cochlear implants on developing children are still unknown. Losses that are *congenital* (present at birth) or that occur prelingually (before the child has learned language skills, the period when the majority of significant hearing losses in children occur) are much more disruptive of the language acquisition process than are losses acquired later in life (see Northern & Lemme, 1986, for a discussion of hearing measurement and impairment.)

Finally, it is important to understand how severe hearing impairment limits the child's access to linguistic input. Not all conversations occur face to face, and the deaf child misses those that take place out of his line of sight. We probably underestimate the degree to which we gain important linguistic insight from language interchanges that occur around us. Thus, even if the deaf child can focus on a speaker's face during conversation, *lipreading* does not automatically guarantee successful interpretation of the conversation. Many sounds are made in the back of the mouth and are not easily visible on the lips, such as velars and liquids. Additionally, there are many sounds in English and in other languages that resemble one another on the lips but are acoustically distinct, such as /p/, /b/, and /m/. Since most deaf children are born to hearing parents (Rawlings & Jensema, 1977), this means that the parents and their young child do not share a mutually intelligible communication system in the crucial early years of language development. Cases of deaf children of deaf parents who use sign language as a preferred method of communication—and thus can include the children in their language system from birth—provide an interesting comparison situation that we address later.

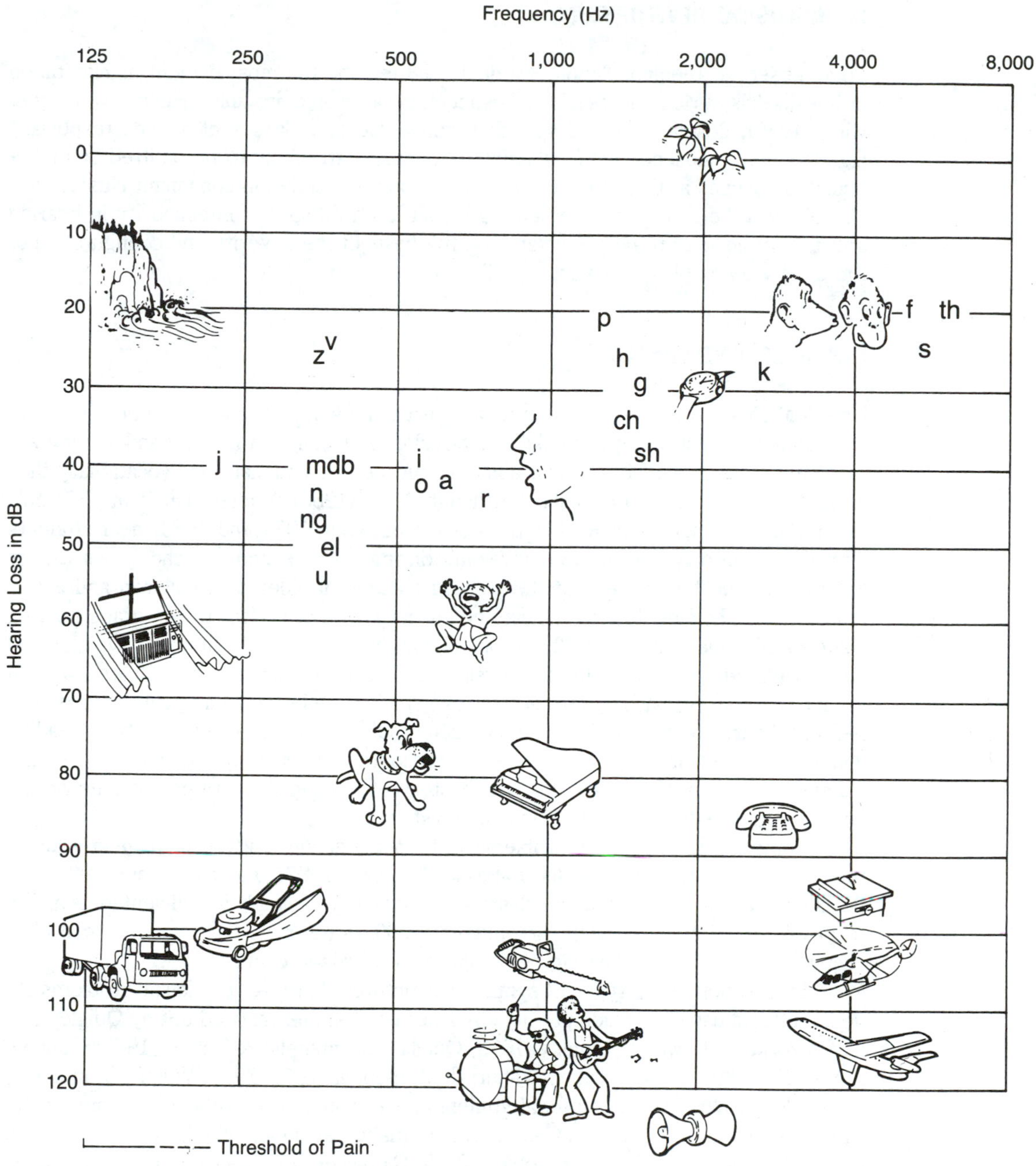

FIGURE 9.1 Frequency spectrum and intensity of everyday sounds, including English-language speech sounds (From *Hearing in Children* (3rd ed.) by J. Northern and M. Downs, 1984, Baltimore: Williams & Wilkins Co. Copyright © 1984 by the Williams & Wilkins Co. Reprinted by permission.)

PHONOLOGICAL DEVELOPMENT

To an observer, the articulation of a deaf child may be the most evident manifestation of her disability. Many deaf children's speech is rated as quite unintelligible (Quigley & King, 1982), despite years of speech training. Certain classes of sounds (especially high-frequency sibilents and less visible phonemes) are likely to be omitted or misarticulated. Sounds at the ends of words and those embedded in consonant clusters are also likely to be missed by the hearing-impaired child. Speech intelligibility in hearing impairment appears to be predictable on the basis of the severity and configuration of the child's hearing loss (Calvert, 1982).

LANGUAGE DEVELOPMENT

The deaf child's problems in acquiring and using the syntactic and semantic aspects of the language and in using such skills to develop proficiency in reading and writing are much more significant factors in his ability to succeed educationally and vocationally than is his typical articulation disability. Although Allen (1986) reports that deaf children's reading achievement improved in the decade between 1974 and 1983, deaf students appear to gain only two grade equivalents during their secondary school years. Furthermore, repeated surveys of the reading abilities of older deaf children and adults suggest that their reading ability may never surpass that of 4th- to 5th-grade hearing children (Hammermeister, 1972; Trybus & Karchmer, 1977). Additionally, Quigley and King (1982) suggest that refined analysis of the receptive grammatical abilities of deaf students indicates that they are less capable readers under certain circumstances than hearing children with equivalent standardized reading achievement scores. Such reading and writing inadequacies can be directly attributed to their limited exposure to the language. Chapter 10 reminds us that mastery of reading and writing are inextricably linked to knowledge of the oral language system.

Some of the deaf child's problems with both oral and written language are due to their depressed vocabulary skills (LaSasso & Davey, 1987; Quigley & Paul, 1984). As deVilliers (1991) observes, overt classroom instruction is simply insufficient in its ability to provide deaf students with the roughly 3,000 words per year that a normal child acquires by merely overhearing or reading new words in context.

Delineation of the types of syntactic structures that pose particular problems for deaf students has been made possible by a series of studies carried out by Quigley and his coworkers (Power & Quigley, 1973; Quigley, Montanelli, & Wilbur, 1976; Quigley, Smith, & Wilbur, 1974; Quigley, Wilbur, & Montanelli, 1974, 1976; Wilbur, Montanelli, & Quigley, 1976). In general, deaf students have trouble comprehending many of the same structures that are troublesome for normally developing children: constructions that violate typical subject–verb–object (S–V–O) patterns in English, such as passives and embedded clauses. Deaf children, however, also have particular problems with modals, verb auxiliaries, infinitives, and gerunds. The deaf child's incomplete grasp of English syntax is made more apparent by errors observed in the following typical writing samples:

We went to family camp today. She will be good family camp dog food. Boy went family fun dog friend car look. The played outuroor camp family good eat afternoon. The played eat fun camp after home. We perttey fun camp after home. The will week fun camp after car. We family will eat and aftrnoon. [10-year-old male, Performance IQ of 129, born deaf, Better Ear Average of 100 dB (ASA).]

We will go to pinic. the woman package. A boy give to a dog eat the bread. The dog barked. the boy look at dog. the boy told a woman stop at car. He carried to the pinic dog sa. the mother told her sister put on the table. She park a car. He was fun. Her brothers played baskeball. the dog played with the boy. after whith. He will go home at 6:45. his mother drive a car. [14-year-old male, Performance IQ of 104, born deaf, Better Ear Average of 90 (ASA).]

Everyone is packing the food in the basket for a picnic. They are very exciting to go to the picnic for their pleasure. A girl gives a sandwich to a little dog to eat. Father carries a bat to play with his girl & boy. Then they have everythings in the car what they want.

After a while the car is leaving out but one boy saw his little dog alone. He told his father to stop to see the dog. He went out of a car. Everyone is laughing. He pats his dog and brings him in the car to go with them too. Then they arrive at a picnic. Mother cooks the food for them. A girl put any dishes on the picnic table. Father and a boy play a softball. Everyone is enjoying today for a picnic. [18-year-old female, Performance IQ of 97, born deaf, Better Ear Average 100 dB (ASA).] (Quigley & King, 1982, pp. 444–445)

Table 9.2 displays some representative patterns of ungrammatical English usage found in the writings of deaf students. While some of the errors resemble those made in the speech of young, normally developing children—such as failure to invert subject and auxiliary for question formation or omission of the copula (the verb *to be*) in sentences—many are unique to hearing-impaired children.

It has been noted by deVilliers (1991) that the repetitive style and overuse of simple sentence types that characterize the writing samples of deaf children may reflect dependence upon classroom drill for the development of syntactic proficiency. Such instruction typically focuses on the grammar of simple sentences. The emphasis upon simple sentence structures affects reading as well as writing ability. Complex sentences are much more common in textual materials than in spoken conversation, and reading proficiency rests upon ability to understand such advanced structures (Perera, 1984). Gormley and Sarachan-Deily (1987) found that deaf children often mastered spelling and punctuation conventions, while possessing poor control over syntax, especially pronominal reference.

■ EDUCATIONAL APPROACHES TO THE DEVELOPMENT OF LANGUAGE IN DEAF CHILDREN

The majority of deaf children, those born into hearing families, are not exposed to ASL early in life. Historically, these children were exposed primarily to oral language models, although this trend has changed over the past two decades (Jordon, Gustason, & Rosen, 1976). Proponents of **oralist** programs have believed that deaf children are best served byinstruction in lipreading, in maximum use of residual hearing (auditory training), and in articulation to improve their speech. Many have feared that such skills might be undermined if children are given the opportunity to learn and use sign language.

TABLE 9.2 Examples of Distinct Syntactic Structures Generated by Deaf Children

Structural environment in which structure occurs	Description of structures	Example sentences
Verb system	Verb deletion	The cat under the table.
	Be or *have* deletion	John sick. The girl a ball.
	Be–have confusion	Jim have sick.
	Incorrect pairing of auxiliary with verb markers	Tom has pushing the wagon.
	By deletion (passive voice)	The boy was pushed the girl.
Negation conjunction	Negative outside the sentence	Beth made candy no.
	Marking only first verb	Beth threw the ball and Jean catch it.
	Conjunction deletion	Joe bought ate the apple.
Complemention	Extra *for*	For to play baseball is fun.
	Extra *to* in POSS-ing complement	John goes to fishing.
	Infinitive in place of gerund	John goes to fish.
	Incorrectly inflected infinitive	Bill like to played baseball.
	Unmarked infinitive without to	Jim wanted go.
Relativization	NPs where *whose* is required	I helped the boy's mother was sick.
	Copying of referent	John saw the boy who the boy kicked the ball.
Question formation	Copying	Who a boy gave you a ball?
	Failure to apply subject–auxiliary inversion	Who the baby did love?
	Incorrect inversion	Who TV watched?
Question formation, negation	Overgeneralization of contraction rule	I amn't tired. Bill willn't go.
Relativization, conjunction	Object-object deletion	John chased the girl and he scared. (John chased the girl and he scared the girl.)
	Object–subject deletion	The dog chased the girl had on a red dress. (The dog chased the girl. The girl had on a red dress.)
All types of sentences	Forced subject–verb–object pattern	The boy pushed the girl. (The boy was pushed by the girl.)

Source: From "The Language Structure of Deaf Children" by S. Quigley, B. Power, and M. Steinkamp, 1977, *Volta Review 79,* p. 80. Copyright 1977 by the Alexander Graham Bell Association for the Deaf, Washington, DC. Reprinted by permission.

Recently, however, a number of **sign systems** (Wilbur, 1987) have been developed to further the linguistic and educational development of the deaf child. These *manual* approaches to deaf education hope to improve the educational outlook of hearing-impaired children, many of whom did not appear to be able to succeed in oral programs.

In general, they attempt to convey manual representations of English sentence structure. That is, the systems translate words and grammatical morphemes used in spoken English into easily visible hand configurations and gestures. Use of manually coded English in combination with speech is called *total communication,* a popular educational approach (Quigley & Paul, 1987). Lou (1988) surveys the history of deaf education in the United States over the past century, and excellent overviews of the half-dozen most commonly used sign systems are provided in Bochner and Albertini (1988), Quigley and King (1982), and Wilbur (1987). Most of the systems share some common features: they generally adapt some ASL signs for vocabulary items, invent new signs to convey grammatical concepts not expressed by discrete signs in ASL (such as articles, auxiliary verbs, and bound affixes for pluralization and tense and number agreement), and produce sentences that duplicate the syntactic structure of English. The result tends to resemble what might occur if one attempted to speak a foreign oral language, such as French, simply by placing French lexical items into an English grammatical framework (i.e., *"mon frère's voiture"* rather than *"la voiture de mon frère"* for the phrase "my brother's car"). For example, the sentence *"The* boy *is* eat*ing"* contains a number of elements not found in ASL (those in italics). While sign systems typically have invented new signs for those elements and would sign the phrase as written, the ASL version would more closely resemble "Boy eat-eat-eat" in English; **reduplicated** movement in ASL signals the progressive aspect, and the article is not necessary.

These sign systems are now an integral part of the curriculum for many if not most hearing-impaired children (Quigley & Paul, 1987). Their use at home by parents is usually highly encouraged in the hope that they may aid deaf students to appreciate the rules that govern correct language use. However, both parents and teachers may find it difficult to communicate fluently in what is, to them, a foreign language, and there is evidence that many adults fail to include a number of the important grammatical features of English in the signed input, thus limiting the child's exposure to the language (Rudser, 1988; Swisher, M., 1985). This problem has been identified as a major need in the development of more effective early intervention initiatives (Moeller & Luettke-Stahlman, 1990).

ACQUISITION OF ASL AS A FIRST LANGUAGE

Many of the relatively few deaf children who are born to deaf parents grow up learning **American Sign Language** (**ASL** or **Ameslan**) as their first language. American Sign Language is a distinct language within the scope of the world's languages, with its own syntactic, semantic, and configurational rules. Klima and Bellugi (1979) and Wilbur (1987) provide excellent descriptions of its grammar. ASL is not based upon English grammar and has rules for expressing S–V–O relationships, tense, pluralization, and so on that are different from the rules for these concepts in English. American Sign Language, like other sign languages of the world, is not transparently meaningful to speakers of English or other sign languages. That is, one cannot easily follow an ASL conversation without knowing the specific rules of ASL. As we discuss more fully in the next section, the language development of children learning ASL from birth closely parallels patterns observed in children acquiring oral languages.

The acquisition of ASL by such children [and by some hearing children exposed to both oral and signed language by one hearing-impaired and one normal hearing parent (Jones & Quigley, 1979; Prinz & Prinz, 1981)] essentially confirms that the language disability demonstrated by hearing-impaired children is one that stems from deficient input rather than other possible causes. That is, children learning ASL as a first language generally develop their first signed words at approximately the same age or even earlier than children who are acquiring oral language (Bonvillian, Orlansky, & Novack, 1983; McIntire, 1977; Wilbur & Jones, 1974). Such a phenomenon suggests that first-word production in speaking children may be constrained by the relatively less rapid development of oral as opposed to manual dexterity in children. However, Pettito (1991) contests the claim that sign usage emerges at an earlier age than verbal language.

There are marked similarities in the courses of ASL and oral language development. The two-word stage in early ASL usage is characterized by semantic relationships similar to those seen in early spoken language productions (Newport & Ashbrook, 1977). Overregularizations of grammatical features and overextensions of vocabulary meaning are noted (Schlesinger & Meadow, 1972). However, accelerated use of vocabulary and combinatorial language may be observed when ASL-using infants are compared to oral language learning infants of similar ages (Bonvillian, Orlansky, & Novack, 1983; McIntire, 1977).

Finally, there is some evidence to suggest that knowing ASL as a first language may aid deaf children in developing better skills with the English language, in much the same way that knowing a first language provides a basis for learning others (Vernan & Koh, 1970). Moores (1987) observes that a subset of more linguistically proficient deaf students come from deaf households.

Geers and Schick (1988) found that children with hearing-impaired parents who were learning manually coded English outperformed their peers with normal hearing parents. Orally educated children of hearing parents also often perform better educationally than the manually educated children of hearing parents, suggesting that parental proficiency with the input language is important to the child's development of linguistic skills.

As Quigley and King (1982) point out, intensive exposure both at school and at home to systems that parallel English may have the potential to be even more facilitative of linguistic progress if parents and teachers can develop good proficiency with the systems. However, any communicative system that maximizes the opportunity for fully developed language interaction between deaf children and those around them is likely to improve their progress in mastering language. Parental SES and active involvement in the child's educational programming also appear to positively affect the development of language proficiency (Moores, 1987).

There is great controversy regarding the relative efficacy of oral and manual educational programs. Some highly intensive oral programs report good English proficiency for their graduates (Geers & Moog, 1987), as do some total communication programs (Delaney, Stuckless, & Walter, 1984; Moores, 1987) and mainstreaming programs (Pflaster, 1980). After surveying their own and previous data, Musselman, Lindsay, and Wilson (1988) concluded that the nature of the hearing loss and the child's intellectual ability had a greater effect on her educational success than did many of the educational programming variables they examined. While there was some suggestion that children in total communication programs had both somewhat better receptive language ability and richer mother–child interaction but that orally educated children had better spoken language, the authors warn that at the present time "unequivocal statements about the value of particular approaches or the consequences of not following one approach or another are unwarranted" (p. 87). Moreover, they report that "one clear conclusion that can be drawn is that no approach has succeeded in reversing the effects on language of severe and profound hearing impairment" (p. 87).

■ MENTAL RETARDATION

COGNITIVE DISABILITY AND THE LANGUAGE ACQUISITION PROCESS

Approximately 2 percent of school-aged children demonstrate some degree of cognitive or mental impairment (U.S. Department of Education, 1987). A good definition of normal intellectual ability is difficult to arrive at, and despite increasing dissatisfaction with the use of intelligence quotients (IQ) to measure mental development, they continue to be used to define and describe this population (Smith & Polloway, 1979). Mental retardation of a mild nature may be indicated by IQ performance falling between 53 and 70; moderate degrees of retardation by IQ scores of approximately 36 to 51; severe retardation by IQ scores between 20 and 35; and profound retardation by scores falling below IQ 20 (Owens, 1985). Jordan (1967) estimates that the vast majority of children with measured IQs falling below 50 will demonstrate severe language problems and that children with higher IQs may still experience language disability. Mental retardation may result from a number of discrete etiologies; however, it is currently unclear whether etiological subgroups of retarded children demonstrate differing patterns of linguistic impairment. Recent evidence suggests that they do not (Miller, Chapman, & Bedrosian, 1978).

The relationship between cognitive development and linguistic development in normal children is still a matter of intense inquiry. While many recent investigations have noted that certain linguistic developments may typically follow mastery of selected cognitive skills in both normally developing children (Corrigan, 1978; Moore & Meltzoff, 1978) and in mentally retarded children (Lobato, Barrera, & Feldman, 1981; Mundy, Seibert, & Hogan, 1984), it is not clear that language development is contingent upon mastery of any specific subset of cognitive abilities, a position first advanced by Lenneberg (1967; see Chapter 7). It is more likely that linguistic and cognitive development may progress in parallel (Gopnik & Meltzoff, 1984) and occasionally present dissociated patterns (Cromer, 1987; Curtiss, 1981; Miller, 1981b). Cromer (1991) argues that possible associations between cognitive and language development may be masked by problems in defining the relevant cognitive skills that might be linked to language acquisition. In particular, he observes that most studies attempt to link Piagetian stage acquisition with the emergence of particular linguistic abilities, and suggests that alternative definitions of cognitive ability may be necessary.

Additionally, it may be that retarded children's profiles of language use and ability do not stem from cognitive deficits at all but rather from a cognitive orientation that results in patterns of social and motivational behaviors distinct from those of normally developing children (Kamhi & Johnston, 1982). Rosenberg (1982) suggests that the quality of *passivity* may best account for the retarded child's slow acquisition of both cognitive and linguistic skills. Miller and Chapman (1984) point out that our current understanding of cognitive prerequisites for language development does not strongly support the practice of teaching specific cognitive skills for the purpose of readying children for language acquisition.

LANGUAGE DEVELOPMENT

No one seriously questions that mentally retarded children typically demonstrate depressed language ability when compared with nonretarded children of the same chronological age. However, researchers are more concerned with discovering the specific patterns of language production and comprehension that characterize this population and identifying possible factors that predict retarded children's mastery of certain linguistic skills. Both questions have important implications for aiding the development of more adequate linguistic ability in retarded individuals.

Examination of patterns of linguistic development has yielded increasing evidence that suggests that retarded children demonstrate language skills best described as *delayed* rather than *deviant.* That is, their patterns of language production and comprehension closely resemble those seen in younger, normal children. Rosenberg (1982) summarizes the general linguistic profile of the mentally retarded child:

> In comparison to nonretarded individuals in the same CA range, language development in the mentally retarded shows the following characteristics: later onset, slower progress, lower final level of achievement, retardation in all aspects of language functioning, but similar stages of acquisition. Thus it appears that the **developmental lag hypothesis** describes not only nonlinguistic cognitive development in the mentally retarded but linguistic cognitive development as well. (p. 339)

In general, mentally retarded children's mental ages (MAs) are a fairly good predictor of their language abilities (Cromer, 1974; Graham & Graham, 1971; Lackner, 1968); however, differences may be seen between normal and retarded children with identical MAs and even between retarded children matched for MA in their global language profiles (Kamhi & Johnston, 1982; Lobato, Barrera, & Feldman, 1981). Additionally, there are some indications that retarded individuals may experience relatively disproportionate difficulty with morphological skills (Lovell & Bradbury, 1967; McLeavey, Toomey, & Dempsey, 1982; Newfield & Schlanger, 1968) and less relative difficulty with pragmatic linguistic abilities (Abbeduto & Rosenberg, 1987; Bedrosian & Prutting, 1978) than would be expected from general estimates of their linguistic development. A lengthy review by Barrett and Diniz (1989) concludes that early lexical development begins at similar mental ages for normal and retarded children. However, retarded children soon begin to lag behind, showing a depressed rate of vocabulary learning.

TEACHING LANGUAGE TO RETARDED CHILDREN

Owens (1985) summarizes some of the relevant considerations and approaches to language intervention with mentally retarded children. *Generalization* of language skills

Children with mental retardation benefit from language programs that emphasize the uses of language in daily life.

outside the clinical setting to spontaneous everyday usage may be particularly troublesome for this group of children (Guess, Keogh, & Sailor, 1978; Salzberg & Villani, 1983). McLean and Snyder-McLean (1978) suggest that therapy will be most effective with this group, as with other groups of language-handicapped children, if it is pragmatic in orientation, emphasizing functional communication as a primary goal. In other words, careful attention should be paid to selecting vocabulary and syntax needed to communicate in the daily environment. In severe cases of communicative impairment, the use of *augmentative communication systems* or devices may be suggested (for reviews of considerations in such a therapeutic approach, see Owens, 1985; Reichle & Karlan, 1988; Romski, Lloyd, & Sevcik, 1988). Examples of such alternatives to oral communication are the use of **communication boards,** which allow children to select symbols or pictures to communicate with others (Cohen & Shane, 1982), and the use of *sign systems,* discussed previously (see Wilbur, 1987, for a discussion of using sign systems with communicatively handicapped persons who are not deaf). While not symbolically or cognitively less complex than spoken language, sign systems may provide somewhat of a "teachability" advantage; that is, the child's hands may be shaped and his production reinforced more easily than his attempts at intelligible vocalizations.

■ LANGUAGE DEVELOPMENT IN VISUALLY HANDICAPPED CHILDREN

Many blind or severely visually impaired children have concomitant problems, such as hearing loss, retardation, and cerebral palsy, which make evaluation of the effects of visual impairment on language development difficult to evaluate (Bigelow, 1987). However, a small proportion of children demonstrate visual impairment as their single developmental disability.

Though the language of such blind children is not noticeably disordered, certain patterns of interest emerge. Early research with this population had suggested developmental delays in the acquisition of speech and language milestones (Fraiberg, 1977); more recent study of children carefully selected to avoid multiple handicapping conditions does not support the notion that blindness *per se* adversely affects language development (Bigelow, 1987; Mulford, 1988).

Most of the research on the language development of blind children has concentrated on analysis of their lexical development. Because their experiential basis for vocabulary development limits exposure to certain referents, one might expect some words not to be common in the early speech of blind children, and this has generally been found to be the case (Andersen, Dunlea, & Kekelis, 1984; Bigelow, 1987; Landau & Gleitman, 1985). Thus, words referring to outdoor items, concepts usually learned from books rather than direct experience, and color terms are notably absent from the early lexicons of visually handicapped toddlers. Additionally, Bigelow (1987) suggests that blind children are less likely to generalize words learned to refer to a given referent to other examples of the same concept.

Many researchers observe that the heavily nominal style of blind children's early language may stem both from the child's perceptual limitations and from parents' styles of interaction, which emphasize calling the child's attention to and labeling of new items in the immediate environment (Urwin, 1977, 1978). Landau and Gleitman (1985) attribute delays in the acquisition of verb auxiliaries to less frequent questioning and more frequent use of imperatives in parental speech to blind children.

Mills (1983) and Dodd (1983) have noted that blindness may influence the course of phonological development, and create patterns of articulation that differ from those of sighted children. Articulation errors made by blind children tend to preserve manner of articulation but change place of articulation (a more visual cue), whereas sighted children in these studies were more likely to attempt to preserve place of articulation cues.

In summary, some aspects of language development are affected by severe visual impairment. However, little work has been done with this population to date, and few children demonstrate blindness as their sole handicapping condition. Garman (1983) draws the distinction between *linguistic* and *communicative* handicap when considering the visually handicapped population. He finds little evidence that the outcome of language development is markedly aberrant in blind individuals, although different strategies may be used to attain language proficiency.

■ AUTISM

GENERAL CHARACTERISTICS

Kanner (1943, 1946) first described a small group of children who displayed extremely aberrant patterns of communicative interaction. Since then, an autistic syndrome has been defined and the following criteria for its diagnosis established (Rutter & Schopler, 1987; Simmons & Tymchuk, 1973):

1. The child demonstrates a striking deficit in the ability to establish and maintain social relationships; he shows a marked lack of responsiveness to those around him and displays *gaze aversion* (avoidance of eye contact with others) and a lack of desire for physical contact, among other socially inappropriate behaviors.
2. The child's language is characterized by an extremely slow course of development and by *echolalia* (repetition of the speech of others); in almost half of all diagnosed cases, expressive language ability is essentially absent (*mutism*). In addition, available language is not used for social communication. Expressive speech is often characterized by *flat* or inappropriate *prosodic contour.* There appears to be a unique pattern of pronoun errors: the autistic child often interchanges *you* and *I*.
3. The child demonstrates an obsession with sameness in her environment, engages in *ritualistic behavior,* and is apparently incapable of dealing with changes in daily routine.
4. The child displays inabilities to play independently or cooperatively and may be incapable of performing self-care activities.
5. The child often evidences intellectual impairment. Freeman and Ritvo (1977) and Rutter (1979) suggest that almost three-quarters of autistic children may be classified as mentally retarded.
6. The onset of symptoms occurred before the child was two-and-a-half years old. This particular criterion is necessary to distinguish between autism and a closely related syndrome, *childhood schizophrenia,* which appears in older chil-

dren after years of apparently normal development. Additionally, in rare cases, children with apparently normal early histories experience language regression and loss (Rutter & Lockyer, 1967).

CAUSATION

When first described years ago, autism was presumed by many to have its origins in a disturbance of the parent–child relationship; since then, there has been growing agreement that the disorder probably has an *organic* (physical) basis (Wetherby, 1984). The precise nature of the underlying neuropsychological deficit is still, however, a matter for great dispute. Among the hypotheses that continue to be entertained are those that posit that autism stems from a disorder of the neurotransmitter system (Yuwiler, Geller, & Ritvo, 1976) or from left hemisphere impairment (Hier, LeMay, & Rosenberger, 1979), to name just two. Recently, Courchesne, Yeung-Courchesne, Press, Hesselink, and Jernigan (1988) discovered underdevelopment of cerebellar structures in a sample of autistic patients who underwent magnetic resonance scanning. Rutter and Schopler (1987) point out that while many studies continue to suggest that autistic children demonstrate abnormal neurophysiological findings, there is great inconsistency in the types of deficits noted. Attempts to delineate gross abnormalities in brain structure and function by either computerized axial tomography (CAT scans) or positron emission tomography (PET scans) have often been unsuccessful (Prior, Tress, Hoffman, & Boldt, 1984; Rosenbloom, Campbell, George, Kricheff, Taleporos, Anderson, Reuben, & Korein, 1984; Herold, Frackowiak, LeCouter, Rutter, & Howlin, 1988). Additionally, those subtle differences that have been noted in neurological functioning between children without disability and those with autism do not readily predict why autistic children demonstrate the particular behaviors that they do. That is, we do not currently have adequate models of the relationships between specific aspects of neurological function and human behavior. Attempts to attribute autism to a specific cognitive dysfunction, such as the inability to construct internal symbolic representations (Hermelin, 1978), for example, suffer from the same problems—how does one locate the neurological substrates of such a cognitive inability, and how would such an impairment produce the specific social, linguistic, and cognitive symptoms that so classically describe autism?

LANGUAGE

Researchers have examined the language of autistic children in detail in an attempt to ascertain whether their communicative difficulties stem from impairment of isolated linguistic skills or from more global patterns of either linguistic or cognitive deficiency. In this light, some have noted that children with autism may display relatively uneven language abilities. For example, Boucher (1976) and Baltaxe and Simmons (1981) suggest that phonological development in autism appears to exceed accomplishments noted in other areas of language knowledge and use. Conversely, most observers have viewed the language deficits in autism as lying primarily in the pragmatic or social domains (Laughton & Hasenstab, 1986; Rutter & Schopler, 1987; Tager-Flusberg, 1981). Rutter and Schopler (1987) comment that

> [while at] one time these [abnormalities in communication] . . . tended to be framed in terms of speech or language impairment, . . . it is clear that the characteristic features involve deviance rather than delay (although delay in development is also usual), and the abnormalities extend beyond speech to many aspects of the communicative process. (p. 165)

The authors point out that abnormalities in communicative development precede the appearance of oral language. Children with autism apparently do not engage in prelinguistic conversations with their caretakers (using body movement, facial expression, or babbling) as do normal children.

ECHOLALIA

The echolalic behavior of children with autism is particularly fascinating. **Echolalia** is the act of repeating language heard in the speech of others. It may take a number of forms. *Immediate echolalia* occurs relatively soon after the model has been presented. Even normal children may repeat a caretaker's utterance before responding, perhaps as a review of what they have just heard. *Delayed echolalia,* on the other hand, is the repetition of utterances or phrases hours, days, or even weeks after the model was first heard. It is particularly common in the speech of echolalic children with autism. Additionally, one can also speak of echolalia as being either *exact* or *mitigated* in nature; mitigated repetitions contain minor changes in structure from the original model. An estimated 75 percent of verbal autistic children demonstrate echolalic speech at one time or another (Ricks & Wing, 1975).

Echolalia potentially provides us with an opportunity to answer some questions about the nature of the language deficit in autism. For example, one can ask if echolalic speech, even if structurally and/or semantically inappropriate to a given situation, contains some elements of pragmatic appropriateness. We can illustrate the problem in the following way. Chris, a four-year-old boy with autism, was having great difficulty in performing a task for his teacher. Frustrated, he swept the puzzle pieces to the floor and yelled, "Chrissy, eat your oatmeal, or I'll spank you!" His mother later reported that Chris had been throwing his cereal on the floor that morning, which had prompted her to threaten him to get him to stop, using exactly those words. Was Chris's utterance totally inappropriate to the situation?

Many researchers have also noted that a great deal of autistic echolalia is somewhat mitigated. Since children's abilities to repeat adult models have often been viewed as an estimate of their own grammatical capacity (Menyuk, 1969; Slobin, 1968), it can be argued that changes that children with autism make in their echolalic renditions of utterances may provide some insight into the degree to which language input is being processed rather than simply stored for playback as *unanalyzed wholes.*

There is some evidence that echolalia is more likely to occur when children with autism show signs of comprehension difficulty (Paccia & Curcio, 1982) and that its frequency in an autistic child's speech is likely to diminish as he develops more spontaneous communicative speech (Howlin, 1982; Prizant, 1978). Baltaxe and Simmons (1977) analyzed echolalic utterances in the bedtime soliloquies of a child with autism. They noted patterns of utterance breakdown, constituent replacement, and phrase recombination similar to those reported for a normal child by Weir (1962). They hypothesized that such behavior reflected knowledge of some basic linguistic rules and structures. Additionally, they suggested that although normal children appear to build up longer utterances from small linguistic units, children with autism may attempt to master language by gradually breaking down long, relatively unanalyzed strings into smaller syntactic components.

After comparing patterns of performance on imitation tasks by normal, retarded, and autistic children, Tager-Flusberg and Calkins (1990) suggested that autistic children may imitate to maintain a conversational role, rather than to foster their grammatical development. They found no evidence that imitated utterances were appreciably longer or more advanced than autistic children's spontaneous speech. Tager-Flusberg and Calkins also advanced the possibility that imitation might aid lexical and phonological development.

TREATMENT

As Tiegerman (1985) notes, *operant training* procedures were commonly used in the past for children with autism, perhaps as an outgrowth of the treatment of their concomitant behavioral problems (Lovaas, 1977). However, as many clinicians begin to emphasize language *function* over language form (pragmatic over syntactic considerations in language use), shifts have occurred to other approaches. A typical problem in the educational management of some children with autism is instituting the notion of interpersonal interaction—the child appears to have little use for language because she has little use for interaction with others in general. An elevated board program (Miller & Miller, 1973), which attempts to instill a dependency on others in these children, is just one approach to this problem. In this treatment approach, the child is placed on a balance beam; in order to obtain assistance in moving across or down from it, she must make requests, which are modeled for her using a combination of manual signs and speech. Other training approaches exist as well.

There is some dispute as to whether the echolalic speech of verbal autistic children should be extinguished as inappropriate or used as a springboard for more spontaneous language use. Prizant and Duchan (1981) noted that the echolalic utterances of the children they studied often appeared to serve important pragmatic functions, such as turn-taking, requesting, and self-regulation. As such, echolalia may be evidence of a desire to communicate that should be reinforced. Scherer and Olswang (1989) demonstrated the efficacy of the clinician's expansion of autistic children's spontaneous and imitative speech in teaching early semantic combinations.

Finally, some clinicians and educators have attempted to train children with autism in the use of *sign systems*. Fay and Mermelstein (1982) suggest that while a number of individual cases of success have been reported, no widespread consensus about the utility of such an approach can yet be documented. Additionally, they note that it is not clear why such an approach should work when the teaching of oral language has failed. Fay and Schuler (1980) provide an overview of approaches and therapeutic considerations in teaching language to children with autism.

Prizant and Wetherby (1987) indicate that when autistic children are taught how to communicate more effectively, their use of aggressive or socially inappropriate behaviors may diminish. Thus, language use is not only a symptom of the autistic syndrome, but an important tool in its management.

Though this section has addressed the specific problems of autistic children, many children who show emotional and behavioral disorders demonstrate concomitant speech and language problems. For more on this topic, see Prizant, Audet, Burke, Hummel, Maher, and Theadore (1990), who surveyed the broader population of children who display both psychiatric and communicative impairments.

■ SPECIFIC LANGUAGE IMPAIRMENT

GENERAL IDENTITY AND PREVALENCE

A large proportion of children who demonstrate language delay or disorder are not hearing impaired, cognitively impaired, or autistic. Moreover, they show no gross signs of brain dysfunction, although minor brain dysfunction may be suspected (Rapin, 1977) or probable (Miller, 1991). Such children demonstrate language impairment as their single obvious developmental disability. As Leonard (1987) points out, the diagnosis of *specific language impairment* (*SLI*) is one of exclusion; that is, alternative explanations for the child's failure to learn language have been sought and not found. Over the years, a number of terms have been used to identify this population: *infantile speech* (Menyuk, 1969), *developmental aphasia* (Benton, 1964) or *childhood aphasia* (Eisenson, 1972), and *deviant language* (Leonard, 1972). A survey of studies referenced in Leonard (1987) suggests that currently these children are often referred to simply as *language delayed* or *language disordered*. Estimates of the number of children who may be classified as SLI vary between 1 and 3 percent of the preschool population (Leske, 1979; Stevenson & Richman, 1976). Tallal (1987), however, points out that estimates of the prevalence of this condition are extremely variable and that the true incidence may be much higher.

It has become apparent that this group of children represents an extremely heterogeneous population, as might be expected when the primary basis of inclusion is that the child does *not* suffer from other identifiable conditions or syndromes (Leonard, 1982). This fact has confounded interpretation of the many studies that have examined such children's functioning (McCauley & Demetras, 1990; Miller, 1991) and made generalized descriptions of the exact nature of the linguistic development and abilities of these children virtually impossible. Some common findings of language behavior are presented in the discussion that follows. The reader should keep in mind, however, that a child carrying the diagnosis of SLI is very likely to present his own unique array of linguistic strengths and weaknesses.

THE NATURE OF LANGUAGE IMPAIRMENT

In general, studies of the language abilities of SLI children seem to suggest that their linguistic development is best characterized as *delayed* in quality rather than disordered, though this characterization is still disputable (Leonard, 1989; Miller, 1991). That is, SLI children appear to use structures and strategies similar to those employed by younger, normal children in most cases. However, this term should not be taken to imply that the SLI child can be expected to "outgrow" her language problem, simply achieving major milestones at later ages. A growing body of evidence suggests that such children do not "catch up"; rather, they demonstrate continued language problems and are at risk for reading and general educational failure (Aram, Ekelman, & Nation, 1984; Silva, Williams, & McGee, 1987; Stevenson, 1984; Tallal, 1987). The evidence increasingly suggests that the language-delayed preschooler of today may well become the *learning-disabled* student of tomorrow (Snyder, 1980). Padgett (1988) and others estimate that over half of all language-delayed preschoolers eventually show depressed reading achievement.

Many investigators have noted that subsets of the SLI population may be identified on the basis of relative areas of strength and weakness. Silva, Williams, and McGee (1987) describe children who show primary deficits in language production, language comprehension, or both production and comprehension. Aram and Nation (1982) and Bates and Thal (1991) also caution that children may show uneven language proficiency.

It sometimes appears that SLI children perform less well at all language tasks than their normal language peers. A few studies suggest that their language development is delayed from the outset, with emergence of single words trailing behind expectations (Morley, Court, Miller, & Garside, 1955; Weeks, 1974). More recent work has specifically targeted a subpopulation of toddlers who show good comprehension but poor expressive vocabulary and lack of combinatorial speech at age two. A fairly high proportion of such *early language delay (ELD)* children continue to demonstrate language and articulation delays as they mature (Rescorla & Schwartz, 1990; Scarborough & Dorrich, 1990).

Older SLI children continue to be slow "word mappers" (Rice, 1987), although possible reasons for this problem are not clear (Dollaghan, 1987; Leonard, 1988). A subset of SLI children are described as *anomic;* that is, they experience marked difficulty in retrieving words for common concepts that they do seem to comprehend (Aram & Nation, 1982; Eisenson, 1972). This *confrontation naming* or *word retrieval* problem may result in speech characterized by *circumlocutions,* or efforts to get around the blockage. A mother of one SLI child reported that her son requested "something round and English (*an English muffin*)" for his breakfast; another SLI child labeled pictures on an articulation test in the following manner: "on my brother's pants (*zipper*)" and "you eat breakfast with it (*spoon*)."

Language Sample: "The Three Little Pigs"
Student: Becky, age seven years, four months
One little pig was making the straw of the house. Was happy because it was fixed up and he was so happy. Then he went to 'nother house. The first pig went to 'nother house. Two pigs and two pigs were running, singing, dancing. The fox was hungry and the third little pig was so busy. O-O-O-O-O, he was so busy. The little pigs—they talking to him. And say "Want to play with us?" He was so busy. They went running, dancing, singing. The pig said, "not my chinny chin." And the fox say, "I'll blow your house." And he puff, puff, and he blow it. He went running he could. And the first little pig went the second little pig. And they peek outside and look out the door and they sing and dance in the stick house.
The fox is . . . fox is lamb. "Not my chinny chin." He hide under the lamb. And he is a fox. And he blow and blow and puff and puff and it broke. He puff, puff, puff, and it so strong. They went to the third pig and he puff and puff and puff, and was too strong. And he went down and he got the soup—inside the soup and he say, "OW! That hurts!" And they was so happy and dancing.

FIGURE 9.2 A language-disordered child retells a familiar story (Source: *Effective Intervention with the Language Impaired Child* (p. 30) by M. Cole and J. Cole, 1981, Rockville, MD: Aspen. Reprinted by permission).

The vast majority of SLI children are identified by their failure to achieve normal syntactic production with or without accompanying deficits in comprehension (Ludlow, 1980). Their abilities to use grammatical morphemes and to utilize a wide array of simple and complex sentence structures are depressed when compared to those of normal peers (see Figure 9.2). This morphological deficit is striking, and has caused some to question whether SLI children are evenly delayed in their language development (Leonard, 1988).

Much current research has investigated less structural and more functional deficits that SLI children may display. As Leonard (1982) concludes, SLI children appear to experience difficulty with many pragmatic functions. They may produce less appropriate requests or respond less appropriately to the requests of others (Brinton & Fujiki, 1982; Prinz & Ferrier, 1983). Older learning-disabled (LD) children, even when not overtly disordered in syntactic or lexical use or comprehension, demonstrate a broad variety of pragmatic impairments (see Donahue, 1987, for review). For example, LD children display less sensitivity to their conversational partners' needs for information or clarification (Donahue, Pearl, & Bryan, 1980; Spekman, 1981), are less adept at guiding conversations (Bryan, Donahue, Pearl, & Sturm, 1981), display depressed narrative abilities (Roth & Spekman, 1986), and are less persuasive speakers (Donahue, 1981). They additionally demonstrate a tendency to interpret language very literally. Wood (1982) describes the child standing in the front of the room who, when cautioned by his teacher, "John, the children can't see the board," replied, "Oh, what's the matter with their eyes?" (p. 71).

As Donahue (1987) points out, it is unclear whether pragmatic and syntactic deficits arise separately in such children, whether their pragmatic deficits may be attributable to subtle linguistic deficiencies, or whether pragmatic deficiency actually constrains the development or display of certain syntactic skills. Evidence exists to support each position in part, and it may well be that different SLI children demonstrate different patterns of relative pragmatic–syntactic disorder. Fey (1986) presents a similar, though distinct viewpoint. He argues that children may differ both in their relative degrees of structural impairment and in their social-conversational tendencies. Some children appear to maximize limited syntactic and lexical skills in attempts to be conversationally adequate. Other children appear to be responsive but nonassertive. And still a third subgroup of children seems to be somewhat conversationally unresponsive to those around them. Finally, a number of SLI children also demonstrate articulation disorders in concert with their language difficulties (Paul & Shriberg, 1982; Tallal, Ross, & Curtiss, 1989). From an opposite perspective, Shriberg, Kwiatkowski, Best, Hengst, and Terselic-Weber (1986) found that a high proportion of children referred for articulation problems demonstrated concurrent language disorder.

CAUSATIVE EXPLANATIONS

A few researchers have proposed that SLI children merely represent the low end of the normal distribution of language talents in children (Leonard, 1991a). In this sense, they might be viewed as no more disordered than are children who lack musical or artistic prowess, if these differing abilities are considered examples of "multiple intelligences" (Gardner, 1983).

However, there is a broader consensus that SLI reflects underlying brain dysfunction at some level, even though it may not be grossly manifest (Cohen, Campbell, & Yaghmai, 1989; Stefanatos, Green, & Ratcliff, 1989; L. Swisher, 1985; Tallal, 1987). In many cases, there appears to be a familial, genetic component (Tallal, Ross, & Curtiss, 1989; Tomblin, 1989). But this assumption does not necessarily explain how such dysfunction disrupts the normal acquisition and use of linguistic abilities. Some researchers have suggested that SLI children suffer from underlying deficits in auditory processing. Tallal and her coworkers (Tallal & Piercy, 1973, 1974, 1975; Tallal & Stark, 1981) demonstrated that SLI children have difficulty in processing rapid acoustic events. The possible implications of such findings for a coherent model of SLI children's actual difficulties with language are still a matter of dispute. However, Leonard (1988), comparing data from English- and Italian-speaking SLI children, observed some common patterns of language formulation that suggest that SLI children are limited in their ability to process low phonetic substance (short, unstressed) morphemes in both languages.

Other researchers suggest that SLI children's language deficiencies reflect subtle cognitive skill deficits, specifically those that support symbolic behavior (Brown, Redmond, Bass, Liebergott, & Swope, 1975; Lovell, Hoyle, & Siddall, 1968). However, results from additional investigations tend to support the same dissociations between cognitive functioning and language development seen in retarded children. Terrell, Schwartz, Prelock, and Messick (1984) found that some SLI children were more adept at symbolic play than younger, linguistically matched controls, and Roth and Clark (1987) noted that it was possible for some of their study children to demonstrate symbolic play impairment that exceeded their language disabilities. Finally, some researchers report that SLI children demonstrate deficits in *information coding,* processing, or memory that might account for their language problems (Kirchner & Klatsky, 1985; Nelson, Kamhi, & Appel, 1987).

Growing interest has been expressed in comparing patterns of language disability in SLI children from different language communities. This cross-linguistic approach to the study of specific language impairment, recently initiated by Leonard, Sabbadini, Volterra, and Leonard (1988) and Clahsen (1989), has the potential to greatly improve our understanding of the basic deficit in SLI. Miller (1991) outlines relevant hypotheses about specific language impairment that might be more fully evaluated by examining children who are experiencing difficulty in learning particular types of languages.

An increasing body of evidence suggests that the term *SLI* may in fact be a misnomer (Leonard, 1987) because SLI children do, upon close examination, appear more likely to have *motor deficits* and/or subtle *cognitive deficits* (King, Jones, & Lasky, 1982; Stark & Tallal, 1981). If we do assume that language impairment arises from brain dysfunction (Benton, 1964; Rapin, 1977), it should not be inconceivable that such children might display varied patterns of linguistic and nonlinguistic performance, depending upon the extent and location of this hypothetical cerebral damage.

While the actual mechanisms responsible for deficient language development in SLI children have yet to be discovered, work has begun to identify certain factors that may place children at risk for the development of disordered language. Current research suggests that a variety of factors, some of which are amenable to preventive measures, may predispose certain children to language and learning disability. Among the possibilities currently being evaluated are *genetic factors* (Ludlow & Cooper, 1983), ingestion of *toxic substances* by the child or mother (e.g., alcohol, drugs, or lead), and chronic bouts of *otitis media* (middle-ear infections) in early childhood (Friel-Patti & Finitzo, 1990).

LANGUAGE INTERVENTION WITH SLI CHILDREN

In a retrospective analysis of reported treatment approaches to SLI, Nye, Foster, and Seaman (1987) noted that language intervention with such children definitely has the potential to improve their syntactic skills substantially, although success in remediating pragmatic deficits appears to be much more limited. In terms of specific therapeutic techniques, modeling has been reported to be most effective and general "language stimulation" least effective. Figure 9.3 provides an example of a modeling paradigm designed by Leonard (1975). However, Connell (1987) found that, while normal children learned an invented experimental morpheme most quickly through

1. The child, the clinician, and a confederate of the clinician, the model, are seated at a table.
2. A pretest is administered by showing the child action pictures or by performing actions and requesting the child to "Tell me what's happening here."
3. The clinician tells the child to listen to the model, who is going to talk in a special way when a picture is presented or an action is performed. The child is told that the model will earn chips (redeemable tokens) only when she talks in the special way (e.g., subject–verb constructions).
4. The clinician gives a picture to the model and asks "What's happening here?" Pretest stimuli are *not* included in training. Tokens are provided on a continuous schedule when the model correctly produces the target structure (e.g., "Boy drink").
5. To enhance the child's awareness of the pattern underlying the models, intentional errors are made on 20 percent of the model's utterances (e.g., "boy" or "drink"). These utterances receive no reinforcement. This procedure is sometimes referred to as developing an attentional set.
6. This procedure is followed until 10 models have been presented.
7. The child is then encouraged to talk like the model in response to the same types of verbal and nonverbal stimuli. The pictures or actions themselves differ from the modeled stimuli, however.
8. The model and the child alternate productions until the child produces three consecutive correct subject–verb sentences. Then the child continues on her own until criterion of 10 consecutive novel sentences containing the target structure is reached.
9. The pretest stimuli are then re-presented to the child without models to determine the extent of the child's acquisition of the structure.

FIGURE 9.3 An example of Leonard's modeling procedure (*Source:* Language intervention with young children *[p. 151] by M. Fey, 1986, San Diego, College-Hill Press. Based on L. Leonard, 1975. Reprinted by permission.)*

modeling procedures (see Figure 9.4 for another example of this technique), SLI children made more rapid progress when taught to imitate their clinician. He concluded that SLI children may differ from normal children not only in the amount of language knowledge they have mastered but also in the ways in which they most efficiently learn language. Rice (1991) concurs. In a series of studies, she and her colleagues found that SLI children were poor *"incidental learners."* Unlike normal children, SLI subjects learned few new words merely by hearing them embedded in a novel cartoon show.

A key problem facing SLI and other language-impaired children is that of *generalization*. Normal children find it very easy to create new sentences by analogy to the large variety of grammatical examples they have heard; most language-disordered children do not. This is the crux of the challenge for language teachers—to teach children

Clinician: This doll is the father. This is the mother. This is the boy, and this is the girl. They are going to get up and get ready to go to work and school. The doll, Harlan, is going to try to guess what they're doing. He's going to talk in a special way. You listen to Harlan's questions. Later, you'll get a chance to guess just like Harlan.

(The barrier is placed between the child and the materials which will be manipulated by the clinician. Harlan takes a position on the child's side.)

Clinician: Ding-a-ling-a-ling.
Harlan: Is the alarm going off?

Clinician: Yes, it is. (Makes a yawning sound.)
Harlan: Is the mother waking up?

Clinician: Nope.
Harlan: The boy waking up?

Clinician: Use your special talk.
Harlan: Is the boy waking up?

Clinician: No, he isn't.
Harlan: Is the father getting up?

Clinician: Yes, he is. (Removes barrier and shows father getting out of bed.) I wonder what he is gonna do now? (Makes a sound like flowing water.)
Harlan: He turning on the water?

Clinician: I didn't hear your special talk.
Harlan: Is he turning on the water?

Clinician: Yes, he is. Do you know why?
Harlan: Is he taking a bath/taking a shower/brushing his teeth?

Clinician: Yes, he is. Mother is doing something now.
Harlan: Is she getting up?, etc.

Next, the child gets a turn to ask questions using "special talk."

FIGURE 9.4 A sample training sequence to illustrate a modeling procedure (*Note:* This procedure exemplifies a way in which a realistic need to communicate can be created in a structured setting. The target structure is the use of auxiliary *is* in questions. Materials include several dolls representing family members, toy bedroom, bathroom, and kitchen furniture, and a large doll or puppet to be used as a model. (*From Language intervention with young children* (p. 178) by M. Fey, 1986, San Diego. College-Hill Press. Reprinted by permission).

to be able to create utterances they have not specifically been taught to say. Numerous specific procedures and discussion about approaches to language remediation with young language-disordered children may be found in Fey (1986) and Leonard (1975), among others. Rice (1991) provides a classroom model for SLI remediation with preschoolers. Following principles detailed in the *learnability* literature (Pinker, 1984, 1989), theoretical issues underlying the *"teachability"* of language are discussed in Rice and Schiefelbusch (1989) and Rice (1991).

Motor impairment prevents this child from speaking and writing, but he is able to use a device that allows him to communicate effectively.

■ ATYPICAL SPEECH DEVELOPMENT

We have described in some detail four major forms of language disorders. There are, in addition, many conditions that lead to atypical speech development. Speech disorders constitute another field of inquiry altogether, and we mention them here only briefly. As in the case of disordered language development, disordered speech development may evolve both from known organic causes and syndromes or from unknown etiology. For instance, significant hearing impairment in children typically results in poor articulation ability; motor disorders in children, such as **cerebral palsy,** often affect the ability to articulate normally. Children with cerebral palsy often demonstrate problems with respiratory support for speech and difficulty producing or controlling the rapid movements of the larynx, jaw, tongue, and lips necessary for the normal rapid rate of conversational speech (see Hardy, 1983, for a general discussion). It is important to point out that in many, if not most, cases of cerebral palsy, receptive language ability and intellectual functioning are relatively unimpaired.

Cleft palate is a condition in which various facial structures, particularly the hard and soft palates, fail to develop properly during the *first trimester* of gestation. A typical result is the inability to control the *intra-oral air pressure* necessary for normal speech development. Air leaks cut through the palatal defect and the nostrils, producing a nasal speech quality and an inability to produce certain classes of phonemes, such as sibilants and high-pressure stops and fricatives (e.g., /p/, /b/, /f/, /v/). Like the child with cerebral palsy, the child with cleft-palate speech often mistakenly elicits listener perceptions of linguistic or cognitive deficiency. The vast majority of cleft-palate children, however, possess normal linguistic and intellectual ability. Cleft-palate speech can usually be substantially improved by a combination of surgical and speech therapy intervention (for a comprehensive overview, see McWilliams, Morris, & Shelton, 1984).

A large proportion of articulation disorders in children have traditionally been termed *functional* (i.e., their etiology is unknown). There is growing evidence that **chronic otitis media** may predispose some children to delayed or disordered speech development, but this possible etiological factor has yet to be firmly established. At one point, problems with *auditory discrimination* were suspected in this population; that is, it was hypothesized that children did not articulate sounds properly because they could not discriminate the difference between their defective productions and the correct model. However, this theory has been criticized by a number of researchers (see Locke, 1980, for discussion), who find that the majority of articulation disordered children appear to have normal perceptual abilities.

In general, children whose articulation development is perceived to be either slow or defective demonstrate phonological patterns similar to those exhibited by younger, normal children (see Chapter 3). Thus, phonemes that emerge late in normal child phonology may be missing or misarticulated in the speech of articulation-impaired children. Additionally, phonological processes common in very young children's word productions—such as consonant cluster reduction, final consonant deletion or devoicing, stopping of continuant sounds, or gliding of liquids—may persist in the speech of older, speech-disordered children (Shriberg, 1991). A number of articulation-disordered children appear to have concurrent language problems (Shriberg et al., 1986). Additionally, syntax and phonology may interact to create varying degrees of difficulty with both articulation and grammar for individual children (Paul & Shriberg, 1982).

Articulation therapy can be effective in remediating articulation disorders of *unknown etiology* (Shriberg & Kwiatkowski, 1987). Some children are aided by a "semantic" approach; here, for example, they would be made aware that failure to include final consonants results in inability to distinguish among words in the language (e.g., *bead, beat, beach, beak*). Other children are helped by direct instructions regarding placement of the articulators for the correct production of problematic sounds. For instance, an /s/ can be produced if the child is told to say /t/, then gradually slide the tongue back. Other approaches exist as well. Overviews of the major issues involved in assessing and remediating children's articulation disorders are provided by Elbert and Gierut (1986), Newman, Creaghead, and Secord (1985), and Stoel-Gammon and Dunn (1984).

CHILDHOOD STUTTERING

A small percentage of children fail to develop normal *fluency* skills. As with language and articulation ability, fluent speech evolves over the course of child development. Thus, even normal children demonstrate a tendency to hesitate, to repeat or prolong sounds, syllables, and words, or to insert fillers such as *um* and *well* between words in utterances. Starkweather (1987) provides a comprehensive overview of changes in these tendencies during childhood.

However, some children's fluency appears to differ both quantitatively and qualitatively from that seen in normal development; they may demonstrate greater degrees of disfluency, such as more than 10 repeated words, syllables, or sounds per 100 words (Adams, 1984). More of their disfluencies are part-word repetitions than one would expect in normal child speech. There are likely to be more repetitions of a repeated segment than in normal speech. Most children occasionally repeat a syllable or word once, such as "but-but I don't want to," but the stuttering child may produce "b-b-b-but I don't want to." Prolonged segments are of excessive duration, and the quality of the prolongation appears tense. Finally, as the child continues to experience difficulty in producing fluent utterances, he may begin to demonstrate signs of self-awareness and frustration.

Most children experience *"developmental disfluency,"* or periods during which their developing capacity to produce fluent speech appears strained by their emerging linguistic abilities. Consultation with a speech pathologist versed in distinguishing between normal disfluency and stuttering is helpful when parents become concerned.

As with many of the disorders surveyed in this chapter, the cause of stuttering is presently not known. There is some suggestion that there may be a genetic predisposition to develop stuttering (see Andrews, Craig, Feyer, Hoddinott, & Neilson, 1983, for a review). Additionally, some research concludes that stutterers show less well-defined lateralization of brain functions. Other investigators have posited that stuttering may result from problems in motor planning or coordination (Kent, 1982; Zimmerman, 1980). Finally, because of known linguistic influences on the frequency and location of stuttering in children's speech (Bernstein, 1981; Bernstein Ratner & Sih, 1987; Wall,

1980; Wall, Starkweather, & Cairns, 1981), some researchers have either posited an underlying linguistic basis for stuttering (Perkins, Kent, & Curlee, 1991), or suggested that stuttering reflects an inability of the child's system to deal with simultaneous language formulation and motor speech production demands (Starkweather, 1987).

More than half of all children who stutter as preschoolers recover before the age of seven (Andrews & Harris, 1964). For those children who continue to experience fluency failure, therapy can be extremely helpful in both teaching more fluent speech style and helping to avoid the development of counterproductive responses to the fear of stuttering, such as speaking fears and distracting ancillary behaviors. Peters and Guitar (1991) provide guidelines for the diagnosis and treatment of fluency disorders in children.

EVALUATION OF SUSPECTED SPEECH AND LANGUAGE DISORDERS IN CHILDREN

Parents are usually the first to suspect that a child may not be developing language skills normally. The child may not have begun to use understandable words by 18 months of age, although other children they know began to acquire language as early as nine months or one year of age. Or the child may not appear to hear well. Or she may appear to use sentence structures that seem too immature for her age.

How does one determine whether a child's communicative development appears normal or disturbed? What is the difference between individual variation (Chapter 8) and atypical variation that places the child at a communicative disadvantage? Evaluation of the communicative competence of children with suspected language disorders is the task of *speech-language pathologists.* Before appraising the child's language skills, hearing acuity is usually evaluated by an *audiologist* to ensure that the child will be able to comply with assessment demands and to rule out hearing impairment as the possible basis for the suspected speech-language delay.

A variety of assessment devices and procedures exists to aid in the identification of children who will need therapeutic intervention to develop adequate communication skills. A number of articulation tests (e.g., the Goldman-Fristoe Test of Articulation, 1986, and the Khan-Lewis Phonological Analysis, 1987) compare both the number and pattern of a child's articulation errors against expected performance for her age. The measurement of a child's language skills may be both theoretically and practically more difficult, however (McCauley & Swisher, 1984). It is difficult to appraise the full range of morphological, syntactic, and pragmatic skills needed to be an effective and age-appropriate communicator in the limited time of a diagnostic session.

Because language skills encompass such a large and varied domain, tests of language ability in children are extremely numerous and diverse, and we cannot easily describe them in this chapter. Aram and Nation (1982) and Wiig and Semel (1986), however, provide extensive overview descriptions of many of the commonly used tests of child language ability. We will note that many tests of language performance can be faulted for limited *content validity*—they are able to sample only a small range of possible language skills and usually do so in ways that do not duplicate real-world communicative situations. Additionally, most standardized language tests are not designed to evaluate the performance of children younger than three years. There has been increased interest in the use of parental report measures, which appear to reliably identify language-delayed and normal children as young as 20 to 24 months (Dale, 1991; Rescorla, 1989). Such measures utilize parental estimates of specific vocabulary, grammatical morphemes, and sentence patterns used by the child, rather than actual samples of the child's speech.

It is widely acknowledged that structured tests of language comprehension and production should be supplemented by structural and pragmatic analysis of spontaneous language samples. Miller (1981a), Tyack and Gottlesben (1974), Scarborough (1990), and MacWhinney (1991) all provide guidelines for syntactic evaluation of spontaneous language; Lund and Duchan (1988) and Roth and Spekman (1984) additionally suggest procedures for assessing the degree to which children appear to be pragmatically competent. These are more time-consuming appraisal techniques, but yield a more complete and representative picture of a child's expressive grammatical ability.

SUMMARY

While the vast majority of children appear to master language skills easily, other children may be comparatively slow language learners and, in some cases, fail to acquire normal adultlike language abilities. Four major conditions adversely affect both the speed and success of language learning. *Hearing impairment* limits the child's exposure to a sufficiently large and intelligible language model. *Mental retardation* is usually accompanied by a slower rate of language development and less proficient final language ability, although it is not clear whether cognitively impaired children's problems with language stem directly from specific cognitive skill deficiencies or from other, more global patterns of behavior.

Autistic children's language is often described as severely deviant in quality, demonstrating a lack of pragmatic appropriateness as well as structural deficiencies. The nature of the underlying deficit in autism has yet to be determined; however, analysis of the striking language patterns seen in autistic children may help to answer questions about the origins of the aberrant behaviors of this unusual syndrome.

Many children appear to have weak or delayed language skills when compared to their peers, but they do not suffer from obvious neurological, cognitive, or perceptual impairment. These *specifically language-impaired* children are thought to demonstrate poor ability to abstract and learn language rules and skills. Many children showing such a pattern of depressed language functioning during early development apparently also go on to experience difficulty with academic skills during their school years.

Though blind children without additional handicapping conditions are not language-disordered in the usual sense, their language development does reflect the influence of limited visual information during the language-learning process. Failure to learn and use certain types of words, and to develop more typical phonological patterns, may be linked both to the absence of visual cues and to the compensating behaviors of caretakers.

Language impairment—which affects the child's ability to use the *lexicon, syntax,* and *pragmatic* systems of language—needs to be differentiated from *speech impairment,* which affects the child's ability to *articulate* the *phonological component* of language. Some speech impairment is due to defects in *oral structure* (such as *cleft palate*); other forms may be due to problems in *motor coordination* of the structures necessary for speech production (such as in the case of *cerebral palsy*). Still other children may misarticulate because they do not *hear* language models correctly (in the case of *hearing impairment*). However, many children demonstrate delayed patterns of articulation development that are not easily explained by these considerations.

Finally, while all children are occasionally disfluent during the language-learning years, some children demonstrate patterns of sound and syllable repetition, prolongation of sounds, and tense pauses between sounds and words in utterances that lead them to be perceived as *stutterers.* The cause of stuttering is, like so many of the disorders we have considered in this chapter, basically unknown, although *motor planning* (or timing disturbance) and *linguistic encoding* difficulty are two of the more commonly considered current approaches to its understanding and treatment.

Treatment of children with communicative handicaps is most effective when it considers the normal sequence of language development and attempts to integrate current beliefs about environmentally facilitating factors in normal language acquisition into the therapeutic process. Success in speech and language teaching appears to be guided in large part by knowledge of when children are ready to learn certain skills, given what they already seem to know. Additionally, the degree to which the language skills being taught can be made pragmatically relevant to everyday communicative needs is extremely important. Finally, the manner in which linguistic skills are introduced and reinforced appears extremely important, although current research does not indicate a single most effective way to teach language skills to children.

SUGGESTED PROJECTS

1. View the evening news or another television program with the sound off. Attempt to transcribe what the speakers are saying and to summarize the content of the news stories or program plot. How successful are you? Write a paper that discusses the degree to which a lack of auditory information makes following spoken conversation difficult.
2. View a videotape of the movie *Children of a Lesser God;* turn off the sound. How easy is it to follow the signing of the deaf actors when the oral narration is missing? Some people claim that sign languages are *transparent,* that they can be easily interpreted without knowing the specific rules for using a given sign language. Discuss your experience. Do you agree or disagree?
3. Try to arrange a visit to one of the following: a school or class for the hearing-impaired, cognitively impaired, autistic, or language-delayed. Write up and share your observations with others in your class. Be sure to address the children's patterns of communicative ability, as well as the techniques that are being used to remediate and augment their language skills.
4. If you can, arrange to observe a speech-language pathologist's therapeutic interaction with a communicatively impaired child. (Many universities operate speech-language and hearing

clinics, as do many hospitals and schools. Additionally, some pathologists work in individual practice.) In a short report, summarize your impressions of the child's communicative problem. Then discuss and analyze the techniques used by the pathologist to teach a particular language skill.

SUGGESTED READINGS

Andrews, G., Craig, A., Feyer, A-M., Hoddinott, H., & Neilson, M. (1983). Stuttering: A review of research findings and theories circa 1982. *Journal of Speech and Hearing Disorders, 48,* 226–245.

Aram, D., & Nation, J. (1982). *Child language disorders.* St. Louis, MO: C. V. Mosby.

Baltaxe, C., & Simmons, J. (1981). Disorders of language in childhood psychosis: Current concepts and approaches. In J. Darby (Ed.), *Speech evaluation in psychiatry.* New York: Grune and Stratton.

Cohen, C., & Shane, H. (1982). An overview of augmentative communication. In N. Lass, L. McReynolds, J. Northern, & D. Yoder (Eds.), *Speech, language and hearing.* Philadelphia: Saunders.

Cromer, R. (1974). Receptive language in the mentally retarded: Processes and diagnostic distinctions. In R. Schiefelbusch & L. Lloyd (Eds.), *Language perspectives: Acquisition, retardation and intervention.* Baltimore: University Park Press.

Cross, T. (1984). Habilitating the language-impaired child: Ideas from studies of parent-child interaction. *Topics in Language Disorders, 4,* 1–14.

Donahue, M. (1987). Interactions between linguistic and pragmatic development in learning-disabled children: Three views of the state of the union. In S. Rosenberg (Ed.), *Advances in applied psycholinguistics: Vol. 1. Disorders of first-language development.* Cambridge: Cambridge University Press.

Fay, D., & Mermelstein, R. (1982). Language in infantile autism. In S. Rosenberg (Ed.), *Handbook of applied psycholinguistics: Major thrusts of research and theory.* Hillsdale, NJ: Erlbaum.

Fay, W., & Schuler, A. (1980). *Emerging language in autistic children.* Baltimore: University Park Press.

Fey, M. (1986). *Language intervention with young children.* San Diego: College-Hill Press.

Johnston, J. (1982). The language disordered child. In N. Lass, J. Northern, D. Yoder, & L. McReynolds (Eds.), *Speech, language and hearing.* Philadelphia: Saunders.

Klima, E., & Bellugi, U. (1979). *The signs of language.* Cambridge, MA: Harvard University Press.

Lahey, M. (1988) *Language disorders and language development.* New York: MacMillan.

Leonard, L. (1982). Specific language impairment. In S. Rosenberg (Ed.), *Handbook of applied psycholinguistics: Major thrusts of research and theory.* Hillsdale, NJ: Erlbaum.

Leonard, L. (1987). Is specific language impairment a useful construct? In S. Rosenberg (Ed.), *Advances in applied psycholinguistics: Vol. 1. Disorders of first-language development.* Cambridge: Cambridge University Press.

McLean, J., & Snyder-McLean, L. (1978). *A transactional approach to early language training.* Columbus, OH: Merrill/Macmillan.

Miller, J. (1991). Research on language disorders in children: A progress report. In J. Miller (Ed.), *Research on child language disorders: A decade of progress.* Austin, TX: Pro-Ed.

Quigley, S., & King, C. (1982). The language development of deaf children and youth. In S. Rosenberg (Ed.), *Handbook of applied psycholinguistics: Major thrusts of research and theory* (pp. 429–476). Hillsdale, NJ: Erlbaum.

Quigley, S., & Paul, P. (1987). Deafness and language development. In S. Rosenberg (Ed.), *Advances in applied psycholinguistics: Vol. 1. Disorders of first language development.* Cambridge: Cambridge University Press.

Rice, M. (1983). Contemporary accounts of the cognitive/language relationship: Implications for speech-language clinicians. *Journal of Speech and Hearing Disorders, 48,* 347–359.

Rosenberg, S. (1982). The language of the mentally retarded. In S. Rosenberg (Ed.), *Handbook of applied psycholinguistics: Major thrusts of research and theory.* Hillsdale, NJ: Erlbaum.

Rutter, M., & Schopler, E. (1987). Autism and pervasive developmental disorders: Concepts and diagnostic issues. *Journal of Autism and Developmental Disorders, 17,* 159–186.

Starkweather, C. W. (1987). *Fluency and stuttering.* Englewood Cliffs, NJ: Prentice-Hall.

Stoel-Gammon, C., & Dunn, C. (1984). *Normal and disordered phonology in children.* Baltimore: University Park Press.

Swisher, L. (1985). Language disorders in children. In J. Darby (Ed.), *Speech and language evaluation in neurology: Childhood disorders* (pp. 33–97). New York: Grune & Stratton.

Wall, M., & Myers, F. (1984). *Clinical management of childhood stuttering.* Baltimore: University Park Press.

Wilbur, R. B. (1987). *American Sign Language: Linguistic and applied dimensions.* San Diego: College-Hill Press.

REFERENCES

Abbeduto, L., & Rosenberg, S. (1987). Linguistic communication and mental retardation. In S. Rosenberg (Ed.), *Advances in applied psycholinguistics: Vol. 1. Disorders of first-language development.* Cambridge: Cambridge University Press.

Adams, M. (1984). The young stutterer: Diagnosis, treatment and assessment of progress. In W. Perkins (Ed.), *Stuttering disorders.* New York: Thieme-Stratton.

Allen, T. (1986). Patterns of academic achievement among hearing-impaired students. In A. Schildroth & M. Karchmer (Eds.), *Deaf children in America.* Austin, TX: Pro-Ed.

Andersen, E., Dunlea, A., & Kekelis, L. (1984). Blind children's language: Resolving some differences. *Journal of Child Language, 11,* 645–664.

Andrews, G., Craig, A., Feyer, A-M., Hoddinott, H., & Neilson, M. (1983). Stuttering: A review of research findings and theories circa 1982. *Journal of Speech and Hearing Disorders, 48,* 226–245.

Andrews, G., & Harris, M. (1964). *The syndrome of stuttering.* London: William Heinemann.

Aram, D., Ekelman, B., & Nation, J. (1984). Preschoolers with language disorders: 10 years later. *Journal of Speech and Hearing Research, 27,* 232–244.

Aram, D., & Nation, J. (1982). *Child language disorders.* St. Louis, MO: C. V. Mosby.

Baltaxe, C., & Simmons, J. (1977). Bedtime soliloquies and linguistic competence in autism. *Journal of Speech and Hearing Disorders, 42,* 376–393.

Baltaxe, C., & Simmons, J. (1981). Disorders of language in childhood psychosis: Current concepts and approaches. In J. Darby (Ed.), *Speech evaluation in psychiatry.* New York: Grune & Stratton.

Barrett, M., & Diniz, F. (1989). Lexical development in mentally handicapped children. In M. Beveridge, G. Conti-Ramsden, & I. Leudar (Eds.), *Language and communication in mentally handicapped people.* London: Chapman and Hall.

Bates, E., & Thal, D. (1991). Associations and dissociations in language development. In J. Miller (Ed.), *Research on child language disorders: A decade of progress.* Austin, TX: Pro-Ed.

Bedrosian, J., & Prutting, C. (1978). Communicative performance of mentally retarded adults in four conversational settings. *Journal of Speech and Hearing Research, 21,* 79–95.

Benton, A. (1964). Developmental aphasia and brain damage. *Cortex, 1,* 40–52.

Bernstein, N. (1981). Are there constraints on childhood disfluency? *Journal of Fluency Disorders, 6,* 341–350.

Bernstein Ratner, N., & Sih, C. (1987). The effects of increases in utterance complexity on stuttering and dysfluency in children. *Journal of Speech and Hearing Disorders, 52,* 278–287.

Bigelow, A. (1987). Early words of blind children. *Journal of Child Language, 14*(1), 47–56.

Bochner, J., & Albertini, J. (1988). Language varieties in the deaf population and their acquisition by children and adults. In M. Strong (Ed.), *Language learning and deafness.* Cambridge: Cambridge University Press.

Bonvillian, J., Orlansky, M., & Novack, L. (1983). Developmental milestones: Sign language acquisition and motor development. *Child Development, 54,* 1435–1445.

Boothroyd, A., Geers, A., and Moog, J. (1991). Practical implications of cochlear implants in children. *Ear and Hearing, 12*(4), 81s–89s.

Boucher, J. (1976). Articulation in early childhood autism. *Journal of Autism and Childhood Schizophrenia, 6,* 297–302.

Brasel, K., & Quigley, S. (1977). The influence of certain language and communication environments in early childhood on the development of language in deaf individuals. *Journal of Speech and Hearing Research, 20,* 95–107.

Brinton, B., & Fujiki, M. (1982). A comparison of request-request sequences in the discourse of normal and language disordered children. *Journal of Speech and Hearing Disorders, 47,* 57–62.

Brown, J., Redmond, A., Bass, K., Liebergott, J., & Swope, S. (1975, June). Symbolic play in normal and language-impaired children. Paper presented at the Annual Convention of the American Speech-Language and Hearing Association, Washington, DC.

Bryan, T., Donahue, M., Pearl, R., & Sturm, C. (1981). Learning disabled children's conversational skills. *Learning Disability Quarterly, 4,* 250–259.

Calvert, (1982). Articulation and hearing impairment. In N. Lass, L. McReynolds, J. Northern, & D. Yoder (Eds.), *Speech, language and hearing.* Philadelphia: Saunders.

Carroll, D. (1986). *Psychology of language.* Monterey, CA: Brooks-Cole.

Clahsen, H. (1989). The grammatical characterization of developmental dysphasia. *Linguistics, 27,* 897–904.

Cohen, C., & Shane, H. (1982). An overview of augmentative communication. In N. Lass, L. McReynolds, J. Northern, & D. Yoder (Eds.), *Speech, language and hearing.* Philadelphia: Saunders.

Cohen, M., Campbell, R., & Yaghmai, F. (1989). Neuropathological abnormalities in developmental dysphasia. *Annals of Neurology, 25,* 567–570.

Connell, P. (1987). An effect of modeling and imitation teaching procedures on children with and without specific language impairment. *Journal of Speech and Hearing Research, 30,* 105–113.

Corrigan, R. (1978). Language development as related to stage six object permanence development. *Journal of Child Language, 5,* 173–190.

Courchesne, E., Yeung-Courchesne, B., Press, G., Hesselink, J., & Jernigan, T. (1988). Hypoplasia of cerebellar vermal lobules VI and VII in autism. *New England Journal of Medicine, 318,* 1349–1354.

Cromer, R. (1974). Receptive language in the mentally retarded: Processes and diagnostic distinctions. In R. Schiefelbusch & L. Lloyd (Eds.), *Language perspectives: Acquisition, retardation and intervention.* Baltimore: University Park Press.

Cromer, R. (1987, August). Active and creative language in some severely retarded children: Dissociations between language and cognition. Paper presented at the Fourth International Congress of the International Association for the Study of Child Language, Lund, Sweden.

Cromer, R. (1991). *Language and thought in normal and handicapped children.* Cambridge, MA: Basil Blackwell.

Cross, T. (1984). Habilitating the language-impaired child: Ideas from studies of parent-child interaction. *Topics in Language Disorders, 4,* 1–14.

Curtiss, S. (1981). Dissociations between language and cognition: Cases and implications. *Journal of Autism and Developmental Disorders, 11,* 15–30.

Dale, P. (1991). The validity of a parent report measure of vocabulary and syntax at 24 months. *Journal of Speech and Hearing Research, 34,* 565–571.

Delaney, M., Stuckless, E., & Walter, G. (1984). Total communication effects: A longitudinal study of a school for the deaf in transition. *American Annals of the Deaf, 129,* 481–486.

deVilliers, P. (1991). English literacy development in deaf children. In J. Miller (Ed.), *Research on child language disorders: A decade of progress.* Austin, TX: Pro-Ed.

Dodd, B. (1983). The visual and auditory modalities in phonological acquisition. In A. Mills (Ed.), *Language acquisition in the blind child: Normal and deficient.* San Diego: College-Hill Press.

Dollaghan, C. (1987). Fast mapping in normal and language-impaired children. *Journal of Speech and Hearing Disorders, 52,* 218–222.

Donahue, M. (1981). Requesting strategies of learning disabled children. *Applied Psycholinguistics, 2,* 213–234.

Donahue, M. (1987). Interactions between linguistic and pragmatic development in learning-disabled children: Three views of the state of the union. In S. Rosenberg (Ed.), *Advances in applied psycholinguistics: Vol. 1. Disorders of the first-language development.* Cambridge: Cambridge University Press.

Donahue, M., Pearl, R., & Bryan, T. (1980). Conversational competence in learning-disabled children: Responses to inadequate messages. *Applied Psycholinguistics, 1,* 387–403.

Eisenson, J. (1972). *Aphasia in children.* New York: Harper & Row.

Elbert, M., & Gierut, J. (1986). *Handbook of clinical phonology: Approaches to assessment and treatment.* San Diego: College-Hill Press.

Fay, D., & Mermelstein, R. (1982). Language in infantile autism. In S. Rosenberg (Ed.), *Handbook of applied psycholinguistics: Major thrusts of research and theory.* Hillsdale, NJ: Erlbaum.

Fay, W., & Schuler, A. (1980). *Emerging language in autistic children.* Baltimore: University Park Press.

Fey, M. (1986). *Language intervention with young children.* San Diego: College-Hill Press.

Fraiberg, S. (1977). *Insights from the blind: Comparative studies of blind and sighted infants.* New York: Basic Books.

Freeman, B., & Ritvo, E. (1977). Diagnostic and evaluation systems: Helping the advocate cope with the "state of the art." In J. Budde (Ed.), *Advocacy and autism.* Lawrence, KS: University of Kansas Press.

Friel-Patti, S., and Finitzo, T. (1990). Language learning in a prospective study of otitis media with effusion in the first two years of life. *Journal of Speech and Hearing Research, 33,* 188–194.

Gardner, H. (1983). *Frames of mind: The theory of multiple intelligences.* New York: Basic Books.

Garman, M. (1983). The investigation of vision in language development. In A. Mills (Ed.), *Language acquisition in the blind child: Normal and deficient.* San Diego: College-Hill Press.

Geers, A., & Moog, J. (1987). Predicting spoken language acquisition of profoundly hearing-impaired children. *Journal of Speech and Hearing Disorders, 52,* 84–94.

Geers, A., & Schick, B. (1988). Acquisition of spoken and signed English by hearing-impaired children of hearing-impaired or hearing parents. *Journal of Speech and Hearing Disorders, 53,* 136–143.

Goldman, R., & Fristoe, M. (1986). *The Goldman-Fristoe Test of Articulation.* Circle Pines, MN: American Guidance Service.

Gopnik, A., & Meltzoff, A. (1984). Semantic and cognitive development in 15- to 21-month-old children. *Journal of Child Language, 11,* 495–513.

Gormley, K., & Sarachan-Deily, A. (1987). Evaluating hearing-impaired students' writing: A practical approach. *Volta Review, 89,* 157–170.

Graham, J., & Graham, L. (1971). Language behavior of the mentally retarded: Syntactic characteristics. *American Journal of Mental Deficiency, 75,* 623–679.

Guess, E., Keogh, W., & Sailor, W. (1978). Generalization of speech and language behavior: Measurement and training tactics. In R. Schiefelbusch (Ed.), *Bases of language intervention.* Baltimore: University Park Press.

Hammermeister, F. (1972). Reading achievement in deaf adults. *American Annals of the Deaf, 116,* 25–28.

Hardy, J. (1983). *Cerebral palsy.* Englewood Cliffs, NJ: Prentice-Hall.

Harper, J. (1975). Age and type of onset as critical variables in early infantile autism. *Journal of Autism and Childhood Schizophrenia, 5,* 25–36.

Hermelin, B. (1978). Images and autism. In M. Rutter & E. Schopler (Eds.), *Autism: A reappraisal of concepts and treatment.* New York: Plenum Press.

Herold, S., Frackowiak, R., LeCouter, A., Rutter, M., & Howlin, P. (1988). Regional cerebral blood flow, oxygen and glucose metabolism in young autistic adults. *Journal of Cerebral Blood Flow and Metabolism.*

Hier, D., LeMay, M., & Rosenberger, P. (1979). Autism and unfavorable left–right asymmetries of the brain. *Journal of Autism and Developmental Disorders, 9,* 153–159.

Howlin, P. (1982). Echolalic and spontaneous phrase speech in autistic children. *Journal of Child Psychology and Psychiatry, 23,* 281–293.

Johnston, J., & Schery, T. (1976). The use of grammatical morphemes by children with communication disorders. In D. Morehead & A. Morehead (Eds.), *Normal and deficient child language.* Baltimore: University Park Press.

Jones, M., & Quigley, S. (1979). The acquisition of question formation in English and American Sign Language by two hearing children of deaf parents. *Journal of Speech and Hearing Disorders, 44,* 196–208.

Jordan, T. (1967). Language and mental retardation. In R. Schiefelbusch, R. Copeland, & J. Smith (Eds.), *Language and mental retardation: Empirical considerations.* New York: Holt, Rinehart & Winston.

Jordon, I., Gustason, G., & Rosen, R. (1976). Current communication trends in programs for the deaf. *American Annals of the Deaf, 121,* 527–532.

Kamhi, A., & Johnston, J. (1982). Towards an understanding of retarded children's linguistic deficiencies. *Journal of Speech and Hearing Research, 25,* 435–445.

Kanner, L. (1943). Autistic disturbances of affective contact. *The Nervous Child, 2,* 217–250.

Kanner, L. (1946). Irrelevant and metaphorical language in early infantile autism. *American Journal of Psychiatry, 103,* 242–246.

Kent, R. (1982). Stuttering as a temporal programming disorder. In R. Curlee & W. Perkins (Eds.), *Nature and treatment of stuttering: New directions.* San Diego: College-Hill Press.

Khan, L, & Lewis, N. (1987). *Khan-Lewis Phonological Analysis.* Circle Pines, MN: American Guidance Service.

King, R., Jones, C., & Lasky, E. (1982). In retrospect: A fifteen year follow-up report of speech-language disordered children. *Language, Speech and Hearing Services in the Schools, 13,* 24–32.

Kirchner, D., & Klatsky, R. (1985). Verbal rehearsal and memory in language-disordered children. *Journal of Speech and Hearing Research, 28,* 556–564.

Klima, E., & Bellugi, U. (1979). *The signs of language.* Cambridge, MA: Harvard University Press.

Lackner, J. R. (1968). A developmental study of language behavior in retarded children. *Neuropsychologia, 6,* 301–320.

Landau, B., & Gleitman, L. R. (1985). *Language and experience: Evidence from the blind child.* Cambridge, MA: Harvard University Press.

LaSasso, C., & Davey, B. (1987). The relationship between lexical knowledge and reading comprehension for prelingually, profoundly hearing-impaired students. *Volta Review, 89,* 211–220.

Laughton, J., & Hasenstab, M. (1986). *The language learning process: Implications for management of disorders.* Rockville, MD: Aspen.

Lenneberg, E. (1967). *Biological foundations of language.* New York: Wiley.

Leonard, L. (1972). What is deviant language? *Journal of Speech and Hearing Disorders, 37,* 427–446.

Leonard, L. (1975). Facilitating linguistic skills in children with specific language impairment. *Applied Psycholinguists, 2,* 89–118.

Leonard, L. (1982). Specific language impairment. In S. Rosenberg (Ed.), *Handbook of applied psycholinguistics: Major thrusts of research and theory.* Hillsdale, NJ: Erlbaum.

Leonard, L. (1987). Is specific language impairment a useful construct? In S. Rosenberg (Ed.), *Advances in applied psycholinguistics: Vol. 1. Disorders of first-language development.* Cambridge: Cambridge University Press.

Leonard, L. (1988). Lexical development and processing in specific language impairment. In R. Schiefelbusch & L. Lloyd (Eds.), *Language perspectives: Acquisition, retardation and intervention* (2d ed.). Austin, TX: Pro-Ed.

Leonard, L. (1989). Language learnability and specific language impairment in children. *Applied Psycholinguistics, 10,* 179–202.

Leonard, L. (1991a). Specific language impairment as a clinical category. *Language, Speech and Hearing Services in Schools, 22,* 66–68.

Leonard, L. (1991b). The cross-linguistic study of language-impaired children. In J. Miller (Ed.), *Research on child language disorders: A decade of progress.* Austin, TX: Pro-Ed.

Leonard, L., Sabbadini, L., Volterra, V., & Leonard, J. (1988). Some influences on the grammar of English- and Italian-speaking children with specific language impairment. *Applied Psycholinguistics, 9,* 39–57.

Leske, C. (1979). *Incidence and prevalence in communication disorders.* Report to the National Advisory Neurological and Communicative Disorders and Stroke Council (Report No. 79–1914). Washington, DC: National Institutes of Health.

Lobato, D., Barrera, R., & Feldman, R. (1981). Sensorimotor functioning and prelinguistic communication of severely and profoundly retarded individuals. *American Journal of Mental Deficiency, 85,* 489–496.

Locke, J. (1980). The inference of speech perception in the phonologically disordered child: Part I. A rationale, some criteria, the conventional tests. Part II. Some clinically novel procedures, their use, some findings. *Journal of Speech and Hearing Disorders, 45,* 431–468.

Lou, M. (1988). The history of language use in the education of the deaf in the United States. In M. Strong (Ed.), *Language learning and deafness.* Cambridge: Cambridge University Press.

Lovaas, O. (1977). *The autistic child: Language development through behavior modification.* New York: Irvington.

Lovell, K., & Bradbury, B. (1967). The learning of English morphology in educationally subnormal special school children. *American Journal of Mental Deficiency, 72,* 609–615.

Lovell, K., Hoyle, H., & Siddall, M. (1968). A study of some aspects of the play and language of young children with delayed speech. *Journal of Child Psychology and Psychiatry, 9,* 41–50.

Ludlow, C. (1980). Children's language disorders: Recent research advances. *Annals of Neurology, 7,* 497–507.

Ludlow, C., & Cooper, J. (Eds.). (1983). *Genetic aspects of speech and language disorders.* New York: Academic Press.

Lund, N., & Duchan, J. (1988). *Assessing children's language in naturalistic contexts* (2d ed.). Englewood Cliffs, NJ: Prentice-Hall.

MacWhinney, B. (1991). *Computational tools for analyzing talk.* Hillsdale, NJ: Erlbaum.

McCauley, R., & Demetras, M. (1990). The identification of language impairment in the selection of specifically language-impaired subjects. *Journal of Speech and Hearing Disorders, 55,* 468–475.

McCauley, R., & Swisher, L. (1984). Use and misuse of norm-referenced tests in clinical assessment: A hypothetical case. *Journal of Speech and Hearing Disorders, 49,* 338–348.

McIntire, M. (1977). The acquisition of American Sign Language hand configurations. *Sign Language Studies, 16,* 247–266.

McLean, J., & Snyder-McLean, L. (1978). *A transactional approach to early language training.* Columbus, OH: Merrill/Macmillan.

McLeavey, B., Toomey, J., & Dempsey, P. (1982). Nonretarded and mentally retarded children's control over syntactic structures. *American Journal of Mental Deficiency, 86,* 485–494.

McWilliams, B. J., Morris, H., & Shelton, R. (1984). *Cleft palate speech.* Philadelphia: B. C. Decker.

Menyuk, R. (1969). *Sentences children use.* Cambridge, MA: MIT Press.

Miller, A., & Miller, E. (1973). Cognitive developmental training with elevated boards and sign language. *Journal of Autism and Childhood Schizophrenia, 3,* 65–85.

Miller, J. (1981a). *Assessing language production in children: Experimental procedures.* Baltimore: University Park Press.

Miller, J. (1981b, June). Individual differences in the language acquisition of retarded children. Paper presented at the Second Annual Symposium for Research in Child Language Disorders, University of Wisconsin, Madison.

Miller, J. (1991). Research on language disorders in children: A progress report. In J. Miller (Ed.), *Research on child language disorders: A decade of progress.* Austin, TX: Pro-Ed.

Miller, J., & Chapman, R. (1984). Disorders of communication: Investigating the development of language of mentally retarded children. *American Journal of Mental Deficiency, 88,* 536–545.

Miller, J., Chapman, R., & Bedrosian, J. (1978). The relationship between etiology, cognitive development and communicative performance. *New Zealand Speech Therapists Journal, 13,*(2), 2–17.

Mills, A. (1983). Acquisition of speech sounds in the visually-handicapped child. In A. Mills (Ed.), *Language acquisition in the blind child: Normal and deficient.* San Diego: College-Hill Press.

Moeller, M., & Luettke-Stahlman, B. (1990). Parent's use of Signing Exact English: A descriptive analysis. *Journal of Speech and Hearing Disorders, 55,* 327–338.

Moog, J., & Geers, A. (1985). EPIC: A program to accelerate academic progress in profoundly deaf children. *Volta Review, 87,* 259–277.

Moore, K., & Meltzoff, A. (1978). Object permanence, imitation and language development in infancy: Toward a neo-Piagetian perspective on communicative development. In F. Minifie & L. Lloyd (Eds.), *Communicative and cognitive abilities—Early behavioral assessment.* Baltimore: University Park Press.

Moores, D. (1987). *Factors predictive of literacy in deaf adolescents.* NIH–NINCDS–83–19. NIH Report.

Morley, M., Court, D., Miller, H., & Garside, R. (1955). Delayed speech and developmental aphasia. *British Medical Journal, 2,* 463–467.

Mulford, R. (1988). First words of the blind child. In M. Smith & J. Locke (Eds.), *The emergent lexicon: The child's development of a linguistic vocabulary.* New York: Academic Press.

Mundy, P., Seibert, J., & Hogan, A. (1984). Relationship between sensorimotor and early communication abilities in developmentally delayed children. *Merrill-Palmer Quarterly, 30,* 33–48.

Musselman, C., Lindsay, P., & Wilson, A. (1988). An evaluation of trends in preschool programming for hearing-impaired children. *Journal of Speech and Hearing Disorders, 53,* 71–88.

National Institutes of Health. (1990). Consensus development conference statement, cochlear implants.

Nelson, L., Kamhi, A., & Appel, K. (1987). Cognitive strengths and weaknesses in language-impaired children: One more look. *Journal of Speech and Hearing Disorders, 52,* 36–43.

Newfield, M., & Schlanger, B. (1968). The acquisition of English morphology by normals and educable mentally retarded children. *Journal of Speech and Hearing Research, 11,* 693–706.

Newman, P., Creaghead, N., & Secord, W. (1985). *Assessment and remediation of articulatory and phonological disorders.* Columbus, OH: Merrill/Macmillan.

Newport, E., & Ashbrook, E. (1977). The emergence of semantic relations in ASL. *Papers and Reports on Child Language Development, 13,* 16–21.

Northern, J., & Lemme, M. (1986). Hearing and auditory disorders. In G. Shames & E. Wiig (Eds.), *Human communication disorders: An introduction.* Columbus, OH: Merrill/Macmillan.

Nye, C., Foster, S., & Seaman, D. (1987). Effectiveness of language intervention with the language-learning disabled. *Journal of Speech and Hearing Disorders, 53,* 348–357.

Owens, R. (1985). Mental retardation: Difference or delay? In D. Bernstein & E. Tiegerman (Eds.), *Language and communication disorders in children.* Columbus, OH: Merrill/Macmillan.

Paccia, J., & Curcio, F. (1982). Language processing and forms of immediate echolalia in autistic children. *Journal of Speech and Hearing Research, 25,* 42–47.

Paden, E., Novak, M., & Beiter, E. (1987). Predictors of phonologic inadequacy in young children prone to otitis media. *Journal of Speech and Hearing Disorders, 52,* 232–242.

Padgett, S. (1988). Speech- and language-impaired three and four year olds: A five year follow-up study. In R. Masland & M. Masland (Eds.), *Preschool prevention of reading failure.* Parkton, MD: York Press.

Paul, R., & Shriberg, L. (1982). Associations between phonology and syntax in speech-delayed children. *Journal of Speech and Hearing Research, 25,* 536–547.

Perera, K. (1984). *Children's writing and reading.* Oxford: Blackwell.

Perkins, W., Kent, R., & Curlee, R. (1991). A theory of neuropsycholinguistic function in stuttering. *Journal of Speech and Hearing Research, 34,* 734–752.

Peters, T., & Guitar, B. (1991). *Stuttering: An integrated approach to its nature and treatment.* Baltimore: Williams & Wilkins.

Pettito, L. (1991). Babbling in the manual mode: Evidence for the ontogeny of language. *Science, 251,* 1493–1496.

Pflaster, G. (1980). A factor analysis of variables related to academic performance of hearing-impaired children in regular classes. *Volta Review, 82,* 71–84.

Pinker, S. (1984). *Language learnability and language development.* Cambridge, MA: Harvard University Press.

Pinker, S. (1989). Learnability paradox in verb lexicon acquisition. In M. Rice and R. Schiefelbusch (Eds.), *The teachability of language.* Baltimore: Brookes.

Power, D., & Quigley, S. (1973). Deaf children's acquisition of the passive voice. *Journal of Speech and Hearing Research, 16,* 5–11.

Prinz, P., & Ferrier, L. (1983). "Can you give me that one?": The comprehension, production and judgment of directives by language-impaired children. *Journal of Speech and Hearing Disorders, 48,* 44–54.

Prinz, P., & Prinz, E. (1981). Acquisition of ASL and spoken English by a hearing child of a deaf mother and a hearing father: Phase II. Early combinatorial patterns. *Sign Language Studies, 30,* 78–88.

Prior, M., Tress, B., Hoffman, W., & Boldt, D. (1984). Computed tomographic study of children with classic autism. *Archives of Neurology, 41,* 482–484.

Prizant, B. (1978). *An analysis of the functions of immediate echolalia in autistic children.* Unpublished doctoral dissertation, SUNY Buffalo, NY.

Prizant, B., Audet, L., Burke, G., Hummel, L., Maher, S., & Theadore, G. (1990). Communication disorders and emotional/behavioral disorders in children and adolescents. *Journal of Speech and Hearing Disorders, 55,* 179–192.

Prizant, B., & Duchan, J. (1981). The functions of echolalia in autistic children. *Journal of Speech and Hearing Disorders, 46,* 241–249.

Prizant, B., & Wetherby, A. (1987). Communicative intent: A framework for understanding social-communicative behavior in autism. *Journal of the American Academy of Child and Adolescent Psychiatry, 26,* 472–479.

Quigley, S., & King, C. (1982) The language development of deaf children and youth. In S. Rosenberg (Ed.), *Handbook of applied psycholinguistics: Major thrusts of research and theory* (pp. 429–476). Hillsdale, NJ: Erlbaum.

Quigley, S., Montanelli, D., & Wilbur, R. B. (1976). Some aspects of the verb system in the language of deaf students. *Journal of Speech and Hearing Research, 19,* 536–550.

Quigley, S., & Paul, P. (1984). *Language and deafness.* Austin, TX: Pro-Ed.

Quigley, S., & Paul, P. (1987). Deafness and language development. In S. Rosenberg (Ed.), *Advances in applied psycholinguistics: Vol. 1. Disorders of first language development.* Cambridge: Cambridge University Press.

Quigley, S., Smith, N., & Wilbur, R. B. (1974). Comprehension of relativized sentences by deaf students. *Journal of Speech and Hearing Research, 17,* 325–341.

Quigley, S., Wilbur, R. B., & Montanelli, D. (1974). Question formation in the language of deaf students. *Journal of Speech and Hearing Research, 17,* 699–713.

Quigley, S., Wilbur, R. B., & Montanelli, D. (1976). Complement structures in the language of deaf students. *Journal of Speech and Hearing Research, 19,* 448–457.

Rapin, I. (1977). Language disability in children. In M. Blaw, I. Rapin, & M. Kinsbourne (Eds.), *Topics in child neurology.* Toronto: Spectrum.

Rawlings, B., & Jensema, C. (1977). *Two studies of the families of hearing impaired children.* Washington, DC: Office of Demographic Studies.

Reichle, J., & Karlan, G. (1988). Selecting augmentative communication interventions: A critique of candidacy criteria and a proposed alternative. In R. Schiefelbusch & L. Lloyd (Eds.), *Language perspectives: Acquisition, retardation and intervention* (2d ed.). Austin, TX: Pro-Ed.

Rescorla, L. (1989). The language development survey: A screening tool for delayed language in toddlers. *Journal of Speech and Hearing Disorders, 54,* 587–599.

Rescorla, L., & Schwartz, E. (1990). Outcome of toddlers with specific expressive language delay. *Applied Psycholinguistics, 11,* 393–407.

Rice, M. (1983). Contemporary accounts of the cognitive/language relationship: Implications for speech-language clinicians. *Journal of Speech and Hearing Disorders, 48,* 347–359.

Rice, M. (1987). Preschool children's fast mapping of words: Robust for most, fragile for some. Paper presented at the Fourth Congress of the International Association for the Study of Child Language, Lund, Sweden.

Rice, M. (1991). Children with specific language impairment: Toward a model of teachability. In N. A. Krasnegor, D. M. Rumbaugh, R. L. Schiefelbusch, and M. Studdert-Kennedy (Eds.), *Biobehavorial foundations of language development,* 447–480. Hillsdale, NJ: Erlbaum.

Rice, M., & Schiefelbusch, R. (Eds.). (1989). *The teachability of language.* Baltimore: Brookes.

Ricks, D., & Wing, L. (1975). Language, communication and the use of symbols in normal and autistic children. *Journal of Autism and Childhood Schizophrenia, 5,* 191–221.

Romski, M., Lloyd, L., & Sevcik, R. (1988). Augmentative and alternative communication issues. In R. Schiefelbusch & L. Lloyd (Eds.), *Language perspectives: Acquisition, retardation and intervention* (2d ed.). Austin, TX: Pro-Ed.

Rosenberg, S. (1982). The language of the mentally retarded. In S. Rosenberg (Ed.), *Handbook of applied psycholinguistics: Major thrusts of research and theory.* Hillsdale, NJ: Erlbaum.

Rosenbloom, S., Campbell, M., George, A., Kricheff, I., Taleporos, E., Anderson, I., Reuben, R., & Korein, J. (1984). High resolution CT scanning in infantile autism: A quantitative approach. *Journal of the American Academy of Child Psychiatry, 23,* 72–77.

Roth, F., & Clark, D. (1987). Symbolic play and social participation abilities of language-impaired and normally developing children. *Journal of Speech and Hearing Disorders, 52,* 17–29.

Roth, F., & Spekman, N. (1984). Assessing the pragmatic abilities of children: Part 1. An organizational framework and assessment parameters. Part II. Guidelines, considerations and specific evaluation procedures. *Journal of Speech and Hearing Disorders, 49,* 2–17.

Roth, F., & Spekman, N. (1986). Narrative discourse: Spontaneously generated stories of learning-disabled and normally achieving students. *Journal of Speech and Hearing Disorders, 51,* 8–23.

Rudser, S. (1988). Sign language instruction and its implications for the deaf. In M. Strong (Ed.), *Language learning and deafness.* Cambridge: Cambridge University Press.

Rutter, M. (1979). Language, cognition and autism. In R. Katzman (Ed.), *Congenital and acquired cognitive disorders.* New York: Raven Press.

Rutter, M., & Lockyer, L. (1967). A five to fifteen year follow-up study of infantile psychosis: Part II. Social and behavioral outcome. *British Journal of Psychiatry, 113,* 1169–1182.

Rutter, M., & Schopler, E. (1987). Autism and pervasive developmental disorders: Concepts and diagnostic issues. *Journal of Autism and Developmental Disorders, 17,* 159–186.

Salzberg, C., & Villani, T. (1983). Speech training by parents of Down syndrome toddlers: Generalization across settings and instructional contexts. *American Journal of Mental Deficiency, 87,* 403–413.

Scarborough, H. (1990). Index of productive syntax. *Applied Psycholinguistics, 11,* 1–22.

Scarborough, H., & Dorrich, W. (1990). Development of children with early language delay. *Journal of Speech and Hearing Research, 33,* 70–83.

Scherer, N., & Olswang, L. (1989). Using structure discourse as a language intervention technique with autistic children. *Journal of Speech and Hearing Disorders, 54,* 383–394.

Schlesinger, H., & Meadow, K. (1972). *Sound and sign: Childhood deafness and mental health.* Berkeley: University of California Press.

Shriberg, L. (1991). Directions for research in developmental phonological disorders. In J. Miller (Ed.), *Research on child language disorders: A decade of progress.* Austin, TX: Pro-Ed.

Shriberg, L., & Kwiatkowski, J. (1987). A retrospective study of spontaneous generalization in speech delayed children. *Language, Speech and Hearing Services in the Schools, 18,* 144–157.

Shriberg, L., Kwiatkowski, J., Best, S., Hengst, J., & Terselic-Weber, B. (1986). Characteristics of children with phonologic disorders of unknown origin. *Journal of Speech and Hearing Disorders, 51,* 140–160.

Silva, P. (1980). The prevalence, stability and significance of developmental language delay in preschool children. *Developmental Medicine and Child Neurology, 22,* 768–777.

Silva, P., Williams, S., & McGee, R. (1987). A longitudinal study of children with developmental language delay at age three: Later intelligence, reading and behavior problems. *Developmental Medicine and Child Neurology, 29,* 630–640.

Simmons, J., & Tymchuk, A. (1973). Learning deficits in childhood psychosis. *Pediatric Clinics of North America, 20,* 665–679.

Slobin, D. (1968). Imitation and grammatical development in children. In N. Endler, L. Boulter, & H. Osser (Eds.), *Contemporary issues in developmental psychology.* New York: Holt, Rinehart & Winston.

Smith, J., & Polloway, E. (1979). The dimension of adaptive behavior in mental retardation research: An analysis of recent practices. *American Journal of Mental Deficiency, 84,* 203–206.

Snyder, L. (1980). Have we prepared the language-disordered child for school? *Topics in Language Disorders, 1,* 29–46.

Spekman, N. (1981). A study of the dyadic verbal communication abilities of learning disabled and normally achieving fourth and fifth grade boys. *Learning Disability Quarterly, 4,* 139–151.

Staller, S. (Ed.). (1991). Multichannel cochlear implants in children. Supplement to *Ear and Hearing, 12*(4).

Stark, R., & Tallal, P. (1981). Selection of children with specific language deficits. *Journal of Speech and Hearing Disorders, 46,* 114–122.

Starkweather, C. W. (1987). *Fluency and stuttering.* Englewood Cliffs, NJ: Prentice-Hall.

Stefanatos, G., Green, G., & Ratcliff, G. (1989). Neurophysiological evidence of auditory channel anomalies in developmental dysphasia. *Archives of Neurology, 46,* 871–875.

Stevenson, J. (1984). Predictive value of speech and language screening. *Developmental Medicine and Child Neurology, 26,* 528–538.

Stevenson, J., & Richman, M. (1976). The prevalence of language delay in a population of three-year-old children and its association with general retardation. *Developmental Medicine and Child Neurology, 18,* 431–441.

Stoel-Gammon, C., & Dunn, C. (1984). *Normal and disordered phonology in children.* Baltimore: University Park Press.

Swisher, L. (1985). Language disorders in children. In J. Darby (Ed.), *Speech and language evaluation in neurology: Childhood disorders* (pp. 33–97). New York: Grune and Stratton.

Swisher, M. (1985). Characteristics of hearing mothers' manually coded English. In W. Stokoe & V. Volterra (Eds.), SLR '83: *Sign Language Research.* Silver Spring, MD: Linstok Press.

Tager-Flusberg, H. (1981). On the nature of linguistic functioning in early infantile autism. *Journal of Autism and Developmental Disorders, 11,* 45–56.

Tager-Flusberg, H., & Calkins, S. (1990). Does imitation facilitate the acquisition of grammar? Evidence from a study of autistic, Down's syndrome and normal children. *Journal of Child Language, 17,* 591–606.

Tallal, P., (1987). Developmental language disorders. In *Learning Disabilities: A report to the U.S. Congress.* Washington, DC: Interagency Committee on Learning Disabilities.

Tallal, P., & Piercy, M. (1973). Defects of non-verbal auditory perception in children with developmental aphasia. *Nature, 241,* 468–469.

Tallal, P., & Piercy, M. (1974). Developmental aphasia: Rate of auditory processing and selective impairment of consonant perception. *Neuropsychologia, 12,* 83–93.

Tallal, P., & Piercy, M. (1975). Developmental aphasia: The perception of brief vowels and extended stop consonants. *Neuropsychologia, 13,* 69–74.

Tallal, P., Ross, R., & Curtiss, S. (1989). Familial aggregation in specific language impairment. *Journal of Speech and Hearing Disorders, 54,* 167–173.

Tallal, P., & Stark, R. (1981). Speech acoustic-cue discrimination abilities of normally developing and language-impaired children. *Journal of the Acoustical Society of America, 69,* 568–574.

Terrell, B., Schwartz, R., Prelock, P., & Messick, C. (1984). Symbolic play in normal and language-impaired children. *Journal of Speech and Hearing Research, 27,* 424–429.

Terrell, S., & Terrell, F. (1983). Distinguishing linguistic differences from disorders: The past, present & future of non-biased assessment. *Topics in Language Disorders, 3,* 1–7.

Tiegerman, E. (1985). Autism: Learning to communicate. In D. Bernstein, & E. Tiegerman (Eds.), *Language and communication disorders in children.* Columbus, OH: Merrill/Macmillan.

Tomblin, B. (1989). Familial concentration of developmental language impairment. *Journal of Speech and Hearing Disorders, 54,* 287–295.

Trybus, R., & Karchmer, M. (1977). School achievement scores of hearing impaired children: National data on achievement status and growth patterns. *American Annals of the Deaf, 122,* 62–69.

Tyack, D., & Gottlesben, R. (1974). *Language sampling, analysis and training: A handbook for teachers and clinicians.* San Francisco: Consulting Psychologists Press.

Urwin, C. (1977). "I'm going to get you: Ready, steady, go!" The development of communication between a blind infant and his parents. In G. Butterworth (Ed.), *The child's representation of the world.* New York: Plenum.

Urwin, C. (1978). The development of communication between blind infants and their parents. In A. Lock (Ed.), *Action, gesture and symbol: The emergence of language.* New York: Academic Press.

U.S. Department of Education. (1987). *Learning Disabilities: A Report to the U.S. Congress.* Washington, DC: Interagency Committee on Learning Disabilities.

Vernon, M., & Koh, S. (1970). Effects of early manual communication on achievement of deaf children. *American Annals of the Deaf, 115,* 527–536.

Wall, M. (1980). A comparison of syntax in young stutterers and nonstutterers. *Journal of Fluency Disorders, 5,* 345–352.

Wall, M., Starkweather, C. W., & Cairns, H. (1981). Syntactic influences on stuttering in young child stutterers. *Journal of Fluency Disorders, 6,* 283–298.

Weeks, T. (1974). *The slow speech development of a bright child.* Lexington, MA: Heath.

Weir, R. (1962). *Language in the crib.* The Hague: Mouton.

Wetherby, A. (1984). Possible neurolinguistic breakdown in autistic children. *Topics in Language Disorders, 4,* 19–33.

Wiig, E., & Semel, E. (1986). *Language assessment and intervention for the learning disabled* (2nd ed.). Columbus, OH: Merrill/Macmillan.

Wilbur, R. B. (1987). *American Sign Language: Linguistic and applied dimensions.* San Diego: College-Hill Press.

Wilbur, R. B., & Jones, M. (1974). Some aspects of the bilingual/bimodal acquisition of sign language and English by three hearing children of deaf parents. In M. LaGaly, R. Fox, & A. Bruck (Eds.), *Papers from the Tenth Regional Meeting of the Chicago Linguistic Society.* Chicago: Chicago Linguistic Society.

Wilbur, R. B., Montanelli, D., & Quigley, S. (1976). Pronominalization in the language of deaf students. *Journal of Speech and Hearing Research, 19, 120–140.*

Wilbur, R. B., Quigley, S., & Montanelli, D. (1975). Conjoined structures in the language of deaf students. *Journal of Speech and Hearing Research, 18,* 319–335.

Wood, M. L. (1982). *Language disorders in school-age children.* Englewood Cliffs, NJ: Prentice-Hall.

Yuwiler, A., Geller, E., & Ritvo, E. (1976). Neurobiochemical research. In E. Ritvo (Ed.), *Autism: Diagnosis, current research and management.* New York: Spectrum.

Zimmerman, G. (1980). Stuttering: A disorder of movement. *Journal of Speech and Hearing Research, 23,* 122–136.

10

Words Move: The Interwoven Development of Oral and Written Language

David Dickinson *Clark University*
Maryanne Wolf *Tufts University*
Sandra Stotsky *Harvard Graduate School of Education*

■ INTRODUCTION

Anna Mudd, the first-grade author of "The Devl and the Babe Goste," is six years old and has been writing stories for at least two years. In its striking use of poetic images, sophisticated syntax, and vocabulary, her written language reflects both the advanced level of her oral language and the fact that her written language now possesses a life of its own—one that will, in turn, influence her oral language, reading, and future writing. This year Anna reads back her stories with great aplomb; last year she could not. It deterred her not a whit.

What we see in Anna's example are the complex interrelationships that exist among early oral language, emergent literacy, and writing development. This chapter is about each of these and the interwoven story of their development. We look closely at what prepares the child in cognitive, linguistic, and social development to move from a world of predominantly *oral language* to a world where written language is stressed and oral language becomes more complex. We examine the nature of written language in *reading* and the changes its acquisition threads through development. We consider the *writing system* and the unique requirements it places upon the developing child. Finally, we come full circle to reflect upon how reading and writing change the oral system from which both emerged.

■ EMERGENT LITERACY

EARLY SOURCES

For children growing up in literate societies, the emergence of written language is a long, gradual process. It begins in infancy with the child's first baby book and is steadily elaborated upon by parents, siblings, and caretakers as they enjoy the closeness that comes from sharing books and telling stories. During these reading times children establish emotional bonds to books as well as to caretakers as they acquire the language of books (Snow & Goldfield, 1983) and begin to learn how print functions. Toddlers and preschool children from diverse cultural and economic backgrounds also learn that reading and writing are culturally valued activities as they observe the many occasions when parents and others read and write (Heath, 1983; Taylor, 1983; Taylor & Dorsey-Gaines, 1989). Literacy-related knowledge is acquired as part of daily routines when children watch television programs such as "Reading Rainbow" and "Sesame Street." As a result of these and many other experiences, children begin constructing knowledge about the uses and nature of written language long before they begin decoding unfamiliar words and writing in a conventional manner. This knowledge is called **emergent literacy** (Sulzby & Teale, 1991).

AWARENESS OF PRINT USES AND CONVENTIONS

By the age of four many children are exuberant consumers and producers of print. Liza is a four-year-old whose room is littered with messages that she has scrawled on scraps

"The Devl and the Babe Goste"

of paper and incorporated into her pretend play. Generally, these consist of marks that contain few if any conventional letters but which are distinctly different from her drawings. Liza also takes part in creating and using different kinds of conventional written products (e.g., letters to Santa Claus, birthday party invitations, grocery lists). She is also beginning to read **environmental print,** print found on packages and signs. Since she was two, Liza has recognized her name and familiar logos such as those of Burger King and McDonald's. Expectations about relationships between speech and print are also developing. When she was three, Liza believed that print on objects labels them. For example, she informed her father that the word *Follensbee* printed on a bar of soap said *soap*. She also knows that one reads print, not pictures, because her small fingers placed on print make it difficult for her father to read her bedtime story.

These competencies are typical. Prior to learning to read, children develop *general concepts* about print, learning such things as the distinction between print and pictures (Harste, Woodward, & Burke, 1984), grasping how books work (e.g., directionality, print can be translated into speech in consistent ways, and books create their own time frame) (Clay, 1979; Snow & Ninio, 1986), and formulating hypotheses about relationships between speech and print (Ferreiro & Teberosky, 1982). Children from all backgrounds in literate societies begin to learn to read environmental print (Dickinson & Snow, 1987; Goodman, 1986; Morgan, 1987) and attempt to convey meaning with print even before they learn to form conventional letters (Harste, Woodward, & Burke, 1984). It is also typical for young children to adopt unconventional ways of writing (e.g., using squiggles, loops, etc.) that they use consistently for months or years (Clay, 1975; Harste, Woodward, & Burke, 1984; Sulzby, 1986). Thus, preschoolers' reading and writing reflect organized conceptions about printed language that affect how they interpret instruction they will receive in school (Dyson, 1984).

SPECIALIZED LANGUAGE SKILLS

When children begin to read and write fluently, they encounter a set of language demands that are more typically associated with reading and writing than with informal conversations: (1) *information* must be conveyed that is new to the hearer, (2) *background knowledge* necessary for the hearer to interpret the message needs to be provided, and (3) the information must be communicated through words and *syntax,* not by relying on intonation and extra-linguistic resources such as gestures. These communicative challenges can occur on written tasks (e.g., reports, memos) and oral tasks (e.g., lectures, telling a story about a past experience to someone who was not present), with the extent to which these characteristics are present falling on a continuum. The skills that arise to cope with these challenges have been called **decontextualized language skills** (Snow & Dickinson, 1991). Research into the origins of abilities to deal with these communicative challenges is just beginning, and this label may prove to be an umbrella term that refers to a set of genres (e.g., narrative, explanation, description) that share similar features and develop in parallel.

NARRATIVE DEVELOPMENT

Language strategies associated with written language become evident in the emerging narrative abilities of children. During the preschool years, children begin to create make-believe tales that include *literary devices* such as *narrators* and *distinct voices* for characters (Rubin & Wolf, 1979). As they move into the primary grades, especially around age six, the structure of their narratives becomes more conventional; children familiar with Western middle-class storytelling norms often include important information such as the *setting,* the *identities* of characters, and clear-cut *shifts* in *time* or *place* (Peterson & McCabe, 1983).

Storytelling is a social act that also involves a multitude of cognitive demands. These two aspects of narrative—the social and the cognitive—are nicely exemplified in the way children use connectives (e.g., *then, because*). Connectives serve semantic functions, indicating the relationships among events in stories (e.g., *but* denotes an opposition between two pieces of information). They also serve social, pragmatic functions, informing the listener of the relationship between previous and upcoming information. For example, *because* can be used to mark the beginning of narratives or episodes within a narrative. Children as young as four use connectives for both purposes, but during the elementary school years show increasing sophistication in *pragmatic* uses (Peterson & McCabe, 1991).

Narrative development shows regular age-related changes, indicating the importance of maturational factors, but culture also plays a major role in shaping the form of children's narratives. The narratives of African-American children (girls especially) tend to have a structure distinct from that of middle-class white children. They use an approach referred to as **topic-associating,** which juxtaposes thematically related incidents to make a point implicitly. These stories can be quite artful, but are hard for teachers to understand because they often lack explicit indications of shifts in time, character, and place (Gee, 1989; Michaels, 1981, 1991). The narratives of Japanese children also take a distinctive form, being extremely succinct and including sets of three episodes. The source of this structure appears to be *haiku* (a traditional Japanese poetry form) and quasi-haiku forms that play an important role in Japanese society, including parent–child language games and reading materials used with young children (Minami & McCabe, in press).

LINKING ORAL DISCOURSE TO READING

There is growing evidence that, for children who attend American preschools and schools, producing oral skills and understanding extended texts emerge in concert with print skills and may play an important role in supporting later literacy skills. One way these linkages can be seen is in subtle ways that children demonstrate their awareness of the differences between the language of books and conversational language. Much to the amusement of adults, children who cannot yet read conventionally enjoy "reading" favorite books aloud. These playful performances include uses of vocabulary and syntax associated with books but not with the child's spoken language (Pappas & Brown, 1987; Purcell-Gates, 1988, in press). Furthermore, there is a developmental progression in these emergent readings that reveals children's growing grasp of how print functions. Initially, children may engage listeners in discussions about books or may label pictures, but later they move away from conversational reproductions toward re-creation of texts that closely approximate the story as it is written (Sulzby, 1985; Sulzby & Zecker, 1991).

Other evidence of the links between oral *discourse skills* and literacy comes from correlational research that has found that, in kindergarten, print-related skills such as the ability to name letters and write are correlated with the ability to understand stories and communicate novel information (Dickinson & Snow, 1987; Dickinson & Tabors, in press). By the middle elementary grades, children's conversational skills can be distinguished from decontextualized skills, with only the latter correlating with reading (Davidson, Kline, & Snow, 1986; Snow, Cancino, Gonzalez, & Shriberg, 1989). Similarly, at this age there is a correlation between reading ability and use of connectives in stories children tell (Weber, 1990). Oral skills are extended to writing, because the ability to tell temporally sequenced narratives that explicitly mark time, scene, and character shifts is transferred to writing tasks (Michaels & Collins, 1984). Furthermore, reading ability is also correlated with children's use of connectives in their written stories (Cox, Shanahan, & Sulzby, 1990).

Further evidence of the intimacy of the linkages between discourse skills and reading comes from the finding that narrative skills lag in children with severe reading problems. Disabled readers have problems with tasks that require the recall and production of narratives, with their problems being most evident at the intersentential level. These problems are indicated by the fact that, when reading-disabled children recall stories, they tend to omit causal and temporal connectives (Roth & Spekman, 1986; Weaver & Dickinson, 1982; reviewed by Dickinson & McCabe, 1991).

METALINGUISTIC AWARENESS

Preschool children typically use language as a tool to communicate thoughts, wishes, and feelings; they give no thought to the tool itself. Reading and writing require a fundamental shift in children's orientation to this tool. Suddenly they must attend to it directly; they must develop **metalinguistic awareness.**

Children are naturally encouraged to develop metalinguistic awareness when there are failures of communication (Clark, 1978). For example, when a child does not get a requested toy, she may be prodded to reflect on the words used to convey her request. As a result, she may alter her wording or syntax. Perhaps as a result of such experiences, beginning in the preschool years, children begin to become aware of syntax (deVilliers & deVilliers, 1972, 1974; Smith & Tager-Flusberg, 1982) and varied features of messages, such as word choices that reduce comprehensibility (Revelle, Wellman, & Karabenick, 1985).

The level of awareness required for preschool children to make themselves more comprehensible may be relatively minimal; children may make adjustments without being fully aware of the changes they have made. Demands for conscious awareness increase dramatically when children begin attempting to read and write. Written symbols capture otherwise ephemeral words and sentences. Print depicts divisions between words and roughly reveals distinctions between phonemes. But in order to read and write, children need to map units of speech onto the correct symbols. In order to

Literate households help prepare children to read.

do this mapping, children first must be able to focus on the correct units in their own speech. This mapping is difficult because words and phonemes are not clearly marked in speech and young children often are not aware that they are distinct units. The psychologist Goodglass (personal communication, 1982) provides a lighthearted example of the problem some children have identifying word units: for a long time in his childhood, he thought that *elemeno* was the long letter in the middle of the alphabet!

Children as young as three may display ***phonemic awareness*** by producing and identifying rhymes. A later manifestation of this skill is the ability to isolate initial and final consonants in words. Many children develop a high level of phonemic awareness during the early school years as a result of reading instruction in alphabetic systems that stress sound-symbol correspondences (Bertelson, 1986; Content, Kolinsky, Morais, &

Bertelson, 1986; Morais, Bertelson, Cary, & Alegria, 1986; Read, Yun-Fei, Hong-Yin, & Bao-Qing, 1986). On the other hand, some children experience great difficulty attending to phonemes. This fact is reflected in the finding that measures of phonemic awareness have repeatedly been found to be strongly related to reading in first grade (Bertelson, 1986; Shankweiler & Crain, 1986).

A longitudinal study of the emergence of reading skills has traced the roots of phonemic awareness back into the third year of life, with a relationship found between three- and four-year-olds' knowledge of nursery rhymes and ability to detect alliteration and their later reading success as six-year-olds (Bryant, Bradley, MacLean, & Crossland, 1989). These researchers argue that nursery rhyme knowledge is important to later reading because of its relationship to later skill at detecting phonemes (Bryant, MacLean, & Bradley, 1990). Bowey and Frances (1991) agree that skill analyzing words into units is related to later reading, but argue persuasively that prior to receiving reading instruction, children only detect the differences between *onsets* and *rimes,* not phonemes. An onset is an initial consonant or consonant cluster (e.g., *pl* in *plan*); a rime is the vowel nucleus and a final consonant or consonant cluster (e.g., *an* in *plan*). It may be that exposure to rhymes and word play enables children to focus on rimes and onsets; this skill supports initial progress in learning to read, and reading instruction leads to full phonemic awareness (Bowey & Frances, 1991).

MOVING TOWARD CONVENTIONAL READING

The construction of the language skills and understanding of the uses and nature of print that began during the first year is the result of a complex weaving together of spontaneous insights and knowledge learned through explicit instruction. The evolution of early literacy abilities can be seen as *hierarchically organized* systems (Lomax & McGee, 1987). Children first construct concepts about books and how print works, and then begin to attend to aspects of the print that surrounds them. This is followed by growth of phonemic awareness and acquisition of phoneme–grapheme knowledge. As children construct knowledge about print and the relationship between print and speech, they also are building oral language skills that support their progress as they encounter the demands of first grade and begin to move into conventional forms of reading and writing (Mason, 1991; Snow & Dickinson, 1991).

It is not uncommon for children reared in literate homes to begin to read and write without explicit instruction (Bissex, 1980; Durkin, 1974–75). However, many others need reading instruction to help them learn to attend to the letters in words instead of treating them as graphic patterns (Ehri & Wilce, 1985; Masonheimer, Ehri, & Drum, 1985). Some children stumble because they have grown up in homes where books are not shared and opportunities to hear and produce complex extended discourse are limited. They arrive at school with weaker emotional bonds to books, less confidence that they will become literate, and fewer of the important psycholinguistic building blocks (Dickinson & Snow, 1987; Warren-Leubecker & Carter, 1988). Other children stumble because cognitive-processing deficiencies block the growth of their reading skills. In the following section we examine theoretical models of the reading process that help explain why some children falter as they attempt to learn to read and write. We then examine some of the sources of variability affecting children's reading development.

THE READING PROCESS

In the neurosciences, the neuronal system of the lowly squid has received a wealth of attention because the squid's long neurons make more visible the complex circuitry of neurons in general. The reading process is something like that for cognitive scientists. Reading represents one of the most interesting and cognitively complex systems and, as such, has a great deal to teach us about cognition in general. Perhaps the single most quoted statement about reading is Sir Edmond Huey's belief that an understanding of all that is involved in the reading system would be "the acme of a psychologist's achievement" (1908, p. 6). And indeed there have been many increasingly sophisticated attempts in the last two decades. There are certain basic assumptions about reading that are shared across most of these accounts and, remarkably, some central ones were first articulated by Huey at the turn of the century.

1. Reading is a complex network of various components or processes whose smooth integration is necessary for fluent reading.
2. The development of fluent reading involves the steady accumulation and synthesis of "more and more complex constituent acts as these are progressively welded together by practice" (1908/1968, p. 105). An integral aspect of this synthesis is the development of a rate of processing, which through "repetition progressively frees the mind from attention to details, makes facile the total act, shortens the time, and reduces the extent to which consciousness must concern itself with the process" (1908/1968, p. 104). In other words, Huey is describing what contemporary scientists term **automaticity** in reading, where the reader is freed from directing much conscious attention to early perceptual subprocesses in order to attend to the more complex work of comprehending the meaning of the text. Further, this growth in rapidity proceeds through a sequence of *developmental stages*.
3. The act of reading is continuous and constructive, where the reader engages in an ongoing interaction with the printed message.
4. Depending on development, manner of instruction, and such individual factors as expertise and psychological and physiological problems, there will be individual differences in the ability to read and the approach to acquisition.

In other words, according to Huey, reading is a fluent, multicomponential, constructive process that changes with development and is influenced by instruction and individual differences in the reader. Few reading theorists would argue with this view; rather, the major shifts in our understanding of reading in the last 80 years are the uncovering of the centrality of *linguistic processes* in reading and our increased ability to specify the complexity and individual components of reading. These changes came about in large part through reading theory in the cognitive and neurosciences. In this three-part section on reading, we first look at the significance of the shift in perspective to reading as a language-based process. Next, via a brief examination of several cognitive accounts of reading's underlying structure, we examine several of Huey's assumptions about reading and give them contemporary specificity. Finally, we discuss reading development and how children master all this complexity.

READING AS A LANGUAGE-BASED ACTIVITY

As late as 1975, reading would not have been referred to with such easy understanding as written language. For most of this century reading was considered a primarily *perceptual,* visually based activity, and theories of instruction and remediation were predicated on this assumption. For example, children with reading disorders were assumed to have visual problems and treated accordingly. During the 1960s and 1970s, however, researchers within the then new paradigm of psycholinguistics (Kavanagh & Mattingly, 1972; Kolers, 1970) challenged this assumption and replaced it with a whole new view. They stated that the nature of reading was language-based (Vellutino, 1979) and that the role of the visual system within reading was limited and should be conceptualized as an entry into more central language systems.

From within this view emerged a wide range of positions. For example, Liberman (in Kavanagh & Mattingly, 1972) stated that reading was "parasitic" on language. Elaborating upon this notion, Mattingly stated,

> Reading is seen not as a parallel activity in the visual mode to speech perception in the auditory mode; there are differences between the two activities that cannot be explained in terms of difference of modality. They can be explained only if we regard reading as a deliberately acquired, language-based skill, dependent upon the speaker-hearer's awareness of certain aspects of primary linguistic activity. (1972, p. 145)

As this view of reading became more articulated, a central question concerned the specific role of phonological processing in reading. Conrad (1972), who studied how the deaf learn to read, summarized this position by suggesting that reading may be possible without phonology but is made considerably easier with it. (See more recent discussion in Shankweiler & Crain, 1986.)

The impact of this view not only on theoretical direction but also on diagnosis, remediation, and instruction cannot be overemphasized. On the one hand, children with reading impairments—long suspected of language dysfunction by neurologists (Denckla, 1972; Kinsbourne & Warrington, 1963)—began to be perceived by the wider community as exhibiting a variety of very different disorders, with various *language problems* at the root of most pathology, and with visual disturbances only one small subgroup (Mattis, French, & Rapin, 1975). Although much work remains to be done in classification (Doehring, 1983; Fletcher & Morris, 1985), the subgroup or cluster approach to reading disorders and emphasis on the connections with language dramatically changed clinical and diagnostic work in this area.

On the other hand, the incorporation of psycholinguistic contributions into reading instruction became the forefront of a controversy whose historical roots (Chall, 1967; Matthews, 1966) are centuries old: what should be emphasized in learning to read? In the 1970s, two research groups—Goodman and Goodman (1977), as well as Smith (1972); and Liberman and Shankweiler and their colleagues (Shankweiler & Liberman, 1972; Liberman, Shankweiler, Fischer, & Carter, 1974)—presented psycholinguistic accounts of reading that were very different in emphases and in implications for teaching. The Goodmans and Smith focused then and now almost exclusively on the extraction of meaning, context, and inference, what are often called the *higher-level* linguistic processes. Major textbooks today under their direction stress these processes in reading acquisition and deemphasize phonic skills, which they believe most children learn without direct instruction.

In contrast, Liberman, Shankweiler, and their colleagues emphasized the relationship between reading and phonological skills like segmentation and phonemic awareness, often referred to as *lower-level skills.* Their research continues to provide strong support for instructional programs that encourage early phonic skills and awareness of the speech stream (Brady & Shankweiler, in press). Differences between these accounts are not trivial; neither have they been reconciled over time (see Adams, 1990; McKenna, Robinson, & Miller, 1990; Vellutino, in press). Instead, the differences have become more visible in later research, especially in *word-recognition models* of reading in the cognitive sciences that we will now describe.

READING MODELS

Huey's first assumption about reading is that it is made up of many parts that must work rapidly together—what is now referred to as the *componential nature* of the reading process. Within such a view reading is considered to be a continuum of related perceptual, linguistic, cognitive, and motor subprocesses, whose integration is affected by both general, cognitive factors (particularly automaticity, attention, and memory capacities) and external variables (syntactic construction, lexical ambiguity, and nature of the material to be read). *Automaticity* here refers to the potential of a process or component after much practice to be completed with extreme rapidity (Sternberg & Wagner, 1982).The term has been treated with some caution by current researchers (Perfetti, in press; Stanovich, 1990). It is used in this discussion to mean that some processes become very fast and are *obligatory;* in addition, they require only limited use of general cognitive resources. Thus, we take a more relativistic, continuum-like view of automaticity: the more automatic an act is, the faster it will be done; the less effortful, then the more automatic the performance (Logan, 1988, p. 515).

Researchers in the cognitive sciences attempt both to specify the function of each of reading's subprocesses and to understand how the subprocesses work together to give information, that is, to make meaning. To facilitate their work, many cognitive scientists use models to depict the underlying microstructure of reading and to make predictions about what happens when some or all of these subparts are activated.

We can bring the cognitive scientists' task to life by constructing a very simple model of the basic subprocesses involved in reading aloud the simple word *cat.*

Figure 10.1 presents a schematic look at some of the processes that would be involved if a first grader looked at *cat.* Our young reader must attend to the print

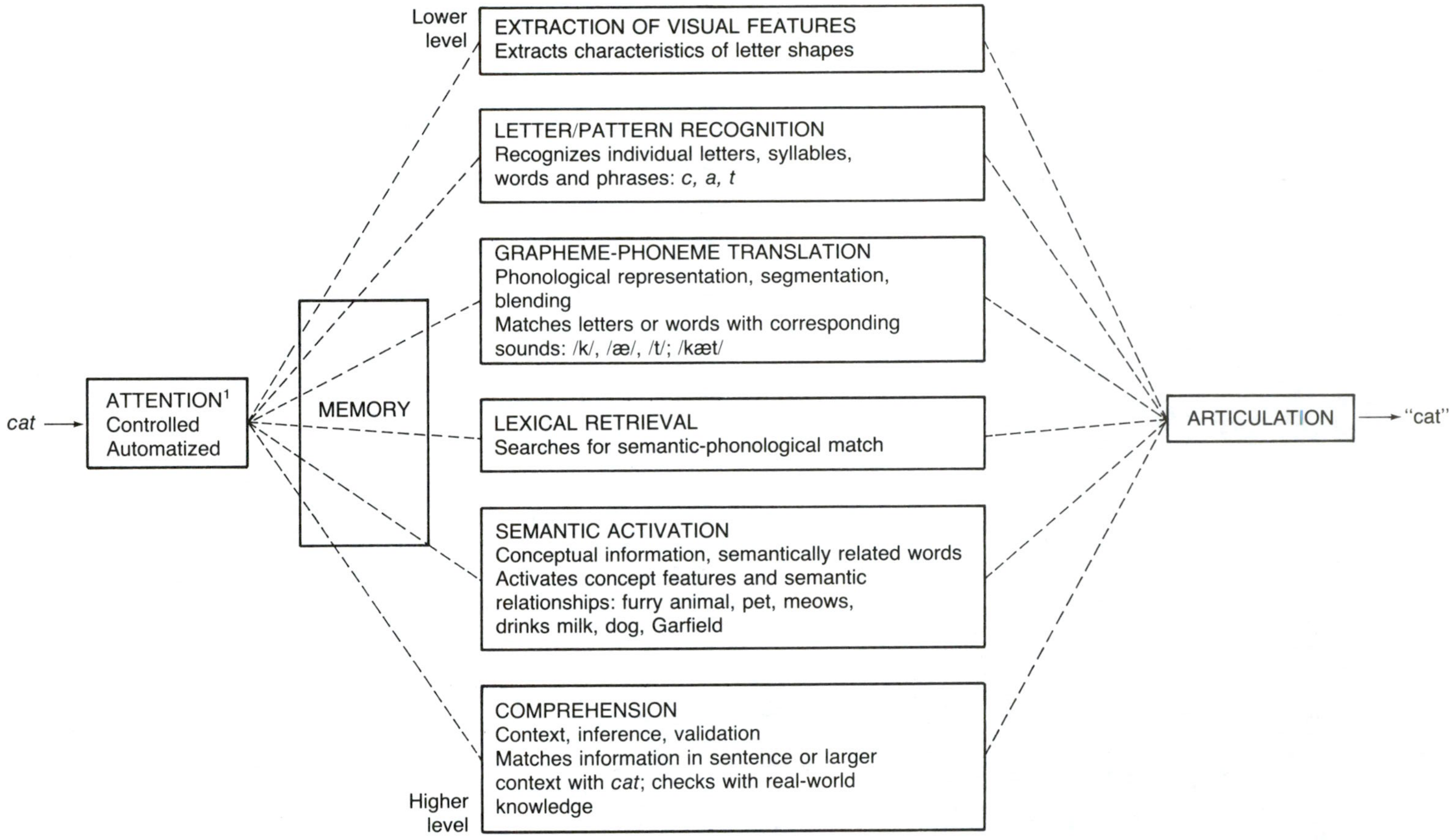

1. Direction, type, and amount of attention are influenced by external factors: development, orthography, reading method, individual differences, and type of material.

FIGURE 10.1 Overview of processes in first reading *cat* (*controlled attention*), extract the visual features (*visual perception* and *analysis*), recognize the letters or graphemes (*letter recognition*), translate the graphemes into their corresponding sounds or phonemes (*grapheme–phoneme correspondence rules*) using knowledge of *phonology* and *orthography* (more grapheme–phoneme rules), *search* and *retrieve lexical information* (phonological and semantic) about the word, *integrate* any available contextual information, *draw inferences, validate* or *refute* the targeted word accordingly, and *articulate* the word within 500 milliseconds (250 milliseconds, if adult). With reference to our model, the processes from attention to lexical access and retrieval are all involved in *word recognition* and are generally referred to as *lower-level processes*. The rest of the operations are involved in *comprehension* and are generally called *higher-level processes*.

But what does it mean to learn to extract visual features (see Crowder, 1982; Gibson & Levin, 1975), and why do children experience difficulties in learning to match the resulting grapheme with a phoneme? What happens when one piece of the process is not learned, is slower to develop, or breaks down? What occurs when *cat* is embedded in a *cat in a hat* or in *The cat's catatonic stare predicted dire catastrophe every time?* How does the stored knowledge in the comprehension processes affect word-recognition processes? In other words, how do all these components or operations work together with and without sentence contexts?

In the following sections we present a simplified history of several comprehensive accounts of reading and reading development. In addition, we refer the reader to more in-depth treatments wherever possible (see overviews by Ellis, 1984; Just & Carpenter, 1987; Perfetti, 1985, in press; Vellutino, 1982; Wolf & Vellutino, in press).

INFORMATION-PROCESSING APPROACHES

A very important contribution to our understanding of reading comes from the information-processing tradition. Researchers working in this tradition attempt to account for how the human brain manages to attend, perceive, match, store, access, and retrieve various kinds of information.

One of the earliest attempts to apply such an approach to reading is found in the **logogen** theory of word recognition by Morton (1969, 1980). Briefly, Morton posited that every known word possesses a logogen, which, for all purposes, is like a switchboard that activates all the features belonging to a word (e.g., visual, auditory, semantic). If the mental logogen unit has sufficient information from its activated features, then a *threshold* is automatically reached, and all of this information is processed and leads to word recognition. The speed of recognition is influenced by many external factors, such as stimulus strength and word frequency. Logogen theory, with its introduction of such information-processing concepts as *feature activation, threshold,* and *automatic word recognition,* was pivotal in the development of later models of word recognition (see Vellutino, 1982; Wolf & Vellutino, in press) and also for later explanations of the adult-acquired dyslexias (Coltheart, Patterson, & Marshall, 1980).

Since Morton's work, information-processing accounts of various aspects of reading have grown in number and sometimes staggering complexity (see Frederiksen,

1981; Stanovich, 1991; Vellutino, 1982). Many researchers have attempted to describe the underlying structure of reading through the use of computer simulation models (Lesgold & Perfetti, 1981; McClelland & Rumelhart, 1986; Rumelhart & McClelland, 1986; Seidenberg & McClelland, 1989). Major differences in these models revolve around the actual organization of the components, the nature of their interaction, and the subprocesses or components that should be indicated in reading breakdown.

Bottom-Up and Top-Down Accounts

To delineate these organizational differences, terminology from artificial intelligence is often employed, specifically the distinction between a direction of processing that is **bottom-up (or data driven)** and one that is **top-down (or concept driven)**. Theories that are bottom-up emphasize that lower-level processes critically influence all further stages of processing. Top-down theories emphasize the influence that higher-level functions like context have upon all other parts of the reading process. A primitive example may be helpful before proceeding. If a reader cannot readily distinguish *b* from *d,* a bottom-up account would predict problems recognizing such words as *bog, dog,* and *boondoggle!* But if the reader must read the sentence "She fell into the bog," top-down theorists would hold that the contextual constraints help the reader make the lower-level distinctions. There is evidence from technically sophisticated experiments for both views, and, predictably, a third, *interactive* type of model has emerged.

The best early example of a bottom-up account, where each stage of data is necessary for the next, is LaBerge and Samuels' (1974) *serial stage processing model of automaticity* in reading. In this model, visual information goes through various lower-level visual, phonological, and episodic memory systems before it is finally comprehended in higher-level semantic systems. The greatest difference between this model and other serial models (cf. Gough, 1972) was that any process could be emphasized or relatively unused, depending on how automatic a particular stage had become. In addition, according to LaBerge and Samuels, with sufficient learning certain stages might become necessary for the automatic activation of meaning.

Closely related to the role of automaticity in bottom-up accounts of reading are the notions of *time allocation* and a *limited capacity* mechanism for processing information. For example, Perfetti and Hogoboam (1975) suggested that all reading processes "must share a limited capacity mechanism . . . which [if] heavily demanded by one process essentially becomes less available for other processes" (p. 461). Perfetti (1985) and others hypothesized that poor readers who require far more time and attention in their nonautomatic, lower-level processes have less processing time available for higher-level comprehension skills.

Let us take a step outside of our theoretical accounts and examine a concrete example of a lower-level problem often found in severely disabled, dyslexic readers. Dyslexic children display surprising, dramatic deficits in their ability to retrieve simple letters and digits rapidly (see Bowers & Swanson, in press; Denckla & Rudel, 1976; Spring & Davis, 1988; Wolf, 1991; Wolf, Bally, & Morris, 1986) and object names accurately (Wolf & Goodglass, 1986). They see these symbols correctly, but they cannot retrieve or name them as fast and accurately as much younger, average-reading children. These retrieval problems, which endure into adulthood (Wolff, Michel, & Ovrut, 1990), indicate that lower-level retrieval processes—common to both continuous naming and word recognition—are deficient in many dyslexic readers.

Although there is overwhelming evidence for dyslexic readers' problems in lower-level processes, bottom-up models of reading cannot account so readily for contextual effects in reading. Top-down models, which portray the reader as engaging in continuous hypothesis testing, explain these effects more handily. In top-down models, the reader's lower-level processing is constrained by ongoing inferences, deductions, and hypotheses about context.[1] These models have been particularly influential in the area of reading comprehension, especially during the middle school years. An important emphasis in this work is on the process by which the child makes the text meaningful through the use of knowledge of both the world and the story's structure. In order to understand a story, a child must be able to infer the motivations of the different characters (Schank & Abelson, 1977). For example, the actions of the wolf in *Little Red Riding Hood* are best understood if one knows that wolves in folk tales are usually unseemly sorts and like to eat defenseless people—preferably young ones. Children also are better able to understand such stories if they are familiar with the typical way that information is sequenced in such stories (Mandler & Johnson, 1977; Stein & Glenn, 1979).

Interactive Accounts

Motivated at least in part by the unanswered questions in bottom-up and top-down models are the more recent, interactive processing accounts of reading. An underlying assumption of interactive reading models is that components represent independent knowledge sources that operate not serially, but in *parallel* ways (Rumelhart & McClelland, 1986). The reader understands the meaning of a text when a sufficient threshold of information from all knowledge sources is reached.

Unlike either bottom-up or top-down models, this threshold can be attained by various combinations of information from higher- or lower-level processes. To describe the complex interrelationships that are hypothesized within strong and weak versions of interactive models is beyond this chapter's scope (see Lesgold & Perfetti, 1981; Levy, 1981; Perfetti, 1985; Rumelhart & McClelland, 1981, 1986; Stanovich, 1991). Nevertheless, it is important to consider the theoretical and applied implications of interactive accounts. An earlier model by Stanovich (1980) is illustrative of this importance for children. This model combines an interactive account of reading with the notion of *compensatory processing* to explain how individual differences in reading can occur. In this view, depending on individual deficits, the child relies on either higher- or lower-level processing to compensate for loss in the other. For example, Stanovich suggests that the child with poor word recognition skills may compensate for these deficiencies by extensive dependence on contextual variables. He suggests that such a view can also be applied to developmental differences.

1. For a different view on how we comprehend individual words in real time, or ongoing speech with and without context, see Swinney, 1979, 1981.

Another earlier interactive model of reading by Perfetti and his colleagues attempts to account for individual differences in terms of what they call "verbal efficiency theory" (Perfetti, 1985). According to this theory and its more recent versions, reading is the interaction of many processes, most significant of which are *lexical access, propositional encoding* (i.e., an understanding of the salient units of meaning, or propositions, in the text), and the construction of *representations* (i.e., the processes by which we combine information in the text with our previous knowledge; see Perfetti, in press). There will be differences in ability according to the relative efficiency or inefficiency in these areas. More recently, both Perfetti (in press) and Stanovich (1991) have placed particular emphasis both on the role of representation in reading and upon increasingly modular ways of understanding how reading processes are organized. Of special importance to this approach is the quality of lexical representation—how well specified words are in memory.

The implications of various models are important for our understanding of both reading development and reading breakdown. Perfetti suggested one might look at various stages of reading (e.g., Chall, 1983). For example, such interactive accounts could provide a richer understanding of certain syndromes within the developmental dyslexias (see speculations in Wolf, 1991).

DEVELOPMENTAL CHANGE IN READING

Now that we appreciate something of the complexity of the reading process, we are better prepared to understand not only the psychologist's achievement, but also the child's! Recall Huey's last assumption about the developmental sequence in learning to read. Although each of the components of reading may be necessary for the whole, some operations require more processing time, depending on individual development and the level of fluency. For example, because first-grade readers are in the early stages of reading, some processes like letter recognition skills have not yet become fully learned and take a longer time. The concept of developmental periods is useful here as a guide for understanding general reading development.

Influenced by Piaget (1970) and work in current cognitive developmental theory, various theorists have postulated a progression of stagelike changes in reading, based on the consolidation of particular subskills at different times (Chall, 1983; Ehri & Wilce, 1985; Frith, 1985; Marsh & Desberg, 1983; Snowling, 1987). These accounts vary along several dimensions: (1) whether there are strong, hierarchical, Piagetian-like stages (e.g., Chall, 1983) or more permeable phase changes (e.g., Frith, 1985); (2) whether the emphasis is upon the change in reading subskills (e.g., Chall, 1983) or strategies (e.g., Ehri & Wilce, 1985; Frith, 1985; Marsh & Desberg, 1983); (3) the centrality of particular dimensions like spelling (e.g., Frith, 1985; Snowling, 1987), early literacy experiences (e.g., Ehri, 1989; Marsh & Desberg, 1983); and (4) the inclusion of adult development (e.g., Chall, 1983).

We will elaborate Chall's (1983) model here, which is representative of strong-stage accounts because it illustrates a life-span approach. She characterized stages in terms of underlying psychological processes, goals, modes of reading, and material read. In the prereading stage, children up to about six years of age are learning letter and number discrimination, recognition, and scanning, as well as the rudiments of reading (e.g., ability to recognize their own names and a few words). In stage 1 (approximately grades 1.5 to 2.5) decoding is the focus and is applied to single words and simple stories. Attention during this stage begins to be more under the control of the child as efficiency develops in such lower-level skills as letter discrimination. Although comprehension skills are not yet honed, they are beginning to emerge, as evidenced by the fact that meaningful word groups are read faster than random words (Doehring, 1976). By stage 2 (approximately grades 2.5 to 4) reading becomes more fluent, and more attention is directed to understanding the meaning of what is read. More inferential skills are used to analyze unknown words. Lower-level skills are more and more consolidated.

Stage 3 (approximately grades 4 to 8) marks a major turning point in reading, according to Chall, as children move from an emphasis on decoding to the comprehension of increasingly complex material. Attention is now well under the reader's control, and scanning rate improves steadily. Critical here is the variety of materials to be read and the cognitive requirements demanded by them. In stage 4 (approximately secondary school), lower-level processes like scanning and phonological and orthographic rules are firmly established, and the reader's attention is directed primarily to more sophisticated comprehension skills like inference and the recognition of different viewpoints. Reading in stage 5 (college level and beyond) incorporates a whole new set of cognitive goals: the synthesis of new knowledge with one's own. It proceeds beyond most decoding and comprehension skills, now long established, and moves into an area where conceptual integration, critical judgment, and new thinking are emphasized.

There are many themes that run through developmental approaches to reading. Two of the most prevalent differ in emphasis. The first theme is that with development, automaticity or efficiency is established through practice; less attention, therefore, is needed in many lower-level subprocesses. As a result, the older the child, the more processing time can be devoted to understanding the meaning of text.

Yet another way of looking at development is similar to Hakes's (1980) findings about earlier metalinguistic abilities: development enables children to have increasing control over how they allocate cognitive processing efforts. Specifically, the more fluent the reader is, the more control he has over where attention should be focused. For example, with unusual script the reader could direct attention to lower-level visual feature extraction, whereas with conceptually difficult material the reader could direct more effort to higher-level comprehension areas, like making inferences.

Neither of these themes explains development for some individuals, for example, children with reading disability. Many reading-disabled children have great difficulty with grapheme–phoneme correspondence and lexical retrieval (lower-level skills), and their entire reading development is disrupted as a result. Other children have no early lower-level difficulties, but later have poor comprehension skills. The end result appears the same—reading failure—but it has emerged from very different sources, at different times, and requires different instructional methodologies and treatments over time. In the following section we take a closer look at problems in reading development.

■ VARIATION IN THE DEVELOPMENT OF READING SKILLS

The study of reading development is made especially challenging by the many factors that affect it. In the following section we explore both cognitive factors associated with learning disabilities and an area in reading development that is not as well understood—gender differences. We then consider external factors such as home experiences and features of children's classrooms that may affect their reading development.

THE DEVELOPMENTAL DYSLEXIAS

The term **developmental dyslexia** (or **dyslexias**) refers to a continuum of severe impairments in the acquisition and development of written language (Rudel, 1985; Vellutino, 1979). These childhood disabilities result in reading and spelling performance that is usually one-and-a-half to two years or more below an age-appropriate level, depending on the age of the child. We prefer the term *developmental dyslexias* to depict the plurality or *heterogeneity* of the syndrome: there are a number of typologies or major subgroups (for discussions of subgroups, see especially Lovett, 1984; Mattis, French, & Rapin, 1975). Table 10.1 depicts a partial listing of all the names that have been used to describe the dyslexias. The heterogeneity of the names themselves is indicative of the very different aspects that caught the attention of researchers over the past century.

Many current definitions of dyslexia are intentionally exclusionary and further define the syndrome as having no instructional, environmental, intellectual, emotional, or gross neurological problems as the basis for impairments. The incidence of dyslexia in the population is estimated to be between 5 and 10 percent, depending on the definition used. The sex ratio has traditionally been believed to be heavily biased toward males, with estimates ranging between 3:1 and 10:1. Recently, however, there is controversy suggesting that females are more frequently dyslexic than past research

TABLE 10.1 Various Names for Reading Impairment since 1896

wortblindheit or word blindness	analphabetia partialis	specific reading disability
congenital dyslexia	linear dyslexia	specific dyslexia
congenital alexia	script blindness	primary and secondary reading retardation
psycholexia	cortical wordblindness	retarded reading
bradylexia	subcortical wordblindness	agnosic alexia, aphasic alexia
legasthenia	asymbolia	auditory dyslexia
word amblyopia	strephosymbolia	dyspraxic dyslexia
amnesia visualis verbalis		developmental dyslexia

indicated. Common (although not universal) characteristics include specific speech and language problems (e.g., speech segmentation, word-finding and phonological-based problems), delayed speech development, familial history of dyslexia, short-term memory problems (e.g., following verbal commands, remembering spelling patterns), directional confusions, and such neurological soft signs as abnormal reflexes and coordination problems. Thus, the profile of an average dyslexic child would be a child of average to superior intelligence who experiences great difficulty in learning to read, spell, and often to write despite adequate instruction and opportunities to learn (see Ellis, 1985; Snowling, 1987; Vellutino, 1991, for reviews).

Theoretical accounts of reading structure and reading pathology have an ongoing reciprocal relationship to each other. Two important principles drive the efforts of many researchers in the field. First, if one can identify the specific subprocesses and/or factors that cause reading to break down, one can infer that such subprocesses are necessary components in the intact process. Thus, the discovery of anomalies in the system that lead to dysfunction gives us important information about the microstructure of reading. The second principle is somewhat similar: if one can watch the early development of individual components in the system, then the structural make-up can be revealed before automaticity yields it impervious to investigation (Wolf, 1991). A third, most recent principle, based on what Lovett (1991) calls *remedial outcome research,* is that we can increase our understanding of reading failure by studying the individual's response (the outcome) to a carefully selected remediation program. Experimental intervention research (e.g., Levy & Stewart, 1991; Lovett, 1991; Segal & Wolf, in press) is one of the most promising new directions in dyslexia research.

GENDER AND LITERACY DEVELOPMENT

The influence of gender on the development of written language skill is something of a mystery story that keeps unfolding and is anything but resolved. Although there always is more variation within one gender than between the two, gender research throughout the school years has found girls to be better writers than boys. For example, in the NAEP (1990) assessment of writing, females wrote significantly better than males at grades 4, 8, and 11, the three grade levels assessed. They also have consistently slightly outperformed boys in reading. To the extent that some oral language skills are more advanced in females than in males (Maccoby & Jacklin, 1974; Myklebust, 1973; see a more differentiated picture in Wolf & Gow, 1986), these findings are understandable. Recent gender studies in language development show that, while girls appear more fluent and automatic in their ability to perform various linguistic tasks, boys seem to be better in receptive and expressive vocabulary (Berninger, personal correspondence, April 1991; Wolf & Gow, 1986). There is, therefore, no simple story based on cognitive/linguistic propensities.

Other factors must be investigated more. For example, in his early research, Graves (1973) found that boys tend to like informational writing, while girls tend to prefer personal and imaginative writing. The value placed on imaginative writing by most elementary school teachers and the relative lack of meaningful content-area writing at the secondary level (Applebee, 1981) may hinder the developing male writer.

Yet another factor affecting writing development is frankly biological. As we see in dyslexia research, many remedial readers at all ages are male; the situation is similar in writing. The questions emerge: do the same biological factors that underlie severe reading disability also underlie severe writing disability and/or less severe writing problems? One of the hypotheses why some boys acquire reading later than most girls is based on such biological reasons as different brain myelination schedules (Geschwind, 1974). Can we assume that writing is similarly affected? One problem is that such biological variation is generally over by grade 3. What sustains the writing variation shown from grades 4 to 11? Are there emotional blocks to reading and writing laid down in some boys during the frustration of these early years when others are budding forth? Is our instruction flexible enough to sustain interest in writing through the years when boys may experience more difficulty? What role do sociocultural factors play? For example, are literacy-related skills considered "girl's stuff" by some boys? Much more research is needed to understand gender differences.

HOME SUPPORTS FOR LITERACY DEVELOPMENT

We now shift our focus from sources of variability primarily rooted in biological factors to those clearly of environmental origin. Studies conducted by the National Assessment of Educational Progress (1985, 1990) have made clear the importance of environmental factors for reading achievement. Consistent differences are associated with the type of community in which the child lives (advantaged urban children perform better than rural children, who, in turn, outperform disadvantaged urban children). Small differences have even been found among different regions of the country (the Northeast and Central regions do somewhat better than the West and South). Of course, these findings reflect only general averages, but they do point to the impact of homes and schools on children's reading growth.

The experiences a child has with print at home have a major impact on reading development. Early experiences with books is especially important: children who find the transition into reading easy have typically been read to during the preschool years (Wells, 1985b; reviewed by Goldfield & Snow, 1984). These experiences are especially powerful if they include opportunities for children to engage in discussions about the meaning of the stories (Heath, 1982), with open-ended questions and talk about word meanings being especially useful for encouraging vocabulary development (Whitehurst et al., 1987).

The language environment of the home also plays an early and important role in supporting children's literacy development. Children from different social and economic backgrounds have adequate opportunities to acquire comparable levels of syntactic abilities by the time they enter school (Wells, 1985a), but there are dramatic differences in support for the kinds of discourse skills associated with literacy. These differences can be seen in how families handle daily routines. For example, some families are able to gather for an evening meal during which they discuss the day's activities and engage in lively conversations that include numerous narratives and explanations. Children who participate in such mealtimes when they are four years old benefit by acquiring larger vocabularies. They subsequently perform better on language comprehension and production tasks in kindergarten (Beals, 1991; De Temple & Beals, in press).

Parents also differ in the extent to which they are able and willing to engage in extended conversations with children throughout the day. Heath (1986) traced the frequency with which three children—a middle-class white girl, a working-class white girl, and a working-class black boy—talked with an adult for at least five minutes. She did this when the children were between 16 to 24 months old and 40 to 48 months old. At both times, the middle-class girl had more conversations. Astonishingly, when they were three years old, the middle-class child has 1,533 such interactions when Heath was present or tape-recording conversations. Each of the working-class children had fewer than 60 such interactions (but for less dramatic class-related differences, see Tizard & Hughes, 1984).

During these extended conversations, children have opportunities to develop and extend ideas, fostering growth of literacy-related discourse skills. Perhaps limited experiences with extended discourse results in some low-income children's difficulties in comprehending narratives (Dickinson & Snow, 1987; Feagans & Farran, 1981). Although low-income families do, on average, show certain differences in discourse practices from middle-class families, it is critical to note that there is great variation within this group. Indeed, one approach to identifying sources of support for literacy development is to study only low-income families and to isolate those experiences in these homes that foster children's literacy development (Snow et al., 1991).

After the preschool years, parents continue to provide important supports for children's literacy development by providing a structured and emotionally supportive environment (Clark, 1983). In addition, specific practices are especially beneficial: listening to their children read (Tizard, Schofield, & Hewison, 1982; Topping & Wolfendale, 1985), maintaining contact with their child's teacher, taking children on trips, and providing reading materials (NAEP, 1990; Snow et al., 1991). The importance of parental involvement during the school years is illustrated by a longitudinal study by Snow and her colleagues (1991) of home and school factors that enhance the literacy development of low-income children. They found that parents' provision of literacy opportunities for their elementary school-aged children (buying books, reading to them, taking them to the library) was strongly related to reading comprehension four years later when their children were in junior and senior high school.

SCHOOL SUPPORTS FOR ORAL DISCOURSE DEVELOPMENT

Once children enter the primary grades, the most important factor affecting the continuing development of their reading skills is classroom instruction. It is encouraging to report that there has been improvement since the early 1970s, with the greatest gains being seen among groups who initially had the lowest scores (NAEP, 1985). Because of the immense amount of research that has been done in an attempt to identify links between instruction and the development of reading skills, we will not review that work

Children from all backgrounds pay attention to environmental print.

here; instead, we will discuss features of classrooms that have an impact on development of literacy-related oral language skills (for reviews of research dealing with instructional practices, see Adams, 1990; Barr, Kamil, Mosenthal, & Pearson, 1991).[2]

2. A current instructional issue generating much controversy is the debate concerning the whole language approach to literacy instruction. Recent work bearing on this can be found in the November 1990 issue of the *Educational Researcher.* Other key readings are Edelsky, Altwerger, and Flores (in press); Edelsky and Draper (in press); Stahl and Miller (1989); and responses in *The Review of Educational Research, 1,* 1990.

Preschool classrooms vary greatly in the extent to which they provide environments conducive to language development. One source of variability is the extent to which teachers actively help children express themselves. Some teachers are quick to tune into children's immediate interests and help them talk about them, while others are more concerned with maintaining control or teaching selected concepts (Smith, 1990; Tizard & Hughes, 1984). For example, Dickinson (1991) contrasted the talk that occurred during lunch at the tables of two teachers with different orientations. One teacher stressed manners and good eating habits. During her lunch with children there were no discussions initiated by children; there were two requests for food and one request to move to a neighboring table where children were pretending. In contrast, another teacher who worked in the same classroom created an atmosphere conducive to talk during the lunch conversation by responding to and extending children's topics. As a consequence, at her table children initiated and developed several extended conversations about past experiences (e.g., pillow fights, the movie *Dumbo,* play fighting).

Teachers can also support literacy-related discourse skills by providing children time and materials for pretend play. As they pretend, children construct imaginary worlds with language, using language in a manner similar to that required for reading. Evidence of the continuity between such uses of language and literacy is the fact that there is a strong correlation between the amount of time children spend pretending in preschool as three-year-olds and later kindergarten measures of vocabulary, story understanding, and print skills (Dickinson & Tabors, in press). Furthermore, careful examination of the content of the talk during pretend play reveals the importance of particular kinds of talk. Children who use many verbs that refer to mental states (e.g., *think, know*), words that suggest children are engaging in sophisticated language use, are likely to perform better on emergent reading tasks over a year later (Pellegrini, Galda, Dresden, & Cox, 1991).

A third avenue for providing oral experiences that support early literacy development is book reading. Two studies conducted in Israel have found that reading aloud series stories (i.e., several books with a constant character) to kindergarten and first-grade children resulted in enhanced abilities to produce and understand extended discourse (Feitelson, Goldstein, & Iraqi, 1990; Feitelson, Kita, & Goldstein, 1986). Similarly, book reading using an approach known as *shared reading,* a technique that includes high levels of group participation, has been found to be a more effective means of helping Pacific Islander children learn English than the standard English as a Second Language approach (Elley & Mangubhai, 1983).

Although reading aloud in itself has beneficial effects on language development, the way teachers engage children in thinking about books also is important. Preschool teachers vary in how they read and discuss books with children: some lead extended discussions about books, others encourage children to chime in with familiar portions of stories, while still others treat book reading more as a performance, reading with only occasional breaks for discussion (Dickinson & Keebler, 1989; Dickinson & Smith, 1991). Variation in the amount and type of talk about stories influences what children gain from book reading, affecting gains both in vocabulary and story understanding (Elley, 1989; Mason & Allen, 1986a; Morrow & Smith, 1990). In general, children benefit from opportunities to talk about stories, with most improvement coming on those aspects of stories that teachers emphasize (e.g., word meanings, recall of story lines).

Although there are varied ways that teachers support children's language growth, teachers face special challenges as they strive to support development of children from varied cultures and from lower socioeconomic backgrounds. In preschools, compared with children from economically advantaged homes, children from less advantaged backgrounds ask teachers fewer questions and interact less with teachers, perhaps because of differences in norms governing communicative behavior linked to social class (Tizard & Hughes, 1984). Cultural differences in rules governing interaction in group events also may impede some children's participation, limiting their chances to develop their discourse skills. Group meetings are organized by explicit and implicit rules, with one typical rule being the "one-speaker-at-a-time" rule (DeStefano, 1984; Eder, 1982). Although this is a common school expectation, it can result in a mismatch between home and school discourse, because this rule does not hold for group discussions in all homes (Schultz, Florio, & Erickson, 1982). One-at-a-time participation also can be problematic for children from non-Western homes where display of knowledge in front of one's peers is not socially acceptable (Boggs, 1972; LeVine, 1978; Mohatt & Erickson, 1981; Phillips, 1972). Yet other challenges arise from the fact that cultural variability in how children tell stories can result in mismatches between teachers' expectations and children's narrative skills (Michaels, 1991; Michaels & Cazden, 1987).

As we gain understanding of those features of classroom language environments that support children's discourse development and of the sources of variability in language use that are culturally and economically based, we increase our ability to create classrooms that support all children's learning. Some progress has been made in creating classrooms that build on and extend the discourse skills that children bring with them to school, but much work remains to be done (O'Connor & Michaels, 1990; Tharp & Gallimore, 1989).

■ DIMENSIONS OF THE DEVELOPMENT OF WRITTEN LANGUAGE

Young children's initial development as writers is similar in many ways to their oral language development. Just as all children develop oral language naturally if they have opportunities to hear others and to talk meaningfully with them, so, too, do they begin to develop naturally as writers well before they receive formal instruction if they have opportunities to see and practice literacy activities. So long as paper, crayons, or pencils are available, most children try to express themselves through scribbles and drawings even if the meaning of their scribbles is not clear to others. Writing extends their spoken language in the same way that reading or being read to expands their world of meaning. And if teachers, other adults, or peers respond chiefly to the meaning, not the form, of what young writers are trying to express, then young children are apt to persevere in their efforts to use written language to communicate with others.

In some ways learning to write is also like learning to read. Children draw upon the same oral language resources whether they read or write, and they use the same intellectual processes for both. As readers or writers, they make associations, compare, contrast, analyze, synthesize, and evaluate. Whether reading or writing, they draw heavily upon prior knowledge and create meaning by using symbols.

However, there are some important differences between beginning writing and early language development. Unlike speaking, writing is a consciously developed language activity, and its development does not directly parallel that of oral language, nor is its pattern of development identical to that of oral language (Stotsky, 1986, 1987a). While in the beginning writers depend heavily upon their spoken language skills, developing writers become increasingly less dependent on spoken language and more directly influenced by their experiences with written language. There are also important differences between reading and writing. While readers and writers are both engaged in the process of constructing meaning, reading and writing are also not identical activities, nor are their patterns of development identical. As Rosenblatt (1989) points out, they are activities with very different goals. While writers seek to create their own written texts, readers seek to construct the meaning of already existing texts. Readers and writers are also stimulated in different ways; for the reader, the ideas of others are the first stimulus for thinking; for the writer, thinking is stimulated by the writer's own ideas as well as by those of others.

How does writing evolve? How do young writers change as they develop? In this section, we examine some of the dimensions of writing development in young writers: the purposes for which they write, the factors influencing fluency, the forms and organizational features of their writing, changes in vocabulary and syntax, and their growth in controlling such surface features as spelling and handwriting.

PURPOSES AND GENRES

From the time that children begin to display a "graphic" urge, their scribbles can represent their efforts to write as well as to draw (Harste, Woodward, & Burke, 1984). The connections between writing and drawing are quite close for young children because both symbol systems involve the use of the same implements—pencils, crayons, and paper. On the basis of their case studies, Graves (1983) and Calkins (1986) suggest that beginning writers plan their stories through their drawings and that drawing is thus a "rehearsal" for writing. On the other hand, Dyson (1986) found in her case study research that drawing did "not necessarily contribute extensively" to children's development of their texts. Whether or not drawing facilitates writing, young writers may spend much more time illustrating their work than actually writing (Bissex, 1980).

Two somewhat different theories of development have been proposed to account for what children write. Moffett (1968) claims that *narrative writing* is the "natural" mode for young writers. This theory appears to be the implicit one held by many early primary grade teachers, who strongly encourage narrative writing by their children as well as the reading of stories. Britton and his associates (1975) hold the somewhat different view that *expressive writing*—informal personal writing to others or for oneself—is the "natural" mode of writing for beginners and underlies the development of both expository and literary writing.

However, Newkirk (1987) found a great deal of nonnarrative writing occurring naturally in primary grade children's lives, and other recent research has shown a diversity of purposes for which young children compose nonnarrative writing. Beginning writers write messages to parents or neighbors (Bissex, 1980; Gundlach, 1981). For example, Bissex's five-year-old son was trying to attract her attention while she was engrossed in reading. Finally, he slipped her this note: "RUDF." She easily interpreted it as "Are you deaf?" Needless to say, he got her attention. Young writers also make lists (Dyson, 1987; Gundlach, 1982), signs like "DO NOT RK!" ("Do not wreck") to warn off intruders in classroom block areas or "KEEP OUT!" to ensure privacy at home; and they even write recipes (Read, 1981). Thus, young children seem to use writing for more than telling stories and know how to exploit its special powers—its capacity for serving as a medium of communication across space and time and as an enduring record of something one wants oneself or others to remember.

During the elementary school years, children learn to compose in such diverse genres of writing as plays, poems, letters, reports, and journals. They also write for a variety of purposes in both their *self-sponsored writing* (writing of their own choice) and *school-sponsored writing* (Hudson, 1986). In her research with children in grades 1 to 5, Hudson found that their range of purposes may be even greater in their self-sponsored writing than in their school assignments. Moreover, older children in her study mentioned more purposes and genres for their writing than did younger children. Children continue to write in a variety of forms and for a variety of purposes throughout their school years, according to a nationwide assessment of writing by the National Assessment of Educational Progress (NAEP) at grades 4, 8, and 11, although students report doing more academic writing and less imaginative literary writing in higher grades (Applebee, Langer, Mullis, and Jenkins, 1990).

FLUENCY, MOTIVATION, AND AUDIENCES

As young writers develop, they spontaneously write longer texts. In the primary grades, children tend to compose very brief texts, perhaps partly because of the physical demands of the act of writing and perhaps partly because of the time needed to determine how to spell words. Also, according to Bereiter and Scardemalia (1982), children do not do efficient memory searches to discover all the ideas they have about a topic. The amount that children write may be affected by their interest in the topic and whether they have selected the topic themselves. In a case study of a small group of second-graders, Graves (1973) found that when children were able to choose their own topics, they wrote more and for longer periods of time than when they were given topics by the teacher. He also found that boys preferred to write about such topics as space, war, or sports, while girls preferred more personal topics. On the other hand, Hudson's (1986) study suggests that students may need only a personal investment in a piece of writing, whether or not the topic was selected by the teacher. Hudson asked the 20 children in her study to tell her whether written pieces they had done at home and at school over the course of several months were self-sponsored or school-sponsored; she found that often children did not distinguish between assignments given by the teacher and those they wrote on their own, remembering many school assignments as self-sponsored. Hudson concluded that children's interest in the topic was probably more important than its source.

Fluency may also be affected by genre. Hidi and Hildyard (1983) compared stories and opinion "essays" written by children in grades 3 and 5 and found the stories almost three times as long as the essays. Finally, fluency may be influenced by having real readers beyond the classroom for one's writing and by receiving responses from these readers. A study by Greenlee, Hiebert, Bridge, and Winograd (1986) found that second-graders who wrote regularly to pen pals and received replies from them wrote longer and more complex letters than children who wrote only to imaginary readers and received comments only from teachers.

To promote fluency, many teachers now encourage children to write their experiences and imaginative stories in journals (Dyson, 1989). Kindergarten students may dictate their stories for the teacher to write in the journals (Dyson, 1986). Some teachers also encourage children to write informal entries in subject-focused journals in math (Evans, 1984), science (Matthews, 1985), and social studies (Rief, 1985; Sowers, 1985) in order to help them begin using writing for learning in the content areas.

Teachers may also enhance children's interest in writing by providing them with authentic audiences, for instance, by encouraging them to share their work with one another and to publish selected finished pieces by copying them neatly in booklet form, illustrating them, and placing them in classroom or school libraries. Calkins (1986) and Hansen (1983) reported dramatic increases in children's interest in writing when teachers adopted these practices. Teachers may also use *dialogue journals,* in which children write to their teacher about their reactions to the literature they are reading and the teacher responds (Atwell, 1987), or they may send messages to which the teacher replies (Kreeft, 1984). Dialogue journals encourage writing by building on natural conversational patterns, ensuring an interested audience and providing a personalized response.

HANDWRITING AND SPELLING

For young writers, fluency very much depends upon their control of graphic forms—letters and punctuation symbols. Graves (1983) noted several stages in handwriting development as children were taught composition. First, children showed a left-to-right orientation in their writing, with little concern for spacing. They then began to show a concern for aesthetics—the shapes of letters or words, word placement, and clean paper. This phase was followed by an interest in imitating conventional spacing, margins, and letter size. As students learned about the temporary nature of their first drafts, they began to deemphasize aesthetic concerns in these drafts. (Aesthetic concerns emerged later in their final copy.) The control that young students gain over their handwriting system is an important factor in their early writing and contributes to their progress in spelling.

As we noted in our discussion of "The Devl and the Babe Goste," many young writers exhibit a highly unconventional spelling system. Preschool writers spell on the basis of the sounds they hear in a word and the sounds they hear in the name of the alphabet letter itself. This combination can produce "creative" but quite readable writing, as we suggested when describing Paul's "RUDF" note. Many young writers who employ invented spelling are unable to reread exactly what it is they have composed (Sulzby, Barnhart, & Hieshima, 1989); conventional rereading is apparently a sign of growth in literacy.

A striking feature of children's invented spelling is its highly rule-governed nature. Read (1971) and Chomsky (1971) found that children tend to resemble one another in the spelling systems they create. These similarities exist in invented spelling systems in part because young children often hear and represent phonetic elements that we literate adults no longer hear (e.g., *prede* for *pretty*). Preconsonantal nasal sounds like /m/ and /n/ are very difficult to hear and are often omitted (e.g., *bet* for *bent,* or *nubrs* for *numbers*). Similarities also result because children commonly use letter names to represent letter sounds (e.g., *y* is often used in place of *w* because the letter name for *y* begins with the sound /w/; thus *win* is often spelled *yn*).

Once children begin formal reading instruction, their judgments about which symbols to use are based on a combination of their phonetic knowledge, phonics, and their experience with written language. Soon, visual spelling patterns begin to replace much of their phonetic spelling—a stage that Ehri (1989) refers to as "morphemic" spelling. But sometimes even this development results in unusual-looking words that, nevertheless, are still spelled logically from the child's perspective. For example, a story by an able fifth-grade writer about his school cafeteria contained a puzzling reference to a *newnade.* Further inquiry revealed the presence of a "noon-aide" in the cafeteria, a person whose title the children had apparently never seen in print. Since the beginning of *noon-aide* sounded like *new* and rhymed with *blew* and *threw,* while the second part rhymed with *lemonade,* the child's spelling was eminently reasonable.

Eventually, invented spelling is replaced by "lexical" spelling, the correct spelling of words that are etymologically related. For example, even though the spoken words *photograph* and *photographer* have different vowel sounds, students who have broad experience with written language know these words are members of the same family and spell them according to their lexical (or dictionary) spelling (Chomsky, 1970). As Hodges (1982) points out, learning to spell is a continuously developing process in the English language that depends on increasing visual, phonological, and morphological knowledge. The more experience that students have with written language, the better the generalizations they can make. Nevertheless, reading experience and maturation alone may not be sufficient for students to make the transition from phonetic to lexical spelling unaided. Peters (1970) found in her research that "rational, systematic teaching" plays a major role in helping young writers with English spelling.

VOCABULARY

Lists of words used by elementary school children show that their written vocabulary is typically very simple (Hillerich, 1978; Rinsland, 1945). In Hillerich's study of the "creative" writing of children in grades 2 to 6, 100 common words accounted for 60 percent of all the words used. Further, Rinsland's study of 6,000,000 running words in the writing of children from grades 1 to 8 showed that such morphologically complex words as prefixed words (e.g., *irregular, indirect, uninhabited*) did not begin to appear with any frequency until grades 6 to 8, even though the base word was used at much earlier grades. The relative simplicity of the writing vocabulary of elementary schoolchildren stands in sharp contrast to the complexity of the vocabulary they find in their reading material. The difference between a reading and a writing vocabulary may span as much as five or more grade levels (Lazdowski, 1976).

As children mature, they not only write more, they use a greater variety of words to convey their ideas. In fact, diversity of vocabulary is highly related to writing quality (Evanechko, Ollila, & Armstrong, 1974). The discrepancy between a reading and writing vocabulary may diminish considerably by high school if students regularly read well-written literature and academic materials. Nagy and Anderson (1984) found that during the elementary school years, children's spoken vocabulary grows by about 3,000 words a year, with much of this growth resulting from increased reading (Nagy, Herman, & Anderson, 1985).

SYNTAX

Children's control of syntax also continues to develop during their school years, and, as with vocabulary growth, the speed of their progress is affected by their reading experiences (Chomsky, 1972). Both reading experience and reading achievement seem to be related to better and more syntactically mature writing (Stotsky, 1984). Several large cross-sectional studies (Hunt, 1965, 1970) and a 13-year longitudinal study by Loban (1976) showed that syntactic growth continues until grade 12 or beyond. Hunt (1965) developed a quite useful measure for his research—the *T-Unit,* a single main clause that includes all the dependent clauses attached to or embedded in it. Studies using the T-Unit have found that, as young writers develop, their sentences become progressively longer, chiefly by means of increases in the number of dependent clauses per T-Unit. From grade 8 on, the best indicator of syntactic growth in writing is the length of the dependent clause in a T-Unit, that is, the number of words within a clause rather than the number of clauses in a sentence. According to Hunt's (1977) research, major growth occurs in nominal structures—the subjects and objects of predicate verbs, and the objects of prepositions. Of special interest is the finding of numerous studies (Golub & Fredrick, 1971; Loban, 1976; O'Donnell, Griffin, & Norris, 1967) that by the end of the elementary school years, students' written language becomes syntactically more complex than their spoken language.

In some ways, oral language may be considered more grammatically complex than written language, as Halliday (1987) points out. But he is referring to what he calls "grammatical intricacy," the long, mazelike sentences whose main thoughts speakers eventually complete despite many parenthetical expressions. Halliday suggests that it is the *lexical density* of written language that is its distinguishing feature. That is probably why such grammatical constructions as participles, nominalizations, attributive adjectives and nouns, and prepositional phrases (constructions that create lexical density within clauses) are more characteristic of academic writing than of conversation (Chafe & Danielewicz, 1987).

ORGANIZATION

As children try to write longer stories, poems, letters, and reports, they draw upon a variety of strategies and discourse structures to help them produce a coherent sequence of ideas. Pictures, literary forms or genres, and informal plans or outlines help them meet the cognitive demands of organizing their thoughts over extended stretches of writing.

Drawings that precede writing provide the first organizational device because the drawings symbolize their ideas, making it easier to organize and remember them as they create the accompanying text. Children may also organize their writing according to their memories of familiar experiences. The order in which an experience is recalled dictates the order in which the child writes it down, as the following story illustrates.

> Yesterday my mother and I went to Lexington senter alone, and I got a new pare of Belly slippers and my mom Bot me a choclet Ice cream cone. (Donnelly & Stevens, 1980, p. 739)

The natural order of time—*chronological order*—is an easy organizing principle, and children rely on it for both their experience stories and imaginative narratives. They may also use such conventional text forms as letter form or the different forms for poems if they are made available to them; these forms provide more advanced ways to organize their writing.

One of the major difficulties with mature forms of **expository writing** is that it requires students to organize large quantities of information in *hierarchical form,* that is, according to logical relationships that have to be reasoned out. Developing writers cannot rely on the natural organizational principle of chronological order for this kind of writing. That is probably why Bereiter and Scardemalia (1982) found in their research that young writers used a "what next" strategy for "organizing" their informational writing, producing "associative writing." However, Newkirk (1987) suggests that very early, even primitive, forms of nonnarrative writing may to some extent develop naturally and serve as the seeds of more developed expository writing. In his study, Newkirk analyzed 100 pieces of nonnarrative writing from first-, second-, and third-grade classrooms and identified eight categories into which he could group them. The categories ranged from labels, lists, and attribute series to coherently arranged paragraphs. The following is an example of an *attribute series* by a second-grader:

> i like birds, cats, dogs, cubs, and some bears, some water anmals are nice to me I loke them and I think they are very, very, cute. Sharks are fish if you didn't know that now you know that. The whale shark is very harmless to people. A shark does not have any bones. Baby sharks are called pups. The largest fish in the world is the whale shark. It can weigh more than an elephant. It's very long. White sharks are the most dangerous sharks of all. When scientists want to learn more about sharks they get close to them. (Newkirk, 1987, pp. 129–130)

The following is an example of a *coherent paragraph* by a third-grader:

> Melissa and Champion are my cows. I raise beef cattle to show. I love to show cows. That is why I wrote this piece. The reason I named Melissa Melissa is that I have a good friend named Melissa. She has beef cattle and taught me everything I know about beef cattle. (Newkirk, 1987, p. 136)

From grades 1 to 3, Newkirk found an increasing use of more organized types and a decreasing use of less structured types. None of the third-grade pieces were *labels* (i.e., a word or phrase naming a pictured item), while only 15 percent of the first-grade pieces were coherent paragraphs. Because Newkirk's data were cross-sectional, he could not determine whether children whose informational writing was more developed and coherent actually went through earlier "stages." Nevertheless, he suggests that mature forms of expository writing, such as the essay or research report, may have their roots in these early forms, not in narrative or personal writing. He also suggests that much of the well-documented difficulty that students have with expository writing in secondary school may reflect limited instruction in intermediate forms of exposition in the middle school years.

In contrast to narrative writing or even the informal nonnarrative writing studied by Newkirk, expository writing requires logical thinking about the relationships among ideas. As students' ideas become more complex, the effort to work out and organize them becomes more difficult. The incorporation of new concepts can pose formidable problems. Often the first attempt to use new vocabulary results in stilted, artificial prose. Similarly, at the secondary school level, initial efforts to organize ideas in a logical way may disintegrate rapidly. For example, when attempting expository writing, many students revert to chronology—a more familiar and easier organizing principle—and complete their papers as narratives, as Durst (1987) found in a study of high school students who had been asked to write an analytic essay about a history excerpt.

No ready-made organizational scheme completely eliminates the need for writers to think through the logical development of their ideas. That is why many college students create an outline to organize their ideas, especially for long pieces of expository writing (Sommers & McQuade, 1984). However, it is likely that written planning may be a late-developing cognitive skill: the latest NAEP assessment of writing (Applebee, Langer, Mullis, and Jenkins, 1990) found that less than 20 percent of students in grades 8 and 11 made notes in planning their responses in a writing task, even though they were explicitly given the opportunity to do so (p. 66).

Extensive, or deep, revising of writing may also be a feature of late cognitive development. In a review of composition research, Hillocks (1986) found few studies that provided evidence of the effectiveness of revision *per se* on the quality of writing. The few he found used high school students. Many studies show that young writers and poor writers of all ages are capable of adding information and making word changes and other minor changes in the phrasing of a sentence. However, in some studies, the revisions young students made sometimes rendered their texts worse rather than better. It may not be possible for most young writers to rethink and reorganize ideas in their writing: the ability to critically read one's own writing may require many years of experience.

THINKING AND WRITING

There is complex interplay between the emerging intellectual capacities of secondary school writers and the broadening range of ways in which they are asked to express their ideas. Writing comes to serve as a major force, both propelling intellectual growth and reflecting it. Older students begin to become aware of the multiple demands to which they must respond (e.g., clarity and logic of argument, elegance of prose, comprehensibility to audience) and explore new ways to generate and organize ideas. Evidence of how writing tasks can facilitate deeper thought comes from such studies as Durst (1987) and Matsuhashi (1982). Durst analyzed the language produced by high school students who were asked both to summarize and analyze a history passage. They did much more complex thinking in the analytic writing task than when producing a narrative summary. Similarly, Matsuhashi found that high school students, who had written both a personal narrative and an essay about what makes a successful communicator, wrote freely, with little time for reflection, when writing the narrative, but wrote more slowly, with frequent pauses to think, when writing the essay. Both studies demonstrate the thought-inducing function of the essay, a form of writing that is usually not taught until the secondary years.

■ SOURCES OF VARIATION IN WRITING DEVELOPMENT

Although it is possible to discern certain broad patterns in writing development over the years, all children of the same age do not develop as writers in a similar way or at a similar pace. The best way to appreciate the extent of variation in writing growth at any one age is to examine writing performance that represents the range of skill that a teacher might encounter in one classroom. Figure 10.2 displays representative samples of writing by students in an elementary school that reflects the entire range of the population of the city. This writing was part of a holistic assessment of writing in grade 5, with ratings of writing quality by the children's teachers that ranged from the lowest (1) to the highest (4) (see Stotsky, 1980, for details). These samples suggest the tremendous variability that may be found in one grade.

As the figure shows, the children have no shortage of ideas, but their ability to communicate as writers varies along all the dimensions discussed earlier. The children are the same age, have the same teachers, and have experienced the same curriculum for five years. Thus, the variation in their writing samples suggests that other factors also affect the development of skill in using written language. Biological and gender differences are discussed on pp. 387–388. In this section, we discuss two other sources of influence that research suggests could account for this variation: instructional and home experiences, and reading experience itself.

INSTRUCTIONAL AND HOME EXPERIENCES

What teachers do to encourage writers and how they respond to the texts their students compose can influence writing development. Hillocks (1986) compared results of 70 studies that used students in grades 6 to 13. He found that experimental studies featuring small-group activities structured around specific objectives, with both peer- and teacher-given criteria for evaluating writing, produced greater gains in writing quality than other patterns of instruction. He concluded that students' development as writers might be best facilitated by teachers who developed carefully thought-out objectives, planned small-group activities to achieve these objectives, and helped students learn how to apply criteria for good writing to their own writing in order to revise and improve their writing.

1. If only I could I would be a teacher and a clown I would be take a trip to south carolina and stay there for my life time and i would be a principal and I would be a nurse.
2. If I only Could beat Dr. J. in a gane of basketball. I Could play NBA all the teams will want me. I will be a star in my own time. Basketball teans was want me to play for them. I will a super star n my own time I will make six million a year. My tean will win the championship. Your star (Child's Name) p s If I Could play for 10 year thay will me the 60 million doller. man
3. If only I could drive a car I would go over some of my friends house. Take them places and go places and do stuff like go to Paragon Park and other places. I'll go to the movies and just drive around. But that would run into a lot of money. The gas money, the repairs. I don't have that kind of money. I would have to get a job. But where could I get a job my age? Well I guess having a car is to much responsibility. Maybe I could get a job playing the guitar and I know I will get a lot of money doing that. But then again I would and probley not want a car.
4. If only I could be a cat, I would sleep all day and prowl around at night. I wouldn't have to bother about school, or careers, or money. I could stay out all night, and make friends with other neighborhood cats. I wouldn't have to eat, or sleep at a particular time. I would sometimes be a homely cat, purring on my master's lap, and sometimes be an alley cat, dependant on only me, killing mice and fighting other cats. I would go on many adventures with other cats, or just by myself. I would sometimes be a sneaky cat, stepping in my master's car when he (or she) wasn't looking, and then, when they got to their dinner party, (or place, etc) I would run out and mess it up. Or, sometimes, I would just sit and think about how much I would like to be—a human, just like, Me.

FIGURE 10.2 Examples of variation in fifth-graders' writing assessed using a holistic rating scheme (*Source: Stotsky, 1980.*)

However, before students come to school, the value that those they respect or love attach to writing of any kind powerfully shapes children's own attitudes (Heath, 1983). They are also influenced by the encouragement they receive in their homes, by having writing implements, and by having interested audiences to listen to the stories they compose or to read the messages they send. Thus, a supportive environment in school, such as the classroom described by Florio and Frank (1982), and the presence of models—people who write—is critical for children whose families or local community may offer them little encouragement as writers.

READING EXPERIENCE

Development in writing is clearly related to development in reading. Research on reading/writing relationships (Stotsky, 1984) suggests that better writing and more syntactically mature writing are associated with reading achievement and reading experience. The results of all the NAEP assessments of writing corroborate the findings of this body of research: better readers are better writers. Reading provides the developing writer with the syntactic structures of written language, a knowledge of various genres and organizational schemes, and a well-developed writing vocabulary. What writers implicitly know about written language comes primarily from their exposure to the mature written language of others. This seems to be as true for young writers (Eckhoff, 1984) as for more mature writers. Even differences in the quality of the written language may matter. In research with fifth-graders, Dressel (1990) found that students who listened to and discussed well-written works of literature later wrote higher-quality stories than students who listened to and discussed less well-written literary works, as judged by professionals. Vygotsky (1962, 1978) and his associates saw reading and writing as activities that developed the higher mental processes. Clearly, the more reading that students do, the more they can enhance the development of their writing and their thinking.

■ CONTINUING LANGUAGE AND LITERACY DEVELOPMENT

We have traced the development of children's conquest of print and the language used to communicate using it, and we have discussed some of the complexities of the continuing effects of these systems upon each other. With growing control of the powerful tools of reading and writing, children now may use literacy to assist further acquisition of oral language. Literate children also stand in a new relationship to language itself, because of the emergence of new metalinguistic skills. In this section we discuss the continuing interplay between language and literacy and point to controversial ideas about the possible effect of literacy upon the mind and upon society.

USING LITERACY TO ACQUIRE ORAL LANGUAGE

Many children enter school speaking languages other than English. For these children, second-language acquisition must occur in parallel with efforts to learn to read and write the language. Naturally this is a challenging feat. Many argue it imposes unnecessary burdens on children; better, they say, to teach literacy skills in the child's first language because these skills will transfer into English once it is mastered. Such transfer has been demonstrated for reading, writing [(e.g., the ability to write in Spanish translates into better English writing (Edelsky, 1982)], and oral decontextualization skills (Davidson, Kline, & Snow, 1986; Lanauze & Snow, 1989; Velasco & Snow, under review). We cannot review the complex arguments related to bilingual education (for reviews see Baker & deKantor, 1981; Hakuta, 1986, in press; Willig, 1985); rather, we wish to point out that the road to literacy for bilinguals has much in common with the paths we have traced for monolingual children and that many of the impediments encountered by poor readers are similar for both mono- and bilingual children (Novoa & Wolf, 1984).

For example, discovery of the units of language called *words* is as perplexing a problem for bilinguals as monolinguals. Not surprisingly, bilingual children arrive at inventive solutions to the segmentation problem (e.g., *meamo* for *me llamo,* or *my name is*). Analysis of English and Spanish writing of children whose first language is Spanish found similar types of segmentation problems in both languages but somewhat fewer such errors in English (Edelsky, 1982). This asymmetry might partly reflect differences in linguistic structures. However, most interesting for our purposes, better segmentation in English also may reflect the fact that printed English was a primary source of language input to these children. We noted earlier that books can provide important oral input that may help children who are learning English as a first (Chomsky, 1970) and as a second language (Elley & Mangubhai, 1983). Acquisition of language through reading may also help children construct an understanding of language units.

COGNITION AND SOCIETY

When we discussed children's initial reading acquisition, we noted the facilitative role of reading instruction on language awareness. Even more profound effects of literacy on cognition can be seen once literate skills have been acquired and the learner has become part of a literate community. Far-reaching attempts have been made to trace changes in society after the introduction of literacy. Critical periods when changes may have occurred have been explored, including ancient Greece (Havelock, 1976), the middle ages, and the age of Enlightenment (Olson, 1977, 1986). Olson has attempted to locate similar changes in the mind of the child (Olson, 1977, 1986). He has argued that the introduction of literacy into culture has resulted in a profound shift in the ability to distinguish between the text uttered by a speaker and the meaning intended and to distinguish between a text and its interpretation. With literacy the words of a speaker become permanent, inviting people to become aware of the distinction between the intention of the speaker and the meaning of the words. Olson (1986) argues that creation of a culture in which literacy plays a fundamental role was causally linked to the emergence of a scientific approach to the world:

> My hypothesis is that the contrast between texts and their interpretations provided the model, or more than that, the precise cognitive categories or concepts needed for the description and the interpretation of nature, that is, for the building of modern science. (pp. 112–113)

This argument has been translated from phylogenetic to ontogenetic history by research that attempts to relate improvement in children's understanding of words that refer to intellectual states (e.g., *say* and *mean*) to children's acquisition of literacy (Olson, 1986). A fascinating longitudinal study is extending this hypothesis into the preschool years, examining the effects of the ways that parents talk about language as they read books on their children's subsequent logical thinking and metalinguistic skills (Reeder, Wakefield, & Shapiro, 1988; Watson, 1989).

Olson's position emphasizes the effects of reading and writing on cognition when they are embedded in a literate culture (Olson, 1986). This position has not gone unchallenged. Others argue that cognitive changes thought to be associated with literacy actually result from changes in the cultural and economic contexts in which people acquire (e.g., in schools) and use literacy (Scribner & Cole, 1981; Street, 1984). In either case, it is clear that literacy equips children with new tools for reflecting on language and action and with new capacities for social action.

SUMMARY

Words move . . .
Words, after speech, reach
Into the silence. Only by the form, the pattern,
Can words or music reach
The stillness,

—T. S. Eliot, *Four Quartets*

We have come no small distance from our six-year-old author's tale of a baby ghost. We have traced the development of reading from first exposure to print through learning the demanding correspondence rules of English to making critical judgments about what is written. In writing we have moved from first scribbles through stories in invented spelling to essays that go well beyond the first communicative purposes of writing. And in oral language, we have seen children change into beings powerfully influenced by both the ever-broadening world of literacy and their own writing.

The cognitive and linguistic accomplishments described did not simply emerge in a vacuum; nothing in language does. Rather, the development of oral and written language systems is profoundly interactive and interwoven. What occurs in early phonological and metalinguistic development affects the acquisition and level of achievement in early reading. The development of reading with its thrust toward understanding and evaluating previously unknown thought affects the ability to communicate in oral and in written forms. The development of writing with its emphasis on expressing, refining, and at times changing our thoughts affects how we speak, read, and think. Finally, the language context with its different codes, expectations, and modes of encouragement can make the difference between evolving within these patterns of interaction between oral and written language or never making the ongoing transitions between them.

Within these transmissions between oral and written language is that property of language captured by both the psychologist (Vygotsky, 1962) and the poet (Eliot, 1971) and alluded to in our chapter title: the movement of words. Words move; they do not stand still; and in their motion they move us as human beings to words never thought and in so doing, to thoughts never spoken.

SUGGESTED PROJECTS

1. In recent years there has been growing concern that reading instruction focuses too heavily on the bottom-up skills required for decoding. Not enough time is spent helping children learn to understand and reflect on what they have read. The neglect of comprehension skills seems to be most noteworthy in low reading groups.

   To find out whether this characterization of reading instruction is true for your area, visit one or two classrooms. Note how much time is spent helping children in different reading groups think about what they have read. Compare the amount of time spent on reading comprehension with the amount of time spent on decoding or testing information recall. Be sure not to confuse testing recall or understanding with guiding children to develop skills for interpreting written text. Read at least one of the appropriate references listed in Suggested Readings to help you organize your observations. Durkin's article (1974–75) is a classic that includes a complete discussion of the coding system she used.
2. For many years parents have been urged to read to their children. Whereas this activity helps foster early reading skill (Goldfield & Snow, 1984), ethnographic studies also point to the importance of the many varied uses of reading and writing in middle-class homes (Heath, 1983; Taylor, 1983) and exciting classrooms (Florio & Clark, 1982; Staton, 1982). Develop a description of a classroom or home as a literate environment. Consider all the types and uses of print in the environment. If you are examining a classroom, think about additional functions for reading and writing that could be introduced into the room.
3. Examine children's metalinguistic awareness. You can look at children's understanding of the concept *word,* their awareness of phonemes, and/or their knowledge of print and the relation of spoken words to print. No one project could include all these issues, but you might select two issues to study in preschool to elementary school children.

   Children's understanding of what a word is undergoes important changes during the preschool and early school years. Two kinds of techniques can be used to determine children's grasp of this concept. You can ask children to segment sentences into units they think are words or you can have them make judgments about words. The segmentation task can be done by having children listen to a sentence and then clap for each word or place a marker for each word. Language judgment questions include asking children to decide which things from a list are *words.* The list should include at least nouns, verbs, conjunctions, articles, noises (e.g., door closing), single phonemes, and phrases. You might also ask children for examples of different kinds of words such as hard words, long words, and short words. For examples of such tasks see Downing and Oliver (1974), Papandropoulou and Sinclair (1974), or Templeton and Spivey (1980).

   For beginning reading, children must learn that words are composed of units. One source of evidence of children's ability to focus on phonemes comes from tasks that require children to decide which words rhyme. You can also have children tap out the number of sounds they hear in a word (e.g., Liberman, Shankweiler, Fischer, & Carter, 1974). Finally, you can ask children to spell a series of words and see how many and which sounds they include (e.g., Morris, 1983).

There is a strong relationship between children's awareness of words and phonemes and their understanding of print (Clay, 1979; Morris, 1983). Clay (1979) has developed a normed test for assessing children's print awareness that requires using special books and a testing manual. Sulzby (1986) has developed another tool for assessing children's print knowledge. It is less formalized than Clay's test and may be easier to use, but it does not provide group norms. In contrast to Clay's and Sulzby's complete interviews, Morris (1983) presents a more limited technique for testing children's ability to match print to words. His technique would be the best to use if you wish also to test other aspects of children's metalinguistic knowledge.

4. The act of reading requires the rapid integration of many lower- and higher-level perceptual, cognitive, and linguistic subprocesses. The smooth functioning of the entire process depends on the development of *automaticity* in individual subprocesses like letter recognition (cf. Gibson & Levin, 1975). The study of automaticity in cognitive functions like reading has received considerable attention, especially in adult cognition. For representative research in this area, review work by LaBerge & Samuels (1974) and Shiffrin & Schneider (1977).

There have also been many studies investigating the development of automaticity (Doehring, 1976) and the effects of its delay or disruption. For example, Denckla and Rudel (1974, 1976) have shown how the failure to achieve rapidity or automaticity in the recognition and retrieval of early symbols (e.g., letters, numbers, and colors) differentiates average and impaired readers. Wolf, Bally, and Morris (1986) have shown that there are stages to the normal development of automaticity in symbol recognition and that some impaired readers have a different sequence of development, whereas others are simply delayed.

Review the studies mentioned here and construct your own rapid, automatized naming test for letters and colors following the explicit instructions in Denckla and Rudel or Wolf et al. Test two adults and a few children at three different ages—five, seven, and ten—and note the changes in rate before, during, and after reading is acquired. How much faster is the adult than the ten-year-old? Is there a greater difference between the adult and the ten-year-old's latency than between the five- and the ten-year-olds'? What are the differences between letter and color naming speed at different ages? Explain what you find, based on the literature you have read.

5. The history of the dyslexias stretches back to ancient Egypt, where a recently found tract records a man with a head injury losing his capacity to read hieroglyphs. Today we would call such a syndrome acquired dyslexia or alexia since it occurs from proven brain injury and after reading is already acquired. See Geschwind (1974) and Coltheart, Patterson, and Marshall (1980) for lively discussions and classifications of adult syndromes. Definitions for the developmental dyslexias are far less straightforward and cause considerable difficulty in research, diagnosis, and remediation. See Benton & Pearl (1978), Ellis (1985), and Vellutino (1979).

The first problem is deciding if and when a child has a serious reading impairment. Is an immature seven-year-old boy who can't read yet reading impaired or dyslexic? What if he is eight years old? What if he is bilingual? What if he has profound visual loss? What if he is in a family undergoing divorce? What if he is in a crowded inner city classroom with no or few adjunct services? All of these hypothetical situations might prompt serious difficulties in learning to read, but it would be rare if the child was what most researchers label *dyslexic.*

In this activity you should first review several thoughtful discussions of the dyslexias in childhood beginning with Vellutino's classic review of the literature (1977) and proceeding through three attempts at definition by Doehring (1983), Rudel (1985), and Morrison (1984). Based on these works, what criteria would you use for selection of subjects if you were to design a study of differences between average readers and children with developmental dyslexia for ages six to twelve? What problems would you foresee and why? How might you circumvent those problems?

Now that you have experienced some of the theoretical difficulties surrounding research in the dyslexias, turn to several clinical realities. If it is possible in your area, arrange to observe (i.e., follow through testing) two children who have been referred to a hospital clinic for neuropsychological testing for reading disabilities. (If no clinic is available, observe in close detail characteristics of several children in a reading group of reading impaired children.) Prepare a brief profile of the similarities and dissimilarities seen in the children. What do both sets of characteristics contribute to your understanding of developmental reading pathology?

6. You can study children's invented spellings if you have access to school children who are encouraged to spell words the best way they can on their own. This project would be most interesting if you could compare a child's spelling over time.
7. The differences between essay-style language and conversational language can be experienced by contrasting the language you use in different situations. Get two sets of six or seven wooden blocks. Erect a screen between yourself and another person; one of you should construct a building. The builder should then describe her construction so that her partner can replicate it. Try doing this with and without responses from your partner. Next, simply talk about what you did the past weekend.

   Afterward discuss how your language changed in the two situations. Consider how your syntax and vocabulary choice changed. Also, discuss the role of the listener in facilitating the communication. Finally, consider how the building description task is like or unlike writing an essay to an unknown audience. Are there similar demands placed on the communicator? What kinds of shifts in language are required in both cases? When children must communicate written information, do you think they might experience some of the same kinds of discomfort you experienced when giving directions to an unresponsive partner?

SUGGESTED READINGS

Adams, M. J. (1990). *Beginning to read.* Cambridge, MA: MIT Press.

Atwell, N. (1987). *In the middle: Writing, reading, and learning with adolescents.* Portsmouth, NH: Heinemann.

Bowey, J. A., & Frances, J. (1991). Phonological analysis as a function of age and exposure to reading instruction. *Applied Psycholinguistics, 12,* 91–121.

Calkins, L. M. (1986). *The art of teaching writing.* Portsmouth, NH: Heinemann.

Cazden, C. B. (1988). *Classroom discourse: The language of teaching and learning.* Portsmouth, NH: Heinemann.

Chomsky, C. (1970). Reading, writing, and phonology. *Harvard Educational Review, 40,* 287–309.

Chomsky, C. (1971). Stages in language development and reading exposure. *Harvard Educational Review, 42,* 1–33.

Chomsky, C. (1972). Write now, read later. *Childhood Education, 47,* 296–299.

Heath, S. B. (1983). *Ways with words.* New York: Cambridge University Press.

Hillocks, G. (1986). *Research on written composition: New directions for teaching.* Urbana, IL: ERIC-NCRE.

Snowling, M. (1987). *Dyslexia: A cognitive-developmental perspective.* Oxford: Basil Blackwell.

Sulzby, E., & Teale, W. (1991). Emergent literacy. In R. Barr, M. L. Kamil, P. Mosenthal, & P. D. Pearson. (1991). *Handbook of reading research (Vol. II)* (pp. 727–758). New York: Longman.

Wolf, M., & Vellutino, F. (in press). A psycholinguistic account of reading. In J. Berko Gleason & N. Bernstein Ratner (Eds.), *Psycholinguistics*. Forth Worth, TX: Harcourt Brace Jovanovich.

REFERENCES

Adams, M. J. (1990). *Beginning to read*. Cambridge, MA: MIT Press.

Altwerger, B., Edelsky, C., & Florers, B. M. (1987). Whole language: What's new? *Reading Teacher, 41,* 144–154.

Applebee, A. (1981). *Writing in the secondary school: English and the content areas* (Research Report No. 21). Urbana, IL: National Council of Teachers of English.

Applebee, A., Langer, J., Mullis I., & Jenkins, L. (1990). *The writing report card, 1984–88. Findings from the nation's report card*. The National Assessment of Educational Progress. Princeton, NJ: Educational Testing Service.

Atwell, N. (1987). *In the middle: Writing, reading, and learning with adolescents*. Portsmouth, NH: Heinemann.

Baker, K. A., & deKanter, A. A. (1981, September). *Effectiveness of bilingual education: A review of the literature*. Washington, DC: U.S. Department of Education, Office of Planning, Budget and Evaluation.

Barr, R., Kamil, M. L., Mosenthal, P., & Pearson, P. D. (1991). *Handbook of reading research* (Vol. II). New York: Longman.

Beals, D. (1991). *'I know who makes ice cream': Explanations in mealtime conversations of low-income families of preschoolers*. Unpublished doctoral dissertation, Harvard Graduate School of Education.

Benton, A. L., & Pearl, D. (Eds.). (1978). *Dyslexia: An appraisal of current knowledge*. New York: Oxford.

Bereiter, C., & Scardemalia, M. (1982). From conversation to composition: The role of instruction in a developmental process. In R. Glaser (Ed.), *Advances in instructional psychology* (Vol. 2). Hillsdale, NJ: Erlbaum.

Bertelson, P. (1986). The onset of literacy: Liminal remarks. *Cognition, 24,* 1–30.

Bissex, G. (1980). *Gyns at wrk*. Cambridge, MA: Harvard University Press.

Boggs, S. T. (1972). The meaning of questions and narratives to Hawaiian children. In C. B. Cazden, V. P. John, & D. Hymes (Eds.), *Functions of language in the classroom* (pp. 299–330). New York: Teacher's College Press.

Bowers, P., & Swanson, L. (in press). Naming deficits in reading disability: Multiple measures of a singular process. *Journal of Experimental Child Psychology*.

Bowey, J. A., & Frances, J. (1991). Phonological analysis as a function of age and exposure to reading instruction. *Applied Psycholinguistics, 12,* 91–121.

Brady, S., & Shankweiler, D. (Eds.). (in press). *Phonological processes in literacy: A tribute to Isabelle Liberman*. Hillsdale, NJ: Erlbaum.

Britton, J., Burgess, T., Martin, N., McLeod, A., & Rosen, A. (1975). *The development of writing abilities (11–18)*. London: Macmillan.

Bryant, P., MacLean, M., & Bradley, L. (1990). Rhyme, language, and children's reading. *Applied Psycholinguistics, 11,* 237–252.

Calkins, L. M. (1986). *The art of teaching writing*. Portsmouth, NH: Heinemann.

Cazden, C. B. (1988). *Classroom discourse: The language of teaching and learning.* Portsmouth, NH: Heinemann.

Chafe, W., & Danielewicz, J. (1987). Properties of spoken and written language. In R. Horowitz & S. J. Samuels (Eds.), *Comprehending oral and written language* (pp. 83–116). Orlando, FL: Academic Press.

Chall, J. S. (1967). *Learning to read: The great debate.* New York: McGraw-Hill.

Chall, J. S. (1983). *Stages of reading development.* New York: McGraw-Hill.

Chomsky, C. (1970). Reading, writing, and phonology. *Harvard Educational Review, 40,* 287–309.

Chomsky, C. (1971). Stages in language development and reading exposure. *Harvard Educational Review, 42*(1), 1–3.

Chomsky, C. (1972). Write now, read later. *Childhood Education, 47,* 296–299.

Clark, E. (1978). Awareness of language: Some evidence from what children say and do. In A. Sinclair, R. J. Javella, & W. J. M. Levelt (Eds.), *The child's conception of language* (pp. 17–44). New York: Springer-Verlag.

Clark, R. (1983). *Family life and school achievement: Why poor black children succeed or fail.* Chicago: University of Chicago Press.

Clay, M. (1975). *What did I write?* Portsmouth, NH: Heinemann.

Clay, M. (1979). *The early detection of reading difficulties: A diagnostic survey with recovery procedures.* Portsmouth, NH: Heinemann.

Coltheart, M., Patterson, K., & Marshall, J. C. (1980). *Deep dyslexia.* London: Routledge & Kegan Paul.

Conrad, R. (1972). Speech and reading. In J. Kavanagh & I. Mattingly (Eds.), *Language by ear and by eye* (pp. 205–240). Cambridge, MA: MIT Press.

Content, A., Kolinsky, R., Morais, J., & Bertelson, P. (1986). Phonetic segmentation in prereaders: Effect of corrective information. *Journal of Experimental Child Psychology, 42,* 49–72.

Cox, B. E., Shanahan, T., & Sulzby, E. (1990). Good and poor elementary readers' use of cohesion in writing. *Reading Research Quarterly, XXV,* 47–65.

Crowder, R. (1982). *The psychology of reading: An introduction.* New York: Oxford University Press.

Cziko, G. A. (in press). The evaluation of bilingual education: From necessity and probability to possibility. *Educational Researcher.*

Davidson, R. G., Kline, S. B., & Snow, C. E. (1986). Definitions and definite noun phrases: Indicators of children's decontextualized language skills. *Journal of Research in Childhood Education, 1,* 37–48.

Denckla, M. B. (1972). Clinical syndromes in learning disabilities: The case of "splitting" vs. "lumping." *Journal of Learning Disabilities, 5,* 401–406.

Denckla, M. B., & Rudel, R. (1974). Rapid "automatized" naming of pictured objects, colors, letters, and numbers by normal children. *Cortex, 10,* 186–202.

Denckla, M. B., & Rudel, R. (1976). Naming of object drawings by dyslexic and other learning disabled children. *Brain and Language, 3,* 1–16.

DeStefano, J. S. (1984). Learning to communicate in the classroom. In A. Pellegrini & T. Yawkey (Eds.). *The development of oral and written language in social contexts* (pp. 155–165). Norwood, NJ: Ablex.

De Temple, J., & Beals, D. (in press). Family talk: Sources of support for the development of decontextualized language skills. *Journal of Childhood Education.*

deVilliers, J. G., & deVilliers, P. A. (1974). Competence and performance in child language: Are children really competent to judge? *Journal of Child Language, 1,* 11–22.

deVilliers, P. A., & deVilliers, J. G. (1972). Early judgments of semantic and syntactic acceptability by children. *Journal of Psycholinguistic Research, 1,* 299–310.

Dickinson, D. K. (1991). Teacher stance and setting: Constraints on conversation in preschools. In A. McCabe & C. Peterson (Eds.), *Developing narrative structure* (pp. 255–302). Hillsdale, NJ: Erlbaum.

Dickinson, D. K., & Keebler, R. (1989). Variation in preschool teachers' styles of reading books. *Discourse Processes, 12,* 353–376.

Dickinson, D. K., & Smith, M. W. (1991, April). Styles of reading books in preschool. Paper presented at the annual conference of the American Educational Research Association, Chicago.

Dickinson, D. K., & Snow, C. E. (1987). Interrelationships among prereading and oral language skills in kindergartners from two social classes. *Early Childhood Research Quarterly, 1,* 1–26.

Dickinson, D., & McCabe, A. (1991). A social interactionist account of language and literacy development. In J. Kavanaugh (Ed.), *The language continuum.* Parkton, MD: The York Press.

Dickinson, D., & Tabors, P. (in press). Early literacy: Linkages between home, school, and literacy achievement at age five. *Journal of Childhood Education.*

Doehring, D. (1976). Acquisition of rapid reading responses. *Monographs of the Society for Research in Child Development, 41*(2).

Doehring, D. (1983). What do we know about reading disabilities? Closing the gap between research and practice. *Annals of Dyslexia, 33,* 175–183.

Donnelly, D., & Stevens, G. (1980). Streams and puddles: A comparison of two young writers. *Language Arts, 57,* 735–741.

Downing, J., & Oliver, P. (1974). The child's conception of "a word." *Reading Research Quarterly, 9,* 568–582.

Dressel, J. H. (1990). The effects of listening to and discussing different qualities of children's literature on the narrative writing of fifth graders. *Research in the Teaching of English, 24*(4), 397–414.

Durkin, D. (1974–75). A six-year study of children who learned to read in school at the age of four. *Reading Research Quarterly, 10,* 9–61.

Durst, R. (1987). Cognitive and linguistic demands of analytic writing. *Research in the teaching of English, 21,* 347–376.

Dyson, A. (1986). Transitions and tensions: Interrelationships between the drawing, talking, and dictating of young children. *Research in the Teaching of English, 20,* 379–409.

Dyson, A. (1987). Individual differences in beginning composing: An orchestral vision of learning to compose. *Written Communication, 9,* 411–422.

Dyson, A. (1989). *Multiple worlds of child writers: Friends learning to write.* NY: Teachers College Press.

Dyson, A. H. (1984). Emerging alphabetic literacy in school contexts: Toward defining the gap between school curriculum and child mind. *Written Communication, 1,* 5–55.

Eckhoff, B. (1984). How reading affects children's writing. In J. Jensen (Ed.), *Composing and comprehending,* 105–114. Urbana, IL: NCRE.

Edelsky, C. (1982). Writing in a bilingual program: The relation of L1 and L2 texts. *TESOL Quarterly, 16,* 211–228.

Edelsky, C., Altwerger, B., & Flores, B. (in press). *Whole language: What's the difference?* Portsmouth, NH: Heinemann.

Eder, D. (1982). The impact of management and turn-allocation activities on student performance. *Discourse Processes, 5,* 383–421.

Ehri, L. (1989). Movement into word reading and spelling: How spelling contributes to reading. In J. M. Mason (Ed.), *Reading and writing connections* (pp. 65–82). Boston: Allyn & Bacon.

Ehri, L. C., & Wilce, L. S. (1985). Movement into reading: Is the first stage of printed word learning visual or phonetic? *Reading Research Quarterly, 20,* 163–179.

Eliot, T. S. (1971). *Four Quartets.* New York: Harcourt Brace Jovanovich, Inc.

Elley, W. (1989). Vocabulary acquisition from listening to stories. *Reading Research Quarterly, XXIV,* 174–187.

Elley, W. B., & Mangubhai, F. (1983). The impact of reading on second language learning. *Reading Research Quarterly, 19,* 53–67.

Ellis, A. (1984). *Reading, writing and dyslexia: A cognitive analysis.* London: Erlbaum.

Ellis, A. W. (1985). The cognitive neuropsychology of developmental (and acquired) dyslexia: A critical survey. *Cognitive Neuropsychology, 2,* 169–205.

Evanechko, P., Ollila, L., & Armstrong, R. (1974). An investigation of the relationships between children's performance in written language and their reading ability. *Research in the Teaching of English, 8,* 315–326.

Evans, C. S. (1984). Writing to learn in math. *Language Arts, 61,* 828–835.

Feagans, L., & Farran, D. C. (1981). How demonstrated comprehension can get muddled in production. *Developmental Psychology, 17,* 718–727.

Feitelson, D., Kita, & Goldstein. (1986). Effects of listening to series stories on first graders' comprehension and use of language. *Research in the Teaching of English, 20,* 339–356.

Feitelson, Goldstein, & Iraqi (1990, December). Effects of story reading on literary language acquisition. Paper presented at the annual meeting of the National Reading Conference, Miami.

Ferreiro, E., & Teberosky, A. (1982). *Literacy before schooling.* Exeter, NH: Heinemann.

Fletcher, J., & Morris, R. (1985). Classification of disabled learners: Beyond exclusionary definitions. In S. Ceci (Ed.), *Handbook of cognitive, social, and neuropsychological aspects of learning disabilities,* Vol. 1, 55–80. Hillsdale, NJ: Erlbaum.

Florio, S., & Clark, C. M. (1982). The functions of writing in an elementary classroom. *Research in the Teaching of English, 16,* 115–130.

Florio, S., & Frank, J. (1982). Literacy and community in the classroom: A case study of Betterburg. In B. Beyer & R. Gilstrap (Eds.), *Integrating writing and social studies* (pp. 31–42). Boulder, CO: Social Science Education Consortium.

Frederiksen, J. (1981). Sources of process interactions in reading. In A. Lesgold & C. Perfetti (Eds.), *Interactive processes in reading.* Hillsdale, NJ: Erlbaum.

Frith, U. (1985). Beneath the surface of developmental dyslexia: Are comparisons between developmental and acquired disorders meaningful? In K. E. Patterson, J. C. Marshall, & M. Coltheart (Eds.), *Surface dyslexia: Neuropsychological and cognitive studies of phonological reading* (pp. 301–330). Hillsdale, NJ: Erlbaum.

Gee, J. P. (1989). Commonalities and differences in narrative construction. *Discourse Processes, 12,* 287–307.

Geschwind, N. (1974). Disconnexion syndromes in animals and man. In N. Geschwind (Ed.), *Selected papers on language and the brain.* Boston: Reidel.

Geschwind, N., & Galaburda, A. (1987). *Cerebral lateralization.* Cambridge, MA: MIT Press.

Gibson, E., & Levin, H. (1975). *The psychology of reading.* Cambridge, MA: MIT Press.

Goldfield, B. A., & Snow, C. E. (1984). Reading books with children: The mechanics of parental influence on children's reading achievement. In J. Flood (Ed.), *Understanding reading comprehension* (pp. 204–218). Newark, DE: International Reading Association.

Golub, L., & Fredrick, W. (1971). *Linguistic structures in the discourse of fourth and sixth graders* (Tech. Rep. No. 166). Madison, WI: University of Wisconsin, Wisconsin Research and Development Center for Cognitive Learning.

Goodman, K., & Goodman, Y. (1977). Learning about psycholinguistic processes by analyzing oral reading. *Harvard Educational Review, 47,* 317–333.

Goodman, Y. (1986). Children coming to know literacy. In W. H. Teale & E. Sulzby (Eds.), *Emergent literacy: Writing and reading* (pp. 1–14). Norwood, NJ: Ablex.

Gough, P. B. (1972). One second of reading. In J. F. Kavanagh & I. G. Mattingly (Eds.), *Language by eye and ear* (pp. 331–358). Cambridge, MA: MIT Press.

Graves, D. H. (1973). *Children's writing: Research directions and hypotheses based upon an examination of the writing processes of seven-year-old children.* Unpublished doctoral dissertation, State University of New York at Buffalo.

Graves, D. H. (1983). *Writing: Teachers and children at work.* Exeter, NH: Heinemann.

Greenlee, M., Hiebert, E., Bridge, C., & Winograd, P. (1986). The effects of different audiences on young writers' letter writing. In J. Niles & R. Lalik (Eds.), *Solving problems in literacy: Learners, teachers, and researchers, 35th Yearbook* (pp. 281–289). Rochester, NY: National Reading Conference.

Gundlach, R. A. (1981). On the nature and development of children's writing. In C. H. Frederiksen & J. F. Dominic (Eds.), *Writing: The nature, development, and teaching of written communication* (Vol. 2, pp. 133–152). Hillsdale, NJ: Erlbaum.

Gundlach, R. A. (1982). Children as writers: The beginnings of learning to write. In M. Nystrand (Ed.), *What writers should know: The language, process, and structure of written discourse* (pp. 129–148). New York: Academic Press.

Hakes, D. (1980). *The development of metalinguistic abilities in children.* New York: Springer-Verlag.

Hakuta, K. (1986). *Mirror of language: The debate on bilingualism.* New York: Basic Books.

Hakuta, K. (Ed.). (in press). Special issue on bilingual education. *Educational Researcher.*

Halliday, M. A. K. (1987). Spoken and written modes of meaning. In R. Horowitz & S. J. Samuels (Eds.), *Comprehending oral and written language* (pp. 55–82). Orlando, FL: Academic Press.

Hansen, J. (1983). Authors respond to authors. *Language Arts, 60,* 970–976.

Harste, J., Woodward, V., & Burke, C. (1984). *Language stories and literacy lessons.* Portsmouth, NH: Heinemann.

Havelock, D. (1976). *Origins of Western literacy.* Toronto: Ontario Institute for Studies in Education.

Heath, S. B. (1982). What no bedtime story means: Narrative skills at home and school. *Language in Society, 11,* 49–76.

Heath, S. B. (1983). *Ways with words: Language, life and work in communities and classrooms.* New York: Cambridge University Press.

Heath, S. B. (1986). Separating "things of the imagination" from life: Learning to read and write. In W. H. Teale & E. Sulzby (Eds.), *Emergent literacy: Writing and reading* (pp. 156–172). Norwood, NJ: Ablex.

Hidi, S., & Hildyard, A. (1983). The comparison of oral and written productions of two discourse types. *Discourse Processes, 6,* 91–105.

Hillerich, R. (1978). *A writing vocabulary of elementary children.* Springfield, IL: Charles C. Thomas.

Hillocks, G. (1986). *Research on written composition: New directions for teaching.* Urbana, IL: ERIC-NCRE.

Hodges, R. (1982). *Improving spelling and vocabulary in the secondary school.* Urbana, IL: ERIC-NCTE.

Hudson, S. (1986). Context and children's writing. *Research in the Teaching of English, 20,* 294–316.

Huey, E. B. (1908). *The psychology and pedagogy of reading.* New York: Macmillan. (Republished in 1968 by MIT Press, Cambridge, MA.)

Hunt, K. (1965). *Grammatical structures written at three grade levels* (Research Report No. 3). Urbana, IL: National Council of Teachers of English.

Hunt, K. (1970). Syntactic maturity in school children and adults. *Monographs of the Society for Research in Child Development, 35* (3, Serial No. 134).

Hunt, K. (1977). Early blooming and late blooming syntactic structures. In C. Cooper & L. Odell (Eds.), *Evaluating writing: Describing, measuring, judging* (pp. 91–106). Urbana, IL: National Council of Teachers of English.

Just, M. A., & Carpenter, P. A. (1987). *The psychology of reading and language comprehension.* Boston: Allyn & Bacon.

Kavanagh, J., & Mattingly, I. G. (1972). *Language by ear and by eye.* Cambridge, MA: MIT Press.

Kinsbourne, M., & Warrington, E. (1963). Developmental factors in reading and writing backwardness. *British Journal of Psychology, 54,* 145–156.

Kolers, P. (1970). Three stages of reading. In H. Levin & J. Williams (Eds.), *Basic studies on reading.* New York: Basic Books.

Kreeft, J. (1984). Dialogue writing—bridge from talk to essay writing. *Language Arts, 61,* 141–150.

LaBerge, D., & Samuels, S. J. (1974). Toward a theory of automatic information processing in reading. *Cognitive Psychology, 6,* 293–323.

Lanauze, M., & Snow, C. E. (1989). The relation between first- and second-language writing skills: Evidence from Puerto Rican elementary school children in bilingual programs. *Linguistics and Education, 1,* 323–337.

Lazdowski, W. (1976). *Determining reading grade levels from analysis of written composition.* Unpublished doctoral dissertation, New Mexico State University, Las Cruces.

Lesgold, A., & Perfetti, C. (Eds.). (1981). *Interactive processes in reading.* Hillsdale, NJ: Erlbaum.

LeVine, R. A. (1978). Western schools in non-Western societies: Affective and cognitive responses. *Teachers College Record, 79,* 749–755.

Levy, B. (1981). Interactive processing during reading. In A. Lesgold & C. Perfetti (Eds.), *Interactive processes in reading.* Hillsdale, NJ: Erlbaum.

Levy, B. A., & Stewart, L. (1991, April). Early diagnosis and treatment of reading problems. Presented in the symposium, Cognitive and Neuropsychological Advances in the Prediction and Intervention of Severe Reading Disabilities, at the meeting of the Society for Research in Child Development, Seattle, WA.

Liberman, I. Y., Shankweiler, K., Fischer, R. N., & Carter, B. (1974). Explicit syllable and phoneme segmentation in the young child. *Journal of Experimental Child Psychology, 18,* 201–212.

Loban, W. (1976). *Language development: Kindergarten through Grade 12.* Urbana, IL: National Council of Teachers of English.

Logan, G. D. (1988). Toward an instance theory of automatization. *Psychological Review, 95,* 492–527.

Lomax, R. G., & McGee, L. M. (1987). Young children's concepts about print and reading: Toward a model of word reading acquisition. *Reading Research Quarterly, 22,* 237–256.

Lovett, M. (1984). A developmental perspective on reading dysfunction: Accuracy and rate criteria in the subtyping of dylexic children. *Brain and Language, 22,* 67–91.

Lovett, M. (1991, April). A remedial outcome approach to the treatment of developmental dyslexia. Presented in the symposium, Cognitive and Neuropsychological Advances in the Prediction and Intervention of Severe Reading Disabilities, at the meeting of the Society for Research in Child Development, Seattle, WA.

Maccoby, E., & Jacklin, C. (1974). *The psychology of sex differences.* Stanford, CA: Stanford University Press.

Mandler, J. M., & Johnson, N. S. (1977). Remembrance of things passed: Story structure and recall. *Cognitive Psychology, 9,* 111–151.

Marsh, G., & Desberg, P. (1983). The development of strategies—The acquisition of symbolic skills. In D. A. Rogers & J. A. Sloboda (Eds.), *The acquisition of symbolic skills.* New York: Plenum.

Mason, J. M. (1991). Reading stories to preliterate children: A proposed connection to reading. In P. Gough, L. Ehri, & R. Treiman (Eds.), *Reading acquisition.* Hillsdale, NJ: Erlbaum.

Mason, J. M., & Allen, J. (1986a). A review of emergent literacy with implications for research and practice in reading. In C. Z. Rothkopf (Ed.), *Review of research in education* (Vol. 13, pp. 3–48). Washington, DC: American Educational Research Association.

Masonheimer, P. E., Ehri, L. C., & Drum, P. A. (1985). Does environmental print identification lead children into word reading? *Journal of Reading Behavior, 12,* 257–272.

Matsuhashi, A. (1982). Explorations in the real-time production of written discourse. In M. Nystrand (Ed.), *What writers know: The language, process, and structure of written discourse.* New York: Academic Press.

Matthews, K. (1985). Beyond the writing table. In J. Hansen, T. Newkirk, & D. Graves (Eds.), *Breaking ground: Teachers relate reading and writing in the elementary school* (pp. 63–72). Portsmouth, NH: Heinemann.

Matthews, M. (1966). *Teaching to read: Historically considered.* Chicago: University of Chicago Press.

Mattis, S., French, J., & Rapin, I. (1975). Dyslexia in children and young adults: Three independent neuropsychological syndromes. *Developmental Medicine and Child Neurology, 17,* 150–163.

McClelland, J. L., & Rumelhart, D. E. (1986). *Parallel distributed processing: Explorations in the microstructure of cognition* (Vol. 2). Cambridge, MA: Bradford Books.

McKenna, M., Robinson, R., & Miller, J. (1990). Whole language: A research agenda for the nineties. *Educational Researcher, 19,* 3–6.

Michaels, S. (1981). "Sharing time": Children's narrative styles and differential access to literacy. *Language in Society, 10,* 423–442.

Michaels, S. (1991). The dismantling of narrative. In A. McCabe & C. Peterson (Eds.), *Developing narrative structure* (pp. 303–352). Norwood, NJ: Ablex.

Michaels, S., & Cazden, C. B. (1987). Teacher/child collaboration as oral preparation for literacy. In B. B. Schieffelin (Ed.), *Acquisition of literacy: Ethnographic perspectives.* Norwood, NJ: Ablex.

Michaels, S., & Collins, J. (1984). Oral discourse styles: Classroom interaction and the acquisition of literacy. In D. Tannen (Ed.), *Coherence in spoken and written discourse.* Norwood, NJ: Ablex.

Minami, M., & McCabe, A. (in press). *Haiku* as a discourse regulation device: A stanza analysis of Japanese children's personal narratives. *Language in Society.*

Moffett, J. (1968). *Teaching the universe of discourse.* Boston: Houghton Mifflin.

Mohatt, G., & Erickson, F. (1981). Cultural differences in teaching styles in an Odawa school: A sociolinguistic approach. In H. T. Trueba, G. P. Guthrie, & K. H. Au (Eds.), *Culture and the bilingual classroom: Studies in classroom ethnography* (pp. 105–119). Rowley, MA: Newbury House.

Moll, L. C. (in press). Bilingual classroom studies and community analysis: Some recent trends. *Educational Researcher.*

Morais, J., Bertelson, P., Cary, L., & Alegria, J. (1986). Literacy training and speech segmentation. *Cognition, 24,* 45–64.

Morgan, A. L. (1987). The development of written language awareness in black preschool children. *Journal of Reading Behavior, XIX,* 49–67.

Morris, D. (1983). Concept of word and phoneme awareness in the beginning reader. *Research in the Teaching of English, 17,* 359–373.

Morrison, F. (1984). Reading disability: A problem in rule learning and word decoding. *Developmental Review, 4,* 36–47.

Morrow, L. M., & Smith, J. K. (1990). The effects of group setting on interactive storybook reading. *Reading Research Quarterly, XXV,* 213–231.

Morton, J. (1969). Interaction of information in word recognition. *Psychology Review, 76,* 165–178.

Morton, T. (1980). Two auditory parallels to deep dyslexia. In M. Coltheart, K. Patterson, & T. C. Marshall (Eds.), *Deep dyslexia.* London: Routledge & Kegan Paul.

Myklebust, H. (1973). *Development and disorders of written language* (Vols. 1 & 2). New York: Grune and Stratton.

Nagy, W., & Anderson, R. (1984). The number of words in printed school English. *Reading Research Quarterly, 19,* 304–330.

Nagy, W., Herman, P. A., & Anderson, R. C. (1985). Learning words from context. *Reading Research Quarterly, 20,* 233–253.

National Assessment of Educational Progress. (1985). *The reading report card: Progress toward excellence in our schools. Trends in reading over four national assessments, 1971–1984* (Report No. 15–R–01). Princeton, NJ: Educational Testing Service.

National Assessment of Educational Progress. (1990). *Learning to read in our nation's schools: Instruction and achievement in 1988 at grades 4, 8, and 12* (Report No. 19–R–02). Princeton, NJ: Educational Testing Service.

Newkirk, T. (1987). The non-narrative writing of young children. *Research in the Teaching of English, 21,* 121–144.

Novoa, L., & Wolf, M. (1984). Word-retrieval and reading in bilingual children. Paper presented at the Boston University Conference on Language Development, Boston, MA.

O'Connor, M. C., & Michaels, S. (1990). *Literacy as reasoning within multiple discourses: Implications for policy and educational reform* (Technical Report #10). Newton, MA: Literacies Institute.

O'Donnell, R., Griffin, W., & Norris, R. (1967). *Syntax of kindergarten and elementary school children: A transformational analysis* (Research Report No. 8). Urbana, IL: National Council of Teachers of English.

Olson, D. R. (1977). From utterance to text: The bias of language in speech and writing. *Harvard Educational Review, 47,* 257–281.

Olson, D. R. (1986). The cognitive consequences of literacy. *Canadian Psychology, 27,* 109–121.

Papandropoulou, I., & Sinclair, H. (1974). What is a word? Experimental study of children's ideas on grammar. *Human Development, 17,* 240–258.

Pappas, C., & Brown, E. (1987). Learning to read by reading: Learning how to extend the functional potential of language. *Research in the Teaching of English, 21,* 160–184.

Patterson, K. E., Marshall, J. C., & Coltheart, M. (Eds.). (1985). *Surface dyslexia: Neuropsychological and cognitive studies of phonological reading.* Hillsdale, NJ: Erlbaum.

Pellegrini, A. D., Galda, L., Dresden, J., & Cox, S. (1991). A longitudinal study of the predictive relations among symbolic play, linguistic verbs, and early literacy. *Research in the Teaching of English, 25,* 219–235.

Perfetti, C. A. (1985). *Reading ability.* New York: Oxford University Press.

Perfetti, C. (in press). The representation problem in reading acquisition. In P. Gough, L. Ehri, & R. Treiman (Eds.), *Reading acquisition.* Hillsdale, NJ: Erlbaum.

Perfetti, C., & Hogoboam, T. (1975). Relationship between single word decoding and reading comprehension skill. *Journal of Educational Psychology, 4,* 461–469.

Peters, M. (1970). *Success in spelling: A study of the factors affecting improvement in spelling in the junior school.* Cambridge, England: Cambridge Institute of Education.

Peterson, C., & McCabe, A. (1983). *Developmental psycholinguistics: Three ways of looking at a child's narrative.* New York: Plenum.

Peterson, C., & McCabe, A. (1991). Linking children's connectives use and narrative macrostructure. In A. McCabe & C. Peterson (Eds.), *Developing narrative structure* (pp. 29–54). Hillsdale, NJ: Erlbaum.

Phillips, S. U. (1972). Participant structures and communicative competence: Warm Springs children in community and classroom. In C. B. Cazden, B. P. John, & D. Hymes (Eds.), *Functions of language in the classroom.* New York: Teacher's College Press.

Piaget, J. (1970). *Structuralism.* New York: Basic Books.

Purcell-Gates, V. (1988). Lexical and syntactic knowledge of written narrative held by well-read-to kindergartners and second graders. *Research in the Teaching of English, 22,* 128–160.

Purcell-Gates, V. (in press). Roots of response. *Journal of Narrative and Life History.*

Read, C. (1971). Preschool children's knowledge of English phonology, *Harvard Educational Review, 41,* 1–34.

Read, C. (1981). Writing is not the inverse of reading for young children. In C. H. Frederiksen & J. F. Dominic (Eds.), *Writing: The nature, development, and teaching of written communication.* Hillsdale, NJ: Erlbaum.

Read, C., Yun-Fei, Z., Hong-Yin, N., & Bao-Qing, D. (1986). The ability to manipulate speech sounds depends on knowing alphabetic writing. *Cognition, 24,* 31–44.

Reeder, K., Wakefield, J., & Shapiro, J. (1988). Children's speech act comprehension strategies and early literacy experiences. *First Language, 8,* 29–48.

Revelle, G. L., Wellman, H. M., & Karabenick, J. (1985). Comprehension monitoring in preschool children. *Child Development, 56,* 653–663.

Rief, L. (1985). Why can't we live like the monarch butterfly? In J. Hansen, T. Newkirk, & D. Graves (Eds.), *Breaking ground: Teachers relate reading and writing in the elementary school* (pp. 133–146). Portsmouth, NH: Heinemann.

Rinsland, H. (1945). *A basic vocabulary of elementary school children.* New York: Macmillan.

Rosenblatt, L. (1989). Writing and reading: The transactional theory. In J. M. Mason (Ed.), *Reading and writing connections.* Boston: Allyn & Bacon.

Roth, F., & Spekman, N. (1986). Narrative discourse: Spontaneously generated stories of learning-disabled and normally achieving students. *Journal of Speech and Hearing Disorders, 51,* 8–23.

Rubin, S., & Wolf, D. (1979). The development of maybe: The evolution of social roles into narrative roles. *New Directions for Child Development, 6,* 15–28.

Rudel, R. G. (1985). Definition of dyslexia: Language and motor deficits. In F. Duffy & N. Geschwind (Eds.), *Dyslexia, current status and future directions.* Boston: Little, Brown.

Rumelhart, D. E., & McClelland, J. (1981). Interactive processing through semantic activation. In A. Lesgold & C. Perfetti (Eds.), *Interactive processes in reading.* Hillsdale, NJ: Erlbaum.

Rumelhart, D. E., & McClelland, J. (1986). *Parallel distributed processing: Explorations in the microstructure of cognition* (Vol. 1). Cambridge, MA: Bradford Books.

Schank, R., & Abelson, R. (1977). *Scripts, plans, goals and understanding: An inquiry into human knowledge structures.* New York: Wiley.

Schultz, J., Florio, S., & Erickson, R. (1982). Where's the floor? Aspects of the cultural organization of social relationships in communication at home and in school. In P. Gilmore & A. Glatthorn (Eds.), *Children in and out of school: Ethnography and education.* Washington, DC: Center for Applied Linguistics.

Scribner, S., & Cole, M. (1981). *The psychology of literacy.* Cambridge, MA: Harvard University Press.

Segal, D., & Wolf, M. (in press). Automaticity, word-retrieval, and vocabulary development in reading-disabled children. In L. Meltzer (Ed.), *Strategy, assessment, and instruction for students with learning disabilities: From theory to practice.* Boston: Little, Brown.

Seidenberg, M., & McClelland, J. (1989). A distributed, developmental model of word recognition and naming. *Psychological Review, 96,* 523–568.

Shankweiler, D., & Crain, S. (1986). Language mechanisms and reading disorder: A modular approach. *Cognition, 24,* 139–168.

Shankweiler, D., & Liberman, I. (1972). Misreading: A search for causes. In J. Kavanagh & I. Mattingly (Eds.), *Language by ear and by eye: The relationships between speech and reading* (pp. 293–308). Cambridge, MA: MIT Press.

Shiffrin, R. M., & Schneider, W. (1977). Controlled and automatic human information processing. *Psychological Review, 84,* 127–190.

Smith, C. L., & Tager-Flusberg, H. (1982). Metalinguistic awareness and language development. *Journal of Experimental Child Psychology, 34,* 449–468.

Smith, F. (1972). *Understanding reading.* New York: Holt, Rinehart & Winston.

Smith, M. W. (1990). Dimensions of variation in preschool teachers' discourse. Unpublished master's thesis, Tufts University.

Snow, C. E., Barnes, W. S., Chandler, J., Goodman, I. F., & Hemphill, L. (1991). *Unfulfilled expectations.* Cambridge, MA: Harvard University Press.

Snow, C. E., Cancino, H., De Temple, & Schley, S. (in press). Giving formal definitions: A linguistic or metalinguistic skill? In E. Bialystok (Ed.), *Language processing and language awareness by bilingual children.* New York: Cambridge University Press.

Snow, C. E., Cancino, H., Gonzalez, P., & Shriberg, E. (1989). Giving formal definitions: An oral language correlate of school literacy. In D. Bloome (Ed.), *Classrooms and literacy* (pp. 233–249). Norwood, NJ: Ablex.

Snow, C. E., & Dickinson, D. K. (1991). Skills that aren't basic in a new conception of literacy. In A. Purves & E. Jennings (Eds.), *Literate systems and individual lives: Perspectives on literacy and schooling.* Albany, NY: SUNY Press.

Snow, C. E., & Goldfield, B. A. (1983). Turn the page please: Situation-specific language acquisition. *Journal of Child Language, 10,* 551–570.

Snow, C. E., & Ninio, A. (1986). The contracts of literacy: What children learn from learning to read books. In W. H. Teale & E. Sulzby (Eds.), *Emergent literacy: Writing and reading* (pp. 116–138). Norwood, NJ: Ablex.

Snowling, M. (1987). *Dyslexia: A cognitive-developmental perspective.* Oxford: Basil Blackwell.

Sommers, N., & McQuade, D. (1984). *Student writers at work: The Bedford prizes.* New York: St. Martin's Press.

Sowers, S. (1985). The story and the "all about" book. In J. Hansen, T. Newkirk, & D. Graves (Eds.), *Breaking ground: Teachers relate reading and writing in the elementary school* (pp. 73–82). Portsmouth, NJ: Heinemann.

Spring, C., & Davis, J. (1988). Relations of digit naming speed with three components of reading. *Applied Psycholinguistics, 9,* 315–334.

Stahl, S., & Miller, P. D. (1989). Whole language and language experience approaches for beginning reading: A quantitative research synthesis. *Review of Educational Research, 59,* 87–116.

Stanovich, K. (1990). Concepts in developmental theories of reading skill: Cognitive resources, automaticity, and modularity. *Developmental Review, 10,* 72–100.

Stanovich, K. (1991). Word recognition: Changing perspectives. In R. Barr, M. L. Kamill, P. Mosenthal, & P. D. Pearson (Eds.), *Handbook of reading research* (Vol. II) (pp. 418–452). New York: Longman.

Stanovich, K. E. (1980). Toward an interactive-compensatory model of individual differences in the development of reading fluency. *Reading Research Quarterly, 16,* 32–71.

Staton, J. (1982). *Dialogue journal writing.* Washington, DC: Center for Applied Linguistics.

Stein, & Glenn. (1979). An analysis of story comprehension in elementary school children. In R. O. Freedle (Ed.), *Discourse processes: Advances in research and theory* (Vol. 2). Norwood, NJ: Ablex.

Sternberg, R., & Wagner, R. (1982). Automatization failure in learning disabilities. *Topics in Learning and Learning Disabilities, 2,* 1–11.

Stotsky, S. (1980). *Evaluation of the writing program at the William M. Trotter School, Boston: September, 1978–January, 1980.* Report prepared for the Boston Public Schools and Curry College, Milton, MA.

Stotsky, S. (1984). Research on reading/writing relationships: A synthesis and suggested directions. In J. Jensen (Ed.), *Comprehending and composing* (pp. 7–22). Urbana, IL: ERIC-NCRE.

Stotsky, S. (1986). On learning to write about ideas. *College Composition and Communication, 37,* 276–293.

Stotsky, S. (1987a). A comparison of the two theories about development in written language: Implications for pedagogy and research. In R. Horowitz & S. J. Samuels (Eds.), *Comprehending oral and written language.* Orlando, FL: Academic Press.

Street, B. V. (1984). *Literacy in theory and practice.* New York: Cambridge University Press.

Sulzby, E. (1985). Children's emergent reading of favorite storybooks: A developmental study. *Reading Research Quarterly, 20,* 458–481.

Sulzby, E. (1986). Writing and reading: Signs of oral and written language organization in the young child. In W. H. Teale & E. Sulzby (Eds.), *Emergent literacy: Writing and reading* (pp. 50–89). Norwood, NJ: Ablex.

Sulzby, E., Barnhart, J., & Hieshima, J. (1989). Forms of writing and rereading from writing: A preliminary report. In J. M. Mason (Ed.), *Reading and writing connections.* Boston: Allyn & Bacon.

Sulzby, E., & Teale, W. (1991). Emergent literacy. In R. Barr, M. L. Kamil, P. Mosenthal, & P. D. Pearson. (1991). *Handbook of reading research* (Vol. II) (pp. 727–758). New York: Longman.

Sulzby, E., & Zecker, L. B. (1991). The oral monologue as a form of emergent reading. In A. McCabe & C. Peterson (Eds.), *Developing narrative structure* (pp. 175–214). Hillsdale, NJ: Erlbaum.

Swinney, D. (1979). Lexical access during sentence comprehension: (Re) consideration of context effects. *Journal of Verbal Behavior, 18,* 645–659.

Swinney, D. (1981). Lexical processing during sentence comprehension: Effects of higher order constraints and implications for representation. In T. Myers, J. Laver, & J. Anderson (Eds.), *The cognitive representation of speech.* Amsterdam: North-Holland.

Taylor, D. (1983). *Family literacy: Young children learning to read and write.* Exeter, NH: Heinemann.

Taylor, D., & Dorsey-Gaines, A. (1989). *Learning to read in the inner city.* Norwood, NJ: Ablex.

Templeton, S., & Spivey, E. M. (1980). The concept of word in young children as a function of level of cognitive development. *Research in the Teaching of English, 14,* 265–278.

Tharp, R., & Gallimore, R. (1989). *Rousing minds to life.* New York: Cambridge University Press.

Tizard, B., & Hughes, M. (1984). *Young children learning.* Cambridge, MA: Harvard University Press.

Tizard, J., Schofield, W. N., & Hewison, J. (1982). Collaboration between teachers and parents in assisting children's reading. *British Journal of Educational Psychology, 52*(1), 1–15.

Topping, K., & Wolfendale, S. (1985). *Parental involvement in children's reading.* New York: Nichols.

Velasco, P., & Snow, C. (under review). *Cross-language relationships in oral language skills of bilingual children.*

Vellutino, F. (1977). Alternative conceptualization of dyslexia: Evidence in support of a verbal-deficit hypothesis. *Harvard University Review, 47,* 334–354.

Vellutino, F. (1979). *Dyslexia.* Cambridge, MA: MIT Press.

Vellutino, F. (1982). Theoretical issues in the study of word recognition. In S. Rosenberg (Ed.), *Handbook of applied psycholinguistics.* Hillsdale, NJ: Erlbaum.

Vellutino, F. (1991). *Dyslexia.* In W. S-Y. Wang (Ed.), *The emergence of language: Development and evolution.* New York: Freeman.

Vellutino, F. (in press). Review of M. J. Adams' *Beginning to read: Thinking and learning about print. Merrill-Palmer Quarterly.*

Vernon, M. D. (1977). Varieties of deficiency in the reading process. *Harvard Educational Review, 47,* 396–410.

Vygotsky, L. S. (1962). Thought and language. Cambridge, MA: MIT Press.

Vygotsky, L. S. (1978). *Mind in society: The formation of higher psychological processes.* Cambridge: Harvard University Press.

Warren-Leubecker, A., & Carter, B. W. (1988). Reading and growth in metalinguistic awareness: Relations to socioeconomic status and reading readiness skills. *Child Development, 59,* 728–742.

Watson, R. (1989). Literate discourse and cognitive organization: Some relationships between parent's talk and 3-year-olds' thought. *Applied Psycholinguistics, 10,* 221–236.

Weaver, P. A., & Dickinson, D. K. (1982). Scratching below the surface structure: Exploring the usefulness of story grammars. *Discourse Processes, 4,* 225–243.

Weber, R. (1990). The construction of narratives by good and poor readers. In J. Zutell, S. McCormick, M. Connolly, & P. O'Keefe (Eds.), *Literacy theory and research: Analyses from multiple perspectives* (pp. 295–302). *Thirty-ninth yearbook of the National Reading Conference.* Chicago: National Reading Conference.

Wells, G. (1985a). *Language development in the pre-school years.* New York: Cambridge University Press.

Wells, G. (1985b). *Language, learning and education.* Philadelphia, PA: NFER-Nelson.

Whitehurst, G. J., Falco, F. L., Lonigan, C. J., Fischel, J. E., De Baryshe, B. D., Valdez-Menchacha, M. C., & Caulfield, M. (1987). Accelerating language development through picture book reading. *Developmental Psychology, 24,* 552–559.

Willig, A. (1985). A meta-analysis of selected studies on the effectiveness of bilingual education. *Review of Educational Research, 55,* 269–317.

Wolf, M. (1991). Naming speed and reading: The contribution of the cognitive neurosciences. *Reading Research Quarterly, 26,* 123–141.

Wolf, M., Bally, H., & Morris, R. (1986). Automaticity, retrieval processes, and reading: A longitudinal investigation of average and impaired readers. *Child Development, 57,* 988–1000.

Wolf, M., & Goodglass, H. (1986). Dyslexia, dysnomia, and lexical retrieval: A longitudinal investigation. *Brain and Language, 28,* 154–168.

Wolf, M., & Gow, D. (1986). A longitudinal investigation of gender differences in language and reading development. *First Language, 6,* 81–110.

Wolf, M., & Vellutino, F. (in press). A psycholinguistic account of reading. In J. Berko Gleason & N. Bernstein Ratner (Eds.), *Psycholinguistics.* Fort Worth, TX: Harcourt Brace Jovanovich.

Wolff, P., Michel, G., & Ovrut, M. (1990). Rate and timing precision of motor coordination in developmental dyslexia. *Developmental Psychology, 26,* 349–359.

Language Beyond Childhood

11

Loraine K. Obler *Graduate School of the City University of New York and Emerson College*

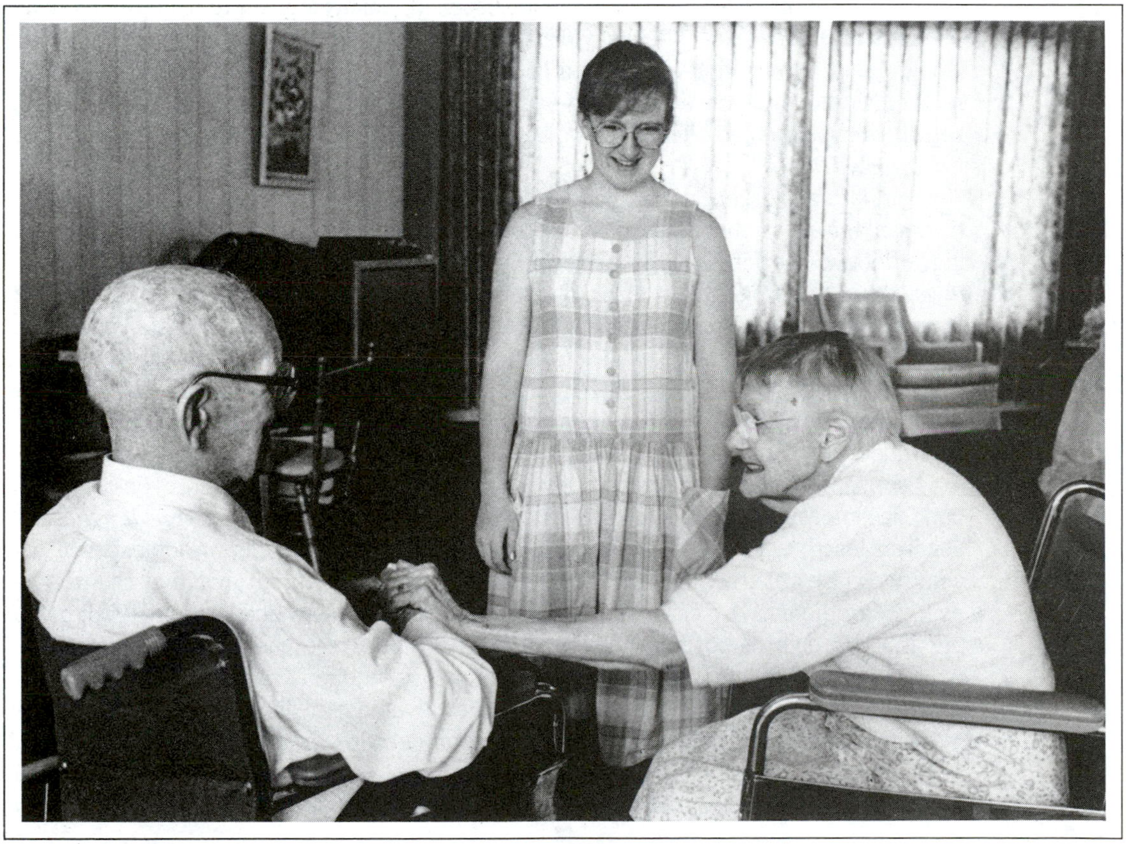

■ INTRODUCTION

Why do we assume that language learning is virtually complete by age six? Probably because most aspects of spoken language and oral comprehension are mastered by then. Yet there is much language acquisition that goes on after age six. In the Chipewyan Indian community, Scollon and Scollon (1979) report (cited in Romaine, 1984, p. 164), it is simply assumed that the Chipewyan grammar is so difficult that only older adults will be able to speak correctly.

Certain syntactic forms are learned in later childhood (Chomsky, 1969; Menyuk, 1977); and of course, the process of learning to read takes place after the primary language skills are learned (see Chapter 10). Acquisition of a second language also often occurs after the primary language development period; indeed, postchildhood learning of a second language is institutionalized in American schools. Further, in those cultures that have a *literary* or "correct" *language,* quite different from the *colloquial language* spoken daily, the literary language is not taught until children are in school. For example, children learn the colloquial Arabic of their own country at home; this might be Syrian Arabic or Egyptian Arabic or one of numerous other local languages. They are taught to read and write classical and modern standard Arabic only after they enter school. In school, and perhaps especially during adolescence, children begin to acquire and make use of different *registers*. They may display somewhat different phonology when reading aloud or in a formal interview with a linguist stranger than they do among their classmates. Moreover, appreciation of the subtle phonological and lexical differences among registers appears, and children can discuss what is "correct" language and what is not (Romaine, 1984).

In late adolescence and adulthood one can still acquire language skills. Consider the many business concerns that teach foreign language fluency, typing, coherent writing, effective speaking, and most recently, effective listening. For *bilinguals* and *polyglots,* there are programs to teach simultaneous translation. And etiquette books teach "correct" forms of address for use in formal social situations. Thus, linguists know there exists the potential for long-term acquisition of language, but we do not usually treat all these postchildhood language skills within the developmental framework. This chapter pulls together the work that has been done on language development in adolescence and adulthood.

In some sense the language development of early childhood and even late childhood is different from that of adulthood since there is probably a *core language* all children learn, whereas the special language registers and skills of adolescence and adulthood are relatively optional—only people who need them and find themselves exposed to them have a chance to acquire them. As Grimshaw and Holden (1976, p. 41) put it, "the bulk of postchildhood learning . . . appears to be in the enrichment of repertoires and the acquisition of appropriateness systems."

Although little is known about language development in middle age, somewhat more work has been done over the last several decades on the language of advanced age. This research has been almost entirely on the language deficits that develop with aging. It is possible, for example, to demonstrate that elderly people as a group have more trouble on *naming tasks* after age 70 (Goodglass, 1980), perform worse on vocabulary definition subtests of the Wechsler Adult Intelligence Scale (Wechsler, 1955), and do less well on comprehension tasks in general (Bergman, 1980; Corso, 1977). These findings fit in too nicely with Western society's belief that old age is a time of decline; the research focus is unbalanced. Research must also look for changes in *linguistic strategy* and try to dissociate from one another the various levels of cognitive deficit that may underlie apparent changes in language use. For example, one would obviously want to distinguish between the poor comprehension that results from impaired hearing and the poor comprehension that results from changes in the brain: the first is a relatively peripheral problem that can be partially remedied, whereas the second involves an essential brain-based language skill, namely the ability to understand language.

The guiding structure of this chapter is chronological. For each stage different questions are most compelling and require different research approaches. First, we consider the adolescent acquisition of first and second languages as it relates to the *critical age hypothesis* (see also Chapters 6 and 7). Then we turn to the language abilities and styles acquired in adolescence and adulthood, for which a sociolinguistic approach is most appropriate. When we turn to the language developments of advanced age, a more strictly linguistic framework is useful to see the way separate language subsystems change differently. At that point we also discuss what is known about changes in brain dominance for language across the life span. Finally, we focus on language patterns that result from brain damage in order to distinguish those changes resulting from disease from the changes linked to healthy aging.

■ IS THERE A CRITICAL AGE FOR NORMAL LANGUAGE ACQUISITION?

Since virtually all children learn one or more languages through daily exposure in early childhood, it is not easy to know whether there is a biological need to acquire language at an early age or whether children could start producing language at any age if for some reason they were delayed. There are two sorts of research that speak to this question. One asks about learning a second language: is it possible to learn one fluently at any age? The other looks at **feral children,** who for some reason were not exposed to language in early childhood. Since none of these children has learned language like a native speaker, we must consider the possibility that there is what Lenneberg calls a critical age for language acquisition (1967), after which (at puberty or younger) a human being is no longer prepared to learn language fully. Of course, it then becomes of interest to ask what the physiological mechanisms underlying language acquisition are and which aspects of language can be learned at a later age even if other aspects cannot be.

When Lenneberg (1967) proposed that there was a **critical period** for language learning, he reasoned that **lateralization** for language has taken place by puberty and the brain's left hemisphere is no longer able to acquire language. Later researchers such as Krashen (1973) and Molfese (1972) have argued that lateralization for language is complete by the age of five. Part of Lenneberg's argument relied on the fact that children who had brain damage and became **aphasic** before puberty recovered language virtually intact, whereas people who had brain damage after puberty never again sounded like native speakers of the language. However, both Genie and Victor, the two best-studied feral children, who had been exposed to virtually no language before their discovery, were found and exposed to language prior to puberty (for discussion of Genie see Chapter 7; see also Curtiss, 1977; Lane, 1976). Thus, if it was not autism that prevented their speech, then we are led with Krashen and Molfese to believe that it is lateralization of language, rather than some neurological concomitant of puberty, that prevents the left hemisphere from acquiring new language. Yet this cannot be entirely true because we know that many people learn a second or third or fourth language after puberty.

Young children who are exposed to more than one language have little difficulty in acquiring both languages and eventually speaking each of them with no interference from the other. By late childhood a child exposed to a new language displays some elements of interference between the two languages, although eventually he will speak the language with no accent. At a certain as yet undetermined time in late childhood or adolescence, it becomes substantially more difficult for a child to learn a new language like a native speaker. Indeed, Scovel (1969) has estimated that only 5 percent of speakers can acquire such mastery. Some researchers attribute this inability to an ego link with accent; Guiora, Brammer, and Dull (1972) maintain that individuals who have a hard time learning a second language without accent have a strong ego identification in the phonological system of their first language. Others maintain that motivation to learn a second language becomes more crucial with age; the child is motivated to learn in order to communicate, but for the adult it is more complex. Clearly, there are motivational features involved; in some cultures—such as that of French Canada, where there is great incentive to speak French like a native speaker—a substantially greater percentage of *anglophones* can sound like native speakers of French despite postpubertal acquisition. Other researchers such as Snow (1987) argue that the child has more time to devote to acquiring a language, whereas the adult is never able to focus energy solely on acquisition. Snow found the speed of language acquisition in younger children to be slower actually than that in older children and adults when syntactic abilities were compared.

Indication that brain organization for language may also influence the ability to acquire a second language comes not only from lateralization studies, but also from research on sex differences: girls are substantially better second language learners than are boys (in U.S. studies at least). One could postulate that the greater *bilateral* organization of a first language in girls renders them better able to acquire a second language. This corresponds with work by Albert and Obler (1978) suggesting that right hemisphere abilities are involved in the early stages of second language acquisition. Also of interest are studies just beginning of exceptional second language learners. The first case identified by Novoa, Fein, and Obler (1988) happens to be a left-hander, who may have the unusual organization that suggests.

Thus, there may be a critical stage for certain aspects of language acquisition. In order to learn a first language like a native speaker, it is crucial that acquisition start before lateralization is fixed. Puberty is too late. However, in order to acquire a second language like a native speaker, there appears to be somewhat more leeway, although the majority of individuals will do substantially better before puberty. Certain individuals—perhaps those with greater bilateral organization for language—may acquire a second language with native accent well into adulthood.

■ LANGUAGE IN ADOLESCENCE AND ADULTHOOD

Much of adult language acquisition is not formally learned but is acquired in context. There are *registers* or styles of speech we need to acquire in our work and in our social relationships. Many of these have been described by sociolinguists, and there has been some focus on the process of acquiring these skills in adolescence. Let us consider briefly what some of these adult language skills are and then turn to the natural acquisition process.

THE LANGUAGE OF PEER AND SOCIAL GROUPS

Special registers are mastered starting in childhood, exploited in adolescence, and refined in adulthood for social activities and for many aspects of interpersonal relationships. One of the primary divisions in our society, of course, is that between females and males. Thus, as one grows to adulthood, one acquires gender-appropriate speech styles. Tannen (1990) has documented how women and men differ in their styles of language use. Women use language more for rapport, while men use it more for competition. Such language mechanisms as interruption and holding the floor have been studied to see how they indicate subtle differences in power (Edelsky, 1981). As a rule, for instance, males interrupt females much more than females interrupt males.

Even in school-age children who have gender-based play groups, differences in the use of standard language can be seen. Although it has generally been thought that girls and women are more likely to use the "correct" forms, instances are also reported where the opposite is the case. For example, Wolfram and Christian (1976) report girls using *liketa* and *supposeta* more than boys (cited in Romaine, 1984). Adolescent male groups often employ distinctly nonstandard language forms as a sign of their group solidarity. Labov (1980) and Cheshire (1982) report that more specific nonstandard forms can be seen in the speech of children and adolescents who belong to peer groups than in the speech of those who do not (cited in Romaine, 1984).

Of course, one may choose deliberately to take on speech characteristics of the other gender, and in certain situations one is expected to. For example, as women have become news "anchors" on television, a certain subtype of women's language has evolved, a style deemed more "listenable" than the style often associated with nonprofessional women in our society. Professional women, in general, learn to lower their *fundamental frequency* somewhat and also to lessen the range of pitch variation in their speech (Kramer, 1975). Likewise, men who participate in child rearing learn the sociolinguistic ways of talking with children and talking about children with other parents.

Bonding language serves not only to identify members within a group but also to distinguish members from outsiders. One of the experimental paradigms that demonstrates this is the **matched guise model** of Lambert (1972). Lambert used it first with respect to French–English bilinguals, but it has been used in all sorts of other situations since. In this paradigm the same speaker is recorded in two separate segments, speaking in two separate languages. Listeners are not told that they are hearing the same speaker more than once; they are simply asked to listen to each passage and to comment on various characteristics of the speaker. Thus, their responses betray the stereotypes they have about the subgroups with which the speakers can be identified. For example, in the 1972 study, French–English Canadian bilinguals judge a male to be taller, more intelligent, and more handsome when he is speaking English than when he is speaking French. And a lecturer with an upper class pronunciation is deemed more intelligent than the same lecturer with a lower class accent. Indeed Romaine has demonstrated that even school-age children are aware of social class differences in language use, and in adolescence they become more sophisticated in identifying their features and sometimes in switching between different dialects for different purposes.

Another sociolinguistic skill that can be mastered during adolescence is that of expressing relative power through language. Anonymous linguistic putdowns have great power to frighten members of racial and ethnic subgroups and sexual minorities, as recent incidents on college campuses have demonstrated. While groups of girls are learning to use language in supportive and interactional ways, the stereotypic boys learn to use language to assert themselves (Maltz & Borker, 1982, cited in Romaine, 1984). One way of asserting power is through ritual insults. Labov and his colleagues have reported on this form of distinctive speech style among African-American male adolescents: it is called "dealing (or "doing" or "running") the dozens" and involves a competitive slandering of the participants or their parents [e.g., "Your mother raised you on ugly milk" (Labov, 1972, p. 311)]. Among adults the ritual putdowns in the gay community and the Jewish community have a different focus [e.g., "Nice car, but where do you put it when they lock the park?" (Murray, 1979, p. 215)]. As Murray stresses, not all members of a given community participate in these ritual insults; indeed, not all members participate in the larger community's use of subdialects or registers.

Special registers are also used to create bonds among members of larger subgroups of society. Chaika (1980) has detailed the special vocabulary of bowlers, noting that in order to be considered an expert bowler, one must be able not only to bowl well but also to use special terminology and idioms. In the same article Chaika details elements of the special register used to communicate by citizen band radio. Not only do CB-radio users have a special vocabulary, they also have a phonology that is apparently free of regional dialects, and they use syntactic structures that are markedly different from standard English (e.g., "I be pushin' an 18-wheeler"). In addition, there are certain subtopics that are heavily used in the CB register: not only the obvious discussion of traffic and police patrol, but also explicit sexual topics encouraged by the anonymity of CB communication and perhaps by boredom.

Language in intimate relationships takes on quite different registers, also. Couples often develop special terminology to refer to private jokes and intimate functions, and they learn to employ language in stimulating ways at intimate times. They may also develop pet names for one another, and it is of interest to note how these evolve over time. Intimate conversations are structured differently from conversations with acquaintances or strangers, Hornstein (1983) has observed. Hornstein recorded 60 telephone conversations, one-third between close friends, one-third between strangers, and one-third between acquaintances. Even in telephone conversations the procedures used for opening a conversation and for negotiating its conclusion are distinctly different for close friends. In particular, with close friends some people feel no need to identify themselves when they call. And conversations between friends can be less goal-oriented or structured; sometimes they are simply for keeping in touch. Between strangers or even acquaintances a phone conversation needs to have a more practical purpose.

Formal social relations are maintained by a highly refined set of skills called *manners*. Through experience we learn what to say in specific adult situations and what not to say. One learns the appropriate way to congratulate someone or to express condolence. In her "Miss Manners" book and syndicated columns, Judith Martin (1983), has enjoined readers to employ conventional expressions, rather than being spontaneous. Spontaneity leads to remarks such as "I'm surprised you're able to keep yourself going like this"; she recommends "I'm terribly sorry. You have my deepest sympathy." In response to an announced pregnancy she requires "Oh, how wonderful! When is it to be?" and not "Was this planned?" or "Aren't you concerned about population growth?"

Teenagers' talk often contains terms that mark their generation, such as "keen" or "awesome."

Different communities and different times require different styles of expressing the same message. For example, in certain circles it is appropriate to boast about one's accomplishments, whereas in others one must diminish them. Furthermore, one may learn the appropriate label by which a particular subgroup prefers to be identified and then may be asked to change this as society changes. Many adult females today prefer to be called *women* although a subgroup prefers to be called *girls*. It is not acceptable to call black people *Negroes;* indeed, some prefer the terms *Afro-American* or *African-American*. The term *Asians* is slowly replacing *Orientals* in the United States.

We may also observe that in different communities certain topics are taboo for discussion and others are taboo for humor. These topics change with the sensitivity of society to given issues. Thus, in many circles ethnic jokes, which were appropriate 30 years ago, are no longer amusing, and the person who uses them is considered thoughtless and ill-mannered.

Certain language skills are highly valued in some subcultures. In some, conversation is considered a valuable asset; in others, the ability to draw people out. In some the ability to debate or argue or tell stories is important, whereas in others the ability to express one's feelings and to involve other people is considered skillful language use. In some it is cleverness that counts; in others it is quick repartee and ritual insult.

LANGUAGE AT WORK

Consider the catalog of special language skills that much adult work requires. For many people, work involves the ability to talk on the telephone, which requires an estimation of another person's behavior even though one cannot see nonverbal responses. Other jobs require the ability to produce certain forms of scientific writing, communicative but nonemotional. The ability to type has long been a requirement for many positions, and now even higher-level workers must acquire typing skills in order to operate word processors and computers. Some jobs require knowledge of specific "languages," particularly the computer fields.

In addition, there are special jobs that involve skills in more than one natural language. For example, there are those who prepare translations for a living. Some translate scientific texts and need a particular set of skills; others translate literary texts and need another, overlapping set of skills. Then there are the *simultaneous translators*—people who accompany monolingual officials to foreign countries and provide immediate translations of their interactions. People who work at the United Nations are responsible for translating as the delegates speak. In order to perform this work, one must have mastered at least two languages and must have the ability to listen and speak at practically the same time.

In theater performance, special language skills are required of the actors—in particular, the ability to speak memorized lines as if they were spontaneous and to use a louder than usual voice as if it were natural. Many members of the clergy employ a special meter and voice modulations in delivering their sermons (Rosenberg, 1970). Another occupation that requires extensive specialized language abilities is that of psychotherapist. Therapists and counselors must hear what their clients and patients are really saying. Sometimes they must decode a message that says one thing on the surface but means another. And therapists must learn to respond in ways that will help effect change in the client (Haley, 1963; Rosen, 1982).

Then there are professional editors, who do not necessarily create written language themselves but who take the efforts of others and mold them into effective written pieces. Good editing requires more than knowing where to use *that* and where to use *which;* it requires an ability to impose logical and artistic structure on someone else's thoughts. And there are the creative writers in our society, from the journalists to the novelists and poets. Even though certain people may have special language skills at an early age, writers develop their talents through hard work. Creative writers often attend workshops and seminars to discuss their work and improve their skills; their style may evolve over many years. Edel (1953–69) gives a picture of the novelist Henry James's development of a more elaborate or convoluted writing style during his adult years. James was undoubtedly influenced by many things, including the typewriter, which was invented during the course of his life, and his shift to dictation that accompanied it. As Gardner has pointed out (1982), dictation requires certain additional skills, such as the ability to concentrate on what one is saying.

Even in work realms that do not focus on language, there is a certain amount of *jargon* to be acquired. Best studied are the special jargons of health care, the legal field, and the political arena with its bureaucratic and administrative language. Medical jargon is used to enable health care workers to communicate effectively with one another; it may also be used to ensure their sense of expertise and power in relation to the clients who come to them without knowledge of this jargon (Elgin, 1983; Shuy, 1979). For example, what the lay person calls senility, the health care worker may call SDAT (senile dementia of the Alzheimer's type) or OBS (organic brain syndrome). Ideally, the health care worker should be able to use the appropriate jargon with colleagues but converse in lay terms with clients.

Medical jargon, it should be noted, is not mere mastery of Latin and Greek vocabulary. As Elgin points out (1983), learning to communicate as a physician includes mastering large structures of discourse and many elements of nonverbal conversations. Paget (personal communication, 1982), for example, studied the way physicians use silence in conversations with patients in order to maintain professional status. The use of professional jargon in the medical setting also lends a certain amount of dignity to procedures that are embarrassing.

Similar phenomena exist in the legal community, with initiates becoming quite fluent in the lexicon, syntax, and idioms of legal language, while lay people flounder unless translations are made. Studies of the difficulties that jurors have in understanding their instructions (Charrow, 1982) have resulted in greater awareness within the legal community of a responsibility to avoid legal jargon in dealing with the noninitiate. Similar studies of bureaucratic and administrative language (Charrow, 1982) have demonstrated that jargon can be useful for communication within a community and for preserving a sense of identity within that community, but it can be ineffective when it is not translated for people who have not had an opportunity to master it.

In addition to these particular professions, most other work situations have their own special linguistic requirements. These may be a few specialized lexical items that refer to elements of the job, or ways of creating terms—abbreviation use can become a special skill. Special items of syntax must be mastered in most jargons. And many professions require the ability to lecture, a style of discourse that demands sensitivity to the audience and redundancy that would be inappropriate if the same material were written. For certain professions in which practitioners assume that a distance must be maintained from the listener, special language skills are required to maintain a careful balance between appearing to say something but not committing oneself to it entirely.

■ ACQUISITION OF ADULT REGISTERS

There are some studies on acquisition of different registers and even dialects in late childhood and adolescence but virtually none on the acquisition of register by adults. We may assume that, as with the language skills of childhood, exposure to the language in question is crucial. Probably it is best to hear the register spoken; reading it or reading about it is a poor substitute. In many ways this parallels the recommended modes for learning a second language. Hearing a social register in context should enable the listener to pick up certain meanings; the adult's ability to explicitly question other meanings is also of use. Again this is analogous to learning a second language, which Snow (1987) points out, adults can do as well as children if they have the time to focus on it. Nevertheless, adolescents and adults have different styles from those of children because they have different cognitive structures that permit them to think about learning and to question in ways that young children cannot.

Exposure to the language is perhaps sufficient for passive use, that is, for comprehension. More exposure brings about better abilities. Sankoff (1970) demonstrated that in Papua, New Guinea, the ability to understand language spoken in a related dialect increased from adolescence through young adulthood and grew further in the 30- to 40-year-olds (cited in Grimshaw & Holden, 1976).

In order to produce the language, some practice is necessary. No doubt there is much rehearsal of language among adolescents as well as adults, practicing what one would say in an expected situation or reviewing what one *did* say and could have said differently (Grimshaw & Holden, 1976). Additionally, adolescents' and adults' ability to criticize themselves, to observe variation in others' usage, and to select among possible styles contributes to speaking an adult register. It is probably also the case that if one has acquired a register and then does not use it for a while in adulthood, both production and comprehension abilities can be diminished or lost.

Why some individuals choose (deliberately or unconsciously) to master the registers and others do not is less clear. It may be that people choose more or less to identify with the subgroups in question. And it is possible that certain people have a particular verbal talent and can acquire styles and change among them at will. Role conflict can also be involved in register choice; for example, a woman who sees herself as very feminine may not acquire the register associated with a male occupation even if she chooses to go into that occupation.

■ LANGUAGE DEVELOPMENTS WITH ADVANCED AGE

Although it is assumed that phonology does not change with advanced age, most people believe that lexical abilities diminish (in particular, people have trouble remembering the names of things and of other people), that comprehension is impaired with age, and that discourse in the elderly tends to run on. In fact, these stereotypes are too simplistic to explain the diversity of language behaviors associated with advanced age. From recent research we learn that there are language changes that result both from direct changes in language areas of the brain and from strategies to compensate for memory or attentional deficits associated with aging.

PHONOLOGY

Phonology does not change substantially with increasing age. Nevertheless, one way in which languages themselves change is through phonological change over time. This may occur between or within generations, so the extent to which speakers vary their phonology as they age is worth studying longitudinally. Bilingualism may also play a role. Clyne (1977) has described a woman who reverted to a heavy German accent (German was her first language) in her second language, English, with advanced age. It is unclear whether the patient was demented; if so, her language development was not indicative of healthy aging. Indeed, de Bot and Clyne (1989) have demonstrated that such behavior is not the rule for immigrants with a similar history.

LEXICON

Psychologists and psycholinguists have studied lexical items because they are quite discrete and easy to specify, unlike syntax, semantics, discourse, and pragmatics. Early studies of word associations (Riegel, 1968) suggested that older subjects had a more varied range of associations than did younger subjects. Riegel pointed out the interesting fact that in his study younger adults were more likely to choose words that fit into the same word class as the stimulus item (*table* and *chair,* for example), whereas older adults were more likely to choose words that co-occur syntactically (*sit* and *chair*). Critics of his interpretation have reminded us that the younger adults in his study had undergone more education, with its standardizing effects. Indeed, in a more recent study to verify this finding, Lovelace and Cooley (1982) did not find that older and younger adults perform differently on this free association task. They concluded that semantic networks are not likely to operate differently because of age differences *per se,* but because of differences in education level. It is worth recalling that there is development in childhood from **syntagmatic** responses in younger children to more **paradigmatic** responses in older children in similar word association studies.

When given certain sorts of lexical tasks, in particular *confrontation-naming* tasks, there is no question that some 70-year-olds perform substantially worse than younger adults. In a confrontation-naming task subjects are shown a picture (or an object) and are asked to tell its name. In a series of studies from our laboratory (e.g., Nicholas, Obler, Albert, & Goodglass, 1985), 30-year-olds performed somewhat worse than 50-year-olds on confrontation-naming of both nouns and verbs. There was a slight decline for 60-year-olds on the average and a substantial decline among 70-year-olds. Longitudinal study of the same subjects (Au, Obler, Albert, Rosen, & Joung, in preparation) indicates scores decline several points for *all* subjects after six years.

Studies of passive access to lexicon, however, seem to show no decrement with aging. That is, if older adult subjects are not asked to produce the label for a concept but rather to recognize that label or name, they perform just as well or better than younger adult subjects. And when they are asked to define words, as on the vocabulary subtest of the Wechsler Adult Intelligence Scale, there are differential results depending on the scoring method. As Botwinick, West, and Storandt (1975) have reported, if one uses a modification of the standard scoring system and requires a single word synonym as a good definition, there are decrements with age starting at age 40. However, by the standard scoring, whereby definitions consisting of more than one word are as good as single word synonyms, older adults perform as well as younger adults. Thus, we suspect that lexical items are not actually lost in older adults; rather, the ability to access them in order to produce them spontaneously is impaired.

With regard to this question of active and passive access to the lexicon, consider Moscovitch's study with Landowski (personal communication, 1983). They found that even though older subjects were more likely to use old fashioned terminology, they recognized current terminology as well or as quickly as younger subjects. The methodology of that study is worth noting: they compared two word-frequency lists, the Thorndike & Lorge list created in the 1940s and the Kucera and Francis list used in the 1970s, and they looked specifically for lexical items that had changed frequency between the two lists. They found that the older adult subjects were more familiar with the 1940s speech and were more likely to use it than were the younger adults. Note that Wingfield, Goodglass, Gleason, Bowles, and Hyde (1988) have seen in their studies with the Boston Naming Test that older subjects may "fail" to name a picture because they use a word that is no longer common. However, the older adults recognized the test items as well as the younger subjects.

Older adults do not have different strategies on these tasks from those of younger adults. Nicholas et al. (1985) looked at whether older adults made different sorts of errors. Although the older adults did use relatively more circumlocutions of the correct items ("moving on his hands and knees, crawling" for "crawling") and did tend to comment on the task more (as a way of avoiding response or buying time), it was clear that for all subjects the most common errors were semantically related items (e.g., *elevator* for *escalator*). Thus, the authors concluded that the different styles were related not to different strategies in response but to the greater difficulty of the task. It is also interesting to note that there appeared to be no distinction among different word classes; essentially the same patterns of lexical access were found for verbs, common nouns, and proper nouns.

However, individual differences on naming tasks may be explained by one's experiences in using language. Barresi, Obler, Au, and Albert (in preparation) have demonstrated that older adults who engage in conversation more perform better on a naming test, while those who watch television more perform worse.

Thus, it would appear that the inner lexicon itself does not change structure with advanced age, except that more items are acquired over the life span; but access for production may be modified. The ability to access the lexicon for comprehension probably does not change. It is possible, however, that the ability to learn new words decreases in advanced age.

COMPREHENSION

In Western society, virtually all people are exposed to enough noise over their lifetime that their hearing deteriorates with age. Relatively good hearing is required for comprehension of spoken language. Thus, on any comprehension test, whether testing on a low level the ability to repeat individual words or on a high level the ability to understand sentences and paragraphs, healthy older subjects will perform worse than healthy younger subjects. The questions of interest to the linguist, however, focus primarily on any change in the brain *substrate* for comprehension with advanced age and secondarily on different comprehension strategies used to deal with hearing loss.

Let us consider the question of special comprehension strategies first. It has been assumed that healthy elderly people who comprehend fairly well despite impaired hearing must have developed special strategies. In a study conducted in Boston (Obler, Nicholas, Albert, & Woodward, 1985), it was hypothesized that older adults rely more heavily on lip reading and face reading than younger people and also that they rely more on semantics, that is, guessing what someone is saying. Neither of these hypotheses proved to be true. Face reading was tested by giving 120 healthy adults aged 30 to 79 a battery of comprehension tests under two conditions. In one they saw the speaker on a TV screen at the same time they heard comprehension questions like "The lion was killed by the tiger; who died?" In the second they heard the same sorts of questions over the same earphones, but did not see the speaker's face. The same difference between the two conditions was found for all four age groups tested, suggesting that all subjects relied equally heavily on face reading, regardless of their age.

In similar fashion subjects' reliance on semantic context was tested. Subjects heard the sentences from the Speech Perception in Noise Test (Kalikow, Stevens, & Elliot, 1977). In half of the sentences the last word is highly predictable from the context of the earlier part of the sentence (e.g., The rose bush had prickly *thorns*); in the other half of the sentences the final word is not easily predictable from the earlier words (e.g., The boy liked to talk about *thorns*). Subjects are asked to write down the final word of each sentence, but the sentences are made harder to hear by having a babbling noise imposed over them. Naturally, scores were higher for everybody in the predictable condition than in the nonpredictable condition. But again there was no greater differential between the two conditions for the 60- and 70-year-old subjects than for the 30- and 50-year-old subjects. Older and younger adults seem to rely equally on guessing the meaning of a word from its semantic context.

In a later study, however, Obler, Fein, Nicholas, and Albert (in press) demonstrated that older adults do rely more heavily than younger adults on plausibility. That is, responding to "The doctor who helped the patient who was sick was healthy; was the doctor healthy?" was easier than "The guide who drove the tourist who was bored was excited; was the guide bored?"

We cannot conclude on the basis of these studies what differences there are in comprehension strategy for younger and older adults. There may be other differences that we have not yet thought of. In fact, Bergman (1980) reviewed the literature on comprehension of synthetically distorted speech and found that older adults do worse on both slowed-down and speeded-up speech than do younger adults. But it is unclear whether this is due to overall hearing impairment or whether it reflects changes in the cognitive processes of comprehension.

Actually, it is important to note that the task Bergman used was a task requiring repetition of the sentence. Thus it could be memory factors rather than strictly linguistic comprehension that causes subjects' problems in his study. Indeed tasks asking for paragraph recall consistently show older adults to perform worse than younger subjects in number of items, concepts, or themes retrieved (Cohen, 1979). On a similar task, however, Kemper (1987) was able to demonstrate that certain syntactic structures posed particular difficulties for older subjects. Left-branching structures, where modifiers pile up before the structures they modify (e.g., *the tall, skinny, greedy* aristocrat) caused the greatest difficulty, as compared to right-branching structures (e.g., the aristocrat *who was tall, skinny, and greedy*). Such a finding suggests that syntactic structure at least interacts with memory load in rendering comprehension progressively difficult with increasing age.

The most provocative suggestion of different strategies derives from a set of studies done by Warren and Warren (1966). They developed a methodology to elicit what is called the **verbal transformation effect,** in which subjects listen to a single word presented over and over on a tape loop. The phenomenon that occurs for all subjects at some time is that they think they are hearing a different word. Subjects are instructed to raise their hand whenever they think they hear something new on the tape. Of interest for our discussion is the fact that older people hear new items less frequently than younger people. Moreover, there are qualitative differences in the types of responses people of different ages are prone to make. In particular, older adults hear only real words (e.g., *stress, tress, rest*), whereas younger adults may hear words that are not English but could be in terms of phonology and morphology (e.g., *res, trest*). Young children, it should be noted, identify words that are not even possible in English (e.g., *rster*). Thus, we are led to believe that older adults may be doing the most efficient processing in terms of what is possible in a given language, without permitting themselves to be distracted by impossible sequences. This may reflect a certain **automaticity** of language processing that develops across the life span.

DISCOURSE

There are a variety of popular beliefs in Western culture about discourse in the elderly: older people tend to run on or to go off on tangents; older people tend to tell stories over and over again without realizing it; bilingual elders can no longer limit themselves to the language appropriate to the listener. According to research these beliefs hold true only for patients with *dementia,* a disease-induced loss of intellectual function. In healthy aging language use either does not change or becomes more elaborate with age. Hints of this have occurred in studies referred to earlier; for example, older people are more likely than 30-year-olds to give definitions consisting of more than one word, and older people are more likely to give comments and circumlocutions on naming tasks.

In research on written discourse in aging, Obler (1980) collected written paragraphs from healthy subjects aged 30 through 79. Subjects were all shown the same picture, the cookie theft picture from the Boston Diagnostic Aphasia Exam (Goodglass & Kaplan, 1972), and were asked to describe it. The 50-year-olds were more likely to use an abbreviated style (e.g., "Boy standing on stool. Mother washing dishes"), whereas the older adults were more likely to use an elaborate style with articles and **deictics** as well as various modifying words and phrases. Moreover, they were likely to link their sentences (e.g., "The boy is standing on the stool while the mother is carefully drying dishes, unaware that the water is running over"). Thus, by word count within several categories and within each theme, one could see a development between the 50s and the 70s toward more elaborate speech. It is worth noting, however, that the 30-year-olds resembled the 70-year-olds in this use of elaborate speech. Thus, it may be that younger adults use an elaborate style naturally, which becomes more abbreviated in the 50s and then elaborates again near the older end of the life span.

In cultures that value tale-telling, it is the older storytellers who are considered the most skilled performers. In Obler's (1980) research in Beit Safafa, a Palestinian village outside Jerusalem, the best tale-tellers were all in their 60s and older. It is precisely the ability to use elaborate speech that makes a tale effective entertainment. This elaboration includes not only details and connections between sentences and larger units, but also personalization and an ability to create rhythm.

Some research on oral discourse shows deficits with increasing age. Kynette and Kemper (1986) found less varied syntactic use in the older subjects (aged 70 and 80) when they analyzed their spontaneous speech in a 20-minute interview. Also, these older subjects made more actual errors than did the 50- and 60-year-olds in the use of morphological markers such as past tense and subject–verb agreement. Ulatowska, Cannito, Hayashi, and Fleming (1985) found intradiscourse referencing via pronouns to be less unambiguously communicative in the group aged over 76 as compared to middle-aged and "young-old" groups (i.e., subjects between the ages of 60 and 75). Thus certain subtle markers of discourse may be seen to decline with age, even while overall more elaborate structures may be used in certain tasks.

SPEECH MONITORING

Older adults have been reported to produce more **dysfluencies**, such as stuttering, word repetition, and sentence fragments (Ehrlich, 1990) in speech, but they are able to repair speech errors as well as younger adults (McNamara, Obler, Au, & Albert, in press).

Narrative skills increase with age.

LATERALITY

Lateralization for a cognitive task means that one or the other of the two halves of the brain is primarily responsible for that task. It has been known for almost a century that language is lateralized in the left hemisphere for most people. More recently, it has become clear that some visual-spatial abilities are lateralized in the right hemisphere. Brown and Jaffe (1975) have hypothesized that laterality intensifies over the life span.

The studies of brain damage and changes in aphasia across the life span speak to this hypothesis. In particular, Brown and Jaffe maintain that lateralization for language in the left hemisphere develops not only during the first five years of life, but in fact during the entire life span. They base this claim on the different types of aphasia resulting from the same lesion to a child and to an older adult. Thus, one would expect that in advanced age left hemisphere dominance for language would be even more marked than it is in the 30s.

Several studies of lateralization have now been undertaken (Borod & Goodglass, 1980; Clark & Knowles, 1973; Johnson et al., 1979; Obler, Woodward, & Albert, 1984) that look at language both in the visual modes and in the auditory modes. These studies suggest that there are not changes in gross lateralization. That is, the left hemisphere would appear to be dominant for language from an early age, and it becomes no more dominant in later ages.

However, there is a second element of the Brown and Jaffe hypothesis, suggesting that there might be changes *within* the left hemisphere language area for organization of language across the life span. This suggestion is more plausible, given our current understanding, and may shed light on increased automaticity of language use with age, as evidenced in the studies of the Warrens and their colleagues (1966).

LANGUAGE STRATEGIES WITH AGING

We have referred to the possibility that older adults use different strategies for language processing. On naming tasks we have noted that older adults may use more words in the course of getting to a correct answer. On vocabulary tasks, where they are asked to define words, older adults also use more words (Botwinick, West, & Storandt, 1975). On comprehension tasks, by contrast, the two strategies tested so far have proven not to change with aging. The behavioral psychologist B. F. Skinner wrote on the ways he used language for "intellectual self-management" (Skinner, 1983). For example, when he needed to remember the name of someone, he found it helpful to recall the original use of the name and then go through the alphabet, trying each letter as the initial letter of the name. He and his wife had also developed some pragmatic routines that made it possible for him to avoid remembering names socially. For example, when he had to introduce his wife to someone whose name he had forgotten and there was a chance that the two had met previously, Skinner said to his wife, "Of course you remember . . . ?" and she quickly interrupts, "Yes, of course. How are you?" The Skinners assumed that acquaintances may or may not have remembered meeting Mrs. Skinner but probably did not trust their own memories, either.

Skinner also developed numerous uses of written language to facilitate diminished memory and attention: "In place of memories, memoranda" was his motto. Thus, he would carry around a notepad so that he would jot down thoughts as they occurred to him and assure that they would not be lost. He also used detailed outlines to plan papers in advance and kept a written index of what he had said so that he would not repeat himself or go off on a tangent. His general strategy was that one can do nothing about the actual accessibility of language, but one can enhance the conditions under which verbal behavior must occur. For example, he suggested a deliberate adoption of new intellectual styles and new ways of thinking to prevent being bogged down in older ones that will no longer be used as well.

Auditory verbal abilities can also be deliberately maintained. One way of keeping records of what one has said or thought is to carry around a tape recorder. Skinner also recommended setting up conversations with colleagues, since the ability to talk to a thoughtful, responsive audience helps stimulate one's own thinking. Of course, Skinner pointed out, any of these strategies would be helpful at any age, but he found them particularly useful in his old age to compensate for difficulties he would otherwise have. Skinner could write and speak articulately about these strategies, but it may be that many older people develop such strategies unconsciously—thus explaining the fact that language abilities in daily life do not appear to change substantially with age.

■ ADULT LANGUAGE AND BRAIN DAMAGE

Damage to the adult's brain brings about several different sorts of language and communication disturbance. In particular, we consider **aphasia** (essentially, language disturbance from left hemisphere damage), language disturbance from right hemisphere damage, and the language disturbance of the **dementias.**

APHASIA

Traditionally, aphasia has been divided into several major types, which have to do not with age but with the type of language disturbance a patient shows. Thus, in **Broca's aphasia** the patient produces speech with effort and *telegrammatically,* but her comprehension is relatively good. In **Wernicke's aphasia,** by contrast, production of speech is quite fluent, but comprehension is very poor. In **global aphasia** both comprehension and production are impaired; in **conduction aphasia** spontaneous production is all right and comprehension is relatively good, too, but the ability to repeat is impaired. In **anomic aphasia** only the ability to name items is lost. Aphasia may occur suddenly in childhood as a result of either stroke or accident (**childhood aphasia**), or children with **developmental dysphasia** may have difficulties over the course of learning language, with no sudden change in their brains. Aphasia can be seen in young adults who have suffered traumatic injuries from vehicle accidents or war wounds. However, the primary population of aphasic individuals in the Western world today is found among older adults who have suffered strokes.

There are several points to be made about how the language disturbances of aphasia relate to age. First, the ability to recover from aphasia differs substantially across the life span. In young children, perhaps up until the age of puberty, the recovery from even severe aphasia is likely to be nearly complete. Only with the most sophisticated testing can these subjects be seen to have language deficits (Dennis & Whitaker, 1976; Guttman, 1942). After brain damage in young adulthood, as well, there is often substantial recovery. Although there are also older adults who recover from aphasia, recovery is much less frequent in this population, and it is hard to predict which aphasic patients will recover. Patients with certain types of aphasia in the early stages are much more likely than other aphasics to recover, but beyond that individual differences are hard to predict.

One question to ask is whether older or younger adults recover better, either spontaneously or in response to speech therapy. There is some debate as to whether older and younger people recover differently when given speech therapy. Bartlett et al. (in preparation) report functional communication recovers variably but with no regard for age in adult aphasics over the first year post-onset. Sarno (1980) argues that if one omits all patients who are thought to have dementing diseases from a population of aphasics, recovery is not significantly related to age. However, the tendencies in all her measures are for older subjects to recover less completely than younger adults. We must not assume on the basis of these findings that there are changes in brain substrate for language with advanced age; even if older adults tend to have more limited recoveries in response to therapy, this tendency may be due to age-related changes in nonlanguage areas subserving the language areas, such as memory or learning ability.

Let us define aphasia as the explicit language disturbance resulting from localized or delimited impairment of the language areas of the brain (see Figure 1.1). For most individuals these areas are primarily in the *cortex,* the exterior part of the brain, and in the central area of the left hemisphere. The type of aphasia resulting from a given lesion changes markedly across the life span. In particular, as Brown and Jaffe (1975) and others have observed, in the young child a lesion to the posterior sections of the language area never results in a *fluent aphasia,* whereas the same lesion in an older adult almost invariably results in a fluent aphasia. (For our purposes the fluent aphasia is similar to Wernicke's, and a *nonfluent aphasia* is similar to Broca's.) In an epidemiological study of the relation between aphasia type and age, aphasic patients' charts for the past decade at the Boston Veterans Administration Medical Center were checked. Certain classic forms of aphasia clustered around different ages in advanced adulthood. In particular, the nonfluent abbreviated-language style aphasia with good comprehension evidenced a mean age of 52 and occurred in 30-year-olds through 60-year-olds, whereas the fluent aphasia with poor comprehension occurred with a mean age of 63 in 40-year-olds through 80-year-olds. This finding, that Broca's aphasics are on the average a decade or more younger than Wernicke's aphasics, has been verified at numerous centers throughout the world. This effect does not seem to relate to a predilection to get strokes in different parts of the brain at different ages, since Miceli et al. (1981) found the same pattern in aphasics whose language disorder resulted from tumors. We may tentatively speculate that there are actual changes in brain substrate organization for language throughout older adulthood as throughout the life span.

RIGHT HEMISPHERE DAMAGE AND LANGUAGE

Until recently it was assumed that the left hemisphere was dominant for language and the right hemisphere had little if anything to do with language. Only recently has the study of various language and communication functions considered right hemisphere damage. Although basic language skills like phonology and lexicon and syntax are not impaired when patients suffer right hemisphere damage, the abilities to use language appropriately in broader, pragmatic senses are affected. For example, Brownell, Michel, Powelston, and Gardner (1983) studied the ability to appreciate humor and discovered that it is impaired in right hemisphere subjects. Bloom, Borod, Obler, and Gerstman (1992) demonstrated that discourse involving emotional content was particularly impaired in patients with right hemisphere damage.

Foldi (1983) studied the ability to appreciate indirect discourse in brain-damaged adults. When we see a picture of a man and a boy standing by a dirty car and the man says to the boy, "That car certainly does look dirty," we understand that the man is not only commenting on the way the car looks, but he may be requesting the boy to clean it. Although the left hemisphere-damaged subjects appropriately selected the underlying meaning, the right hemisphere-damaged subjects were unable to appreciate such underlying pragmatic meanings.

LANGUAGE IN THE DEMENTIAS

The onset of aphasia is usually sudden, particularly in the case of aphasia resulting from stroke or accident. In the case of a tumor there is a progressive onset of aphasia, but the *lesion,* or area of damage, is still relatively delimited. In the **dementing diseases** like Alzheimer's, by contrast, there is more widespread damage to the brain. This damage may be subtle enough in any individual location that it is not revealed by our current methods of x-raying the brain. Nevertheless, after a person with one of these diseases has died, postmortem study of the brain shows changes at the cellular level that have been reflected in the progressive deterioration of cognitive abilities. These abilities include memory, problem-solving ability, and learning ability, as well as the language abilities on which we are focusing.

There are a number of diseases that include dementia. Many of them are only now beginning to be well studied from a medical viewpoint, and the neurobehavioral and neurolinguistic studies have started only recently. Compared to the studies of aphasia, which have been going on for the last century, studies of dementia are in an early, descriptive phase. We must first distinguish among the various sorts of dementia, and then we can describe the language behaviors associated with them.

One basic distinction to be made is whether the brain structures involved in the dementia are primarily *cortical* (on the surface of the brain) or *subcortical* (beneath the surface of the brain). In diseases such as **Parkinson's disease** and *progressive supranuclear palsy,* it is predominantly subcortical structures that are impaired, whereas in diseases such as **Alzheimer's disease**, it is predominantly cortical structures that are impaired. Thus, it is in Alzheimer's disease in particular that we see language disturbance that mimics that of the aphasias. Specifically, the language disturbance of early Alzheimer's disease looks like anomic aphasia, where the primary deficit is in the ability to name things. By the mid- to late stage, the language disturbance looks like Wernicke's aphasia: patients produce fluent, poorly monitored speech with syntactically correct usage of some words and occasional *jargon* items (which in this terminology means nonsense words). Patients with Alzheimer's disease also have difficulty in comprehension of language and in repeating sentences of substantial length and/or low probability.

By the late stages of the disease, most patients produce little language and are sometimes taken to be mute. Other patients may produce language inappropriately—talking when no one is around and/or not talking when people are present. The language produced at this stage is almost entirely stereotypic, with nothing that is propositional. Thus, late Alzheimer's patients may look like global aphasic patients, who produce and comprehend very little language. Even in the late stages, however, some pragmatic competence remains. Patients may still maintain eye contact appropriately or respond to formulaic questions like "How are you today?" (Causino, Obler, Knoefel, & Albert, in preparation).

In the early stages of the disease the ability to read may actually be better for Alzheimer's patients than the ability to understand spoken language, because spoken language requires more consistent attention. However, the ability to write deteriorates fairly rapidly. In the early and midstages, problems in writing are simply misspellings and an occasional omission or inappropriate addition of an inflectional suffix (Au, Albert, Freedman, Obler, & Litter, submitted). By the later stage, however, patients produce nonsense words and incomplete sentences and eventually refuse to write altogether.

In those dementias that co-occur with subcortical disease, in particular Parkinson's disease, it is the speech faculties that are most impaired rather than underlying language abilities. Patients tend to speak very softly, and their speech is inarticulate, speeding up to a mumble after the first several words. When one asks these patients to write, however, or listens carefully to their oral language production, one can note certain mild errors of syntax, particularly the deletion of morphemes or the inappropriate addition of morphemes. For example, the patient may write, "The grandchildren comes around." In subcortical as in cortical impairment, the incorrect use of grammatical forms may also occur. For example, in telling us the story of Little Red Riding Hood, one patient said, "The wolf took a liking *toward* the basket," instead of "The wolf took a liking *to* the basket." Such examples suggest a certain lack of monitoring on the part of the patients and are of interest to the theoretician because they suggest that idioms are not necessarily represented in unitary fashion in the brain, but may be broken up. Further evidence of this is seen in the work of Kempler and Van Lancker (1988), who showed that for patients with Alzheimer's disease, comprehension is impaired for high-frequency idioms whose meanings are not transparent (e.g., a *blue mood*).

In addition to the broader, descriptive studies, specific studies of naming and discourse abilities in Alzheimer's disease have been undertaken. Rochford (1971) maintained that affected subjects show primarily visual misperception errors on a naming task. Thus, they label a picture of flippers as the visually similar aprons more frequently than healthy elderly individuals do. However, Bayles and Tomoeda (1983) have shown results analogous to those found by Nicholas et al. (1985) for healthy subjects of all ages; as with healthy individuals, semantic substitutions are the most frequent error that demented patients make on a naming task. Thus, these results contradict earlier findings, which may have represented a particular subpopulation of Alzheimer's patients with predominantly visual–spatial difficulties rather than language difficulties.

If naming is impaired, researchers have asked, is it because the lexicon itself is losing its internal structure, or is it rather that access into the lexicon is impaired?

Schwartz, Marin, and Saffran (1979, 1980) found that the demented subject they studied extensively (WLP) was able to read words aloud and demonstrate their meaning via gesture when she heard them. Nevertheless she had trouble distinguishing pictures of dogs from those of cats in a sorting task; distinguishing pictures of birds, however, was not difficult. Thus they conclude that aspects of the linguistic lexicon and its connection to meaning are spared, but some strictly semantic categories are starting to break down. Nebes, Martin, and Horn (1984), in apparent contradiction, present evidence that certain aspects of semantic structure are still effective in mid- to moderately demented patients. Verbal priming via a semantically related word (e.g., *nurse* for *doctor*) facilitates the patients' ability to read a word aloud relatively faster than an equivalent unprimed word, as it does for normals, even though overall it takes the demented patients longer in both conditions. The apparent contradiction can perhaps be resolved if we consider that it is possible for some aspects of the semantic system to disintegrate while others do not, a point made quite effectively by Bayles and Kaszniak (1987).

Aspects of pragmatic abilities break down over the course of Alzheimer's dementia. One that has been most studied can occur in bilingual patients who lose the ability to choose the right language to address their listener. They may also mistakenly code-switch between their two or more languages when their listener only speaks one (de Santi, Obler, Sabo-Abramson, & Goldberger, 1989; Hyltenstam & Stroud, 1989).

Since aphasia is the most studied of the language and communication disturbances resulting from brain damage, it is understandable that therapies have been developed only for aphasia. Because the incidence of dementia is increasing in Western populations as people live longer, researchers and clinicians are currently at work developing therapies to improve or at least forestall the deficits in patients who have both language disturbances and learning difficulties. This work is on the cutting edge of current research.

Of the numerous ways to study both the language changes that take place over the healthy life span and adult language impaired by brain damage, there is one that we have not yet touched on that provides a good conclusion: the **regression hypothesis.**

Roman Jakobson suggested in 1941 that the language deficits of aphasia occur in the reverse order of the process of development of language in childhood. In doing this, he was extending the theory of Ribot (1882), which proposed that, across a broad range of psychological skills, the first learned elements were the last to be lost, whether from brain damage or advanced age. Jakobson's hypothesis, which he presented brilliantly with regard to the phonological systems, although appealing in its symmetry, has not held up to close scrutiny (see Gleason in Caramazza & Zurif, 1978, and Menn & Obler, 1990). Patients who lose the ability to produce plurals and past tenses do not have the same morphological systems as children just acquiring those inflections. For instance, a Broca's aphasic may be able to make an /-əz/ plural like *nurses* but unable to make a possessive of the same word. This is a pattern not seen in children. So acquisition of language, when studied in detail, is not the reverse of aphasia. In part, this is evident from the fact that there are different sorts of aphasia but essentially only one hierarchy for childhood acquisition of language.

Obler (1981) has suggested that dementia be considered a more appropriate field for looking at the regression hypothesis, since in dementia one sees a progressive deterioration that is more strictly a reversal of language and cognitive development than the sudden impairment of aphasia. Moreover, as with the child, in whom language development is closely linked to other cognitive development, in the patient suffering from dementia the progression of language deficits is closely linked to the progression of nonlanguage cognitive deficits. However, even with the demented patients there are more differences to be seen than similarities. In particular, these revolve around automatic abilities, which are not yet developed in the child but which may remain until a very late stage in the demented patient. Very demented patients may retain only swear words or politeness routines acquired in later childhood. Children at the one- or two-word stage are quite different from older people at these stages.

SUMMARY

Language development after childhood can be relatively subtle. Older children continue to acquire expertise in pragmatic linguistic behaviors, such as those pertaining to power differences (e.g., gender and social class differences). Also, as adolescents and adults join different subcultures, they may acquire language registers appropriate to those subcultures. Many work situations require distinctive language use as well.

Learning a second language may occur at any age. It appears, however, that there is a critical period around puberty after which it is much more difficult for most people to acquire phonological proficiency in a new language.

In late adulthood, certain language changes are obvious, while other areas of language remain unchanged. Access to the lexicon becomes problematic for many elderly subjects who must search for a specific word or idiom. We can deduce, however, that the lexicon itself remains unchanged, since when they are given a word to define, the elderly can do this with the proficiency of any young adult. Learning new words continues throughout the life span, but it is possible that it becomes somewhat more difficult with older adulthood.

Studies of comprehension in the elderly suggest that in addition to the obvious difficulties brought on in Western society by peripheral hearing loss, there are changes in the ability to process complex materials for comprehension. Whether these are strictly linguistic changes based in the brain or whether they are secondary to memory and attentional changes remains unclear. Moreover, many elderly adults develop successful strategies to get around these problems.

The data on possible changes of discourse with aging are controversial. Some have reported increased elaborateness, while others have reported less varied syntax. In any event, discourse does not appear to suffer the same degree of decline that lexical access and comprehension manifest. Nor are changes seen for lateral brain organization for language.

Two forms of brain damage are likely to affect the elderly population in Western cultures; these result in aphasia and dementia. Of all the aphasia types, fluent aphasias (such as Wernicke's aphasia) are most likely to occur in older subjects. There is debate as to whether recovery from aphasia becomes more difficult with increasing age.

Specific language disorders associated with dementing diseases such as Alzheimer's disease have recently been described. Overall, the language and communication behavior looks similar to what is seen in the fluent aphasias: anomia in the early stages and Wernicke's aphasia in mid- to late stages. With subcortical dementias, by contrast, primarily speech and not language problems are seen. Even in the cortical dementias, where general cognitive loss accompanies the language and communication deficits, Jakobson's regression hypothesis does not hold: the quality of language changes in Alzheimer's disease is markedly different at every stage of the progressive decline from that of language in early childhood.

SUGGESTED PROJECTS

The ideal projects to be suggested from a study of lifespan development of language are longitudinal studies. In a semester or even a year it is simply not possible to see natural language change in adults, except in language learners and in a limited number of demented or aphasic patients. The following projects can give some sense of language change with time by using a cross-sectional approach or a post-hoc longitudinal approach.

1. Find an older friend who agrees that he forgets the names of things more than previously. Go through some of his photograph books, and see what sort of strategies he uses when he cannot remember specific names. You could also discuss the things he has noticed that are called something different today from what they were called when he learned the names. See whether you can find which idioms have changed.
2. The next time you are the client of a professional (a physician or a lawyer or a plumber), note the words and idioms that are used that you do not understand or understand but would not use. Question the professional about these words; consider the extent to which she is able to translate and the extent to which these words are an unexplainable part of her jargon. Also observe how she feels about your questioning her use of jargon. You could also bring together a friend who is in the first year of professional school and a friend who is completing professional school or practicing in the field. Note how the two of them converse on common topics and see what differences there are in their abilities to use their professional jargon and to translate it for you as a noninitiate.
3. Find someone who wrote journals at the age of 20 and continued writing them through the age of 60 or 70, and who is prepared to share the journals with you. Note how the language changes over the years, not only in terms of content, but also in the vocabulary and idioms used and in the form of sentences and paragraphs. A similar project would be to compare the writing styles of a poet or novelist who has produced very different works in early and late career (e.g., W. B. Yeats, W. H. Auden, Colette, Shakespeare, Racine, Plato, Drabble).
4. Spend a day with someone who has several children of different ages. Observe how the adult has developed different language registers appropriate to the age of each child. Detail what the differences are.
5. List the special language skills you have learned in college or graduate school. Consider what you have been taught and also what you have learned about constructing a composition, using speech appropriately in different classes, and acquiring the jargon of your major field.

6. If you are a member of an intimate relationship that employs creative pet names, write these down and study their development over the course of a semester.

SUGGESTED READINGS

Bergman, M. (1980). *Aging and the perception of speech.* Baltimore: University Park Press.

Brown, J., & Jaffe, J. (1975). Hypothesis on cerebral dominance. *Neuropsychologia, 13,* 107–110.

Melvold, J., Au, R., Obler, L., & Albert, M. L. (n.d.). Language in aging and dementia. In M. L. Albert (Ed.), *Neurology of aging* (2d. ed., in preparation). New York: Oxford University Press.

Skinner, B. F. (1983). Intellectual self-management in old age. *American Psychologist, 38,* 239–244.

REFERENCES

Albert, M. L., & Obler, L. K. (1978). *The bilingual brain: Neuropsychological and neurolinguistic aspects of bilingualism.* New York: Academic Press.

Au, R., Albert, M., Freedman, M., Obler, L., & Litter, J. (n.d.). *Writing disorders in dementia.* Manuscript submitted for publication.

Au, R., Obler, L. K., Albert, M., Rosen, J., & Joung, P. (n.d.). *Longitudinal naming loss in aging.* Manuscript in preparation.

Barresi, B., Obler, L. K., Au, R., & Albert, M. L. (n.d.). *Language use practices and naming abilities.* Manuscript in preparation.

Bartlett, C., Rubens, A., Holland, A., Barresi, B., & Satake, E. (n.d.). *Recovery of functional communication in aphasia: Effects of age and severity.* Manuscript in preparation.

Bayles, K., & Kaszniak, A. (1987). *Communication and cognition in normal aging and dementia.* Boston: Little, Brown.

Bayles, K., & Tomoeda, L. (1983). Confrontation naming impairment in dementia. *Brain and Language, 19,* 98–114.

Bergman, M. (1980). *Aging and the perception of speech.* Baltimore: University Park Press.

Bloom, R., Borod, J., Obler, L. K., & Gerstman, L. (1992). Impact of emotional content on discourse production in patients with unilateral brain damage. *Brain and Language, 42,* 153–164.

Borod, J., & Goodglass, H. (1980). Hemispheric specialization and development. In L. Obler & M. Albert (Eds.), *Language and communication in the elderly: Clinical, therapeutic, and experimental issues.* Lexington, MA: D. C. Heath.

Botwinick, J., West, R., & Storandt, M. (1975). Qualitative vocabulary responses and age. *Journal of Gerontology, 30,* 574–577.

Brown, J., & Jaffe, J. (1975). Hypothesis on cerebral dominance. *Neuropsychologia, 13,* 107–110.

Brownell, H., Michel, D., Powelston, J., & Gardner, H. (1983). Surprise but not coherence: Sensitivity to verbal humor in right hemisphere patients. *Brain and Language, 18,* 20–27.

Caramazza, A., & Zurif, E. (1978). *Language acquisition and language breakdown: Parallels and divergencies.* Baltimore: Johns Hopkins University Press.

Causino, M., Obler, L., Knoefel, J., & Albert, M. (n.d.). *Spared pragmatic abilities in late-stage Alzheimer's disease.* In L. K. Obler, R. Bloom, S. de Santi, & J. Ehrlich (Eds.), *Discourse in Clinical Populations.* Manuscript in preparation.

Chaika, E. (1980). Jargons and language change. *Anthropological Linguistics, 22,* 77–96.

Charrow, V. (1982). Linguistic theory and the study of legal and bureaucratic language. In L. Obler & L. Menn (Eds.), *Exceptional language and linguistics.* New York: Academic Press.

Cheshire, J. (1982). *Variation in an English dialect.* Cambridge: Cambridge University Press.

Chomsky, C. (1969). *The acquisition of syntax in children from five to ten.* Cambridge, MA: MIT Press.

Clark, L., & Knowles, J. (1973). Age differences in dichotic listening performance. *Journal of Gerontology*, 28, 173–178.

Clyne, M. (1977). Bilingualism of the elderly. *Talanya, 4,* 45–56.

Cohen, G. (1979). Language comprehension in old age. *Cognitive Psychology, 11,* 412–429.

Corso, J. (1977). Auditory perception and communication. In J. Birren & K. W. Schaie (Eds.), *The psychology of aging.* New York: Van Nostrand Reinhold.

Curtiss, S. (1977). *Genie: A psycholinguistic study of a modern-day "wild child."* New York: Academic Press.

de Bot, K., & Clyne, M. (1989). Language reversion revisited. *Studies in Second Language Acquisition, 11,* 167–177.

Dennis, M., & Whitaker, H. (1976). Language acquisition following hemi-decortication: Linguistic superiority of the left over the right hemisphere. *Brain and Language, 3,* 404–433.

de Santi, S., Obler, L., Sabo-Abramson, H., & Goldberger, J. (1989). Discourse abilities and deficits in multilingual dementia. In Y. Joanette & H. Brownell (Eds.), *Discourse abilities in brain damage: Theoretical and emperical perspectives.* New York: Springer.

Edel, L. (1953–69). *Henry James* (4 vols.). London: Hart-Davis.

Edelsky, C. (1981). Who's got the floor? *Language in Society, 10,* 383–421.

Ehrlich, J. (1990). *Influence of structure on the content of oral narrative in adults with dementia of the Alzheimer's type.* Unpublished doctoral dissertation, CUNY Graduate School.

Elgin, S. (1983). *The gentle art of verbal self-defense.* Englewood Cliffs, NJ: Prentice-Hall.

Foldi, N. (1983). Sensitivity to indirect commands by right- and left-hemisphere brain-damaged adults (Doctoral dissertation, Clark University, 1983). *Dissertation Abstracts International, 44,* 1958B.

Gardner, H. (1982). Dictated by necessity, or every man his own Boswell. In *Art, mind, and brain* (pp. 257–261). New York: Basic Books.

Gleason, J. Berko. (1978). The acquisition and dissolution of the English inflectional system. In A. Caramazza & E. Zurif (Eds.), *Language acquisition and language breakdown.* Baltimore: Johns Hopkins University Press.

Goodglass, H. (1980). Naming disorders in aphasia and aging. In L. K. Obler and M. L. Albert (Eds.), *Language and communication in the elderly: Clinical, therapeutic, and experimental issues.* Lexington, MA: D. C. Heath.

Goodglass, H., & Kaplan, E. (1972). *Assessment of aphasia and related disorders.* Philadelphia: Lea and Febiger.

Grimshaw, A., & Holden, L. (1976). Postchildhood modifications of linguistic and social competence. *Social Science Research Council Items, 30,* 33–42.

Guiora, A., Brammer, R., & Dull, C. (1972). Empathy and second language learning. *Language Learning, 22,* 111–130.

Guttman, E. (1942). Aphasia in children. *Brain, 65,* 205–219.

Haley, J. (1963). *Strategies of psychotherapy.* New York: Grune & Stratton.

Horner, J., Heyman, A., Kanter, J., Royall, J., & Aker, C. R. (1983). Longitudinal changes in spoken discourse in Alzheimer's dementia. Paper presented to the International Neuropsychological Society, Mexico City.

Hornstein, G. (1983). Intimate conversations among women. Paper presented at the Association for Women in Psychology Conference, Seattle.

Hyltenstam, K., & Stroud, C. (1989). Bilingualism in Alzheimer's dementia: Two case studies. In K. Hyltenstam and L. K. Obler (Eds.), *Bilingualism across the lifespan: Aspects of acquisition, maturity, and loss.* Cambridge: Cambridge University Press, 1989.

Jakobson, R. (1941, 1968). *Child language, aphasia, and phonological universals.* The Hague: Mouton.

Johnson, R., Cole, R., Bowers, J., Foiles, S., Nakaido, A., Patrick, J., & Woliver, R. (1979). Hemispheric efficiency in middle and later adulthood. *Cortex, 15,* 109–119.

Kalikow, D., Stevens, K., & Elliot, L. (1977). Development of a test of speech intelligibility in noise using sentence materials with controlled word predictability. *Journal of the Acoustic Society of America, 61,* 1337–1351.

Kemper, S. (1987). Syntactic complexity and the recall of prose by middle-aged and elderly adults. *Experimental Aging Research, 13,* 47–52.

Kempler, D., & Van Lancker, D. (1988). Proverb and idiom comprehension in Alzheimer's disease. *Alzheimer's Disease and Associated Disorders, 2,* 38–49.

Kramer, C. (1975). Women's speech: Separate but unequal? In C. Thorne & N. Henley (Eds.), *Language and sex: Difference and dominance.* Rowley, MA: Newbury House.

Krashen, S. (1973). Lateralization, language learning, and the critical period: Some new evidence. *Language Learning, 23,* 63–74.

Kucera, H., & Francis, W. N. (1967). *Computational analysis of present-day American English.* Providence, RI: Brown University Press.

Kynette, D., & Kemper, S. (1986). Aging and the loss of grammatical forms. *Language and Communication, 6,* 65–72.

Labov, W. (1972). *Language in the inner-city: Studies in the black English vernacular.* Philadelphia: University of Pennsylvania Press.

Labov, W. (1980). The social origins of sound change. In W. Labov (Ed.), *Locating language in time and space* (pp. 251–264). New York: Academic Press.

Labov, W., & Fanshel, D. (1977). *Therapeutic discourse: Psychotherapy as conversation.* New York: Academic Press.

Lambert, W. (1972). *Language, psychology, and culture.* Palo Alto, CA: Stanford University Press.

Lane, H. (1976). *The wild boy of Aveyron.* Cambridge, MA: Harvard University Press.

Lenneberg, E. (1967). *Biological foundations of language.* New York: Wiley.

Lovelace, E. A., & Cooley, S. (1982). Free association of older adults to single words and conceptually related words and triads. *Journal of Gerontology, 37,* 432–437.

Maltz, D., & Borker, R. (1982). A cultural approach to male–female miscommunication. In J. Gumperz (Ed.), *Language and social identity* (pp. 195–217). Cambridge: Cambridge University Press.

Martin, J. (1983, March 28). Miss Manners. *Boston Globe.*

McNamara, P., Obler, L., Au, R., & Albert, M. (n.d.). *Speech repair processes in the elderly.* Manuscript submitted for publication.

Menn, L., & Obler, L. K. (Eds.). (1990). Summary chapter. *Agrammatic aphasia: A cross-language narrative sourcebook.* Amsterdam: Benjamins.

Menyuk, P. (1977). *Language and maturation.* Cambridge, MA: MIT Press.

Miceli, G., Caltagirone, C., Gianotti, G., Masullo, C., Silveri, M., & Villa, G. (1981). Influence of age, sex, literacy and pathologic lesion on incidence, severity and type of aphasia. *Acta Neurologica Scandinavica, 64,* 370–382.

Molfese, D. (1972). Cerebral asymmetry in infants, children and adults: Auditory evoked responses to speech and music stimuli (Doctoral dissertation, Pennsylvania State University, 1972). *Dissertation Abstracts International, 34,* 1298B.

Murray, S. (1979). The art of gay insulting. *Anthropologial Linguistics, 21,* 211–223.

Nebes, R. D., Martin, D. C., & Horn, L. C. (1984). Sparing of semantic memory in Alzheimer's disease. *Journal of Abnormal Psychology, 93,* 321–330.

Nicholas, M., Obler, L., Albert, M., & Goodglass, H. (1985). Lexical retrieval in healthy aging and in Alzheimer's dementia. *Cortex, 21,* 595–606.

Novoa, L., Fein, D., & Obler, L. (1988). A neuropsychological study of an exceptional second language learner. In L. Obler & D. Fein (Eds.), *The exceptional brain: The neuropsychology of talent and special abilities.* New York: Guilford Press.

Obler, L. (1980). Narrative discourse style in the elderly. In L. Obler & M. Albert (Eds.), *Language and communication in the elderly.* Lexington, MA: D. C. Heath.

Obler, L. (1981). Review of *Le Langage des Déments* by Luce Irigaray. *Brain and Language, 12,* 375–386.

Obler, L., Fein, D., Nicholas, M., & Albert, M. L. (in press). Auditory comprehension and aging: Decline in syntactic processing. *Journal of Applied Psycholinguistics.*

Obler, L., Nicholas, M., Albert, M. L., & Woodward, S. (1985). On comprehension across the adult lifespan. *Cortex, 21,* 273–280.

Obler, L., Woodward, S., & Albert, M. (1984). Lateralization in aging? *Neuropsychologia, 22,* 235–240.

Ribot, T. (1882). *Diseases of memory: An essay in the positive psychology.* London: Paul.

Riegel, K. (1968). Changes in psycholinguistic performance with age. In G. Talland (Ed.), *Human aging and behavior.* New York: Academic Press.

Rochford, G. (1971). A study of naming errors in dysphasic and in demented patients. *Neuropsychologia, 9,* 437–443.

Romaine, S. (1984). *The language of children and adolescents: The acquisition of communicative competence.* Oxford: Blackwell.

Rosen, S. (Ed.). (1982). *My voice will go with you: The teaching tales of Milton H. Erickson.* New York: Norton.

Rosenberg, B. A. (1970). *The art of the American folk preacher.* New York: Oxford University Press.

Sankoff, G. (1970). Mutual intelligibility, bilingualism and linguistic boundaries. In *International days of sociolinguistics* (pp. 839–848). Rome: Institut Luigi Sturzo.

Sarno, M. T. (1980). Language rehabilitation outcome in the elderly aphasic patient. In L. K. Obler & M. L. Albert (Eds.), *Language and communication in the elderly: Clinical, therapeutic, and experimental issues.* Lexington, MA: D. C. Heath.

Schwartz, M., Marin, O., & Saffran, E. (1979). Dissociations of language function in dementia: A case study. *Brain and Language, 7,* 277–306.

Schwartz, M., Saffran, E., & Marin, O. (1980). Fractionating the reading process in dementia: Evidence for word specific print-to-sound associations. In M. Coltheart, K. Patterson, & J. Marshall (Eds.), *Deep dyslexia* (pp. 259–269). London: Routledge & Kegan Paul.

Scollon, R., & Scollon, S. (1979). *Linguistic convergence: An ethnography of speaking at Fort Chipewyan.* Alberta, NY: Academic Press.

Scovel, T. (1969). Foreign accents, language acquisition, and cerebral dominance. *Language Learning, 19,* 245–254.

Scovel, T. (1979). The effects of neurological age on nonprimary language acquisition. In R. Anderson (Ed.), *New dimensions in second language acquisition research.* Rowley, MA: Newbury House.

Shuy, R. (1979). Language policy in medicine: Some emerging issues. In J. Alatis & G. R. Tucker (Eds.), *Language in public life* (pp. 126–136). Washington, DC: Georgetown University Press.

Skinner, B. F. (1983). Intellectual self-management in old age. *American Psychologist, 38,* 239–244.

Smith, M. (1957). Relation between word variety and mean letter length of words with chronological and mental ages. *Journal of General Psychology, 56,* 27–43.

Snow, C. (1987). Relevence of the notion of a critical period to language acquisition. In M. Bornstein (Ed.), *Sensitive periods in development* (pp. 183–209). Hillsdale, NJ: Erlbaum.

Tannen, D. (1990). *You just don't understand: Women and men in conversation.* New York: William Morrow.

Thorndike, E., & Lorge, I. (1944). *The teacher's word book of 30,000 words.* New York: Teacher's College Press.

Ulatowska, H., Cannito, M., Hayashi, M., & Fleming, S. (1985). Language abilities in the elderly. In H. Ulatowska (Ed.), *The aging brain: Communication in the elderly.* San Diego: College-Hill Press.

Warren, R. M., & Warren, R. P. (1966). A comparison of speech perception in childhood, maturity, and old age by means of the verbal transformation effect. *Journal of Verbal Learning and Verbal Behavior, 5,* 142–146.

Wechsler, D. (1955). *Manual for the Wechsler Adult Intelligence Scale.* New York: Psychological Corporation.

Wingfield, A., Goodglass, H., Gleason, J. Berko, Bowles, N., & Hyde, M. R. (1988). *A process model for naming and its aberrations.* Unpublished manuscript.

Wolfram, W., & Christian, D. (1976). *Appalachian speech.* Washington, DC: Center for Applied Linguistics.

Glossary

This glossary defines words as they are used in this textbook. Many of the words (i.e., *competence, assimilation*) are technical terms here that have very different meanings in other contexts.

Acoustic phonetics The study of the types of sound waves produced by different shapes of the vocal tract when making speech sounds. This knowledge allows scientists to synthesize speech by reproducing the acoustic patterns.

Adapted speech Speech adapted to the social context or listener needs.

Affix A bound morpheme. Affixes can be placed before the word stem (prefixes such as *un-*); they can be suffixes, such as *-ed*; they can appear within the word as infixes, such as the *o,* which signals past tense in the English "sold."

Affricate A sound that is a combination of a stop and fricative, such as the voiced sound at the beginning of *judge* or the unvoiced sound at the beginning of *church.*

Allomorph Any one of the possible phonetic forms of a morpheme; for example, the English possessive ending, spelled *s,* has three allomorphs: /s/, /z/, and /əz/. Which allomorph is used depends on the final sound of the word.

Alveolar Refers to any consonant made with the tongue near or touching the alveolar ridge, which is behind the upper front teeth. English alveolar consonants include /t/, /d/, /n/, /s/, and /z/.

Alzheimer's disease A progressive dementia characterized by the presence of neuronal plaques and tangles in the cerebral cortex.

American Sign Language See *ASL.*

Ameslan See *ASL.*

Amplification The use of hearing aids to improve impaired hearing ability.

Anaphoric Referring to previous discourse through the use of pronouns, definite articles, and other linguistic devices. For example, "I saw a rainbow. It was beautiful."

Anomia Aphasic difficulty in producing nouns.

Aphasia Loss of impairment of language ability because of brain damage. Aphasic syndromes vary, depending on the site of the damage.

Arcuate fasciculus A band of subcortical fibers connecting Broca's area and Wernicke's area in the left hemisphere of the human brain. See *Conduction aphasia.*

Articulators General term for the parts of the mouth (lips, areas of the tongue, teeth, areas of the roof of the mouth, et al.) involved in the production of speech sounds.

ASL American Sign Language. A complete language, related historically to French, this is the manual language used by the deaf community in the United States.

Aspect A modification of the verb found in some languages, such as Black English, that indicates whether an activity was completed, or is ongoing.

Assimilation Changing a sound in a word to make it more similar to an adjacent or nearby sound in that word or a neighboring word. *Assimilation* leads us to pronounce "greenbeans" as "greembeans."

Augmentative communication system Any of a number of ways, such as communication boards, designed to help disabled individuals to communicate.

Autism A childhood disorder, probably neurological in origin, characterized by stereotypic behavior, and a broad range of social, communicative, and intellectual deficiencies.

Automaticity The potential of a process to be completed with great speed after long practice, without allocating to it conscious attention. When a cognitive process becomes automatic, it does not require extra time or processing capacity.

Back channel Feedback from the addressee, commonly in the form of nonverbal nods and eye contact or verbal signals of comprehension.

Babbling Prespeech consisting of relatively long strings of syllables that may be used communicatively or as solo sound-play.

Baby talk One of many names for the speech register used with young children. The term is sometimes used to refer to the speech of young children. See *CDS.*

Basic level category The level of abstraction most generally appropriate in a given situation or for the given speaker, for instance *dog,* rather than *animal* or *puli.*

Behavioral regulation Guiding one's own or another's overt behavior, which is one of the many uses of language.

Behaviorist One who believes generally that the principles of learning can be used to explain most behavior, and that observable events, rather than mental activity, are the proper objects of study.

Bidialectal Having control of two dialects in a language.

Bilabial A sound made with both lips, e.g., /b/ and /p/ in English.

Biological capacity Innate factors, which are those present in the organism by virtue of its genetic makeup.

Black English A dialect associated with black speakers, or working class speakers; used by many Southern speakers, regardless of race.

Bottom-up processing A term taken from artificial intelligence to depict the direction of processing. *Bottom-up* indicates that a process begins with the most basic level data and is driven upward. This is contrasted with *top-down processing* that begins with the concepts and then proceeds downward to the most basic level of data.

Bound morpheme A morpheme that occurs only bound to other morphemes—it cannot stand alone (e.g., the *s* in *cats*).

Broca's aphasia See *Broca's area.*

Broca's area Area of the left hemisphere in the frontal region. Damage to this area results in aphasia characterized by difficulty in producing speech.

CA Chronological age. Actual age; in child language research, typically reported in years and months. Two years and three months is noted as 2;3.

Canonical form A sequence of phonological features expressing the properties that a group of highly similar words have in common.

Categorical perception Two sounds with the same magnitude of acoustic difference are heard as different sounds if they fall into different phonemic categories, but they are heard as the same sound if they are from the same phonemic category.

CDS Child-directed speech. The special speech register used when talking to children, including short sentences, greater repetition and questioning, and higher and more variable intonation than that of speech addressed to adults. See *Baby talk.*

Cerebral palsy A congenital motor disability that can affect an individual's ability to produce oral language. Various subgroups of cerebral palsied individuals exist (i.e., ataxic, spastic), reflecting damage to distinct areas of the brain before or at birth.

Child-directed speech See both *CDS,* and *Baby talk.*

Childhood aphasia An acquired aphasia occurring in children, usually as a result of stroke or accident. Contrasted with developmental dysphasia, q.v.

Chronic otitis media Middle-ear infection that may be present for months or years. See *Otitis media.*

Classical concept A concept that can be characterized by unchanging criteria. For example, a "bachelor" can be defined as one who is not married.

Classical conditioning A form of learning in which previously neutral stimuli (i.e., words) through repeated pairings with other stimuli come to elicit similar responses. First described by Pavlov.

Cleft Palate A congenital disability (caused by defects in the bone or tissue separating the oral and nasal cavities) that impairs control of the oral air pressure necessary for the articulation of many speech sounds.

Closed-class word In language, this is one of a small group of words with a role that is basically grammatical in nature, such as articles and prepositions in English. Also called *function word,* q.v.

Cochlear implant Device that is surgically implanted in the inner ear to stimulate the acoustic/auditory nerve of a person suffering from deafness.

Code oriented One kind of style exhibited by children learning language. Code-oriented children emphasize references to things in their language.

Code switching Switching from one language, or dialect, to another in the course of a conversation.

Collective monologue A type of childhood conversation in which two speakers appear to take turns but the content of their messages is completely unrelated, or related only by accident.

Color term Any word that refers to a color, e.g., "magenta."

Communication boards Devices that allow speech-impaired individuals to gesture toward written or pictorial images to assist their communication efforts.

Communicative competence Linguistic competence plus knowledge of the social rules of language use. The speaker has phonological, morphological, syntactic, and semantic knowledge and the knowledge of pragmatics necessary to use language in its social context.

Communicative temptation tasks Tasks designed to elicit communication efforts from an infant.

Competence Linguist's term for the inner knowledge one has of language and all of its linguistic rules and structures.

Competition model A model of language development based on PDP networks that assumes that various cues in the language environment compete with one another. The most available and reliable cues will be learned first. Developed by Bates & MacWhinney.

Compound word A word that is made up of two free morphemes, such as "blackbird" or "candlestick."

Conduction aphasia An aphasic syndrome characterized by inability to repeat; typically resulting from damage to the arcuate fasciculus.

Confrontation naming The ability to name items when provided with visual stimuli.

Consonant Any speech sound made by constricting the vocal tract enough to impede air flow through the mouth. Consonants include stops, affricates, fricatives, nasal stops, and liquids. Glides (semivowels) are sometimes grouped with consonants.

Content word Also called *open class word*. Nouns, verbs, and modifiers within a language are considered content words; words such as articles and auxiliary verbs are considered function words or functors.

Conversational asymmetry Degree of unbalance in a conversation, in which speakers do not have equal numbers of turns, time on the floor, and so on.

Conversational babble Babble in which intonation contour, eye contact, and gesture strongly resemble those used in adult conversational interaction. See *Expressive jargon*.

Critical period A period in development during which certain events must take place if they are to take place at all.

Cue availability In the competition model, a measure of the frequency of appearance of any particular cue in the language environment.

Decibel (dB) A measure of a sound's loudness.

Decontextualized language Language that can be understood apart from the context in which it is used, and can successfully communicate information that is new to the hearer; lies on one end of a continuum, with contextualized (e.g., face-to-face conversation) language being at the other end.

Deictic terms From the Greek "deiktikos" (able to show), words that are used as linguistic pointers, e.g., "here," "there." Also called *deixis*.

Dementia Loss of mental ability, typically through neurological impairment, such as Alzheimer's disease.

Dementing disease Any disease that causes loss of mental ability.

Derivational morpheme A morpheme that can be used to derive a new word. See *Derived word.*

Derived word A complex word made from a base morpheme to which various affixes have been added. For instance, "unhappiness" is derived from "happy" by the addition of the affixes *un* and *ness*.

Descriptive adequacy Characteristic of a model or theory that assures that it is capable of describing and cataloging all relevant behaviors and distinguishing them from those that are not relevant.

Development dysfluency A stage of normal child language development during which many children demonstrate stuttering-like behaviors.

Developmental dyslexia Difficulty in learning to read, in the absence of other handicapping conditions.

Developmental dysphasia Congenital language disability in the absence of obvious cognitive, perceptual, or neurological deficits. A more current term is *specific language impairment*.

Developmental lag hypothesis The theory that a mentally retarded child's linguistic and cognitive development follows the same order seen in normally developing children, but at a slower rate, and beginning later.

Dialect A systematic subvariety of a language spoken by a group of speakers sharing certain characteristics, such as geographical origin or social class.

Discourse accent A kind of problem often encountered by older learners of a second language, in which they do not gain complete control of pragmatic rules, and thus may have an *accent* in choosing topics appropriately, etc.

Down syndrome A congenital condition, usually caused by trisomy of the 21st chromosome, often characterized by short stature, typical epicanthic eyefolds, and varying degrees of mental retardation.

Dramatist One kind of individual style displayed by children learning language, who prefer to represent human interaction in their symbolic play.

Dummy syllable A place holder, or empty phonological form. Some children learning language use a dummy syllable in place of all unstressed initial syllables.

Dysfluency Breaks in the ongoing rhythm of speech, such as those caused by hesitations, repetitions, or the use of fillers like "um," "well," etc.

Dyslexia Any one of a number of conditions that lead to a specific impairment in learning to read; dyslexias are typically linguistic processing problems, rather than difficulties with perception.

Dyslexics Individuals with dyslexia.

Echolalia Repetition of all or part of another's utterance as one's turn in a conversation; common in autistic children.

Egocentrism; egocentric speech Speech not adapted to listener needs, e.g., using complex language to speak to young children, or using color terms to direct the action of a blindfolded (or blind) listener.

Emergent literacy Children's understanding about reading and writing before they actually acquire these skills; this understanding is enhanced in households that engage in many reading and writing activities.

Empiricism A theoretical approach emphasizing observable, environmental explanations of behavior.

Environmental print Writing found on traffic signs, food and household goods, packaging, in buildings, et al. Often the first words a child recognizes.

Exophoric Using the nonlinguistic context of a conversation in order to make a linguistic referent clear. For example, saying, "the man" when only one man is in the room.

Expository writing Writing that is dependent on logic, rather than on chronology, as its organizational principle.

Expressive jargon Babbling consisting of strings of sounds uttered with a variety of stress and intonation patterns. See *Conversational babble.*

Expressive style A speech style observed in toddlers that is characterized by the use of many personal-social terms.

Fast mapping The ability of some children to *map* a word onto its meaning with only one or two examples/exposures.

Feral children So called "wild" children (*homo ferus* of Linnaeus). These children are supposedly raised by wolves or other animals, walk on all fours, and have no language when they are found.

Folk etymology An explanation of a word's origin that is not based on the actual historical record, but rather on common sense or custom: "It's called *Friday* because it is the day you eat fried fish."

Format/scaffold In Vygotskyian theory, adults are thought to provide intellectual interaction that serves as a scaffold, or format, that makes it possible for children to develop at a much faster rate than they could without this helpful intervention.

Formulaic expressions Expressions that are acquired and used as unanalyzed wholes (e.g., "lookit," "wazat," "lemme see").

Free morpheme A morpheme that can stand alone (e.g., "cat"), as opposed to a bound morpheme.

Free word association A word association in which the subject responds freely with the first word that comes to mind.

Free variation Allophones that can appear in the same environment without changes in meaning are said to be in *free variation.* For instance, /t/ can be released, unreleased, aspirated, unaspirated at the end of the word "hat."

Fricative A speech sound produced partly or wholly by airstream friction, such as /s/ or /v/.

Function words Words that fulfill a solely grammatical function (e.g., "what," "for," "where"). See *Closed-class word.*

Functional core According to some theorists, a functional core underlies children's early words. This implies that early meanings are based on how objects are used, and that the labels are later extended to similar objects.

Functionalism A theoretical approach emphasizing the functions or uses of any behavior (e.g., the function of requesting) rather than the structure of the behavior itself.

Genderlect The dialects associated with men's and women's speech variants.

Given/new principle Pragmatic rule that one can only use a definite article when referring to a noun if the hearer shares the speaker's knowledge; one can only say "the man," if the hearer knows who the man is. Otherwise it is "a man."

Glide A speech sound made with slightly more vocal tract constriction than a vowel and having shorter duration than a vowel. The sounds /j/ and /w/ are *glides.* They are also referred to as semivowels.

Global aphasia Aphasia resulting from extensive brain damage; the patient has poor comprehension and little voluntary language.

Glottal fricative Speech sound made by friction in the glottis.

Government and binding theory (GB) A model of grammar descended from earlier Transformational Generative models. It proposes only one type of transformation (movement of elements), the specification of possible grammatical frames for lexical items and their mapping onto the syntax of sentences, and universal constraints on possible syntactic rules, among many other notions.

Grapheme The written symbol of a particular writing system (e.g., a letter in the alphabet).

High amplitude sucking (HAS) A technique used to study infant perceptual abilities. Typically involves recording an infant's sucking rate as a measure of its attention to various stimuli.

Higher-level processes A term used in information processing accounts that refers to more cognitively complex processes like comprehension, inference, et al. These conceptual processes are contrasted with *lower-level* processes that refer to more basic cognitive processes like letter recognition.

Holophrastic Said of infants' one word speech that is thought to embody a complete intention.

Illocutionary intent The goal of a speaker, such as persuading, informing, or requesting.

Immersion Settings in which a group of learners are all taught a new language through the medium of the second language

Index of Productive Syntax, IPsyn A method of evaluating children's spontaneous language that relies upon scoring a sample for the presence of various grammatical forms.

Input language Specially modified language directed to young children. See *CDS,* and *Baby talk.*

Intentional communication Any communicative act that an individual engages in purposefully.

Interdental Speech sound made by placing the tongue between the teeth: The initial sounds of "this" or "thing" in English.

Internalized representation The mental, or inner cognitive image of external reality.

International phonetic alphabet See *IPA.*

Intonation contour The pattern of rhythmic stress and pitch across an utterance. In English, a falling pitch at the end of an utterance typically indicates a statement, whereas a final rising pitch usually marks an interrogative.

IPA International phonetic alphabet. A set of characters that can be used to represent any speech sound unambiguously. Unlike the English alphabet, *IPA* characters have only one value.

IPsyn See *Index of Productive Syntax.*

Intelligibility The degree to which an individual's speech is understandable by others.

Irony Using words to convey the opposite of their literal meaning, e.g., "It's so clean in here," said of a messy dorm room.

Joint attention Situation in which two individuals are paying attention to the same thing at the same time, as in reading a book together.

Kinship term Word that refers to familial relationships (e.g., "aunt," "cousin").

Labial Any speech sound made by bringing the lips close together or making them touch one another. The English labials are /p/, /b/, and /m/.

Labiodental Any speech sound made by bringing the lower lip close to, or in contact with, the upper teeth. The English labiodentals are the fricatives /f/ and /v/.

LAD Language acquisition device. The innate mental mechanism that, according to linguistic theorists, makes language acquisition possible.

Language standardization Process whereby a language becomes the official or standard language used in a community.

Lateralization The process whereby one side of the brain becomes specialized for particular functions; for instance, the left side becomes *lateralized* for language.

Learnability theories Various models of language acquisition based on several assumptions concerning the nature of children, known learning mechanisms, and the structure of language and the logical inferences that can be drawn from these assumptions. Developed by Pinker, Wexler, and others.

Lexicalization The process of attaching words to meanings.

Linguistic chauvinism The attitude that one language or dialect is superior or more correct than others.

Linguistic competence See *Competence.*

Liquid A consonantal speech sound made with less oral constriction than a fricative but more constriction than a glide. The English *liquids* are /l/ and /r/.

Locutionary act The actual form of an utterance (syntactic construction, semantics, etc.), regardless of speaker's intent or effect on a listener.

Logogen Central unit of a theory of word recognition by John Morton (1969). The *logogen* is like an individual switchboard for each word's components, i.e., the visual, phonological, and semantic aspects of a word.

Lower-level processes A term used in information processing accounts that refers to more basic cognitive processes like letter-number recognition, grapheme-phoneme correspondence. Contrasted with *higher-level* processes that refer to more complex, conceptual operations like comprehension.

Low-structured observation A method of studying young children that often relies upon free play with a standard set of toys.

MA Mental age. A measure of an individual's cognitive functioning, which can be greater or less than chronological age. If a child of 10 can solve problems that are typically only solved by average 12-year-olds, the child is said to have a mental age of 12.

Main clause first strategy A way of interpreting sentences in which the hearer assumes that the event described in the main clause of a sentence is the event that occurred first.

Matched guise model An experimental paradigm in which listeners make judgments about the characteristics of speakers of different languages or dialects, without knowing that the "speakers" are just one person who is multilingual. This makes it possible to show attitudes toward the language, since the speaker is constant.

Mean Length of Utterance See *MLU.*

Means-ends concept Children at Stage 4 of the Piaget's sensorimotor phase begin to understand causality, have a concept of *means-ends,* and learn to communicate intentionally, lending support to the notion that certain cognitive developments might be prerequisites to language acquisition.

Message oriented An individual style of language acquisition that emphasizes the social situation, rather than reference to things.

Metalinguistic awareness Knowledge about language, that is, an understanding of what a word is and a consciousness of the sounds of language. The ability to think about language.

Metaphor Figure of speech in which one thing is called by the name of another to indicate the similarities between them: "This room is a pig pen."

Minimal pair A pair of words that differ in meaning and whose sounds are the same except for one phonetic segment. For example, "ram/ran" form a minimal pair differing only in the final consonant; "ram/rim" form a *minimal pair* differing only with respect to the vowel.

MLU Mean length of utterance. A measure applied to children's language to gauge syntactic development; the average length of the child's utterances is calculated in morphemes.

Model An attempt to explain any currently unexplained phenomenon by reference to a possibly similar, but understood phenomenon.

Model adequacy Characteristic of a theory or model that includes principles that can account for the relevant behaviors.

Modulated babble Babble with intonation contours strongly resembling those of adult speech. Because intonation carries some aspects of meaning, *modulated babble* can be used (especially in conjunction with gesture) for communicative purposes even though the sound sequences themselves are meaningless.

Monologue Speech by one person. See *Collective monologue.*

Morpheme A minimal meaningful unit of language. A free morpheme (e.g., "cat") can stand alone. A bound morpheme (e.g., the plural *s* on "cats") must always be connected to another morpheme.

Morphology The rules that govern the use of morphemes in a language; for instance the *morphology* of English requires that plural endings vary according to the last sound of the word stem.

Mutual exclusivity A cognitive bias shown by children, who typically avoid labeling anything at more than one level of generality. Hence, they may refer to their pet as a "dog," but not also as an "animal."

Nasal, nasal stop A speech sound made with the velum lowered so that air can escape through the nose. English *nasals* include /m/, /n/ and /ŋ/.

Nativism A theoretical approach emphasizing the innate, possibly genetic contributions to any behavior.

Nativist One who believes that language (or other development) is preprogrammed in the individual, not the product of learning.

Neologism A new, made-up word, often not a word in the language, as when a Wernicke's aphasic patient refers to an ashtray as a "fremser."

Negative evidence Evidence concerning language errors or unacceptable combinations of sounds or words.

Nominalist fallacy The belief that simply naming a phenomenon also sufficiently explains that phenomenon.

Nonreduplicated babbling Babbling in which the consonant-vowel syllables are quite varied within an utterance. Also called *variegated babbling.*

Object permanence The understanding that an infant gains during the latter part of the first year that objects continue to exist even though they may no longer be visible.

Obstruent Any speech sound that constricts the vocal tract enough to cause air-stream friction or closes if off entirely. The *obstruents* of a language consist of the stops, affricates, and fricatives.

Open-class word See *Content word.*

Operating principles Cognitive strategies that a child might employ in learning language, such as, "Pay attention to the ends of words."

Oralism An approach to deaf education that emphasizes auditory training, articulation ability, and lipreading.

Order of mention strategy A way to interpret sentences used by children, in which they assume that the first thing mentioned is the first thing that occurred.

Ostension Pointing to referent; a technique used by mothers in teaching basic level categories. ("That's a taxi over there.")

Otitis media Infections of the middle ear, which may, if chronic, affect a child's speech and language development.

Overextension Used here to refer to a child's use of a word in a broader context than is permissible in the adult language; for instance, an infant may call all men "daddy." Parents who call tigers "kitty" are also producing overextensions.

Overlaid function Said of most speech functions, because the organ systems on which they depend have a different primary function; thus, articulation of phonemes is *overlaid* on the tongue, an organ with a primary function involving eating.

Overregularization A common tendency among children and second language learners, *overregularization* involves applying regular and productive grammatical rules to words that are exceptions: "hurted" and "mouses," for example.

Palatal A speech sound made on the hard palate. In English, the initial sound of "shirt" is a *palatal.*

Paradigmatic In word association tests, said of a word that is the same part of speech as a stimulus word.

Paralinguistic Nonphonemic aspects of language, such as some prosodic features, that convey information about the speaker's mood, affect, and so on.

Parameter According to current theory, a parameter is a kind of linguistic switch that the young learner "sets" after exposure to the language; one of a finite number of values along which languages are free to vary. For example, the so-called Pro-drop parameter distinguishes languages such as English and German, which do not permit omission of lexical subjects, from languages such as Spanish or Italian, which do.

Parkinson's disease A progressive disease, subcortical in nature, with primary effects in speech, rather than language.

Patterner A child who displays a style of early language acquisition that emphasizes physical characteristics and patterns in the world of objects.

PCF See *Phonetically consistent form.*

PDP Parallel distributive processing. Part of a computer-based model that explains grammatical development by analogy with the kinds associative links that computers can forge.

Performance Linguist's term for the production of speech. Contrasts with competence, which is almost always greater than *performance.*

Performative Early meaningful vocalization-gesture pattern closely tied to a specific context.

Perlocutionary effect The effect that any particular utterance has on its recipient. See *Locutionary act,* and *Illocutionary intent.*

Personal-Social items Words that express affect, social relationships; also conventional social expressions (e.g., "want," "please," "whoops!" "thank you").

Phone An individual speech sound; the realization of a phoneme in a particular context.

Phoneme A speech sound that can signal a difference of meaning; two similar speech sounds *p* and *b* represent different phonemes in English because there are pairs of words with different meanings that have the same phonetic form except that one contains *b* where the other contains *p*, e.g., "pet" and "bet." See *Minimal pair.*

Phonetically consistent form (PCF) A consistent sound pattern used in a consistent situation, not derived from the adult language. See also *Vocable,* and *Protoword.*

Phonology Study of the sound system of language. The sounds the language uses, as well as the rules for their combination.

Phonotactics The study of the permissible sequences of sounds in a language.

Place of articulation The point or points in the vocal tract where the upper and lower articulators come closest together in the production of a particular phone.

Pragmatics The rules for the use of language in social context, and in conversation, or the study of these rules.

Preverbal Occurring before the infant can speak.

Principle of contrast Children's assumption that no two words have the same meaning. Hence they assume that a new word will not refer to something for which they already have a name.

Principle of relevance A conversational maxim that holds that what a speaker says is supposed to be relevant to the conversation.

Probabilistic concept A concept characterized by a variable set of criteria, unlike a classical concept. For instance, "bird" is a probabilistic concept, because no criterion defines it exclusively, that is, a creature need not fly, have a beak, feathers, et. al., to qualify as a bird.

Procedural rules Rules or procedures to follow to ensure successful communication. These include "listener rules," such as how to modify your speech for younger listeners.

Production The process of speaking.

Productive Said of the regular forms of a language that are used in the formation of new words, regular plural endings, for instance.

Productive ending A grammatical ending that can be added to all or most new words in a language, including made-up words like new product names or borrowed words like names of animals from distant places.

Progressive phonological idiom A word in a child's vocabulary that is pronounced more accurately than most other words of the same general adult target form. Idioms are an exception to the child's current set of rules, and are progressive in the sense that they anticipate the ability the child will soon have.

Prosodic features Aspects of the speech stream, such as stress and intonation, that convey differences in the meaning of words or sentences.

Protoimperative An early expression used by children, that has imperative intent, but does not have the structure of an imperative in the adult language. At the one-word stage, for instance, "cookie!" might be a *protoimperative.*

Prototype An instance of a category that best exemplifies it; for example, a "robin" is a *prototypical* member of the category "bird," because it has all of the important defining features.

Protoword A sequence of sounds (used by a child) that has a relatively consistent meaning but is not necessarily based on any adult word. The terms "phonetically consistent form" and "vocable" are also used for this general notion.

Rate of acquisition The time course of the child's acquisition of language.

Reduplicated babbling Babbling in which consonant-vowel combinations are repeated, such as "bababa." Also called *repetitive babbling.*

Referent The actual thing to which a particular word alludes—an actual cat, for instance, as opposed to the meaning of the word, which is a mental construct.

Referential style A speech style observed in toddlers that is characterized by the use of nouns, and few personal social terms. See *Expressive style.*

Reflexive vocalization A sound made involuntarily, such as a vegetative sound, a burp, cough, newborn cry, and so on.

Register Special forms of speech used for particular listeners or social settings, such as CDS.

Regression A change backward from behavior that is more adult-like to behavior that is a poorer approximation of the adult model and representative of earlier stages of development.

Regression hypothesis The theory (not currently upheld) that in aphasia speech is lost in mirror image fashion to the order of acquisition.

Regular allomorph An allomorph whose use is stable in terms of general phonological patterns. For example, the /s/, /z/, and /əz/ allomorphs of the English plural are regular—which one is used depends on the sound of the end of the noun it is added to. Irregular allomorphs of the plural include endings particular to certain words, such as the *en* plural of words as in *oxen*.

Regularization The process of making language forms conform to regular patterns.

Routine A speech form that occurs predictably in particular situations (e.g., greetings and conversational closings such as "hello" and "bye").

Scaffold A supportive linguistic/communicative context supplied by mothers and other adults to young children. See *Format.*

Script Refers to a known scheme or structure of knowledge. A story's *script,* therefore, refers to our previous knowledge about the organization, plot, characters, and so on.

Semantic feature One of the criteria by which a concept is defined and distinguished from other concepts. For instance, + male and + relative are two features of the concept *brother*.

Semantic network A word and all of the words that are related to it through various hierarchies of meaning.

Semantics The study of the meaning system of language.

Semantic softener A word such as "please" that modulates the possible harshness of a statement.

Semantic transparency Obvious meaning. One of the principles children use in making new words, "plant man" for "gardener," for instance.

Semivowel See *Glide.*

Sensitive age A period in which an organism is particularly vulnerable, or in which certain developments can optimally take place. There may be a sensitive age, rather than a critical period, for language acquisition.

Sensorimotor stage In Piagetian theory, the first 18 months of a child's life, when the major mode of cognition is through the senses and the action of the body.

Set test A word association or production test in which the subject is asked to respond with only a particular category of words, such as words beginning with a certain letter.

Sign language A rule-governed manual language system, containing its own lexical, syntactic and conversational constraints.

Sign system An educational communication system that translates an oral language into a manual code. In general, the syntax of *sign systems* is borrowed from that of the oral language upon which they are based.

Simplified register A modified speech style that contains features thought to aid a listener who is immature or otherwise not fully competent in the language—baby talk, for instance, or speech to foreigners.

SLI, Specific language impairment Delayed or deviant language development in a child who exhibits no cognitive, neurological, or social impairment.

Social routine Routinized speech used in social settings, such as "bye bye."

Sociolinguistics An approach to the study of language variation and adaptation that considers the ways social constructs (class, gender, role, status, et al.) influence language, and which makes use of observation of natural conversations.

Sound play See *Babbling.*

Species specific Refers to the fact that language as we know it is specific to our species, and not to others.

Species uniform Refers to the observation that the major milestones of language occur in the same way and at the same general time in all members of the species.

Speech acts Aspects of the pragmatic system, such as requesting, apologizing, and so forth.

Standard dialect or language The preferred form of a language, in which pronunciation, word meaning, and grammar rules have been explicitly described, such that it becomes the form used in schools and taught to foreigners.

Stem allomorphy A change in the sound (regardless of the spelling) of the stem of a word when an affix is added. For example, the /d/ at the end of "allude" becomes /z/ when *-ion* is added.

Stress Greater prominence on one or more syllables in a word; this may be due either to greater actual loudness, a marked change (usually a rise) in pitch, or greater length of the syllable.

Structuralism A theoretical approach emphasizing the organization or structure of a behavior as opposed to its use or function.

Submersion Language learning setting in which one second language learner is surrounded by native speakers.

Syntagmatic Reflecting a linearly ordered relationship between sentential constituents; in word association, a word that typically follows the stimulus word in sentence.

Syntax The rules by which sentences are made, such forms as passives, declaratives, interrogatives, imperatives.

Telegraphic speech Speech that consists of content words, without functors, much like a telegram.

Test question A question to which the questioner knows the answer. Used by some parents to test or demonstrate their children's linguistic, and other, knowledge.

TGG Transformational generative grammar, developed by Noam Chomsky, a grammar in which surface structure is derived from deep structure by the application of transformational rules.

Theoretical adequacy Characteristic of a theory or model that contains principles that not only account for observed behaviors, but are the actual principles individuals use to attain those behaviors.

Theory of mind Assumptions individuals hold about the state of knowledge of others. Children must develop a *theory of mind* in order to speak to others at an appropriate level.

Top-down A term taken from artificial intelligence research to depict the direction of processing. *Top-down* (or concept-driven) indicates that processing moves from the level of concepts downward to basic level data. This direction is in contrast to data-driven or bottom-up accounts that proceed upward.

Topic associating Narrative style that juxtaposes topics without the use of many devices that provide coherence.

Topic coherence Narrative style that includes conjunctions and other markers that help show the relationship between topics.

Transformational syntax see *TGG.*

Underextension Use or understanding of a word that does not include its full range; assuming, for instance, that "dog" refers only to collies.

Universal grammar Hypothetical set of restrictions governing the possible forms all human languages may take.

Universal Property assumed to characterize all human languages.

Unvoiced sound A speech sound (fricative, stop, et al.) produced without vocal cord vibration, for example, /s/, /t/.

Variegated babble See *Nonreduplicated babbling.*

Velar Any speech sound produced by having the back of the tongue touch or come near the underside of the *velum,* or soft palate. The English velars are the consonants /k/, /g/, and /ŋ/. See *Velum.*

Velum Also called the soft palate; the soft extension of the hard palate. The *velum* plays two major roles as an articulator: first, it can be raised to close off the passage from the pharynx into the nasal cavity and lowered to open this passage; second, the back of the tongue rises to touch the *velum* in the production of the velar stops.

Verbal transformation effect Phenomenon that occurs after a given word has been listened to repeatedly. The listener begins to hear new words.

Vernacular The common, everyday language of a community.

Vocable A consistent sound pattern used in a consistent situation, not derived from the adult language (also called *protoword* or *phonetically consistent form*).

Voiced sound A speech sound (stop, fricative, et al.) produced with vocal cord vibration, for example, /a/, /z/. In the case of English, this term is usually also extended to the stops /b, d, g/.

VOT Voice onset time. A measure that describes the point during the production of a speech sound at which vocal cord vibration, or voicing, begins.

Vowel A speech sound made with a relatively unobstructed flow of air. Semivowels have some restriction but the air is not stopped and there are no friction sounds (e.g., /w/ or /y/).

Well formed Acceptable in grammatical structure to native speakers of a language.

Wernicke's aphasia Aphasia characterized by fluent but relatively empty speech, poor comprehension, and neologisms in severe cases.

Wernicke's area Speech area in the posterior region of the left hemisphere. Damage to *Wernicke's area* results in Wernicke's aphasia.

Wh/question A question preceeded by a *wh-* word, such as who, what, why, where, when, (or how) that requires specification of the missing element in the answer.

Whole word method A method of teaching reading that emphasizes recognition of the entire contour of a word, rather than its phonological elements.

Yes/no question A question that may be responded to by saying "yes" or "no."

Zone of proximal development In Vygotskyian theory, the range of behaviors available to a child in the helpful presence of a guiding adult.

Name Index

Subject Index